Handbook of In

C000051133

W
DE
G

Handbooks of Applied Linguistics

Communication Competence
Language and Communication Problems
Practical Solutions

Editors
Karlfried Knapp and Gerd Antos

Volume 7

Mouton de Gruyter · Berlin · New York

Handbook of Intercultural Communication

Edited by
Helga Kotthoff and Helen Spencer-Oatey

Mouton de Gruyter · Berlin · New York

Mouton de Gruyter (formerly Mouton, The Hague)
is a Division of Walter de Gruyter GmbH & Co. KG, Berlin.

⊗ Printed on acid-free paper which falls within the guidelines
of the ANSI to ensure permanence and durability.

Library of Congress Cataloging-in-Publication Data

Handbook of intercultural communication / edited by Helga Kotthoff,
Helen Spencer-Oatey.
  p. cm. −   (Handbooks of applied linguistics ; 7)
Includes index.
ISBN 978-3-11-021431-4 (pbk. : alk. paper)
1. Intercultural communication.   I. Kotthoff, Helga.   II. Spencer-
Oatey, Helen, 1952−
P94.6.H356   2009
303.48'2−dc22
                                                     2009030971

Bibliographic information published by the Deutsche Nationalbibliothek

The Deutsche Nationalbibliothek lists this publication in the Deutsche Nationalbibliografie;
detailed bibliographic data are available in the Internet at http://dnb.d-nb.de.

ISBN 978-3-11-021431-4

© Copyright 2009 by Walter de Gruyter GmbH & Co. KG, D-10785 Berlin.
All rights reserved, including those of translation into foreign languages. No part of this book
may be reproduced in any form or by any means, electronic or mechanical, including photo-
copy, recording, or any information storage and retrieval system, without permission in writing
from the publisher.
Cover design: Martin Zech, Bremen.
Cover photo: LaRae/morgueFile.
Typesetting: Dörlemann Satz GmbH & Co. KG, Lemförde.
Printing and binding: AZ Druck und Datentechnik GmbH, Kempten (Allgäu).
Printed in Germany.

Introduction to the handbook series
Linguistics for problem solving

Karlfried Knapp and Gerd Antos

1.   Science and application at the turn of the millennium

The distinction between "pure" and "applied" sciences is an old one. According to Meinel (2000), it was introduced by the Swedish chemist Wallerius in 1751, as part of the dispute of that time between the scholastic disciplines and the then emerging epistemic sciences. However, although the concept of "Applied Science" gained currency rapidly since that time, it has remained problematic.

Until recently, the distinction between "pure" and "applied" mirrored the distinction between "theory and "practice". The latter ran all the way through Western history of science since its beginnings in antique times. At first, it was only philosophy that was regarded as a scholarly and, hence, theoretical discipline. Later it was followed by other leading disciplines, as e.g., the sciences. However, as academic disciplines, all of them remained theoretical. In fact, the process of achieving independence of theory was essential for the academic disciplines to become independent from political, religious or other contingencies and to establish themselves at universities and academies. This also implied a process of emancipation from practical concerns – an at times painful development which manifested (and occasionally still manifests) itself in the discrediting of and disdain for practice and practitioners. To some, already the very meaning of the notion "applied" carries a negative connotation, as is suggested by the contrast between the widely used synonym for "theoretical", i.e. "pure" (as used, e.g. in the distinction between "Pure" and "Applied Mathematics") and its natural antonym "impure". On a different level, a lower academic status sometimes is attributed to applied disciplines because of their alleged lack of originality – they are perceived as simply and one-directionally applying insights gained in basic research and watering them down by neglecting the limiting conditions under which these insights were achieved.

Today, however, the academic system is confronted with a new understanding of science. In politics, in society and, above all, in economy a new concept of science has gained acceptance which questions traditional views. In recent philosophy of science, this is labelled as "science under the pressure to succeed" – i.e. as science whose theoretical structure and criteria of evaluation are increasingly conditioned by the pressure of application (Carrier, Stöltzner, and Wette 2004):

Whenever the public is interested in a particular subject, e.g. when a new disease develops that cannot be cured by conventional medication, the public requests science to provide new insights in this area as quickly as possible. In doing so, the public is less interested in whether these new insights fit seamlessly into an existing theoretical framework, but rather whether they make new methods of treatment and curing possible. (Institut für Wirtschafts- und Technikforschung 2004, our translation).

With most of the practical problems like these, sciences cannot rely on knowledge that is already available, simply because such knowledge does not yet exist. Very often, the problems at hand do not fit neatly into the theoretical framework of one particular "pure science", and there is competition among disciplines with respect to which one provides the best theoretical and methodological resources for potential solutions. And more often than not the problems can be tackled only by adopting an interdisciplinary approach.

As a result, the traditional "Cascade Model", where insights were applied top-down from basic research to practice, no longer works in many cases. Instead, a kind of "application oriented basic research" is needed, where disciplines – conditioned by the pressure of application – take up a certain still diffuse practical issue, define it as a problem against the background of their respective theoretical and methodological paradigms, study this problem and finally develop various application oriented suggestions for solutions. In this sense, applied science, on the one hand, has to be conceived of as a scientific strategy for problem solving – a strategy that starts from mundane practical problems and ultimately aims at solving them. On the other hand, despite the dominance of application that applied sciences are subjected to, as sciences they can do nothing but develop such solutions in a theoretically reflected and methodologically well founded manner. The latter, of course, may lead to the well-known fact that even applied sciences often tend to concentrate on "application oriented basic research" only and thus appear to lose sight of the original practical problem. But despite such shifts in focus: Both the boundaries between disciplines and between pure and applied research are getting more and more blurred.

Today, after the turn of the millennium, it is obvious that sciences are requested to provide more and something different than just theory, basic research or pure knowledge. Rather, sciences are increasingly being regarded as partners in a more comprehensive social and economic context of problem solving and are evaluated against expectations to be practically relevant. This also implies that sciences are expected to be critical, reflecting their impact on society. This new "applied" type of science is confronted with the question: Which role can the sciences play in solving individual, interpersonal, social, intercultural, political or technical problems? This question is typical of a conception of science that was especially developed and propagated by the influential philosopher Sir Karl Popper – a conception that also this handbook series is based on.

2.   "Applied Linguistics": Concepts and controversies

The concept of "Applied Linguistics" is not as old as the notion of "Applied Science", but it has also been problematical in its relation to theoretical linguistics since its beginning. There seems to be a widespread consensus that the notion "Applied Linguistics" emerged in 1948 with the first issue of the journal *Language Learning* which used this compound in its subtitle *A Quarterly Journal of Applied Linguistics*. This history of its origin certainly explains why even today "Applied Linguistics" still tends to be predominantly associated with foreign language teaching and learning in the Anglophone literature in particular, as can be seen e.g. from Johnson and Johnson (1998), whose *Encyclopedic Dictionary of Applied Linguistics* is explicitly subtitled *A Handbook for Language Teaching*. However, this theory of origin is historically wrong. As is pointed out by Back (1970), the concept of applying linguistics can be traced back to the early 19th century in Europe, and the very notion "Applied Linguistics" was used in the early 20th century already.

2.1.   Theoretically Applied vs. Practically Applied Linguistics

As with the relation between "Pure" and "Applied" sciences pointed out above, also with "Applied Linguistics" the first question to be asked is what makes it different from "Pure" or "Theoretical Linguistics". It is not surprising, then, that the terminologist Back takes this difference as the point of departure for his discussion of what constitutes "Applied Linguistics". In the light of recent controversies about this concept it is no doubt useful to remind ourselves of his terminological distinctions.

Back (1970) distinguishes between "Theoretical Linguistics" – which aims at achieving knowledge for its own sake, without considering any other value –, "Practice" – i.e. any kind of activity that serves to achieve any purpose in life in the widest sense, apart from the striving for knowledge for its own sake – and "Applied Linguistics", as a being based on "Theoretical Linguistics" on the one hand and as aiming at usability in "Practice" on the other. In addition, he makes a difference between "Theoretical Applied Linguistics" and "Practical Applied Linguistics", which is of particular interest here. The former is defined as the use of insights and methods of "Theoretical Linguistics" for gaining knowledge in another, non-linguistic discipline, such as ethnology, sociology, law or literary studies, the latter as the application of insights from linguistics in a practical field related to language, such as language teaching, translation, and the like. For Back, the contribution of applied linguistics is to be seen in the planning of practical action. Language teaching, for example, is practical action done by practitioners, and what applied linguistics can contribute to this is, e.g., to provide contrastive descriptions of the languages involved as a foundation for teaching methods. These contrastive descriptions in turn have to be based on the descriptive methods developed in theoretical linguistics.

However, in the light of the recent epistemological developments outlined above, it may be useful to reinterpret Back's notion of "Theoretically Applied Linguistics". As he himself points out, dealing with practical problems can have repercussions on the development of the theoretical field. Often new approaches, new theoretical concepts and new methods are a prerequisite for dealing with a particular type of practical problems, which may lead to an – at least in the beginning – "application oriented basic research" in applied linguistics itself, which with some justification could also be labelled "theoretically applied", as many such problems require the transgression of disciplinary boundaries. It is not rare that a domain of "Theoretically Applied Linguistics" or "application oriented basic research" takes on a life of its own, and that also something which is labelled as "Applied Linguistics" might in fact be rather remote from the mundane practical problems that originally initiated the respective subject area. But as long as a relation to the original practical problem can be established, it may be justified to count a particular field or discussion as belonging to applied linguistics, even if only "theoretically applied".

2.2.   Applied linguistics as a response to structuralism and generativism

As mentioned before, in the Anglophone world in particular the view still appears to be widespread that the primary concerns of the subject area of applied linguistics should be restricted to second language acquisition and language instruction in the first place (see, e.g., Davies 1999 or Schmitt and Celce-Murcia 2002). However, in other parts of the world, and above all in Europe, there has been a development away from aspects of language learning to a wider focus on more general issues of language and communication.

This broadening of scope was in part a reaction to the narrowing down the focus in linguistics that resulted from self-imposed methodological constraints which, as Ehlich (1999) points out, began with Saussurean structuralism and culminated in generative linguistics. For almost three decades since the late 1950s, these developments made "language" in a comprehensive sense, as related to the everyday experience of its users, vanish in favour of an idealized and basically artificial entity. This led in "Core" or theoretical linguistics to a neglect of almost all everyday problems with language and communication encountered by individuals and societies and made it necessary for those interested in socially accountable research into language and communication to draw on a wider range of disciplines, thus giving rise to a flourishing of interdisciplinary areas that have come to be referred to as hyphenated variants of linguistics, such as sociolinguistics, ethnolinguistics, psycholinguistics, conversation analysis, pragmatics, and so on (Davies and Elder 2004).

That these hyphenated variants of linguistics can be said to have originated from dealing with problems may lead to the impression that they fall completely into the scope of applied linguistics. This the more so as their original thematic focus is in line with a frequently quoted definition of applied linguistics as "the theoretical and empirical investigation of real world problems in which language is a central issue" (Brumfit 1997: 93). However, in the recent past much of the work done in these fields has itself been rather "theoretically applied" in the sense introduced above and ultimately even become mainstream in linguistics. Also, in view of the current epistemological developments that see all sciences under the pressure of application, one might even wonder if there is anything distinctive about applied linguistics at all.

Indeed it would be difficult if not impossible to delimit applied linguistics with respect to the practical problems studied and the disciplinary approaches used: Real-world problems with language (to which, for greater clarity, should be added: "with communication") are unlimited in principle. Also, many problems of this kind are unique and require quite different approaches. Some might be tackled successfully by applying already available linguistic theories and methods. Others might require for their solution the development of new methods and even new theories. Following a frequently used distinction first proposed by Widdowson (1980), one might label these approaches as "Linguistics Applied" or "Applied Linguistics". In addition, language is a trans-disciplinary subject par excellence, with the result that problems do not come labelled and may require for their solution the cooperation of various disciplines.

2.3.   Conceptualizations and communities

The questions of what should be its reference discipline and which themes, areas of research and sub-disciplines it should deal with, have been discussed constantly and were also the subject of an intensive debate (e.g. Seidlhofer 2003). In the recent past, a number of edited volumes on applied linguistics have appeared which in their respective introductory chapters attempt at giving a definition of "Applied Linguistics". As can be seen from the existence of the Association Internationale de Linguistique Appliquée (AILA) and its numerous national affiliates, from the number of congresses held or books and journals published with the label "Applied Linguistics", applied linguistics appears to be a well-established and flourishing enterprise. Therefore, the collective need felt by authors and editors to introduce their publication with a definition of the subject area it is supposed to be about is astonishing at first sight. Quite obviously, what Ehlich (2006) has termed "the struggle for the object of inquiry" appears to be characteristic of linguistics – both of linguistics at large and applied linguistics. It seems then, that the meaning and scope of "Applied Linguistics"

cannot be taken for granted, and this is why a wide variety of controversial conceptualizations exist.

For example, in addition to the dichotomy mentioned above with respect to
whether approaches to applied linguistics should in their theoretical foundations
and methods be autonomous from theoretical linguistics or not, and apart from
other controversies, there are diverging views on whether applied linguistics is
an independent academic discipline (e.g. Kaplan and Grabe 2000) or not (e.g.
Davies and Elder 2004), whether its scope should be mainly restricted to language teaching related topics (e.g. Schmitt and Celce-Murcia 2002) or not (e.g.
Knapp 2006), or whether applied linguistics is a field of interdisciplinary synthesis where theories with their own integrity develop in close interaction with
language users and professionals (e.g. Rampton 1997/2003) or whether this
view should be rejected, as a true interdisciplinary approach is ultimately impossible (e.g. Widdowson 2005).

In contrast to such controversies Candlin and Sarangi (2004) point out that
applied linguistics should be defined in the first place by the actions of those
who practically *do* applied linguistics:

> [...] we see no especial purpose in reopening what has become a somewhat sterile
> debate on what applied linguistics is, or whether it is a distinctive and coherent
> discipline. [...] we see applied linguistics as a many centered and interdisciplinary
> endeavour whose coherence is achieved in purposeful, mediated action by its prac-
> titioners. [...]
> What we want to ask of applied linguistics is less what it is and more what it does, or
> rather what its practitioners do. (Candlin/Sarangi 2004:1–2)

Against this background, they see applied linguistics as less characterized
by its thematic scope – which indeed is hard to delimit – but rather by the
two aspects of "relevance" and "reflexivity". Relevance refers to the purpose
applied linguistic activities have for the targeted audience and to the degree that
these activities in their collaborative practices meet the background and needs
of those addressed – which, as matter of comprehensibility, also includes taking
their conceptual and language level into account. Reflexivity means the contextualization of the intellectual principles and practices, which is at the core of
what characterizes a professional community, and which is achieved by asking
leading questions like "What kinds of purposes underlie what is done?", "Who
is involved in their determination?", "By whom, and in what ways, is their
achievement appraised?", "Who owns the outcomes?".

We agree with these authors that applied linguistics in dealing with real
world problems is determined by disciplinary givens – such as e.g. theories,
methods or standards of linguistics or any other discipline – but it is determined
at least as much by the social and situational givens of the practices of life.
These do not only include the concrete practical problems themselves but also

the theoretical and methodological standards of cooperating experts from other disciplines, as well as the conceptual and practical standards of the practitioners who are confronted with the practical problems in the first place. Thus, as Sarangi and van Leeuwen (2003) point out, applied linguists have to become part of the respective "community of practice".

If, however, applied linguists have to regard themselves as part of a community of practice, it is obvious that it is the entire community which determines what the respective subject matter is that the applied linguist deals with and how. In particular, it is the respective community of practice which determines which problems of the practitioners have to be considered. The consequence of this is that applied linguistics can be understood from very comprehensive to very specific, depending on what kind of problems are considered relevant by the respective community. Of course, this participative understanding of applied linguistics also has consequences for the Handbooks of Applied Linguistics both with respect to the subjects covered and the way they are theoretically and practically treated.

3.   Applied linguistics for problem solving

Against this background, it seems reasonable not to define applied linguistics as an autonomous discipline or even only to delimit it by specifying a set of subjects it is supposed to study and typical disciplinary approaches it should use. Rather, in line with the collaborative and participatory perspective of the communities of practice applied linguists are involved in, this handbook series is based on the assumption that applied linguistics is a specific, problem-oriented way of "doing linguistics" related to the real-life world. In other words: applied linguistics is conceived of here as "linguistics for problem solving".

To outline what we think is distinctive about this area of inquiry: Entirely in line with Popper's conception of science, we take it that applied linguistics starts from the assumption of an imperfect world in the areas of language and communication. This means, firstly, that linguistic and communicative competence in individuals, like other forms of human knowledge, is fragmentary and defective – if it exists at all. To express it more pointedly: Human linguistic and communicative behaviour is not "perfect". And on a different level, this imperfection also applies to the use and status of language and communication in and among groups or societies.

Secondly, we take it that applied linguists are convinced that the imperfection both of individual linguistic and communicative behaviour and language based relations between groups and societies can be clarified, understood and to some extent resolved by their intervention, e.g. by means of education, training or consultancy.

Thirdly, we take it that applied linguistics proceeds by a specific mode of inquiry in that it mediates between the way language and communication is expertly studied in the linguistic disciplines and the way it is directly experienced in different domains of use. This implies that applied linguists are able to demonstrate that their findings – be they of a "Linguistics Applied" or "Applied Linguistics" nature – are not just "application oriented basic research" but can be made relevant to the real-life world.

Fourthly, we take it that applied linguistics is socially accountable. To the extent that the imperfections initiating applied linguistic activity involve both social actors and social structures, we take it that applied linguistics has to be critical and reflexive with respect to the results of its suggestions and solutions.

These assumptions yield the following questions which at the same time define objectives for applied linguistics:

1. Which linguistic problems are typical of which areas of language competence and language use?
2. How can linguistics define and describe these problems?
3. How can linguistics suggest, develop, or achieve solutions to these problems?
4. Which solutions result in which improvements in speakers' linguistic and communicative abilities or in the use and status of languages in and between groups?
5. What are additional effects of the linguistic intervention?

4.   Objectives of this handbook series

These questions also determine the objectives of this book series. However, in view of the present boom in handbooks of linguistics and applied linguistics, one should ask what is specific about this series of nine thematically different volumes.

To begin with, it is important to emphasize what it is not aiming at:

– The handbook series does not want to take a snapshot view or even a "hit list" of fashionable topics, theories, debates or fields of study.
– Nor does it aim at a comprehensive coverage of linguistics because some selectivity with regard to the subject areas is both inevitable in a book series of this kind and part of its specific profile.

Instead, the book series will try

– to show that applied linguistics can offer a comprehensive, trustworthy and scientifically well-founded understanding of a wide range of problems,
– to show that applied linguistics can provide or develop instruments for solving new, still unpredictable problems,

- to show that applied linguistics is not confined to a restricted number of topics such as, e.g. foreign language learning, but that it successfully deals with a wide range of both everyday problems and areas of linguistics,
- to provide a state-of-the-art description of applied linguistics against the background of the ability of this area of academic inquiry to provide descriptions, analyses, explanations and, if possible, solutions of everyday problems. On the one hand, this criterion is the link to trans-disciplinary co-operation. On the other, it is crucial in assessing to what extent linguistics can in fact be made relevant.

In short, it is by no means the intention of this series to duplicate the present state of knowledge about linguistics as represented in other publications with the supposed aim of providing a comprehensive survey. Rather, the intention is to present the knowledge available in applied linguistics today firstly from an explicitly problem solving perspective and secondly, in a non-technical, easily comprehensible way. Also it is intended with this publication to build bridges to neighbouring disciplines and to critically discuss which impact the solutions discussed do in fact have on practice. This is particularly necessary in areas like language teaching and learning – where for years there has been a tendency to fashionable solutions without sufficient consideration of their actual impact on the reality in schools.

5.   Criteria for the selection of topics

Based on the arguments outlined above, the handbook series has the following structure: Findings and applications of linguistics will be presented in concentric circles, as it were, starting out from the communication competence of the individual, proceeding via aspects of interpersonal and inter-group communication to technical communication and, ultimately, to the more general level of society. Thus, the topics of the nine volumes are as follows:

1. Handbook of Individual Communication Competence
2. Handbook of Interpersonal Communication
3. Handbook of Communication in Organisations and Professions
4. Handbook of Communication in the Public Sphere
5. Handbook of Multilingualism and Multilingual Communication
6. Handbook of Foreign Language Communication and Learning
7. Handbook of Intercultural Communication
8. Handbook of Technical Communication
9. Handbook of Language and Communication: Diversity and Change

This thematic structure can be said to follow the sequence of experience with problems related to language and communication a human passes through in the course of his or her personal biographical development. This is why the topic areas of applied linguistics are structured here in ever-increasing concentric circles: in line with biographical development, the first circle starts with the communicative competence of the individual and also includes interpersonal communication as belonging to a person's private sphere. The second circle proceeds to the everyday environment and includes the professional and public sphere. The third circle extends to the experience of foreign languages and cultures, which at least in officially monolingual societies, is not made by everybody and if so, only later in life. Technical communication as the fourth circle is even more exclusive and restricted to a more special professional clientele. The final volume extends this process to focus on more general, supra-individual national and international issues.

For almost all of these topics, there already exist introductions, handbooks or other types of survey literature. However, what makes the present volumes unique is their explicit claim to focus on topics in language and communication as areas of everyday problems and their emphasis on pointing out the relevance of applied linguistics in dealing with them.

Bibliography

Back, Otto
　1970　　Was bedeutet und was bezeichnet der Begriff 'angewandte Sprachwissen-schaft'? *Die Sprache* 16: 21–53.
Brumfit, Christopher
　1997　　How applied linguistics is the same as any other science. *International Journal of Applied Linguistics* 7(1): 86–94.
Candlin, Chris N. and Srikant Sarangi
　2004　　Making applied linguistics matter. *Journal of Applied Linguistics* 1(1): 1–8.
Carrier, Michael, Martin Stöltzner, and Jeanette Wette
　2004　　*Theorienstruktur und Beurteilungsmaßstäbe unter den Bedingungen der Anwendungsdominanz.* Universität Bielefeld: Institut für Wissenschafts- und Technikforschung [http://www.uni-bielefeld.de/iwt/projekte/wissen/anwendungsdominanz.html, accessed Jan 5, 2007].
Davies, Alan
　1999　　*Introduction to Applied Linguistics. From Practice to Theory.* Edinburgh: Edinburgh University Press.
Davies, Alan and Catherine Elder
　2004　　General introduction – Applied linguistics: Subject to discipline? In: Alan Davies and Catherine Elder (eds.), *The Handbook of Applied Linguistics*, 1–16. Malden etc.: Blackwell.
Ehlich, Konrad
　1999　　Vom Nutzen der „Funktionalen Pragmatik" für die angewandte Linguistik. In: Michael Becker-Mrotzek und Christine Doppler (eds.), *Medium Sprache im Beruf. Eine Aufgabe für die Linguistik*, 23–36. Tübingen: Narr.

Ehlich, Konrad
 2006   Mehrsprachigkeit für Europa – öffentliches Schweigen, linguistische Distanzen. In: Sergio Cigada, Jean-Francois de Pietro, Daniel Elmiger, and Markus Nussbaumer (eds.), *Öffentliche Sprachdebatten – linguistische Positionen. Bulletin Suisse de Linguistique Appliquée/VALS-ASLA-Bulletin* 83/1: 11–28.

Grabe, William
 2002   Applied linguistics: An emerging discipline for the twenty-first century. In: Robert B. Kaplan (ed.), *The Oxford Handbook of Applied Linguistics*, 3–12. Oxford: Oxford University Press.

Johnson, Keith and Helen Johnson (eds.)
 1998   *Encyclopedic Dictionary of Applied Linguistics. A Handbook for Language Teaching.* Oxford: Blackwell.

Kaplan, Robert B. and William Grabe
 2000   Applied linguistics and the Annual Review of Applied Linguistics. In: W. Grabe (ed.), *Applied Linguistics as an Emerging Discipline. Annual Review of Applied Linguistics* 20: 3–17.

Knapp, Karlfried
 2006   Vorwort. In: Karlfried Knapp, Gerd Antos, Michael Becker-Mrotzek, Arnulf Deppermann, Susanne Göpferich, Joachim Gabowski, Michael Klemm und Claudia Villiger (eds.), *Angewandte Linguistik. Ein Lehrbuch.* 2nd ed., xix–xxiii. Tübingen: Francke – UTB.

Meinel, Christoph
 2000   Reine und angewandte Wissenschaft. In: *Das Magazin.* Ed. Wissenschaftszentrum Nordrhein-Westfalen 11(1): 10–11.

Rampton, Ben
 1997 [2003]   Retuning in applied linguistics. *International Journal of Applied Linguistics* 7 (1): 3–25, quoted from Seidlhofer (2003), 273–295.

Sarangi, Srikant and Theo van Leeuwen
 2003   Applied linguistics and communities of practice: Gaining communality or losing disciplinary autonomy? In: Srikant Sarangi and Theo van Leeuwen (eds.), *Applied Linguistics and Communities of Practice*, 1–8. London: Continuum.

Schmitt, Norbert and Marianne Celce-Murcia
 2002   An overview of applied linguistics. In: Norbert Schmitt (ed.), *An Introduction to Applied Linguistics.* London: Arnold.

Seidlhofer, Barbara (ed.)
 2003   *Controversies in Applied Linguistics.* Oxford: Oxford University Press.

Widdowson, Henry
 1984 [1980]   Model and fictions. In: Henry Widdowson (1984) *Explorations in Applied Linguistics* 2, 21–27. Oxford: Oxford University Press.

Widdowson, Henry
 2005   Applied linguistics, interdisciplinarity, and disparate realities. In: Paul Bruthiaux, Dwight Atkinson, William G. Egginton, William Grabe, and Vaidehi Ramanathan (eds.), *Directions in Applied Linguistics. Essays in Honor of Robert B. Kaplan*, 12–25. Clevedon: Multilingual Matters.

Acknowledgements

We would like to thank the many people who have played a part in this book. We are grateful to the general editors, Gerd Antos and Karlfried Knapp for conceptualizing this series of handbooks and for inviting us to edit this volume. We are also grateful to the chapter authors for the time and effort they have put into their writings, and for the numerous ways in which they have worked so collaboratively with us.

We would like to thank Barbara Karlson and Wolfgang Konwitschny at Mouton de Gruyter for their efficient handling of the publication process, and for their speedy responses to our queries. We are grateful to Sue Lightfoot for indexing the volume for us so efficiently.

Finally, we would like to thank our families and friends for their support and encouragement throughout the project.

A big 'thank you' to all of you!

July 2007   Helga Kotthoff and Helen Spencer-Oatey

Contents

V. Assessing and developing intercultural competence

1. Introduction

Helen Spencer-Oatey and Helga Kotthoff

The focus of this series of Handbooks of Applied Linguistics is 'linguistics as problem solving', and this particular volume explores the topic of intercultural communication. In this introductory chapter we briefly consider a few fundamental questions and outline the scope of the volume.

1. What is Intercultural Communication?

Intercultural communication, as the name indicates, is concerned with communication across cultures. Gudykunst (2000), a communication studies scholar, distinguishes it from cross-cultural studies of communication as follows:

> 'Cross-cultural' and 'intercultural' are often regarded as interchangeable. They are, nevertheless, different. Cross-cultural research involves comparing behaviour in two or more cultures (e.g. comparing self-disclosure in Japan, the USA and Iran when individuals interact with members of their own culture). Intercultural research involves examining behaviour when members of two or more cultures interact (e.g. examining self-disclosure when Japanese and Iranians communicate with each other). ... Understanding cross-cultural differences in behaviour is a prerequisite for understanding intercultural behaviour.
>
> Gudykunst 2000: 314

This is a useful distinction, but it immediately raises a more fundamental issue: how can cultures be defined and how can intercultural communication thus be distinguished from intracultural communication? This is a very complex question, which requires in-depth theoretical discussion and which some of the authors in this volume address (see, for example, Žegarac).

It is now widely accepted that cultures cannot simply be reduced to nationality, nor even to a homogeneous speech community, which ethnographers of communication assumed until recently (Hymes 1974). Today we can see that many people live in ephemeral social formations, that they simultaneously belong to several cultures and that they can change their memberships. We can assume with less certainty than ever that there are separate local cultures. Various international influences reach, for example through the mass media, even the most remote village communities and influence their feeling, thinking and acting (see, for example, Hinton in this volume). But this does not necessarily mean that they will become increasingly globalized. After all, it is precisely in contact that a need for distinction arises, and ethnicity can be created as a relevant feature for differences in contacts (Barth 1969). Whether or not this in fact happens depends on complex historical preconditions.

Nevertheless, we still speak of intercultural and intracultural communication, well aware that the boundaries between the one and the other cannot be clearly drawn. Schütz (1972, 53–69) drew attention to the fact that every type of communication includes experience of otherness. The experiences of various individuals coincide only partially, and each person processes new information within their own horizon. Although understanding operates on the assumption of reciprocity of perspectives; that does not mean that it actually occurs. Understanding is not dependent on complete reciprocity; it is sufficient that a shared meaning can be developed.

Our "idealizations of homogeneity" – to use a further expression of Schütz's (1972, 12) – are different, depending on whom we find ourselves in contact with, and in what manner. The tradition of interactional sociolinguistics has shown that very subtle refinements of orientation to one another in conversation determine whether people will experience and define themselves as belonging more to an "in-group" or as belonging more to an "out-group." If the subtle interactional orientations to one another in the area of prosody, gesture, facial expression, distance, sequencing of conversational contributions, negotiation of interaction modalities, levels of directness and so on do not succeed, we are prone to experience someone else as not "one of us."

In compiling this handbook, we have taken a pragmatic approach, which is in line with the aims of the series: we have started with the assumption that people regard themselves as belonging to different social groups, and that group members, through contact and socialization processes, develop 'family resemblances' in their behavioural practices, beliefs and values. These family resemblances, which individual members acquire to greater or lesser extents in relation to different aspects, do not simplistically determine their behaviour; on the contrary, interaction is a dynamic process through which people jointly construct (consciously and/or unconsciously) their complex and multiple identities. It is the study of this dynamic process that the field of intercultural communication is concerned with.

As Gudykunst points out, we need cross-cultural studies to inform intercultural studies, and so within this Handbook of Intercultural Communication we have included both cross-cultural and intercultural perspectives. The chapters focus on different types of social groups, including national groups (e.g. Chapter 9 by Kotthoff and Chapter 13 by Franklin), ethnic minorities (e.g. Chapter 12 by Roberts and Chapter 14 by Eades), and communities of practice (e.g. Chapter 8 by Marra and Holmes, and Chapter 21 by Corder and Meyerhoff). These types of groups are by no means exhaustive; they represent important types of cultural groups, but other types, such as professional groups, could equally well have been included.

2.   What are the 'problems' that need to be addressed?

Needless to say, intercultural communication can proceed very smoothly and successfully, and conversely, intracultural communication can be fraught with difficulties. Moreover, not every misunderstanding in intercultural encounters relates to cultural backgrounds. Sometimes social conflicts can be 'culturalized', in that the notion of culture is used as an excuse to mask political or economic conflicts or asymmetries. For example, in many Western countries, children with migration backgrounds are low achievers at school (see Scherr and Thielmann in this volume), and this often has more to do with insufficient language training programmes than with cultural problems.

Many social issues remain largely covert within a society, because they are regarded as normal within that culture. These include, for example, the fact that women and foreigners in many fields less often advance to the centre of power, and that they rarely reach the executive suites anywhere. Admission is not explicitly denied to them; rather, they are impeded in access through a low evaluation of their habitus (Bourdieu 1984), to which speech behaviour belongs. In the evaluation of a communication-stylistic habitus, conflicts of historicity and interests come into play. Not all social institutions necessarily value equality of opportunity. Culture is a system of diversities and tensions, and includes differences of power, differences in access to legitimate means of expressing power, and struggles over these means. This is especially true of the media. In the USA, for example, the state has almost completely withdrawn from Afro-American ghettos; in France the state likewise only very sporadically intervenes in big-city immigrant ghettos (to name only two examples). The schools in such districts scarcely deserve the name (Bourdieu 1997). The ghetto-worlds form their own subsystems, with a low standard of living, higher criminality, much violence and their own interactional norms and networks of connections. It makes little sense simply to confront such situations with a plea for recognition of diversity, because underlying many interethnic communication conflicts there are dynamics of inequality that are inscribed in the specific social order of that culture, with very different consequences for the participants.

So, then, what are the frequent 'real-world problems' in intercultural communication that the field, and hence this Handbook, need to address? The chapters in this volume deal with a very wide range of issues, including the following:

– Misunderstandings and the impact of cultural factors on the making of meaning;
– Conflict and the impact of cultural factors on relationship management and development;
– Gatekeeping and discrimination;
– The impact of unequal power relations on communication;

–   Business and management success in intercultural contexts;
–   Media impact in a globalized world;
–   Identity perception and communication;
–   Intercultural competence and assessment;
–   Intercultural adjustment and training.

There are no easy procedures for either understanding or dealing with these 'problems'. Instead, the authors in this volume explore the complex factors involved and suggest helpful ways of framing and addressing the challenges that the various 'problems' pose.

3.   What theories, data and research methods are needed to explore the 'problems'?

Even a cursory glance at these real-life intercultural communication 'problems' indicates that the discipline of applied linguistics is insufficient for addressing them adequately. A multidisciplinary approach is essential. Concepts and theories need to be based not only on (applied) linguistic research, but also on work in psychology, anthropology, sociology, political science, communication studies, and management studies in particular. Moreover, since intercultural communication can affect many different sectors of life, such as education, health, business, management, law, tourism, politics and diplomacy, the concerns and insights of these various sectors also need to be incorporated, and data needs to be collected from all such settings.

Different disciplines tend to focus on different issues, seek different kinds of data, and use different research methods to obtain and analyze that data. Such variation is reflected in the chapters of this volume. Many authors rely exclusively on discourse data (interpersonal and/or media discourse), some analyze self-report questionnaire data, and yet others refer to interview data. Others again use a combination of methods and data types.

Unfortunately, up to now, most intercultural communication research has tended to occur within a small number of disciplinary groupings: psychology and communication studies, business and management, and linguistics and anthropology/sociology. There has been a tendency to look down on the approaches used by the 'others', with the result that there is ignorance (either wilful or inadvertent) of each other's research. For example, many handbooks and manuals of intercultural communication training include no mention of applied linguistic research at all, even though there are many relevant insights for such training. This poses a challenge to applied linguists to communicate their findings more effectively to people from other disciplines. Non-linguists are often not interested in the intricate details of linguistic analysis, yet they may benefit from the thrust of the findings and may want just this 'thrust' to be com-municated.

As Madeleine Brabant, Bernadette Watson and Cindy Gallois argue at the end of their chapter (chapter 4) in relation to psychology and applied linguistics, there is great potential for more and deeper interactions between scholars of all fields who are interested in intercultural communication. This volume aims to help promote this process.

4.   What is the scope of this volume?

In the light of all the above, we have developed the following sections:

Section 1: Multidisciplinary perspectives on intercultural communication
Section 2: Intercultural perspectives on communicative practices and processes
Section 3: Intercultural communication in different sectors of life
Section 4: Issues and debates
Section 5: Assessing and developing intercultural competence

We introduce the foci and component chapters of Sections 1–5 at the beginning of each of the sections.

Notes:

1. Fredrik Barth has frequently shown in his research (1969) that cultural contact by no means suffices to minimize differences.

References:

Barth, Fredrik
    1969   *Ethnic Groups and Boundaries.* New York
Bourdieu, Pierre
    1984   *Distinction: A Social Critique of the Judgement of Taste.* Cambridge, Mass.: Harvard Univ. Press.
Bourdieu, Pierre
    1997   "Ortseffekte," in: Pierre Bourdieu (ed.), *Das Elend der Welt.* Konstanz, 159–169.
Gudykunst, William B.
    2000   Methodological issues in conducting theory-based cross-cultural research. In: Helen Spencer-Oatey (ed.), *Culturally Speaking. Managing Rapport through Talk across Cultures*, 293–315. London: Continuum.

Hymes, Dell
    1974   "Ways of Speaking." In: Richard Bauman und Joel Sherzer (eds.), *Explorations in the Ethnography of Speaking*, 433–451. Cambridge University Press.
Alfred Schütz
    1972   "Der Fremde." In A. Schütz (ed.), *Gesammelte Aufsätze*. Band 2. Den Haag: Nijhoff 53–69.
Schütz, Alfred
    1972   (ed.), *Gesammelte Aufsätze*. Band 2. Den Haag: Nijhoff.

I. Multidisciplinary perspectives on intercultural communication

Editors' introduction

Research on intercultural communication is a multidisciplinary endeavour. As early as the 18th century, researchers in disciplines such as psychology and anthropology were exploring how culture and language mutually influence each other and how this in turn impacts on thinking. Wilhelm von Humboldt (1767–1835) argued that language was the soul of a nation and that we could discover national characteristics by means of language analysis (von Humboldt 1997).

Section 1 of this handbook demonstrates the range of disciplines that contribute to research on intercultural communication, along with the variety of research methods that are used. The authors' areas of expertise include cultural anthropology, discourse analysis/interactional sociolinguistics, cognitive pragmatics, social/cross-cultural psychology, applied linguistics, social pragmatics and organizational behaviour. The types of data the researchers gather for analysis include questionnaire responses, interactional discourse and interview comments, and the foci of their interests range from the understanding of intercultural communication processes to the challenges of intercultural adjustment and the management of conflict.

In chapter 2, Gumperz and Cook-Gumperz, who are cultural anthropologists as well as linguists, focus on the question of how culture influences communication. They argue for a perspective which distinguishes between grammatical and semantic structures and the historical knowledge they encapsulate, on the one hand, and broader communicative processes, on the other hand. They use a number of interaction sequences to demonstrate what kinds of cultural knowledge are needed for appropriate inferences to be drawn and for cooperative interaction to take place. The authors outline developments within interactional sociolinguistics, a branch of applied linguistics that has, for more than thirty years, focused on the analysis of conversations in which participants have very different repertoires. The analytical methods used are empirical, and usually involve several steps: the recording of relevant situations followed by interviewing of key participants and checking with them about the researcher's interpretations of how local actors handle the problems they encounter. Building on the tradition of the ethnography of communication, which these two authors have strongly influenced, Gumperz and Cook-Gumperz maintain that researcher participation in cultural events is of vital importance for identifying the implicit knowledge of 'insiders'. With this empirical procedure, it has been found that contextualization cues, such as prosody, are highly important. When interpreted along with other grammatical and lexical signs, they construct a contextual ground for situated interpretation and thereby affect how particular messages are (mis)understood.

In chapter three, Vladimir Žegarac takes a cognitive pragmatic approach to explore similar questions to Gumperz and Cook-Gumperz: how culture contributes to context and how it influences communication. Starting from the concept of situation, he draws on the same key researchers (Goffman, Hymes) who inspired interactional sociolinguistics, and he also regards cultural variation as a result of diverse ecological circumstances. However, Žegarac interprets context in cognitive terms – as the set of assumptions exploited in utterance interpretation – and maintains that the concept of *mutual cognitive environment* can be relativized to culture in a way which brings us closer to an understanding of its role in communication. He discusses the distinction between intra-cultural and inter-cultural communication, arguing that there is a fluid transition between the two, and he demonstrates the explanatory value of cognitive pragmatics for analysing clashes of cultural assumptions and situation-based expectations. However, he acknowledges that knowing which assumptions will be in the mutual cultural environment of individuals from particular cultures is an empirical matter of the sort that social approaches to pragmatics are concerned with. This highlights a major difference in research approach: cognitive pragmatics pays less attention to the gathering of extensive discourse/interaction data, and tends to theorize from a small number of examples.

The next chapter, chapter 4, explores the contribution of psychology to the field of intercultural communication. Madeleine Brabant, Bernadette Watson and Cindy Gallois provide a succinct overview of the vast psychological literature in this area, and distinguish two major psychological approaches to the study of intercultural communication: one that focuses on intercultural communication competence and the skills that are needed for this, and one that focuses on intergroup communication. The authors briefly describe some well-known theories within each approach, including Gudykunst's anxiety and uncertainty management theory, Kim's cross-cultural adaptation theory, Tajfel's social identity theory, and Gallois' communication accommodation theory. Unlike linguistic approaches to intercultural communication, where the focus is on the details of the communicative interaction, both of these major psychological approaches focus primarily on the factors influencing people's behaviour in intercultural contexts, including cultural values (such as individualism–collectivism), attitudes, identity, and motivation to accommodate. The authors point out that psychologists' most frequently used instrument for data collection is the questionnaire, and in studies of intercultural communication processes where discourse data is analysed, they use simulated interaction data more commonly than authentic data. Brabant et al. conclude their chapter by calling for more and deeper interactions between psychologists and applied linguists, so that they can learn from each other, and complement each other's approaches to the field.

Chapter 5 is also written by psychologists, but deals with a more specific topic. David Matsumoto, Seung Hee Yoo and Jeffrey A. LeRoux focus on the issue of intercultural adjustment and the role that emotions play in this process. They see emotions as transient reactions to events or situations, involving cognitive, physiological, expressive and behavioural components. They argue that adjustments to new cultures often involve negative outcomes (e.g. emotional distress, dysfunctional communication, depression, anxiety, diminished school and work performance, and difficulties in relationships) and that an important goal of intercultural adaptation should be to minimize these negative outcomes and to maximize positive ones. The authors maintain that there are four psychological skills that can help this process and lead to personal growth: emotion regulation, critical thinking, openness and flexibility. They identify emotion regulation as the gatekeeper of this growth process. They then present a tool for assessing and predicting people's potential for intercultural adjustment – the intercultural adjustment potential scale (ICAPS) – and empirical evidence for its validity. They report findings from several studies which show that people who score high on emotion regulation have high positive social skills, more success in life, and are less likely to withdraw from active involvement with the social world. The authors conclude by arguing that emotion regulation is one of the most important psychological skills in our lives, and that it is vital for combating ethnocentric and stereotypic ways of dealing with people and for handling more effectively the increasing cultural diversity of our world.

The last chapter in this section, chapter 6, also deals with a specific topic. Nathalie van Meurs and Helen Spencer-Oatey take a multidisciplinary approach in exploring the issue of intercultural conflict. They incorporate frameworks, models and research findings from management studies, cross-cultural psychology, communication studies, and applied linguistics/social pragmatics. The authors start by discussing two classic frameworks for analyzing conflict: Thomas' 'grid' framework of conflict management orientations, and Brown and Levinson's face model of politeness. They consider the relative strengths and weaknesses of these two models, and the extent to which they can be synthesized. The authors then turn to the impact of culture on conflict. They describe the widely reported links between conflict and cultural values, but point out that one of the weaknesses of this macro level research is that it ignores a lot of contextual variation. Next, van Meurs and Spencer-Oatey explore the interconnection between conflict and communication. They critically discuss the widely cited link between directness–indirectness and the instigation and management of conflict, and point out that most research within the fields of management, cross-cultural psychology and communication studies use self-report data. They maintain that there is a great need for more discourse-based research into intercultural conflict, and they briefly review some applied linguistic studies on this topic. Throughout the chapter, the authors point out how little interchange there has been so far between applied linguistic researchers of conflict, and those working within organizational behaviour, communication studies and psychology. They conclude by calling for greater interdisciplinary sharing and discussion of ideas, of concepts and of findings.

Humboldt, Wilhelm von
  1997   On the national character of languages. In: T. Harden and D. Farrelly (ed.), 52–68. *Essays on Language*. Frankfurt: Peter Lang.

2. Discourse, cultural diversity and communication: a linguistic anthropological perspective

John J. Gumperz and Jenny Cook-Gumperz

1. Language difference and cultural relativity

Anthropology's critical contribution to intercultural communication is the insight that language differences affecting interpretation in everyday life are not just matters of semantics and grammar. Speaking and understanding also depend on the social situations in which verbal exchanges take place. Over the past four decades the developing field of linguistic anthropology has refined these initial insights into a theory of communicative practice that accounts for both universals of contexts and cultural differences in interpretation. The early post World War Two research on intercultural communication was bedeviled by the commonsense assumption that since language shapes the way we classify our experiential worlds and therefore think, communicating across cultural boundaries becomes inherently problematic. Popular writings on this issue appear in many forms, from undergraduate term papers to political arguments for language and immigration policies and reflect a "language myth" of essentialized cultural difference that many scholars have attempted to argue against e.g. Agar (2002); Bauer and Trudgill (1998).

While ideas akin to what we now call relativity have been debated at various times throughout history, particularly in the 18th and 19th centuries, it was not until the early part of the 20th century that the notion was systematized and integrated into the then prevailing empiricist academic tradition of linguistic and anthropological analysis of Boas, Sapir, Whorf. In particular, Whorf's popular writings (1956) and the striking examples he cited from his own professional experience as an insurance investigator, illustrated how semantic and grammatical inter-language differences may bring about potentially serious, sometimes fatal misunderstandings. This work brought linguistic and cultural relativity to the attention of a wider public. A second generation of scholars set out to test Whorf's findings by combining ethnographic fieldwork on culture with systematic linguistic research (Carol and Casagrande 1959). But as Lucy (1992) argues, these early attempts to validate Whorf's insightful and suggestive arguments through comparative analysis were theoretically and empirically flawed and unsuccessful. Following these failures, scholarly interest turned away from relativity to focus on universals of language and thought.

In their recent re-examination of the Sapir–Whorf hypothesis of linguistic and cultural relativity, Gumperz and Levinson (1996) argue that to the extent that linguistic categorization reflects cultural codes, these codes must be treated as historically created conventional ways of referring which do not necessarily determine what people do or think at any given time. To show how language can affect thought and lead to action we need to take a different and more detailed perspective on communication, a perspective which distinguishes between grammatical and semantic structures and the historical knowledge they encapsulate, on the one hand, and broader communicative processes that rest on language yet have special, often metaphoric, significance in evoking contexts and constructing social personae, on the other.

Take the following illustrative example:

Example 1
[Brief exchange between two women in an office, also discussed in Gumperz 1982]
A: Are you going to be here for ten minutes?
B: Go ahead and take your break. Take longer if you want.
A: I'll just be outside on the porch.
B: OK don't worry.

To make sense of this brief exchange we must begin from a position which assumes that communication in face-to-face encounters can be seen as constituted by interactive exchanges of moves and countermoves involving speakers and listeners who actively cooperate in the joint production of meaningful interaction (see Corder and Meyerhoff in this volume). The cultural knowledge that is needed to understand this exchange is common to many workplace situations that occur globally. In the present case we may begin by asking how we know that B's comment is a response to A's question? The assumptions that make these exchanges both appropriate, and in accord with accepted politeness conventions reveal an awareness of the relations between the two women that requires us to know a series of culturally specific details, such as that most offices are expected to have someone on duty during working hours, and that in this particular situation, office workers can determine their own break-times. The lexico-grammatical or denotational content of this exchange is simple, but inferences necessary to understand it rest on familiarity with a complex body of social relational assumptions that reveal culturally specific knowledge acquired through participation. The approach we illustrate here departs from established notions of culture as an abstract unitary set of community wide beliefs and norms, showing how human action depends on a variety of interactionally established cultural practices (see also Günthner in this volume). The challenge for the researcher/analyst interested in intercultural communication is to discover how these practices can be located in action by pursuing ethnographic investigations that relate to specific communicative situations.

2.   Ethnography of communication

The ethnography of communication approach introduced new perspective that focused on how language functions in actual ethnographically documented speech events, rather than on relations between community wide cultural norms and linguistic structures abstracted from talk. Begun in the 1960s, the ethnography of communication provided the insight that culture was essentially a communicative phenomenon, constituted through talk. It thus gave the impetus for the emerging linguistic anthropology of the 1980s and onward (Duranti 2001). Although as anthropologists we also speak of culture in quite general terms, we argue that we can study how culture works by observing or participating in a range of culturally distinct events. Building on the 1960s writings of Dell Hymes and others, the *Ethnography of Communication* (Hymes 1974; Gumperz and Hymes 1964, 1972; Bauman and Sherzer 1974) laid out an initial program of comparative research on language use that combines participant ethnographic field work with linguistic analysis. Roman Jakobson's notion of the speech event was adopted as an intermediate level of analysis that provides more access to the interpretive processes motivating participants' actions. Events are units of analysis in terms of which interpretive practices can be examined in detail. At the same time, events are also valorized entities that frequently enter into public sphere discussions about the event.

The early writings on speech events stimulated a great deal of comparative ethnographic research in various parts of the world on the relevant underlying cultural assumptions and structures of event performances, such as who could participate, what topics could be discussed, and on the social norms governing participation. Later on, as more empirical data became available, work began to focus on in-depth interpretive examination of the discourse that constitutes the event. The basic insight here is that the traditional analysts' community-level cultural categories neither demonstrably reflect what motivates account for speakers' actions ins everyday encounters. So far, however, most researchers have been concerned with specifying what such implicit knowledge is, not with how it enters into interpretations.

Examples of speech events typically described in the literature of the time are ritual performances, ceremonies, or magical rites such as are found in small, traditional, largely face-to-face societies, or encounters in urban minority speech events and routines. Most of the everyday encounters that are part of contemporary bureaucratic life, as many of the chapters in this volume demonstrate, such as the job interviews, counseling sessions, committee meetings, classroom lectures, medical encounters, and other informal encounters that we typically participate in during the course of our lives, also constitute speech events, as many of the chapters in this volume demonstrate. Yet, we also know that many intercultural situations differ from what we know from reading existing ethnographic accounts in that they are less sharply delimited and that we commonly employ event names only after the encounter, to convey something of what was done at the time. Such labels are not sufficiently refined to capture the details of what goes on. In a job interview, for example, a great deal of the time may be spent in casual talk, or narratives may be used to illustrate a point, anecdotes may be told, or elaborate instructions given, and so on.

At this stage it is useful to distinguish between different ways of analyzing interpretations. Initially, linguistic anthropologists relied on ethnographic observations to reveal the cultural assumptions that underlie interpretations. Somewhat later a second approach emerged that focuses directly on the organization of speech exchanges and takes a broader view of language as communicating both content and metapragmatic or indexical information about content. This later approach became known as interactional sociolinguistics (Gumperz 1982).

A new analytic concept that accounts for conversationalists' ability to distinguish among phases of an event and to reach agreement on what is intended at any one time has become established: the speech activity. In this we assume that in the initial phase of interpretive processes listeners seek to relate the ongoing talk to past experiences by categorizing what they see and hear as an instantiation of one or another activity type (Levinson 1983). Whereas speech events exist in time and space, the notion of activity type is used here to refer to mental models or schemata of goal-oriented actions. Such models yield criteria for judging what is expected and for inferring how what is said in the course of an event fits into a coherent whole. Agreement on what activity type is being enacted at any given time thus also implies agreement on culturally grounded inferences such as what the likely communicative outcomes are, what range of topics can be brought up, what information can be expressed in words, and what interpretations should be alluded to indirectly by building on shared understanding (Gumperz 1981, 1982).

The following example will illustrate some of these points.

Example 2
[New research assistant addressing the secretary of the research unit]
A: Good morning.
B: HI JOHN.
A: HOWDI.
B: HOW'RE YA DOIN?
A: Fine ... ah ... do you know – did you get anything back on those forms you had me fill out?

B: Hm ... like what?

A: I wondered if they sent you a receipt or anything or a copy of–

B: ==you mean your employment forms?

A: Yeah.

B: Yeah, I kept a copy. Why, is there a question?

A: Cause I just left it with the anthropology department.

B: Oh, that's OK, they'll just send them over to L. and S. and they'll send them on.

A: I just wanted to make sure they're OK.

B: Oh yeah. Don't worry about it.

This example could be described as a typical event within a university setting where a graduate research assistant enquires about his employment status. However, a single event classification is not sufficient to explain the details of the exchange, which involves a series of speech activities. Note, for example, that B replies to A's initial "neutral" greeting by shifting to a more informal "Hi." This leads to the second pair of greetings confirming the informality of the exchange. A then makes a tentative sounding enquiry leaving the exact nature of his request unspecified, leading B to ask for more information, so that four turns of talk are necessary before the reason for A's request is made clear. B realizes the need to give more information on the employment process.

In this exchange we can see that what is conveyed at any point is significantly affected by preceding talk, and in turn constrains what can follow. One cannot, therefore, assume that communicating is simply a matter of individuals transforming their ideas into signs by means of a culturally acquired code. Instead we concentrate on participants' own context-bound, situated, on-line processing of information. As in example 1, the participants rely on culturally acquired knowledge about institutional goals and procedures to arrive at their interpretations, that are then constantly adjusted during the interaction (see also Roberts in this volume).

In interpreting what they hear, interactants focus not just on the referential content of messages, but on what a speaker intends to communicate, as speech act theorists have already told us (Austin 1962; Searle 1969; Grice 1989). Empirical research on discourse and conversation over the last decades provides ample evidence to document this position. It has become clear in the course of this work that interpretations also rely on perceptions of extralinguistic context, knowledge of the world, as well as on the cultural presuppositions that are brought to the interaction (Atkinson and Heritage 1985). Everyday conversational interpretations are automatically produced, and their underlying mechanisms are not readily subject to conscious recall. They can only be studied by means of deductions based on comparative examination of speakers' and listeners' moves and countermoves, and for analytical purposes it is useful to assume that extralinguistic knowledge is introduced into the interpretive process in a series of stages roughly equivalent to Goffman's notion of frames (1983).

Erving Goffman's notion of frame offers a useful point of departure. In his highly suggestive treatment of interactive exchanges, Goffman argues that the principles that guide action in any given encounter are hierarchically nested in terms of levels of generality operating at various degrees of remove from the situation at hand, with each level acting like a membrane to filter out certain considerations while highlighting others (Goffman 1974). But Goffman did not attempt to present an explicit theoretical framework for empirical work. However, the development of linguistic anthropology around the notion of communicative practice provides a way of integrating cultural knowledge of speech situations and events into a wider approach to analyzing the cultural presuppositions involved in human action.

3.   Communicative practice and conversational inference

Understanding speech events rests on what Hanks (1996), following Silverstein (1992), calls communicative practice. Communicative practice provides a unifying concept for the analysis of context-bound everyday talk that enables us to deal with grammar and semantics as they enter into situated interpretation, along with cultural presuppositions that rely on two types of knowledge: a) grammar and lexical signs that signal via well known grammatical rules and lexical semantics and b) indexical signs, and among them contextualization conventions that signal by direct association between sign and context. Such indexical knowledge can only be acquired through interactive experience within a cultural environment.

Analytical procedures, including those developed and described in previous work at Berkeley in Interactional Sociolinguistics (Gumperz 1981, 1982), have drawn on the concepts of speech event, activity type and conversational analysis of sequential organization, as well as on notions of conversational inference and contextualization to provide a range of analytical tools for understanding communicative practice. Conversational inference is defined as the situated, context-bound process of interpretation by means of which participants in an exchange assess other participants' communicative intentions and on which they base their own responses (Gumperz 1982).

At a more local level of inference, interpretations are made about more immediate communicative tasks, as for example, how to respond to a particular move, how to initiate a topic, how to open or close an interaction, how to shift topics or distinguish main information from subsidiary points, how to make asides and, most importantly, how to allocate turns at talk and claim the floor. It is this level of verbal interaction, which we can refer to as conversational man-

agement, that has received the most attention in the by now well-known sociological research on conversational analysis. In an extensive series of studies of
sequencing phenomena, conversational analysts have provided convincing evidence to document the many hitherto unnoticed and largely unconscious ways
in which the maintenance of conversational involvement depends on active interpersonal cooperation and show the interactional complexity of conversational management (Schegloff 2003; Duranti and Goodwin 1992; Levinson
1983). But the main goal of this tradition of conversational analysis is the discovery of the recurrent sequentially ordered patterns or structures by which conversations are managed. The focus is on what is common to conversational exchanges in general. Conversational analysts do not account for the on-line
processing that individuals must do in maintaining conversational cooperation
with specific persons, nor do they attempt to deal with the role of context and
cultural presuppositions in conversation.

4.   Interpretation in interaction

Much of what has been learned so far about interpretation in discourse applies to
situations where at least some level of conversational cooperation can be taken
for granted and some shared inferences assumed. The aim is to find empirical
ways of showing through discourse analysis whether or not interpretive procedures are shared (see Kotthoff in this volume). What is analyzed is conversational inference, defined as the interpretive procedure by means of which
interactants assess what is communicatively intended at any point in an exchange
and on which they rely to plan and produce their responses. As pointed out
above, individuals engaged in conversation do not just react to dictionary or referential meaning. The analytical problem is to reveal the hypothesis formation
process by which participants assess what others intend to communicate.

To give a further example:

Example 3
Imagine that Bill had just observed Tom talking to Fred, and Bill asked Tom
what he and Fred had been doing. Tom then might answer, "I asked Fred if he
was FREE this evening." Bill might infer that Tom is planning to join Fred in
some activity, although literally speaking this is clearly not what the utterance
"meant."

The process of interpretation here is something like the following: a) based on
his linguistic knowledge, Bill perceives that Tom is putting unusually strong
stress on FREE (here as elsewhere in the paper capitalization marks extra
stress); b) Bill can thus infer that Tom is using stress as a contextualization cue;

and c) his background knowledge tells him that this sort of stress is often used when a speaker has a proposal to make. Therefore he seems justified in drawing the inference that the speaker had some activity in mind. And this is what motivates his inference. Such an interpretation is of course not the only possible one. The background knowledge Bill relied on was acquired through past communicative experience.

Where background knowledge or indexical signaling processes are not shared, interpretations may differ, and this is precisely what tends to go wrong when people who differ in cultural knowledge interact. Focusing on communicative practice does not solve the problem of interpretive ambiguity. The aim is to detect what it is about speakers' linguistic and cultural background that leads them to a particular interpretation. This is of course quite different from assessing the truth or falsity of specific interpretations. Situated on-line interpretation that reveals both what the most likely inferences are and how participants arrive at them can be shown to be useful in studies of inter-cultural and inter-ethnic communication in detecting systematic differences in interpretive practices affecting individuals' ability to create and maintain conversational involvement.

5.   Misunderstandings as a resource for generalizations about communicative practice

Throughout the chapter we use excerpts from urban encounters to show how discourse analysis of the linguistic anthropologists' notion of context-bound communicative practice has begun to reshape our understanding of the complexities of communication in everyday situations. To reiterate: what the presuppositions are that enter into conversational inference and how they are reflected in talk varies among other things with speakers' and listeners' communicative background. The sharing of inferential procedures cannot be taken for granted; it must be demonstrated through ethnographically informed in-depth analysis of what transpires in an encounter. A main purpose of analysis is to show how diversity can affect interpretation. Some of the best known studies in interactional sociolinguistics were in fact carried out in urban workplace settings where laymen who are under great pressure to perform must deal with experts whose interpretive premises are quite different from their own and therefore operate with different background assumptions (Gumperz 1981, 1982; Gumperz and Roberts 1991, Roberts in this volume). Analysis of such situations can reveal the nature of the inferential process.

Now consider the following brief excerpt from a set of selection interviews for individuals who, having lost their positions are applying for paid traineeships at a publicly funded institution offering instruction in skills that are in short supply. In each case R is the interviewer and T the applicant.

Example 4
Electrician
1 R: Have you visited the skills center?
2 T: Yes, I did.
3 R: So you've had a look at the workshops?
4 T: Yes.
5 R: You know what the training allowance is? Do you?
6 T: Yeah.
7 R: Do you know how much you've got to live on for the period of time.

Bricklayer
1 R: Have you visited the skills center?
2 T: Yep. I've been there. yeah.
3 R: So you've had a chance to look around? And did you look in at the brick shop?
4 T: Ah yeah. We had a look around the brick shop and uhm, it looks OK. I mean itsn–
5 R: All right.
6 T: Pretty good yeah.

Note that while the interviewer asks roughly the same questions in each case, the two applicants differ in the way they answer. The electrician provides only minimal replies (e.g. yes, yeah, yes I did), he offers no information on his own. The bricklayer, on the other hand, adds personal comments. And as a result he succeeds in engaging the interviewer in a less formal exchange. For example, in turn 2 he replies with a sentence of his own, which leads the interviewer to suggest that he approves of the facilities. Then in turn four the bricklayer begins as if about to express an opinion, but then he pauses as if searching for the right expression. Whereupon the interviewer helps him by supplying a suitable expression, and the exchange ends on a note of agreement. The electrician, on the other hand, receives no such help. In fact, as R's question in turn 7 suggests, he appears not to be sure how interested the applicant is in the workshop and its facilities.

If it is revealed that the electrician is a non-native born Asian worker, and the bricklayer a British native from the local region, it could be argued that ideological prejudices against non-natives is at work in these interviews. While there is little question that ideology is an important factor in such encounters, the experience referred to as prejudicial is often hidden by the indirectness of interactional exchanges, as in Example 4, where no one utterance appears to directly express any disagreement or negativity. However, neither participant, the interviewer or the interviewee, might infer that the exchange was satisfactory. This and other similar workplace interviews suggest, that the treatment the two applicants receive is also to a significant extent due to the fact that, based on their communicative background, interviewers and applicants draw different inferences from what they see and hear, and taken together these inferences cumulatively lead to different outcomes. Miscommunications of the above type can be detected after the fact through close analysis of the extent to which moves are coordinated in interactional exchanges. We can identify highly cooperative exchanges where listeners readily respond to speakers' moves, where interruptions and repairing or correcting what was said are relatively infrequent, and thematic shifts are smoothly negotiated. The linguistic-pragmatic evidence for cooperation can be found at two levels: a) in the interpretive relationships or semantic ties among successive moves, and in the degree to which second speakers are successful in making the expected inferences from a first speaker's indirect speech acts; b) in the rhythmic synchrony of the conversational exchange (Erickson 2004). Analyses of such inferential processes can provide evidence to show how such differences depend on recognition of contextualization cues (Gumperz 1982).

The potential for miscommunication is a function of differences in taken-for-granted, culturally specific knowledge acquired in the course of socialization experiences and differences in discourse conventions. While grammar plays a role in discourse, it enters into the communicative phenomena we have discussed only inasmuch as it affects our ability to understand what the communicative intent is at a particular point in an utterance. Indexical signs are also essential to discourse level understanding. This suggests that, contrary to what applied linguists and anthropologists have tended to assume, the mere fact that native language differences exist does not necessarily have serious consequences for understanding and the maintenance of conversational cooperation. Both participants in the above example had lived and worked in Western industrial settings for much of their adult lives, but they had brought with them different linguistic and cultural background experiences that continue to resonate in these encounters.

6.   Interactional sociolinguistics' contribution to intercultural communication

The contribution of interactional sociolinguistics to inter-cultural communication involves the unraveling of instances of interpretative ambiguity at the level of discourse like those that have been discussed in this chapter. The aim is to find plausible interpretations, i.e., solutions that are plausible in that they show how constituent actions cohere in the light of the event as a whole, and the assumptions in terms of which we assess its significance. This is of course quite different from determining the truth or falsity of specific interpretations. The method resembles the conversational analyst's procedures of reconstructing the strategies members employ in formulating specific actions, but it differs from conversational analysis in that the concern is with the situated interpretation of communicative intent, not with strategies as such, and in that analysis is not confined to overtly lexicalized information. Instead of taking interpretive processes for granted, it suggests a) what the most likely interpretations are and b) what the assumptions are and the inferential processes by which they are achieved.

Empirical studies employ the following procedures to deal with the problem of interpretive ambiguity. First, there is an initial period of ethnographic research designed to: a) provide insight into local communicative conventions; b) discover the recurrent types of encounters most likely to yield communicative data relevant to the research problem at hand; c) find out through observation, interviewing key participants and checking one's own interpretations with them of how local actors handle the problems they encounter and what their expectations and presuppositions are. In the second stage, the ethnographic findings provide the basis for selecting events reflecting representative sets of interactions for recording. Analysis begins with the scanning of the recorded materials at two levels of organization: a) content and b) pronunciation and prosodic organization. The aim is to isolate sequentially bounded units, marked off from others in the recorded data by some degree of thematic coherence and by beginnings and ends detectable through co-occurring shifts in content, prosody, or stylistic and other formal markers. Extending the ethnography of communication practice somewhat, the term event is used to refer to such temporally organized units. The aim is to discover segments of naturally organized interaction containing empirical evidence to confirm or disconfirm the analyst's interpretations, evidence against which to test assumptions about what is intended elsewhere in the sequence.

Once isolated, event recordings are transcribed, and interactional texts (that is transcripts that account for all the communicatively significant, verbal and non-verbal signs perceived) are prepared by setting down on paper all those perceptual cues: verbal and nonverbal, segmental and non-segmental, prosodic, paralinguistic and other cues that, as past and on-going research shows, speakers and listeners demonstrably rely on as part of the inferential process. This procedure enables us not only to gain insights into situated understandings, but also to isolate recurrent form–context relationships and show how they contribute to interpretation. Relationships can then be studied comparatively across events to yield more general hypotheses about members' contextualization practices.

Contextualization can take many linguistic forms. Among the most important are the choice among permissible linguistic options at the level of pronunciation, morphology, syntax or lexicon – as in code or style switching, the use of intonation or tone of voice, speech rhythm or pausing, and the use of formulaic phrases or idiomatic expressions that have particular interactional import. It follows that shared knowledge of contextualization conventions is a precondition for conversational cooperation. Where conventions are not shared, participants are unable to agree on what activity or communicative task is being enacted. They might, but need not necessarily, find themselves unable to predict where the conversation is going or how to integrate what is said into a coherent whole, so that the interaction becomes unpredictable. If attempts at turn allocation or topic shift negotiation fail, conversationalists are in the position of strangers lost in a foreign city who must try to find their way without being able to rely on road signs (Gumperz 1992).

In interactional analysis, speaking is treated as a reflexive process such that everything said can be seen as either directly reacting to preceding talk, reflecting a set of immediate circumstances or responding to past events, whether directly experienced or indirectly transmitted. To engage in verbal communication, therefore, is not just to express one's thoughts; speaking ties into a communicative ecology that significantly affects the course of an interaction. We use the term 'contextualization' cue to refer to any linguistic sign which, when processed in co-occurrence with symbolic grammatical and lexical signs, serves as an indexical sign to construct the contextual presuppositions that underlie situated interpretation and thereby affects how constituent messages are understood. Code switching is one type of contextualization cue; others include phonetic enunciation, along with prosody (i.e. intonation and stress), rhythm, tempo and other such supra-segmental signs (Gumperz 1991: 229–252). Contextualization cues, when interpreted along with other grammatical and lexical signs, construct the contextual ground for situated interpretation and thereby affect how particular messages are understood (Gumperz 1982). As metapragmatic signs, contextualization cues represent speakers' ways of signaling and providing information to interlocutors and audiences about how language is being used at any point in the ongoing exchange. What sets them apart from communicatively similar indexical signs like "here" and "there" is that they are for the most part intrinsically oral forms. Since no utterance can be made without such signs, contextualization cues are ever present in talk, and to the extent that they can be shown to affect interpretation, they provide direct evidence for the necessary role that indexicality plays in talk. In conversation we could not possibly express all the information that interlocutors must have to plan their own contributions and adapt their talk to that of their interlocutors, so that it is easy to see the reason for this indexical signaling.

Finally, and perhaps most importantly, indirect (not overtly lexicalized) signaling mechanisms are for the most part culturally specific. That is, they reflect conventions that speakers and listeners have learned over time by cooperating and living with others, and in that sense they are cultural conventions (see Coder and Meyerhoff in this volume).

How interactional sociolinguistics views the identification of contextualization cues as a process of understanding can be illustrated in the following way:

"Sometime ago, while driving to the office, my radio was tuned to a classical radio station. At the end of the program, the announcer, a replacement for the regular host, who was scheduled to return the next day, signed off with the following words: I've enjoyed being with "*YOU these last two weeks." I had not been listening very carefully, but the unusually strong focal accent on "*you" in a syntactic position where I would have expected an unaccented pronoun caught my attention. It sounded as if the announcer were talking to someone else. Yet there was no other person with him on the program. This led me to search my memory of past communicative experience to construct an alternative, more plausible scenario that might suggest an interpretation. The speaker's words reminded me of a leave taking exchange where a first speaker might begin with "I've enjoyed being with you," and the second might respond with "It was fun being with you." I therefore inferred that the announcer, by accenting the personal pronoun as one would in the second part of the exchange, was actually implicating the first" (p. 222: Gumperz 2001).

A second, somewhat more complex example comes from an analysis of the cross-examination transcript of a victim in a rape trial (Gumperz 1992):

Example 5
Counsel: You knew at the time that the defendant was interested in you, didn't you?
Victim: He asked me how I'd BEEN ... just stuff like that.

Our interpretation of the above exchange relies on what is known about cross-examinations as adversarial proceedings where the defense attorney attempts to expose weaknesses in the victim's testimony to explain what happened (see Eades in this volume). But while general knowledge of such courtroom practices tells us something about participants' motives in courtroom situations, we need to turn to what they actually said to understand what they intended to convey. By means of the words he used and by the way he contextualized his talk, that is choosing to begin with an assertion and following it with a tag question, the attorney was attempting to induce the audience to infer that the victim had had a prior relationship with the defendant. The victim's move, on the other hand, positioned and pronounced as it is immediately after the attorney's question, argues for a different scenario. Her phrase "how I'd been" with the accent on "been," is a form of reported speech which in this context evokes the intertextually related formulaic expression "how've you BEEN," commonly employed by people who have not met recently. We thus infer that she is suggesting that she and the attacker were merely casual acquaintances. In this way she managed indirectly to contest the attorney's argument, without openly challenging him and running the risk of appearing overly aggressive.

In each of the above cases the interpretations relied on the retrieval of the background knowledge necessary to construct possible scenarios or envisionments, or in some instances to inter-textually recall specific expressions in terms of which the speaker's words made sense. Both "activity type" and "activity" refer to such evoked envisionments, and the interpretation of communicative intent rests on these envisionments. They can be seen as abstract representations of the actions of actors engaged in strategically planning and positioning their moves in order to accomplish communicative ends in real life encounters. In the envisioning process actors rely, among other things, on ideologically based and contextually specific presuppositions about mutual rights and obligations, assumptions about individuals' personal characteristics apart from their knowledge of grammar and the indexical function of specific signs to get their message across. This implies that, in addition to meaning assessments in the established sense of the terms, inferencing always depends on constantly negotiated and renegotiated interpersonal relationships by means of the same verbal signaling process with which content is assessed.

Note that we have used the term 'activities' rather than 'genre' in this chapter to highlight our emphasis on ongoing communicative practices as the main object of analysis. The notion of genre has become a part of many recent analyses of texts, largely as the result of the influence of Bakhtin's writings, known in English through two key compendium translations (1981; 1986). As we see it, Bakhin's use of genre was intended as part of his critique of early structuralist linguistics, and as such can be seen as having some commonality with the idea of speech activities. A fuller discussion of this point must wait for a later paper (see Günthner and Kotthoff's preface to section II for the use of 'genre')

By revealing the underlying interpretive process at work in an encounter, which is otherwise bound to remain hidden, such analyses of key situations in institutional life can provide insights into the interpretive bases of communicative assessments. At the same time, such analyses can enable participants to learn from the difficulties that arise in an encounter.

7.   Conclusion

The encounters discussed here constitute a range of settings that are marked by historically and linguistically quite distinct traditions. Examples like these are useful in illustrating how inferential processes are grounded in both linguistic and other background knowledge. They also show how the social outcomes and consequences of communicative alignment or misalignment can be far more extensive than any one analysis can show. Over time such miscommunication can seriously affect individuals' ability to adapt to new communicative circumstances and therefore their life chances. Discourse conventions are learned through interpersonal contact. Learning requires a great deal of feedback, and it is the quality of the learning situation that determines learning. Most favorable to learning are peer situations, where speakers can give each other the benefit of the doubt and feel that they can make mistakes without fear of being misjudged. Hierarchical situations, where feedback opportunities are constrained by norms governing conduct, are less conducive to learning. This means that not all individuals of a certain ethnic background encounter communication problems. Those who enter a new society as individuals are more likely to learn the new discourse conventions than those who migrate to live with others who share their background. When people settle in groups, they may adopt a new language but, in their interpersonal contacts, they are likely to develop discourse conventions based on previous communicative experience that are perceived as discrepant by other outsiders. As some of the examples cited here show, analysis of communicative practice can serve as a means of monitoring and thereby gaining ordinarily unavailable insights into those everyday life communication processes that have become so important in today's diverse communicative environments (Cook-Gumperz and Gumperz 2002).

References

Atkinson, Maxwell and John Heritage
  1985   *Structures of Social Action.* Cambridge and New York: Cambridge University Press.
Agar, Michael
  2002   *Language Shock.* New York: William Morrow.
Austin, John. L.
  1962   *How to do Things with Words.* London and New York: Oxford University Press.
Bakhtin, Mikhail M
  1981   *The Dialogic Imagination. Four essays.* Ed. by Michael Holquist. Transl. C. Emerson & M. Holquist. Austin, Texas: University of Texas Press
Bakhtin, Mikhail M
  1986   *Speech Genres and other late essays.* Ed by Carl Emerson & Michael Holquist. Transl. V. McGee. Austin, Texas: University of Texas Press.
Bauer, Laurie and Peter Trudgill
  1998   *Language Myths.* London: Penguin Books.
Bauman, Richard and Joel Sherzer
  1974   *Exploration in the Ethnography of Speaking.* Cambridge and New York: Cambridge University Press.
Carrol, John B. and Joseph Cassagrande
  1958   The function of language classifications. I. Behaviour. In: Eleanor E. Maccoby, Theredore M. Newcomb and Elizabeth L. Hartley (eds.), *Readings in Social Psychology,* 18–31. New York: Henry Holt.
Cook-Gumperz, Jenny and John J. Gumperz
  2002   Gatekeeping interviews: intercultural differences or common misunderstandings? *Language and Intercultural Communication* 2(1): 25–37.

Corder, Saskia and Miriam Meyerhoff
this volume Communities of practice in the analysis of intercultural communication.
Duranti, Alessandro
    2001   *Linguistic Anthropology: a Reader.* Oxford and Malden, MA: Blackwell
        Publishers.
Duranti, Alessandro and Charles Goodwin
    1992   *Rethinking Context: Language as an Interactive Phenomenon.* Cambridge
        and New York: Cambridge University Press.
Eades, Diana
this volume Understanding Aborginial Silence in Legal Contexts. Chapter 14.
Erickson, Frederick
    2004   *Talk and Social Theory.* Cambridge and Malden, MA: Polity.
Goffman, Erving
    1974   *Frame Analysis, an Essay on the Organization of Experience.* New York:
        Harper Row.
Goffman, Erving
    1983   The interaction order. *American Sociological Review* 48: 1–17.
Grice, Paul
    1989   *Studies in the Way of Words.* Cambridge, MA and London: Harvard Univer-
        sity Press.
Günthner, Susanne
this volume Intercultural Communication and the Relevance of Culture Specific Reper-
        toires of Communicative Genres
Gumperz, John J.
    1978   The conversational analysis of interethnic communication. In: E. Lamar
        Ross (ed.), *Interethnic Communication.* Athens, GA: University of Georgia
        Press.
Gumperz, John J.
    1981   *Discourse Strategies.* Cambridge and New York: Cambridge University
        Press.
Gumperz, John J.
    1982   *Language and Social Identity.* Cambridge and New York: Cambridge Uni-
        versity Press.
Gumperz, John J.
    1992   Context and understanding. In: Alessandro Duranti and Charles Goodwin.
        Rethinking Context: Language as an Interactive Phenomenon, 229–252.
        Cambridge and New York: Cambridge University Press.
Gumperz, John J.
    2001   Interactional Sociolinguistics: a personal perspective in *The Handbook of
        Discourse Analysis.* Ed. by D.Schiffrin, D.Tannen H. E. Hamilton. Oxford
        & Malden MA: Blackwells Publishing.
Gumperz, John J. and Jenny Cook-Gumperz
    2005   Language standardization and the complexities of communicative practice.
        In: Susan Mackinnon and Sydel Silverman (eds.), *Complexities: Beyond
        Nature and Nurture,* 268–288. Chicago and London: University of Chicago
        Press.
Gumperz, John J. and Dell H. Hymes
1972/1986 *Directions in Sociolinguistics.* Oxford and Boston: Blackwell.

Gumperz, John J. and Stephen C. Levinson
  1996   *Rethinking Linguistic Relativity.* Cambridge and New York: Cambridge
            University Press.
Gumperz, John J. and Celia Roberts
  1991   Understanding in intercultural encounters. In: Jef Verschueren and Jan
            Blommaert (eds.), *Proceedings of the 1987 International Pragmatics As-
            sociation Meetings*, 51–90. Amsterdam and Philadelphia: John Benjamins.
Hanks, William
  1996   *Language and Communicative Practice.* Boulder, CO: Westview Press.
Hymes, Dell H.
  1974   *Foundations of Sociolinguistics.* Philadelphia: University of Pennsylvania
            Press.
Kotthoff, Helga
this volume Ritual and Style in Intercultural Communication.
Levinson, Stephen C.
  1983   *Pragmatics.* Cambridge and New York: Cambridge University Press.
Lucy, John
  1992   *Language, Diversity,and Thought: a reformulation of the linguistic relativ-
            ity hypothesis.* Cambridge&New York: Cambridge University Press.
Roberts, Celia
this volume Intercultural Communication in Healthcare Settings.
Schegloff, Emmanuel
  2003   *Discussing Conversation Analysis.* Edited by Paul T. Thibaut and Carlo L.
            Prevignano. Amsterdam and Philadelphia: John Benjamins.
Searle, John
  1969   *Speech Acts: an Essay in the Philosophy of Language.* Cambridge and New
            York: Cambridge University Press.
Silverstein, Michael
  1992   In: John A. Lucy (ed.), *Metapragmatic Discourse and Metapragmatic
            Function*, 33–58. Cambridge: Cambridge University Press.
Whorf, Benjamin Lee
  1956   *Language, Thought and Reality:selected writings of Benjamin Lee Whorf.*
            ed. J.B.Caroll Cambridge MA: MIT Press.

3.   A cognitive pragmatic perspective on communication and culture[1]

Vladimir Žegarac

1.   Introduction

> I would define a social situation as an environment of mutual monitoring possibilities, anywhere within which an individual will find himself accessible to the naked senses of all others who are 'present', and similarly find them accessible to him.
>
> Goffman ([1964] 1972: 63)

The impact of Erving Goffman's work on the development of social approaches to human interaction has been immense, but the fundamentally cognitive character of his definition of "social situation" – clearly reflected in the notion of "mutual monitoring" – has been largely ignored. This is apparent in the way the term *situation* is characterized within Fishman's (1972: 48) sociolinguistics (as "the co-occurrence of two (or more) interlocutors related to each other in a particular way, communicating about a particular topic, in a particular setting"), in Halliday's (see Halliday and Hasan 1976: 22) functionalist view of language (where *field*, *mode* and *tenor* are the key determinants of situations), in Hymes' (1972) ethnographic approach to communication (in which the categories of *setting, participant, end, act sequence, key, instrumentalities, norms of interaction and interpretation*, and *genre* provide a template for analysing communicative events) and in much other work in the loosely defined field of (social) pragmatics. To be sure, these authors are aware of the psychological nature of *situation*. Thus, Halliday and Hasan (1976) observe:

> The term SITUATION, meaning the 'context of situation' in which a text is embedded, refers to all those extra-linguistic factors which have some bearing on the text itself. A word of caution is needed about this concept. At the moment, as the text of this Introduction is being composed, it is a typical English October day in Palo Alto, California; a green hillside is visible outside the window, the sky is grey, and it is pouring with rain. This might seem to be part of the 'situation' of this text; but it is not, because it has **no relevance** to the meanings expressed, or to the words or grammatical patterns that are used to express them [emphasis VŽ].
>
> Halliday and Hasan (1976: 21)

Despite the general awareness that the concept of (*communication*) *situation* calls for a psychological explanation, existing definitions of this term tend to have a distinctly externalist-descriptive, rather than an internalist-explanatory flavour. The main aim of this article is to provide an introductory internalist, cognitive-psychological, account of communicative interaction in the context of culture. The lack of anything approximating a universally accepted theory of communication or a universally accepted theory of culture inevitably makes this endeavour possible only with some radical corner-cutting.

Although several natural points of contact between communication and culture have been identified in commonsense terms, the indissoluble link between the two has defied explanation. The following passage provides some intuitive support for the cognitive, Relevance-theoretic approach (Sperber and Wilson 1986/95) on which this article is based:

> Over time, the habitual interactions within communities take on familiar forms and structures, which we will call *the organization of meaning*. These structures are imposed upon the situations which people confront and are not determined by the situation itself. For example, the wink of an eye. Is it a physical reflex from dust in the eye? Or an invitation to a prospective date? Or could it be someone making fun of you to others? Perhaps a nervous tick? The wink itself is real, but its meaning is attributed to it by observers. The **attributed** meaning may or may not coincide with the **intended** meaning of the wink. Effective social interaction, though, depends on the **attributed** meaning and **intended** meaning coinciding [emphasis VŽ].
>
> Trompenaars and Hampden-Turner (1997: 24)

This passage suggests the following view: culture is a stable system of relations between (visible) things in the environment of people ("forms and structures") and their (invisible) significances, shared by a social group. (Note that the terms *cultural* and *social* are nearly synonymous. Following the common practice in social psychology and anthropology, I will call *cultural* those social things which are relatively stable and widespread.) This view of culture as a phenomenon suggests that particular cultures should be thought of as having fuzzy boundaries and that they can be identified in terms of indefinitely many various characteristics of social groups (such as: ethnicity, nation, profession, age group, sexual orientation).

Communication is different from other forms of social interaction in that it involves making evident the intention to convey information by integrating the evidence of this intention with the context. (It should be noted that the term *context* is used more broadly in social than in cognitive approaches to pragmatics. In social approaches *context* is the total linguistic and non-linguistic background to an act of communication. In Sperber and Wilson's (1986/95) cognitive account of communication, this term refers to a set of mentally represented assumptions which interacts with new information from various sources, including communication.) It is this communicative intention (i.e. the intention to make evident the intention to inform) that crucially distinguishes a (deliberate) wink from an involuntary twitch, which is also informative because it may provide evidence for various conclusions, such as: *the twitch was caused by dust in the eye*. The concept of *communicative intention* is important, because people generally pay attention to those phenomena which are evidently produced with the intention to convey information. For example, we tend to pay attention and attribute meanings to blinks, which we recognize as deliberate, rather than to twitches, which are likely to remain unnoticed, because they are not perceived as produced with the intention to convey information. Whilst culture is characterized by meanings shared within a social group, communication is a mode of social interaction through which new meanings can come to be shared. However, communication is generally at risk of failure, because the attribution of meaning depends on the interlocutors' ability to reason in the way intended by the communicator and to select the right context for the interpretation of the communicative act. As there is no guarantee that the addressee will interpret the communicative act in the way intended by the communicator, there can be no guarantee that the attributed and the intended meanings will coincide. Since a person's cultural knowledge crucially determines the contexts which are available to them, the risk of miscommunication is generally higher in interactions between people from different cultural backgrounds. Therefore, a plausible account of *inter*-cultural communication should provide answers to the following questions:

– What is cultural knowledge?
– How does cultural knowledge contribute to context?

I try to show that the theoretical backbone of Sperber's (1996) epidemiological approach to culture and Sperber and Wilson's (1986/95) Relevance-theoretic approach to communication provide explicit and well-motivated answers to these questions. The article is structured as follows: first, some of the main tenets of Relevance Theory are illustrated with a few examples of (inter-cultural) communication. Second, the epidemiological approach to culture is introduced, and a way of characterizing the distinction between *intra-* and *inter*-cultural communication is suggested. Finally, the framework of Relevance Theory is outlined in order to show how the contribution of cultural background to the context can be integrated with this approach to communication in a principled way.

2.   Examples of a Relevance-theoretic account of (inter-cultural) communication

In Relevance Theory terms, human cognition is geared towards improving the belief system of individuals and the most important type of social interaction through which this goal is pursued is called ostensive-inferential communication. On this view, an act of ostensive behaviour (such as a pointing gesture, a [deliberate] wink, or an utterance) makes evident the communicator's intention to inform the addressee/audience of something. Comprehension is an inference (i.e. reasoning) process which takes the evidence presented by the communicative act (i.e. an ostensive stimulus) and the context as inputs, and yields interpretations as outputs. These tenets of Relevance Theory are illustrated by the following examples of (*inter*-cultural) communication:

(1) A British family had lived in an African country for several years. They had become familiar with the local language and culture. After the break-out of civil war in the region, they were forced to leave the country. Before leaving, they accepted the local peoples' offer of help and asked them to try and "rescue" some of their "special things". Quite some time later, they were somewhat surprised to find that their TV set and video recorder were the main rescued items.

In this case, the British participants did not take account of the context (i.e. the set of assumptions) in which their interlocutors would interpret the phrase "special things", despite their knowledge of the local culture (most likely, because they had to divide their attention between several pressing concerns, which made them revert to their more intuitive cultural mindset).[2]

In other instances of miscommunication, the intended interpretation is recognized, but it is not accepted. Consider Example (2):

(2) [The following is an extract from an interview with Haldun Aydingün, the author of the book *The Divorced Man*, described in the Cyprus Turkish Airlines' in-flight magazine *Caretta* (September 2005) as "an entertaining look at the institution of marriage, how the institution and, more importantly, a break with this institution, affects men and their behaviour".]

Interviewer:
You make allusions to the male make-up and even say, "I wish the male body had a control button that would suppress sexual impulses". On the other hand, it is clear that you value faithfulness and the institution of marriage. Aren't these two somewhat contradictory?

Interviewee:
No, not in the manner you have just described. What I was trying to communicate here was the fact that the male sexual impulse was very basic, a need that had to be met. If sexuality is expressed in a healthy way in marriage then there is a chance that marriage and faithfulness can be non-contradictory.

The interviewee's intention to communicate that he holds modern views on gender relations is very salient in the interview from which this excerpt is taken. However, rather than accepting this message, many (Western European) readers will be more convinced by the inadvertently produced evidence of the interviewee's old-fashioned views which may easily appear sexist, or, at least, not politically correct, in the modern Western world (e.g. *A man's sexual needs are naturally stronger – more basic – than a woman's*; *Men are not able, or they are less able than women, to control their sexual impulses*, etc.). So, in this instance, communication will be less than successful in case the communicator has inadvertently conveyed some belief-assumptions which contradict those that he evidently intends to convey.

Miscommunication may also arise because some evidence of the communicative intention has not been recognized by the addressee:

(3) At a meeting recently held in Japan, an American was discussing two alternative proposals with his colleagues, all of whom were native speakers of Japanese. The American was well schooled in the Japanese language and was, indeed, often called "fluent" by those around him. At this meeting, proposal A was contrasted to proposal B, and a consensus was reached about future action, and the meeting then dismissed. Upon leaving the room the American commented, "I think the group made a wise choice in accepting proposal A". A Japanese colleague, however, noted, "But proposal B was the group's choice". The American continued: "But I heard people say that proposal A was better". The Japanese colleague concluded, "Ah, you listened to the words but not to the pauses between the words".

Brislin (1978: 205), quoted in Gutt (2000: 78)

In this situation, pauses were intended to be recognized as produced with the intention to convey something important for the interpretation of the words used (i.e. that the speaker merely acknowledges the hearer's view, whilst rejecting it politely). The hearer misunderstood the utterance because he had overlooked the communicative intent behind the pauses due to his lack of appropriate contextual cultural knowledge about the way pauses are used as ostensive stimuli.

The success of genuine communicative acts, such as (1) to (3), depends on the informative intention being recognized. However, in many situations the fulfilment of the informative intention depends on the informative intention not being recognized. Consider:

(4) Situation: Zoë, a final year undergraduate, was waiting to see one of her lecturers to discuss her dissertation topic with him. After the lecturer had asked her a couple of times to wait a little bit longer, Zoë came up with an alternative action plan, and said, roughly:

"That's alright. I'll come to see you later this week. I'll first go and talk about it with Chloë. She's already started working on her dissertation, so she can help me with the topic".

What did Zoë intend to communicate to her lecturer? She overtly communicated that she did not mind coming another time and that she would come to see him much better prepared as a result of talking first to a fellow student. That was the informative intention that Zoë made evident (i.e. her communicative intention). But the lecturer drew a further conclusion on the basis of what Zoë had said. In his opinion, Zoë's friend Chloë had been going about her dissertation project in a way which did not provide the best example to follow, so he insisted that Zoë should stay and discuss her topic with him. As Zoë had not said (or otherwise made evident) anything that would indicate a negative attitude towards the lecturer, she did not communicate that she disapproved of waiting, that she did not think much of the help the lecturer would give her, that she would like to know what the lecturer thought about Chloë's work, and so on. A couple of years after she had graduated, the lecturer saw Zoë. He asked her if she remembered this incident and he told her how she had inadvertently made him change his mind, so he decided to talk to her without further delay. But Zoë corrected him: "No! That worked!" She explained that she had had the intention to inform the lecturer that it was desirable that he should see her promptly, but rather than making this intention evident, she had concealed it, hoping that he might reason in the way he actually did.

This example illustrates an important general point: in instances of overt communication, the communicator makes the informative intention evident and, in doing so, takes responsibility for what is communicated. There are various reasons for not wanting to convey information overtly, but people generally resort to covert social interaction when they do not wish to take responsibility for what they are trying to convey or when making the informative intention evident would jeopardize its fulfilment. In the situation described in (4), Zoë's informative intention (that the lecturer should change his mind and see her promptly, possibly also that he should reveal his opinion of Chloë's work) was fulfilled because it was concealed successfully.

Covert forms of information transmission are particularly important in intercultural social settings. For example, what might be a successful way to conceal the evidence of a particular informative intention in one culture, may seem transparent in the context of another. The following excerpt, taken from an open letter by the Cyprus Turkish Airlines' Acting Manager, published in the airline's in-flight magazine *Caretta* (September 2005), clearly illustrates this point:

(5) Welcome Aboard

> The hot summer season will soon be a thing of the past. Unfortunately, the aviation sector has experienced some uncomfortably hot moments this summer as well. The accident involving a plane from Southern Cyprus saddened all of us deeply. We would like to take this opportunity to convey our condolences to the people of Southern Cyprus and the aviation community.

> This accident, which grieved all of us so deeply, has shown once again just how seriously the aviation sector must take its responsibilities.
>
> [...]
>
> The Helios crash has been yet another reminder to the entire sector that there must not be negligence in even the smallest details.
> Our company has always operated with this mindset, constantly increasing and strengthening its precautions and efforts regarding flight safety and will continue to host its passengers with confidence.

The text from which this excerpt is taken makes evident the informative intention to express solidarity with another airline and the people affected by the accident, but many readers will reject this informative intention, because of what they take to be compelling evidence for the conclusion that the writer has a covert aim, a hidden agenda, as it were: to put down a rival company in order to promote his own. What must have seemed a clever and legitimate marketing move to the writer of the letter, is seen as a transparent, hypocritical and insensitive marketing ploy in the cultural context of many people in the intended readership.

These examples point to the importance of culture in context selection. Therefore, an explanatory approach to *inter*-cultural communication should provide an account of the way cultural knowledge is represented and used in communication.

3.   The epidemiological approach to culture

Like some other animals, humans represent mentally various aspects of the world they live in. Unlike any other animals, humans have the ability to form *metarepresentations*, i.e. belief-representations (*beliefs* hereafter) about the mental representations of their physical and psychological environments. Their ability to do this is evidenced by all things which are part of culture: a given thing is a hammer, not in virtue of the representation we form of its shape, form and other visible features, but because we make such representations the objects of various beliefs (e.g. that the thing in question is used for a particular purpose). To give another example, consider the mental representation of a particular thing (let's call it *A*) as a small stone. It is easy to think of circumstances which may lead one to make the mental representation: *A is a small stone* the object of beliefs, such as: *A is a small stone which can be used to keep the door open*, or *A is a small stone which can be used to prevent paper from flying off the desk when the window is open*. When such beliefs about the representation of *A as a small stone* become accepted by the members of a social group, A becomes an artefact: a doorstop or a paperweight. Of course, a typical artefact is a thing which has been designed and produced with a specific purpose in mind. However, what makes it a cultural thing is the existence of widespread and stable beliefs about (mental representations of) it, rather than the fact that it has been consciously designed and produced. It should also be noted that, when a mental representation of a psychological phenomenon, say, the emotional experience of anger, is metarepresented – in other words, when the representation of the direct experience of this emotion is made the object of some beliefs (such as: [this] *is the way one feels when something unpleasant one does not want to happen happens, although its occurrence could/should have been avoided*) – the direct emotional experience of anger becomes "visible" to the mind, and, therefore, available for symbolic representation and communication. In sum: the metarepresentational capacity is the human mind's capacity to think about itself and it is the biological prerequisite for the emergence of cultural categories.

Some important differences between the communicative behaviour of people and animals suggest that the metarepresentational capacity is unique to humans. For example, it is often observed that animals engage in complex forms of social behaviour: bees pass on to other bees information about the location of pollen-rich fields and lions hunt in groups by ambushing their prey. But a bee which "reads" another bee's dance gets the information content directly, as it were, without making the dance or its information content the object of beliefs (see von Frisch 1967). To give another example, we can realistically imagine a group of lions preparing for the hunt by taking positions through monitoring each other's movements and coordinating their actions in remarkably complex ways. However, the idea of lions planning the hunt by drawing lines in the sand and indicating with pebbles their respective positions relative to their prey is rather far-fetched. The ability to do this would involve the lions making representations such as: *A is a pebble*, the object of beliefs, such as: *A is a pebble which represents that antelope over there that we could hunt down*. But lions, bees and other animals do not have the metarepresentational capacity (i.e. the capacity to form beliefs about mental representations). That is why they are not capable of reasoning feats which even young children find easy and intuitive, or of the type of symbolic communication that comes naturally to humans. (This account of the role of *metarepresentations* in explaining culture simplifies greatly. For a more detailed discussion, see articles in Sperber 1996, 2000.)

While the metarepresentational capacity provides the basis for explaining our ability to think about our own and other people's minds and for the possibility of symbolic action, the theory of culture needs to explain how particular cultural representations emerge and spread. For example, we ought to be able to give an account of the way small wedge-shaped objects come to be thought of as doorstops, or how a given symbol, such as the expression "special things" in (1), comes to denote different sets of objects in different societies. In a series of publications Dan Sperber (see Sperber 1985, 1996) has developed the idea that explanations in the domain of culture should focus on a particular relation between psychological and ecological influences. On his view, a defining feature of social-cultural things is the relation between forms and structures, which are by and large in the environment of people, and mental representations, which are in individual people's minds/brains. Therefore, cultural categories should be seen as resulting from interactions between *intra*-individual, cognitive-psychological, mechanisms responsible for our ability to interpret the world, and *inter*-individual, social-cultural, mechanisms, such as communication, which enable us to disseminate these representations within and across human populations (see Sperber 1996: 49). On this view, cultures are not natural kinds. Rather, they consist of relatively stable patterns of a particular type of metarepresentation, which I will call *cultural representation*:

> Cultural representation: a metarepresentation which involves a stable three place relation between:
> – a mental representation (of a physical entity, event, direct emotional experience, etc.);
> – a belief about this mental representation (e.g. hammer, doorstop, love, anger); and
> – a sizable population made up of individuals (a nation, an ethnic group, an age group, a professional group, etc.) who share the same, or very similar, beliefs about particular types of mental representations over significant time spans.

Cultural representations emerge and spread through causal chains which involve mental representations and public productions (utterances, texts, pictures, artefacts in the environment of individuals) which are reproduced repeatedly and reasonably faithfully, thus achieving stability and wide distribution, through a process (very sketchily) illustrated in figure 1.

Figure 1. Schema of the causal chain involved in the spreading of cultural representations.

This approach is articulated in the context of an analogy between the study of culture and the study of epidemics. Just as there is no epidemic without individual organisms being infected by particular viruses or bacteria, there is no culture without representations being distributed in the brains/minds of individuals. This analogy is very suggestive in several ways. For instance, it is often observed that culture is both an individual and a social construct (see Matsumoto 1996: 18). There is no epidemic without diseased individuals, but the study of epidemics cannot be reduced to the study of individual pathology. By the same token, a culture cannot exist without some cultural representations being in the brains/minds of individuals, but it does not follow that the study of culture can be reduced to the study of individual psychology. Just as infections are in individual people's bodies, mental representations are in their minds/brains. And, just as the spreading of diseases is explained by investigating the interaction between strains of micro-organisms with the environment that they live in, the distribution of cultural representations is explained in terms of communicative, as well as other types of, interaction between people and their environment. From this perspective, the boundaries of a given culture are not any sharper than those of a given epidemic. An epidemic involves a population with many individuals being afflicted to varying degrees by a particular strain of micro-organisms over a continuous time span on a territory with fuzzy and unstable boundaries. And a culture involves a social group (such as a nation, ethnic group, profession, generation, etc.) defined in terms of similar cultural representations held by a significant proportion of the group's members. In other words, people are said to belong in the same culture to the extent that the set of their shared cultural representations is large. This characterization of a culture naturally accommodates the existence of multicultural nations, professions, etc. It also suggests a straightforward characterization of sub-culture, as a set of cultural representations within a given culture which are shared (mainly) by a subset of its members (e.g. teenagers, members of particular professions, different social classes within a national or ethnic cultural group, and so on).

On this view, individual cultures are epiphenomenal, rather than natural, things which owe their identities to the joint influences of a range of historical, political, economic, and various other factors. Therefore, *intra*-cultural communication could be characterized as communication between participants who share most cultural representations, and *inter*-cultural communication, as communication between participants who share few cultural representations. This raises the following questions: how similar does the shared set of cultural representations of two individuals need to be, for communication between them to be considered *intra*-cultural? And conversely, how small should their shared set of cultural representations be, for communication between them to be considered *inter*-cultural? Plausible answers to these questions can be given in the context of two observations. First, some cultural representations are intuitively more important, or central, than others. This intuition seems to be based on two facts: (a) some cultural representations are more causally efficacious than others in terms of the extent to which they inform the beliefs and guide the actions of those who hold them, and (b) some of the beliefs and actions which are informed by cultural representations pertain to a greater number of spheres of social life than others. Therefore, the *centrality* of a cultural representation could be characterized as follows:

Centrality of a cultural representation
A cultural representation is central to the extent that it is causally efficacious across many spheres of social life.

For example, a system of religious beliefs may influence virtually all aspects of social life, whilst fashions tend to be, not only relatively short-lived, but they may also be confined to relatively isolated social-cultural domains (e.g. how to dress when going to a party). Therefore, cultural proximity/distance is a joint function of the number and the centrality of cultural representations:

Cultural proximity/distance
Two or more individuals/groups are culturally close to the extent that their shared set of cultural representations is large and to the extent that the centrality of these cultural representations is high.

OR:

Two or more individuals/groups are culturally distant to the extent that their shared set of cultural representations is small and to the extent that the centrality of these cultural representations is low.

Clearly, the greater the cultural closeness between people, the more able they will be to make accurate estimates of each other's cognitive resources (e.g. about the contextual assumptions available to other members of the same cultural group), and the better the chances of communicative success between them will be. Thus, in examples (1), (2), (3) and (5) cultural distance played a major role in the communicators' failure to achieve their goals.

Second, the shared cultural knowledge of two or more people may be adequate for communication in some situations, whilst being inadequate for communication in other situations. Therefore, the distinction between *intra*- and *inter*-cultural communication should be related to situations of communication:

Situation of intra-cultural communication
A situation of communication in which the cultural distance between the participants is not significant enough to have an adverse effect on communicative success, so it need not be specially accommodated by the participants.

Situation of inter-cultural communication
A situation in which the cultural distance between the participants is significant enough to have an adverse effect on communicative success, unless it is appropriately accommodated by the participants.

This approach has a clear implication for the way in which research in the field of inter-cultural communication might proceed:

(i)   establish the extent to which the intended and the attributed meanings of a given communicative act coincide;
(ii) find out the similarity between the context in which the communicative act was actually interpreted, and the context intended by the communicator;
(iii) find out the extent to which cultural representations have contributed to the gap between the actual and the intended context, and
(iv) assess the impact of those cultural representations on communicative success (taking account of their centrality).

An important methodological aspect of research along these lines is that it is informed by robust intuitions about interpretations of communicative acts and by empirical findings based on evidence from a range of different sources. Note that these findings are independent of, and more reliable than, any of the theoretical concepts which guide the research, so they can provide a reasonably solid basis for testing hypotheses about the impact of culture on communication between participants from particular cultural groups in particular situations.

The importance of this methodological observation is further highlighted by a major difference between cultures and epidemics. Epidemics result from the replication of micro-organisms designed to multiply by producing virtually identical copies of themselves. What needs to be explained are the circumstances in the environment which favour the emergence and the success of strains of micro-organisms which are different from, rather than being identical copies of, their ancestors. In contrast to bacteria and viruses, human brains/minds are designed to transform, rather than to replicate, representations in the normal mode of operation. We generally synthesize information forming new representations on the basis of perceptual inputs from the environment and already held representations. The outputs of such processes are new representations which are more or less similar, rather than identical, to the input ones. For example, reports of what a person has said only exceptionally preserve the exact form of the speaker's original utterance, and back-translation seldom results in a text identical to the source-language original. Only in exceptional circumstances do representations with highly similar forms and contents replicate without significant changes over long time spans, thus becoming part of culture.

This observation has two important consequences for the study of culture. On the one hand, it suggests that cross-cultural similarity is more surprising than cultural diversity. Since people live in vastly different physical environments, we might expect that cultures should differ rather more widely than they actually do. So, the main task for a theory of culture is to explain systematic cross-cultural similarities. On the other hand, cultural variation is the result of the diverse ecological circumstances in which human populations live. Therefore, it is extremely unlikely that these cultural variations fall in the scope of a general theory. Instead, descriptions and explanations in the social-cultural domain ought to be concerned with the study of the distribution of various cultural categories (e.g. artefacts, genres, art forms, "codes" of behaviour, etc.) in the context of a handful of fairly simple universal cognitive mechanisms and of myriad ecological factors. To give but one example, we are used to thinking of carrots as being of an orangey colour. In fact, the orange carrot is largely a cultural innovation which originated in Holland only several centuries ago, when the Dutch made their national colour the colour of the carrot. Before that time carrots, apparently, used to be of a dark-purplish hue. But this is not sufficient to explain the lasting (cross)-cultural success of this designer vegetable. It seems plausible to assume that our biological disposition to associate some colours, such as orange, with edible things, more readily than others, such as dark-purple, is a universal psychological factor which most likely played an important role in the appeal of orangey carrots to people. Of course, the cross-cultural success of the orange carrot also owes a great deal to other ecological factors, including cultural achievements, such as the advent of fairly effective means of transportation, international travel, and so on. In other words, orangey carrots were successful because they were persistently intuitively perceived as more desirable than their purplish ancestors, and because their production and transportation were relatively economical. This is a general point: successful cultural things are those which preserve an appreciable degree of perceived *relevance* in relatively large human populations over relatively significant time spans. Clearly, the term *relevance* can be used as a measure of (likely) cultural success only provided it is given explicit theoretical content.

4.   Relevance in cognition

The stability of representations over time and their geographical distribution owe much to a general functional feature of human cognition: its orientation towards improving the belief system of individuals. If this is indeed a major function of human cognition, then it should be characterized in terms of an efficiency measure, a cost benefit relation of some sort. This is true of any thing that has a function, as the following analogy with purposeful artefacts illustrates:

> Efficiency is some measure of benefit divided by cost. The benefit of a pot could be measured as the quantity of water that it holds. Cost can conveniently be measured in equivalent units: the quantity of material of the pot itself. Efficiency might be defined as the volume of water that a pot can hold divided by the volume of material that goes to make the pot itself.
>
> Dawkins (1996: 7)

Since the function of both communication and cognition is to bring about improvements in individuals' belief systems, cognitive gain constitutes the benefit side of the equation. As humans have finite cognitive resources and limited time for reasoning, planning and decision making, it seems plausible to assume that processing effort is the cost parameter in this cognitive efficiency measure. Sperber and Wilson (1986/95) call this measure relevance and define it as follows:

> Relevance
>
> A phenomenon is relevant to an individual:
> (a) to the extent that the cognitive effects achieved when it is processed in context are large, and
> (b) to the extent that the processing effort required for achieving the effects is small.
> Adapted from Sperber and Wilson (1986/95: 153)

On this view, the effect–effort ratio is not measured by mapping values on a numerical scale. People's estimates of effect and effort are based on the monitoring of symptomatic physico-chemical changes, and, when they are represented mentally, they take the form of judgements which are intuitive and comparative, rather than consciously calculated and absolute. These intuitive judgments are not merely retrospective but prospective: people have intuitions about how relevant the processing of a phenomenon is likely to be, not merely about how relevant a phenomenon which has been processed has turned out to be (cf. Sperber and Wilson 1986/95: 130–131). This characterization of relevance provides the basis for the following law-like generalization about human cognition:

> The Cognitive Principle of Relevance:
> Human cognition tends to be geared to the maximization of relevance.
> Sperber and Wilson (1995: 260)

The human cognitive system's orientation towards relevance provides one part of the explanation for the emergence and the success of cultural categories, including artefacts. On this approach, a plausible account of the success of the orange carrot might go, roughly, as follows: orangey carrots seemed more edible than purplish ones. Clearly, the assumption that a particular plant is edible generally interacts with other assumptions in more productive ways than the assumption that it is not likely to be edible (e.g. how to include it in various recipes). So, representations of orangey carrots seemed more relevant than those of purplish ones on the cognitive effects side. Moreover, if we assume that the two types of carrot are known to be equally beneficial foods, then representations of orangey carrots, which are more readily (that is, more intuitively) thought of as edible, will seem more relevant on the mental effort side as well: other things being equal, the more desirable a thing looks, the more cognitively salient it will be. And, the more cognitively salient something is, the less processing effort will be required for its mental representation and processing. It is interesting to note that the supremacy of orangey carrots is currently being challenged by research which shows that various types of non-orangey carrots (still grown in some parts of the world) are rich in natural substances which reduce the threat of cancer.[3] In light of general knowledge about the link between cancer and food, as well as the growing awareness of the increasing incidence of cancer, non-orangey carrots are likely to begin to seem more and more relevant to more and more people, largely as a result of the dissemination of representations of their beneficial properties by means of communication.

5.   Relevance in communication

Most of the time a vast range of stimuli impinge on our senses at a fairly high rate. Some of these stimuli pre-empt our attention (e.g. loud noises, flashes of light, etc.), thus creating an expectation that processing them will yield significant cognitive effects. Finally, some attention pre-empting stimuli are designed to create – and to be recognized as designed to create – the expectation that they are worth paying attention to (e.g. a [deliberate] wink, the sound of a door bell, a pointing gesture, an utterance, an unexpected silence or pause in speech, etc.). This last type of stimuli are called *ostensive stimuli*, and as mentioned in section 2, their use in conveying information is called ostensive-inferential communication. To recognize a stimulus as ostensive entitles the addressee to presume that whoever produced it did so because they thought this stimulus was worth paying attention to. Consider the following exchange from Chekhov's play *Three Sisters*:

6) Vershinin: … It's nice living here. But there's one rather strange thing, the station is fifteen miles from the town. And no one knows why.
    Soliony: I know why it is. [*Everyone looks at him*] Because if the station were nearer, it wouldn't be so far away, and as it is so far away, it can't be nearer [*An awkward silence*].

    Chekhov, *Three Sisters,* Act One

Soliony's conversational contribution is likely to meet with his interlocutors' disapproval because they have been made to expend gratuitous processing effort. By engaging in communication, Soliony creates the expectation that what he has to say deserves the attention of the others. In other words, he issues a promissory note to the effect that his interlocutors' expectation of cognitive reward will be fulfilled. As his remark is clearly irrelevant, he fails, not merely to fulfil an expectation that his interlocutors happen to have formed, but to honour a promise that he has made.

To sum up: human communication involves the production and interpretation of ostensive stimuli, which make evident the communicator's intention to convey some belief-assumptions. The communicator, by making evident her intention to inform the addressee, effectively issues a kind of promissory note to the effect that the utterance (or other ostensive stimulus) is worth paying attention to. The Cognitive Principle of Relevance makes it possible to spell out the conditions under which this promise has been honoured: an act of communication is worth paying attention to, provided that doing so will lead to the derivation of enough cognitive effects to warrant at least some attention, without gratuitous expenditure of processing effort.

These observations on the role of the Cognitive Principle of Relevance in ostensive-inferential communication are more formally captured by the following generalization, known as the Communicative Principle of Relevance:

Communicative Principle of Relevance:
Every act of ostensive communication communicates a presumption of its own optimal relevance.

Sperber and Wilson (1995: 260)

Presumption of Optimal Relevance:
(a) The ostensive stimulus is relevant enough for it to be worth the addressee's while to process it.
(b) The ostensive stimulus is the most relevant one compatible with the communicator's abilities and preferences/goals.

Adapted from Sperber and Wilson (1995: 270)

The principle of relevance provides the basis for a production strategy (followed by the communicator) and a comprehension strategy (followed by the addressee):

Relevance-Theoretic Production Strategy
Given your preferences/goals, choose the least effort-demanding option for the hearer.

Žegarac (2004: 203)

Relevance-Theoretic Comprehension Strategy
(a) construct interpretations in order of accessibility (i.e. follow a path of least effort)
(b) stop when your expectation of relevance is satisfied.

Adapted from Carston (2002: 380)

The communicator's choice of signal is guided by two factors: their assumptions about the addressee (the addressee's knowledge and reasoning abilities) and the communicator's own preferences or goals. Thus, in examples (1) to (3), the communicator's poor assessment of the addressee's/audience's cognitive resources (more specifically, the availability and salience of particular contextual assumptions to the addressee/audience) is the cause of miscommunication. In (4) and (5), communicators try to manipulate the addressee/audience by concealing their informative intentions. Overt (i.e. ostensive) communication is a particularly efficient means for spreading representations, precisely because ostensive stimuli are presumed to come from a helpful source: if the addressee can assume that the ostensive stimulus is the best one that the communicator could have chosen in order to convey a particular set of belief-assumptions, they are in a position to narrow their search for cognitive effects. The interpretation (i.e. the set of cognitive effects) which is most salient in the addressee's immediate context, is also the most likely to be optimally relevant. If it is not, the context is suitably adjusted (by discarding some assumptions and introducing others) until enough effects are derived for the communicative act to be found consistent with the Principle of Relevance (or until processing is abandoned and communication fails). Such adjustments to the context draw freely on the addressee's world knowledge, more technically, their cognitive environment:

> Cognitive environment (of an individual)
> The set of assumptions that are manifest to an individual at a given time.
>
> Carston (2002: 376)

Informally, the term "manifest" means "salient". In Relevance Theory, manifestness is defined as follows:

> Manifestness (of an assumption to an individual)
> The degree to which an individual is capable of mentally representing an assumption and holding it as true or probably true at a given moment.
>
> Carston (2002: 378)

The concept of cognitive environment is crucial in explaining ostensive-inferential communication, because a person's cognitive environment sets a limit on the contexts which are available to them. The concept of manifestness points to the fact that the cognitive environments of two (or more) people may differ, not only with respect to which assumptions are available to them at a given time, but also in terms of the extent to which they are able to represent them mentally and to use them in mental processing. Therefore, in deciding which ostensive stimulus to use, the communicator needs to assess which contextual assumptions are available to the addressee and how manifest they are to them. These judgements are based on the communicator's presumptions about the participants' shared cognitive environment. More technically, they are based on their mutual cognitive environment:

> Mutual cognitive environment
> A cognitive environment which is shared by a group of individuals and in which it is manifest to those individuals that they share it.
>
> Carston (2002: 378)

The notion of mutual cognitive environment is important because it sets a limit on the possibilities of communication, as illustrated in (7):

(7) Situation: Kiki, a mutual acquaintance/friend of Maria's and Peter's, had told Peter in April that Maria would be coming to England in May, and that she was planning to see a few people, including him. She also asked him not to tell Maria that she had informed him of her planned visit. Peter was surprised, but he kept the "secret". He did not meet up with Maria in England as he was away on business at the time of her visit. However, unknown to Peter, Kiki disclosed to Maria what she had told him. So, for the next few months, he remained under the impression that Maria was unaware of his knowledge of her visit to England. The following is an excerpt from their chat on the internet in which the assumption that Maria visited England in May, which was already in Peter's and Maria's shared cognitive environment, became mutually manifest to them:

[1] Peter: Are you going on holiday for the New Year and Christmas?
[2] Maria: Haven't quite made up my mind yet, but I'm probably going to Barbados to see Sharon and visit some other friends as well.
[3] Peter: Sounds good. Are you planning to visit England again?
[4] Maria: No, I did last June.
[5] Peter: Yeah, when I was in Beijing!
[6] Maria: Yes, when Kiki told you. I almost killed her!

People have clear intuitions about the distinction between assumptions which are mutually manifest (i.e. presumed shared) and those which are merely shared. For example, prior to the exchange in (7), the assumption *Maria visited England in June* was in Peter's and Maria's shared cognitive environment, but it was not in their mutual cognitive environment. Peter's affirmative response, [5], indicates that a previously shared assumption has now become mutually manifest to Maria and to him, and this opened up the possibility of communication on the topic of her visit to England earlier in the year.

It is important to note that the term (mutual) "manifestness" refers to the psychological disposition for mental representation. In (7), the assumption that Peter and Maria had known all along that Maria had visited England in June, became highly (mutually) manifest to them. Therefore, they represented it mentally, becoming fully conscious of it. However, the mutual cognitive environment that people draw upon in communication largely consists of background assumptions which are presumed shared by all people, or, at least, by all members of a particular community or group. Following Searle (1980), Carston (2002) refers to this set of assumptions as Background (with a capital *B*) and characterizes it as follows:

We might usefully think of Background as a set of assumptions and practices that maintains a fairly steady degree of not very high manifestness, across time, in an individual's cognitive environment. A subset of the Background consists in assumptions/practices which make up the mutual cognitive environment of all (non-pathological) human beings – the deep Background; other subsets are the mutual cognitive environments of what can loosely be termed culturally defined groups of human beings – local Backgrounds.

Carston (2002: 68)

Background is a useful technical term in that it identifies a subset of the interlocutors' presumed shared beliefs which play an important role in communication. For example, if any of the Background assumptions do not hold, the speaker should indicate this clearly. Failure to do so inevitably goes against the Principle of Relevance. Consider Example (8):

(8) Mary: I saw Peter yesterday.

Given our Background knowledge about people, it would not be rational for Mary to say: *I saw Peter yesterday* in order to convey the idea that she saw parts of Peter scattered round the room. According to the Principle of Relevance, the hearer is entitled to treat certain assumptions about the physical properties of people as taken for granted. These Background assumptions are not communicated, because they are already (presumed) held at maximal strength. Therefore, they do not need to be represented consciously in a given situation of communication.

Many cultural representations are an important part of the local (i.e. cultural) Background. They too are generally mutually manifest to the members of particular groups. They can be, and often are, taken for granted in communication between people who presume that they belong in the same culture. These cultural representations tend to be so intuitive to those who hold them that they often appear natural, rather than conventional, so they too are seldom consciously represented. That is why they are typically the loci of miscommunication in situations of inter-cultural communication, which suggests that cross-cultural training should focus primarily on the differences between the trainee's and the host group's local Backgrounds.

In light of these observations, the notions of cognitive environment and mutual cognitive environment can be related to cultural knowledge as follows:

Cultural environment (of an individual)
The set of cultural representations which are manifest to an individual at a given time.
(In other words, the proper subset of an individual's cognitive environment which consists only of cultural representations.)

Mutual cultural environment
A cultural environment which is shared by two or more individuals and in which it is
manifest to those individuals that they share it.
(In other words, the proper subset of the mutual cognitive environment of two or
more people, which consists only of cultural representations.)

On this view, the cultural environment of an individual is a subset of that individual's cognitive environment, and the mutual cultural environment of two or more people, is a subset of their mutual cognitive environment. The terms *cultural environment* and *mutual cultural environment* are useful because they provide a principled basis for distinguishing between issues relating to context selection in *inter-* and *intra*-cultural communication. Thus, in examples (1), (2), (3) and (5) miscommunication is largely due to the communicators' incorrect estimates of their and the addressee's/audience's mutual cultural environments. Of course, which assumptions will be in the mutual cultural environment of individuals from particular cultures is an empirical matter of the sort that social approaches to pragmatics are concerned with.

In Relevance Theory terms, communication involves the production and the interpretation of evidence of the communicative and the informative intentions. This evidence may be more or less conclusive. The more conclusive the evidence for some belief-assumptions presented by a communicative act, the more strongly those assumptions are communicated by that act. The Relevance-theoretic notion of communicative *strength* provides the basis for explaining the commonsense notions of *direct* and *indirect* communication. A particular assumption, or set of assumptions, has been communicated directly to the extent that the communicative act presents the addressee with conclusive evidence of the communicator's intention to make that assumption, or set of assumptions, more manifest. And conversely, the less conclusive the evidence of the communicator's intention to communicate a particular assumption, or set of assumptions, is, the more indirectly, i.e. *weakly*, that assumption, or set of assumptions, is communicated. It should be clear that what counts as sufficiently conclusive evidence of a particular communicative (or informative) intention in one culture, may be hopelessly poor evidence of this intention in the context of another. For example, in the situation described in (3), the Japanese participants presumed that pauses in their speech presented sufficiently strong evidence of their communicative intentions to be noticed by the American participant, whilst presenting suitably weak evidence of their informative intention to convey a rejection of the American participant's chosen plan. In Relevance-theory terms, the comprehension of a communicative act which presents less conclusive evidence for a particular informative intention requires more processing effort than one which presents more conclusive evidence for that informative intention. Therefore, a communicator aiming at optimal relevance should always choose the ostensive stimulus which provides the most conclusive evidence of their informative intention. It follows from this, that a communicative act which communicates a particular set of assumptions more weakly than is necessary for communicating that set of assumptions, will prompt the addressee to derive further contextual (i.e. cognitive) effects in order to offset the extra processing effort required for the interpretation. In other words, the addressee will assume that the informative intention is also somewhat different from that which would have been communicated by a more direct communicative act. Thus, the pauses in (3) communicate, not merely the rejection of the American colleague's chosen plan, but also some degree of concern on the part of the communicators for his positive face (see Brown and Levinson 1987). This suggests that cultural differences in the appropriate degree of (in)directness in communication, such as the one illustrated in (3), receive a natural explanation within the epidemiological approach to culture and the framework of Relevance Theory. The pervasive use of subtle ostensive stimuli within a society depends on the extent to which the mutual cultural environment of its members includes representations about their appropriate use. As Kate Berardo has impressed upon me, such a mutual cultural environment is more likely to be established in a relatively close-knit isolated society, such as Japan, which went through a period of two hundred and fifty years of cultural isolation. In contrast to the Japanese culture, the US culture emerged in a melting pot of diverse cultural influences in which the mutual cultural environment of its members was rather restricted, and this explains why the use of subtle ostensive stimuli, and various forms of communicative indirectness which depend on such stimuli, could not have developed and stabilized in US culture to the same extent as they did in Japan.

6.   Conclusion

In this article I have tried to show how Sperber's (1996) epidemiological approach to culture and Sperber and Wilson's (1986/95) Relevance-theoretic account of human communication and cognition jointly provide an intuitive, simple and effective framework for analysing situations of *inter*-cultural communication. In particular, I have argued that the concept of *mutual cognitive environment* – in effect, a theoretically motivated equivalent of what Goffman ([1964] 1972: 63) termed "an environment of mutual monitoring possibilities" – can be related to culture in a way which brings us closer to an understanding of culture's role in communication.

Notes

1. In writing and rewriting this article I have benefited greatly from the help of many people. Special thanks to Robyn Carston and Helen Spencer-Oatey who always had time for my frequent queries, and also to Kate Berardo, Joy Caley and Anna Mantzouka who have in various ways directly contributed to the content of this text. The responsibility for all the remaining flaws is mine.
2. Of course, whether the denotation of a particular expression, in this case "special things", is determined culturally or by individual people's values, attitudes etc. needs to be established on the basis of appropriate (ethnographic) evidence. In the situation described in (1), the evidence, which for space reasons cannot be presented here, strongly supports the view that electrical goods were considered particularly precious in the local culture.
3. See http://www.cals.wisc.edu/media/news/02_00/carrot_pigment.html for more information.

References

Brislin, Richard W.
  1978   Contributions of cross-cultural orientation programmes and power analysis to translation/interpretation. In: David Gerver and Wallace H.W. Sinaiko (eds.)/ *Language, Interpretation and Communication*. Proceedings of the NATO Symposium on Language and Communication, Venice, 26 Sept–1 Oct 1977. New York: Plenum Press.
Brown, Penelope and Steven Levinson
  1987   *Politeness*. Cambridge: Cambridge University Press.
Carston, Robyn
  2002   *Thoughts and Utterances: The Pragmatics of Explicit Communication*. Oxford: Blackwell Publishing.
Dawkins, Richard
  1996   *Climbing Mount Improbable*. London: Penguin Press.
Fishman, Joshua
  1972   The sociology of language. In: Pier P. Giglioli (ed.), *Language and Social Context*, 45–58. London: Penguin Books.
Goffman, Erving
  1964   The neglected situation. *American Anthropologist* 66 (6–2): 133–136. Reprinted in: Pier P. Giglioli 1972 (ed.), *Language and Social Context*, 61–66. London: Penguin Books.
Gutt, Ernst-August
  2000   *Translation and Relevance*. Manchester: St Jerome Publishers.
Halliday, Michael Alexander Kirkwood and Ruqaiya Hasan
  1976   *Cohesion in English*. London: Longman.
Hymes, Dell
  1972   Models of the interaction of language and social life. In: John Gumperz and Dell Hymes (eds.), *Directions in Sociolinguistics: the Ethnography of Communication*, 35–71. New York: Holt, Reinhart and Winston.

Matsumoto, David
    1996   *Culture and Psychology*. Pacific Grove, CA: Brooks/Cole.
Searle, John
    1980   The background of meaning. In: John Searle, Ferenc Keifer and Manfred
            Bierwisch (eds.), *Speech Act Theory and Pragmatics*, 221–32. Dordrecht:
            Reidel.
Sperber, Dan
    1985   *On Anthropological Knowledge*. Cambridge: Cambridge University Press.
Sperber, Dan
    1996   *Explaining Culture*. Oxford: Blackwell.
Sperber, Dan (ed.)
    2000   *Metarepresentations: A Multidisciplinary Perspective*. Oxford: Oxford
            University Press.
Sperber, Dan and Deirdre Wilson
    1986/95 *Relevance: Communication and Cognition*. Oxford: Blackwell. 2nd edition
            (with postface) 1995.
Sperber, Dan and Deirdre Wilson 1995. Postface. In: Dan Sperber and Deirdre Wilson
    1995   *Relevance: Communication and Cognition*, 2nd edn, 255–279. Oxford:
            Blackwell.
Trompenaars, Fons and Charles Hampden-Turner
    1997   *Riding the Waves of Culture: Understanding Cultural Diversity in Business*.
            London: Nicholas Brealey Publishing.
von Frisch, Karl
    1967   *The Dance Language and Orientation of Bees*. Cambridge, MA: Belknap
            Press of Harvard University Press.
Žegarac, Vladimir
    2004   Relevance theory and "the" in second language acquisition. *Second Language Research* 20(3): 193–211.

4. Psychological perspectives: social psychology, language, and intercultural communication

Madeleine Brabant, Bernadette Watson and Cindy Gallois

1. Introduction

Intercultural communication has a long history in social psychology and in many other fields. Indeed, the tradition of language and social psychology (LASP: e.g. Giles and Coupland 1991) emerged from studies of intercultural communication, as social psychologists in the 1960s and 70s aimed to add their own insights to research in linguistics and anthropology. Today, most scholars in language and social psychology consider intercultural encounters to be at the heart of their field (see Gallois, McKay and Pittam 2004).

Because the literature from psychology is so large, we can barely scratch its surface in a single chapter, and we have been very selective. Readers wanting more detail might wish to explore the series of volumes on intercultural communication published since the early 1980s by Sage, in particular the volumes on theories in intercultural communication (Gudykunst 2005; Kim and Gudykunst 1988; Wiseman 1995), as well as other chapters in this volume. In addition, there are many books (particularly Robinson and Giles 2001) and two major journals (*Journal of Cross-Cultural Psychology* and *International Journal of Intercultural Relations*) that have a largely psychological approach to intercultural communication. In this chapter, we attempt to describe the major features of the social-psychological perspective which distinguish it from other approaches, along with a critique of this perspective and some suggestions for the future.

We examine two major traditions in the study of intercultural communication in social psychology. The first of these traditions, the larger in terms of numbers of scholars and studies, is generally known as 'intercultural communication competence' (ICC). Key assumptions underpinning this research are, first, that intercultural communication is essentially interpersonal communication where interactants may not be using the same set of social and communication rules, and secondly, that if interactants acquire the relevant skills and knowledge, competent and effective communication will follow. The second tradition takes as its point of departure that intercultural communication is primarily 'intergroup' communication. Researchers in this tradition emphasize the socio-historical context and the intergroup relations between cultures. They argue that these factors are the main determinants of the motivations and behaviours in an intercultural encounter.

By critiquing these two social-psychological traditions, we highlight the following issues: (1) they address different aspects of intercultural interactions; (2) by themselves they are too limited; (3) theories that combine the two (e.g. Communication Accommodation Theory: see Gallois, Ogay and Giles 2005) provide powerful models for predicting and explaining communication success and failure, and (4) the perspective of psychology in understanding intercultural communication complements those of related disciplines.

1.1.   Distinctive features of the psychological perspective

From its earliest days, psychology emphasized individual behaviour. Even social psychology, which took as its core territory the study of group and larger processes, still starts with the individual as its unit of analysis and moves thence to explore the impact of other people and larger social variables on individuals. Not surprisingly, then, the interest of social psychologists in intercultural communication has tended to focus on individuals' attitudes and behaviour, with larger forces being encapsulated in terms of their impact on individual speakers and listeners. For intercultural communication, this has had consequences both for theory and methodology.

1.1.1.   Theory

1.1.1.1. Focus on motivation

Giles (1973) argued for the inclusion of motivation as a driving factor in all intergroup communication, rather than constructing speakers as (he argued) sociolinguistic automata. Since then, social psychologists have emphasized the motivational drivers in intercultural encounters. For example, Giles noted the capacity of speakers to change sociolinguistic style depending upon whether they liked and admired their interlocutor (or disliked the other person); this was the initial basis for Speech Accommodation Theory. Likewise, Lambert et al. (1960) noted the impact of language spoken (French or English) on listeners' evaluations of speakers, and argued that this process was anchored in the attitudes triggered by language. Psychological work in intercultural communication has always been based on the assumption that the attitudes, interactional goals, and motives of interlocutors determine their choice of language and non-verbal behaviour (with an emphasis on variables that are partly or fully under voluntary control), as well as their evaluation of it.

1.1.1.2. Focus on reception and evaluation

If motivation drives the way interactants approach an intercultural encounter, it also drives the way they perceive such an encounter. Thus, social psychologists have been interested largely in the impact of communication, rather than in the characteristics of communication *per se*. Thus, theory has highlighted the role of the attribution process in interpreting communication from members of another culture. Most psychological theory in this area, for example, has posited the value of an ethno-relative or intercultural perspective (e.g. Kim 1995, 2001; Triandis 1996) to more effective intercultural encounters. Whereas scholars in other fields may study in great detail the specific features of language and non-verbal communication, with little regard for the subtleties of their impact, social psychologists have tended to do the opposite.

1.1.1.3. Focus on identity

Perhaps the most distinctive feature of the social-psychological approach to intercultural communication is the central role given to identity, especially social identity. As the discussion below indicates, intercultural communication can be conceptualized almost entirely in terms of identity management (cf. Ting-Too-mey 1993). The underlying assumption is that interactants bring their identity into an encounter, and may (or may not) negotiate a change in personal or social identity depending upon their evaluation of the encounter. In recent years, social psychologists have begun to explore the extent to which identity may emerge as a result of the communication process itself (e.g. Hecht 1993; Hecht et al. 2001), but there is still a tendency to construct identity as primary and communication as flowing from it.

1.1.2.   Methodology

1.1.2.1. Questionnaires

The favourite measure of social psychologists is undoubtedly the questionnaire, and this method is probably the most common in the social-psychological study of intercultural communication. The advantage is that questionnaires are easy to administer and analyse, and a wide variety of attitude questions, norms, and knowledge of social variables can be tapped efficiently. The disadvantage is that they may not have much to do with situated behaviour in intercultural encounters. In a classic example of this, Bourhis (1983) asked French Canadians in Montreal whether they would change to English if a stranger asked them for help or directions. In his questionnaire study, the majority said they would not accommodate. When he observed actual behaviour in shops in Montreal, however, he noted that the vast majority of French speakers did accommodate to an English-speaking stranger. Work like this has highlighted the importance of tailoring the method to the research question. Questionnaires are excellent devices for studying overt attitudes, norms, and social rules, but they may be poor predictors of communication in context.

1.1.2.2. Simulated intercultural communication: matched guise technique

Lambert and colleagues (1960) pioneered a uniquely social-psychological technique for the study of intercultural communication. The Matched Guise Technique (MGT) in its earliest form involved a single bilingual or multi-lingual speaker who recorded two or more monologues of relatively neutral content (e.g. giving directions in a city) in each of his languages (speakers were always male). The passages were exact translations of each other, so that speaker characteristics and content were controlled as much as possible. Later work (see Giles and Powesland 1975) used the same technique to measure different accents within a language (e.g. RP, London, Scottish, Welsh accents in English). The idea was that differences in evaluations of the speaker could be attributed to the impact of the language or accent.

The MGT had the great advantage of being a fairly unobtrusive measure of reception, and thus arguably less susceptible to social desirability and other biases than direct techniques like questionnaires. On the other hand, it came under fairly stringent critiques from within and outside psychology. First, there had been an almost exclusive reliance on male speakers. Gallois and Callan (1981) replicated some of the early work in Australia for male speakers, but results were nearly reversed when the speakers were female. As it turns out, other social group memberships (gender, age, professional role) and other features of the context are extremely important influences on evaluations of speakers, so that the decontextualized aspect of the MGT was called into question. On another front, Nolan (1983) pointed to the danger in assuming that the same speaker across guises had the same characteristics. He noted that speaker stereotypes about language (and even more, about accent) have a significant impact on vocal style. In addition, the diglossic nature of many bilingual environments means that speakers are unlikely to be equally at home in both or all their languages for any particular content; once again, the impact of contextual features cannot be ignored. In recent years, researchers have tended to return to more direct measures of evaluation, but the MGT is still seen regularly in the literature.

1.2.   Interpersonal and intergroup approaches to intercultural
        communication

After World War II, the interest of researchers in intercultural communication
and miscommunication grew rapidly because of the negative reactions received
by Western sojourners and diplomats. In addition, large-scale immigration and
human rights movements in many countries made communication effectiveness
and prejudice more salient than previously. During this period, researchers concentrated on topics like social and display rules and communication effectiveness between cultures.

Hall (1959, 1966, 1981) proposed that most miscommunication across cultures results from the operation of different rules or norms (e.g. interpersonal
distance, where social norms are tied to values about aggressiveness and sexuality). Interactants miscommunicate by interpreting the behaviour of others using
different rules as if the others were using their own rules. Hall argued that if social rules could be brought to the surface and made explicit, much of the heat
would disappear from intercultural encounters, and communication would be
more effective and positive. In a similar vein, Argyle, Furnham and Graham
(1981) defined social rules as socially shared expectations about appropriate
and inappropriate behaviour in situations. They argued that, while there are
many cultural similarities in communication, especially nonverbal communication, the differences still cause a great deal of misunderstanding. Argyle and
colleagues proposed training people to use the social rules of another culture, to
reduce the chance of miscommunication in an intercultural encounter. Triandis
and Schwartz also argue for understanding intercultural dynamics from an interpersonal perspective (e.g. Schwartz 1999; Triandis 1996; Triandis and Suh
2002).

It is hard to overestimate the impact of this approach, particularly for communication skills training (see Matsumoto in this volume for a detailed discussion of the role of these variables in psychological adjustment in intercultural contexts). Almost all intercultural communication training conducted by
psychologists takes Hall's and Argyle's work as its starting point. Only in very
recent times has a serious critique of this approach appeared, arguing among
other things that both interpersonal and intergroup factors are significant influences in many or all intercultural encounters (e.g. Gallois and Pittam 1996).

2.   Intercultural communication competence (ICC)

The most direct descendant of Hall's and Argyle's work in social psychology is
the tradition of intercultural communication competence (cf. Prechtl and Davidson-Lund in this volume). Researchers have posited a measurable level of effec-

tiveness in an intercultural encounter but have not necessarily followed through with measurement. This approach focuses on the training of immigrants and sojourners who are motivated to attain a satisfactory level of communication competence in their host country (cf. Newton in this volume). We discuss three ICC models here, but there are many others (e.g. Singelis and Brown 1995; Matsumoto in this volume).

2.1.   Anxiety and uncertainty management

Gudykunst's (1988, 1995) theory of anxiety and uncertainty management (AUM) gives priority to cultural traditions, values and norms over socio-political factors. He posits that individuals must experience optimal levels of anxiety and uncertainty to communicate effectively in intercultural encounters. The extent to which they experience uncomfortable or optimal levels of anxiety and uncertainty depends on their level of communication skills, motivation, and knowledge of general and specific cultural factors. The process of anxiety and uncertainty reduction through acquiring intercultural communication competence is performed by individuals qua individuals. To adapt to the ambiguity of a new situation, individuals perform tension-reducing and information seeking behaviours (Ball-Rokeach 1973). Gudykunst (1988) notes that much behaviour is habitual, and individuals are often not conscious of their behaviour (see Triandis 1996). Thus, when interacting with people from a different culture who do not share the same implicit theory of behaviour, sojourners become more conscious of their own behaviour.

Gudykunst (1988) posits individualism–collectivism (Hofstede 1983) as the major dimension of cultural variability influencing intergroup processes. People in individualistic cultures tend to apply the same value standards to all, while those in collectivistic cultures tend to apply different value standards to members of their ingroups and outgroups. Triandis (1996) suggests that collectivistic cultures emphasize the goals, needs and views of the ingroup rather than individual pleasure, shared ingroup beliefs rather than unique individual beliefs, and value cooperation with ingroup members rather than individual outcomes. Gudykunst, thus, suggests that an increase in collectivism results in an increase in the differences in uncertainty reduction processes (attributional confidence) between ingroup and outgroup communication. Gudykunst (1995) proposes that the anxiety and uncertainty management processes underlying both interpersonal and intergroup communication are the same, highlighting the conceptualization of intercultural communication as interpersonal communication across different social rules and values. Hubbert, Gudykunst and Guerrero's (1999) results, in a study of international students in the US, supported AUM theory.

2.2.   Cross-cultural adaptation theory

Kim's (1995, 2001) cross-cultural adaptation theory is based on the systems concept that change is the consequence of stress and adaptation in a new cultural environment. The linkages in her model indicate mutual causations, reflecting the open-systems principle of reciprocal functional relationships among a system, its parts, and its environment. Kim proposes that a predisposition by sojourners to communicate, in terms of personality and cultural factors, is linked to more competent acquisition of the host communication system, through interaction with the mass media and host individuals, along with a loss or refocusing of interactions in the old culture. Thus, she assumes that sojourners are differently motivated to become part of the new culture or to adopt an intercultural identity. This process of adaptation is moderated by the host environment, in that some environments are more tolerant of strangers and new behaviours and value systems.

Kim places a strong emphasis on sojourners acquiring what she refers to as an intercultural identity; that is, an identity that is based in neither culture but that sits between them. She describes this as an emerging identity that develops out of the challenging and painful experiences of self-reorganization under the demands of the new milieu. This intercultural identity is achieved through prolonged experiences of trial and error; it is a new expanded identity that is more than either the original identity or the identity of the host culture (cf. Shibutani and Kwan 1965). The pressure on newcomers to conform comes from the dominant group. As new learning occurs, deculturation from the old culture also occurs. Kim describes a transformative process of stress–adaptation, where disequilibrium brought about by stress, uncertainty, and anxiety allows self-reorganization and self-renewal.

Kim's (1995, 2001) theory identifies six dimensions that facilitate or impede the process of cross-cultural adaptation. These dimensions reflect the experiences that individuals face in a new environment, through which they change toward greater functional fitness and psychological health in the host environment and toward an intercultural identity. In Kim's view, adaptation by an individual to a cultural environment occurs almost entirely in and through communication. Kim (2001) also highlights the practical issues that sojourners encounter, and her model provides a framework for the development of training programs.

2.3.   Identity negotiation process model

Ting-Toomey's (1993) identity negotiation process model proposes that identification is mediated by a dialectic of security–vulnerability and inclusion–differentiation, as well as by identity coherence and individual and collective self-esteem. The result of this dialectic determines cognitive, affective, and be-

havioural resourcefulness, and thus the extent to which the identity negotiation process in intercultural encounters is effective. The model posits that
individuals in all cultures desire to be competent communicators in a diverse
range of interactive situations, becoming competent through repeated practice.
They also learn to deal with others appropriately and effectively through habitual routines. Ting-Toomey assumes that people desire positive group- and per-
son-based identities in all types of communicative situations. According to the
identity negotiation model, satisfactory outcomes include feelings of being
understood, respected, and supported. As in most other models, outcome is contingent on the perceptions of the communicators in the interaction. Outcome
also depends crucially on the willingness of interactants to practice mindfulness
(i.e. thoughtful rather than automatic communication) with dissimilar others. To
the extent that this happens, interactants should experience a high sense of identity satisfaction.

Identity understanding begins with gathering accurate identity information
and being culturally sensitive in probing identity based-details. In addition, it
involves the willingness to share facets of one's own self-conception with others
in a culturally sensitive manner. A feeling of being respected and supported
requires the mindful monitoring of one's verbal and nonverbal behaviour and
norms in interacting with dissimilar others, and treating other salient social and
personal identities with consideration and dignity. The consequences of the
identity negotiation process affect the quality of relationships. Ting-Toomey's
model provides the principles for training individuals to manage intercultural
conflict.

2.4.   Summary

Across all the ICC models described above, there are several common factors.
The first is ethno-relativism (i.e. the ability of a stranger to take on the perspective of the unknown or new culture). The second is the need for the sojourner
to obtain some education and knowledge about the new culture. The third
is mindfulness, or the need for sojourners to engage with the new culture and to
be constantly aware of their own as well as the new culture's values, norms, and
behaviours. The final factor involves the belief that appropriate communication
skills and knowledge will result in more effective communication.

This approach to intercultural communication and competence training has
had a successful record in a number of contexts. Business travellers in particular
have experienced increased self-confidence and better results in encounters with
new cultures. Many students and immigrants have also benefited, and immigrants often speak positively of training in this tradition. Underlying the whole
approach, however, are several key assumptions: that people are unproblemati-
cally motivated to communicate well; that hosts are at least tolerant of the ef-

forts of sojourners; and that most intercultural interactions have mainly inter-personal salience. In brief, that there is no reason why communication should not proceed smoothly if people are mindful and communicate skilfully. The ICC tradition does not try to explain contexts in which miscommunication between two cultural groups may be inevitable despite the best intentions of well-trained communicators. The intergroup approach we describe below is aimed to explain and predict when intercultural communication is likely to fail.

3.   Intercultural interactions as intergroup encounters

The second main socio-psychological approach to intercultural communication comes mainly from scholars in language and social psychology (LASP). These researchers have been especially interested in contexts where two or more cultures co-exist, often in a state of social or power inequality, for many years (or permanently). These include diglossic and other bilingual communities, long-term immigrants, and intercultural contexts where interactants come from different groups but use a common language (e.g. the countries of the UK). Be-cause of this, whereas the goal of ICC theories is communication competence, for this approach it is to understand prejudice, discrimination, conflict between cultures, and how rivalry and antagonism can be reduced.

3.1.   Second-language acquisition and use

One of the earliest models in this tradition comes from Gardner and his col-leagues (see Gardner 1985), and explores the intrinsic and extrinsic motivations for learning a second language. Extrinsically motivated learners attempt to learn a second language for instrumental reasons (e.g. economic advantage, job pros-pects), while those with intrinsic motivation have a genuine desire to learn about and if possible become part of the new linguistic community. A key assumption of this model is that the quality of interactions and the motivation for language learning are based primarily on intergroup history, and driven as much by moti-vation as by communication skill. In most contexts, one or more communicative communities are advantaged and dominant, with prejudice marked by negative, hostile or patronizing communication. The assumption is that this is the norm in most intergroup encounters, so that less account is taken of interpersonal re-lations between participants.

Clément and Gardner (2001) characterize second-language acquisition as making the second language part of the individual's very being (i.e. they posit intrinsic motivation as essential to effective L2 learning). This process involves at least some degree of identification with the other language community. Gardner and Clément (1990) distinguish three individual-difference variables in second-language acquisition that influence how well or quickly individuals learn another language: cognitive characteristics (language aptitude and language learning strategies), attitudes and motivation, and personality characteristics.

Contact with the second-language speaking group in naturalistic contexts is a key part of L2 acquisition (as it is for Kim 1995, 2001, albeit for different reasons). Positive benefits from language acquisition can only be achieved if the first language and culture are well established within the individual (Carey 1991; Clément 1984; Cummins and Swain 1986, Hamers and Blanc 1988; Landry and Allard 1992). The familial, educational, and social context should allow the development and transmission of the first language and culture. Ethnolinguistic vitality (Giles, Bourhis and Taylor 1977; Prujiner et al. 1984) is a closely related concept that is also relevant to second-language acquisition and use, as well as to the maintenance of the original ethnic identity. Ethnolinguistic vitality refers to the power and viability of an ethnic group in a specific context, as measured by the demographic representation of the community, its institutional representation and socio-economic status, and its position in the media and cultural landscape of the larger society. Vitality is important in second-language acquisition and use, as well as in maintenance of the original ethnic identity.

Research has also shown a consistent relationship between demographic, political, economic, and cultural capital factors and first-language retention and competence (Landry and Allard 1992; Landry, Allard and Henry 1996). The gap between structural or objective vitality and psychological vitality is bridged by recasting structural factors as subjective perceptions by individuals, so that vitality is now commonly measured through self-report questionnaire indices of perceptions (Bourhis, Giles and Rosenthal 1981). Researchers have found a relationship between objective and subjective ethnolinguistic vitality (Bourhis and Sachdev 1984; Landry and Allard 1992). Self-confidence in using the second language has been shown to be positively related to the degree of identification with the second-language group, and in the case of minority group members it is negatively correlated with identification to the first-language group (Noels and Clément 1996; Noels, Pon and Clément 1996). Competence in and preference for using the second language may entail, or may be perceived to entail, the loss of first language and culture (Cameron and Lalonde 1994; Clément, Gauthier and Noels 1993). Better adjustment and well-being are often correlated with greater self-confidence in using the second language and greater social support from the second language network (Clément, Michaud and Noels 1998; Noels and Clément 1996; Noels, Pon and Clément 1996), so that learning a second language may be a vector of individual psychological adjustment and collective language and culture loss (see Clément and Gardner 2001). Clearly, the socio-psychological understanding of second-language acquisition in this model is driven not by skills training (although ability and training are important), but by individual motivation and attitudes.

3.2.   Social identity theory

Social identity theory was developed in part to explain the ways in which socio-cultural factors affect interaction (and thus communication) between different social groups and cultures (cf. Spreckels and Kotthoff in this volume). The theory rests on the assumption that the socio-historical context is the first factor influencing social behaviour, and thus the primary influence on interpersonal communication (Tajfel 1979; Tajfel and Turner 1979; Turner et al. 1987). The history of relations between two groups alone is sometimes enough to produce stereotypes about people in those groups, even though people who hold the stereotypes may be reluctant to admit this. The process of categorizing ourselves and others into groups or categories is ubiquitous and may be arbitrary (see Tajfel 1979). The process of stereotyping begins in the physical world, and stereotypes help to simplify and control judgments about strange situations. Individuals belong to a wide range of group memberships, ethnic and cultural groups, large-scale social categories (sex, race, age, social class, religion, etc.), occupational and other groups (Turner et al. 1987). When there is a history of conflict or social inequality between two groups, people tend to rationalize discriminatory behaviour through stereotypes.

In general, the theory posits that people describe their own group (ingroup) using dimensions on which it appears positive and salient, and describe the other groups (outgroups) in negative terms. Where there is social inequality, the dominant group may nevertheless be perceived as more intelligent, beautiful, and so forth, while the disadvantaged group is seen as submissive, uneducated, poor, but friendly by people in both groups (Lambert et al.'s work in 1960 was one of the first studies to show this clearly in an existing community, Montreal). Many structural features, including the differential use of dominant and non-dominant languages, reinforce such inequalities. For example, members of dominated groups are rarely given credit for their language abilities by members of the dominant group, but are stereotyped as stupid or criticized for their lack of perfect fluency by monolinguals. Much of social identity theory concerns the ways that structural inequalities influence the ways in which people construct and communicate their social identities, and how they use stereotypes and identity management to change or maintain the status quo (Taylor and McKirnan 1984).

3.3.   A typology of intercultural adaptation

Another approach that focuses on motivation is Berry's (1997) typology of intercultural adaptation. Berry (1980) was the first to propose that immigrant and host
cultural identity could be portrayed as independent dimensions, rather than as extreme points of a single bipolar continuum. According to Berry's acculturation
model, there are two dimensions yielding four acculturation strategies: 'integration', 'assimilation', 'separation' and 'marginalization' (Berry 1980). Integration reflects a desire to maintain key features of the immigrant cultural identity
while adopting aspects of the majority culture (i.e. a high value placed on the
original culture and the new culture). Assimilation reflects a desire by immigrants
to relinquish their own cultural identity for the sake of adopting the cultural identity of the host majority (high value on the new culture but not the old one). Separation is characterized by the immigrant's desire to maintain all features of the
original cultural identity while rejecting relationships with members of the majority host culture (high value on the old but not the new culture). Marginalization
(more recently called *individualism*) characterizes individuals who reject both
their own and the host community culture and emphasize another social identity
(e.g. occupation), thereby losing contact with both their heritage culture and that
of the host majority (low value placed on both the old and the new culture).

   Acculturation orientations such as maintenance of the immigrant culture can
be mediated by the extent to which immigrants feel accepted or discriminated
against by host community (Bourhis and Gagnon 1994; Moghaddam, Taylor
and Wright 1993). Bourhis et al. (1997) extended Berry's model to the societal
level (see also Moïse and Bourhis 1994), positing that the match between individual and societal orientations determines the effectiveness of intercultural
communication. Their model aims to present a more dynamic account of immigrant and host community acculturation in multicultural settings.

3.4.   Summary

The second theory discussed here takes an intergroup approach to intercultural
communication. From this perspective, researchers address the concept of ethnocentrism (a preference for all aspects of one's own culture relative to other
cultures) as opposed to ethno-relativism. Good communicative outcomes may
come out of the reduction in discriminatory language or harmful speech, more
effective learning of the other culture's language, dialect, or style by members
of both (all) cultures, better accommodation to the communication needs and
behaviours of others, and better language and cultural maintenance by minority
groups. Communication is viewed not so much as a skill but rather as the result
of a motivation (identity maintenance or negotiation, reduction of prejudice,
etc.), based on intergroup history. Miscommunication is construed not as a defi-

ciency of the individual but rather as based on the motivations that underlie one or both interactants in an intercultural encounter.

This approach to intercultural communication acknowledges that because of the socio-historical context and intergroup relations, people may not be motivated to communicate well. Members of the dominant group may not be tolerant of the efforts made by members of a less dominant group, and in any case intergroup relations are salient in most interactions. In addition, in this approach there is an understanding that some encounters will not proceed smoothly and these encounters may be better avoided. One weakness of this perspective lies in the inherent complexities in these theoretical approaches that attempt a comprehensive explanation of intercultural encounters. By including so many variables, it is difficult to tease out when particular elements are salient in the model and when they are not.

3.5.   Communication accommodation theory

Communication Accommodation Theory (CAT: e.g. Gallois et al. 1995; Giles, Coupland and Coupland 1991) is a theory of both intergroup and interpersonal communication, invoking the dual importance of both factors in predicting and understanding intergroup interactions. In our introduction, we noted that CAT proposes that communication has both interpersonal and intergroup elements. It is this combination that makes CAT such a powerful model. For example, Jones et al. (1999) used CAT to explain differences in the communication dynamics between Australian and Chinese students studying at an Australian university. Specifically, the cultural differences between these two cultural groups led to differing communication strategies and behaviours, as well as different perceptions of others' behaviour. In a different context, Watson and Gallois (1998) were able to explain why independent observers who watched a number of videotaped interactions between health professionals and their patients rated some as more satisfying and positive than others.

CAT developed from speech accommodation theory (Giles 1973) and provides communication scholars with an intergroup theory of intercultural communication. It has been influenced by both social identity theory and ethnolinguistic identity theory (see Gallois, Ogay and Giles 2005). CAT recognizes the importance of power and of macro-level societal factors. The theory posits that speakers orient towards interlocutors at varying levels of intergroup and interpersonal salience. Socio-historical factors and the goals of each interactant play a critical role in the levels of intergroup and interpersonal salience. In an intercultural context, therefore, intergroup rivalry may be a major but not the only influence on a speaker's choice of communication behaviours.

The primary thesis of CAT is that individuals interacting with others use communication strategies to achieve a desired social distance between themselves and interacting partners (Giles 1973; Giles et al. 1987). The goals of interactants drive the communication strategies that they exhibit. These strategies include approximation (convergence, divergence, and maintenance of language, accent, or other behaviours), discourse management (sharing or not of topics, register, etc.), interpretability (making communication clearer or more obscure), interpersonal control (more or less equal role relations), and emotional expression (more or less reassurance, etc.). As noted above, an interactant may perceive at certain times during the encounter that salience is simultaneously high intergroup and high interpersonal. In recent years (e.g. Gallois and Giles 1998; Gallois, Ogay and Giles 2005), the focus has been on summarizing the sociolinguistic strategies and goals into an overall accommodative stance (accommodation or reducing social distance, or non-accommodation or increasing it).

Approximation focuses on a speech partner's productive management of an interaction and refers to changes in speech patterns. Convergence is driven by a motivation to identify with or gain approval from an interlocutor (Bourhis and Giles 1977; Street and Giles 1982). Convergence may also arise out of the concern of ensuring the interaction flows more smoothly, which improves the effectiveness of communication (Gallois, Ogay and Giles 1995). Divergent behaviours are motivated at two levels to display distinctiveness from one's interlocutor. At the individual level, divergence may serve to accentuate differences or display disdain for the other. At the group level, divergence may emphasize a valued group identity (Cargile, Giles and Clément 1996; Tajfel 1979; Yaeger-Dror 1991). When there is a history of rivalry and inequality or the intergroup relationship is in flux, interactants tend to emphasize intergroup salience.

The other, non-approximation, strategies are also driven by each speech partner's goals. Interpretability refers to the extent to which conversational competence is focal and whether there exists understanding between interactants. Discourse management focuses on the conversational needs of each interactant and is concerned with the communication process rather than content. Interpersonal control concerns with issues of role and power relations between interactants and the extent to which one or other of the speech partners is constrained to a particular role. Where interactants' emotional and emotional needs are salient, emotional expression serves to reassure.

By situating intergroup encounters in a socio-historical context, CAT takes account of intergroup and interpersonal history, along with societal norms and values. CAT tracks an interaction between individuals, starting with the intergroup and interpersonal history and orientation they bring to the interaction, communication behaviours during the interaction, and perceptions and subsequent evaluations of the interaction. These evaluations then become part of the larger context that is taken to the next similar interaction. Gallois, Ogay and Giles (2005) suggest that intercultural encounters take place in the context of intergroup as well as interpersonal history, and in the context of different and sometimes contradictory social norms. Effective communication depends crucially on these factors. For this reason, ICC training models are likely to fail in certain contexts, because interactants are not motivated to communicate well or because intergroup norms restrict or prohibit the possibility of serious interpersonal communication (see Gallois 2003). It is essential for both theory development and applications that researchers take full account of the intergroup aspect of intercultural communication. CAT provides a comprehensive way to do this, without neglecting the interpersonal and idiosyncratic aspects of conversation.

4.   Future directions for the socio-psychological approach to intercultural communication

As can be seen, these two major traditions in psychology about the study of intercultural communication have separate and complementary strengths and areas of application. The first one has fared well in contexts where speakers are motivated to communicate well and where intergroup history is either not salient (as in the case of individual travellers without strong views about the new culture) or not negative. Contrary to earlier predictions from Hall's (1959) work, cultural distance has proved less of a factor in communication and miscommunication than has intergroup history (see Gallois and Pittam 1996). The second tradition has aimed to explain interactions in settings of social inequality or intergroup rivalry. In general, researchers in this tradition are pessimistic about the possibility of effective communication and the potential of intercultural communication competence training. Instead, they concentrate on the description and explanation of settings of long-term and problematic intergroup contact.

Clearly it is important to theorize and address all these contexts, and no one theory of intercultural communication or training program presently does that (see Gallois 2003; Hajek and Giles 2003). A first step involves the careful analysis of a context in terms of intergroup relations, interpersonal relations, cultural values and norms, and skills and knowledge, in that order. A theory like CAT is well placed to do this. Gallois (2003) notes that in some situations, intergroup relations are so negative as to undermine any attempt to interact, no matter how skilled the interactants are. In such situations it may be better to attempt to alter social identity to embrace a larger, shared identity. In other contexts, individual orientation, the behaviours that occur in an interaction and the way they are perceived are the most important determinants of communication effectiveness. The very concept of effective communication is challenged by CAT and similar theories, because communication outcomes are posited as being as much in the eye of the beholder as in the actual behaviour of interactants (see Gallois and Giles 1998; Hajek and Giles 2003).

To conclude, there is much potential for more and deeper interactions between psychologists, emphasizing perceptions and motivations, and applied linguists, attending more to production. There are good examples of this kind of collaboration. One striking example is the collaboration between Coupland, Giles and their colleagues. This resulted among other things in their model (Coupland, Wiemann and Giles 1991) of miscommunication and problematic talk, which theorizes six causes of miscommunication ranging from inherent and unrecognized flaws in discourse through to socio-structural power imbalances (also likely to be unrecognized, albeit for different reasons). Models like this one, and theories like CAT, can provide a basis for understanding intercultural communication in context and as influenced by larger social and psychological factors. We hope that in another decade the research literature will reflect this amalgam.

References

Argyle, Michael, Adrian Furnham and Jean Ann Graham
    1981   *Social Situations*. Cambridge: Cambridge University Press.
Ball-Rokeach, Sandra
    1973   From persuasive ambiguity to definition of the situation. *Sociometry* 36: 378–389.
Berry, John W.
    1980   Acculturation as varieties of adaptation. In: Amado Padilla (ed.), *Acculturation Theory, Models and Some New Findings,* 9–25. Boulder, CO: Westview.
Berry, John W.
    1997   Immigration, acculturation, and adaptation. *Applied Psychology: An International Journal* 46: 5–68.
Bourhis, Richard
    1983   Language attitudes and self-reports of French-English usage in Quebec. *Journal of Multilingual and Multicultural Development* 4: 163–179.
Bourhis, Richard Y. and André Gagnon
    1994   Préjugés, discrimination et relations intergroupes. In: Robert J. Vallerand (ed.), *Les Fondements de la Psychologie Sociale*, 707–773. Boucherville, Québec: Gaëtan Morin.
Bourhis, Richard Y. and Howard Giles
    1977   The language of intergroup distinctiveness. In: Howard Giles (ed.), *Language, Ethnicity and Intergroup Relations*, 119–135. London: Academic Press.
Bourhis, Richard and Itesh Sachdev
    1984   Vitality perceptions of language "attitudes": some Canadian data. *Journal of Language and Social Psychology* 3: 97–126.
Bourhis, Richard, Howard Giles and Doreen Rosenthal
    1981   Notes on the construction of a "Subjective Vitality Questionnaire" for ethnolinguistic groups. *Journal of Multilingual and Multicultural Development* 2: 144–155.

Bourhis, Richard Y., Léna C. Moïse, Stéphane Perreault and Sascha Sénécal
1997   Towards an interactive acculturation model: a social psychological approach. *International Journal of Psychology* 32: 369–386.

Cameron, James E. and Richard N. Lalonde
1994   Self-ethnicity and social group memberships in two generations of Italian Canadians. *Journal of Personality and Social Psychology* 20: 514–520.

Carey, Stephen T.
1991   The culture of literacy in majority and minority language schools. *Canadian Modern Language Review* 47: 950–976.

Cargile, Aaron, Howard Giles and Richard Clément
1996   The role of language in ethnic conflict. In: Joseph B. Gittler (ed.), *Research in Human Social Conflict, Vol.1*, 189–208. Greenwich, CT: JAI Press.

Clément, Richard
1984   Aspects socio-psycologiques de la communication inter-ethnique et de l'identité culturelle. *Recherches sociologiques* 15: 293–312.

Clément, Richard and Robert C. Gardner
2001   Second language mastery. In: Howard Giles and W. Peter Robinson (eds.), *The New Handbook of Language and Social Psychology*, 489–504. London: Wiley.

Clément, Richard, Renée Gauthier and Kimberley Noels
1993   Choix langagiers en milieu minoritaire: attitudes et identité concomitantes. *Revue Canadienne des Sciences du Comportement* 25: 149–164.

Clément, Richard, C. Michaud and Kimberley A. Noels
1998   Effets acculturatifs du support social en situation de contact intergroupe. *Revue Québecoise de Psycologie* 19: 189–210.

Coupland, Nikolas, John M. Wiemann and Howard Giles
1991   Talk as "problem" and communication as "miscommunication". An integrative analysis. In: Nikolas Coupland, Howard Giles and John M. Wiemann (eds.), *"Miscommunication" and Problematic Talk*, 1–17. Newbury Park, CA: Sage.

Cummins, Jim and Merrill Swain
1986   *Bilingualism in Education.* New York: Longman.

Gallois, Cindy
2003   Reconciliation through communication in intercultural encounters: potential or peril? *Journal of Communication* 53: 5–15.

Gallois, Cindy and Victor J. Callan
1981   Personality impressions elicited by accented English speech. *Journal of Cross-Cultural Psychology* 12: 347–359.

Gallois, Cindy and Howard Giles
1998   Accommodating mutual influence in intergroup encounters. In: Mark T. Palmer and George A. Barnett (eds.), *Mutual Influence in Interpersonal Communication: Theory and Research in Cognition, Affect and Behavior* (Vol. Progress in Communication Sciences, 135–162). Stamford, UK: Ablex Publishing Corporation.

Gallois, Cindy and Jeffery Pittam
1996   Communication attitudes and accommodation in Australia: a culturally diverse English-dominant context. *International Journal of Psycholinguistics* 12: 193–212.

Gallois, Cindy, Howard Giles, Elizabeth Jones, Aaron C. Cargile and Hiroshi Ota
  1995   Accommodating intercultural encounters: elaborations and extensions. In:
          Richard L. Wiseman (ed.), *Intercultural Communication Theory*, 115–147.
          Thousand Oaks, CA: Sage.
Gallois, Cindy, Susan McKay and Jeffery Pittam
  2004   Intergroup communication and identity: intercultural, health, and organisa-
          tional communication. In: Kristine Fitch and Robert Sanders (eds.), *Hand-
          book of Language and Social Interaction*, 231–250. Mahwah, NJ: Erlbaum.
Gallois, Cindy, Tania Ogay and Howard Giles
  2005   Communication accommodation theory: a look back and a look ahead. In:
          William Gudykunst (ed.), *Theorizing about Intercultural Communication*,
          121–148. Thousand Oaks, CA: Sage.
Gardner, Robert C.
  1985   *Social Psychology and Second Language Learning: The Role of Attitudes
          and Motivation.* London: Edward Arnold.
Gardner, Robert C. and Richard Clément
  1990   Social psychological perspectives on second language acquisition. In: Ho-
          ward Giles and W. Peter Robinson (eds.), *Handbook of Language and
          Social Psychology*, 495–518. Chichester: John Wiley and Sons.
Giles, Howard
  1973   Accent mobility: a model and some data. *Anthropological Linguistics*
          15(2): 87–109.
Giles, Howard and Nikolas Coupland
  1991   *Language: Contexts and Consequences.* Milton Keynes: Open University
          Press.
Giles, Howard and Peter F. Powesland
  1975   *Speech Style and Social Evaluation.* London: Academic Press.
Giles, Howard, Richard Y. Bourhis and Donald M. Taylor
  1977   Towards a theory of language in ethnic group relations. In: Howard Giles
          (ed.), *Language, Ethnicity and Intergroup Relations*. London: Academic
          Press.
Giles, Howard, Justine Coupland and Nikolas Coupland (eds.)
  1991   *Contexts of Accommodation: Developments in Applied Sociolinguistics*
          (Studies in Emotion and Social Interaction.) Cambridge: Cambridge Uni-
          versity Press.
Giles, Howard, Anthony Mulac, James J. Bradac and Patricia Johnson
  1987   Speech accommodation theory: the first decade and beyond. In: Margaret
          McLaughlin (ed.), *Communication Yearbook*, Vol. 10, 13–48. Beverly
          Hills, CA: Sage.
Gudykunst, William B.
  1988   Uncertainty and anxiety. In: Young Yun Kim and William B. Gudykunst
          (eds.), *Theories in Intercultural Communication*, 123–156. Newbury Park,
          CA: Sage.
Gudykunst, William B.
  1995   Anxiety/uncertainty management theory: current status. In: Richard Wise-
          man (ed.), *Intercultural Communication Theory*, 8–58. Thousand Oaks,
          CA: Sage.

Gudykunst, William B.
  2005   *Theorizing about Intercultural Communication.* Thousand Oaks, CA: Sage.
Hajek, Chris and Howard Giles
  2003   Intercultural communication competence. A critique and alternative model.
          In: Brant Burleson and John Greene (eds), *Handbook of Communicative
          and Social Skills*, 935–957. Mahwah, NJ: LEA.
Hall, Edward T.
  1959   *The Silent Language.* New York: Doubleday and Co.
Hall, Edward T.
  1966   *The Hidden Dimension.* Garden City, NJ: Doubleday.
Hall, Edward T.
  1981   *Beyond Culture.* Garden City, NJ: Doubleday.
Hamers, Josiane F. and Michel Blanc
  1988   *Binguality and Bilingualism.* Cambridge: Cambridge University Press.
Hecht, Michael L.
  1993   2002: a research odyssey toward the development of a communication the-
          ory of identity. *Communication Monographs* 60: 76–82.
Hecht, Michael L., Ronald L. Jackson II, Sheryl Lindsley, Susan Strauss and Karen
          E. Johnson
  2001   A layered approach to ethnicity: language and communication. In: W. Peter
          Robinson and Howard Giles (eds.), *The New Handbook of Language and
          Social Psychology*, 429–449. Chichester: Wiley.
Hofstede, Geert
  1983   Dimensions of national cultures in fifty countries and three regions. In: Jan B.
          Deregowski, Suzanne Dziurawiec and Robert C. Annis (eds.), *Expectations
          in Cross-cultural Psychology*, 335–355. Lisse: Swets and Zeitlinger.
Hubbert, Kimberley N., William B. Gudykunst and Sherrie L. Guerrero
  1999   Intergroup communication over time. *International Journal of Intercultural
          Relations* 23: 13–46.
Jones, Elizabeth, Cindy Gallois, Victor J. Callan and Michelle Barker
  1999   Strategies of accommodation: development of a coding system for con-
          versational interaction. *Journal of Language and Social Psychology* 18:
          125–152
Kim, Young Yun
  1995   Cross-cultural adaptation: an integrative theory. In: Richard L. Wiseman
          (ed.), *Intercultural Communication Theory*, 170–193. Thousand Oaks, CA:
          Sage.
Kim, Young Yun
  2001   *Becoming Intercultural: An Integrative Theory of Communication and
          Cross-cultural Adaptation.* Thousand Oaks, CA: Sage.
Kim, Young Yun and William B. Gudykunst
  1988   *Theories in Intercultural Communication* (International and Intercultural
          Communication Annual, Vol. 12). Newbury Park, CA: Sage.
Kotthoff, Helga
  this volume Ritual and style across cultures, Chapter 9.
Lambert, Wallace E., Richard Hodgson, Robert C. Gardner and Samuel Fillenbaum
  1960   Evaluational reactions to spoken languages. *Journal of Abnormal and So-
          cial Psychology* 60: 44–51.

Landry, Réal and Rodrigue Allard
   1992   Ethnolinguistic vitality and the bilingual development of minority and majority group students. In: William Fase, Koen Jaspaert and Sjaak Kroon (eds.), *Maintenance and Loss of Minority Languages*, 223–251. Amsterdam: John Benjamins.
Landry, Rodrigue, Réal Allard and Jacques Henry
   1996   French in south Louisiana: towards language loss. *Journal of Multilingual and Multicultural Development* 17: 442–468.
Matsumoto, David, Seung Hee Yoo and Jeffrey A. LeRoux
this volume Emotion and intercultural adjustment, Chapter 5.
Moghaddam, Fathali M., Donald M. Taylor and C. Stephen Wright
   1993   *Social Psychology in Cross-cultural Perspective*. New York: Freeman.
Moïse, Léna C. and Richard Y. Bourhis
   1994   Langage et ethnicité: communication interculturelle à Montréal. *Canadian Ethnic Studies* 26: 86–107.
Newton, Jonathan
this volume Adapting authentic workplace talk for workplace communication training, Chapter 24.
Noels, Kimberley and Richard Clément
   1996   Communicating across cultures: social determinants and acculturative consequences. *Canadian Journal of Behavioural Science* 28: 214–228.
Noels, Kimberley, Gordon Pon and Richard Clément
   1996   Language, identity, and adjustment: the role of linguistic self-confidence in the adjustment process. *Journal of Language and Social Psychology* 15: 246–264.
Nolan, Francis
   1983   *The Phonetic Basis of Speaker Recognition*. Cambridge: Cambridge University Press.
Prechtl, Elisabeth and Anne Davidson Lund
this volume Intercultural competence and assessment: perspectives from the INCA project, Chapter 22.
Prujiner, Alain, Denise Deshaies, Josiane Hamers, Michel Blanc, Richard Clément and Réal Landry
   1984   *Variation du Comportement Langagier lorsque deux Langues sont en Contact*. Québec: International Centre for Research on Language Planning.
Robinson, W. Peter and Howard Giles (eds.)
   2001   *The New Handbook of Language and Social Psychology*. Chichester: Wiley and Sons.
Schwartz, Shalom H.
   1999   A theory of cultural values and some implications for work. *Applied Psychology: An international Review* 48: 23–47.
Shibutani, Tamotsu and Kian M. Kwan
   1965   *Ethnic Stratification: A Comparative Approach*. New York: Macmillan.
Singelis, Theodore M. and William J. Brown
   1995   Culture, self, and collectivist communication: linking culture to individual behavior. *Human Communication Research* 21: 354–389.
Street, Richard L. and Howard Giles
   1982   Speech accommodation theory: a social cognitive approach to language and

speech behavior. In: Michael E. Roloff and Charles R. Berger (eds.), *Social Cognition and Communication*, 193–226. Beverly Hills, CA: Sage.

Tajfel, Henri
1979   Individuals and groups in social psychology. *British Journal of Social Psychology* 18: 183–190.

Tajfel, Henri and John C. Turner
1979   An integrative theory of intergroup conflict. In: W.G. Austin and S. Worchel (eds.), *The Social Psychology of Intergroup Relations*, 33–53. Belmont, CA: Wadsworth.

Taylor, Donald and David J. McKirnan
1984   A five-stage theory of intergroup behaviour. *British Journal of Social Psychology* 23: 291–300.

Ting-Toomey, Stella
1993   Communicative resourcefulness: an identity negotiation perspective. In: Richard L. Wiseman and Jolene Koester (eds.), *Intercultural Communication Competence* (International and Intercultural Communication Annual, Vol. 17, 72–111). Newbury Park, CA: Sage.

Triandis, Harry C.
1996   The psychological measurement of cultural syndromes. *American Psychologist* 51: 407–415

Triandis, Harry C. and Eunkook M. Suh
2002   Cultural influences on personality. *Annual Review of Psychology* 53: 133–160.

Turner, John C., Michael Hogg, Penelope Oakes, Stephen Reicher and Margaret S. Wetherell
1987   *Rediscovering the Social Group: A Self-categorisation Theory*. Oxford: Blackwell.

Watson, Bernadette and Cindy Gallois
1998   Nurturing communication by health professionals toward patients: a communication accommodation theory approach. *Health Communication* 10: 343–355.

Wiseman, Richard
1995   *Intercultural Communication Theory*. Thousand Oaks, CA: Sage.

Yaeger-Dror, Malcah
1991   Linguistic evidence for social psychological attitudes: Hypercorrection or [r] l by singers from a Mizrahi background. *Language and Communication* 11: 309–331.

5.   Emotion and intercultural adjustment

David Matsumoto, Seung Hee Yoo and Jeffrey A. LeRoux

Previous work on intercultural communication effectiveness has generally focused on its cognitive components, including cultural knowledge, language proficiency, and ethnocentrism. In this chapter, we examine the role of emotions in intercultural adjustment, and suggest that the ability to regulate emotion is one of the keys to effective intercultural communication. Our model focuses on the role of emotion in intercultural communication episodes, and particularly on the skills necessary for the resolution of intercultural conflict, arguing that emotion regulation is a gatekeeper ability that allows people to engage in successful conflict resolution that leads to effective, long-term intercultural communication.

Culture plays a large role in the communication process (see Žegarac in this volume). Building on that material, we first describe the concepts of intercultural adaptation and adjustment, then the factors that previous research has identified related to adjustment. We then discuss the role of emotions, but also highlight the importance of critical thinking and openness/flexibility, in a growth model of intercultural adjustment potential that has at its core the ability to regulate emotions. We review empirical support for this model, and then review literature examining cultural differences in emotion regulation. Throughout, we blend literature from both communication and psychology in producing a unique perspective on this topic.

1.   Intercultural adaptation and adjustment

1.1.   Definitions

One of the most important consequences of and processes associated with intercultural communication is intercultural adaptation and adjustment. We have found that it is important to make a distinction between adaptation and adjustment. On one hand we believe that adaptation is based in the sociocultural domain (Ward 2001); that is, it refers to the process of altering one's behaviour to fit in with a changed environment or circumstances, or as a response to social pressure. One of the most well known models of adaptation, for instance, is Berry's (Berry, Kim and Boski 1988) analysis of the interaction styles for sojourners, immigrants, and refugees. In this model, four categories of interaction style are identified: integrators, marginalizers, separators, and assimilators. These refer to behavioural changes made in response to different environments.

On the other hand we define adjustment as the subjective experiences that are associated with and result from attempts at adaptation, and that also motivate further adaptation. Previous researchers have incorporated a wide range of outcome measures as adjustment, including self-awareness and self-esteem (Kamal and Maruyama 1990), mood states (Stone Feinstein and Ward 1990), and health status (Babiker, Cox and Miller 1980; all cited in Ward 2001). Some have developed synthesizing strategies to integrate specific approaches in order to highlight a smaller number of features. For example, Brislin (1993) identified three factors of adjustment, including (1) having successful relationships with people from other cultures; (2) feeling that interactions are warm, cordial, respectful, and cooperative; and (3) accomplishing tasks in an effective and efficient manner. Gudykunst, Hammer and Wiseman (1977) included the ability to manage psychological stress effectively. Black and Stephens (1989) identified general adjustment involving daily activities, interaction adjustment involving interpersonal relations, and work adjustment related to work and tasks.

Adapting to a new culture can have both positive and negative adjustment outcomes. The positive consequences include gains in language competence; self-esteem, awareness, and health (Babiker, Cox and Miller 1980; Kamal and Maruyama 1990); self-confidence, positive mood, interpersonal relationships, and stress reduction (Matsumoto et al. 2001). Clearly when intercultural experiences go well, individuals report evolving in many qualitative, positive ways so that they are different, and better, individuals. These include the development of multicultural identities and multiple perspectives with which to engage the world.

Negative adjustment outcomes include psychological and psychosomatic concerns (Shin and Abell 1999); early return to one's home country (Montagliani and Giacalone 1998); emotional distress (Furukawa and Shibayama 1995); dysfunctional communication (Gao and Gudykunst 1991; Okazaki-Luff 1991); culture shock (Pederson 1995); depression, anxiety, diminished school and work performance, and difficulties in interpersonal relationships (Matsumoto et al. 2001). In extreme cases negative adjustment results in antisocial behaviour (gangs, substance abuse, crime) and even suicide. Fortunately all sojourners do not experience this wide range of psychological and physical health problems, but most have probably experienced *some* of these problems at some point in their sojourn.

Intercultural experience is comprised of continuous adaptation and adjustment to the differences with which we engage every day. This engagement is not easy because of the occurrence of misunderstandings due to cultural differences. Our ethnocentric and stereotypic ways of thinking, which are themselves normal psychological functions, make it easy for us to create negative value judgments about those differences and misunderstandings. Negative emotions are also associated with these judgments. These negative reactions make it difficult for us to engage in more constructive methods of interacting, and keep us from truly appreciating those differences and integrating with people who are different.

One of the goals, therefore, of intercultural adaptation is to adopt an adaptation pattern that minimizes these stresses and negative adjustment outcomes, and maximizes positive ones. Negative adjustment outcomes often serve as important motivators for continued or refined adaptations to the new environment, a concept that is rooted in the notion that emotions are motivational (Tomkins 1962, 1963) and that affect fuels the development of cognitive schemas (Piaget 1952). The development of strategies that deal with potential conflict and misunderstanding is imperative in order to produce successful and effective long-term intercultural communication and relationships.

1.2.   Factors that predict adjustment

Studies have identified a wide range of variables such as knowledge, language proficiency, attitudes, previous experiences, levels of ethnocentrism, social support, cultural similarity, adventure, and self-construals as factors that influence intercultural adjustment (reviewed in Matsumoto et al. 2001; see also Brabant, Wilson and Gallois in this volume) Among these, three factors have consistently emerged as leading contributors: knowledge of host and home culture, ethnocentrism, and language proficiency. In fact it is precisely because of these factors that many intercultural training interventions involve language skill and knowledge training. The underlying assumption of such training is that if people can speak the language of the host culture, and if they know some basic facts about it, they can adjust to life better. Likewise, if people can recognize ethnocentric attitudes, they will have successful adjustments.

Fostering positive intercultural adjustment requires the development of effective intercultural communication competence (ICC). ICC has been studied extensively (Gudykunst and Kim 1984; Littlejohn and Jabusch 1982; Powers and Lowery 1984), and refers to the skills, talents, and strategies in which we engage in order to exchange thoughts, feelings, attitudes, and beliefs among people of different cultural backgrounds (cf. Prechtl and Davidson-Lund in this volume). ICC is reliant on a process that ensures successful and effective communication across cultures.

How can we develop such a process? (cf. Rost-Roth in this volume; Newton in this volume.) One strategy would be to become thoroughly versant in a culture, recording the cultural similarities and differences found in it and building your own 'cultural dictionary'. This is a formidable task, as there is so much about culture to learn and so little time, energy, and storage space available. This approach, however, is not without merit, and certainly many people develop such almanacs in their minds about cultures with which they become intimately familiar through personal experiences. Related processes such as knowledge of and attitude toward host culture, ethnocentrism, social distance, and exposure to host culture members are all related to ICC (Gudykunst and Kim 1984; Samovar and Porter 1995; Wiseman, Hammer and Nishida 1989).

But it is virtually impossible to create that dictionary of culture for all the cultures and peoples we will possibly come in contact with, and many of us do not have the opportunities to become truly culturally fluent in this fashion. Instead, the vast majority of us will need to rely on a *process model* of intercultural growth to engage in effective intercultural communication. As disagreements and misunderstandings based on intercultural communications are inevitable, it becomes important to be able to manage our negative emotional reactions when engaging with those differences. Those who can will then be able to engage in a more constructive intercultural process and open the door to more successful intercultural interactions. Those who cannot will have that door closed to them. Emotion management, therefore, is central to this process, and holds the key to adjustment.

2.   An emotion-focused approach to intercultural adjustment: the psychological engine of adjustment

Emotions, in fact, are a large part of our lives. Emotions are transient reactions to events or situations, and involve a package of cognitive, physiological, expressive, and behavioural components. When emotions are elicited, they affect our thinking, turn on a unique physiology, make us feel certain ways, and motivate us to engage in behaviour. They colour life and experiences, giving them meaning and relevance. Sadness, anger, disgust, fear, frustration, shame, and guilt – while all negative and unattractive – are all significant in that they tell us something important about ourselves and our relationships with other people, events, or situations. Happiness, joy, satisfaction, pleasure, and interest are also important emotions in that they, too, give us important information about our relationships with others. Emotions are 'read-out mechanisms' because they provide information to us about our relationship to the world around us (Buck 1984).

Emotions are important because they motivate behaviours. Sadness and anger make us do something, just as happiness and joy reinforce behaviours. The father of modern day research and theory of emotion in psychology – Sylvan Tomkins – suggested that emotions *are* motivation, and if you want to understand why people behave the way they do, you have to understand their emotions (Tomkins 1962, 1963). For these reasons, it is only natural that we give more consideration to this aspect of our lives vis-à-vis intercultural adjustment.

As mentioned above, we assume that intercultural misunderstandings occur because of cultural differences. We further assume that these misunderstandings are laden with emotion such as anger, frustration, anxiety, or sadness. Thus how well people deal with their negative emotions and resolve conflicts is a major determinant of intercultural adjustment success or failure. While intercultural adaptation inevitably involves many positive experiences as well, one of the keys to successfully adjusting to a different culture is having the ability to re-solve conflicts well.

When negative emotions are aroused during conflict, it is easy for people to be overcome by those feelings because they take over one's thinking and feel-ing. Even people who are usually adept at thinking critically and who can act in perfectly moral and altruistic ways may not be able to think or act in such a manner when overcome by negative emotions. It is these critical moments in the intercultural interaction episode – when negative emotions are aroused be-cause of inevitable cultural differences – that define a key step in personal growth, which is a means to both intercultural success or stagnation. Individuals who can regulate their negative feelings, somehow put them on hold and not act directly upon them, or allow them to overwhelm them, will be able to then en-gage in other processes that will aid them to expand their appraisal and attribu-tion of the causes of the differences. Once emotions are held in check, individ-uals can engage in critical thinking about the origins of those differences and the nature of misunderstandings, hopefully allowing themselves to go beyond their own cultural lenses to entertain the possibility of other causes of the differences that they may not have even been aware of. Once this type of critical thinking can occur, these individuals will have an active choice of accepting or rejecting alternative hypotheses concerning the causes of those differences, and can have the openness and flexibility to accept rival hypotheses if it turns out their initial reactions were inaccurate.

By engaging in critical thinking about cultural differences and being open and flexible to new ways of thinking, people continually add new cognitive schemas in their minds to represent the world. The addition of new schemas adds complexity to the ability to interact with diversity, creating new expec-tations and greater awareness of similarities and differences. All of this is poss-ible only when emotions are regulated and negative emotions are not allowed to get the best of one. This is a growth model of development.

If, however, negative emotions overcome us and dictate how we think, feel, and act, we cannot engage in critical thinking about those differences. People re-vert to a previous way of thinking about those differences that is rooted in their ethnocentric and stereotypic ways of viewing the world and others. Instead of creating rival hypotheses and new schemas that will stimulate growth in ways of thinking, this process reinforces pre-existing, limited ways of thinking. Openness and flexibility to new ideas and to these rival hypotheses are not even options be-cause the new ideas do not exist. Instead there is only a regurgitation of stereo-types and vindication of ethnocentric attitudes. This is a non-growth model.

The four main ingredients to personal growth in relation to dealing with cultural differences in our model, therefore, are Emotion Regulation (ER), Critical Thinking (CT), Openness (OP), and Flexibility (FL). These are psychological skills that are internal, and we call them the *psychological engine* of adaptation and adjustment. They are the psychological mechanisms by which intercultural success or stagnation, personal growth or vindication, will occur. Of these ER is the key ingredient as it is the gatekeeper of the growth process, because if we cannot put our inevitable negative emotions in check, it is impossible to engage in what is clearly higher order thinking about cultural differences.

These psychological processes are crucial to intercultural adjustment. It does not matter how much information about host or home culture, or the degree of language skills one may have; if one cannot regulate emotions, think critically about situations, events, and people, and does not have the openness of mind and flexibility to adopt alternative positions to what one is familiar with and accustomed to, it is difficult to develop ICC. If, however, one has these psychological attributes, then one has the psychological engine that will allow one to use knowledge and language in order to weather the storms of intercultural conflicts, rise above them, become a stronger, wiser, and more multicultural person.

The model we propose is similar to the concepts of assimilation and accommodation proposed by Piaget that explain how cognitive development occurs (Cowan 1978; Dasen 1976; Piaget and Campbell 1976; Piaget, Elkind and Flavell 1969; Piaget, Gruber and Vonèche 1977). Piaget suggested that infants and children attempt to adapt to their environments by first assimilating the environment into their existing cognitive schemas. When the environment does not match their schemas, infants and children accommodate, that is, alter their existing schemas or add to them, thereby increasing cognitive complexity. While Piaget's theory of cognitive development focused on the process of assimilation and accommodation, what fueled accommodation, that is cognitive growth, was the negative affect that occurred when infants attempted to assimilate the environment into their existing schemas and they did not fit; that is, negative affect fueled cognitive development (Cowan 1978; Piaget 1952). In the same vein we propose that negative emotional experiences fuel the need to adapt and readapt to the environment. Those who adapt in positive, constructive ways will experience positive adjustment outcomes while those who do not will experience negative outcomes.

These assumptions sit well with research in other areas of psychology. Marital satisfaction, for instance, which is not unlike intercultural communication, is correlated with the ability of the couple to deal with and resolve differences of opinions and conflicts, and not necessarily by the amount of positive experiences they have together (Carstensen, Gottman and Levenson 1995; Gottman and Levenson 1986, 1992, 1999, 2000; Levenson and Gottman 1983). Conflict resolution skills are one of the keys to a happy marriage, and we believe they are a key to successful intercultural adjustment. Recent research has also demonstrated that there are gender and ethnic group differences in emotion regulation, that individual differences in it are related to regulation success, mood regulation, coping styles and strategies, inauthenticity, interpersonal functioning, and well-being (Gross and John 2003).

The key, therefore, to achieving successful intercultural adjustment is the engagement of a personal growth process model where ways of thinking, person perception, and worldview are constantly being updated by the new and exciting cultural differences with which we engage in our everyday lives. The key to this engagement is the ability to regulate our emotional reactions and the other components of the psychological engine of adjustment. If we can do so, then the increasing cultural diversity of the world is an exciting research laboratory where we can constantly test our hypotheses, explore new hypotheses, throw out theories of the world that do not work, and create theories that do. In this framework the world is an exciting place to be and the challenge of cultural diversity and intercultural episodes and conflicts is a stage for forging new relationships, new ideas, and new people. It is the stage for intercultural success for those individuals who can engage in the processes outlined above. For these individuals, life is an enjoyable journey.

3. Empirical support for the growth model of intercultural adjustment: the intercultural adjustment potential scale (ICAPS)

3.1. Development and validation of the ICAPS

For years the field has struggled with the creation of valid and reliable individual difference measures that will predict intercultural adjustment. The identification of several psychological variables as the keys to intercultural adjustment, however, opens the door to such development. Because there was no measure that could assess individual differences in the potential for intercultural adjustment based on the psychological skills outlined above, we created one, resulting in the development of the Intercultural Adjustment Potential Scale (ICAPS).

Our strategy was to embody the several factors previously suggested in a pool of items and then to empirically test which had the strongest ability to predict intercultural adjustment, rather than to decide on an a priori basis which items should be included. We thus examined item content from a number of valid and reliable personality inventories assessing psychological constructs related to emotion regulation, critical thinking, openness and flexibility; we also included other skills such as interpersonal security, emotional commitment to traditional ways of thinking, tolerance of ambiguity, and empathy. We created items based on the ideas gleaned from our examination of many existing scales, and also constructed our own items. This resulted in the initial development of 193 items.

One issue that arose early in this work was whether this test would be developed for any sojourner of any cultural background, or for those from a single culture. We opted for the latter, assuming that it would be more beneficial to create and validate a measure that has as high a predictive validity as possible for one cultural group, rather than develop a general measure at the sacrifice of predictive validity. The development of a culture-general measure would require the testing of people from multiple home cultures in multiple host cultures, which would be practically infeasible. Moreover a culture-specific measure could serve as the platform for similar method development in other cultures. Thus, we focused on Japanese sojourners and immigrants, because of the literature in the area and our own expertise with this culture.

Because we were concerned about the cross-cultural equivalence of the 193 items, had to take into account that respondents might have different English language capabilities, and had to remove any colloquialism and difficulty of wording, two researchers created the items, reviewing and modifying all items in terms of language and style, rendering the wording appropriate for Japanese students who might possess a limited selection of English idioms commonly in use. Two Japanese research assistants then reviewed the items, ensuring that they were understandable to native Japanese. Items that depended for their utility on a cultural value in which Japanese and U.S. culture differed were excluded. In all cases, items were written to adapt the cultural meaning of an item in the United States to the same cultural context from a Japanese perspective.

To date many studies have demonstrated the internal, temporal, and parallel forms reliability, and convergent, predictive, and incremental validity of the ICAPS to predict intercultural adjustment (Matsumoto et al. 2001, 2003a, 2004). Early on we decreased the number of items from 193 to 55, based on each item's empirical ability to predict intercultural adjustment. Items having little or nothing to do with intercultural adjustment were eliminated, even if elsewhere they reliably measured an aspect of an underlying psychological skill (e.g. openness) that was theoretically related to adjustment. Also, some items predicted adjustment better than others; thus, only items that predicted adjustment the best, according to empirical criteria, were retained. Although the ICAPS was originally developed for use with the Japanese, our studies have also shown that it predicts adjustment in immigrants from all around the world, including India, Sweden, Central and South America, suggesting that it taps a pancultural set of psychological skills relevant to intercultural adjustment.

3.2.   Identifying the psychological skills underlying the ICAPS:
        the importance of emotion regulation

Initial factor analyses using normative data (n approximately 2,300, half of whom were non-U.S. born and raised) suggested that four factors underlie the ICAPS – Emotion Regulation (ER), Openness (OP), Flexibility (FL) and Critical Thinking (CT) (Matsumoto et al. 2001). These findings provided support for our theoretical formulation in which the importance of ER, OP, CT and FL are the key psychological ingredients to intercultural adaptation. These skills were hypothesized as necessary in allowing immigrants and sojourners to cope with stress and conflict that are inevitable in intercultural sojourns, while at the same time allowing for personal growth in understanding, tolerance and acceptance of cultural differences.

To obtain further support for the validity of these four psychological skills to predict adjustment, we created scores for each of these scales and computed correlations between them and various adjustment variables across the studies conducted to determine which psychological constructs predicted adjustment. Individuals who scored high on the ICAPS scales, and especially ER, had less adjustment problems at work, home, during spare time, and in family domains; less somatic, cognitive, and behavioural anxiety; less depression; greater subjective well-being in their adjustment to the US or another country; greater subjective adjustment; higher dyadic adjustments in international marriages; higher life satisfaction; less psychopathology; less culture shock and homesickness; higher language scores; better grades; more tendency to work; higher income; and managerial skills useful in solving the complex problems of running a business. These correlations provided strong support for this conglomeration of skills to predict adjustment.

Conceptually we suggested that ER was a gatekeeper skill because it is necessary for people to manage inevitable intercultural conflict and that once emotions were regulated individuals could engage in critical thinking and assimilation of new cognitive schemas that aid in adjustment. Various outcomes across all studies supported this contention. Across studies, ER predicted most of the adjustment measures relative to the other ICAPS scales. In addition, hierarchical multiple regressions indicated that ER accounted for most of the variance in adjustment outcomes when entered first in the regression; the additional variance accounted for by OP, FL, and CT was always negligible (Matsumoto et al. 2003b). People who score high on ER have high positive social skills and abilities, more success in life, successful coping, achievement, ability, and psychological mindedness. They also have less Neuroticism, and less tendency to withdraw from active involvement with the social world.

Our most recent studies continue to highlight the importance of ER to intercultural adjustment. In one study (Yoo, Matsumoto and LeRoux 2006), international students attending San Francisco State University completed the ICAPS and a variety of adjustment measures at the beginning and end of the academic year (September and May). ER was highly and significantly correlated with all adjustment variables. Individuals with higher ER scores had less anxiety, culture shock, depression, homesickness, and hopelessness, and more contentment and satisfaction with life. Moreover each of these relationships were observed when the ICAPS ER scale at time 1 was correlated with these adjustment variables at time 2, 9 months later, and when demographic variables were controlled. The correlations with time 2 adjustment variables also survived when the same variable's time 1 levels were controlled. Individual differences in ER, therefore, predicted adjustment concurrently, and considerably well into the future as well (Table 1).

Table 1. Correlations between ICAPS emotion regulation scale and adjustment variables in international students assessed at the beginning (time 1) and end (time 2) of school year

| Adjustment variable | Correlations | | | |
	Time 1	Sig	Time 2	Sig
Beck anxiety inventory	–0.39	**	–0.34	*
Contentment	0.31	*	0.41	*
Culture shock	–0.66	***	–0.71	***
Beck depression inventory	–0.40	**	–0.33	*
Homesickness	–0.24	*	–0.37	*
Beck hopelessness inventory	–0.45	***	–0.41	*
Satisfaction with life scale	0.40	**	0.41	*

$*p < 0.05$ $**p < 0.01$ $***p < 0.001$

Many of the findings we have reported have been replicated by other laboratories (Savicki et al. 2004). Thus we are very confident about the ability of ER to predict a variety of intercultural adjustment outcomes. Still there are many questions that remain. For instance, because ER is a skill, we believe that it can be improved with training. It is clear that typical teaching about culture that occurs in didactic classrooms does *not* affect ER (Matsumoto 2001, 2002). But it is also clear that training seminars that are based on experiential learning about culture can improve people's ER scores (Matsumoto et al. 2001, 2003a).

Because the ICAPS reliably and validly assesses individual differences in ER related to intercultural adjustment, there is great potential for the ICAPS to be used as a diagnostic tool. Training programs specially designed to improve ER can aid those with low ER scores in improving their potential for intercultural adjustment. At the same time, individuals with high ER skills can look to other areas of improvement in terms of training needs. The ICAPS as a whole and ER scores in particular can be used as an aid in personnel selection for overseas assignments or work in multinational, intercultural teams.

At the same time, the relationship between ER and adjustment is not perfect. Some people who score very low on ER do adjust well, while some people who score high on ER adjust poorly. While ER is undoubtedly one of the most important psychological skills related to adjustment, it is definitely not the only psychological skill that contributes to adjustment. And psychological skills are only one factor of many that contributes to adjustment. Other factors include situational, environmental, and ecological variables, all of which affect adaptation and adjustment. ER is only one factor that contributes to adjustment outcomes, albeit an important one.

4.   Cultural differences in emotion regulation

Clearly ER is one of the most important skills necessary for intra- and intercultural adjustment. Given that there are individual differences in ER (Gross 1999a, 2002; Gross and John 2003), one question that arises concerns whether or not there are cultural differences in ER. This is an interesting possibility that raises questions not only about intercultural encounters, but about the origins of such skills. And it also leads to the possibility that people of some cultures that are generally higher on ER would be better equipped to adjust well interculturally, while people of cultures typically lower on ER may be less suited for adjustment. These differences also implicate cross-cultural differences in intracultural indices of adjustment, such as subjective well-being or anxiety.

In fact there are a number of previous studies that suggest that there are substantial cultural differences in ER. The earliest systematic cross-cultural data that points in this direction is Hofstede's seminal study on work-related values. One of the cultural dimensions that Hofstede identified was Uncertainty Avoidance (Hofstede and Bond 1984; Hofstede 1980, 2001); this dimension is probably linked to ER. Uncertainty Avoidance (UA) is defined as the degree to which people feel threatened by the unknown or ambiguous situations, and have developed beliefs, institutions, or rituals to avoid them. Cultures high on UA are most likely characterized by low levels of ER, while cultures low on UA have high ER. Individuals high on ER would tend to feel less threatened by unknown or ambiguous situations, and would be able to deal with such situations more constructively than those with low ER, as discussed throughout this chapter. This suggests that people from countries high on UA would have more difficulty in intercultural adjustment, while people from countries low on UA would have relatively less difficulty. In Hofstede's study, the three countries highest on UA were Greece, Portugal and Guatemala; the three lowest were Denmark, Hong Kong and Sweden.

Another source of information concerning cultural differences in ER comes from McCrae's multinational study of the five factor model of personality (Allik and McCrae 2004; McCrae 2002; McCrae et al. 1998). In these studies McCrae and his colleagues have used their Revised NEO-Personality Inventory (NEO-PI-R; Costa and McCrae 1992), a 240 item questionnaire that measures the five personality traits considered to be universal: Extraversion, Openness, Agreeableness, Conscientiousness, and Neuroticism. To date McCrae has reported data on this measure from 36 samples in 32 countries involving both college students and adults (McCrae 2002). Although data are collected from individuals, means on the various facet scores were computed for each sample. The Five Factor Model replicates on the national level as well as the individual (McCrae 2001, 2002). Based on these results McCrae has computed country-level means for each of the five factors (and their facets) for each of the countries studied. Country scores on Neuroticism probably reflect mean levels of ER. Neuroticism is typically defined as emotional lability, and thus high scores on Neuroticism probably reflect low scores on emotion regulation, and vice versa. This suggests that people from countries high on Neuroticism would experience more difficulty in intercultural adjustment, and vice versa. In McCrae's study, the three countries that scored highest on Neuroticism were Portugal, Italy and Spain; the three lowest were Sweden, Denmark and Norway.

The notion that Hofstede's UA and McCrae's Neuroticism are related to each other received empirical support by Hofstede and McCrae (2004), who computed country-level correlations between their respective culture and personality scores. UA was correlated with Neuroticism 0.58 (and negatively with Agreeableness –0.55), suggesting that these dimensions share a common denominator. We suggest that one common denominator is ER.

One of the limitations of using the Hofstede and McCrae data to estimate cultural differences in ER is that neither of them intended to measure ER directly. The ICAPS described earlier in this chapter, however, does, and our current normative database includes data from approximately 11,000 individuals around the world. We computed an exploratory factor analysis of these data, after doubly standardizing both within individuals and countries in order to eliminate positioning effects and to produce a pancultural solution (Leung and Bond 1989). As previously, the first factor to emerge in these analyses was ER. We then created scale scores for the raw data using the highest loading items on this factor (11 items), and computed means on this scale for each country represented in the data set. (Respondents rate each item on a 7-point scale; means therefore range from 1–7.) Like the Hofstede and McCrae data sets, these data (Table 2) also demonstrate considerable variability across cultures in ER. The three countries with the highest ICAPS ER scores were Sweden, Norway, and Finland; the three lowest were Japan, Malaysia, and China.

To examine whether the ICAPS ER scores were empirically related to Hofstede's UA and McCrae's Neuroticism, we computed country-level correlations between them. ICAPS ER was marginally negatively correlated with UA, $r(47) = -0.20$, $p < 0.10$, indicating those countries with higher ER scores had lower UA scores, as expected. ICAPS ER was also negatively correlated with Neuroticism, $r(29) = -0.49$, $p < 0.01$, indicating that countries with higher ER scores had lower Neuroticism scores, as expected.

Several other studies have measured ER or concepts related to it across cultures, and provide further hints as to its cultural variability. Matsumoto and his colleagues (2003b), for instance, reported two studies in which they administered the Emotion Regulation Questionnaire (Gross and John 2003), a ten-item scale that produces scores on two subscales, Reappraisal and Suppression. Americans had significantly higher scores than the Japanese on Reappraisal, while the Japanese had significantly higher scores on Suppression. In that same report, the Americans also had significantly higher scores than the Japanese on the ICAPS ER scale, while the Japanese had significantly higher scores on the Neuroticism scale of the NEO-PI-R. These findings converge with the country listing of ICAPS ER scores described above.

Finally a number of studies have documented cultural differences in display rules (Ekman and Friesen 1969). These are rules learned early in life that govern the modification of emotional displays as a function of social circumstance. Display rules are related to ER because they concern the management of the expressive component of emotion. The first study to document the existence of display rules was Ekman and Friesen's classic study involving American and Japanese participants viewing highly stressful films in two conditions while being videotaped (Ekman 1972; Friesen 1972). When viewing the stimuli alone, both American and Japanese observers showed the same emotions in their faces; when in the presence of a higher status experimenter, however, cultural differences emerged. While the Americans continued to show their facial signs of negative emotions, Japanese observers were more likely to mask their negative feelings with smiles.

Subsequent cross-cultural research has continued to document cultural differences in display rules. Elsewhere we (Biehl, Matsumoto and Kasri in press; Matsumoto 1990) demonstrated how Japanese, Hungarians and Poles tended to deamplify negative emotions to ingroup members but amplify positive ones relative to Americans; they also amplify negative emotions to outgroups and minimize positive ones. We have also documented display rule differences between the US, Russia, South Korea and Japan (Matsumoto et al. 1998), and among different ethnic groups in the US (Matsumoto 1993). In our latest research we have reported cultural differences among the US, Japan, and Russia on display rules (Matsumoto et al. 2005).

Presumably other rules or similar types of mechanisms exist for other emotion components. Hochschild (2001), for instance, has proposed the concept of feeling rules, which concern the regulation of the experiential component of emotion. Gross suggests individuals can regulate their emotions by altering the antecedents that bring forth emotion (selecting or modifying situations, altering attention, or changing cognitions) and the behavioural and physiological responses related to emotion (Gross 1998, 1999a, 1999b, 2002; Gross and John 2003; Gross and Levenson 1993). Cross-cultural studies of these concepts are necessary to examine possible cultural differences in them as well.

Table 2. Country listing of emotion regulation scores from the ICAPS

Country	ICAPS Emotion Regulation score	Standardized Emotion Regulation score
Australia	4.58	0.21
Austria	4.76	0.89
Belgium	4.57	0.16
Botswana	4.43	−0.38
Brazil	4.63	0.39
Bulgaria	4.76	0.89
Canada	4.56	0.10
Chile	4.63	0.39
China	3.96	−2.23
Costa Rica	4.70	0.65
Croatia	4.76	0.89
Denmark	4.93	1.55
El Salvador	4.70	0.65
Estonia	3.36	.
Finland	4.93	1.55
France	4.57	0.16
Germany	4.57	0.16
Greece	4.47	−0.23
Guatemala	4.70	0.65
Hong Kong	4.15	−1.48
Hungary	4.76	0.89
India	4.64	0.42
Indonesia	3.75	.

Country	ICAPS Emotion Regulation score	Standardized Emotion Regulation score
Israel	4.11	−1.62
Italy	4.47	−0.23
Japan	3.87	−2.57
Lebanon	4.57	0.16
Malawi	4.43	−0.38
Malaysia	3.91	−2.41
Mexico	4.50	−0.11
Netherlands	4.57	0.16
Nigeria	4.36	−0.65
Norway	4.93	1.55
New Zealand	4.85	1.25
Peru	4.63	0.39
Philippines	4.33	−0.76
Poland	4.76	0.89
Portugal	4.47	−0.23
Russia	4.41	−0.45
South Africa	4.43	−0.38
South Korea	4.26	−1.04
Spain	4.47	−0.23
Sweden	4.93	1.55
Switzerland	4.76	0.89
Taiwan	4.09	−1.72
Thailand	4.22	−1.19
Turkey	4.67	0.53
USA	4.50	−0.13
Venezuela	4.63	0.39
Yugoslavia	4.76	0.89
Zambia	4.43	−0.38
Zimbabwe	4.43	−0.38

5.   Conclusion

ER is probably one of the most important psychological skills in our lives vis-à-vis intercultural adjustment. With ER, the increasing cultural diversity of the world is an exciting research laboratory, where we can constantly test our hypotheses, explore new hypotheses, throw out theories that do not work, and create theories that do. Without ER, people reinforce and crystallize their pre-existing ethnocentric and stereotypic ways of dealing with the world. With ER, people voyage through life; without it, they vindicate their lives.

While we have focused in our work and in this chapter on the role of ER in interpersonal contexts, there is no reason to believe that the model we propose is not applicable also to intergroup contexts. In the world today there are many contexts in which people may begin an encounter with prejudice and an assumption that the other person will be 'difficult' to communicate or deal with. Although we have done no research on this directly, we would predict that emotion regulation is also important on the intergroup level, where prejudice and history may lead to pre-existing destructive emotions that are not conducive to successful intergroup relationships. Future research will need to delve into the possibility of using our model to explore these issues.

Our views on the role of emotion, critical thinking, and openness in effective intercultural communication fill a void in our understanding of the development of ICC and fostering positive intercultural adjustment outcomes, and provide the field with important new ways of conceptualizing intercultural training. Indeed, our work on ER suggests that one of the primary goals of intercultural communication competence and training programs should be in the improvement of ER skills in trainees. Tools such as the ICAPS can be used to assess individuals on their ER levels, providing important diagnostic information about strengths and weaknesses, as well as for documenting the efficacy of training. The emotional impact of typical training devices such as role plays, simulations, and the like can be analysed for their emotional impact and the ways they foster the development (or not) of ER. Tools such as Description, Interpretation, and Evaluation (DIE) can be complemented by incorporating emotions and their evaluation (what we call the Description, Feeling, Interpretation, and Evaluation – DFIE – model). No matter how complex or advanced our cognitive understanding of culture and communication is, this understanding does no good if we cannot regulate emotions that inevitably occur in intercultural communication episodes.

References

Allik, Juri and Robert R. McCrae
   2004   Toward a geography of personality traits: patterns of profiles across 36 cultures. *Journal of Cross-Cultural Psychology* 35: 13–28.
Babiker, Isam E., John L. Cox and Patrick M. Miller
   1980   The measurement of cultural distance and its relationship to medical consultations, symptomatology and examination of performance of overseas students at Edinburgh university. *Social Psychiatry* 15: 109–116.
Berry, John. W., Uichol Kim and Pawel Boski
   1988   Psychological acculturation of immigrants. In: Young Yun Kim and William B. Gudykunst (eds.), *Cross-Cultural Adaptation: Current Approaches.* (*International and Intercultural Communication Annual*, Vol. 11, 62–89). Newbury Park, CA: Sage.
Biehl, Michael, David Matsumoto and Fazilet Kasri
   in press   Culture and emotion. In: Uwe Gielen and Anna Laura Comunian (eds.), *Cross-Cultural and International Dimensions of Psychology.* Trieste, Italy: Edizioni Lint Trieste S.r.1.
Black, J. Stewart and Gregory K. Stephens
   1989   The influence of the spouse on American expatriate adjustment and intent to stay in Pacific rim overseas assignments. *Journal of Management* 15: 529–544.
Brabant, Madeleine, Bernadette Watson and Cindy Gallois
In this volume Psychological perspectives: social psychology, language and intercultural communication, Chapter 4.
Brislin, Richard
   1993   *Understanding Culture's Influence on Behavior.* Fort Worth, TX: Harcourt Brace Jovanovich.
Buck, Ross W.
   1984   *The Communication of Emotion.* New York: Guilford Press.
Carstensen, Laura L., John M. Gottman and Robert W. Levenson
   1995   Emotional behavior in long-term marriage. *Psychology and Aging* 10: 140–149.
Costa, Paul T. and Robert R. McCrae
   1992   *Revised Neo-Personality Inventory (NEO-PI-R) and Neo Five Factor Inventory (NEO-FFI).* Odessa, FL: Psychological Assessment Resources.
Cowan, Philip A.
   1978   *Piaget: With Feeling: Cognitive, Social, and Emotional Dimensions.* New York: Holt Rinehart and Winston.
Dasen, Pierre R.
   1976   *Piagetian Psychology: Cross Cultural Contributions.* New York: Gardner Press (distributed by Halsted Press).
Ekman, Paul
   1972   Universal and cultural differences in facial expression of emotion. In: J.R. Cole (ed.), *Nebraska Symposium on Motivation 1971*, 207–283. Lincoln, NE: Nebraska University Press.

Ekman, Paul and Wallace Friesen
  1969   The repertoire of nonverbal behavior: categories, origins, usage, and coding. *Semiotica* 1: 49–98.
Friesen, Wallace V.
  1972   Cultural differences in facial expressions in a social situation: an experimental test of the concept of display rules. Unpublished Doctoral dissertation, University of California, San Francisco.
Furukawa, Toshiaki and Tadashi Shibayama
  1995   Factors including adjustment of high school students in an international exchange program. *Journal of Nervous and Mental Disease* 182(12): 709–714.
Gao, Ge and William Gudykunst
  1991   Uncertainty, anxiety, and adaptation. *International Journal of Intercultural Relations* 14: 301–317.
Gottman, John M. and Robert W. Levenson
  1986   Assessing the role of emotion in marriage. *Behavioral Assessment* 8: 31–48.
Gottman, John M. and Robert W. Levenson
  1992   Marital processes predictive of later dissolution: behavior, physiology, and health. *Journal of Personality and Social Psychology* 63: 221–223.
Gottman, John. M. and Robert W. Levenson
  1999   Rebound from marital conflict and divorce prediction. *Family Process* 38: 287–292.
Gottman, John M. and Robert W. Levenson
  2000   The timing of divorce: predicting when a couple will divorce over a 14-year period. *Journal of Marriage and the Family* 62: 737–745.
Gross, James J.
  1998   The emerging field of emotion regulation: an integrative review. *Review of General Psychology* 2: 271–299.
Gross, James J.
  1999a   Emotion and emotion regulation. In: Lawrence A. Pervin and Oliver P. John (eds.), *Handbook of Personality: Theory and Research*, 2nd edn, 525–552. New York: Guilford.
Gross, James J.
  1999b   Emotion regulation: past, present, future. *Cognition and Emotion* 13(5): 551–573.
Gross, James J.
  2002   Emotion regulation: affective, cognitive, and social consequences. *Psychophysiology* 39: 281–291.
Gross, James J. and Oliver P. John
  2003   Individual differences in two emotion regulation processes: implications for affect, relationships, and well-being. *Journal of Personality and Social Psychology* 85: 348–362.
Gross, James J. and Robert W. Levenson
  1993   Emotional suppression: physiology, self-report, and expressive behavior. *Journal of Personality and Social Psychology* 64: 970–986.
Gudykunst, William B. and Young Yun Kim
  1984   *Communicating with Strangers: An Approach to Intercultural Communication*. New York: McGraw Hill.

Gudykunst, William B., Mitchell R. Hammer and Richard Wiseman
1977   An analysis of an integrated approach to cross-cultural training. *Inter-national Journal of Intercultural Relations* 1(2): 99–110.
Hochschild, Arlie
2001   Emotion work, feeling rules, and social structure. In: Ann Branaman (ed.), *Self and Society*, 138–155. Malden, MA: Blackwell Publishers.
Hofstede, Geert H.
1980   *Culture's Consequences: International Differences in Work-related Values.* Beverly Hills: Sage Publications.
Hofstede, Geert H.
2001   *Culture's Consequences: Comparing Values, Behaviors, Institutions and Organizations across Nations*, 2nd edn. Thousand Oaks, CA: Sage Publications.
Hofstede, Geert H. and Michael H. Bond
1984   Hofstede's cultural dimensions: an independent validation using Rokeach's value survey. *Journal of Cross-Cultural Psychology* 15(4): 417–433.
Hofstede, Geert H. and Robert R. McCrae
2004   Personality and culture revisited: linking traits and dimensions of culture. *Cross-Cultural Research* 38: 52–88.
Kamal, Abdulaziz A. and Geoffrey Maruyama
1990   Cross-cultural contact and attitudes of Qatari students in the United States. *International Journal of Intercultural Relations* 14: 123–134.
Leung, Kwok and Michael H. Bond
1989   On the empirical identification of dimensions for cross-cultural comparisons. *Journal of Cross-Cultural Psychology* 20: 133–151.
Levenson, Robert W. and John M. Gottman
1983   Marital interaction: physiological linkage and affective exchange. *Journal of Personality and Social Psychology* 45: 587–597.
Littlejohn, S.W. and David M. Jabusch
1982   Communication competence: a model and application. *Journal of Applied Communication Research* 10: 29–37.
Matsumoto, David
1990   Cultural similarities and differences in display rules. *Motivation and Emotion* 14: 195–214.
Matsumoto, David
1993   Ethnic differences in affect intensity, emotion judgments, display rule attitudes, and self-reported emotional expression in an American sample. *Motivation and Emotion* 17: 107–123.
Matsumoto, David
2001   Teaching culture in the classroom: Does it really produce differences in behaviors? Paper presented at the Regional Conference of the International Association of Cross-Cultural Psychology, Winchester, UK, July 2001.
Matsumoto, David
2002   Culture, psychology, and education. In: Walter J. Lonner, Dale L. Dinnel, Susanna A. Hayes and D.N. Sattler (eds.), *Online Readings in Psychology and Culture*. Bellingham, WA: Western Washington University, Department of Psychology, Center for Cross-Cultural Research. Available at http://www.ac.wwu.edu/~culture/readings.htm [Accessed 31 January 2007]

Matsumoto, David, Sachiko Takeuchi, Sari Andayani, Natalia Kouznetsova and Deborah Krupp
1998   The contribution of individualism–collectivism to cross-national differences in display rules. *Asian Journal of Social Psychology* 1: 147–165.
Matsumoto, David, Jeffrey A. LeRoux, Charlotte Ratzlaff, Haruyo Tatani, Hideko Uchida, Chu Kim and Shoko Araki
2001   Development and validation of a measure of intercultural adjustment potential in Japanese sojourners: the intercultural adjustment potential scale (ICAPS). *International Journal of Intercultural Relations* 25: 483–510.
Matsumoto, David, Jeffrey A. LeRoux, Mariko Iwamoto, Jung Wook Choi, David Rogers, Haruyo Tatani and Hideko Uchida
2003a   The robustness of the intercultural adjustment potential scale (ICAPS). *International Journal of Intercultural Relations* 27: 543–562.
Matsumoto, David, Jung Wook Choi, Satoko Hirayama, Akihiro Domae and Susumu Yamaguchi
2003b   Culture, display rules, emotion regulation, and emotion judgments. *submitted*.
Matsumoto, David, Jeffrey A. LeRoux, Roberta Bernhard and Heather Gray
2004   Personality and behavioral correlates of intercultural adjustment potential. *International Journal of Intercultural Relations* 28: 281–309.
Matsumoto, David, Seung Hee Yoo, Satoko Hirayama and Galina Petrova
2005   Validation of an individual-level measure of display rules: the display rule assessment inventory (DRAI). *Emotion* 5: 23–40.
McCrae, Robert R.
2001   Trait psychology and culture: exploring intercultural comparisons. *Journal of Personality* 69: 819–846.
McCrae, Robert R.
2002   NEO-PI-R data from 36 cultures: further intercultural comparisons. In: Robert R. McCrae and Juri Allik (eds.), *The Five-factor Model of Personality across Cultures*, 105–125. New York: Kluwer Academic/Plenum Publishers.
McCrae, Robert R., Paul T. Costa, Gregorio H. del Pilar, Jean-Pierre Rolland and Wayne D. Parker
1998   Cross-cultural assessment of the five-factor model: the revised neo personality inventory. *Journal of Cross-Cultural Psychology* 29: 171–188.
Montagliani, Amy and Robert A. Giacalone
1998   Impression management and cross-cultural adaptation. *Journal of Social Psychology* 138: 598–608.
Newton, Jonathan
In this volume Adapting authentic workplace talk for workplace communication training, Chapter 24.
Okazaki-Luff, Kazuko
1991   On the adjustment of Japanese sojourners: beliefs, contentions, and empirical findings. *International Journal of Intercultural Relations* 15: 85–102.
Pederson, Paul
1995   *The Five Stages of Culture Shock: Critical Incidents around the World.* Westwood, CT: Greenwood Press.

Piaget, Jean
  1952   *The Origins of Intelligence in Children*. London: International Universities Press.
Piaget, Jean and Sarah F. Campbell
  1976   *Piaget Sampler: An Introduction to Jean Piaget through his own words*. New York: Wiley.
Piaget, Jean, David Elkind and John H. Flavell
  1969   *Studies in Cognitive Development; Essays in Honor of Jean Piaget*. New York: Oxford University Press.
Piaget, Jean, Howard E. Gruber and Jacques Vonèche
  1977   *The Essential Piaget*. New York: Basic Books.
Powers, William and David Lowery
  1984   Basic communication fidelity. In: Robert Bostrom (ed.), *Competence in Communication*, 57–71. Beverly Hills, CA: Sage.
Prechtl, Elisabeth and Anne Davidson Lund
In this volume Intercultural competence and assessment: perspectives from the INCA project, Chapter 22.
Rost-Roth, Martina
In this volume Intercultural training, Chapter 23.
Samovar, Larry A. and Richard E. Porter
  1995   *Communication between Cultures*. Belmont, CA: Wadsworth.
Savicki, Victor, Rick Downing-Burnette, Lynne Heller, Frauke Binder and Walter Suntinger
  2004   Contrasts, changes, and correlates in actual and potential intercultural adjustment. *International Journal of Intercultural Relations* 28: 311–329.
Shin, Heajong and Neil Abell
  1999   The homesickness and contentment scale: Developing a culturally sensitive measure of adjustment for Asians. *Research on Social Work Practice* 9: 45–60.
Stone Feinstein, E. and Colleen Ward
  1990   Loneliness and psychological adjustment of sojourners: new perspectives on culture shock. In: Daphne Keats, Donald Munro and Leon Mann (eds.), *Heterogeneity in Cross-cultural Psychology*, 537–547. Lisse, Netherlands: Swets and Zeitlinger.
Tomkins, Sylvan S.
  1962   *Affect, Imagery, and Consciousness* (Vol. 1: The positive affects). New York: Springer.
Tomkins, Sylvan S.
  1963   *Affect, Imagery, and Consciousness* (Vol. 2: The negative affects). New York: Springer.
Ward, Colleen
  2001   The A, B, Cs of acculturation. In: David Matsumoto (ed.), *Handbook of Culture and Psychology*, 411–446. New York: Oxford University Press.
Wiseman, Richard, Mitchell R. Hammer and Hiroko Nishida
  1989   Predictors of intercultural communication competence. *International Journal of Intercultural Relations* 13: 349–370.
Yoo, Seung Hee, David Matsumoto and Jeffrey A. LeRoux
  2006   Emotion regulation, emotion recognition, and intercultural adjustment. *International Journal of Intercultural Relations* 30: 345–363.

6. Multidisciplinary perspectives on intercultural conflict: the 'Bermuda Triangle' of conflict, culture and communication

Nathalie van Meurs and Helen Spencer-Oatey

1. Introduction

A few decades ago, managers spent more than 20% of their time trying to resolve conflicts (Thomas and Schmidt 1976). Nowadays, conflicts are probably even more complex and time consuming to resolve, because technological advances, the world's exponential growth rate, and globalization have led to increased contact between culturally diverse people. Different norms, values, and language can make negotiating more stressful and less satisfactory (Brett and Okumura 1998), and conflict cannot be managed effectively without simultaneously considering both culture and communication. In fact, the three concepts of conflict, culture and communication are like a Bermuda Triangle – hazardous conditions will emerge unless the three are simultaneously handled appropriately.

Conflict processes are studied by researchers in a range of disciplines, including organizational behaviour, management studies, (intercultural) communication studies, peace studies, and applied linguistics. Unfortunately, research in these various disciplines tends to exist in parallel fields, with infrequent passages across theoretical and empirical divides. In this chapter we provide an overview of key theoretical frameworks, explore some of the main views as to the impact of culture, and consider the interrelationships between conflict, culture and communication. We call for more interdisciplinary research, so that boundaries can be broken down and illuminating new insights can emerge.

2. The concept of conflict

Conflict is an unavoidable element of interaction; it takes place between friends and family, and within and between groups and organizations. It occurs "when two or more social entities (i.e. individuals, groups, organizations, and nations) come in contact with one another in attaining their objectives" and when some kind of incompatibility emerges between them (Rahim 1992: 1). It is often regarded as undesirable, and much attention is typically focused on how to prevent or resolve it. However, conflict need not necessarily be undesirable. It can contribute to the maintenance and cohesion of groups, and it can stimulate reflection and change. So in these senses, it can be positive.

According to Hammer (2005: 676), conflict entails two key elements: (a) perceived (substantive) disagreement and (b) strong, negative emotions. The source of the disagreement or incompatibility can be various, of course. It could be that people have incompatible attitudes, values, and beliefs; or it could be that two parties require the same resource, or need to engage in incompatible activities to acquire a goal. In terms of affective experience, Rahim (1992: 17) argues that the incompatibilities, disagreements, or differences must be sufficiently intense for the parties to experience conflict. Yet, there can be differences in people's threshold of conflict awareness or tolerance, and this can sometimes be a cause of conflict in itself.

Conflict can be classified into two basic types, according to whether its predominant basis or source is cognitive or affective. Cognitive conflict results from differences of opinion on task-related issues such as scarce resources, policies and procedures, whereas affective, psychological, or relational conflict stems from differences in emotions and feelings (De Dreu 1997, Rahim 1992, Thomas 1976). Of course, these sources are not mutually exclusive, in that a conflict can start by being about a task-related issue and then develop into a personality clash.

What, then, do intercultural researchers want to find out through their study of conflict? There are three fundamental issues:

- What are the procedural characteristics of conflictive episodes? What tactics, communicative styles and linguistic strategies can be used to manage them?
- What factors influence the preferences, styles and tactics that people may choose, and what positive and negative impacts do they have on the outcomes? How may cultural differences impact on the emergence and management of conflict?
- What role does communication play in the emergence and management of conflict?

The following sections explore some of the main approaches that researchers have taken in addressing these questions.

3.   Classic frameworks for analysing conflict

3.1.   Thomas' (1976) models of dyadic conflict

Kenneth Thomas (1976), in a classic paper, proposed two complementary models of conflict – a process model and a structural model. The process model focuses on the sequence of events within a conflict episode, whilst the structural model focuses on the underlying factors that influence the events.

In his process model, Thomas (1976) proposes that a conflict episode comprises five main events from the viewpoint of one of the parties: frustration, conceptualization, behaviour, other's reaction, and outcome, with the outcome of a given episode setting the stage for subsequent episodes on the same issue. Thomas' specification of the behavioural element in this process is particularly well known. He applied Blake and Mouton's (1964) classic managerial grid to the study of conflict, arguing that people may hold different orientations towards a given conflict, depending on the degree to which they want to satisfy their own concerns and the degree to which they want to satisfy the other's concerns. He identified five orientations: neglect, appeasement, domination, compromise and integration (see Figure 1). Neglect reflects avoidance or indifference, in that no attention is paid to the concerns of either self or other. Appeasement reflects a lack of concern for self, but a high concern for the other, whilst domination represents a desire to win at the other's expense. Compromise is intermediate between appeasement and domination, and is often the least satisfactory for the two parties. Integration represents a problem-solving orientation where there is a desire to integrate both parties' concerns.

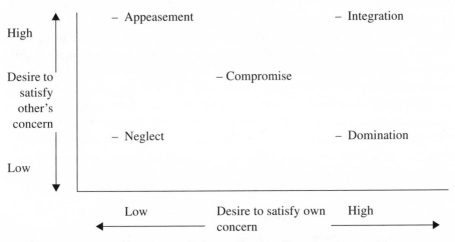

Figure 1. Thomas' 'grid' framework of conflict management orientations
(Based on Thomas 1976: 900)

A number of different terms are now in widespread use for these five orientations, and these are shown in Table 1. In the rest of this chapter, the terms used are: collaborative, competitive, compromising, accommodative and avoiding.

Table 1. Main terms used as labels for the five conflict management orientations

High self/high other concern	High self/low other concern	Medium self/ medium other concern	Low self/high other concern	Low self/low other concern
– Integrating (Thomas 1976; Rahim 1992) – Collaborative (Thomas 1976) – Problem solving (De Dreu 1997)	– Dominating (Thomas 1976; Rahim 1992) – Competitive (Thomas 1976) – Contending (De Dreu 1997)	– Compromising (Thomas 1976; Rahim 1992) – Sharing (Thomas 1976)	– Appeasing (Thomas 1976) – Accommodative (Thomas 1976) – Obliging (Rahim 1992) – Yielding (De Dreu 1997)	– Neglecting (Thomas 1976) – Avoidant/ avoiding (Thomas 1976; Rahim 1992; De Dreu 1997)

Thomas and Kilmann (1974) developed the Thomas–Kilmann conflict MODE instrument to measure people's conflict handling orientations. However, Rahim (1983) criticized its validity and reliability, and developed the 'Rahim Organizational Conflict Inventory-II' (ROCI-II Instrument). It achieved higher reliability scores, and this instrument has been widely used by researchers in management studies and intercultural communication. However, Sorenson, Morse and Savage (1999) actually measured the underlying concerns particular to the dual concern model (i.e. self vs. others) and found that only dominating and appeasement strategy choice correlated with these concerns; the more integrative strategies (i.e. problem solving and obliging) shared little variance and seemed subject to other contextual variables.

3.2.   Intercultural perspectives

In his structural model, Thomas (1976) maintains that people's response styles are hierarchically ordered, in that they have a dominant style, a back-up style, a least-preferred style and so on. He suggested that this hierarchy could be influenced by factors such as personality, motives and abilities. Could culture, therefore, influence this hierarchy, with some orientations being more prevalent in certain societies than in others? Many cross-cultural researchers have explored this question, and a widespread finding (e.g., Bond and Hwang 1986; Morris et al. 1998; Ohbuchi and Takahashi 1994; Trubinsky, Ting-Toomy and Lin 1991) is that a neglect style (that is also labeled avoidance) is more common among East Asians than among Americans. Yet, van Meurs (2003) found there were also differences between British and Dutch managers in this respect. Her results showed that although managers preferred a collaborative approach, the British managers were more avoiding than the Dutch managers, both in their own eyes and in those of the Dutch. While Britain and the Netherlands are often grouped together in terms of cultural values, they differ in terms of their need to avoid uncertainty, with the Dutch having a greater aversion to uncertainty and ambiguity (Hofstede 1991, 2001). This is a value that could have a major impact on preferences for handling conflict.

These findings could be regarded as conceptually problematic, because according to Thomas' orientation framework, neglect is an ineffective orientation, in that it reflects a lack of concern for the interests of either self or other and entails withdrawal. In fact, other researchers have found that avoiding is motivated by a concern for the relationship with the people involved (e.g., De Dreu 1997; Leung et al. 1990; Markus and Kitayama 1991; Morris et al. 1998). Friedman, Chi and Liu (2006) proposed that far from reflecting lack of concern, an avoiding style could result from concern for others. They hypothesized that it could reflect three possible concerns: (a) concern that a direct approach will damage the relationship, (b) concern that a direct approach will be more costly in cost–benefit terms, and (c) genuine concern for others based on personal values. They also hypothesized that the hierarchical status of the people involved in the conflict would have an impact. Using respondents from Taiwan and the USA, their results show a greater tendency for Taiwanese to use avoidance than Americans do. They found that this was explained by higher Taiwanese expectations that direct conflict will hurt the relationship with the other party, and by greater intrinsic concern for others. They found that it was not explained by differences in expected career costs/benefits of good/bad relations with others. In addition, their Taiwanese respondents showed more sensitivity to hierarchy than their American respondents did, in that avoidance behaviour was even more important for them when the other party was of higher status.

Superficially these studies suggest that Thomas' (1976) grid framework has limited cross-cultural validity. In fact, however, it is important to distinguish people's orientations (i.e. the degree to which they want to satisfy their own desires and those of the opposing party) and the tactics that people use to pursue them. This is a distinction that Thomas himself originally made, and Friedman, Chi and Liu's (2006) qualitative data illustrate its importance. They found that their Chinese respondents often displayed a long-term orientation, reporting tactics such as 'do nothing right now, but draw a lesson for future actions' and 'say nothing but collect more data on my own'. In other words, they found that avoidance was a tactic for achieving a satisfactory resolution of the conflict in the longer-term.

Van Meurs (2003) wanted to assess the motivations for conflict styles by measuring individual's concern for clarity, control and inconvenience without the focus on self vs. other. She found that managers were equally concerned about clarity but that British managers were more concerned than Dutch managers about inconvenience (i.e., to prevent awkward and uncomfortable situations from happening or difficult questions from being asked). They are unlikely to do so because they care for the other party, so it may be that the Dutch managers are extremely unconcerned about inconvenience, mainly because they care more about clarity and control regardless of harmony. Indeed, a concern for inconvenience significantly predicted managers' use of avoiding.

From an intercultural point of view, it is vital, therefore, to explore the tactics that people use, as well as people's desired outcomes for a particular conflict episode and their generally preferred style or orientation for handling it. Lytle (1999), for example, in her study of Chinese conflict management styles, reports several categories of behaviour that cannot easily be linked with the grid framework, because they are tactics rather than orientations or styles. They include group-oriented behaviour (such as consulting with the group to solve a problem, reframing the problem as a group problem and appealing to the group for help) and relational behaviour (including building up the relationship with the other party, and building up 'guanxi' or social connections with others).

3.3.   Brown and Levinson's face model

A second classic study that has had a major impact on studies of conflict is Brown and Levinson's (1987) face model of politeness. These authors start with the basic assumption that "all competent adult members of a society have (and know each other to have) 'face', the public self-image that every member wants to claim for himself" (Brown and Levinson 1987: 61). They further propose that face consists of two related aspects: negative face and positive face. They define negative face as a person's want to be unimpeded by others, the desire to be free to act as s/he chooses and not be imposed upon. They define positive face as a person's want to be appreciated and approved of by selected others, in terms of personality, desires, behaviour, values, and so on. In other words, negative face represents a desire for autonomy, and positive face represents a desire for approval. The authors also draw attention to another important distinction: the distinction between self-face and other-face.

Brown and Levinson (1987) point out that face is something that is emotionally invested; it can be lost, maintained or enhanced in interaction, and so interlocutors constantly need to pay attention to it. They assume that people typically cooperate with each other in maintaining face in interaction, because people are mutually vulnerable to face attack: if one person attacks another person's face, the other is likely to retaliate. Moreover, they argue that some speech acts (such as criticism and directives) are inherently face-threatening, and that conflict can be avoided by managing those speech acts in contextually appropriate ways. They claim that there are five super-strategies for handling face-threatening acts:

- bald on-record performance (clear, unambiguous and concise speech)
- positive politeness (language that is 'approach-based' and treats the hearer as an in-group member)
- negative politeness (language that is 'avoidance-based' and respects the hearer's desire for freedom and autonomy)
- off-record performance (indirect and comparatively ambiguous speech)
- non-performance of the face-threatening act.

People choose which super-strategy to use by assessing the 'weightiness' of the speech act. According to Brown and Levinson (1987) this entails assessing the power differential between the interlocutors, the distance–closeness between them, and the degree of imposition (or face-threat) of the message itself.

3.4.   Limitations of Brown and Levinson's face model

Brown and Levinson's (1987) face model has been hugely influential. Numerous studies have used it as an analytic framework and many others have investigated one or more of its elements. Nevertheless, there have also been widespread criticisms of it, and here we consider those that are most pertinent to the study of conflict.

As explained in section 3.3, Brown and Levinson's (1987) framework starts with the assumption that harmony is the desired option, because we all want our own face needs to be upheld. Culpeper (2005, Culpeper, Bousfield and Wichmann 2003), on the other hand, argues that people may sometimes want to be deliberately offensive or face-threatening, and that Brown and Levinson's (1987) framework is not broad enough to cater for this. He therefore proposes a set of 'impoliteness' super-strategies that are mirror images of Brown and Levinson's politeness super-strategies. When speakers use these strategies, their intention is to attack the hearer's face, rather than to uphold it. Culpeper (2005, Culpeper, Bousfield and Wichmann 2003) draws on a variety of data sources to provide authentic examples of the use of these various super-strategies.

Other researchers have questioned whether Brown and Levinson's (1987) focus on the performance of (face-threatening) speech acts provides a broad enough basis for analysing the complexities of (dis)harmony in interaction. Spencer-Oatey (2005), for example, argues that rapport is dependent on the participants' dynamic management of three main factors: interactional wants (both task-related and relational), face sensitivities, and perceived sociality rights and obligations. She maintains that relational conflict is likely to emerge if the various participants' expectations over each of these factors are not handled appropriately, and that a pre-requisite for maintaining positive rapport is thus for each of the participants to be aware of and/or sensitive to the interactional wants, face sensitivities, and perceived sociality rights and obligations that they each hold. Spencer-Oatey (2000: 29–30) also proposes that people may have different orientations towards positive rapport:

1. Rapport-enhancement orientation: a desire to strengthen or enhance harmonious relations between interlocutors;
2. Rapport-maintenance orientation: a desire to maintain or protect harmonious relations between the interlocutors;
3. Rapport-neglect orientation: a lack of concern or interest in the quality of relations between the interlocutors (perhaps because of a focus on self);
4. Rapport-challenge orientation: a desire to challenge or impair harmonious relations between the interlocutors

She points out that people's motives for holding any of these orientations could be various.

3.5.   A synthesized summary

Building on the theorizing of Thomas (1976), Brown and Levinson (1987), Spencer-Oatey (2000), along with Friedman, Chi and Liu's (2006) and van Meurs' (2003) findings, it seems that the motivations underlying these conflict-handling tactics can be multiple, and can include the following (interrelated) concerns:

- Cost–benefit considerations (the impact of the handling of the conflict on the instrumental concerns of self and/or other)
- Rapport considerations (the impact of the handling of the conflict on the smoothness/harmony between the parties)
- Relational considerations (the impact of the handling of the conflict on the degree of distance–closeness and equality–inequality between the parties)
- Effectiveness considerations (the impact of the handling of the conflict on the degree of concern for clarity, control, and inconvenience between parties)

Thomas' five conflict-handling orientations or styles cannot be mapped in a straightforward manner onto these underlying concerns, and thus cannot be explained simply in terms of concern for self versus concern for other, as Thomas's (1976) and Rahim's (1983, 1992) frameworks suggest. Similarly, styles and tactics do not have a one-to-one relationship. Let us take avoidance as an example. If I avoid handling a conflict, it could be that I want to withdraw from the problem (as indicated by Thomas' grid), but there could also be several other possibilities. It could be that I want to maintain or build rapport with the other person; it could be that I want to show respect for the superordinate status of the other person; or it could be that my long-term goal is to dominate my opponent, and that I feel the best way of achieving this is to initially avoid conflict whilst I muster my arguments and/or gain support from elsewhere. Alternatively, I may feel uncomfortable avoiding the problem, because I have a low tolerance for uncertainty, and prefer to maintain clarity and control. Finding an effective solution may be more important to me, even if it risks damaging the relationship, because I believe I can amend that at a later date. Or I may feel that by NOT avoiding the problem, I will be able to resolve it and thus maintain good relations.

Brown and Levinson's (1987) politeness super-strategies, and Culpeper's (2005, Culpeper, Bousfield and Wichmann 2003) impoliteness super-strategies are potential verbal tactics that primarily relate to rapport considerations (although naturally they can have a knock-on effect on both relational and cost–benefit considerations). Analysis of the verbal tactics that people use in conflict episodes is an area where applied linguistics can make a valuable contribution to the study of conflict (see section 5.2).

The studies discussed in section 3.2 highlight the importance of considering culture in the Bermuda Triangle of conflict, and we explore this in detail in the next section.

4.   Conflict and culture

4.1.   Conflict and cultural values

Hofstede (1991, 2001) identified five dimensions of cultural values (individualism–collectivism, high–low power distance, masculinity–femininity, high–low uncertainty avoidance, and long/short-term orientation), and many researchers have focused on the impact of individualism–collectivism on conflict management styles and preferences. Hofstede defines this dimension as follows:

> Individualism stands for a society in which the ties between individuals are loose: everyone is expected to look after him/herself and her/his immediate family only. Collectivism stands for a society in which people from birth onwards are integrated into strong, cohesive in-groups, which throughout people's lifetime continue to protect them in exchange for unquestioning loyalty.
>
> Hofstede 2001: 225

Leung (1987) found that respondents from an individualist society (the USA) differed in their conflict-handling preferences from those from a collectivist society (China), although he also found some culture-general results. Ting-Toomey (1999: 211–212) argues that individualist and collectivist values are reflected in independent and interdependent self-construals respectively, and that these can impact on conflict as shown in Table 2.

Table 2. Cultural Values, Self-Construals and the Conflict Process
(Derived from Ting-Toomey 1999: 211–212)

Individualist Values and Independent Self-Construals	Collectivist Values and Interdependent Self-Construals
1. Conflict is perceived as closely related to the goals or outcomes that are salient to the respective individual conflict parties in a given conflict situation.	1. Conflict is weighted against the face threat incurred in the conflict negotiation process; it is also interpreted in the web of ingroup/outgroup relationships.
2. Communication in the conflict process is viewed as dissatisfying when the conflict parties are not willing to deal with the conflict openly and honestly.	2. Communication in the conflict process is perceived as threatening when the conflict parties push for substantive discussion before proper facework management.
3. Conversely, communication in the conflict process is viewed as satisfying when the conflict parties are willing to confront the conflict issues openly and share their feelings honestly (i.e. assertively but not aggressively).	3. Communication in the conflict interaction is viewed as satisfying when the conflict parties engage in mutual face-saving and face-giving behaviour and attend to both verbal and nonverbal signals.
4. The conflict outcome is perceived as unproductive when no tangible outcomes are reached or no plan of action is developed.	4. The conflict process or outcome is perceived as unproductive when face issues are not addressed and relational/group feelings are not attended to properly.
5. The conflict outcome is perceived as productive when tangible solutions are reached and objective criteria are met.	5. The conflict process or outcome is defined as productive when both conflict parties can claim win–win results on the facework front in addition to substantive agreement.
6. Effective and appropriate management of conflict means individual goals are addressed and differences are dealt with openly, honestly, and properly in relation to timing and situational context.	6. Appropriate and effective management of conflict means that the mutual 'faces' of the conflict parties are saved or even upgraded in the interaction and they have dealt with the conflict episode strategically in conjunction with substantive gains or losses.

Not all studies have completely supported the link between individualism–collectivism and conflict-handling preferences. For example, Gire and Carment (1992) investigated Canadian (individualist) and Nigerian (collectivist) preferences and found there were various similarities. Moreover, others have explored the influence of other values. Leung et al. (1990), for instance, investigated the impact of masculinity–femininity using respondents from Canada and The Netherlands (masculine and feminine societies respectively but both highly individualistic, according to Hofstede's data), and found that their Dutch respondents preferred more harmony-enhancing procedures than their Canadian respondents did.

Other researchers have used Schwartz's (1992; Schwartz et al. 2001) framework of cultural values to examine the interrelationship between values and conflict management styles. Schwartz's framework has the advantage that it can be measured easily and reliably at the individual level, whereas Hofstede's figures are culture level measures; moreover, the other main individual level measure, independent–interdependent self-construal (as referred to by Ting-Toomey 1999), may be too broad and also of dubious validity (Kim 2005: 108).

In Schwartz's (1992; Schwartz et al. 2001) individual-level framework, there are ten universal value constructs, and they fall into four main groupings: Self-Enhancement, Self-Transcendence, Openness to Change, and Conservation. Morris et al. (1998) analysed the extent to which Schwartz's cultural values could predict two of the grid framework conflict handling styles: avoidance and competition. In a study of Chinese and US managers in joint venture firms, they predicted that the Chinese managers would have a greater preference for avoidance than the US managers, and that the US managers would have a greater preference for competition than the Chinese managers. These predictions were confirmed. They also hypothesized that (a) an avoiding style would reflect an individual's orientation towards Conservation values, and that any Chinese–US differences in avoiding style would be mediated by country differences in preference for Conservation; and that (b) a competition style would reflect an individual's orientation towards Self-Enhancement, that any Chinese–US differences in competition style would be mediated by country differences in preference for Self-Enhancement. Both of these hypotheses were confirmed.

Bilsky and Jehn (2002), in a study using German students, found that avoiding behaviour was negatively correlated with Self-Direction (a component value of Openness to Change), and since Schwartz (1992) argues that Openness to Change and Conservation (with the latter comprising the component values Security, Conformity and Tradition) are polar opposites, this fits in with Morris et al.'s (1998) findings. In other words, the studies found that Conservation was important to Chinese MBA students and this was linked with a preference to avoid conflict, whereas the polar opposite value Openness to Change was important to German students and this was linked with a preference NOT to avoid conflict.

Van Meurs (2003) suggests that the role of Uncertainty Avoidance needs to be researched further, as Germanic clusters have been found to be more uncertainty avoidant than Anglo clusters (Ashkanasy, Trevor-Roberts and Earnshaw 2002; House et al. 2002) and this could affect, these groups' preferences for avoiding conflict. Unfortunately, to date, Uncertainty Avoidance is not adequately represented by individual-level value measures.

4.2.   Conflict, culture and context

One of the weaknesses of this macro level research is that it ignores a lot of contextual variation. Although there may be differences (such as between Americans and Chinese) in preferred styles for managing conflict, such generalizations can gloss over the rich complexity and variation that exists in real-life situations. Davidheiser's (2005) study of mediation practices in southwestern Gambia illustrates this point very vividly. He observed and recorded 121 live conflict mediation events, conducted 54 ethnographic interviews and 39 semi-structured interviews, and held panel sessions with Gambian mediation experts. He draws the following conclusions:

> Shared values have a profound effect both on how mediation is practiced and on the nature of the process itself. However, this impact is multi-dimensional and resists easy generalization. … Whilst it is true that there appear to be meta-level normative differences in orientations to mediation in the West and elsewhere, there is also great heterogeneity in both of these areas. Dichotomizing mediation praxis according to whether the practitioners are Western or non-Western, traditional or modern, high- or low-context communicators, glosses over the multiplicity of practice found outside the realm of theory and dramatically over-simplifies a complex picture.

> Mediation practices can be described as 'embedded', or linked to macro- and micro-level influences and varying according to the specific context and characteristics of each case. Peacemaker behaviour was influenced by numerous factors, including the sociocultural perspectives of the participants and situational variables such as the type of dispute in question, the nature of the social relations between the parties, and the participants' personalities.

> Davidheiser 2005: 736–7

If we are to gain an in-depth understanding, therefore, of intercultural conflict in real-life situations, it is vital to consider contextual variability. In fact, as Bond, Žegarac and Spencer-Oatey (2000) point out, culture can be manifested in a variety of ways, in addition to cultural values, including perception of contextual variables. Spencer-Oatey's (2005) rapport management framework identifies some features that can be subject to cultural variation yet that are also contextually sensitive. These include (but are not limited to) the behavioural norms, conventions and protocols of given communicative events (e.g., how formal they 'should' be), the 'scripts' as to how given communicative events should be enacted; the rights and obligations associated with given role relationships; and the contractual/legal agreements and requirements (written and unwritten) that apply to a given organization, profession or social group. When people's expectations are not fulfilled, they may perceive this as 'negatively eventful' (Goffman 1963: 7), and this can (but, of course, need not necessarily) be a source of interpersonal conflict. Many cross-cultural and intercultural pragmatic studies aim to unpack and illuminate these processes through careful analysis, as section 5.2 reports.

5.   Conflict and communication

5.1.   Communicative conflict styles

Much of the argumentation on conflict and cultural values (see section 4.1) touches on the role of communication. Directness–indirectness is seen as having a particularly important impact on both the instigation and the management of conflict. It has been found that different cultures may endorse the same conflict management orientation (e.g., collaborative) yet vary in the way they handle it verbally. Pruitt (1983) found that both direct and indirect information exchange correlated with socially desirable, collaborative agreements. Similarly, Adair, Okumura and Brett (2001) showed that Americans achieve collaborative integration of ideas through direct communication but that Japanese do so through indirect communication which allows people to infer preferences. They concluded that "facility in direct or indirect communications may not lead to joint gains if parties do not also have a norm for information sharing", and that collaborative behaviour is based on different motivations, dependent on the culture (Adair, Okumura and Brett 2001: 380). Similarly, van Meurs (2003) found that Dutch managers equated directness with being consultative, whereas the British preferred to use indirectness and be consultative.

In much intercultural research, directness–indirectness is assumed to be associated with individualism–collectivism and/or independent–interdependent self-construal, and it is linked with concern for face. Unfortunately, however, the majority of studies (in management, cross-cultural psychology and in communication studies) conflate the measurement of the two, using, for example, a questionnaire item on directness both as a measure of Individualism/Independence and as a measure of communicative directness–indirectness. This, of course, is circular and unsatisfactory. In addition, there is a need to consider whether other communicative styles are important.

Hammer (2005) proposes two fundamental dimensions (directness–indirectness, emotional expressiveness–restraint), and four types of conflict styles: Discussion Style (direct but emotionally restrained), Engagement Style (direct and emotionally expressive), Accommodation Style (indirect and emotionally restrained), and Dynamic Style (indirect and emotionally expressive) (cf. Kott-hoff in this volume, on communication style). Hammer has developed an Inter-cultural Conflict Styles Inventory [ICSI] in relation to this, and has used it, along with his four-quadrant model, in a variety of applied contexts. He reports that it has been of practical benefit in his mediation sessions.

> In one mediation I conducted, both parties completed the ICSI prior to the initial mediation session. After reviewing the mediation process with the parties, I then re-viewed with them their ICSs. One of the disputants–' style was 'engagement' while the other was 'accommodation.' A large part of the conflict between these individ-uals had involved misperceptions each held of one another, based on differences in intercultural conflict resolution style. For example, the accommodation style indi-vidual felt the other party was 'rude and aggressive' while the engagement individ-ual characterized the accommodation style person as deceptive and lacking in com-mitment. After discussing these misperceptions in terms of differences in conflict resolution styles (rather than personal traits), the disputants were better able to ad-dress their substantive disagreements.
>
> Hammer 2005: 691–2

However, one very major weakness of virtually all the research into the role of communication in conflict processes that is carried out in management, cross-cultural psychology and communication studies is that it is nearly always based on self-report data, using Likert-style responses to questionnaire items. There is a very great need for discourse-based research, of the kind reported in the next section.

5.2.   Conflict and discourse research

One very significant contribution that applied linguistics can make to our under-standing of conflict processes is the identification of the types of linguistic tac-tics that people may use to implement the conflict management styles that Tho-mas (1976) identified. For example, how may people avoid conflict? What insights does applied linguistic research offer on this question? Most linguistic research does not attempt to draw any explicit links with frameworks in busi-ness and communication studies, but an exception is Holmes and Marra (2004). Using their New Zealand workplace data (see Marra and Holmes in this vol-ume), these researchers explored the role that leaders may play in managing conflict in meetings. They argue that the effective management of conflict be-gins well before any actual conflictual episodes occur, and demonstrate how 'as-sertion of the agenda' is one effective technique that skillful leaders use to avoid conflict. They provide several examples of actual discourse to illustrate ways in which chairpersons achieve this, including moving talk on to the next agenda item, and directing people's attention back to a key point, when disparate views begin to be expressed. They also identify a second tactic that could be regarded as an avoidance strategy: diverting a contentious issue to another venue for discussion. Saft (2004) also found that the ways in which meetings are chaired has a major impact on conflict behaviour. He analyses two different sets of university faculty meetings in Japan, in which arguments were frequent in one set but rare in the other. Saft demonstrates how the chairpersons' control and organization of turn-taking in the meetings was crucial, in that it either constrained the expression of opposition or enabled it.

In both of these studies, the researchers demonstrate how conflict can be avoided through skillful management of meetings. This data thus indicates that far from being a negative strategy that shows lack of concern both for self and for other (see Figure 1 above), promoting conflict avoidance can be a very effective and positive management strategy. This applied linguistic research thus supports other work in organizational behaviour and cross-cultural psychology (e.g., De Dreu 1997; Gire and Carmet 1992; Leung et al. 1990; Markus and Kitayama 1991; Morris et al. 1998; Ohbuchi and Takahashi 1994) that maintains that conflict avoidance in fact can be motivated by a concern (rather than lack of concern) for others.

Context is important in terms of the choice of strategy (Rahim 1992). A crisis situation may need a dominating strategy, whereas a complex problem may require an integrating (i.e. problem solving) approach, and a relational issue may require people to avoid each other for the short term. Holmes and Marra's (2004) study of workplace discourse confirmed the impact that context can have on conflict management tactics. They found the following factors to be important in influencing leaders' choices of strategy:

- Type of interaction (e.g., workplace meeting), its level of formality, number of participants, and so on;
- Workplace culture, including organizational culture and community of practice culture;
- Importance/seriousness of the issue;
- Leadership style.

In relation to avoidance, they point out that the seriousness of the issue is a key contextual factor. They found that, in their data, good chairpersons and effective leaders tended to encourage 'working through conflict' when a decision was serious or when it was an important one, such as one that set a precedent for subsequent decisions.

Much linguistic research focuses on analysing the detailed linguistic strategies that occur in conflictive discourse, and does not attempt to link them to the macro styles identified in business and communication studies. For example, Günthner (2000) analyses the ways in which German participants in a German–Chinese conversation maximize the expression of dissent, and ways in which the participants end a confrontational frame. She identifies three strategies in her discourse data that the German participants used for signaling dissent in a focused and maximized way:

- 'Dissent-formats': the speaker provides a (partial) repetition of the prior speaker's utterance and then negates it or replaces parts of it with a contrasting element.
- 'Dissent-ties': the speaker latches her disagreeing utterance to the prior turn, and thus produces a syntactic and lexical continuation of the preceding utterance, but then in continuing it demonstrates consequences which contradict the argumentative line of the first speaker.
- Reported speech: the speaker reproduces the opponent's prior utterance (maybe several turns later) in order to oppose it.

She also identifies three strategies that the participants use to (try to) end a confrontational frame:

- Concession, when one participant 'gives in'.
- Compromise, where a speaker moves towards the other party's position and proposes a possible 'middle ground'.
- Change of activity, where a speaker introduces a new verbal activity, such as focusing on the situation at hand (e.g., by enquiring 'what kind of tea is this?')

These last three strategies could, in fact, be linked with the macro styles of avoiding, obliging, competing, sharing and problem solving. Concession is an obliging strategy, compromise is a sharing strategy, and change of activity could be regarded as an avoiding strategy.

Another example of the detailed analysis of linguistic strategies in conflictive encounters is Honda (2002). She analyses Japanese public affairs talk shows, and examines the ways in which oppositional comments are redressed or downplayed. Table 3 shows the classification of strategies that she identifies.

Table 3. Redressive Strategies identified by Honda (2002) in her Analysis of Japanese Public Affairs Talk Shows

Redressive Strategy	Gloss	Example
Mollifiers	Remarks that precede the expression of opposition, and downplay its directness	- Initial praise - Initial token agreement - Initial acceptance of the opponent's point of view - Initial denial of disagreement or one's own remark

Redressive Strategy	Gloss	Example
Mitigators	Features within the expression of opposition that downplay its directness	– Pauses – Discourse markers that show hesitation – Minimizers such as a little, maybe
Untargeted opposition	Expression of opposition that does not make it clear whether or not it is targeted at a specific person or viewpoint	– Remark that contradicts or differs from the opponent's view but the opposition is attributed as being with a third party rather than with the opponent – Remark that contradicts or differs from the opponent's view but is not directed at the opponent, or made in response to the opponent's previous remarks

Honda (2002) also demonstrates how some confrontations in her data initially proceed in an unmitigated fashion, but later the opposing parties take restorative action and end their argument in a seemingly cooperative fashion. In other words, as with Günthner's study, different tactics were used at different points in the conflict. This suggests once again that context (in this case, discourse context) can influence choice of strategy, and that macro designations of people's conflict management styles will only be able to provide indicative generalizations of their normative preferences.

A second major contribution that applied linguistics can make to our understanding of conflict processes, especially in intercultural contexts, is to reveal how conflicts may arise by carefully analysing authentic interactions. Bailey (1997, 2000), for example, analyses service encounters between Korean retailers and African-American customers to help throw light on the longstanding conflict between these two groups that had been widely reported in the media. Analysing video recordings of the service encounters, he found that there were noticeable differences in the ways that Korean and African-American customers interacted with the Korean retailers, such as in terms of length of the encounter, overall quantity of talk, inclusion of personable topics and small talk, and the amount of affect displayed. Follow-up interviews with the customers and the retailers indicated that both the Korean retailers and the African-American customers evaluated the other negatively, interpreting the other's behaviour as disrespectful, and as racist (in the case of the Korean retailers) and as intimidating (in the case of the African-American customers). Bailey draws the following conclusion:

... divergent communicative patterns in these everyday service encounters simultaneously represent (1) an on-going *source of tensions*; and (2) a *local enactment of pre-existing social conflicts.*

Bailey 2000: 87 (italics in the original)

Another example is Spencer-Oatey and Xing (2003). These researchers compare two Chinese–British business welcome meetings which were very similar in many respects, yet were evaluated very differently by the participants. One of them was part of a very successful business visit, whilst the other led to a very problematic visit which came to a climax on the final day when there was a heated dispute that lasted for nearly two and a half hours. The authors analyse the reasons for the differences in outcomes, and identify the following: the role of the interpreter (see also Spencer-Oatey and Xing in this volume), the role of the chairperson, mismatches between British and Chinese culturally-based and contextually-based assumptions and expectations, confusion over the roles and relative status of the participants, and a confounding effect between all of these factors.

6.   Concluding comments

The various approaches to studying and analysing conflict reported in this chapter each have their own strengths and weaknesses. In terms of research methodology, most organizational psychological and communication researchers use either simulated role play in experimental-type conditions, or self-report questionnaire items. Whilst these approaches are useful in many respects, they have some serious limitations and need to be complemented by studies of authentic conflictive encounters and situations. In such studies various types of research data need to be collected including ethnographic, discourse and/or post-event interview data, in order to improve the validity and granularity of research findings on conflict. Applied linguists have a major role to play here. However, it needs to be acknowledged that much applied linguistic research is impenetrable for people from other disciplines. The analyses are often so detailed and so full of linguistic technical terms, that they are difficult for non-linguists to follow. Moreover, it is hard for people (such as intercultural trainers) to pick out the practical relevance of the findings.

Up to now there has been very little interchange of conceptual frameworks and research findings between applied linguistic researchers of conflict and those working within organizational behaviour and communication studies. Findings are typically published in different journals, and people may be unaware of each other's work. We hope that this chapter will help to start breaking down this divide, and that there will be greater interdisciplinary sharing and discussion of ideas, concepts and findings, even if some conflict is a concomitant part of the process!

References

Adair, Wendi L., Tetsushi Okumura and Jeanne M. Brett
    2001   Negotiation behaviors when cultures collide: The U.S. and Japan. *Journal of Applied Psychology* 86: 371–385.
Ashkanasy, Neal M., Edwin Trevor-Roberts and Louise Earnshaw
    2002   The Anglo cluster: Legacy of the British Empire. *Journal of World Business* 37: 28–39.
Bailey, Benjamin
    1997   Communication of respect in interethnic service encounters. *Language in Society* 26: 327–356.
Bailey, Benjamin
    2000   Communicative behavior and conflict between African-American customers and Korean immigrant retailers in Los Angeles. *Discourse and Society* 11: 86–108.
Bilsky, Wolfgang and Karen A. Jehn
    2002   Organisationskultur und individuelle Werte: Belege für eine gemeinsame Struktur [Organizational culture and individual values: evidence for a common structure]. In: Michael Myrtek (ed.) *Die Person im biologischen und sozialen Kontext*, 211–228. Göttingen: Hogrefe
Blake, Robert R. and Jane S. Mouton
    1964   *The Managerial Grid*. Houston, TX: Gulf Publishing.
Bond, Michael H. and Kwang-Kuo Hwang
    1986   The social psychology of Chinese people. In: Michael H. Bond (ed.) *The Psychology of the Chinese People*, 213–266. Hong Kong: Oxford University Press.
Bond, Michael H., Vladimir Žegarac and Helen Spencer-Oatey
    2000   Culture as an explanatory variable: problems and possibilities. In: Helen Spencer-Oatey (ed.) *Culturally Speaking. Managing Rapport through Talk across Cultures*, 47–71. London: Continuum.
Brett, Jeanne M. and Tetsushi Okumura
    1998   Inter- and intra-cultural negotiation: U.S. and Japanese negotiators. *Academy of Management Journal* 41: 410–424.
Brown, Penelope and Stephen C. Levinson
    1987   *Politeness. Some Universals in Language Usage.* Cambridge: CUP. Originally published as Universals in language usage: politeness phenomenon. In: Esther Goody (ed.) 1978 *Questions and Politeness: Strategies in Social Interaction.* New York: CUP.
Culpeper, Jonathan
    2005   Impoliteness and entertainment in the television quiz show: *The Weakest Link. Journal of Politeness Research* 1: 35–72.
Culpeper, Jonathan, Derek Bousfield and Anne Wichmann
    2003   Impoliteness revisited: with special reference to dynamic and prosodic aspects. *Journal of Pragmatics* 35: 1545–1579.
Davidheiser, Mark
    2005   Culture and mediation: a contemporary processual analysis from southwestern Gambia. *International Journal of Intercultural Relations* 29: 713–738.

De Dreu, Carsten K.W.
1997   Productive conflict: The importance of conflict management and conflict issue. In: Carston K.W. De Dreu and Evert van de Vliert (eds.) *Using Conflict in Organizations*, 9–22. London: Sage.
Friedman, Ray, Shu-Cheng Chi and Leigh Anne Liu
2006   An expectancy model of Chinese–American differences in conflict-avoiding. *Journal of International Business Studies* 37: 76–91.
Gire, James T. and D. William Carment
1992   Dealing with disputes: The influence of individualism-collectivism. *Journal of Social Psychology* 133: 81–95.
Goffman, Erving
1963   *Behavior in Public Places.* New York: Free Press.
Günthner, Susanne
2000   Argumentation and resulting problems in the negotiation of rapport in a German–Chinese conversation. In: Helen Spencer-Oatey (ed.) *Culturally Speaking. Managing Rapport through Talk across Cultures*, 217–239. London: Continuum.
Hammer, Mitchell R.
2005   The intercultural conflict style inventory: a conceptual framework and measure of intercultural conflict resolution approaches. *International Journal of Intercultural Relations* 29: 675–695.
Hofstede, Geert
1991   *Cultures and Organizations: Software of the Mind.* London: HarperCollins-Business.
Hofstede, Geert
2001   *Culture's Consequences. Comparing Values, Behaviors, Institutions, and Organizations across Nations.* London: Sage.
Holmes, Janet and Meredith Marra
2004   Leadership and managing conflict in meetings. *Pragmatics* 14(4): 439–462.
Honda, Atsuko
2002   Conflict management in Japanese public affairs talk shows. *Journal of Pragmatics* 34: 573–608.
House, Robert, Mansour Javidan, Paul Hanges and Peter Dorfman
2002   Understanding cultures and implicit leadership theories across the globe: an introduction to project GLOBE. *Journal of World Business* 37: 2–10.
Kim, Min-Sun
2005   Culture-based conversational constraints theory. Individual- and culture-level analyses. In: William B. Gudykunst (ed.) *Theorizing about Intercultural Communication*, 93–117. Thousand Oaks: Sage.
Kotthoff, Helga
this volume Ritual and style across cultures, Chapter 9.
Leung, Kwok
1987   Some determinants of reactions to procedural models for conflict resolution: a cross-national study. *Journal of Personality and Social Psychology* 53(5): 898–908.
Leung, Kwok, Michael H. Bond, D. William Carment, Lila Krishnan and Wim B.G. Liebrand
1990   Effects of cultural femininity on preference for methods of conflict process-

ing: A cross-cultural study. *Journal of Experimental Social Psychology* 26: 373–388.

Lytle, Anne L.
1999   Chinese conflict management styles: an exploratory study. Paper presented at the Twelfth Conference of the International Association for Conflict Management, San Sebastian, Spain, 20–23 June 1999.

Markus, Hazel R. and Shinobu Kitayama
1991   Culture and the self: implications for cognition, emotion, and motivation. *Psychological Review* 98: 224–53.

Marra, Meredith and Janet Holmes
this volume Humour across cultures: joking in the multicultural workplace, Chapter 8.

Morris, Michael W., Katherine Y. Williams, Kwok Leung, Richard Larrick, M.Teresa Mendoza, Deepti Bhatnagar, Jianfeng Li, Mari Kondo, Jin-Lian Luo and Jun-Chen Hu
1998   Conflict management style: Accounting for cross-national differences. *Journal of International Business Studies* 29(4): 729–748.

Ohbuchi, Ken-Ichi and Yumi Takahashi
1994   Cultural styles of conflict management in Japanese and Americans: passivity, covertness, and effectiveness of strategies. *Journal of Applied Social Psychology* 24(15): 1345–1366.

Pruitt, Dean G.
1983   Achieving integrative agreement. In: Max H. Bazerman and Roy J. Lewicki (eds.) *Negotiating in organizations*, 35–50. Beverly Hills, CA: Sage.

Rahim, M. Afzalur
1983   A measure of styles of handling interpersonal conflict. *Academy of Management Journal* 26: 368–376.

Rahim, M. Afzalur
1992   *Managing Conflict in Organizations*. Westport, CT: Preager Publishers.

Saft, Scott
2004   Conflict as interactional accomplishment in Japanese: arguments in university faculty meetings. *Language in Society* 33: 549–584.

Schwartz, Shalom H.
1992   Universals in the content and structure of values: theoretical advances and empirical tests in 20 countries. In: Mark P. Zanna (ed.) *Advances in Experimental Social Psychology* (Vol. 25), 1–65. San Diego: Academic Press.

Schwartz, Shalom H., Gila Melech, Arielle Lehmann, Steven Burgess, Mari Harris and Vicki Owens
2001   Extending the cross-cultural validity of the theory of basic human values with a different method of measurement. *Journal of Cross-Cultural Psychology* 32(5): 59–542.

Sorenson, Ritch L, Eric A. Morse and Grant T. Savage
1999   What motivates choice of conflict strategies? *International Journal of Conflict Management* 10: 25–44.

Spencer-Oatey, Helen
2000   Rapport management: a framework for analysis. In: Helen Spencer-Oatey (ed.) *Culturally Speaking. Managing Rapport through Talk across Cultures*, 11–46. London: Continuum.

Spencer-Oatey, Helen
   2005   (Im)Politeness, face and perceptions of rapport: unpackaging their bases and interrelationships. *Journal of Politeness Research* 1: 95–119.

Spencer-Oatey, Helen and Jianyu Xing
   2003   Managing rapport in intercultural business interactions: a comparison of two Chinese–British welcome meetings. *Journal of Intercultural Studies* 24(1): 33–46.

Spencer-Oatey, Helen and Jianyu Xing
this volume The impact of culture on interpreter behaviour, Chapter 11.

Thomas, KennethW.
   1976   Conflict and conflict management. In: Marvin Dunnette (ed.) *The Handbook of Industrial and Organizational Psychology*, 889–935. Chicago: Rand McNally.

Thomas, KennethW. and Ralph H. Kilmann
   1974   *The Thomas–Kilmann Conflict Mode Instrument.* Tuxedo, NY: Xicom.

Thomas, Kenneth W. and Warren Schmidt
   1976   A survey of managerial interests with respect to conflict. *Academy of Management Journal* 19: 315–318.

Ting-Toomey, Stella
   1999   *Communicating across Cultures.* New York: The Guilford Press.

Trubinsky, Paula, Stella Ting-Toomey and Sung Ling Lin
   1991   The influence of individualism–collectivism and self-monitoring on conflict styles. *International Journal of Intercultural Relations* 15(1): 65–84.

van Meurs, Nathalie
   2003   Negotiations between British and Dutch managers: Cultural values, approaches to conflict management, and perceived negotiation satisfaction. Unpublished doctoral dissertation, University of Sussex, Brighton, East Sussex, UK.

II. Intercultural perspectives on communicative practices and processes

Editors' introduction

Section 2 explores communicative practices and processes, and makes evident how culture and communication are closely interconnected. Research by psychologists such as Schwartz (e.g. 1999) and management scientists such as Hofstede (2001) have focused on the link between culture and values, and that is clearly important. However, culture can be reflected in a range of other ways, and the applied linguistic research reported in this section draws attention to the crucially important ways in which culture is reflected in communicative practices and processes.

The first three chapters of the section focus on discoursal and stylistic conventions: communicative genres (chapter 7), the use of humour (chapter 8), and rituals and style (chapter 9). The last two chapters of the section focus on culture and the processing and negotiation of meaning: lingua franca communication (chapter 10) and interpreter behaviour (chapter 11). The chapters cover a wide range of geographical areas (e.g. New Zealand in chapter 8, Caucasian Georgia and Germany in chapter 9, South Africa in chapter 10), ethnic groups (e.g. Pākehā and Māori in chapter 8, Chinese and English in chapter 11), activity types (e.g. job interviews in chapter 7, workplace meetings in chapter 8, toastings in chapter 9) and professional groups (e.g. medical practitioners and business managers in chapter 11).

The five chapters together provide differing perspectives on the interconnection between culture and communication, each taking a different angle to help build up the picture. To illustrate how this may be achieved, let us take 'talking about troubles' as an example. In terms of discourse structure, a culture may have established certain genres for problem presentation, be it in a psychotherapeutic setting or among friends. Moreover, a person's troubles can be presented seriously or humorously, dialogically or monologically; or they can, in certain contexts, fulfil ritual functions such as demonstrative suffering in order to create intimate bonding. Whereas in one cultural context a genre like telling a story about a problem might demand humorous distancing strategies, in another it might require pathetic emphasis; in yet another it might be presented complainingly and protestingly. The language in which the story is told can determine whether subtle undertones are heard or not; and furthermore, when there is an interpreter, an inexperienced interpreter may underplay sensitivities. Indeed, in medical and therapeutic contexts, experience has shown that interpretation and lingua francas often suppress certain aspects of a problem, so that a patient receives inadequate treatment.

Concepts such as genre, activity type, frame and ritual do not exclude one another, but how do they connect? Whereas the concept of genre, discussed by Susanne Günthner in chapter 7, focuses on compositional structures of verbal interaction, the main focus of ritual theories lies in the symbolization processes that transcend the realm of interpersonal relations. The latter is the topic of chapter 9 by Helga Kotthoff. Many communicative practices are at the same time generic in their structure and ritualized insofar as they communicate various symbolic aims. In using a communicative genre, speakers construct an intertextual relation between the situative text and a canonical pattern.

Similarly, it could be asked how genre and activity type relate to each other. In chapter 2 John Gumperz and Jenny Cook-Gumperz draw on the concept of activity type. A genre normally has a higher degree of internal organization than an activity type, but the main difference is that the two concepts focus on different sides of a communicative practice: within a genre concept the dimension of patterning is highlighted, while in the concept of activity type the focus is on the communication of an intention and how this is interpreted.

Let us now consider each of the chapters in turn.

In chapter 7 Susanne Günthner explores a wide range of oral and written communicative genres, from complaints to academic articles. She sees the notion of genre as a linkage between communicative contexts and cultural speaking practices, and builds on the traditions of Anthropological linguistics and Sociology of Knowledge. Genres are treated as historically and culturally specific conventions, pre-patterned, not only to relieve the speaker, but also to assist the recipients in limiting interpretative possibilities. In using a communicative genre, speakers construct an intertextual relation between the situative 'communicative text' and a canonized pattern. Internal, interactional and external features constitute the patterning of a communicative genre.

Chapter 8 presents findings from the Wellington Language in the Workplace project about cultural underpinnings of humour. Meredith Marra and Janet Holmes explore the shared cultural knowledge, values and beliefs which underlie humorous activities in New Zealand, carried out by Māori people and New Zealanders of British origin (Pākehā). Humour often serves as a relational practice building social cohesion, but it also reinforces boundaries between *them* and *us* in an acceptable way. One example shows how a Māori speaker gives a witty performance about a magic box (which is in reality the micro-wave) and very indirectly makes it clear that the micro-wave should be cleaned after usage. The authors discuss many generic features which make the performance a typical Māori activity, including the speaker's concern for protecting individual face, his teaching strategies, and the implicit respect for superiors. Humour is often overlooked in intercultural research and trainings. The article fills a gap and presents some implications for intercultural education.

In Chapter 9 Helga Kotthoff discusses the relations between ritual and style, from simple rituals such as gift presentation to complex genres such as toasting. Following Goffman, Kotthoff extends the concept of ritual to everyday activities because activities like greetings, dinner conversations, dress or culinary codes contain symbolization processes that transcend the realm of interpersonal relations and communicate honour. Kotthoff shows the interconnection of ritual and style especially in comparing toasting in formerly Soviet republics and in Western Europe. She combines insights from the ethnography of speaking, anthropology, sociolinguistics and conversation analysis to discuss scenes of intercultural stylistic difference, adaptation, and creativity. The performance study of various genres and activity types gives us access to individualistic and sociocentric conceptions of personhood. The concept of style is related to that of face work and to that of contextualization.

Lingua franca communication is the topic of chapter 10. Christiane Meierkord shows it as involving an increased number of communicative conventions and linguistic signs and as, thus, resulting in the participants' heightened insecurity as to what constitutes appropriate behaviour in the interaction. Cultural differences are reflected in genres such as narratives and argumentation, but also in politeness styles. Their admixture can result in new, 'in-between' cultures. Although the focus is on South Africa, where English and Afrikaans serve as the major lingua francas, Meierkord relates information about many multilingual countries in which Esperanto, pidgins and creole languages play a role. A considerable body of literature has developed around several lingua francas. South Africa nowadays promotes multilingualism, whereas the apartheid regime had made Afrikaans and English the sole official languages of South Africa. However, these two languages are still the languages used by the powerful elites, and to date most schools have failed to go beyond the teaching of Bantu as a second language. English is given a special status, which makes the situation diglossic. Meierkord reports many studies which show that speakers tend to carry the conventions of their mother tongue into their second language English. For example, greetings are longer in Xhosa. South African English is in the process of absorbing a variety of conventions that lend a peculiarly idiosyncratic pragmatic dimension to many encounters.

Helen Spencer-Oatey and Jianyu Xing argue in chapter 11 that the interpreter is never a non-person, but is an active participant who influences the ways in which the discourse develops. Culture influences all the roles an interpreter plays: message converter, message clarifier, cultural clarifier, and advocate of the primary interlocutor. They examine authentic intercultural data from various settings in which an interpreter's unsatisfactory performance resulted in a sometimes very problematic encounter for the primary interlocutors. They discuss in detail scenes from a Chinese-British business meeting which were video-taped and discussed with all the participants. The interpreter created confusion because he paid such great attention to perceived cultural conventions that meanings were distorted.

All five chapters of this section draw on authentic conversational material that was to a large extent gathered by the authors themselves. Their methods, inspired by conversation and discourse analysis, demonstrate vividly that applied linguistics has become an indispensable discipline for research in intercultural communication.

References

Hofstede, Geert
    2001   *Culture's Consequences*. 2nd edition. Thousand Oaks: Sage.
Schwartz, Shalom
    1999   A theory of cultural values and some implications for work. *Applied Psychology: An International Review* 48: 23–47.

7. Intercultural communication and the relevance of cultural specific repertoires of communicative genres[1]

Susanne Günthner

1. Introduction

As studies in Intercultural Communication reveal, 'otherness' is not an objective relationship or a given entity between individuals or groups, but is the result of interactive accomplishments and interactive processes of attributions (Schuetz 1944/1972; Hahn 1994). But how is 'otherness' constructed and made relevant in interaction? And what are the situative functions of interactively constructed 'otherness'?

In his phenomenological essay *The Stranger*, Alfred Schuetz (1944/1972) analyzes the typical situation in which 'strangers' find themselves in their attempt to interpret the cultural pattern of a social group which they approach, and to orient themselves within it. In this situation the so far unquestioned and taken for granted schemes for interpreting the social world no longer function as a system of tested 'recipes at hand': The hitherto available recipes and their efficiency, as well as the typical attitudes required by them, are no longer an unquestioned 'matter of course' which give both security and assurance. Instead, the knowledge that has been taken for granted until now and has provided trustworthy recipes for interpreting the social world, becomes unworkable and a 'crisis' arises. Strangers find that neither the schemes of interpretation and expression, brought from their cultural group, nor the underlying basic assumptions concerning the 'thinking as usual' are any longer valid within the approached group (Schuetz 1944/1972: 104).

Situations in which we are confronted with the limits of our taken for granted schemes of interpreting often lead to processes of categorizing into 'us' and 'them', and thus to the interactive construction of cultural 'otherness'.

As research in Anthropological Linguistics has shown, the proper loci for the study of culture, cultural identities and differences – and thus, for studying the construction of cultural 'otherness' – are 'communicative practices' (Voloshinov 1929/1986; Hanks 1996; Günthner 2000a). Within the analysis of 'communicative practices' the concept of 'communicative genres' (Luckmann 1986; Bergmann and Luckmann 1995; Günthner and Knoblauch 1995; Günthner 2000a) plays a major role.

In the following, I will show that two important factors in the interactive construction of cultural differences are culture specific knowledge and the use of 'communicative genres' (e.g. gossip, complaints, lamentos, business negotiations, lectures, narratives, prayers, letters of recommendation, academic articles, personal ads, etc.). On the basis of a review of the research on communicative genres, the present article aims to outline the main issues of genre analysis and point out some of the relevant analytical categories which allow for a description of communicative genres, and thereby demonstrate the significance of this research for the analysis of communicative contexts and cultural speaking practices.

I shall argue that the analysis of communicative genres is not only relevant for the description and explanation of communicative practice in detail, but also by establishing an essential analytic link between communicative activities in the ongoing interaction on the one hand, and the sociocultural context, communicative expectations and ideologies of cultural groups on the other hand, the concept of communicative genre mediates between situatively produced communicative practices and larger sociocultural contexts, as well as between sedimented cultural knowledge and the emergence of (new) practices in the ongoing interaction.[2]

2.   The concept of 'communicative genres'

In communicative situations, meaning is negotiated on the basis of the communicative intentions, inferences and sociocultural knowledge of the participants. A relevant part of this knowledge is knowledge about the use of 'communicative genres'.

The concept of 'communicative genres' as developed within Sociology of Knowledge and Anthropological Linguistics ties back to the work of Bakhtin (1979/1986) and Voloshinov (1929/1986). In accordance with Bakhtin, speaking occurs in speech genres which guide the interaction and which are determined by social structures:

> Speech genres organize our speech in almost the same way as grammatical (syntactical) forms do. We learn to cast our speech in generic forms and, when hearing others' speech, we guess its genres from the very first words; we predict a certain length (...) and a certain compositional structure; we foresee the end; that is, from the very beginning we have a sense of the speech whole, which is only later differentiated during the speech process.
>
> Bakhtin 1979/1986: 78–79

Genres, however, do not appear as complex language structures devoid of the dynamics of interaction but rather as interactive patterns of speech. They not only guide the activities in verbal interaction but are also part of the ideologies of social groups (Bakhtin 1979/1986).

In the last 20 years, studies within the Sociology of Knowledge[3] as well as within Anthropological Linguistics[4] have repeatedly addressed the issue of communicative genres and they provide a theoretical conceptualization which links the notion of 'genre' to the theoretical model of Social Constructivism (Berger and Luckmann 1966). Communicative genres, thus, represent a central communicative means in the construction of social reality.

Empirical investigations of genres have demonstrated that this concept also proves to be a useful analytical tool with respect to the description of communicative patterns in everyday interactions as well as in intercultural communication.[5]

Communicative genres can be defined as *historically and culturally specific, prepatterned and complex solutions to recurrent communicative problems* (Luckmann 1986). On the one hand, they guide interactants' expectations about what is to be said (and done) in the particular context. On the other hand, they are the sediments of socially relevant communicative processes. Thus, communicative genres can be treated as *historically and culturally specific conventions and ideals according to which speakers compose talk or texts and recipients interpret it* (Hanks 1987; Günthner 2000a). In choosing a particular genre, a speaker makes use of culturally segmented solutions to communicative problems, and at the same time – due to their prepatterning – genres not only 'relieve' the speaker, but also assist the recipients in limiting the interpretative possibilities of utterances by relating them to the specific genre. Thus, the knowledge that communicative processes with specific functions occurring in certain social situations take on recurrent forms, not only guides the communicative actions themselves but also their interpretations. An essential element of genre-related knowledge is knowledge about the appropriate use of genres, i.e. when to use or not to use a particular genre.

Members of a cultural group are usually familiar with the communicative genres which are necessary for their particular life-world; e.g. they know how to tell a joke, they recognize when someone else is telling a joke and also know in which situations it is appropriate to tell what kinds of jokes (Günthner and Knoblauch 1994, 1995). There are situations which require the use of a particular genre (e.g. in Caucasian Georgia, when someone dies, 'lamentos' are expected; Kotthoff 1999, 2002b). In other situations, e.g. if speakers intend to criticize the misbehaviour of their co-participants, they might have a choice between various genres, such as complaints, reproaches, teasing, making fun of, etc. The particular choice depends on various aspects, such as the social context, the specific communicative situation, the relationship between the participants, their habitus, the degree of the misbehaviour, etc.

In using a communicative genre, speakers construct an intertextual relation between the situative 'communicative text' and a canonized pattern. In this recontextualization of a generic pattern, speakers might follow the canonized model, deviate from it or create hybrid forms – the possibilities of variations are manifold. In everyday interactions, we frequently meet mixtures and hybridiz-ations of various generic models; e.g. a professor might tell a joke within her lecture, and thus integrate a particular genre (a joke) into a more complex one (a lecture); or she might switch within her lecture into a cermonial tone of voice and thus transform the genre.

As historical and cultural products, communicative genres are open to change and cultural variation. If we take communicative genres as socially con-structed solutions which organize, routinize, and standardize the dealing with particular communicative problems, it seems quite obvious that different cul-tural groups may construct different solutions for specific communicative prob-lems. Thus, the repertoire of communicative genres varies from culture to cul-ture (Günthner 1993, 1995; Günthner and Luckmann 2001, 2002). Culture specific ways of using and interpreting communicative genres can be located on three levels: (i) *the level of internal features*, (ii) *the interactional level* and (iii) *the level of external features*. In the following, I shall introduce these three le-vels and present examples from research on intercultural communication to il-lustrate possible culture specific uses of communicative genres.

2.1.   The level of internal features

The internal structure of communicative genres consists of:

> overall patterns of diverse elements, such as words and phrases, registers, formulas and formulaic blocs, rhetorical figures and tropes, stylistic devices (metrics, rhyme, lists, oppositions), prosodic melodies, specific regulations of dialogicity, repair strat-egies and prescriptions for topics and topical areas.
> Luckmann 1992: 39; (translated by Günthner and Knoblauch 1995)

Rhetorical differences concerning elements on the internal level of communi-cative genres can lead to the interactive construction of cultural differences in communication. An example of how differences in *prosodic features* in service encounters may lead to different interpretations, and thus result in miscommuni-cation, is discussed by Gumperz (1982). Indian and Pakistani women working at a cafeteria of a British airport were perceived as surly and uncooperative by British speakers of English. This interpretation was based on the Indian inton-ation patterns used by these women: When customers in the cafeteria chose meat, they were asked whether they wanted gravy. A British employee would utter 'gravy?' using rising intonation, whereas the Indian employees used fal-ling intonation: 'gravy.'. This prosodic difference turned out to be relevant for the inferences drawn by the British customers: 'gravy.' with a falling intonation contour was "not interpreted as an offer but rather as a statement, which in the context seems redundant and consequently rude" (Gumperz 1982: 173). However, for the Indian speakers, this falling intonation was their conventional way of asking questions in service encounters and did not imply any sign of rudeness or indifference.

Differences in the use of communicative genres and patterns on the internal level also include non-verbal elements (gaze, mimics, gesture, etc.),[6] lexico-semantic elements,[7] phonological devices, and syntactical patterning as well as the selection of specific linguistic varieties. There may be differences in idiomatic expressions, proverbial sayings, routine formulas,[8] etc. – especially differences in the rules governing their incorporation into larger communicative genres. Communicative genres may also vary in their discursive organization:[9] Tyler and Davies' (1990) study of interactions between Korean teaching assistants and American students shows what they call differences in the organizational pattern of argumentation. When American students approached Korean teaching assistants and asked 'How come I got such a low grade?', Korean teaching assistants used an 'inductive/collaborative approach'. They did not start by providing an overall statement but listed various errors, beginning with relatively minor procedural points. This strategy is considered by the Korean participants to be 'less threatening and more face-saving' to the student. The American students, however, expecting a general statement of the problem, interpreted the strategy as a sign of incompetence. As Tyler and Davies (1990: 402) point out:

> (…) what from the Korean Teaching Assistant's perspective is a less confrontational discourse strategy, in this particular context, provides the framework for increased confrontation. The interlocutors appear to be operating from two different sets of expectations as to how the argument should progress. Each of the participants experiences the other's responses as jarring and irritating. As the exchange progresses, the discordant strategies, in concert with other mismatches, contribute to a reciprocal sense of non-cooperation.

Cultural differences on the internal level of genres can also affect stylistic conventions: In their study of the courtroom testimony of Native Americans, Gumperz (2001) and Underwood and Gumperz' (1988) show that in answering an attorney's question, the Native American witnesses generally produce a narrative "which begins with a reference to how the knowledge was acquired and by whom the witness was told, as if the speaker needed to cite authority for each statement. Those parts of the answer that contain material relevant to the question that was asked are embedded in the narrative, as if responsibility for the answer were not the individual's but the group's" (Underwood and Gumperz 1988: 6–7). As the authors point out, narrative forms here serve as a verbal strategy to conform to Native American norms in producing statements that reflect the authority of the group. The speaker foregrounds the fact that what is said reflects the tribe's position, not any one person's belief or opinion. Gumperz

(2001) and Gumperz and Cook-Gumperz (in this volume) show how culturally different speaking practices and stylistic conventions can lead to the conviction of minority speakers.

Thematic features also represent elements of the internal structure of communicative genres. Kotthoff's (1991: 251–253, Kotthoff in this volume) analysis of 'toasts' in Caucasian Georgia shows that toasts make use of a certain thematic canon: "peace, the guests, the parents, the dead, the children, friendship, love, the women whose beauty embellishes the table". Foreigners unaware of canonical themes may cause embarrassment by choosing for their toasts inappropriate subjects.

The interactive construction of 'in-groups' and 'us' vs. 'out-groups' and 'them' may also be evoked by differences in modalizations of genres. There may be different cultural conventions concerning the topics appropriate for jokes and treatment of jocular stories.[10] An example given by von Helmolt (1997) shows the differences between French and German engineers participating in a joint working session. The French participants repeatedly shifted from a serious task-oriented mode of discourse to a light-hearted jocular one (marked both non-verbally by facial expressions, gestures, laughter and by allusion to shared background knowledge, teasing, etc.). For the French this was a phatic activity, 'un clin d'oeil complice', for the Germans a sign of lack of interest or misplaced frivolity.

Although, in this overview I concentrate on oral communication, different conventions concerning rhetorical features in genres cannot be reduced to oral genres; written genres may also reveal culturally different traditions concerning the internal level (Swales 1990, Esser 1997).

2.2.   The level of interactional features

This level consists of those elements which are part of the ongoing interaction, i.e. the interactive organization of conversations, including patterns of turn-taking, preference organizations, strategies for longer stretches of conversation and the participation framework.

In her study of dinner conversations among New Yorkers and Californians, Tannen (1984) shows that because of different ways of managing turn-taking, misunderstandings arise. The New Yorkers have different turn-taking rules and conventions to show conversational involvement: they use much overlap and latching, a fast rate of speech and they avoid internal pauses. The result is that the East Coast speakers continually take the floor, the West Coast participants waiting in vain for a pause they deem long enough for them to start talking. Whereas the 'fast' speakers think that the others have nothing to say, the 'slow' ones feel that they are not given a chance to talk.

Various studies of intercultural encounters demonstrate differences in the signalling of attentive listening. Research in the organization of 'backchannel' activities in different cultural groups reveals that recipients' reactions differ in at least two respects: the frequency of producing 'backchannel' signals and the types of verbal elements employed in specific communicative genres (Clancy et al. 1996, Günthner 1994). Erickson and Schultz' (1982) analysis of interactive strategies used by Black and White students and counsellors in counselling sessions in American colleges also demonstrates culture-specific ways of showing that one is listening attentively in these institutional contexts. White speakers employ specific syntactic and prosodic means to signal 'listening-response relevant-moments' and thereby demonstrate that they expect recipient reactions. Their White co-participants understand these contextualization cues and produce the expected recipient reactions at the 'right' moments. Black speakers, however, who are not familiar with the White speaking style, do not understand these cues and refrain from producing recipient signals. The absence of expected reactions leads the White speakers to reformulate and recycle their utterances, give hyperexplanations and 'talk down' (Erickson and Schultz 1982: 132). White recipients also tend to show more explicitly than Black recipients that they are listening attentively by applying verbal and non-verbal cues. Consequently, White speakers do not notice the subtle signals of Black recipients and provide further explications, repetitions, etc. This leads to the interpretation of the Black participants that their White co-participants are 'talking down' and are not taking them seriously.

Concerning preference organization in communicative genres, various cultural differences are to be observed. Schiffrin's (1984) analysis of Philadelphian Jewish argumentative styles demonstrates that there is a preference for the production of disagreement. In German argumentation, direct disagreement also seems to be preferred (Kotthoff 1993). In intercultural argumentation, however, different preference systems concerning specific genres may lead to irritation. As Naotsuka and Sakamoto (1981: 173–174) remark, in Japanese argumentation direct confrontation is avoided in favor of communicative harmony. Europeans' way of showing direct opposition is considered to be 'rude'.[11]

Culturally different preference structures may also show up in reactions to compliments. As Pomerantz (1984) points out, – in observation of the principle that self-praise is to be avoided – reactions to compliments (in Western cultures) usually downgrade the compliment, shift referent, return the compliment or use appreciation tokens (e.g. 'thanks a lot'). Thus, the response to a compliment for an excellent dinner may contain downgrading (e.g. 'The vegetables were overcooked'), a referent shift (e.g. 'It's a recipe John gave me') or an appreciation (e.g. 'Thank you'). In the Chinese context, however, accepting a compliment with 'feichang xie xie' ('thanks a lot') would be considered inappropriate and be interpreted as a sign of arrogance or 'modern Western ways of speaking'. Instead, the receiver of a compliment for a meal is expected to downgrade the assessment, e.g. by denying the excellence of the food or by refuting his or her capacity to cook ('wo zuo cai, zuo de bu hao, qing yuanliang' 'I didn't cook well, please excuse my bad cooking') (Günthner 1993).[12]

Philips' (1972) analysis of participation structures in classroom interactions in Warm Springs (Oregon) reveals striking differences between Indian and White children. Non-Indian teachers continuously complain that Indian children show a great deal of reluctance to talk and participate in various verbal activities in the classroom. As Philips points out, this 'failure to participate' is based on the 'social condition for participation' which exists in the class situation and which the Indian children are not accustomed to. In traditional Indian learning contexts, the use of speech is notably minimal, and one observes others and starts with private self-testing before one demonstrates one's skills. In Western classroom interactions, however, the prevailing assumption is that one learns more effectively by practising even if it involves making mistakes. As Indian children are neither accustomed to such public 'exhibition' nor to the fact that they cannot choose the proper time for demonstration of their skills, they refrain from participating. A further reason for the absence of participation is that Indian children are not used to interactive structures in which one person (such as the teacher) overtly controls the activity of other people in the interacting group.[13]

2.3.   The level of the external features

The external level reflects the relationship between the use of genres and particular communicative milieus, communicative situations, the selection of types of actors (according to gender, age, status, etc.), and the institutional distribution of genres.

Cultural 'otherness' may be constructed in respect to gender specific uses of particular genres. In Caucasian Georgia 'toasting' is an important, ritualized male genre, its competent use is a mark of masculinity (Kotthoff 1995 and in this volume). Those men who lack the rhetorical abilities of toasting 'are considered unmanly'. If a foreigner refuses to offer a toast or if his toast appears 'too modest', his 'masculinity' is questioned. In informal situations, women may also occasionally take over the role of toast-masters. In formal situations, however, the toastmaster inevitably is a man. In intercultural encounters, when foreign women are invited to formal dinner-parties, they embarrass their hosts when they assume that toasting is expected from all guests and 'usurp' the role of toast-master (Kotthoff 1991).

Miller (1994, 2000) describes intercultural problems arising between Japanese and American business people because of cultural differences in the institutional organization of communicative genres. For American business people meetings are "thought to be the appropriate place in which to persuade people or try to change their minds" (Miller 1994: 224). They expect decision-making and the resolution of conflict in the meeting. This contrasts sharply with the Japanese understanding of business meetings. Consensus is achieved before the formal meeting. The participants meet in bars, cafes, etc., where they argue and try to iron out differences of opinion before the actual meeting. The formal meeting itself is to bestow ritual approval to what went on before it. This kind of pre-meeting activity called 'nemawashi' ('spadework') does not have negative connotations in Japan. As Miller (1994: 226) points out, "interactants often assume that the problem relates to fundamental differences in national character. As a case in point, we are constantly reminded of a difference between Japanese and Americans which is uncritically accepted and habitually repeated: Japanese, we are told, are always indirect and ambiguous, while Americans are presumably unable to be anything but direct and pushy (...)".

Cultural differences in genre related knowledge tend to have particularly grave consequences when they occur in 'gate-keeping' situations of various institutions. Access to education, occupational career, and health are affected by decisions in such situations (Gumperz 1982, 2001; Erickson and Schultz 1982, Scherr, Roberts, and Eades in this volume). As Scollon and Scollon's (1981: 180–182) study of courtroom interactions in Alaskan state courts demonstrates, for certain classes of offences jail sentences were consistently longer for Alaskan Natives than for Whites. On examining pre-sentence reports, the authors found that those for the Natives reported the absence of any plans for the future. White Americans, in contrast, regularly stressed their intention of returning to a job or to school and thus expressed their desire to improve themselves. This culturally approved way of 'putting your best foot forward' seemed to have influenced the White American legal professional assessment of the accused.

Elements located on these three levels (the internal, the interactional and the external level) constitute the patterning of communicative genres. Thus, genres cannot be reduced to specific textual patterning on the internal level, but they are interactive accomplishments between speaker and recipient and are closely tied to larger cultural, political and institutional issues in the construction of social reality.

Furthermore, as work on genre conventions in different cultural communities reveals, knowledge about communicative practices and genres in modern societies regulates the access of individuals to various institutional and private settings. According to Bourdieu (1990), linguistic knowledge is an important part of 'symbolic capital', i.e. ways of speaking symbolize one's belonging to a particular social 'field'. Those who have power, determine the 'legitimate' ways of speaking. Knowledge about 'how to speak' is a powerful means for certain groups to stay in power and also to keep other groups from having power. The power of the words depends on the power of the speaker of the words, which is determined by her/his social location in a particular 'field'. In addition to this view, one should stress that the social location of the speaker is itself constructed communicatively to a large extent, as his/her access to a certain field is built up by communicative activities and by way of communicative genres.

The concept of communicative genres not only allows us to analyze communicative activities, but it also provides a framework for relating particular practices to larger sociocultural contexts, and thus for connecting emerging communicative gestalts to sedimented and culturally conventionalized patterns.

3.   Aspects of instantiating communicative genres within intercultural communication

In portraying the different levels of genre analysis, I have referred to literature on possible cultural variation in the use of features situated on these levels. In the following, I shall portray the possible consequences of culturally specific genre traditions for intercultural encounters.

As communicative genres are historical and cultural products, working as orientation frames to produce and interpret communicative action, different cultural groups may have different repertoires of genres; a given communicative problem (e.g. lamenting for the dead) may be 'institutionalized' as a communicative genre in some cultural groups, but not in others.[14] Lack of knowledge about such differences may lead to problems in some situations. Even more treacherous, however, are situations into which the participants enter with different repertoires of seemingly similar genres (academic discussions, business negotiations, job interviews) and with inadequate knowledge about the differences in the mode of employment of the genre, stylistic variations, etc.

3.1.   Culturally varying repertoires of communicative genres

In intercultural communication participants 'start' with different repertoires of genres. In one cultural group there may be generic ways of handling particular communicative activities, whereas interactants of another group may not be familiar with this routinized pattern.

Birkner and Kern's (2000) work on job interviews between East and West German participants provides a striking example of interactants who are confronted with a so far unfamiliar genre. After German reunification, East Germans were confronted with the genre of job interviews. What Birkner and Kern's empirical investigation shows, is a clash between the demands of the genre (being part of the communicative culture of the West) and the communicative resources available qua membership of the East German communicative culture; whereas job interviews in the West demand displays of one's abilities and prior experiences, East German institutional style encourages modesty and concealment of one's abilities. Whereas Western job interviews expect applicants to show active contributions, East German communicative ideology demands the avoidance of the agent-subject and requires indirectness and vagueness. Furthermore, job interviews in the West are based on a superficial ideology of equality beneath which power relations are hidden, and a superficial atmosphere of informality is constructed; East German institutional styles expose and underline power relations through formality and submission. Thus, in responding to the new communicative expectations and the demanded genre, East German applicants tend to re-activate a formal, institutional 'East German discourse style', mixed with certain elements of what they guess or assume to be adequate for this West German genre.[15]

Besides revealing how participants react in situations in which they are confronted with new genres, Birkner and Kern's (2000), Kern's (2000), Auer and Kern's (2001) as well as Birkner's (2002) studies show that in modern societies the borders between different repertoires of genres do not necessarily go hand and hand with geographical or linguistic borders (such as Germany or the German language).

Also, within the academic world, interactants may be confronted with genres which are not part of their own academic rhetorical tradition (Clyne 1987; Swales 1990; Paltridge 1997; Ehlich 1998; Swales et al. 1998). In German universities (as well as in many other European and North-American universities) 'office hours' are an institutionalized genre (Günthner 2001; Meer 2002). In their socialization at university, students acquire the necessary knowledge about this genre; e.g. knowledge about when to consult professors or lecturers on what kind of problems, about interactive procedures in office hours, knowledge that these consultations take place at scheduled times and fixed locations, etc. In various academic cultures (e.g. Vietnam, China, Russia, Uzbekistan, Kazakhstan, etc.), however, office hours do not exist. Foreign students from these cultures often tend to have problems with the communicative genre of office hours at German universities. The following sequences, stemming from interviews with Chinese students at German universities, illustrate some of these problems.

Fan, a Chinese student of German, states:

Such office hours, we don't have them in China. In China students visit their professor at home. This means: you have a problem, so you want your teacher to help you. Normally. When I came to Germany at first, I did not know what to do in these office hours. I did not know this form 'office hours'. And then I asked other Chinese foreign students what one should talk about in these office hours. And they said: just talk about your studies. One should tell the professors what one has already accomplished. You go there with an aim and you have to achieve this aim before you leave. (own translation; S.G.)

Li, a Chinese student recollects her first experience with 'office hours' at a German university:

> I went to see my professor and brought him a lacquer vase as a gift. And I said to him: 'I want to give you this Chinese vase as a gift'. But he looked at the vase and said: 'Ms. Li, this is very kind of you, but I cannot accept the vase'. And he told that I should take the vase away with me again. I was so shocked. And I thought to myself: 'You are so stupid. Right at the beginning you spoilt everything.' Heeheehee. (...) In China, you must know, it is very important that the professor accepts your present. Only later I understood that here you don't offer presents to your professors. (...) In China one thinks like this: First you offer the present and then you talk about your problem. Then the talk will go much more smoothly. You don't do it the other way round. (own translation; S.G.)

These sequences not only demonstrate the insecurity of Chinese students confronted with the 'new' genre of office hours, but they also show how certain expectations concerning this new genre (e.g. offering a gift from home to the professor) are disappointed.

3.2.   Different uses of seemingly similar communicative genres

Besides having culturally different repertoires of communicative genres, often seemingly similar genres are used differently by members of different communicative cultures.[16]

Li's (1999) analyses of Chinese–Dutch and Chinese–Finnish interactions reveal culture specific expectations towards the genre of business negotiations; Whereas for Chinese participants establishing good interpersonal relations is central in these interactions, for their Dutch and Finnish counterparts the outcome of the negotiation is central. Furthermore, Li's detailed empirical study shows differences in discourse organization: Chinese speakers tend to provide background information before presenting the central argument. Often they just present background information and expect their co-participants to formulate the intended conclusions. Dutch and Finnish participants, who are not used to this way of providing extended background information first, often get frustrated waiting for the main arguments to come. Li argues that culturally different expectations and ways of handling the genre of business negotiations can lead to insecurities and frustrations.

Spencer-Oatey and Xing's (2000) ethnographic study of business visits shows revealing facts about culturally different expectations between Chinese and British business partners concerning such visits. The authors argue that due to different expectations concerning welcome meetings, hotel arrangements, programmes of activities, different ways of judging the importance of the visitors and especially different 'face' concepts, business visits can turn out to be 'acrimonious and unpleasant' experiences (Spencer-Oatey and Xing 2000: 272).[17]

Kotthoff's (2002a) study of German–Russian academic talks (in Arts and Social Sciences) also shows striking differences in dealing with seemingly similar genres. German speakers tend to present some sort of orientation about the topical structure of their talk at the beginning of their presentation. Further, German speakers often explicitly refer to subtopics. Russian speakers usually provide no such orientation. Whereas German academic talks are usually rather focussed on one major topic, the thematic scope of Russian talks is rather wide and resembles more what in German tradition would be a festive talk. Furthermore, whereas German speakers explicitly quote ideas, theses, etc. from other authors, in Russian talks it is difficult to figure out which are the speaker's own theses and which are ideas stemming from other researchers.

Cultural differences in the organization, patterning and further handling of seemingly similar genres cannot be reduced to oral rhetorical tradition; studies within academic discourse reveal profound cultural differences in the organization of written genres, too.[18] Kirkpatrick's (1991) analysis of information sequencing in Mandarin and English 'letters of request' shows how similar communicative genres may vary in their discursive organization. Chinese letters of request reveal a preference for providing reasons first, before the main point (the request) is stated. The Chinese genre of request letters generally conforms to the following schema: salutation, preamble ('face work'), reasons, and then the request itself. Thus, in contrast to English request letters, Chinese not only produce extended face work which forms an integral part of the request, but they also tend to place the reasons before the request itself:

> This appears to be a formalized way of framing requests. That is to say, native speakers are able to identify these requests as well-written, normal, and polite long before they come to the requests themselves, because they are familiar with the structure of requests and the sequence in which the parts of a request are ordered. ... Changing the order, by moving the request to the beginning, results in a letter or request being marked as direct and possibly impolite.
>
> Kirkpatrick 1991: 198

3.3.   Different stylistic assessments of seemingly similar genres

In intercultural communicative situations there may be not only clashes of various communicative genres, but also differences in the stylistic assessment of particular genres.[19] Knowing how to use these genres belongs just as much to communicative competence as does knowing which genre is stylistically appropriate for doing particular interactional work.

Apparently identical genres may also have differing stylistic conventions, they may be used in different social contexts or milieus or have a high prestige in one culture and be associated with lower status groups in another culture. The use of proverbs provides an example for the different assessment of seemingly similar genres. In German, proverbs are treated as the 'wisdom of the little man', and books on style advise against using them (Günthner 1993). In the Chinese context, however, to 'ornament' one's argumentation, academic thesis or speech with quotes from proverbial sayings (especially 'chengyu'; i.e. figurative proverbial sayings in tetragram form) is highly valued and appreciated as a sign of good education. Various studies in spoken Chinese, numerous Chinese language books for foreigners and collections of Chinese proverbs stress the fact that the culture of proverbs in China is very lively. They are considered to be 'shuoguo jiaoyu' – a sign of being well educated. Studies in Chinese rhetoric report that much of Chinese power to convince relies on analogies and on citations of recognized authorities, anecdotes and fables (Granet, 1985: 39–41). In Chinese argumentation, for instance, proverbial sayings fulfil an important function in the backing of arguments: they allow speakers to demonstrate their classical knowledge and to present their own assertions as being part of traditional and still valid collective wisdom. The use of proverbs, however, is not restricted to oral genres. Chinese writers of academic texts often support their arguments by referring to traditional wisdom in the form of a proverbial saying (Günthner 1991, 1993). Furthermore, Chinese students of German often use German proverbs in similar ways (in many Chinese universities the teaching of foreign languages includes teaching of proverbs in the respective languages): German theses or other academic papers written by Chinese students often start with German proverbs such as 'the first step is always the most difficult' ('Aller Anfang ist schwer'), 'you can't teach an old dog new tricks' ('Was Hänschen nicht lernt, lernt Hans nimmermehr'). Chinese teachers of German simply transfer onto the German language their culturally shaped attitudes towards the genre of proverbs which enjoys such a high status in China.

Thus, in intercultural situations we are not only confronted with clashes of various expressions of communicative genres but also with differences in the stylistic assessment of particular genres (Kotthoff in this volume). Knowing how to use these genres belongs just as much to communicative competence as does knowing which genre is appropriate for doing particular interactional work.

3.4.   The emergence of new, hybrid forms in intercultural communication

When members of different cultural groups come to communicate with one another, they hardly ever do so without some knowledge about the other culture and their etiquette of language use. This knowledge may have been acquired from other members of their own culture, it may have been picked up from vague hearsay, or it may stem from previous experiences with members of the other cultural groups. Even if this knowledge is acquired in 'official' instruction – such as intercultural training programs – it is no guarantee of its accuracy.

The following example illustrates how misinstruction can lead to hypercorrection on the level of style and genre. In China, students of German are taught that Germans are very 'direct' themselves and that they prefer 'directness' in others. They are not told, however, what constitutes this peculiar German 'directness' nor when it is to be used. In initial contacts with Germans many Chinese act upon this piece of 'knowledge' in order to meet what they assume to be the expectations of the German addressees. They leave the safe ground of their own conventions and venture upon the thin ice of German 'directness'. This was amply demonstrated by a perusal of letters written by Chinese students and scholars to German professors (Günthner 1993; Günthner and Luckmann 2001, 2002). Hypercorrection prevailed and produced something whose structural features were neither a German nor a Chinese genre, but a kind of hybrid genre whose regular structure bears the mark of an attempted solution of a communicative problem.

Customarily and expectedly, these letters begin with an address. This is followed by an apology for 'imposing' upon the addressee. This is followed abruptly by a list of requests and demands. A typical example:

Dear Prof. Dr. Schmidt,[20]

Pardon me for troubling you with my problem. My name is Liu Xiaobing. I am working at the university in Nanjing as a physics teacher. I would like to work for you. Therefore I need a position in your laboratory. Would you be able to provide this for me? Unfortunately my scholarship from the Chinese government only lasts for one year. But I would like to write my dissertation with you. Please be so kind and arrange a scholarship for my dissertation. Important research material is difficult to come by in China. Therefore I need to get some literature from you. Please send the books to my private address in Nanjing.
Pardon me for my annoyance.
(own translation; S.G.)

This example shows how problematic context-free attributions of seemingly culture-specific communicative practices can turn out to be. They not only tend to reproduce stereotypes but may even have severe consequences.

Furthermore, the example reveals that participants in intercultural communication not only stick to their own genre traditions but also use various strategies of adaptation, compromise etc. Thus, new hybrid forms are emerging. Intercultural communication thus cannot be reduced to the transmission of one's own conventions to the situation at hand; intercultural encounters have their own dynamics and may lead to new forms of communicating (Günthner 1993; Koole and ten Thije 1994).

New forms emerging in intercultural communication may not necessarily lead to negative consequences, as in the examples above, where the Chinese students often received negative answers from the German professors, or in the East–West German job interviews, where East German applicants reacted to the genre requirements by re-activating elements from the formal East German institutional style, mixed with features of what they assumed to be appropriate for this new genre (Birkner and Kern 2000; Auer and Kern 2001). As various studies on 'crossing' and 'mixing' phenomena in Germany reveal, new hybrid forms and genres tend to develop among migrant children of the 2nd and 3rd generation of Turkish immigrants. Turkish genres, such as 'ritual insults' are becoming transformed and mixed with rap songs and routine formulas stemming from German-Turkish comedy-shows (Füglein 2000, Hinnenkamp 2002).

4.   Conclusions

Although this paper only outlines the issues, I hope it has nevertheless shown how genres are part of a cultural system of signs and have "value loadings, social distributions, and typical performance styles according to which they are shaped in the course of utterances" (Hanks 1987: 670).

As this overview shows, research on stylistic-rhetorical conventions for handling particular (oral and written) genres turns out to be a fruitful approach for studying intercultural communication. In combining genre analysis with intercultural communication, the following questions arise:

(1) Do interactants from different cultural groups have similar repertoires of genre?
(2) How are particular genres realized within a specific cultural group?
(3) Do seemingly similar genres have similar functions in these cultural groups?
(4) Are there culturally diverging stylistic evaluations of seemingly similar genres?
(5) What kind of hybrid forms are emerging in what kind of contexts?

The analysis of communicative genres can prove to be an important link between language and culture, as in the actual production of utterances oriented to a specific genre, where speakers not only produce culturally routinized conventions of communication but also reconfirm, recreate or modify typified organizational forms of communicative behavior.

By establishing an analytic link between research of situatively produced communicative practices, culturally conventionalized ways of organizing specific communicative activities (i.e. genres), and larger sociocultural contexts, genre analysis provides an important methodological tool for studying intercultural encounters.

Notes

1. Thanks to Karlfried Knapp and Helga Kotthoff for their comments on an earlier version of this paper. Thanks also to Annemarie Young for checking the English.
2. Cf. Hanks (1987); Günthner and Knoblauch (1994, 1995); Günthner (2000a).
3. Cf. Luckmann (1986, 1987, 1988, 1992); Bergmann (1987); Günthner and Knoblauch (1994); Bergmann and Luckmann (1995); Keppler (1994).
4. Cf. Hanks (1987); Briggs and Bauman (1992); Günthner (1993, 2000a); Kotthoff (1995).
5. Cf. Günthner (1993, 2000b, 2001); Günthner and Luckmann (2001, 2002); Di Luzio, Günthner and Orletti (2001); Kotthoff (1994, 1995, 1999, 2002a, b).
6. Gumperz and Roberts' (1991) study of counselling sessions between British and Indian counsellors and clients in British neighbourhood centers offers an example of culturally different use of gaze: Whereas Indian speakers 'use gaze to monitor interlocutor's reactions, to determine possible turn transition points or to ask for the floor and call attention to new information', British speakers 'seek to meet the interlocutor's gaze when they are addressing them or listening to what they are saying'. These nonverbal differences regularly lead to irritations between the clients and social workers in the analyzed interactions.
7. Cf. Gumperz (1982) on differences in Black and White political speech styles; and Gumperz, Aulakh and Kaltman (1982) on the different use of particles in Indian and British English.
8. Cf. Coulmas (1981), Günthner (1993). Cf. also Duranti (2001) on properties of greetings across languages and speech communities.
9. Cf. also Iwasaki and Horie (1998) on discursive patterns in Japanese and Thai conversations; cf. Günthner (1993), Young (1994) and Li (1999) on different discursive patterns in Chinese and German/US-American and Dutch argumentations.
10. Cf. Vermeer (1989) on different cultural conventions of telling jokes in Chinese-German business negotiations. Cf. also Goodwin and Lee (1994) on cultural variation of taboo topics.
11. The same holds for argumentations in Thai culture (Richards and Sukwiwat 1983). Cf. also Günthner (1993, 2000b) on German–Chinese differences in argumentative styles.
12. Cf. also Spencer-Oatey, Ng and Dong (2000) on British and Chinese responses to compliments.
13. Cf. Erickson and Mohatt (1982) for similar findings on cultural organization of participation structures in classroom situations with Indian and White teachers.
14. Cf. Feld (1990) on ritual lamenting among the Kaluli, Caraveli-Chaves (1980) among Greek women, Urban (1988) and Briggs (1992) among Warao women, Sherzer (1987) among the Kunas, and Kotthoff (1999, 2002b) among Georgian women in the Caucasus.
15. Cf. also Chen (2003) on cultural contrasts between German and Chinese job interviews.
16. Cf. also Anderson's (1994) study of culturally variant accounting practices in English and Italian service encounters. Cf. Rehbein's (2001) work on German-American business negotiations and differences in verbal and non-verbal strategies.
17. Cf. also Scollon and Scollon (1995) on intercultural differences in professional discourse, and Clyne (1994) on intercultural communication in work settings.

18. Cf. Swales (1990) who explores genres of self-presentation and self-marketing within academic discourse (e.g. abstracts, thesis and submission letters; i.e. letters which accompany the article when it is first sent to an editor) and shows problems non-native scientists from Egypt, China, Iran have with English academic genre traditions. Swales et al. (1998) reveal cross-cultural differences in argumentative patterning in student essays. Cf. also Liang's (1991) study on cultural differences in scientific reviews among German and Chinese writers. Cf. also Kniffka's (1994) study of 'letters to the editor across cultures'.
19. Cf. Gumperz (1982) who reveals that the genre of political speeches reveals striking differences in rhetorical strategies used by Black and White speakers. Typical Afro-American rhetorical strategies, such as the metaphoric use of 'to kill someone' for 'destroying someone's political influence' may lead to serious disagreement on the interpretation of what is said. Cf. Günthner (1993) on cultural differences in argumentative styles between German and Chinese speakers; Yamashita (2001) on 'politeness styles' in Japanese and German interactions; Scollon and Pan (2002) on stylistic differences in conflict management strategies between East Asian and North American speakers.
20. All names have been changed.

References

Anderson, Laurie
    1994   Accounting practices in service encounters in English and Italian. In: Heiner Pürschel (ed.), *Intercultural Communication*. Proceedings of the 17th International L.A.U.D. Symposium Duisburg, 99–120. Frankfurt a. M.: Peter Lang.
Auer, Peter and Frederike Kern
    2001   Three ways of analysing communication between East and West Germans as intercultural communication. In: Aldo Di Luzio, Susanne Günthner and Franca Orletti (eds.), *Culture in Communication*, 89–116. Amsterdam: Benjamins.
Bakhtin, Mikhail. M.
    1979/1986   The problem of speech genres. In: Mikhail M. Bakhtin (ed.), *Speech Genres and other Late Essays*, 60–102. Austin: University of Texas Press.
Berger, Peter and Thomas Luckmann
    1966   *A Treatise in the Sociology of Knowledge*. New York: Anchor Books.
Bergmann, Jörg
    1987   *Klatsch. Zur Sozialform der diskreten Indiskretion*. Berlin/New York: de Gruyter.
Bergmann, Jörg and Thomas Luckmann
    1995   Reconstructive genres of everyday communication. In: Uta M. Quasthoff (ed.), *Aspects of Oral Communication*, 289–304. Berlin/New York: de Gruyter.
Birkner, Karin
    2002   Ost- und Westdeutsche im Bewerbungsgespräch: Ein Fall von Interkultureller Kommunikation. In: Helga Kotthoff (ed.), *Kultur(en) im Gespräch*, 301–332. Tübingen: Narr.

Birkner, Karin and Frederike Kern
    2000   Impression management in East and West German job interviews. In: Helen
            Spencer-Oatey (ed.), *Culturally Speaking. Managing Rapport through Talk
            across Cultures*, 255–272. London/New York: Continuum.
Bourdieu, Pierre
    1990   *Was heißt Sprechen? Die Ökonomie des sprachlichen Austausches.* Wien:
            Braumüller.
Briggs, Charles L.
    1992   'Since i am a woman, i will chastise my relatives': Gender, reported speech,
            and the (re)production of social relations in Warao ritual wailing. *American
            Ethnologist* 19(2): 337–361.
Briggs, Charles L. and Richard Bauman
    1992   Genre, intertextuality and social power. *Journal of Linguistic Anthropology*
            2(2): 131–172.
Caraveli-Chaves, A.
    1980   Bridges between worlds: The Greek women's ritual lament as communi-
            cative event. *Journal of American Folklore* 95: 129–158.
Chen, Shing-Lung
    2003   *Kulturelle Kontraste bei deutschen und chinesischen Bewerbungsgesprä-
            chen. Am Beispiel des Berufsbereichs der Informationstechnologie.* Frank-
            furt: Peter Lang.
Clancy, Patricia M., Sandra A. Thompson, Ryoko Suzuki and Hongyin Tao
    1996   The conversational use of reactive tokens in English, Japanese, and Manda-
            rine. *Journal of Pragmatics* 26: 355–387.
Clyne, Michael
    1987   Cultural differences in the organization of academic texts: English and Ger-
            man. *Journal of Pragmatics* 11: 217–247.
Clyne, Michael
    1994   *Inter-cultural Communication at Work.* Cambridge: Cambridge University
            Press.
Coulmas, Florian
    1981   *Routine im Gespräch. Zur pragmatischen Funktion der Idiomatik.* Wies-
            baden: Athenäum.
Di Luzio, Aldo, Susanne Günthner and Franca Orletti (eds.)
    2001   *Culture in Communication. Analyses of Intercultural Situations.* Amster-
            dam: Benjamins.
Duranti, Alessandro
    2001   Universal and Culture-Specific Properties of Greetings. In: Alessandro
            Duranti (ed.), *Linguistic Anthropology. A Reader*, 208–238. New York:
            Blackwell.
Eades, Diane
    this volume Understanding aboriginal silence in legal contexts. Chapter 14
Ehlich, Konrad
    1998   Kritik der Wissenschaftssprachen. In: Lothar Hoffmann, Hartwig Kalver-
            kämper and Herbert Ernst Wiegand (eds.), *Fachsprachen. Ein inter-
            nationales Handbuch zur Fachsprachenforschung und Terminologiewis-
            senschaft (=HSK 14.1)*, 856–866. New York/Berlin: de Gruyter.

Erickson, Fred and Gerald Mohatt
1982   Cultural organization of participation structures in two classrooms of Indian students. In: George Spindler (ed.), *Doing the Ethnography of Schooling*, 133–174. New York: Holt, Rinehart and Winston.

Erickson, Fred and Jeffrey J. Schultz
1982   *The Counselor as Gatekeeper: Social and Cultural Organization of Communication in Counselling Interviews*. New York: Academic Press.

Esser, Ruth
1997   *'Etwas ist mir geheim geblieben am deutschen Referat'. Kulturelle Geprägtheit wissenschaftlicher Textproduktion und ihre Konsequenzen für den universitären Unterricht von Deutsch als Fremdsprache*. München: Iudicium.

Feld, Steven
1990   Wept thoughts: The voicing of Kaluli memories. *Oral Tradition* 5 (2/3): 241–266.

Füglein, Rosemarie
2000   *Kanak Sprak. Eine ethnolinguistische Untersuchung eines Sprachphänomens im Deutschen*. Germanistik. Bamberg: Universität Bamberg.

Goodwin, Robin and Iona Lee
1994   Taboo topics among Chinese and English friends: a cross-cultural comparison. *Journal of Cross-Cultural Psychology* 25(3): 325–338.

Granet, Marcel
1985   *Das chinesische Denken*. Frankfurt: Suhrkamp.

Gumperz, John J.
1982   *Discourse Strategies*. Cambridge: Cambridge University Press.

Gumperz, John J.
2001   Contextualization and ideology in intercultural communication. In: Aldo Di Luzio, Susanne Günthner and Franca Orletti (eds.), *Culture in Communication. Analyses of Intercultural Situations*, 35–55. Amsterdam: Benjamins.

Gumperz, John J. and Celia Roberts
1991   Understanding in intercultural encounters. Manuscript. In: Jan Blommaert and Jef Verschueren (eds.), *The Pragmatics of Intercultural and International Communication*, 51–90. Amsterdam: Benjamins.

Gumperz, John J., Tom C. Jupp and Celia Roberts
1979   *Crosstalk. A Study of Cross-cultural Communication*. Southall: National Centre for Industrial Language Training.

Gumperz, John J., Gurinder Aulakh and Hannah Kaltmann
1982   Thematic structure and progression in discourse. In: John J. Gumperz (ed.), *Language and Social Identity*, 22–56. Cambridge: Cambridge University Press.

Gumperz, John and Jenny Cook-Gumperz
this volume Discourse, cultural diversity and communication: a linguistic anthropological perspective. Chapter 2

Günthner, Susanne
1991   'A language with taste': Uses of proverbial sayings in intercultural communication. *Text* 3: 399–418.

Günthner, Susanne
1993   *Diskursstrategien in der Interkulturellen Kommunikation. Analysen deutsch-chinesischer Gespräche.* Tübingen: Max Niemeyer Verlag.
Günthner, Susanne
1994   Cultural differences in recipient activities: Interactions between Germans and Chinese. In: Heiner Pürschel (ed.), *Intercultural Communication,* 481–502. Frankfurt: Peter Lang.
Günthner, Susanne
1995   Language and culture – An analysis of a Chinese–German conversation. *Beiträge zur Fremdsprachenvermittlung* 28: 3–39.
Günthner, Susanne
1999   Zur Aktualisierung kultureller Differenzen in Alltagsinteraktionen. In: Stefan Rieger, Schamma Schahadat and Manfred Weinberg (eds.), *Interkulturalität. Zwischen Inszenierung und Archiv,* 251–268. Tübingen: Narr.
Günthner, Susanne
2000a   *Vorwurfsaktivitäten in der Alltagsinteraktion. Grammatische, prosodische, rhetorisch-stilistische und interaktive Verfahren bei der Konstitution kommunikativer Muster und Gattungen.* Tübingen: Niemeyer.
Günthner, Susanne
2000b   Argumentation in German–Chinese conversations. In: Helen Spencer-Oatey (ed.), *Culturally Speaking. Managing Relations in Talk across Cultures,* 217–239. London: Cassell.
Günthner, Susanne
2001   Kulturelle Unterschiede in der Aktualisierung kommunikativer Gattungen. *Info DaF Informationen Deutsch als Fremdsprache* 28 (1): 15–32.
Günthner, Susanne and Hubert Knoblauch
1994   'Forms are the food of faith'. Gattungen als Muster kommunikativen Handelns. *Kölner Zeitschrift für Soziologie und Sozialpsychologie* 4: 693–723.
Günthner, Susanne and Hubert Knoblauch
1995   Culturally patterned speaking practices – the analysis of communicative genres. *Pragmatics* 5(1): 1–32.
Günthner, Susanne and Thomas Luckmann
2001   Asymmetries of knowledge in intercultural communication. The relevance of cultural repertoires of communicative genres. In: Aldo Di Luzio, Susanne Günthner and Franca Orletti (eds.), *Culture in Communication. Analyses of Intercultural Situations,* 55–86. Amsterdam: Benjamins.
Günthner, Susanne and Thomas Luckmann
2002   Wissensasymmetrien in der interkulturellen Kommunikation. Die Relevanz kultureller Repertoires kommunikativer Gattungen. In: Helga Kotthoff (ed.), *Kultur(en) im Gespräch,* 213–244. Tübingen: Narr.
Hahn, Alois
1994   Die soziale Konstruktion des Fremden. In: Walter M. Sprondel (ed.), *Die Objektivität der Ordnungen und ihre kommunikative Konstruktion,* 140–166. Frankfurt: Suhrkamp.
Hanks, William F.
1987   Discourse genres in a theory of practice. *American Ethnologist* 14(4): 668–692.

Hanks, William F.
   1996   Language form and communicative practices. In: John J. Gumperz and
            Steven Levinson (eds.), *Rethinking Linguistic Relativity*, 232–270. Cam-
            bridge: Cambridge University Press.
Helmolt, Katharina von
   1997   *Kommunikation in internationalen Arbeitsgruppen: eine Fallstudie über
            divergierende Konventionen der Modalitätskonstituierung.* München: Iu-
            dicium.
Hinnenkamp, Volker
   2002   Deutsch–Türkisches Code-Mixing und Fragen der Hybridität. In: Wolfdiet-
            rich Hartung and Alissa Shethar (eds.), *Kulturen und ihre Sprachen. Die
            Wahrnehmung anders Sprechender und ihr Selbstverständnis*, 123–140.
            Berlin: Trafo Verlag.
Hufeisen, Britta
   2002   *Ein deutsches 'Referat' ist kein englisch-sprachiges 'Essay'. Theoretische
            und praktische Überlegungen zu einem verbesserten textsortenbezogenen
            Schreibunterricht in der Fremdsprache Deutsch an der Universität.* Inns-
            bruck: Studien Verlag.
Iwasaki, Shoichi and Preeya Ingkaphirom Horie
   1998   The 'Northridge Earthquake' conversations: Conversational patterns in
            Japanese and Thai and their cultural significance. *Discourse and Society*
            9(4): 501–529.
Keppler, Angela
   1994   *Tischgespräche.* Frankfurt: Suhrkamp.
Kern, Frederike
   2000   *Kulturen der Selbstdarstellung: Ost- und Westdeutsche in Bewerbungs-
            gesprächen.* Wiesbaden: Deutscher Universitätsverlag.
Kirkpatrick, Andy
   1991   Information sequencing in Mandarin letters of request. *Anthropological
            Linguistics* 33(2): 183–203.
Kniffka, Hannes
   1994   Letters to the Editor across cultures. In: Heiner Pürschel (ed.), *Intercultural
            Communication.* Proceedings of the 17th International L.A.U.D. Sympo-
            sium Duisburg, 383–413. Frankfurt a. M.: Peter Lang.
Koole, Tom and Jan D. ten Thije
   1994   *The Construction of Intercultural Discourse.* Amsterdam: Rodopi.
Kotthoff, Helga
   1991   Der Tamada gibt bei Tisch den Ton an. Tafelsitten, Trinksprüche und
            Geschlechterrollen im kaukasischen Georgien. In: Susanne Günthner and
            Helga Kotthoff (eds.), *Von fremden Stimmen*, 229–260. Frankfurt: Suhr-
            kamp.
Kotthoff, Helga
   1993   Disagreement and concession in disputes. On the context sensitivity of
            preference structures. *Language in Society* 22: 193–216.
Kotthoff, Helga
   1994   Verbal duelling in Caucasian Georgia. In: Uta M. Quasthoff (ed.), *Aspects
            of Orality*, 112–137. Berlin: de Gruyter.

Kotthoff, Helga
1995   The social semiotics of Georgian toast performances. *Journal of Pragmatics* 24: 353–380.
Kotthoff, Helga
1999   Affect and meta-affect in Georgian mourning rituals. In: Jürgen Schläger and Gesa Stedman (eds.), *Representations of Emotion*, 149–172. Tübingen: Narr.
Kotthoff, Helga (ed.)
2002   *Kultur(en) im Gespräch*. Tübingen: Narr.
Kotthoff, Helga
2002a   Vortragsstile im Kulturvergleich: Zu einigen Deutsch–Russischen Unterschieden. In: Eva Maria Jakobs and Annely Rothkegel (eds.), *Perspektiven auf Stil. Festschrift für Barbara Sandig*, 321–351. Tübingen: Niemeyer.
Kotthoff, Helga
2002b   Dein Leid mir: Über die Kommunikation von Gefühlen in georgischen Trauerritualen. In: Helga Kotthoff (ed.), *Kultur(en) im Gespräch*, 99–150. Tübingen: Narr.
Kotthoff, Helga
this volume Ritual and Style in Intercultural Communication. Chapter 9.
Li, Xiangling
1999   *Chinese–Dutch Business Negotiations*. Amsterdam: Rodopi.
Liang, Yong
1991   Zu soziokulturellen und textstrukturellen Besonderheiten wissenschaftlicher Rezensionen. Eine kontrastive Fachtextanalyse Deutsch/Chinesisch. *Deutsche Sprache* 4: 289–311.
Luckmann, Thomas
1986   Grundformen der gesellschaftlichen Vermittlung des Wissens: Kommunikative Gattungen. *Kölner Zeitschrift für Soziologie und Sozialpsychologie*, Sonderheft 27: 191–211.
Luckmann, Thomas
1987   Kanon und Konversion. In: Aleida Assmann and Jan Assmann (eds.), *Kanon und Zensur*, 38–46. München: Fink.
Luckmann, Thomas
1988   Kommunikative Gattungen im kommunikativen 'Haushalt' einer Gesellschaft. In: Gisela Smolka-Koerdt, Peter M. Spangenberg and Dagmar Tillman-Bartylla (eds.), *Der Ursprung der Literatur*, 279–288. München: Fink.
Luckmann, Thomas
1992   Rekonstruktive Gattungen. Manuskript. Universität Konstanz.
Meer, Dorothee
2002   *'Dann jetz Schluss mit der Sprechstundenrallye'* – *Sprechstundengespräche an der Hochschule. Ein Ratgeber für Lehrende und Studierende*. Baltmannsweiler: Schneider Verlag Hohengehren.
Miller, Laura
1994   Japanese and American meetings and what goes on before them: A case study of co-worker misunderstanding. *Pragmatics* 4(2): 221–238.
Miller, Laura
2000   Negative Assessments in Japanese–American workplace interactions. In: Helen Spencer-Oatey (ed.), *Culturally Speaking. Managing Rapport through Talk across Cultures*, 240–254. London/New York: Continuum.

Naotsuka, Reiko and Nancy Sakamoto
1981   *Mutual Understanding of Different Cultures.* Osaka: Taishukan.
Paltridge, Brian
1997   *Genres, Frames and Writing in Research Settings.* Amsterdam: Benjamins.
Philips, Susan
1972   Participant structures and communicative competence: Warm Springs
          children in community and classroom. In: Courtney B. Cazden, Dell Hymes
          and Vera P. John (eds.), *Functions of Language in the Classroom,* 86–127.
          New York: Teachers College Press.
Pomerantz, Anita
1984   Agreeing and disagreeing with assessments: Some features of preferred/
          dispreferred turn shapes. In: J. Maxwell Atkinson and John Heritage (eds.),
          Structures of Social Action: Studies in Conversation Analysis, 57–101.
          Cambridge: Cambridge University Press.
Rehbein, Jochen
2001   Intercultural negotiation. In: Aldo Di Luzio, Susanne Günthner and Franca
          Orletti (eds.), *Culture in Communication. Analyses of Intercultural Situ-
          ations,* 173–208. Amsterdam: Benjamins.
Richards, Jack C. and Mayuri Sukwiwat
1983   Language transfer and conversational competence. *Applied Linguistics*
          4(2): 113–125.
Roberts, Celia
this volume Intercultural Communication in Healthcare Settings. Chapter 12.
Scherr, Albert
this volume Schools and Cultural Difference. Chapter 15.
Schiffrin, Deborah
1984   Jewish argument as sociability. *Language in Society* 13: 311–335.
Schuetz, Alfred
1944/1972 The stranger: an essay in social psychology. *The American Journal of Soci-
          ology* XLIX: 499–512.
Scollon, Ron and Suzanne Scollon
1981   *Narrative Literacy and Face in Interethnic Communication.* Norwood:
          Ablex.
Scollon, Ron and Suzie Scollon
1995   *Intercultural Communication.* Oxford/Cambridge: Blackwell.
Scollon, Suzanne and Yuling Pan
2002   Saa Taaigik: a metaphor for conflict management. In: David C.S. Li (ed.),
          Discourses in Search of Members. In Honor of Ron Scollon, 423–451. Lan-
          ham: University Press of America.
Sherzer, Joel
1987   A diversity of voices: men's and women's speech in ethnographic perspec-
          tive. In: Susan U. Philips, Susan Steele and Christine Tanz (eds.), *Lan-
          guage, Gender and Sex in Comparative Perspective,* 95–120. Cambridge:
          Cambridge University Press.
Spencer-Oatey, Helen and Jianyu Xing
2000   A problematic business visit to Britain: issues of face. In: Helen Spencer-
          Oatey (ed.), *Culturally Speaking. Managing Rapport through Talk across
          Cultures,* 272–288. London/New York: Continuum.

Spencer-Oatey, Helen, Patrick Ng and Li Dong
   2000   Responding to compliments: British and Chinese evaluative judgements.
          In: Helen Spencer-Oatey (ed.), *Culturally Speaking. Managing Rapport*
          through Talk across Cultures, 98–120. London/New York: Continuum.
Swales, John M.
   1990   *Genre Analysis*. Cambridge: Cambridge University Press.
Swales, John M., Ummul K. Ahmad, Yu-Ying Chang, Daniel Chavez, Dacia Dressen and
          Ruth Seymour
   1998   Consider this: the role of imperatives in scholarly writing. *Applied Linguistics* 19(1): 97–121.
Tannen, Deborah
   1984   *Conversational Style. Analyzing Talk among Friends*. Norwood: Ablex.
Tao, Hongyin and Sandra Thompson
   1991   English backchannels in Mandarin conversations: a case study of superstratum pragmatic 'inference'. *Journal of Pragmatics* 16: 209–223.
Tyler, Andrea and Catherine Davies
   1990   Cross-linguistic communication missteps. *Text* 10(4): 385–411.
Underwood, Charles and John J. Gumperz
   1988   The Native American as witness. Manuscript.
Urban, Greg
   1988   Ritual wailing in Amerindian Brazil. *American Anthropologist* 90(2): 385–400.
Vermeer, Manuel
   1989   'Fremde Teufel und blaue Ameisen': Vom Einfluß der Mentalitätsproblematik beim Dolmetschen Chinesisch–Deutsch und Deutsch–Chinesisch. In: Hans J. Vermeer (ed.), *Kulturspezifik des translatorischen Handelns*, 31–49. Heidelberg: Universitätsverlag.
Voloshinov, Valentin N.
   1929/1986 *Marxism and the Philosophy of Language*. Cambridge, MA: Harvard University Press.
Yamashita, Hitoshi
   2001   Höflichkeitsstile im Deutschen und Japanischen. In: Heinz-Helmut Lüger (ed.), *Höflichkeitsstile*, 315–334. Frankfurt: Peter Lang.
Young, Linda Wai Ling
   1994   *Crosstalk and Culture in Sino-American Communication*. Cambridge: Cambridge University Press.

8. Humour across cultures: joking in the multicultural workplace

Meredith Marra and Janet Holmes

1. Humour in multicultural workplaces

The Wellington Language in the Workplace project has been researching communication in New Zealand workplaces since 1996. When the project began we could not have anticipated that so much of our research would be devoted to the analysis and interpretation of humour at work (e.g. Holmes 2000, 2006; Holmes and Marra 2002a, 2002b, 2004). Humour is so prevalent in our data that it was impossible to ignore. One reason for this ubiquity is that humour is a remarkably flexible discourse strategy for achieving a range of communicative objectives, both people-oriented and task-oriented. The effective use of humour and its accurate interpretation by interlocutors is, however, very context-sensitive, and typically relies for its effect on shared understandings and experiences.

In this paper we focus on the use of humour in multicultural workplaces. Our examples illustrate some of the varied functions served by humour, and explore the shared cultural knowledge, values, and beliefs which underlie the appropriate use and interpretation of humour in such workplaces. Until the early 19th century the New Zealand population comprised exclusively indigenous Māori people, but during the 20th century Pākehā New Zealanders (people of mainly British origin) rapidly established themselves as the largest group. Māori people now make up only about 15 % of the total New Zealand population (www.stats.govt.nz). However, immigration from Europe, Asia and the Pacific has also enhanced cultural diversity, and New Zealand workplaces have thus become increasingly multicultural.

Reflecting some of this diversity, we draw on recorded data from two different workplace teams. The first group are employees of a small corporate organization where a large proportion of the team identify as Māori. Moreover, the organization is committed to supporting and promoting Māori issues within a mainstream (and predominantly Pākehā) industry. Their communication patterns and their humour regularly reflect Māori cultural values, and the ethnicity of the speakers is often foregrounded. The second group are a team of shift workers operating in a multicultural factory setting. Many of the team, including the team leader, identify as Samoan, but the team also includes Pākehā, Tongan and Māori workers. In both these workplaces, humour occurs frequently. However, the interactional norms of each workplace are very different, and there are also some very distinctive features of the styles of humour which characterize the interactions of the different workplace teams. In this paper we explore these differences, relating them to the distinctive communities of practice of each group (Wenger 1998), with specific reference to the ethnic and cultural norms that permeate them.

2.   The functions of humour

The most obvious and overt function of humour is to entertain or amuse, but, as many researchers have pointed out, it serves a range of other functions (e.g., Duncan 1985; Murphy 1986; Linstead 1988; Sabath 1990; Cox, Read and Van Auken 1990). Some have proposed taxonomies to categorize the functions of humour. Martineau (1972), for example, identifies three broad functions of humour: humour for consensus, conflict and control. Ervin-Tripp and Lampert (1992) depict humour as equalizing, defending, sharing and coping. Graham, Papa and Brooks (1992) list 24 types of humour and focus on the social-psychological functions. Hay's (1995) taxonomy identifies twelve micro-functions, including insult, fantasy, and self-deprecation. Clearly, humour serves many different and complex functions. Moreover, any specific instance of humour may be multifunctional (e.g., Tracy and Coupland 1990), so that humour often serves multiple goals simultaneously.

Several types of humour are particularly relevant in the workplace context. Firstly, humour may serve as a form of relational practice by 'creating team' (Fletcher 1999) and building solidarity or social cohesion between workers (Blau 1955; O'Quin and Arnoff 1981; Holdaway 1988). Humour has been described as the glue that holds groups together and helps people feel included (a form of 'positive politeness' in Brown and Levinson's (1987) terms). Understanding an in-joke, for example, demonstrates the existence of common ground between co-workers, and reinforces team membership.

Humour also contributes to the ongoing construction of social identity by actively highlighting and reinforcing boundaries between different social groups i.e. creating an *us* and a *them*, but in an acceptable way. In response to specific aspects of the on-going interaction, an individual may use humour to draw attention to their ethnicity or gender, and distinguish it from that of others, as illustrated in Holmes and Marra (2002a). In particular, minority group members often use humour to express, in a socially acceptable way, some degree of resentment at their marginalization, or to contest majority group norms. Poking fun at an outgroup is safe and entertaining when the outgroup members are safely out of range, but challenging outgroup members in face-to-face interaction is a much riskier enterprise; in such contexts the tension-defusing role of humour is very valuable.

Individual goals may also be met through humour. Humour offers the speaker the option of recourse to the 'I was only joking' explanation for an offensive action; humour provides a useful strategy for conveying a negative or critical message in an ostensibly acceptable form. In this way, individuals make use of humour to manage necessary face threatening speech acts such as criticizing, complaining, refusing and disagreeing (Holmes and Stubbe 2003a; Daly et al. 2004).

In addition, humour may also be used to challenge norms such as the taken-for-granted ways of doing things in a particular workplace, and especially to challenge power relationships. Holmes and Marra (2002c) examine a range of ways in which humour may contest or subvert the status quo, at individual, group, and societal levels. Quips, jocular abuse and parodic humour, for example, function as distancing devices to emphasize boundaries between the speaker and the target of the humour, and provide a socially acceptable means of encoding critical intent. Humour provides a socially acceptable 'cover' for criticisms of individuals, or for subverting and challenging established norms and practices. Among friends, humour can provide a means of contesting a group member's status in the group. Between those of different status, humour can be a double-edged weapon, providing a legitimate means of subverting authority, a difficult-to-challenge way of criticizing superiors.

This summary of the various functions of humour is far from exhaustive, but it can serve as a basis for the analysis in this paper.[1]

3.   Researching effective communication in New Zealand workplaces

The Wellington Language in the Workplace Project has been investigating communicative strategies in New Zealand workplaces since 1996. To date, the research team has collected and analysed naturalistic data from 21 different workplaces involving approximately 450 participants. In every case, the basic principles of our methodology have remained the same.

The research team adopts an appreciative inquiry approach, choosing organizations, teams and individuals who are recommended to us (by other organizations, colleagues, or employees) as good models of effective communication. Volunteers record a selection of their everyday workplace conversations using personal Walkmans, and more recently MiniDisc recorders. The interactions thus collected typically include small one-to-one meetings, social talk, phone calls, etc., and each dataset is augmented with video recordings of larger meetings, and ethnographic observations. In factories, the methodology was adapted to accommodate different working patterns, including a good deal of movement about the factory floor by team members, sporadic talk, and noisy equipment (Stubbe 2001). Volunteers were wired with radio microphones in one factory,

for instance, so that they could move about; the recording was monitored re-
motely by a Research Assistant, and editable MiniDiscs were used to remove
large gaps between interactions. In all cases, volunteers have full control of the
recording process, choosing what and when to record, and what to edit out if
they so wish. The resulting database currently comprises approximately 1500
interactions ranging from 30 second phone calls to day-long meetings and 12
hour factory shifts (see Holmes and Stubbe 2003a for a fuller description of the
dataset and methodology).

One particularly important objective of the project is to disseminate findings
back to end-users, whether HR managers, communication trainers, or language
teachers, in order to help improve communication in the workplace. Drawing on
this aspect of our work, the final section of this paper discusses the implications
of the analysis of workplace humour for intercultural and cross-cultural education. First however, we examine selected examples of humour from two
multicultural teams in order to illustrate some of the complex functions of workplace humour, and highlight differences in the way humour is used in different
communities of practice.

4.   Two communities of practice

The concept of a 'community of practice' (Eckert and McConnell-Ginet 1992,
1999; Lave and Wenger 1991; Wenger 1998; Corder and Meyerhoff in this volume) provides a useful starting point for comparing the use of humour in different groups. Evolving from a social constructionist approach, a 'community of
practice' (CofP) refers to the dynamic process whereby groups construct their
group identity through their common practices, verbal and non-verbal; group
identity develops through regular social interaction within ongoing exchanges.

Within this framework Wenger (1998: 73), an important proponent of the
concept of a community of practice, argues that three crucial criteria distinguish
a community of practice from other types of groups (a speech community, social
network or team, for example).[2] Firstly, the community is characterized by mutual engagement; secondly, members share a joint, negotiated enterprise; and
thirdly they have a shared repertoire. Using these criteria, both of the teams on
which we focus in this analysis qualify as communities of practice. Members interact regularly: recordings of one-to-one conversations, as well as informal and
formal meetings, provide substantial evidence of their mutual engagement and
their orientation to progress in a jointly agreed enterprise, as well as their use of
a shared verbal and non-verbal repertoire to constantly negotiate various work
roles and workplace objectives.

As sociolinguists, we focus particularly on ways in which CofPs construct
and enact their shared discursive or linguistic repertoire. Wenger proposes spe-

cific features which help to instantiate the CofP: "sustained mutual relationships – harmonious or conflictual"; "shared ways of engaging in doing things together"; "local lore, shared stories, inside jokes, knowing laughter"; and "certain styles recognized as displaying membership" (1998: 125–126). The way a team makes use of humour as a discourse strategy clearly contributes to the construction of the shared repertoire of the CofP.

The two workplaces described below engage in rather different interactions in the course of their work, reflecting their distinctive daily tasks and workplace objectives. They also conduct their business in different kinds of settings: the Māori organization typically holds meetings and discussions around tables and desks, while the factory team conduct their daily briefing meetings and talk on the factory floor. These two CofPs thus provide interesting case studies for examining the different ways in which humour is used in New Zealand workplace interactions involving minority ethnic groups. In the analysis which follows, we focus especially on types of humour which seem to distinguish the two workplaces.

4.1.   Case study 1: A Māori company in a Pākehā industry

The Māori organization competes in a predominately Pākehā industry and business world, but their corporate values mean that ethnicity is always salient in this workplace. The organization's mission is to contribute towards the promotion of Māori people, knowledge and ideas as they carry out their business. For this team, appropriate communicative behaviour incorporates Māori ways of behaving and interacting, as well as the use of te reo Māori (the Māori language) to varying degrees, reflecting proficiency and appropriateness. However, as a corporate organization in New Zealand, Pākehā ways of doing business inevitably constitute the unmarked way of behaving. Consequently, the specific form of intercultural communication which characterizes this workplace integrates the pressures of conforming to Pākehā business norms with a strong commitment to incorporating Māori values into workplace talk. Patterns of humour in the workplace reflect this complex mix.

Example 1 is an extract from a long section of workplace talk in which Rangi uses humour to soften his complaint about people who do not clean up after themselves in the communal kitchen. To make his point, he has brought a cardboard box as a visual aid to represent the microwave to which he refers, and, adopting a stance more in line with Māori than Pākehā protocol, he stands to deliver his speech.

(1)³ Context: Rangi stands in front of the staff at a monthly staff meeting
1. Rangi: ae kia ora koutou ['hello everyone']
2.   but before we start this is my magic box ngaru iti
      [literally 'little wave']
3.   ngaru meaning wave iti meaning in this context microwave
4.   yes it's twelve o'clock by crikey I'm hungry
5.   I think I'll shoot down the kitchen and make myself a kai ['feed']
6.   grab the plate fill it up put it in the microwave close the lid
7.   ring ring ring the bloody phone I'll have to duck down
8.   and answer the damn thing ring ring ring ring ring ring
9.   pick it up the buggers gone hang it up
10.   in comes a mate yackety yack yackety yack yackety yack
11.   yackety yack <u>ooh</u> my kai ['food'] I'll race down to the kitchen
12.   <u>open the door bugger me days</u>
13.   <u>the damn thing's exploded</u>
14.   doesn't matter I'll clean it later [sings]: I kai ['eat'] away I go:
15.   poor old Yvonne comes down the stairs
16.   open the microwave and someone's spewed inside
17.   so [in funny voice]: please team when it happens
18.   clean it out straight away:

Everyone finds Rangi's performance hilarious. He uses the cardboard box, his voice and his body to great effect, constructing a convincing amusing persona, namely someone who forgets he has left the microwave on with food in it. But as well as being entertained, the team also respond positively to the message that they should clean the microwave out immediately after using it. Rangi effectively makes it clear that leaving the microwave in a mess is socially unacceptable behaviour.

This example illustrates a number of different points. Most relevant is the skilful use of humour to convey a critical message effectively. This is typical in this workplace where good-natured humour plays a significant part in interactions, especially in staff meetings. Rangi's performance (note that he begins by referring to his 'magic box', suggesting he is a magician) will be remembered for some time.

There are many features of Rangi's presentation which mark it as Māori, and also as appropriate to this community of practice, in particular. Most fundamentally, Rangi does not direct his criticism at any individual. In Pākehā workplaces, people often use humour to soften a criticism directed to a specific individual (Holmes 2000). By contrast, Rangi aims his criticism at the group. The problematic issue is presented as a group issue, and the complaint is not targeted at any specific person, a very acceptable way of addressing a controversial issue in Māori contexts. Rangi's strategy – 'if the cap fits' – is not exclusive to Māori, but it is very acceptable and widely adopted in Māori inter-action.

There are a number of other features which also suggest that this is humour in a Māori, rather than a Pākehā workplace. Most obviously, Rangi begins with a Māori greeting *kia ora koutou*, and uses the Māori lexical item *kai* for food (lines 5,11,14). He teaches the Māori phrase *ngaru iti* for 'microwave' (line 2); this is a common feature in this workplace where mutual learning and jointly constructed knowledge are the bread and butter of everyday interactions. He uses reporting devices which have been identified as typifying Māori narratives (Holmes 1998, 2003): e.g. the use of direct speech with no explicit quotative signals for immediacy: e.g. *by crikey I'm hungry I think I'll shoot down the kitchen and make myself a kai* (lines 4–5). He uses subject elision (e.g. lines 6, 9), emphasizing the informality, along with informal lexical items such as *the damn thing* (lines 8, 13), *bugger* (lines 9, 12), *yackety-yack* (line 10), and *spewed* (line 16). Furthermore, the whole monologue is delivered with a steady rhythmic beat, subtly resonating with rhythms familiar from Māori speeches in more formal contexts. These rhythms contribute to the 'performance' quality of Rangi's speech, which is further boosted by audience applause and laughter throughout (cf. Kotthoff in this volume, on rituals and style). Overall, this is a distinctively Māori way of delivering his message.

One other relevant point is the implicit, indirectly expressed respect for Yvonne, the company director, which is apparent in the reference to her finding a disgusting mess in the microwave (lines 15–16). Māori people are generally very sensitive to status differences, and, unlike Pākehā, who typically deliber-ately play down differences of rank, Māori often explicitly indicate respect for superiors. Here Rangi's reference to Yvonne can be interpreted as a subtle rem-inder of her position, usefully serving to strengthen the importance of his mess-age.

Complaining about the state of the kitchen is a common speech act in many workplaces, but it is typically accomplished by a written reminder from an ad-ministrative assistant. Here Rangi, handed the floor to make a substantial con-tribution to workplace business, takes a fair amount of time out to make this strictly off-topic point. His use of humour to convey his message, his concern for protecting individual face, his low key use of Māori language and Māori dis-course features, his teaching strategies, and the implicit respect for superiors, are all features which are consistent with Māori ways of doing things, ways which are very acceptable in this Māori workplace, despite the company's over-all business orientation within the wider Pākehā society.

Example 2 also illustrates a distinctively Māori use of humour in some re-spects, though there are also features which recur in the humour of other ethnic minorities. Fundamental to understanding this example is the Māori concept of *whakaiti*, 'humility' or appropriate modesty: it is inappropriate to talk about one's own achievements, and self-praise is quite unacceptable. It is up to others to provide praise and appreciation (Metge 1995: 160). Thus any reference to activities which reflect well on an individual need to be handled with skill; humour provides one acceptable strategy for managing this problem in the workplace.

(2) Context: monthly staff meeting of Māori organization. Yvonne is the CEO.
1. Yvo: I was with the um I felt the presentation wasn't that good
2.   because my briefing was about a two second phone [laughs]: call:
3.   and so I (didn't) know who was going to be at the conference
4.   and ( ) what's it about I had no programme beforehand
5.   so I was a bit um (/)
6. She: /is this the one you had yesterday
7. Yvo: yeah
8. She: I loved it
9. Yvo: /oh did you
10.   /[general laughter]
11. She: I actually came home raving
12. Yvo: oh that's only because I had a photo of you
13. Ran: /smoking
14.   /[general laughter]

Yvonne begins by reporting on a conference presentation she has given claiming, modestly and in a culturally appropriate way, that her contribution was not good due to lack of preparation (lines 1–5). Again, appropriately, another staff member, Sherie, responds by praising Yvonne's performance *I loved it* (line 8), and *I (actually) came home raving* (line 11). Yvonne first responds with apparent surprise to this praise *oh did you* (line 9), eliciting laughter from her colleagues. She then provides a more pro-active response maintaining the general laughter by teasing Sherie that it was the inclusion of a photo of Sherie in her presentation which influenced her positive assessment of it (line 12). Rangi's contribution *smoking* (line 13) maintains the tease and supports Yvonne by pointing out that Sherie was engaging in socially unacceptable behaviour in the photograph (cf. Hay 1996).

In close-knit groups, teasing is an effective strategy for maintaining and constructing group solidarity (e.g. Hay 1995). Members of this workteam enjoy working together and this kind of teasing and supportive humour is frequent in their interactions. However, the way humour is used in this organization tends to be consistent with Māori cultural norms despite the Pākehā working environment and industry. Thus in example 2, Yvonne uses teasing humour to deflect attention from herself and her achievements, while Rangi supports her with a comment that contributes to the group sense of cohesion and reflects team members' familiarity with each other's strengths and weaknesses.

We turn now to our second case study, a multicultural factory team with very distinctive communication patterns, including distinctive ways of using humour between team members.

4.2.   Case study 2: A multinational factory

Our second community of practice comprises a close-knit team of mainly male shift workers in a Wellington factory. The team includes members from four different ethnic groups, namely Samoan, Māori, Tongan and Pākehā. Most of their communication is in English, although Samoan is also used on occasion, especially between Samoan workers. As described in Holmes and Stubbe:

> "the team enjoys sustained and multiplex mutual relationships". They have daily briefing sessions, individuals have regular contact with one another in the course of their 12-hour shifts, they see one another at 'smoko' (tea/coffee breaks), and there is regular social contact between many team members outside work hours. Moreover, because many of the team members have worked together for a relatively long time, and have developed a strong sense of group identity, they are a very cohesive group. There is a real sense of joint enterprise in this team, which is highly-motivated both in terms of completing the immediate tasks during a shift, as well as meeting longer term goals such as continuing to out-perform other production teams, and meeting quality and safety targets. Teamwork is highly and explicitly valued, something which is further reinforced by the Polynesian cultural background of a majority of the team, which tends to privilege the group over individuals.
>
> Holmes and Stubbe 2003b: 589

One of the more noticeable ways in which these characteristics are reflected in discourse is in a strong orientation to team morale, and a very distinctive sparky communicative style. Team members use many markers of solidarity in their interactions, and there is a good deal of in-group talk and gossip. They also have a well-deserved reputation at the factory for uninhibited swearing, and constantly joking around and 'having each other on' which sits alongside their status as the top-performing team. At the time of the study, their particular blend of verbal humour, jocular abuse and practical jokes contributed to a unique team culture, and generally helped to create positive relationships within the team".[4]

This multicultural team has thus developed a distinctive approach to workplace interaction and humour is an integral component of this style. Expletives and jocular abuse, in particular, distinguished this team as a community of practice from others both within the factory and outside. Team members swore at each other "not only with impunity, but with positive affect. Forms of fuck [for example], appear to act as markers of solidarity and positive politeness for members of this community of practice" (Daly et al. 2004: 954). Moreover, joking around and playing practical jokes on each other were regular events contributing to 'creating team' and constructing camaraderie within the group, as example 3 illustrates (see Stubbe 1999).

(3) Context: factory team members chatting in the control room above the production area
1. Ger: fucking Ginette got Peter a beauty yesterday ...
2. Rob: did you get the message oh yeah what happened
3. Den: oh did she throw that plastic full of water
4. Ger: no +++ told him to call Mr Lion
5. Rob: oh yeah
6. Den: oh yeah
7. Ger: mr lion called for him
8. Den: [laughs]
9. Ger: she gave him the phone number
10. Den: /the zoo
11. Ger: /he called up the Wellington zoo
12.   [laughter]
13. Ger: (only Peter)
14. Rob: yeah (good morning) Wellington zoo ( )
15.   is mr lion there please [laughs]
16.   so did anyone er get Ginette or what
17. Ger: no (everyone's being good today)

This is an account of a classic April Fools' Day trick played by the team supervisor, Ginette, on team members: she fooled several team members into ringing the zoo to ask for 'Mr Lion', much to the mirth of their colleagues. Note the typical use of the intensifier *fucking* (line 1), the supportive feedback from Dennis and Rob (lines 5, 6, 10), and the colloquial style throughout. As in example 1, the reported speech is presented in a direct style, without quotatives *yeah (good morning) Wellington zoo ( ) is Mr Lion there please* (lines 14–15), giving it immediacy and impact.

This kind of joking regularly characterizes this team's interactions (as indicated by Dennis's reference to another practical joke *did she throw that plastic full of water*, line 3), providing relief from the repetitiveness of their daily work, and making their interactions more enjoyable. We have many examples of their interactive style which includes a good deal of good-humoured but challenging 'slagging off' at each other (see for example Holmes and Stubbe 2003a: 109ff).

This in-your-face interactional style could not be more different from the low key style of humour described in case study 1. About a third of the Power Rangers team identify as Samoan and Ginette, the team leader, is Samoan, and so it is not surprising that Samoan styles of humour appear to predominate in the team as a whole. 'Ribbing' one's mates and 'having them on' is a well-accepted style of Samoan interaction in informal contexts, which contrasts markedly with the serious and sober nature of Samoan 'chiefly' talk in formal contexts. In Samoan culture, there is a marked contrast between the dignified and measured style of speech adopted by chiefly leaders in formal tribal contexts and the robust exchanges among others at the informal periphery, where tension is released (Alfred Hunkin pc). Light-hearted jocular abuse and practical joking are well-recognized as features of the style of Pacific Island workers (Daly et al. 2004). The direct, robust and confrontational nature of this style contrasts markedly with the much lower key humour of the Maori team described in case study 1.

Correspondingly, Ginette's style, as team leader, is very different from that of Yvonne. In keeping with her team culture, Ginette is confident, confrontational and direct and does not suffer fools gladly, nor tolerate slack work, or lateness. Though she generally spices her criticisms with sparky humour, she mercilessly focuses on individuals who threaten to undermine the team's high performance levels. And, by contrast to the style which typifies the Māori organization described above, individuals are frequently the target of sarcastic and critical comment as example 4 illustrates.

(4)[5] Context: Ginette, the team manager, is working in the scales area of the packing line and talking to other members of the team.

1. Gin:	dumb eh oh and it wa- I think it was yesterday or the day before +
2.	he had Sam up there there must have been a blockage in the hopper
3.	and Iesia and I were standing (and Sam) was banging away +
4.	I said to Iesia why the fuck is he banging the dust extraction pipe
5.	know that big thick pipe
6. Hel:	yeah
7. Gin:	instead of banging the hopper/he was =
8. Hel:	/[laughs]
9. Gin:	=banging the pipe /[laughs]
10. Hel:	/[laughs]
11. Gin:	[laughs]: and I said to him: what's the matter Sam
12. Hel:	( )
13. Gin:	[mimics Sam]: oh hopper's blocked
14.	powder's not coming through to the head:
15.	so why are you banging the dust extraction pipe
16.	[mimics Sam]: oh:
17. Hel:	[laughs]

Ginette here entertains Helen, her immediate neighbour on the packing line, with a humorous story of Sam's stupidity in banging the extraction pipe which will have no effect on a hopper blockage. She characterizes Sam unmercifully as *dumb eh* (line 1) and then uses a typical expletive to signal her astonishment at his stupid behaviour *why the fuck is he banging the dust extraction pipe* (line 4). Ginette then ruthlessly exposes Sam to ridicule by reproducing the exchange she conducted with him in a way that clearly demonstrates his lack of common sense. Ginette represents herself as asking an apparently innocent question *what's the matter Sam* (line 11). Sam's response *hopper's blocked powder's not coming through to the head* (lines 13–14) is then directly juxtaposed to her devastatingly direct challenge exposing his illogical behaviour *so why are you banging the dust extraction pipe* (line 15), providing much amusement to her audience. Ginette has set Sam a trap into which he neatly falls. Ginette finishes off by wickedly mimicking Sam's dim-witted response as he finally gets the message *oh* (line 16). Sam is thus presented in the final exchange as an idiot who cannot see the stupidity of his behaviour until Ginette spells out for him quite explicitly that his actions are not well directed to solving the problem. Focusing on individual shortcomings is quite acceptable in this community of practice, and is in fact a common strategy for ensuring team members keep up to the mark.

The team works 12 hour shifts which begin with an early 6am briefing meeting. One of Ginette's typical strategies when team members arrive late is to use humour to signal that this has been noted e.g. *good afternoon sue* at a 6am meeting! Dressing down another late-comer she calls out *nice of you to join us, were you busy making babies last night?* Her humour often has this kind of raw edge, as do the interactions among other team members – jocular abuse is the normal coinage of their everyday workplace interaction (Holmes and Marra 2005).

4.3.   The influence of community and ethnicity

Humour contributes to the distinct characteristics of a workplace team. Teams develop different attitudes to humour and tolerate different amounts of humour at work; distinctive topics of amusement develop in different communities of practice; and teams develop regular verbal humour routines, as well as different styles of humour. Holmes and Marra (2002b) identified distinct workplace cultures based on the amount, type (single utterance or extended sequences), style (contestive vs supportive) and construction (collaborative vs competitive) of humour, and found that these dimensions provided a means of constructing a distinctive humour configuration for each workplace. These dimensions also provide the basis for comparing the two workplaces described in this paper. Compared, for example, to many Pākehā government departments we have researched, there is a high level of humour in both these workplaces, especially in regular staff meetings. However, the humour in the Māori workplace is generally relatively supportive and collaborative compared to the more contestive and competitive humour in the predominantly Pacific Island factory community of practice.

Moreover, as the examples have illustrated, the contribution of cultural norms should not be overlooked. While team spirit is important both in the Māori organization and the multicultural factory team, the ways in which this spirit is encouraged differs markedly between the workplaces. In the Māori organization, in accordance with Māori cultural norms, the focus is on the group, even when criticism and complaint is involved; individuals are not singled out for comment. In the Pacific Island factory team, the pressure is on the individual to maintain the team's high performance, and individuals who are not measuring up are an appropriate target for critical comment. Humour is a strategy used in both communities for conveying negative comment in a more acceptable way, but it has a much sharper edge in the factory context.

Another point of contrast is the different ways in which the two team leaders construct themselves as professionals in the workplace (Holmes and Marra 2005; Marra and Holmes 2005). Conforming to Māori norms which emphasize modesty and avoid self-promotion, Yvonne plays down the importance of her presentation in example 2 and deflects attention from the compliment paid by Sherie by teasing her about the reason for it. Ginette on the other hand, in line with Samoan norms of explicit pride in and overt demonstration of one's status and power, presents a sharp-edged story which illustrates her quick wits and her logical skills in argument, and which portrays her as an intelligent as well as a demanding manager.

5.   Implications for cross-cultural and intercultural education

Socio-pragmatic competence is an often under-estimated aspect of workplace success. Learning ways of interacting which are appropriate and acceptable in a workplace is an important aspect of fitting in and becoming an integrated member of the workplace as a community of practice. Understanding, accurately interpreting, and appropriately contributing to workplace humour is one important component of this process. Indeed a sense of humour has been identified as a crucial characteristic in the workplace. Being able to do your job is only part of what is needed for workplace success. Only 15% of workers are fired because of lack of competence, according to a Robert Haft International survey cited in Sultanoff (1993), the remaining 85% are let go because of their inability to get along with fellow employees. Developing appropriate socio-pragmatic skills, including learning to handle humour, often presents a real hurdle for immigrant workers joining new cultures and communities, especially when the language of the workplace is different from their home language (Clyne, 1991, 1994; Gumperz, Jupp and Roberts 1979, Roberts, Davies and

Jupp 1992). Such workers are often skilled at their jobs, but do not always know how to manage the social and interpersonal aspects of workplace interaction. Interpersonal interaction provides a range of challenges for anyone joining a new place of work. Learning to cope with and contribute appropriately to the distinctive style and type of humour of one's new community of practice is an important aspect of this process of integration into the workplace team.

Our research on communication in different workplaces emphasizes the importance of identifying the social, contextual, discursive and cultural norms for interaction in each community of practice. New workers need to be sensitized to the potential for miscommunication. Old patterns will not necessarily transfer to new workplaces. Each community of practice develops its own distinctive patterns and ways of doing things, including preferred styles of humour, as we have briefly illustrated in this paper.

Interestingly, humour is often overlooked in cross-cultural training perhaps precisely because it is so context dependant. However, we have suggested a number of ways in which those involved in assisting new workers can contribute to raising their levels of socio-pragmatic awareness, including their ability to manage the social aspects of workplaces interaction (Newton 2004; Holmes 2004, 2005). Newton (2004) for example, outlines three types of pedagogical task for this purpose: Awareness-Raising Tasks, Interpretation Tasks and Communication Practice Tasks. He provides examples of awareness tasks which pay attention to *explicit knowledge*, and interpretation tasks oriented to *noticing* (Ellis 1999), which encourage learners to attend to and interpret socio-pragmatic meaning in authentic language episodes. Role-play illustrates a communication practice task which provides practice in attending to socio-pragmatic dimensions of language in production contexts (see also Newton in this volume).

As Newton notes "the three task types offer a varied but integrated approach to using authentic talk in language instruction for the workplace" (2004: 59). Using local television programmes can also provide material for raising awareness and learning to interpret humour correctly (Grant 1996; Grant and Devlin 1996; Grant and Starks 2001). Materials from our project are also available for exposing learners to authentic data and for practising interpretive skills and suggesting potential role plays (Stubbe and Brown 2002). Such tasks assist learners to interpret and produce socio-pragmatically appropriate talk in authentic contexts and they are then well placed to adapt this knowledge for their own communicative ends.

6.   Conclusion

As Wenger (1998) has noted, learning how to operate successfully within a particular community of practice is like an apprenticeship involving learning appropriate verbal behaviours that characterize the group and distinguish it from others, and acquiring its shared repertoire. Research which analyses day-to-day interactions in relevant communities of practice can help identify the range of patterns that workers may encounter, and can provide materials to help prepare them to participate and contribute to the on-going interaction, including the humorous exchanges which often seem especially problematic on initial entry. While some lessons can only be learned "on the job", there is an important place for research and education in preparing people for the range of different cultural patterns that they may encounter in a new workplace. Focusing on workplace humour, this paper has provided brief examples of such patterns from authentic talk in New Zealand workplaces.

Appendix: Transcription Conventions

<u>Yes</u>	Underlining indicates emphatic stress
RATION	Small caps for names of organizations
[laughs] : :	Paralinguistic features and editorial comments in square brackets, colons indicate start/finish
+	Pause of up to one second
... /..... ... /.....	Simultaneous speech
(hello)	Transcriber's best guess at an unclear utterance
–	Incomplete or cut-off utterance
... ...	Section of transcript omitted
≡	Speaker's turn continues

All names used in examples are pseudonyms.

Notes

1. See also Holmes (2000), Holmes and Marra (2002a, b, c).
2. See Holmes and Meyerhoff (1999) for further discussion of this point.
3. See appendix for transcription conventions.
4. See also Daly et al. (2004), Stubbe (1999, 2000, 2002, forthcoming), Holmes and Marra (2002b).
5. This example is also discussed from different perspectives in Holmes (2006) and in Stubbe (2002).

References

Blau, Peter M.
  1955   *The Dynamics of Bureaucracy: A Study of Interpersonal Relations in Two Government Agencies*. Chicago: University of Chicago Press.
Brown, Penelope and Stephen C. Levinson
  1987   *Politeness: Some Universals in Language Usage*. Cambridge/New York: Cambridge University Press.
Clyne, Michael
  1991   Patterns of inter-cultural communication in Melbourne factories. *Language and Language Education* 1: 5–30.
Clyne, Michael
  1994   *Inter-Cultural Communication at Work. Cultural Values in Discourse*. Cambridge: Cambridge University Press.
Corder, Saskia and Miriam Meyerhoff
  this volume Communities of practice in the analysis of intercultural communication, Chapter 21.
Cox, Joe A., Raymond L. Read and Philip M. van Auken
  1990   Male–female differences in communicating job-related humor: An exploratory study. *Humor* 3: 287–295.
Daly, Nicola, Janet Holmes, Jonathan Newton and Maria Stubbe
  2004   Expletives as solidarity signals in FTAs on the factory floor. *Journal of Pragmatics* 36: 945–964.
Duncan, W. Jack
  1985   The superiority theory of humor at work: Joking relationships and informal status patterns in small task-oriented groups. *Small Group Behaviour* 16: 556–564.
Eckert, Penelope and Sally McConnell-Ginet
  1992   Think practically and look locally: language and gender as community-based practice. *Annual Review of Anthropology* 21: 461–490.
Eckert, Penelope and Sally McConnell-Ginet
  1999   New explanations in language and gender research. *Language in Society* 28: 185–201.
Ellis, Rod
  1999   The place of grammar instruction in the second/foreign language curriculum. *New Zealand Studies in Applied Linguistics* 5: 1–21.
Ervin-Tripp, Susan and Martin D. Lampert
  1992   Gender differences in the construction of humorous talk. In: Kira Hall, Mary Bucholtz and Birch Moonwomon (eds.), *Locating Power.* Proceedings of the Second Berkeley Women and Language Conference April 4 and 5 1992, 105–117. Berkeley: Berkeley Women and Language Group.
Fletcher, Joyce M.
  1999   *Disappearing Acts: Gender, Power and Relational Practice at Work*. Cambridge, MA: MIT Press.
Graham, Elizabeth E., Michael J. Papa and Gordon P. Brooks
  1992   Functions of humor in conversation: Conceptualization and measurement. *Western Journal of Communication* 56: 161–183.

Grant, Lynn E.
1996   Teaching conversation using a television soap. *Prospect* 11(3): 60–71.
Grant, Lynn E. and Gaylene A. Devlin
1996   *Teaching Conversation: The 'Shortland Street' Way* [video and workbook]. Auckland: South Pacific Pictures.
Grant, Lynn E. and Donna Starks
2001   Screening appropriate teaching materials. Closings from textbooks and television soap operas. *IRAL* 39: 39–50.
Gumperz, John J., T.C. Jupp and Celia Roberts
1979   *Crosstalk: A Study of Cross-Cultural Communication.* Southall, Middx: National Centre for Industrial Language Training.
Hay, Jennifer
1995   Gender and humour: Beyond a joke. MA thesis, Department of Linguistics, Victoria University of Wellington.
Hay, Jennifer
1996   No laughing matter: Gender and humour support strategies. *Wellington Working Papers in Linguistics* 8: 1–24.
Holdaway, Simon
1988   Blue jokes: Humour in police work. In: Chris Powell and George E.C. Paton (eds.), *Humour in Society: Resistance and Control*, 106–122. London: Macmillan.
Holmes, Janet
1998   Narrative structure: some contrasts between Maori and Pakeha story-telling. *Multilingua* 17: 25–57.
Holmes, Janet
2000   Politeness, power and provocation: How humour functions in the workplace. *Discourse Studies* 2: 159–185.
Holmes, Janet
2003   "I couldn't follow her story ...": Ethnic differences in New Zealand narratives'. In: Juliane House, Gabriele Kasper and Steven Ross (eds.), *Misunderstanding in Social Life: Discourse Approaches to Problematic Talk*, 173–198. London: Pearson Education.
Holmes, Janet
2004   Talk at work and "fitting in": A socio-pragmatic perspective on workplace culture. In: Gillian Wigglesworth (ed.), *Marking our Difference: Languages in Australia and New Zealand Universities.* Proceedings of Conference on Language Education in Australian and New Zealand Universities. 2003, 95–115. Melbourne: University of Melbourne.
Holmes, Janet
2005   Socio-pragmatic aspects of workplace talk. In: Yuji Kawaguchi, Susumu Zaima, Toshihiro Takagaki, Kohji Shibanno and Mayumi Usami (eds.), *Linguistics Informatics – State of the Art and the Future:* The First International Conference on Linguistic Informatics, 196–220. Amsterdam: John Benjamins.
Holmes, Janet
2006   Workplace narratives, professional identity and relational practice. In: Anna De Fina, Deborah Schiffrin and Michael Bamberg (eds.), *Discourse and Identity*, 166–187, Cambridge: Cambridge University Press.

Holmes, Janet and Meredith Marra
  2002a   Humour as a discursive boundary marker in social interaction. In: Anna
           Duszak (ed.), *Us and Others: Social Identities across Languages, Dis-
           courses and Culture*, 377–400. Amsterdam: John Benjamins.
Holmes, Janet and Meredith Marra
  2002b   Having a laugh at work: How humour contributes to workplace culture.
           Journal of Pragmatics 34: 1683–1710.
Holmes, Janet and Meredith Marra
  2002 c   Over the edge? Subversive humour between colleagues and friends. *Humor*
           15: 65–87.
Holmes, Janet and Meredith Marra
  2004   Relational practice in the workplace: Women's talk or gendered discourse?
           Language in Society 33: 377–398.
Holmes, Janet and Meredith Marra
  2005   Narrative and the construction of professional identity in the workplace. In:
           Joanna Thornborrow and Jennifer Coates (eds.), *The Sociolinguistics of
           Narrative*, 193–213. Amsterdam: John Benjamins.
Holmes, Janet and Miriam Meyerhoff
  1999   The community of practice: Theories and methodologies in language and
           gender research. *Language in Society: Special Issue: Communities of Prac-
           tice in Language and Gender Research* 28: 173–183.
Holmes, Janet and Maria Stubbe
  2003a   *Power and Politeness in the Workplace. A Sociolinguistic Analysis of Talk
           at Work*. London: Longman.
Holmes, Janet and Maria Stubbe
  2003b   'Feminine' workplaces: Stereotype and reality. In: Janet Holmes and
           Miriam Meyerhoff (eds.), *The Handbook of Language and Gender*, 573–599.
           Oxford: Blackwell.
Kotthoff, Helga
this volume Ritual and style across cultures, Chapter 9.
Lave, Jean and Etienne Wenger
  1991   *Situated Learning: Legitimate Peripheral Participation*. Cambridge: Cam-
           bridge University Press.
Linstead, Steve
  1988   Jokers wild: Humour in organisational culture. In: Chris Powell and George
           E.C. Paton (eds.), *Humour in Society: Resistance and Control*, 123–148.
           London: Macmillan.
Marra, Meredith and Janet Holmes
  2005   Constructing ethnicity and leadership through storytelling at work. Paper
           presented at the ANZCA Conference 2005: Communication at Work, 4–7
           July 2005, University of Canterbury, Christchurch, New Zealand.
Martineau, W.
  1972   A model of the social functions of humor. In: Jeffrey H. Goldstein and Paul
           E. McGhee (eds.), *The Psychology of Humor: Theoretical Perspectives and
           Empirical Issues*, 101–125. New York: Academic Press.
Metge, Joan
  1995   *New Growth From Old: The Whanau in the Modern World*. Wellington,
           New Zealand: Victoria University Press.

Murphy, M.
    1986   The functions of humor in the workplace. PhD thesis, The Fielding Institute.
Newton, Jonathan
    2004   Face-threatening talk on the factory floor: Using authentic workplace inter-
            actions in language teaching. *Prospect* 19(1): 47–64.
Newton, Jonathan
this volume. Adapting authentic workplace talk for workplace intercultural communi-
            cation training, Chapter 24.
O'Quin, K. and J. Arnoff
    1981   Humor as a technique of social influence. *Social Psychology Quarterly* 44:
            349–357.
Roberts, Celia, Evelyn Davies and T.C. Jupp
    1992   Mapping interaction: Practice and theory. In: Celia Roberts, Evelyn
            Davies and T.C. Jupp (eds.), *Language and Discrimination: A Study
            of Communication in Multi-Ethnic Workplaces*, 28–111. London: Long-
            man.
Sabath, Robert E.
    1990   The serious use of humor. *Journal of Management Consulting* 6(3): 40–43.
Stubbe, Maria
    1999   Just joking and playing silly buggers: Humour and teambuilding on a fac-
            tory production line. Paper presented at NZ Linguistic Society Conference,
            Massey, 24–26 November 1999.
Stubbe, Maria
    2000   'Just do it ...!' Discourse strategies for 'getting the message across' in a
            factory production team. In: J. Henderson (ed.), *Proceedings of the 1999
            Conference of the Australian Linguistic Society.* http://www.arts.uwa.edu.
            au/LingWWW/als99/proceedings.
Stubbe, Maria
    2001   *From Office to Production Line: Collecting Data for the Wellington
            Language in the Workplace Project.* Language in the Workplace Occa-
            sional Paper 2. Wellington, New Zealand: Victoria University of Welling-
            ton.
Stubbe, Maria
    2002   Managing the contradictions: gender, ethnicity and power in the discourse
            of a factory team. Symposium on Power and Politics: Talking Gender and
            Race. International Conference on Language and Psychology. ICLASP 8.
            Hong Kong, 14–19 July 2002.
Stubbe, Maria
forthcoming Miscommunication and problematic talk in multicultural workplaces: A
            New Zealand case study. Unpublished PhD thesis, School of Linguistics
            and Applied Language Studies, Victoria University of Wellington.
Stubbe, Maria and Pascal Brown
    2002   *Talk that Works: Communication in Successful Factory Teams: A Training
            Resource Kit.* Wellington: School of Linguistics and Applied Language
            Studies, Victoria University of Wellington.
Sultanoff, Steven
    1993   Taking humor seriously in the workplace. www.humormatters.com/articles/
            workplac.htm.

Tracy, Karen and Nikolas Coupland (eds.)
    1990   *Multiple Goals in Discourse*. Clevedon, Avon, UK: Multilingual Matters.
Wenger, Etienne
    1998   *Communities of Practice: Learning, Meaning and Identity*. Cambridge:
            Cambridge University Press.

9.   Ritual and style across cultures

Helga Kotthoff

1.   Introduction

Ritual and style play an important part in the (re)construction of culture. Rituals are multidimensional, social performances of collective knowledge and sense making. In agreement with Geertz (1973) I see ritual performances as "meta-social commentaries" which can be interpreted in all their shades of meaning by producers and recipients within a community of practice. Various ritual theorists have emphasized that their social functions are more important than the instrumental ones (Leach 1976; Werlen 2001); they bind the group together, inspire joint action and structure the social reality. They have a beginning and an end and thus a time structure. By highlighting expressive and aesthetic dimensions they also stimulate emotional and metaphysical experiences of the participants (Knoblauch and Kotthoff 2001). Style comes into play. Collins (2004: xi) suggests that we can see how variations in the intensity of rituals lead to variations in social membership patterns "not on the global level of 'society' in the large sense but as memberships that are local, sometimes ephemeral, stratified and conflictual". Hence, it is always important to identify how a ritual is carried out stylistically. Style features indexicalize the social meaning of an event and they invite inferencing (see Gumperz and Cook-Gumperz in this volume; Eckert 2000).

In this chapter I will discuss a variety of rituals, from simple rituals such as gift presentation to complex ones such as toasting. I will primarily discuss examples from Germany and countries of the former Soviet Union, especially from Caucasian Georgia. We will take a close look at cultural specificities and the knowledge which is demanded for the performance of toasts at the dinner table. All stylistic shades are interpreted, which sometimes in crosscultural encounters leads to misunderstanding or astonishment. Some rituals are open to everybody; some are exclusive.

Toasts are a genre known in many societies. In the former Soviet Union, however, toasting was of outstanding importance and it continues to be so. In Caucasian Georgia, especially, it is also a way to "do being Georgian" (as ethnomethodologists would put it, see Spreckels and Kotthoff in this volume) because it is often used to confess national values, which are communicated in a very emotional style.

The West likes to see itself as "antiritualistic" (Douglas 1982). Goffman (1967, 1981), more than anyone, has however made us see that our everyday life is full of interaction rituals and that many activities have ritual layers beyond the instrumental one. Soeffner (1991) points out that Western societies are in fact only less ritualistic than more traditional ones in the degree to which they acknowledge their rituals. Consider, for example, the ritual of bringing a gift when one is invited to a private home. All cultures have special social semiotics for behaviour as a guest. In Western Europe a guest would not bring red roses because they are reserved for lovers and could therefore invite such a reading; neither would one bring red cloves because they are reserved for the expression of solidarity on the first of May (Labour Day) or the eighth of March (International Women's Day). In Germany we would not bring white chrysanthemums, either, because they normally express grief relating to a death and are brought to a funeral parlour. Likewise, for hosts with whom one is not on intimate terms, body care products could suggest a veiled complaint against poor hygiene. On the other hand, across most cultures wine or sweets, novels, and musical recordings are accepted without difficulty. Apparently there are areas in which a trans-national standard has emerged for fulfilling the role of guest.

Once the gift is deposited in its wrapper with the host, the next problems in the semiotics of gift-bringing emerge. In contrast to Western Europe, gifts hardly merit a glance in China and Georgia, where they disappear immediately in cupboards or bedrooms (Kotthoff 1991b; Günthner 2000a, b). Germans and most West Europeans, by contrast, expect euphoric gratefulness and enthusiasm. The guest's present must be unpacked and explicitly praised. Such a way of thanking belongs to the strategies of "positive politeness" (as also gift presentation), e.g., "Oh, is that the new CD of Madeleine Peyroux? Wow! I always wanted to buy that for myself." (For the concept of positive politeness, see Brown and Levinson 1987). In China and Georgia, by contrast, the host exercises considerable restraint in expressing thanks for the gift to avoid giving the impression that the guest is welcome mainly because of the gift. Gift presentation is ritualistic because it is a routine social act achieving various symbolic aims (Mauss 1978). The instrumental act, consisting in the presentation of some more or less useful object, is relatively unimportant. In Spencer-Oatey (2000b) a wide variety of intercultural misunderstandings resulting from different politeness practices are discussed.

2.   Goffman's concept of rituality

Drawing on the analogy to theories of religious ritual, Goffman (1967) extends the concept of ritual to everyday activities. Religious rituals are characterized by ceremonial forms of activity which are used as symbols, making reference to a transcendent religious realm of meaning. Similarly, in interaction rituals he sees symbolization processes that transcend the realm of interpersonal relations.

Communicative acts like greeting, expressing well-being, extending greetings to others, expressing interest, etc., all serve to maintain a symbolic order among the participants in a chain of activities. The semiotics of dress and habit, space and presentation of food has ritualistic dimensions. For example, the semiotics of dress is gendered in most cultures and recreates a gendered social cosmos. In Western and many Eastern cultures, the female sex attributes exclusiveness and delicacy to itself by dressing in lace and silk stockings, whereas men's corresponding dress code attributes robustness to the male sex. Many activities arising in social interaction thus carry with them ritual aspects and stand in some relation to membership significance. Just as drinking wine and eating bread at communion in a Christian church fulfill no practical or instrumental function – they neither quench the thirst nor relieve the hunger of the participants – the eating and drinking at a party are not meant entirely to fulfill these functions, either. Goffman (1967) indeed mentions parties as ceremonial events several times. In many parts of the world, alcoholic drinks are obligatory at events to which guests are invited in the evening. Drinking is ritually associated with "loosening up", informality, imbuing cheeriness and suppressing rigidity. In some areas, especially for men, shared drinking is a part of "brotherly" binding. In Caucasian Georgia, whenever a guest appears, he or she must be especially honored, and among men the ritual dimension of drinking always comes into play (Kotthoff 1991b, 1995). To his considerable surprise, a man coming from the West may find himself required to empty a glass of Cognac even when invited to breakfast. Interaction rituals are thus an essential means of symbolizing the quality of relationships.

In this article we will examine the speech genre of toasting to show the interconnection of style and ritual. It will be discussed how a pathetic style of the toasting ritual creates a religious sphere for the dinner table society in Georgia. In other formerly Soviet republics the ritual was also carried out in pathetic style but without prayer formulas. Western people, in contrast, practice toasting as a form of supporting "positive face needs" (i.e., thanking, congratulating, see below).

Goffman's interest in the interaction order is considerably more general than that of, e.g., Brown and Levinson (1987). From a sociological perspective, he assumes that the social order reveals itself in forms of interaction but is also historically grounded in it. Over the span of his career Goffman attempted to establish person-to-person interaction as a separate field of study. In connection with his studies of the interaction order, he also addressed those normative acts which have implications for the social place of individuals. He observed the dramatization of the social order in everyday encounters. Like linguistic anthropologists (see Gumperz and Cook-Gumperz in this volume), Goffman sees the access to social roles, ranks and functions not only as exogenous factors of communication but also as something produced in the social encounter.

Aspects of social interaction are ritualized (symbolically loaded); e.g., a person presents a self. Goffman calls this "communicating a line":

> Every person lives in a world of social encounters, involving him either in face-to-face or mediated contact with other participants. In each of the contacts, he tends to act out what is sometimes called a 'line' – that is, a pattern of verbal and nonverbal acts by which he expresses his view of the situation and through this his evaluation of the participants, especially himself ... The term face can be defined as the positive social value a person effectively claims for himself by the line others assume he has taken during a particular contact. Face is an image of self delineated in terms of approved social attributes – albeit an image that others may share. (1967: 5)

"Face" is an image of the self formed from recognized social attributes that a person claims for her- or himself and that in turn are confirmed by others. A person's "line" refers to the coherence that is expected in the presentation. Every person is involved in confirming the lines of others; hence, their lines are constructions of the same order. Faces of persons must show consistency and they are thus institutionalized in interpersonal encounters. That certain "lines" have been assigned to a person often becomes evident only when the person no longer fulfills the expectations implied in them. Normally one feels emotionally bound to one's personal face; it guarantees security and self-esteem. A personal face, however, comes into being by means of a typification in which both the person and her environment are involved. Within the confines of a culture, both social and situative typifications can be readily identified. We can interpret by which manner of speaking, hair style, style of dress or behavior someone such as a professor presents herself as a progressive and easy going type (communicating a "line" in Goffman's sense), and with what means a conservative habitus (in Bourdieu's [1990] sense) is created. In intercultural contact, by contrast, there is little certainty as to how to interpret such stylistic devices and identify the types they are meant to create.

Goffman mainly described US American and Western face politics, which attributes a sacred value to the individual and her/his autonomy. Other anthropologists (such as Shweder and Bourne 1984) have emphasized that many traditional cultures have a sociocentric conception of personhood. The difference between an individualistic and a sociocentric conception of personhood has an impact on communicative styles. Matsumoto (1988) and Yamada (1997) contrast American ideals of independence to those of Japanese interdependence. With Geertz (1983: 59) we can contrast Western conceptions of egocentric personal autonomy with sociocentric conceptions of personhood:

The Western conception of the person as a bounded, unique, more or less integrated motivational cognitive universe, a dynamic center of awareness with emotion, judgement, and action organized into a distinctive whole, and set contrastively both against such wholes and against the self's social and natural background. We will see that in the former Soviet Union, to a much higher extend than in the West, drinking toasts communicate a sociocentric concept of personhood.

3.   Style, inference and keying

Style plays an important role not only in ritual communication. Tannen (1984) pointed out that style is more than "the frosting on a cake." Style is the particular way in which utterances and activities are performed in their contexts of use. Within a culture we conventionalize stylistic features which thereby become expectable in a certain context. Degrees of (in)directness and (in)formality are, among others, important stylistic dimensions in many social settings. Gumperz (1979) combined insights from ethnography of speaking, anthropology, sociolinguistics and conversation analysis to suggest a way of analyzing speech styles as contextualization cues, i.e., cues that speakers use to suggest the interpretation of what is said within and in relation to particular interpretive frames, e.g., for dimensions such as degree of formality, directness, and intimacy (cf. also Auer 1992). I will use this approach here to discuss scenes of intercultural stylistic difference, adaptation, misinterpretation, and creativity.

Interactants use styles and their alternation in order to signal and constitute various kinds of meaning, e.g., textual, situational, social and/or interactional; recipients, on the other hand, perceive and interpret style as a meaningful cue used to make particular kinds of meaning inferable (Sandig and Selting 1997). Accordingly, important tasks of stylistic research are (a) the description of the ways in which style and stylistic means are used to constitute stylistic meanings and (b) the analysis of the kinds of stylistic meanings that recipients perceive and interpret. Since contextualization cues are the most unconsciously used devices and are interpreted against the background of one's own culturally conventionalized expectations, their misuse often results in unnoticed misinterpretations of communicative intent. Style is often the interplay of verbal and other semiotic cues (Eckert 2000). Language and speech are accompanied by other semiotic procedures, for example clothing, which often indicate at the same time a gender, class and situation marking. The "performative turn" in semiotics and pragmatics points to the necessity of reconstructing bundles of co-occurring style features which are used as constitutive and meaningful cues of holistic styles. Sandig and Selting (1997) write that many typified styles can be conceived of as being organized prototypically, with prototypical kernel features most relevant for the constitution and interpretation of a particular style as against more peripheral features that a style might share with "neighboring" styles. Hence, styles can be realized more or less clearly.

In all areas of intercultural communication style is a relevant dimension which may be the origin of social difficulties and conflicts (Tannen 1984). In her study of German–Chinese interactions, Günthner (1993, 2000b) reports on differing stylistic conventions with respect to differing uses of recipiency tokens like "mhm" or "uhu" by Chinese and German native speakers, differing uses of proverbial sayings, differing levels of directness in topic development and different strategies in handling disagreement. In most Asian cultures disagreement is expressed rather indirectly (Yamada 1997). Levels of directness and tendencies concerning how to support the negative or the positive face have often been identified as significantly different cross-culturally (Foley 1997; Spencer-Oatey 2000b). Sifianou (1992) notes a difference between England and Greece in the significance accorded to the two aspects of face. The English place a higher value on privacy and individuality (negative face), while the Greeks emphasize group involvement and ingroup relationships (positive face). The limits to personal territory among Greeks include all those who belong to the same ingroup, defined as someone concerned with one's welfare. Positive face extends to cover these, so that there is a strong desire that one's companions are also liked and approved. Positive face is, thus, defined over the group of ingroup associates, not with reference to isolated individuals, as is largely the case in England. We will later notice some similarities in the facework strategies of Greeks and Georgians.

Kotthoff (1991a) also demonstrates stylistic differences in dealing with disagreement in German and American office-hour conversations at universities. To a much greater extent than the Germans, the American participants framed their dissent as proposals or suggestions, thereby mitigating the level of directness. Within the United States, Tannen (1984) and Erickson and Shultz (1982) found considerable differences among social groups (ethnic and regional) in the ways conversational signals are perceived. New Yorkers interpret quick, short queries, "machine gun questions," as encouragement to the story-teller to tell more, thus as signs of "high involvement" (Tannen 1984). Californians, on the other hand, interpret them as a signal to the teller to come to the end.

A speech style also creates a certain keying. Following Goffman (1974) and Hymes (1974), keying signifies a process which regulates the particular reality and coherence relations of utterances (Kotthoff 1999b). In humor the relationship to reality is loosened and special inferences are needed to create "sense in nonsense," to use Freud's expression (1985). Loosening the relationship between statement and reality means widening the possible scope of imagination. Laughter particles in utterances are important keying markers; they often indexicalize that a text is to be interpreted as humorous (see Marra and Holmes in this volume for cultural differences in humor). Pathos is another example of keying. It is important in toast rituals. We will show its stylistic markers and different evaluations.

In the conventional understanding of Western cultures, pathos is associated with emotionally laden words, stilted phrases, ponderous speech meant to be emotionally moving, festiveness, with emotionally excessive reception and the uneasy feeling of being all too close to kitsch. In Germany the keying of pathos has fallen into especially deep disfavor, undoubtedly owing to its excessive use in the Nazi period. By contrast, in Caucasian Georgia pathos has a fixed place in everyday communicative genres. No meal takes place, even among good acquaintances, without several elaborate and festive toasts to guests, their families and shared values (Kotthoff 1995, 1998). In Germany the peculiar danger of falling into pathos-laden speech is often avoided with irony and humor, while in other cultures, like that of Georgia, it continues to be practiced in an undiluted way. Responses that nearly lead to tears or to the invocation of religious formulas are not only entirely acceptable, but in some contexts indeed desired.

4.   Formality vs. informality

Particular chosen styles serve, among other things, to mark situations or relationships as formal or as informal. We use a wide variety of forms of expression to negotiate the degree of formality or informality (Irvine 1979). In most situations this degree is in fact negotiable – and not already set, as in institutional discourse, for example, in a court of law. In this sense, stylistics goes beyond the verbal realm, including for example the use of space and body expression. In the West, in general, strong efforts to de-formalize interactions can be observed (Collins 2004). Nowadays in Germany people take leave of one another in nearly any situation with the familiar and informal "tschüss" (an even more informal leave-taking than "bye"). While twenty years ago it would have been unthinkable for German newscasters to leave the television screen using this expression, today it is more or less the rule. Likewise, people can be greeted nearly anywhere with "hallo", (which in formal situations would have been felt as rude a generation ago). In internet chats there is almost a prohibition against formal style, at least in those areas where young people set the tone. To be sure, there is an accepted "netiquette," which, however, mainly concerns gross indecency and tabu words.

In the business world, too, a progressive deformalization is taking place. In smaller information technology firms the familiar address with "Du" is often the rule (Menz 2000) regardless of how well employees in fact know one another. The traditional formal business dinner is giving way to a less formal "enriched apero," as it is called in Switzerland. Much the same can be observed at academic meetings, where appetizers are passed around on trays to guests who, standing at high tables, attempt to engage in relaxing smalltalk in all directions. The ability to make friendly conversation on inconsequential topics is increasingly prized, and a plethora of books offer advice on how best to go about it.

While such trends seem to be firmly established in the West, in Caucasian Georgia, where neither the meals are small nor the talk that accompanies them, a much different use of formal style can be found. The following sections examine ritual and style in the construction of social encounters with guests. I compare such situations in Georgia and Kazakhstan with ones in Germany.

5.   The toast ritual and its style

5.1.   The Georgian ceremony "supra" and the genre of toasts

Guests from the West taking their seats for food and drink at a Georgian table seldom know that they are entering a situation dramatically different from comparable ones in their native country (Kotthoff 1991b). They are immersed in a ceremony, the ancient "supra" or table ceremony, that has little in common with the informal chatting between dishes and drinks familiar to them. The framework of meals shared with guests is something that varies greatly among cultures, and it activates different knowledge schemes. The enacting of a supra is an indispensible act of honoring the guest. But even within close groups like families and neighbours there are many occasions for ceremonial banquets, e.g., marriages, birthdays, examinations, births, returns from trips, funerals and their anniversaries – and everyday visits from neighbours. According to the occasion, "happy" banquets (lxinis supra) are distinguished from "sad" ones (čiris supra), distinctions that are also enacted through the choice of foods and the topics of toasts. But even an ordinary evening spent with friends is formalized insofar as a communicative genre comes into play and sets the frame for the evening's interaction, the toasting genre (see Günthner in this volume on genres).

After the Georgian wine has been poured, the central communicative piece of the supra scenario can begin, the canonical sequence of toasts. No wine is drunk until a toast has been uttered. Thus, with the alcoholic drink, a non-verbal element is incorporated into the structure of the genre sadřegrʒelebi (Chatwin 1997).

The toasts, the sadřegrʒelebi,[1] are generally offered by a man, the tamada, who has been assigned this task beforehand or was specially chosen by the group for this function. Often it is the host himself or a friend of the house who plays the part of the tamada. The tamada ensures that each draught of wine constitutes a gesture of honoring a person. Simply drinking without this function is regarded as impolite.

The toasts follow a variable set of canonic themes, but the canon is adapted to the situation. In this way the conversation is formalized to a high degree and is fitted to a specific temporal structure.

5.2. Drinking to wish God's favor

Between 1988 and 2006 I spent altogether some 27 months in Georgia and collected about 40 hours of sound recordings of toasts, offered mainly in Georgian but also in German and in Russian.

Let us look at a toast made by a man (Coṭne) from the capital city of Tbilisi, who, with four others (including myself) from Tbilisi, was making a visit to the country in the region Pshavi. Coṭne drinks to the neighborhood and to the extended families of the Pshavs who are present. He invokes religious formulas in line 43 ("I bless you all") and in line 44 ("and may God give his favour to everyone") as it is normal. The start of the toast is clearly marked by a formal and ceremonial manner of speech.

Data 1

27 C: აღიღოს იმათი სახელი,
        adidos imati saxeli,
        praised be the names of those,

28   რომელნიც თქვენი ხელიდან ჭიქას ითხოვს,
        romelnic tkveni xelidan čikas itxovs,
        who await from your hands a glass,

29   და თქვენი ენიდან სახელის
        da tkveni enidan saxelis
        and from your tongues mention

30   გაგონებას და სათქმელის თქმას.
        gagonebas da satkmelis tkmas.
        of their own names.

31 V: gaumarǯos ((parallel conversation))

32   იმათ სახელსა და იმათ კაცობას
        imat saxelsa da imat ḳacobas
        to the names and to the humanity,

33   და იმათ ვაჟკაცობას
        da imat važḳacobas
        and to the virility

34   და იმათ ქალობას,
        da imat kalobas,
        and to the femininity of those,

35   ვინც გვერდით დაგიდიან,
        vinc gverdit dagidian,
        that accompany you,

36   ავლილ-ჩავლილნი მრუდე თვალს არ გამოგაყოლებენ,
        avlil-čavlilni mrude tvals ar gamogaqoleben,
        and cast no disparaging looks at you,

37   თქვენ პატივსა სცემთ და ისინიც პატივსა გცემენ.
     tkven paṭivsa scemt da isinic paṭivsa gcemen.
     whom you honor and by whom you are honored.

38   ღმერთმა გაუმარჯოს სუქველას,
     r̄mertma gaumaržos suqvelas,
     God shall give his favor to all.

39   მე ამით დავლოცავ აქ თქვენ სამეზობლობს,
     me amit davlocav ak tkven samezoblobos,
     herewith I drink to your neighbors,

40   საგვარეულოსას.
     sagvareulosas. ((raises the glass))
     to your extended families.

41 N.: საფშავლოს, ((glasses clink))
        sapšavlos,
        to the Pšavs.

42 C: საფშავლოს.
       sapšavlos.
       to the Pšavs.

43   დაგილოცავთ სუქველას,
     dagilocavt suqvelas,
     I bless you all,

44   და ღმერთმა გაუმარჯოს სუქველას,
     da r̄mertma gaumaržos suqvelas,
     and may God give his favor to everyone ((holds the glass))

45   ჩვენ მასპინძლებს.
     čven maspinʒlebs
     to our hosts.

46 E: amin, amin, amin.
       amin, amin, amin.
       amen, amen, amen.

47 V: gaumaržos.

48   ((all drink))

The city-dweller Coṭne begins his toast with a formally polite introduction that reminds us of a prayer: "praised be" (adidos). And indeed, in Georgia prayer is in a way a genre that borders closely on toasting.

27 C: adidos imati saxeli,
       praised be the names of those,

28   romelnic tkveni xelidan čikas itxovs,
     who await a glas from your hands,

29   da tkveni enidan saxelis
     and mention from your tongues

He makes much use of metonomy, as in line 27 ("praised be the names of those" for "praised be those"), in line 28 ("from your hands" for "from you"), and in line 29 ("from your tongues" for "from you"). Metonomy adds pathos to the discourse by elevating the particularity of its contents. Further, we find repeatedly rhetorical three-part lists:

32   imat saxelsa da imat k̲acobas
       to the names and to the humanity,
33   da imat važk̲acobas
       and to the virility
34   da imat kalobas,
       and to the femininity of those,
35   vinc gverdit dagidian,
       that accompany you,
36   avlil-čavlilni mrude tvals ar gamogaqoleben,
       and cast no disparaging looks at you,
37   tkven pat̲ivsa scemt da isinic pat̲ivsa gcemen.
       whom you honor and by whom you are honored.
38   r̲mertma gaumarǯos suqvelas,
       God shall give his favour to all.

Here two such three-part lists follow one another. We encounter important cultural concepts like that of the family name (saxeli); važk̲acoba, which could be translated by "proper virility" (line 33), and of kaloba (34), "proper femininity" (see Kotthoff 1991b and 1995 for a discussion of the gender politics of the Georgian toasts), as well as the term for honor and deference (pativi). Further meanings, that do not need to be made explicit, are associated with these terms; they are invoked by virtue of the shared understanding of the participants.

Again and again there appear religious formulas, as in (38). Hence, it is not surprising that the toast elicits a religious formula as response.

46 E: amin, amin, amin.
       amen, amen, amen.

A round of toasting ends normally when all participants have seconded with "gaumarǯos" (47).

5.3.   Communicating honor and interdependency

The great importance given to formal and pathos-laden communication and to addressing those present as representatives of larger entities, such as their clans, their regions, or their extended families or institutions to which they may belong, marks stylistic and ritual differences to the corresponding genre of toasts in western Europe or North America. In Georgia, the pathos-laden form of presentation is seen as normal and is not felt to be bombastic or pompous.

While raising glasses and clinking them belong internationally to the genre, in Georgian toasts an emotionally laden and sometimes even religious vocabulary plays an important role, as we have just seen, and additionally, speakers use metaphor, metonymy, and threefold lists of parallel structures to achieve aesthetic and emotive effects. Important textual characteristics include a marked framing of the toast, more or less pronounced prosodic and syntactic line structuring, repetitive use of formulas, as well as a special, picturesque and exclusive vocabulary distinct from that of everyday speech; these serve to praise the qualities of the toasted individuals.

In the toast social qualities of persons are often made publicly visible. Georgian guests and their hosts expect positive mention of their families or native regions as signs of politeness, as well as respect for deceased members of their families. Similar to what Sifianou (1992) and Matsumoto (1988) write about politeness standards in Greek and Japanese cultures, in Georgia a person is positioned in relationship to his/her social group and the duties it entails.

Interdependency and reciprocity can be identified as the central ideas in the Georgian concept of "paṭivi." In Georgia the honor of an individual unavoidably extends to that of his family and village (as in many Asian and southern European cultures, as well). Persons who honor others too little place their own honor in jeopardy. In that sense Georgian culture resembles all those which have been characterized as sociocentric (see Foley 1997 for an overview).

Culturally and morally bound conceptions are involved in many ways in encounters with guests. In comparing Western and Oriental[2] styles of communication, we often encounter contrasting values of independence and interdependency. I have analyzed toasts as ways of communicating respect in social networks (Kotthoff 1999a). In toasts culturally specific morals (and the attendant politics of feeling) become evident in the performances.

The repetitiveness of themes and formulas, the pathos-laden manner and the verbal expression of hopes and shared desires remind one of prayer. God and other transcendental forces are addressed directly in the Georgian toast. Hence, it is hardly surprising that the guests respond with "amin" (amen). Indeed, culinary events often combine with religion in all corners of the world, and even in the Western world, within the religious sphere shared eating and drinking play a symbolic role, even if that role is exclusively symbolic.

An often made, explicit compliment in a toast is that someone is a good Georgian. Being Georgian is an omnipresent moral value, which confirms on an everyday level the importance of national independence, won only a few years ago. Throughout Georgia "doing being Georgian" is one ritual layer within the process.

By contrast, in Germany today "Germanness" does not represent a recognized value; at the best, "Europeanness" can fill this role. Persons who proclaim their "good Germanness" unavoidably assume a political stance associated with rightist fringes of the political spectrum. Thus, for many German guests in Georgia the repeated praise of "good Georgianness" seems a little suspicious. Likewise, the praise of qualities like "proper virility" in mixed company gatherings furnishes much material for jokes among guests from the West.

5.4.   Toasts that honor parents

The toast presented in Data 1 is in no way a special or unusual event in Georgia. To make this clear I present as Data 2 a toast recorded in 1990 at an evening gathering of young, well acquainted academics in Tbilisi (the Georgian original can be found in Kotthoff 1995).

Tamada Badri (T), Goča (O), Gia (G) and a young married couple (E:):
Data 2
First toast in a round of young intellectuals in Tbilisi

```
 1 T:  I want to offer you a toast
 2     (–) to our earthly gods,
 3     to our parents, mother and father. (1.0)
 4     anyway I have taken it as a rule
 5     not to ask the participants at this table
 6     if their mother or father is missing. (1.0)
 7     even if a parent is already dead,
 8     he or she is not dead but alive,
 9 ?:  (? ?)
10 T:  as long as a gram of their blood still flows in someone else.
11     because of that they are earthly gods, (––)
12     because their earthly children
13     when they do not dwell on this earth anymore.
14     do not let the memories of them decay.
15     gaumarǯos to our earthly gods,
16     to our parents, to our mother and father.
       [gaumarǯos.
17 ?:  [cheers to them. (? ?) ((everybody drinks))
18 T:  I wish them well-being, health and good luck. (1.0 drinking)
```

19   popular wisdom claims, (–) even if a child for his parents (––)
20   would fry an egg on his or her hand,
21   she could never pay back what her/his parents did for
22   her/him.
23   paying back merits might mean that we should not
24 O: [(? ?)
25 T: [lose or reject the traditions, (–) customs, moral credo,
26   that our parents gave us,
27   we should not lose it and trample on it.
28   this honor will surely be the payment for their caring efforts.
29   in Hegel there is a remarkable statement.
      parents love their children more than children love their parents, and that
      is natural.
32   why? he was asked. (–)
33   because parents are imperfect and see the extension
34   of their own imperfection in their children.
35   therefore they love them more.
36 O: gaumarʒos.
37 T: gaumarʒos. best wishes to all of your parents.
38 O: [gaumarʒos to our earthly gods.
36 E: [gaumarʒos. ((they clink glasses and drink))

As in the toast of Data 1, the conventional formal announcement "I want to offer
you a toast" (me minda šemogtavazot sadřegrʒelo) attracts attention. Here again
the toast-maker (tamada) switches to a formal style and a ceremonious vocabulary such as "earthly gods" (miçieri řmertebi). Further stylistic changes help to
set the toast off from the usual conversation; these include the progressively
specific, three-part list in lines 2–3, "to our earthly gods, to our parents, to our
mother and father."

The third sentence (7–10) contrasts death and life. The expression miçieri
řmertebi (earthly gods) is substantiated in lines 11–15. It is repeated again in
line 16. This line shows again the rhetorical procedure of triple denomination of
the object. In line 17, the group gives a toast reply. The central formula is often
repeated by the audience. The good wishes expressed next in line 18 are also
structured in a three-part list format: "well-being, health and good luck" (kargad
qopna, žanmrteloba vusurvot, bedniereba vusurvot). The one-second pause marks
the time that is given for drinking.

In lines 19 ff., the tamada refers to a popular saying, which is also a typical
procedure. He uses an extravagant, but concrete picture, thereby combining
tradition and creation. From line 23 to 26, he explains the traditional values. The
usage of a three-part grouping can again be observed with the values mediated
by the parents (traditions, customs, moral credo). These lists serve to elaborate

subtopics by way of varied repetition. Triple denomination facilitates both oral composition and memory.

A dialogical dramatization, starring the philosopher Hegel as the main source, then follows in line 29. The small drama is used as the punch line of the toast. The coda is presented in line 33ff., at which point the toast noticeably comes to an end. The closing consists of gaumaržos, expressed by speaker O. Closings are often collaboratively produced. Tamada Badri repeats this formula and another one. Speaker O again repeats the gaumaržos-formula, seconded by everybody present. They all clink glasses and drink.

In the toasts, Georgian value orientations are conspicuously expressed and repeatedly acknowledged. Toasts to participants' parents, "our earthly gods", (miçieri ŕmertebi), are common. In stark contrast to that of western countries, and especially to that of post-war Germany, the Georgian culture of communication emphasizes pathos and religiously flavoured praise of others. To be sure, pathos-laden toasts are not exclusively Georgian; a highly developed culture of toasting can be found throughout the territories of the former Soviet Union. However, the toasts of Russia, Ukraine and Kazakhstan are not so noticeably religious as those of Georgia, which may be traced to the role this genre played during the Soviet era in keeping Georgian religious practices alive outside of the church (Kotthoff 1999a).

5.5.   Comparison of a Russian-Kazakh with a German toast

The toasts which follow below were recorded at a conference on German language and literature at Alma-Ata in 1994. Data 3 is translated from a toast given in German by a Russian scholar of German living in Kazakhstan. Here we see again how the discourse is coloured by pathos-laden strategies. Data 4 illustrates the relative sobriety of a German native offering a comparable toast, more or less within the genre norms of his own culture.

Data 3
K: A Russian scholar of German at a German–Kazakh Conference
 1 K: the (−−) international (−) conference of German scholars (−−)
 2   was (−) for us (−) I don't know how for you (−−)
 3   was for us a (−−) notable, a (−−) a remarkable (−−) event.
 4   (−−) its significance extends far (−) beyond (−−)
 5   the bound of our purely professional,
 6   pedagogic (−−) linguistic (−−) (−−) interests. (−)
 7   linguistics, (−) pedagogy, (−)
 8   these are really only (−) the formal themes of this event.
 9   it was (−) not (−) a (−−) not a simple meeting of German scholars,
10   teachers, (−) of German teachers,

11   (–) who (– –) treat their many problems. (–)
12   no. (–) this meeting (– –) had a greater (–) meaning.
13   (– –) it was an (–) important,
14   it was something more important than a (–) simple meeting.
15   for (–) here (– –) the spiritual forces (–)
16   of differing, (–) powerful cultures came in contact.
17   (–) this meeting has given a strong impulse (–) to our (–) thoughts, (–)
18   our thoughts develop, (–) expand more quickly, (–), more forcefully,
      more intensely (–)
19   our ideas realize themselves (–) in a coherent direction
20   (–) and our hearts (–) now beat (–) as I can (–) well imagine,
21   (–) more in synchrony. (– –) but (–) that does not mean,
22   that we (–) abandon (–) our individual interests,
23   our individual opinions, (–) views and so forth.
24   (– –) no. no. it has to do with the (–) harmony, (–) the synthesis
25   (– –) I mean, (–) the principle (–) will remain (– –) valid,
26   (–) the principle of dialectical unity (–)the SHARED
27 ?: hahahahaha
28 K: and the PARTIcular. (–) then (– –) via German scholarship (–)
29   to the enrichment (–) of different (–) cultures. (– –) thank you.
30   cheers.

Professor K's stylistic elaborations of this short toast speech are more than evident. In particular, the lines 12 to 21 exhalt his theme in a manner that would be hard to imagine as coming from a Western scholar.

12   no. (–) this meeting (– –) had a greater (–) meaning.
13   (– –) it was an (–) important,
14   it was something more important than a (–) simple meeting.
15   for (–) here (– –) the spiritual forces (–)
16   of differing, (–) powerful cultures came in contact.
17   (–) this meeting has given a strong impulse (–) to our (–) thoughts, (–)

The assertion in 20 and following, that as a result of the conference the participants' hearts would synchronize, seems strange and slightly humorous to those from the West.

18   our thoughts develop, (–) expand more quickly, (–), more forcefully,
      more intensely (–)
19   our ideas realize themselves (–) in a coherent direction
20   (–) and our hearts (–) now beat (–) as I can (–) well imagine,
21   (–) more in synchrony.

5.6.   Pathetic keying

A number of rhetorical strategies contribute to the pathos-laden quality of the toast, for example, explicit 'upgrading'.

4   (– –) its significance extends far (–) beyond (– –)
5   the bound of our purely professional,
6   pedagogic (– –) linguistic (– –) (– –) interests. (–)

and the many uses of metonymy, already mentioned.

Pathos certainly is not contextualized exclusively on the verbal level. Like all "keyings" it also makes use of prosodic strategies, like the many pauses and the slow tempo of speech evident throughout data 3.

Keyings are an important subgroup of contextualization which have been as yet little studied. They influence both the meaning of an utterance and its pragmatic function, and they modulate the truth conditions of a discourse, the relation to reality; in humor or in eccentric speech, for example, they are loosened (Kallmeyer 1979); in pathos, as well, but in a different direction. In joking one can play with incongruent double framings, while in pathos the double framing is congruent: value systems (e.g., a current-concrete frame and a general or transcendent one) are brought into alignment. In lines 22–27 the speaker begins with a rather everyday remark ("our thoughts develop") and ends with an eccentric metaphor ("our hearts now beat more in synchrony"). The value of the intensified exchange of thoughts is thus raised.

Kern (1994: 398), one of the few linguists who has written about the "scorned communicative stance" of pathos in recent times, suspects that pathos-laden speech acts undergo, by means of special mechanisms, a paradigmatic mythologizing of everyday affairs. In fact, this is just what Prof. K. attempts. A conference of Germanic scholars, in and of itself no extraordinary occurrence, is elevated to a rare if not impossible (except perhaps in a mythical realm) event: the synchronous beating of hearts. Kern characterizes this second level of the mythological as a diffuse conglomerate of meanings, which can be described here on the level of metaphor, metonomy and rhetorical three-part lists: thoughts develop more strongly, ideas develop more coherently, hearts beat more in synchrony. Pathos presumes a shared frame of values, morals and feelings.

According to Aristotle (Nikomachean Ethics and Rhetoric), pathos touches the emotions (cf. Staiger 1944: 79) and "incites sleepy existence," in Staiger's words (1944: 80).

The Georgian, Russian and Kazakh toasts unify shared, honored objects with expressions of praise. The speakers display high emotional involvement, which is meant to be shared by auditors, and it is affirmed in the clinking of glasses and drinking. The informational value is, in most cases, far less relevant than the evocation of a shared feeling of respect. This is what the ceremony is meant to confirm, renew and strengthen. Those who clothe the objects of shared esteem in the best, most pathos-laden linguistic forms earn the admiration of the entire table society.

By comparison, the toasts of the Germans are usually as compact and to-the-point as the toast given by one of the organizers of the conference in Alma-Ata, which is transcribed and translated below.

Data 4
D: A German philologist
 1 D: the conference (–) was cooperatively prepared and
 2   organized and carried out and brought to a good conclusion,
 3   (–) but let me just say (?briefly?);
 4   (–) the DAAD, (–) the Goethe Institute (–) have worked together,
 5   which functioned on a very good common ground,
 6   (–) we have got a lot,
 7   we have got quite a lot of things (–) set up (––)
 8   and, uh, I'm glad
 9   this conference (–) has been such a great success,
10   it would not (–) have succeeded so well,
11   had not the (–) foreign languages institute
12   (–) contributed (–) in a fundamental way.
13   so for this reason I now want to raise a glass (––)
14   to (–) the future (–) University of Linguistics in Alma Ata.

The philologist D actually only thanks the three organizers who brought the conference together, and then he offers his toast to the host university. He ascribes to it an important role in achieving the conference's success. But he praises neither the university nor its assembled teachers and their families. He does not engage in raising the values of shared goals or achievements. It is thus not surprising that Georgians, Russians and Kazakhs often characterize the speeches of Germans with sober matter-of-factness.

In the West, speeches of praise to persons present are incomparably less frequent, and toasts play a much smaller role in the society's genre household than in the territories of the former Soviet Union. They are, in fact, usual only at certain festivities, like marriages and graduation parties. At the most, two or three are offered, but never a chain of ten to twenty (as is common in Georgia), and even these are often undermined or framed with humour and irony. On German internet pages toasts can be found almost exclusively in humoristic contexts, and even at weddings it is usual for parents and relatives to spice their good wishes for the bride and groom with little jokes and humorously revealing stories. The attitude of pathos is met with scepticism.

In other contexts it is also unusual for Germans to come forth with explicit moral praise for persons present, for example, in the form of "Mr. Giorgi is a wonderful neighbour and a very good person. We love and value Mr. Giorgi greatly!" In Georgia such exclamations are completely normal, not only at the table.

In toasts, values are expressed that can be understood against the background of a specific cultural history. These values are not always shared – and even among Georgians a variety of opinions about them can be found. There are also Georgians who find the rigid toasts too long-winded and who object, above all, to the resulting ample consumption of alcohol.

The positive politeness of the Georgian table culture has a networking character. In contrast to Western cultures, it is oriented to a sphere of contact larger than the individual. It brings esteem to the network in which the vis-à-vis stands, including deceased relatives. To this extent, Georgian politeness has a strong network oriented and even religious component not found in the West.

6.   Handling cultural differences in ritual and style

An often cited dimension of intercultural contact is that the outsider usually interprets foreign behavior, at least at the outset, in the framework of his or her own cultural system (Knapp 2004). In the intercultural situation, the presumed common knowledge about behavioural patterns is problematic (Günthner and Luckmann 2002). In terms of intercultural understanding, misjudgements of culturally differing pragmatic conventions have far greater consequences in their emotional significance than grammatical or lexical mistakes, since they are often ascribed to personality attributes of the speaker, not merely to his or her linguistic knowledge. A further difficulty is that in the realm of politeness it is seldom possible to inquire about how an utterance was meant (Holmes 1995). A possible misinterpretation cannot be clarified on the spot because the rules of politeness forbid going into the unexplicit levels of meaning.

Listening to toasts, differences in values and in the associated structures of social relevance within cultures become visible. These can be brought together under the well-known dichotomy: esteem for interdependence or independence. This does not mean, however, that individuals are forced to choose between the two; in fact, many today are able to move comfortably in both cultural frameworks.

We have seen that, in Georgia and other countries of the former Soviet Union, toasts play a much larger role in communicating honor and respect than they do in western Europe. The toast honors not only the person toasted but his or her entire social network, including deceased relatives. A shared meal thus has an implicit religious dimension in Georgia, which on my view, is a considerable difference to the West. In other countries of the former USSR, as well, a pathetic style that Westeners often smile about is practiced within the genre (as was the case at the conference dinner in Alma Ata). However, for Georgians it was important in the Soviet era to distinguish themselves from other Soviet peoples, and one possibility to communicate this distinction was achieved by including a religious dimension in their toasts.

In the data presented above, we find that a high degree of formality, pathos, the explicit communication of values such as 'clan orientation', expressed in religious undertones and references to transcendent reality, as well as explicit praise of the guests, are dimensions that characterize the Georgian toasts by their presence, and the German toast by their absence.

In Georgia the communciation of honor (pativi) is ominpresent in everyday life and is often directly expressed: I give you pativi. On my view, this is a special case of "positive politeness" as it has been described by Brown and Levinson (1987) and debated by Matsumoto (1988), Foley (1997), Spencer-Oatey (2000a) and others. Giving and receiving pativi takes place not primarily in reference to the individual but to his or her social network. Morally laden networks of social obligation play a large role in all aspects of everyday life. Displays of honor, esteem and deference are part of the give and take of extended families. Thus, the dichotomy of collectivism and individualism often cited in intercultural research is quite plausible. However, some researches, like Hofstede (1991), overlook the need to "do" both, in the sense of ethnomethodology. One should not invoke such concepts in order to essentialize a difference, but rather show how they acquire relevance within a community of practice (which might for some activities extend to the level of a nation), bearing in mind that the dichotomy does not characterize societies absolutely, and that mixed forms are likely to be found.

Goffman, too, has emphasized that the Western concept of "face" is oriented to the concept of the individual, with his particular freedom of action and his personal need for acknowledgment, not as a concept of the collective. Cultures of the East did not, in general, become collective just by virtue of the socialist phases some of them experienced. Rather, one important historical factor was that they did not develop a Weberian "protestant ethic," which in many Western societies brought in an enhanced dose of individualism (Hahn 1994).

In closing, let me summarize some observations that result from the ethnographic study of ritual and style in German–Georgian situations with guests, particularly at meals. In recent times both cultures have had considerable contact, and it is not necessary to expect that their different behavioural norms must lead to irritation and tensions. As has been noted by Bührig and ten Thije (2006), in intercultural encounters a wide variety of perceptions, from positive enrichment to rejection, can be found, varying according to context as well as the type and length of the encounter. In the points below I continue to speak of relations between Georgians and Germans, but in fact most observations would hold for encounters between individuals from the former Soviet Union and those from Western cultures.

Reciprocal enrichment
Germans often express mild amazement at the Georgians' rhetorical prowess and gifts for social observation that they reveal in their toasts. Georgians, on the other hand, enjoy the informality of Western parties and the relative modesty of the hosts.

Partial lack of understanding
When invited to gatherings with Georgian families, Germans often find displeasure in the formalized drinking, in the way that toasts interrupt what, for them, would be the normal flow of conversation, and in the repetition of a small range of themes in the toasts. Georgians object that, in Germany, they are given too little opportunity to honor appropriately the other guests and their families.

Adaptation to the styles of the others
Visitors from the West must learn to formulate toasts in Georgia, Russia, Kazakhstan, Ukraine, etc., while Georgians, Russians and Kazakhs, etc. in Western countries must learn to be flexible in their use of the genre and to find pleasure in practicing informal small talk.

Instances of rejection
Visitors, especially from the West, often object to the long toasts of the Georgians and the accompanying high consumption of alcohol.

Instances of confirming stereotypes
These differing social practices are often cited when Georgians characterize Germans as too sober and dry, or when Germans complain that Georgians are too ceremonious, fussy and long-winded.

Flexible "we" and "you" constructions
Mixed German-Georgian groups in Germany or in Georgia construct situations with guests in a relatively Western, informal style, or in a style that is more "Georgian" and formal, whereby it must be noted that neither the Germans nor the Georgians fully change their style and adopt that of the other group. When Georgians living in Germany invite other Georgians as guests, normally all participants confirm their shared Georgian identity with toasts. They practice "doing being Georgian" (see Spreckels and Kotthoff in this volume). Likewise, Germans meeting only other Germans in Georgia offer no toasts in unmarked situations. However, arising intercultures such as mixed networks also form a "we" from the conglomeration of styles they comprise.

Notes

1. The transliterations from Georgian generally follow scholarly conventions described, for example, in Fähnrich (1987). However, I notate the voiced post-velar fricative as "Ṭ".
2. Such concepts as "Western" and "Oriental" are, of course, vague and problematic, but they are used here to suggest that some of the cultural differences described here make sense for large cultural areas which go beyond a community of practice.

References

Auer, Peter and Aldo di Luzio (eds.)
  1992   *The Contextualization of Language*. Amsterdam: Benjamins.
Bourdieu, Pierre
  1990   *The Logic of Practice*. Stanford: Stanford University Press.
Brown, Penelope and Stephen Levinson
  1987   *Politeness. Some Universals in Language Usage*. Cambridge: Cambridge University Press.
Bührig, Christin and Ja ten Thije
  2006   *Beyond Misunderstanding. The Linguistic Reconstruction of Intercultural Communication*. Amsterdam: Benjamins.
Chatwin, Mary Ellen
  1997   *Socio-cultural Transformation and Foodways in the Republic of Georgia*. New York: Nova Science Publishers.
Collins, Randall
  2004   *Interaction Ritual Chains*. Princeton: Princeton University Press.
Cook-Gumperz, Jenny and John Gumperz
  1976   Context in children's speech. In: *Papers on Language and Context*. (Working Papers No. 46.) Berkeley, CA: Language Behaviour Research Laboratory.
Corder, Saskia and Miriam Meyerhoff
  this volume   *Communities of practice in the analysis of intercultural communication*. Chapter 21
Douglas, Mary
  1982   *Natural Symbols*. New York: Pantheon.
Eckert, Penelope
  2000   *Lingustic Variation as Social Practice*. London: Blackwell.
Erickson, Frederic and Geoffrey Shultz
  1982   *The Counselor as Gate Keeper: Social Interaction in Interviews*. New York: Academic Press.
Fähnrich, Heinz
  1987   *Grammatik der georgischen Sprache*. Jena: Universitätsverlag.
Foley, William A.
  1997   *Anthropological Linguistics. An Introduction*. Malden and Oxford: Blackwell.

Freud, Sigmund
1985   *Der Witz und seine Beziehung zum Unbewußten.* Frankfurt: Fischer. First
        published Vienna [1905].
Geertz, Clifford
1973   *The Interpretation of Cultures.* New York: Basic Books.
Geertz, Clifford
1983   *Local Knowledge.* New York: Basic Books.
Goffman, Erving
1967   *Interaction Ritual.* Garden City, NY: Doubleday.
Goffman, Erving
1974   *Frame Analysis. An Essay on the Organizations of Experience.* New York:
        Harper & Row.
Goffman, Erving
1981   The Interaction Order. *American Sociological Review* 48: 1–17.
Gumperz, John
1979   Cross-cultural communication. In: John Gumperz, Tony Jupp and Celia
        Roberts, *Crosstalk.* London: BBC. Reprinted (2003) in Roxy Harris and
        Ben Rampton (eds.), *The Language, Ethnicity and Race Reader*, 267–276.
        London: Routledge.
Gumperz, John and Cook-Gumperz, Jenny
this volume Discourse, cultural diversity and communication: a linguistic anthropologi-
        cal perspective. Chapter 2
Günthner, Susanne
1993   *Diskursstrategien in der interkulturellen Kommunikation. Analysen deutsch–
        chinesischer Gespräche.* Tübingen: Niemeyer.
Günthner, Susanne
2000a   Höflichkeitspraktiken in der interkulturellen Kommunikation – am Bsp.
        chinesisch–deutscher Interaktionen. In: Heinz-Helmut Lüger (ed.), *Stile
        der Höflichkeit*, 295–313. Frankfurt: Lang.
Günthner, Susanne
2000b   Argumentation and resulting problems in the negotiation of rapport in a
        German–Chinese conversation. In: Helen Spencer-Oatey (ed.), *Culturally
        Speaking. Managing Rapport through Talk across Cultures*, 217–240. Lon-
        don/New York: Continuum.
Günthner, Susanne
this volume *Intercultural communication and the relevance of cultural specific reper-
        toires of communicative genres.* Chapter 7
Günthner, Susanne and Thomas Luckmann
2002   Wissensasymmetrien in interkultureller Kommunikation. In: Helga Kott-
        hoff (ed.), *Kultur(en) im Gespräch*, 213–245. Tuebingen: Narr.
Hahn, Alois
1994   Theorien zur Entstehung der europäischen Moderne. *Philosophische
        Rundschau* Heft 3–4 31: 178–202.
Hofstede, Geert H.
1991   *Cultures and Organizations, Software of the Mind.* New York: McGraw-
        Hill.
Holmes, Janet
1995   *Women, Men and Politeness.* London: Longman.

Hymes, Dell
1974   Ways of speaking. In: Richard Bauman and Joel Sherzer (eds.), *Explorations in the Ethnography of Speaking*, 433–451. Cambridge: Cambridge University Press.

Irvine, Judith
1979   Formality and informality in communicative events. *American Anthropologist* 81(4): 773–790. Reprinted (2001) in Alessandro Duranti (ed.), *Linguistic Anthropology*, 189–208. London: Blackwell.

Kallmeyer, Werner
1979   "(Expressif) Eh ben dis donc, hein' pas bien'". Zur Beschreibung von Exaltation als Interaktionsmodalität. In: Rolf Kloepfer (ed.), *Bildung und Ausbildung in der Romania*, 549–568. München: Fink.

Kern, Peter Christoph
1994   Pathos. Vorläufige Überlegungen zu einer verpönten Kommunikationshaltung. In: Heinrich Löffler, Karlheinz Jakob and Bernhard Kelle (eds.), *Texttyp, Sprechergruppe, Kommunikationsbereich. Studien zur deutschen Sprache in Geschichte und Gegenwart*, 396–411. Berlin: de Gruyter.

Knapp, Karlfried
2004   Interkulturelle Kommunikation. In: Karlfried Knapp et al. (eds.), *Angewandte Linguistik*, 409–431. Tübingen: Francke.

Knoblauch, Hubert and Helga Kotthoff (eds.)
2001   *Verbal Art across Cultures*. Tuebingen: Narr.

Kotthoff, Helga
1991a   Lernersprachliche und interkulturelle Ursachen für kommunikative Irritationen. *Linguistische Berichte* 135: 375–397.

Kotthoff, Helga
1991b   Der Tamada gibt am Tisch den Ton an. Tafelsitten, Trinksprüche und Geschlechterrollen im kaukasischen Georgien. In: Susanne Günthner and Helga Kotthoff (eds.), *Von fremden Stimmen. Weibliches und männliches Sprechen im Kulturvergleich*, 229–261. Frankfurt: Suhrkamp.

Kotthoff, Helga
1995   The social semiotics of Georgian toast performances. Oral genre as cultural activity. *Journal of Pragmatics* 24: 353–380.

Kotthoff, Helga
1998   Irony, Quotation, and Other Forms of Staged Intertextuality. In: *InList-Arbeitspapier* No. 5. University of Potsdam. Reprinted (2002) in Carl Graumann and Werner Kallmeyer (eds.), *Perspectivity in Discourse*. 201–233. Amsterdam: Benjamins.

Kotthoff, Helga
1999a   Mahlzeiten mit Moral: Georgische Trinksprüche zwischen Pathos und Poesie. In: Jörg Bergmann and Thomas Luckmann (eds.), *Kommunikative Konstruktion von Moral*, Volume 2: *Von der Moral zu den Moralen*, 13–50. Opladen: Westdeutscher Verlag.

Kotthoff, Helga
1999b   Coherent keying in conversational humour: Contextualising joint fictionalisation. In: Wolfram Bublitz, Uta Lenk and Eija Ventola (eds.), *Coherence in Spoken and Written Discourse*, 125–150. Amsterdam: Benjamins.

Leach, Edmund
1976   *Rethinking Anthropology.* New York: Athlone Press.
Marra, Meredith and Holmes, Janet
this volume Humour across cultures: Joking in the multicultural workplace. Chapter 8.
Matsumoto, Y.
1988   Reexamination of the universality of face: politeness phenomena in Japanese. *Journal of Pragmatics* 11: 721–736.
Mauss, Marcel
1978   Die Gabe. In: Marcel Mauss (ed.), *Soziologie und Anthropologie*, Bd. 2, 9–114. Berlin: Ullstein. First published Paris [1925].
Menz, Florian
2000   *Selbst- und Fremdorganisation im Diskurs. Interne Kommunikation in Wirtschaftsunternehmen.* Wiesbaden: Deutscher Universitätsverlag.
Sandig, Barbara and Margret Selting
1997   Discourse styles. In: Teun van Dijk (ed.), *Discourse as Structure and Process: A Multidisciplinary Introduction*, 138–156. London: Sage.
Shweder, Richard and E. Bourne
1984   Does the concept of person vary cross-culturally? In: Richard Shweder and Robert A. LeVine (eds.), *Culture Theory: Essays on Mind, Self and Emotion*, 158–199. Cambridge: Cambridge University Press.
Sifianou, Maria
1992   *Politeness Phenomena in England and Greece: A Cross-Cultural Approach.* Oxford: Oxford University Press.
Soeffner, Hans-Georg
1991   Zur Soziologie des Symbols und des Rituals. In: Jürgen Oelkers and Klaus Wegenast (eds.), *Das Symbol – Brücke des Verstehens*, 63–81. Stuttgart/Berlin/Köln: Kohlhammer.
Spencer-Oatey, Helen
2000a   Rapport management: A framework for analysis. In: Helen Spencer-Oatey (ed.), *Culturally Speaking: Managing Rapport through Talk across Cultures*, 11–47. London: Continuum.
Spencer-Oatey, Helen
2000b   *Culturally Speaking: Managing Rapport through Talk across Cultures.* London: Continuum.
Spreckels, Janet and Kotthoff, Helga
this volume Communicating Identity in Intercultural Communication. Chapter 20.
Staiger, Emil
1944   Vom Pathos. Ein Beitrag zur Poetik. *Trivium* 2: 77–92.
Tannen, Deborah
1984   *Conversational Style.* Norwood, NJ: Ablex.
Werlen, Iwar
2001   Rituelle Muster in Gesprächen. In: Klaus Brinker et al. (eds.), *Text- und Gesprächslinguistik*, 1263–1278. Berlin: de Gruyter.
Yamada, Haru
1997   *Different Games, Different Rules: Why Americans and Japanese Misunderstand Each Other.* Oxford: Oxford University Press.

10. Lingua franca communication in multiethnic contexts

Christiane Meierkord

1. Introduction

Lingua francas are languages used for communication between speakers who do not share either of their mother tongues. It is characteristic of lingua franca communication that the constellations of speakers interacting in the lingua franca are ever changing. For example, English may be used for communication between a German and a Japanese, but also between a Xhosa and a white speaker of Afrikaans in South Africa. The community of lingua franca users is, thus, always a heterogeneous one, comprised of individuals from a vast number of different linguistic and cultural backgrounds.

Against this definition, lingua franca communication has been established as one of three types of intercultural communication by Knapp (1991), alongside 'foreign language communication' – interactions between native and non-native speakers, and "mediated communication" – interactions conducted with the help of an interpreter (see Spencer-Oatey and Xing in this volume). Knapp discusses lingua franca communication as involving an increased number of communicative conventions and linguistic signs, and as, thus, resulting in the participants' heightened insecurity as to what constitutes appropriate behavior in the interaction. Other scholars have chosen not to approach lingua franca communication as inherently problematic. Instead, they assume that these interactions result in the construction of a new, in-between, third culture (e.g. Koole and ten Thije 1994). The first part of this article relates lingua franca communication to intercultural communication, language contact, and multilingualism, pointing out the differences from, and similarities with, other forms of intercultural communication. This discussion will be combined with an account of some of the languages used as lingua francas.

Many languages serve as lingua francas for *inter*national communication, either on a global scale (e.g. English) or in a somewhat delineated area (e.g. Russian in Eastern Europe). But several languages also act as *intra*national lingua francas in countries which have a large number of indigenous languages. Often these nations were founded during the era of colonization, and the language used as a lingua franca is commonly the language of the former colonizing power (e.g. English in Nigeria or India). In other countries, such as Papua New Guinea or Haiti, pidgins and creoles developed, following the continuing contact with the European languages (English-based Tok Pisin or French-based

Haitian Creole). In all of the above countries, as Mesthrie et al. (2000: 38) point out, "a speech community comprises people who are in habitual contact with each other by means of speech which involves either a shared language variety or shared ways of interpreting the different language varieties commonly used in the area." Thus, lingua franca communication *within* a particular country seems to differ from international lingua franca communication. *Intra*national lingua franca communication may take place within one speech community sharing linguistic codes and interactional conventions. However, if the use of an intranational lingua franca merely implies an instrumental use of the language, participants in *intra*national lingua franca communication may not be fully aware of the communicative conventions holding in their interlocutors' cultures either. The second part of this chapter will discuss the different strategies which countries choose to deal with their multilingual and multicultural society, and how the use of a lingua franca is related to these strategies.

The third part of the article will present South Africa as a specific case of a multilingual nation.[1] The country has eleven national languages, although the 1991 census[2] reported that more than 23 different languages were spoken in the country.[3] Although English and Afrikaans serve as the major lingua francas in the country, cultural differences are reflected in different discourse conventions such as the construction of narratives or argumentative texts, or in different politeness conventions (Ndoleriire 2000, Chick 1995). This seems to be due to the apartheid system's policy of keeping individual ethnicities apart, both in education as well as in residential areas. Contact between the different languages and cultures was therefore restricted. The chapter will eventually focus on the lingua franca English. It will report on research that has been conducted on intercultural communication in English as a lingua franca in South Africa and relate those findings to the status which is attributed to English by its second language users.

2.   The nature of lingua franca communication

In 1953, the UNESCO defined a lingua franca as "a language which is used habitually by people whose mother tongues are different in order to facilitate communication between them" (UNESCO 1953). This definition embraces two different contexts: the use of a language which is the mother tongue to neither of the speakers involved, or a language which is the mother tongue to some of the participants but not to others. The definition furthermore comprises an infinite number of communicative purposes or contexts in which the lingua franca acts as a facilitator. As such, the definition is in contrast to earlier ones, which were often based on the original meaning of the term *lingua franca*. This initially referred to the pidgin Lingua Franca, which emerged as a language of trade and commerce in the Mediterranean from the 15th century until the 19th (Wans-brough 1996). Since Lingua Franca was a trade language, the term *lingua franca*, when eventually extended to other languages used for communication across linguistic boundaries, was understood as synonymous to *auxiliary language* (Samarin 1987), and the use of a language as a lingua franca was strongly associated with its performing specific purposes.

Samarin (1987) distinguishes three types of lingua francas: natural, pidginized, and planned languages can and do serve as lingua francas. An example of a planned lingua franca is Esperanto, which was designed to enable world-wide communication, but which today mainly serves to unite the community of Esperantists (Fiedler 2002). In this context, Esperanto is used as a spoken language in interpersonal communication and for radio broadcasts. Yet there is also a considerable body of literature, translated and original, as well as the community's own newspaper.

Whereas a planned language such as Esperanto has been engineered and then been spread across a wider community, pidginized languages emerged out of communicative necessity. As Mesthrie et al. (2000: 280) point out, they "arise when groups of people who do not speak a common language come into contact with each other. [...] The need for the rapid development of a means of communication results in a relatively simple type of language which may draw on the languages of the groups involved." Pidgins emerged as lingua francas mainly in the Pacific, in Asia, in the Caribbean, and on the West African coasts. Diverse social conditions favored the development of pidgins, such as slavery (the cause for most Caribbean pidgins and creoles), trade, European settlements, war, and labor migration (for example giving rise to *Gastarbeiterdeutsch*). Many of these pidgins existed for a short time only and never stabilized. By definition, pidgins have no native speakers. However, this does not generally imply that they are used for restricted purposes only, as section 2.2 will explain.

Pidgins emerged whenever individuals did *not* share a language for communication. But frequently speakers can resort to a third, already existing, language which, however, is not the mother tongue of all of them. For example, a Turkish and a Chinese businesswoman may conduct their negotiations in English, if neither of them has sufficient command of the other's mother tongue. This type of lingua franca communication in a natural language has been at the centre of research during the last two decades or so. Largely, however, research has concentrated on the use of English as a lingua franca (see Knapp and Meier-kord 2002, Lesnyák 2004, Pölzl 2003, Seidlhofer 2000, Smit 2003).

Lingua franca communication, then, involves the use of a language which most often is the mother tongue of neither of the speakers participating in the interaction. But no matter whether its speakers are native or non-native speakers, lingua francas have come – due to increased migration and interlingual relationships – to be employed for a variety of functions, which extend well beyond serving for business communication. As Knapp and Meierkord (2002) point out, the different languages used as lingua francas fulfill a range of different functions. Some lingua francas serve highly specialized purposes and function only in very restricted contexts such as airtraffic control. However, others are employed for government purposes, as medium of instruction in schools and tertiary education (Smit 2003) and at universities, and they also play an important role in intimate, personal interactions and as a medium for creative writing.

2.1.   Lingua francas for restricted purposes

Specific, restricted forms of a number of natural languages have been designed to codify and facilitate communication for specific purposes. Basic English (Ogden 1930) is a simplified form of English, engineered for easy international use. Based on a vocabulary of only 850 items and a few straightforward grammatical rules, it a presents an attempt to provide people with an international second language which will take as little of their time as possible to learn. It is used by some aircraft manufacturers and other international businesses to write manuals and to communicate. A Basic English version of the Bible was published in 1965 by Cambridge University Press, and today an online-version in Basic English is available at www.biblekeeper.com/bible-in-english/index.html. The relevance of Ogden's ideas for modern English language teaching is discussed in Seidlhofer (2002).

Ogden's endeavor to simplify English has been adapted by a number of companies and organizations. *Airspeak* is a form of English used for communication between pilots and the airports, and *Seaspeak* enables ship-to-shore communication. *Seaspeak* has recently been used as a basis for a European project aiming at facilitating police interaction (Johnson et al. 1993 and www.prolingua.co.uk). In 1971, the *Caterpillar Tractor Company* developed *Fundamental English*, a 900-words, form of English used to compile product documentation for its international customers. And in 1979, the *Douglas Aircraft Company* devised a 2000-word dictionary it uses for its technical manuals. Similar to *Basic English*, these forms do not contain synonyms or idioms. Sentences are short and simple. As Heuler (1989) points out, many companies have since followed suit and developed their own simplified form of English.

In addition to international companies, some of the broadcast stations aiming at an international listenership have also designed reduced forms of English. For example, *Special English* is a simplified version of English used by the *Voice of America*. Started as an experiment on October 19, 1959, *Special English* today is a program broadcast daily, which addresses "people who are not fluent in English". It uses a core vocabulary of 1500 words. Sentences are short and simple, and they contain only one idea which is generally expressed in the active voice. As *The Voice of America* itself points out: "The goal was to communicate by radio in clear and simple English with people whose native language was not English." [4]

All the above forms of English clearly classify as what Hüllen (1992) has called "languages of communication" (Kommunikationssprachen) as opposed to "languages of identification" (Identifikationssprachen). As a language of communication, in Hüllen's terms, a language is used as a culture-free code, and its individual linguistic signs perform referential functions only (Hüllen 1992: 305). Several authors (e.g. Knapp 1987, 1991, or Lesnyák 2004) hold that "language use in lingua franca situations is limited to functional areas, thus the only demands on speakers are those of intelligibility and function" (Lesnyák 2004: 20). But recently, there has been some debate about whether a language used as a lingua franca can also serve expressive purposes, or, in Hüllen's terms, whether it qualifies as a language of identification under certain circumstances.

Given the extended function of lingua francas, one can hardly hold that lingua franca communication is a culture-free form of interaction. From within the concept of culture as mutually created through interaction (Sherzer 1987), culture in lingua franca communication has been seen as disursively constructed and as having a hybrid character resulting from the different participants' contributing towards it. For the lingua franca English, Hüllen (1982: 86) estimates that interaction in this language will involve the emergence of secondary speech communities (as opposed to macro-societal speech communities), characterized by their own temporary communicative conventions, when he assumes the following: "With every Italian and German, Dutch and Frenchman who uses English as a mediating language, there arises a unique and genuine speech community where the roles and the rules of mutual understanding have to first be established." Hüllen seems to conceive of an inter-community which develops a form of inter-culture of its own, at least with respect to its communicative conventions (see Corder and Meyerhoff in this volume). This idea of an "inter" or "third" culture has occupied research in different frameworks for the last two decades or so (e.g. Koole and ten Thije 1994). However, there is as yet no conclusive evidence for the establishment and existence of such a third culture and how it surfaces in the verbal behavior of lingua franca users.

2.2.   Lingua francas for expressive purposes

The idea that any language, and thus also a language used as a lingua franca, could be culture-free is one which we can hardly imagine if the language is not only used in contexts such as the ones just mentioned above. Increased migration, both compulsory and voluntary, has resulted in an incline of those contexts in which the use of a lingua franca extends well beyond the transactional function of using a language. Migration does not only result in trade and international business but also in interpersonal relations.

Generally, lingua francas of all three types mentioned above allow for the communication of content which goes beyond the mere exchange of transactional phrases used to conduct business. Tok Pisin, a pidgin / creole which has been spoken in Papua New Guinea for more than 120 years (Mühlhäusler 1986), is one of the lingua francas which started out as jargons used by traders in the Pacific region. Today Tok Pisin is one of the official languages[5] used in Papua New Guinea, a country with, currently, 823 living languages.[6] Tok Pisin is used for administrative purposes, in education, and there is a Newspaper (*Wantok*) as well as a broadcast station using Tok Pisin as their medium. The pidgin is also used in interethnic marriages and the offspring of these couples speak Tok Pisin in a creolized form.

Several lingua francas have also developed considerable bodies of literature, both prose and poetry. Meeuwis (2002) discusses the works of the poet Kayo Lampe who uses Lingala, a creole spoken in central Africa, for the poems which he writes and publishes in, and for, the Congolese diaspora community in Belgium. This is in stark contrast to the majority of Congolese writers, who overwhelmingly have chosen French as their working language. Meeuwis also points out that Lingala has come to be used by the majority of the Congolese immigrants as the "lingua franca at levels of informal communication in the diaspora" (2002: 31).[7] With increased access to the internet, individuals have also started to utilize this medium for the dissemination of prose and poetry. For example, writers from across the African continent have found a platform to publish their creative writing across speech community boundaries at www.crossingborders-africanwriting.org. This project aims at opening up "shared creative and cultural space. Our emphasis will be on building a new international community of writers, on new work for a new world." Even the international Esperanto community uses the engineered lingua franca as an expressive medium. As Fiedler (2006) points out, a number of authors have chosen to publish both lyric poetry as well as prose fiction, resulting in a body of approximately ten thousand pieces of original literature in Esperanto.

The discussions of the cultural content of lingua franca communication mainly investigate discourse conventions. However, lingua franca communication is also interaction across speakers of different forms of the language used as the lingua franca. As such it is a form of language contact. In addition to regarding lingua franca communication as involving interaction across ethnicities or cultures, discussions of lingua franca communication also need to take into account that its speakers command at least two languages, albeit not necessarily at equally high levels of proficiency (Meierkord 2005). Thus, lingua franca communication implies language contact both in each individual, bilingual or multilingual, speaker as well as across the speakers participating in an interaction conducted via a lingua franca.

With regard to the first aspect, a large number of studies have documented that bilingual speech is characterized by transfer from one language into the other, by borrowing of lexical material, and by code-switching between the different languages. At the societal level, bilingualism frequently results in diglossia, i.e. the use of two or more different languages or language varieties throughout a single speech community, where each of them performs distinct social functions. The following chapter will discuss a number of natural languages used as lingua francas.

3.   Lingua francas in multiethnic settings

The need for a lingua franca for communication across language boundaries is most easily visible in settings at the international level. International communication involves too many different languages as to always be conducted in the speakers' mother tongues. For practical reasons, participants in international interactions therefore usually choose to communicate in one of the more widespread languages. However, an increasing number of nations comprise speakers of different mother tongues, and as a result a lingua franca is used to enable interaction across speech community boundaries within these countries.

3.1.   International and intranational lingua francas

Most ethnic languages which have come to be used as lingua francas do so either at a regional or at an international level, or for both purposes. Languages frequently used as international lingua francas are Arabic, Chinese, English, French, Russian and Spanish (Meierkord 2006). Their use well beyond their original speech communities is characterized by certain changes to the language: speakers seem to use fewer culture-bound vocabulary items, idioms and speech acts. A number of scholars have taken this to be an indicator of a newly emerging form of English. For example, Crystal (1997) talks about *World Standard Spoken English*, and earlier Quirk (1985) discussed *Nuclear English*. Both are conceived as "neutral" forms of English, not associated with a particular culture or region. However, recent findings in lingua franca communication research indicate that interactions conducted in a lingua franca at an international level are rather characterized by strategies to adapt the English language to the needs emerging in a particular context. For example, Pölzl and Seidlhofer (2006) reveal that speakers insert mainly formulaic phrases of their mother tongues or of the language dominating in their immediate environment, or "habitat" as the authors call it. Thus, Jordanian speakers incorporate the Arabic listener response and discourse marker *ya^{c}ni* into their English utterances. Besides the "habitat", or situational context, groups using English as a lingua franca may also develop their very own discourse conventions. In another study, Pölzl (2003) discusses how for example both Austrian as well as Japanese speakers meeting in Cairo, Egypt, use Japanese and German toasting formulae *prost* and *kanpai* ('Cheers') when interacting in English as a lingua franca. This can not be explained by the "habitat", which is Egypt. Rather the participants in the interaction seem to appreciate each others' cultural identities.

Examples for regionally used lingua francas are, for example, Swahili, which is used in Kenya and Uganda, Sango used in the Central African Republic, or Putonghua, the Mandarin Chinese variety which serves in the People's Republic of China. These lingua francas have also been called 'languages of wider communication' (Stewart 1968). Unfortunately, there is to date no research into the linguistic characteristics of lingua franca communication conducted in these languages. The *intra*national use of lingua francas has often been the result of colonialization, which resulted in arbitrarily drawn nation boundaries that paid little respect to the citizens' mother tongues. As a result, peoples speaking different languages came to constitute one nation, and a language was required to allow for administration of the country as well as for interaction between the different peoples. Many of the post-colonial states are multilingual to such an extent that, for practical reasons, one or several lingua francas need to be decided on to guarantee the feasibility of administration, education etc. The indigenous languages frequently existed in non-standardized oral forms only, and no writing system had been devised for them at the time when a decision for one or more official languages was taken.

When two or more languages are used within one country, this implies bilingualism, both at the level of the society as well as at the individual level. Kachru describes bilingualism as the "linguistic behaviour of the members of a speech community which alternately uses two, three or more languages depending on the situation and function" (Kachru 1986: 159). His quote indicates that the language serving as a lingua franca in these settings is usually chosen to perform specific functions such as the ones outlined above. Furthermore, it is often given the status of the country's national or official language. A national language is "a language which serves the entire area of a nation rather than a regional or ethnic subdivision" (Eastman 2001: 657). In contrast, official languages are those languages used within a nation to conduct the business of its government. As such, there can be regionally used co-official languages.

The following sections discuss a selection of multilingual nations to illustrate the different approaches taken by individual countries.

3.2.   Language policy and intercultural communication in
multilingual settings

Societal multilingualism has many reasons. Recently, increased migration has
led to a mixture of cultures and languages within nations which had previously
been conceived as being largely monolingual[8], e.g. Iceland. Originally, such
countries had established their political boundaries such as to comprise basically one speech community, often confined by geographical boundaries such as
the sea in the case of Iceland, or rivers and mountains in many other cases. However, the historical development of numerous countries was such as to eventually involve the integration of more than one speech community within one
nation. A selection of these is listed in table 1.

Table 1. Language use in a selection of multilingual nations

country	living languages	national language(s)	official language(s)
Australia	231	English	English
Canada	85	English, French	English, French
India	415	Hindi	Hindi, English, Bengali, Telugu, Marathi, Tamil, Urdu, Gujarati, Malaya-lam, Kannada, Oriya, Punjabi, Assamese, Kashmiri, Sindhi, and Sanskrit
Nigeria	510	Edo, Efik, Adamawa Fulfulde, Hausa, Idoma, Igbo, Central Kanuri, Yoruba, English	Hausa, Igbo, Yoruba, English
Switzerland	12	French, German, Italian, Romansh	French, German, Italian

Multilingualism in the individual countries listed in the table has different reasons depending on the socio-historic circumstances of the individual nation's
course of foundation. But all the nations face the problem of having to decide on
a language policy, determining which languages will be chosen to govern and
administer the country and to provide education to its citizens, but also to account for the multilingual society.

Switzerland, or rather the Swiss Confederation, dates back to 1291, when the people of the valley of Uri, the democracy of the valley of Schwyz, and the community of the Lower Valley of Unterwalden decided to succor each other in loose alliance. These three cantons were joined by others in the subsequent years, eventually yielding what is present-day Switzerland when a modern federal state was founded in 1848. Against the background of the country's history, its constitution is designed to balance the interests of the state as a whole with the interests of the individual cantons. As a result, Switzerland acknowledges four languages as national languages, although Romansh is only spoken in the trilingual canton of Graubünden, by approximately 0.5 % of the Swiss population. However, Romansh is not an official language, but Romansh speakers have a right to address the authorities in their mother tongue.[9] Interestingly, neither of the four national languages serves as a nation-wide lingua franca today. Rather, many cantons have opted for English as the first compulsory foreign language to be taught in schools. And as a result, younger Swiss citizens frequently have a better command of English than of the other languages spoken in their country.

Canada and Australia have a different history, characterized by the migration of large British English speaking populations. Originally a British settlement, Canada became self-governing in 1876. It has since been a country attracting immigrants from all over the world, and this is reflected in its population as well as in the linguistic situation pertaining to the country. The *Ethnologue* currently lists 85 living languages spoken in Canada. These include languages as diverse as Dutch, Punjabi, Spanish, Ukrainian, Arabic, and Chinese, all of which have considerable native speaker communities of several hundred thousand individuals. However, the number of national languages in Canada is limited to two: English and French, which is due to the country's history as both a British and a French settlement and the size of the English and French speaking communities.

Similar to Canada, Australia has been an immigration country for centuries. The Australian government presents a very clear outline of the country's multicultural policy. With regard to the languages spoken by its immigrants, Australia has chosen to designate English as its sole national language. As the government itself declares in its section on Australian multicultural policy on its official website,

> All Australians are expected to have an overriding loyalty to Australia and its people, and to respect the basic structures and principles underwriting our democratic society. These principles are: the Constitution, parliamentary democracy, freedom of speech and religion, *English as the national language*, the rule of law, acceptance and equality.[10]

The *Ethnologue* presently lists 235 living languages spoken in Australia. Most of these are Aboriginal languages, which, however, have only very small numbers of mother tongues speakers (the total figure for all speakers of Aboriginal languages is 47,000, according the *Ethnologue*). German, Italian, Arabic and Chinese are the immigrant languages which have the largest speech communities. In Canada and Australia the fact that these were originally British settlements with British citizens and their descendants eventually outnumbering the Aboriginal population is the key factor determining the language policy in these nations. This is not the case in the following two countries: India and Nigeria.

In post-colonial countries, a number of factors have influenced the decisions to choose a European language as the official language. Webb and Kembo-Sure (2000: 11) point out that nation-building is one of these factors, since the process necessitates the choice of an integrative language.

> As a result, political leaders usually decide to promote the ex-colonial language of the pre-independence era (English, French, or Portuguese) as the 'language of national integration', arguing that these languages are socio-culturally neutral and do not have the potential for stirring up conflict, as they are nobody's primary language.

For India, the *Ethnologue* states that approximately 415 languages are in daily use. India's constitution designates Hindi as one of its official languages, together with English. The official language act of 1963 (as amended in 1967) makes provisions for the use of Hindi as the official language of the country. At the same time it allows for the use of the English language alongside Hindi for all the official purposes of the Union for which it was being used immediately before that day and for the transaction of business in Parliament.[11] Also, the languages act makes provisions for the use of additional official languages in the individual states of India. The national languages of the country are Assamese, Bengali, Bodo, Dogri, Gujarati, Hindi, Kannada, Kashmiri, Konkani, Maithili, Malayalam, Manipuri, Marathi, Nepali, Oriya, Punjabi, Sanskrit, Santhali, Sindhi, Tamil, Telugu, Urdu. English has been kept as an associate official language far beyond the originally intended period, i.e. up to 1965, due to the Dravidian south's opposition against Hindi. But English not only serves as a linguistic tool for administering the country. It also functions as a lingua franca for social interaction across speech communities and in education.

Just as India, Nigeria is another example of a post-colonial nation which embraces a large number of ethnicities and, thus, of individual speech communities. The *Ethnologue* currently lists 510 living languages for Nigeria.[12] Hausa, Igbo, and Yoruba are the three indigenous languages which have large speech communities in the country. Their importance is reflected in the fact that these three languages are co-official languages in Nigeria. The Nigerian constitution makes provisions for the use of languages in the National Assembly and the House of Assembly. It gives clear preference to the English language, for example in article 55, which states: "The business of the National Assembly shall be conducted in English …." However, the constitution also states that Hausa, Ibo and Yoruba shall be used "when adequate arrangements have been made".[13]

As the above illustrations indicate, individual countries have found very different ways of dealing with their multiethnic and multilingual population. In all countries, the multilingual situation and the special status given to those languages which serve as the national lingua francas has resulted in a situation which involves language contact and intercultural communication. Speakers of different mother tongues and from different speech communities, potentially each with their own communicative conventions, frequently interact in a variety of social situations. The next section describes the situation pertaining to South Africa to illustrate in more detail the sociolinguistic status which English enjoys as an intranational lingua franca and the resulting issues of intercultural communication.

4.   A case study: lingua francas in South Africa as a multilingual country

4.1.   Languages and language use in South Africa

Originally inhabited by the Khoe and the San, then populated by migrating Bantu tribes, and eventually colonized by the Dutch and the British, South Africa has been characterized by language contact and multilingualism at all times. Today, a large number of the languages used in South Africa have the status of official languages. These are the major Bantu languages Ndebele, Northern Sotho, Southern Sotho, Swati, Tsonga, Tswana, Venda, Xhosa, Zulu, as well as Afrikaans and English. The status of these languages is reflected in the language policy of South Africa. To promote multilingualism, the curriculum stipulates that all children need to learn one of the indigenous Bantu languages in school. However, most white South Africans, who have either English or Afrikaans as their mother tongue, learn one of the Bantu languages in such an educational context only. By contrast, the majority of black South Africans acquire second and/or additional languages informally, through interaction with speakers of these languages. As a result, black South Africans are frequently multilingual in that they speak five or even more languages, as Mesthrie (1995: xvi) points out. The following comment by a 23-year-old male student (taken from Mesthrie 1995: xvi) illustrates several noteworthy aspects of language use in South Africa:

> My father's home language was Swazi, and my mother's home language was Tswana. But as I grew up in a Zulu-speaking area we used mainly Zulu and Swazi at home. But from my mother's side I also learnt Tswana well. In my high school I came into contact with lots of Sotho and Tswana students, so I can speak these two languages well. And of course I know English and Afrikaans. With my friends I also use Tsotsitaal.

The student's first utterance indicates that families are often bilingual, due to intermarriage across the different original tribes. Furthermore, labor migration, which is widespread in South Africa (due to a shortage of labor in the vast rural areas), often implies that speakers need to acquire a further language – Zulu in the case of the 23-year-old and his parents. In multilingual urban areas in general, language contact usually results in black speakers acquiring even more languages. At the end of his comment, the speaker mentions three lingua francas. English and Afrikaans are the two major lingua francas used across South Africa. Depending on the area, either of the two is more widespread than the other. The last language, Tsotsitaal, is of particular interest. It also is a lingua franca, but not an officially recognized one. Tsotsitaal belongs to what are referred to as urban lingua francas: mixed forms of language used in metropolitan areas, mainly by black males.

In addition, there are several languages, sometimes no longer spoken, which serve to unite people of similar religious fate. For example, Arabic is used as a lingua franca for prayer in mosques, and Hebrew and Sanskrit function as the media for the Jewish and the Hindi communities' services. The individual lingua francas serve their functions in clearly defined contexts. As a result, some of them are associated with high social prestige whereas others are used by restricted user communities, nevertheless playing an important role in their users' linguistic repertoire in that they are frequently used for identity construction. Afrikaans and English were the national languages associated with the two colonizing powers, the Dutch and the British. Prior to the present constitution, the apartheid regime had made Afrikaans and English the sole official languages of South Africa. However, the two languages occupied different domains. Traditionally, English has dominated the business and industrial sector, and higher education. Afrikaans, on the other hand, has been associated with the civil service and government (during apartheid), and it was the dominant language of the police, army and navy. Given the wide acceptance of both languages in these important domains, both languages have been valued by all citizens as indispensable. As a result, both languages have been used by large numbers of second language speakers, allowing for interaction between speakers of different mother tongues, in the past with Afrikaans having even more second language speakers than English (see McCormick 2006). Today, English is gradually attracting increasing numbers of second language users, despite the multilingual language policy of the government. The reasons for this preference of English are manifold. But in particular, English is regarded as a guarantee to socio-economic empowerment by the still disadvantaged black and colored communities. As a consequence, many colored families have chosen to shift from Afrikaans towards English as their home language. And black families make enormous efforts to send their offspring to multiethnic, traditionally English-medium schools.

Besides using the two former colonial languages, speakers have established other forms of language which proved useful for interactions in multilingual settings. On the sugar-cane plantations of South Africa, a pidgin, Fanakalo, originated and has, since, stabilized through continuous use in the gold and diamond mines. Fanakalo "probably originated from contacts between English people and Afrikaners with Zulus in the province of Natal in the mid-nineteenth century" (Mesthrie et al. 2000: 288). Its status, however, is often associated with exploitation, since its use for efficient communication among mine workers of diverse linguistic background also meant "that, as workers were not given the opportunity to learn English (or Afrikaans) adequately, they were severely restricted with respect to job prospects" (Webb and Kembo-Sure 2000: 10).

4.2.   The status of English in South Africa

Although South Africa's constitution provides the necessary background for an appraisal of all languages, the historical position of English and Afrikaans is difficult to alter in practice. The two languages are, at present, still the languages used by the economically powerful white upper middle and upper class. And also those black citizens who have managed to establish their own businesses often value English highly. But the public sector has a policy of providing equal opportunities for coloreds and blacks, which may eventually lead to a better representation of the indigenous Bantu languages in governmental offices and enterprises. Also, a number of financial institutions have started to use the Bantu languages for their information leaflets and for the instruction screens displayed on automated teller machines.

The use of English in South Africa and the status which the language has gained as a lingua franca throughout the country's population has been discussed with reference to both its positive and negative aspects. Although a very large number of black South Africans report to have a speaking knowledge of English, the individual proficiency levels range from a basic knowledge of formulaic utterances only through to full grammatical and communicative competence.

The problem of language choice is particularly pronounced in the education sector. As Mesthrie et al. (2001: 413) point out, the Curriculum 2005, which has been effective since the mid 1990s, promotes the use of more than one medium of instruction in schools. This would be in fulfillment of the constitutional provisions, but up to date most schools have failed to go beyond mere teaching of the Bantu languages as second languages and to truly provide multilingual classrooms with more than one medium of instruction. Mesthrie et al. (2000: 413) state that "so far there are few teachers adequately prepared for the teaching practice in such multilingual schools, and teaching materials are not yet available for higher grades".

The promotion of multilingualism is also crucial since is has been discussed as a factor for facilitating intercultural understanding. The apartheid policy of race segregation has frequently resulted in a mutual unawareness of the other ethnicities' cultural conventions. The following excerpt from the data collected in a research project on identity construction in South African Englishes illustrates this lack of knowledge or awareness. Here, a Xhosa and a colored speaker discuss how they gain a better understanding of each others' cultural backgrounds from watching soaps which are set against South Africa's multicultural background.

example (1):

```
S1    Isidingo, this it's more/ it's more interesting from
      there as well. (..) You know at sometimes you know when
      you get two wives. (.) It's not, so easy [it's not easy
S2                                             [to ... satis-
S1    to (XX) both] of them.
S2    fy    both.]
S2    Ja, that is what [I also learnt now, yes.]
S1                     [ (  X  X  X  X  X  )  ]
S2    All that is [happening in Isidingo.]
S1                [That    is    what    I] learned about their
      culture now. And and and for for for me like we like we
      say eh coloureds and black. So that soapies, teach you
      a lot about/ when I watched Kaslam now recently, it was
      about this um (..) lady's hu- husband, who passed away.
      [But she was] staying, she was staying in Joburg.
S2    [Okay.]
S1    Now they've got their own land, ne? What do you call it,
      the/ the own/ the own countries like Transkei or Ciskei
      that is their home/ you call it your homelands, ne? so
      when, his body had to go to his homeland, his paren[ts
S2                                                        [To get
S1    never/]
S2    burried.]
S1    Ja, to get buried. So his parents never knew [that he was
S2                                                 [That he has
S1    married,] he's got a wife
S2    got a wife.]
S1    You understand? So they wanted to control everything. But
      only his brother knew (..) uh knew the wife. And so when
      (.) they did/ his parents didn't want to accept her.
      Because she came with a a short skirt, she didn't have
      this thing (.) over her shoulder. And and (..) and then,
      (..) well, then he told them that (.) um this was his
      wife and that was his way of living eh with her in
      Johannesburg. So they ei/ either they gonna accept her or
```

```
he's also leaving with her. (..) So they/ so (she) (.)
the mother/ his mother like (.) er (..) taught her more
about their culture.
```

As Ndoleriire (2000) points out, this lack of knowledge does not only involve customs and practices, but it also includes awareness of communicative conventions. Ndoleriire discusses the use of English as a lingua franca as one possible approach to avoiding intercultural miscommunication, albeit emphasizing the problems associated with the promotion of an intranational lingua franca in African countries. He concludes that in these nations "the majority of the people, however, experience difficulty communicating in the 'official' language, or are totally incapable of doing so" (2000: 283). However, Kasanga (1995) indicates that using English as a lingua franca would not necessarily help avoid misunderstanding in intercultural communication. He reports that speakers tend to transfer their mother tongue conventions into their second language English when performing requests. "In standard native forms of English (especially British English), indirectness is paramount in achieving politeness [...], whereas in Sepedi (and, by the same token, in BSAfE [black South African English, cm], indirectness is not a determining factor" (1995: 223). And Cuvelier (2002: 78) finds that greeting routines in Xhosa are usually longer than those in English: "If the person you are greeting has children and a partner (wife/husband), you are supposed to ask about their health. And then to continue to create some common ground", a convention which speakers may transfer into their way of using English as a second language. Whether users of English as a lingua franca in South Africa in fact use culturally flavored language in their interactions has, however, not yet been adequately researched.

5.   Conclusion

As is the case in South Africa, the use of a particular language as lingua franca in a multiethnic setting or nation often implies a diglossic situation. That is, the language chosen as a lingua franca is often given the special status of an official language, used in administration, government and education. Such situations frequently involve problems such as the exclusion of sometimes significant parts of the population from political, social and economic participation, when the lingua franca is not mastered by population at large.

At the same time, a lingua franca is often regarded as a welcome addition to an individual's communicative repertoire in that it sometimes allows for the use of conversational strategies that are not appropriate in the speakers' mother tongues (see also Spencer – Oatey and Xing in this volume). In sum, the negative aspects may be compensated by implementing a multilingual language policy as advocated by Ndoleriire (2000: 283): "The multilingualism option, on the other hand, implies that all citizens of a (highly multilingual) state will need to learn at least three languages, and that these languages will also become the languages of official use". Such an approach would establish the language used as a lingua franca as one element of the community's linguistic repertoire. It might also help avoid intercultural communication problems, since learning several of a country's languages would also increase the specific knowledge about, as well as a general awareness of, culturally determined conventions of language use.

Notes

1. This part of the article is based on a research project funded by the VolkswagenStiftung under grant nos. II/79 388 and II/82 052.
2. www.statssa.gov.za/census01/html/default.asp, accessed 15. 12. 2005
3. The more recent 2001 census asked respondents what language they spoke most often in their household, but only listed the eleven official languages and an additional category labelled "other" as response options.
4. www.voanews.com/specialenglish/about_special_english.cfm, accessed 08. 12. 2005
5. The other official languages are Hiri Motu, another pidgin / creole, and English.
6. www. ethnologue.com, accessed 15. 12. 2005
7. For more formal and official contacts, immigrants use French (Meeuwis 2002: 30).
8. However, in most nations there have always been minority languages spoken by a small proportion of the population. In Iceland, Danish is recognized as a minority language.
9. www.swissworld.org, accessed 15. 12. 2005
10. www.immi.gov.au/living-in-australia/a-diverse-australia/government-policy/australians-together/current-policy/in-brief.htm. – accessed 13. 02. 2007, italics mine
11. www.languageinindia.com/april2002/officiallanguagesact.html, accessed 24. 11. 2005)
12. www.ethnologue.com/show_country.asp?name=NG, accessed 15. 12. 2005
13. www.nigeria-law.org/ConstitutionOfTheFederalRepublicOfNigeria.htm, accessed 15. 12. 2005

References

Chick, Keith J.
    1995   Interactional sociolinguistics and intercultural communication in South Africa. In: Rajend Mesthrie (ed.), *Language and Social History*, 230–241. Cape Town/ Johannesburg: David Philip.
Corder, Saskia and Meyerhoff, Miriam
in this volume Communities of practice in the analysis of intercultural communication. Chapter 21.

Crystal, David
1997   English: How one language is uniting the world. *Spotlight* 7: 12–16.
Cuvelier, Pol
2002   *Intercultural Communication in the Classroom: Educator's Guide.* Antwerp: UFSIA – Universiteit Antwerpen.
Eastman, Carol M.
2001   National Language / Official Language. In: Rajend Mesthrie (ed.), *A Concise Encyclopedia of Sociolinguistics*, 657–662. Oxford: Elsevier.
Fiedler, Sabine
2002   On the main characteristics of Esperanto-communication. In: Karlfried Knapp and Christiane Meierkord (eds.), *Lingua Franca Communication*, 53–86. Frankfurt a.M.: Lang.
Fiedler, Sabine
2006   Standardization and self-regulation in an international speech community: the case of Esperanto. *International Journal of the Sociology of Language* 177, 67–90.
Heuler, Martina
1989   *Prinzipien sprachlicher Vereinfachung in der technischen Dokumentation am Beispiel des Englischen.* Hildesheim: University of Hildesheim Press.
Hüllen, Werner
1982   Teaching a foreign language as 'lingua franca'. *Grazer Linguistische Studien* 16, 83–88.
Hüllen, Werner
1992   Identifikationssprachen und Kommunikationssprachen: Über Probleme der Mehrsprachigkeit. *Zeitschrift für Germanistische Linguistik* 20(3), 298–317.
Johnson, Edward, Mark Garner, Steve Hick and David Matthews
1993   *PoliceSpeak – Police Communications and Language – Speech and Text Recommendations.* Cambridge: PoliceSpeak Publications.
Kachru, Braj B.
1986   *The Alchemy of English: The Spread, Functions and Models of Non-Native Englishes.* Oxford: Pergamon.
Kasanga, Luanga A.
1995   'I am asking for a pen': Framing of requests in black South African English. In: Kasia M. Jaszczolt and Ken Turner (eds.), *Meaning through Language Contrast*, Volume 2, 219–235. Amsterdam: Benjamins.
Knapp, Karlfried
1987   English as an international lingua franca and the teaching of intercultural communication. In: W. Lörscher and R. Schulze (eds.), *Perspectives on Language in Performance: Studies in Linguistics, Literary Criticism, and Foreign Language Teaching to Honour Werner Hüllen on the Occasion of his Sixtieth Birthday*, 1022–1039. Tübingen: Narr.
Knapp, Karlfried
1991   Linguistische Aspekte interkultureller Kommunikationsfähigkeit. Unpublished habilitation thesis submitted to the Faculty of Philosophy of the Heinrich-Heine-university Düsseldorf, in May 1991.
Knapp, Karlfried and Christiane Meierkord
2002   *Lingua Franca Communication.* Frankfurt a.M.: Peter Lang.

Koole, Tom and Jan D. ten Thije
1994 *The Construction of Intercultural Discourse.* Amsterdam: Rodopi.
Lesznyák, Ágnes
2004 *Communication in English as an International Lingua Franca: An Explora-tory Case Study.* Norderstedt: Books on Demand.
McCormick, Kay
2006 Afrikaans as a lingua franca in South Africa: the politics of change. *Inter-national Journal of the Sociology of Language* 177, 91–106.
Meeuwis, Michael
2002 The sociolinguistics of Lingala as a diaspora lingua franca: Historical and language-ideological aspects. In: Karlfried Knapp and Christiane Meierkord (eds.), *Lingua Franca Communication*, 29–52. Frankfurt a.M.: Peter Lang.
Meierkord, Christiane
2005 Interactions across Englishes and their lexicon. In: Claus Gnutzmann and Frauke Intemann (eds.), *The Globalisation of English and the English Lan-guage Classroom*, 89–104. Tübingen: Narr.
Meierkord, Christiane
2006 Lingua francas as second languages. In: Keith Brown(ed.), *Encyclopedia of Language and Linguistics 2nd Edition*, entry 641. Oxford: Elsevier.
Meierkord, Christiane and Karlfried Knapp
2002 Approaching lingua franca communication. In: Karlfried Knapp and Christiane Meierkord (eds.), *Lingua Franca Communication*, 9–28. Frank-furt a. M.: Peter Lang.
Mesthrie, Rajend
1995 Introduction. In: Rajend Mesthrie (ed.), *Language and Social History*, xv-xx. Cape Town/Johannesburg: David Philip.
Mesthrie, Rajend et al.
2000 *Introducing Sociolinguistics.* Edinburgh: Edinburgh University Press.
Mühlhäusler, Peter
1986 *Pidgin and Creole Linguistics.* Oxford: Blackwell.
Ndoleriire, Oswald K.
2000 Cross-cultural communication in Africa. In: Vic Webb and Kembo-Sure (eds.), *African Voices: An Introduction to the Languages and Linguistics of Africa*, 268–285. Oxford: Oxford University Press.
Ogden, Charles K.
1930 *Basic English: A General Introduction with Rules and Grammar.* London: Kegan Paul.
Pölzl, Ulrike
2003 Signalling cultural identity: the use of L1/Ln in ELF. *Views* (Vienna English Working Papers) 12(2), 3–23. <www.univie.ac.at/Anglistik/views/03_2/POEL_SGL.PDF, accessed April 26, 2005>
Pölzl, Ulrike and Barbara Seidlhofer
2006 In and on their own terms: the "habitat factor" in English as a lingua franca interactions. *International Journal of the Sociology of Language* 177, 151–176.
Quirk, Randolph
1985 International communication and the concept of Nuclear English. In: Larry

E. Smith (ed.), *English for Cross-Cultural Communication*, 151–165. London: Macmillan.

Samarin, William J.
  1987   Lingua franca. In: Ulrich Ammon, Norbert Dittmar and Klaus J. Mattheier (eds.), *Sociolinguistics: An International Handbook of the Science of Languages and Society.* Volume 1, 371–374. Berlin: Mouton de Gruyter.

Seidlhofer, Barbara
  2000   Mind the gap: English as a mother tongue vs. English as a lingua franca. *Vienna English Working Papers* 9 (1), 51–68.

Seidlhofer, Barbara
  2002   The shape of things to come? Some basic questions about English as a lingua franca. In: Karlfried Knapp and Christiane Meierkord (eds.), *Lingua Franca Communication*, 269–302. Frankfurt a.M.: Lang.

Sherzer, Joel
  1987   A discourse-centered approach to language and culture. *American Anthropologist* 89, 295–309.

Smit, Ute
  2003   English as lingua franca (ELF) as medium of learning in a hotel management education program: an applied linguistic approach. *Views* (Vienna English Working Papers) 12(2), 40–74. <www.univie.ac.at/Anglistikviews/03_2/SMI_SGLE.PDF, accessed April 26, 2005>

Spencer-Oatey, Helen and Jianyu Xing
  in this volume The impact of culture on interpreter behaviour. Chapter 11.

Stewart, William
  1968   A sociolinguistic typology for describing national multilingualism. In Joshua A. Fishman (ed.), *Readings in the Sociology of Language*, 531–545. The Hague: Mouton.

UNESCO
  1953   *The Use of Vernacular Languages in Education.* Paris: UNESCO.

Wansbrough, John
  1996   *Lingua Franca in the Mediterranean.* Richmond, UK: Curzon Press.

Webb, Vic and Kembo-Sure
  2000   Language as a problem in Africa. In: Vic Webb and Kembo-Sure (eds.), *African Voices: An Introduction to the Languages and Linguistics of Africa*, 1–25. Oxford: Oxford University Press.

11.   The impact of culture on interpreter behaviour

Helen Spencer-Oatey and Jianyu Xing

1.   Introduction

This chapter explores the impact that cultural factors can have on interpreters' performance in intercultural interactions. Of course, all interactions that involve interpreters are inevitably intercultural interactions, but many intercultural interactions can (and very frequently do) take place without the involvement of interpreters.

In interpreter-mediated intercultural interactions, there are at least three parties: the two or more (groups of) primary interlocutors who want to communicate with each other but who cannot converse in a language that is mutually intelligible to everyone, and the interpreter(s). The interpreter is frequently regarded as a 'non-person', in that s/he is expected to contribute nothing to the substance of the interaction. However, as Wadensjö (1998: 67) points out, there are aspects of an interpreter's role that do not fit that of a non-person. In formal settings where simultaneous or consecutive interpreting occurs, such as at major international conferences and diplomatic visits, the interpreter's function is certainly constrained by the event, and the impact that the interpreter can have on the primary interlocutors (although not on the message conveyed) is limited. However, there are numerous other situations where the interpreter's function is potentially more flexible, and it is on these less controlled settings that this chapter focuses. We argue that the interpreter is never a non-person in such contexts; on the contrary, s/he is an active participant who dynamically influences the ways in which the discourse develops.

We maintain that cultural factors have a major impact on the interpreters' active involvement and this influences their effectiveness as mediators of meaning. In the first part of the chapter we focus on professional interpreters and in the second part we consider the use of untrained interpreters. In both cases, we explore the ways in which cultural factors influence the effectiveness of interpreters' behaviour. The first section focuses on the various roles that an interpreter needs to play, and illustrates the (potential) impact of cultural factors on the effective performance of these various roles. The second section focuses on the use of untrained interpreters and examines some authentic intercultural data in which an interpreter's unsatisfactory performance partly resulted in a very problematic encounter for the primary interlocutors, to a large extent because of inappropriate handling of cultural factors.

2.   Culture and interpreter roles

The California Healthcare Interpreters Association (2002) identifies four main roles for interpreters: message converter, message clarifier, cultural clarifier, and patient advocate. We use this categorization as a framework for considering the impact of cultural factors on the interpreter's task. Gulliver (1979; cited by Wadensjö 1998: 64) argues that a third party who is present at a negotiation will always exert some influence on the process, and we maintain that this applies to interpreters. In fact, we argue that in all their roles, professional interpreters are active participants who need to be consciously aware of the importance of managing cultural factors effectively (see also Thielmann in this volume and Roberts in this volume).

2.1.   Interpreter as message converter

All professional interpreters are required to adhere to a code of ethics established by the regional, national or international organization to which they belong. 'Accuracy' is one of the ethical principles that almost all organizations identify, and the Office of Ethnic Affairs in Te Tari Matawaka, New Zealand (1995), explains it as follows: "The interpreter shall, to the best of their ability, interpret faithfully and accurately between the parties; omitting nothing said by either party nor adding anything which the parties did not say".

Superficially, this may seem a straightforward principle to adhere to; however, in practice it can be quite complex, with cultural factors playing a role, as can be seen from the California Healthcare Interpreters Association's (2002) performance measures for this principle:

> Interpreters demonstrate accuracy and completeness by acting to:
> a.   Convey verbal and non-verbal messages and speaker's tone of voice without changing the meaning of the message;
> b.   Clarify the meaning of non-verbal expressions and gestures that have a specific or unique meaning within the cultural context of the speaker;
> c.   Maintain the tone and the message of the speaker even when it includes rudeness and obscenities. *Note:* different cultural understandings and levels of acceptance exist for the usage of obscene expressions and profanities, and we understand the resistance most interpreters have towards uttering such expressions, although interpreters need to honor the ethical principle of 'Accuracy and Completeness' by striving to render equivalent expressions;
> d.   Reveal and correct interpreting errors as soon as recognized;
> e.   Clarify meaning and verify understanding, particularly when there are differences in accent, dialect, register and culture;
> f.   Maintain the same level of formal/informal language (register) used by the speaker, or to request permission to adjust this level in order to facilitate understanding when necessary to prevent potential communication breakdown.

g. Notify the parties of any medical terms, vocabulary words, or other expressions which may not have an equivalent either in the English or target languages, thus allowing speakers to give a simplified explanation of the terms, or to assist speakers in doing so.

California Healthcare Interpreters Association (2002: 30–31)

Let us consider the case of explicit and implicit information. In low context cultures, a large proportion of the message is encoded explicitly in the words and structures, whereas in high context cultures, a smaller proportion is verbally encoded, with a greater proportion of the meaning needing to be inferred from the context. In court contexts, it is unacceptable for interpreters to change implicit language into a more explicit version, for as Wadensjö explains, "It would obviously be a challenge to the court if interpreters were ... allowed to clarify an attorney's deliberately ambiguous question" (Wadensjö 1998: 75). However, in many contexts, this issue can give rise to genuine interpreting dilemmas. Suppose a Western company makes a proposal to a Chinese company and receives the response *kaolu kaolu*. This literally means 'I/we (implied) will (implied) think it over', but in this context it is generally understood as signifying polite refusal (Kondo et al. 1997). How should this be interpreted? Rendering it as, 'we'll think it over' could give the wrong impression, and lead the Western representative to expect a response later. On the other hand, saying 'I'm afraid we cannot agree at this time' might be too specific, especially if the Chinese company wanted to be deliberately ambiguous. Clearly, the interpreter's decisions on such matters can have a major impact on the interaction.

Similarly, the issue can give rise to major dilemmas in healthcare contexts, as Kaufert's (1999) research illustrates. Kaufert researched the experiences of Aboriginal health interpreters in Canada, and one of the examples he reports is as follows. A 72-year-old Aboriginal man was admitted to hospital for diagnostic evaluation of urinary tract problems. He spoke only Ojibway, and on his admission, his son acted as interpreter. The next day he was scheduled for a cystoscopic examination, and so arrangements were made for a male interpreter to come to help explain the procedure and get the patient's signature of consent. Unfortunately the male interpreter was called away, and the only interpreter available was a 28-year-old woman. The urologist started his explanation, but soon became frustrated because he felt the interpreter was hesitating too much and seemed unable to get his message across. After several unsatisfactory exchanges, he drew a sketch of the male urinary system, and eventually the patient agreed to the procedure, saying that although he didn't understand everything, he would sign because he trusted them to do the best for him. Why was the interpreter so hesitant and seemingly incompetent? Kaufert explains it as follows:

> After the consent agreement was signed, the interpreter returned to her office and discussed the encounter with her supervisor. She explained how the direct translation of the physician's explanation of the procedure would have forced her to violate fun-

damental cultural prohibitions against references to urinary and reproductive anatomy in cross-gender communication. She added that her reluctance in this case was strongly influenced by the patient's age and by his status as a respected elder. The Director of the Aboriginal Services Program told her that professional medical interpreters must translate stigmatized concepts objectively and accurately. The interpreter agreed, but said that the elder would not have understood that her role as an interpreter had given her the privilege of using words which he saw as disrespectful in a conversation between a male elder and a young woman. The program Director conceded the validity of her point and agreed that the interview should have been delayed until a male interpreter was available.

Kaufert (1999: 415–417)

2.2.   Interpreter as message clarifier

An interpreter may need to intervene during an interpreting session in order to clarify a message. This can arise in the following ways:

- the interpreter has not fully understood the concept she/he is being asked to interpret and needs to ask for clarification;
- the interpreter realizes that the client or practitioner has misunderstood (or failed to understand) the message, even though the interpreter was correct;
- the interpreter needs to alert one of the principal interlocutors that a missed inference has occurred, or that a different inference has been drawn.

Cultural factors can often play a major role in such circumstances, as the following examples given by the Northern Ireland Health and Social Services Interpreting Service (2004) illustrate:

Different meaning inferred:
A Health Visitor in attempting to determine a date of birth may ask to see a passport. Yet such a request to some clients could imply that their status was being questioned, so an interpreter may intervene by explaining to the client why the request is being made and suggesting that any form containing a date of birth will do, this can then be reported back to the Health Visitor.

Inferred but not stated and knowledge assumed:
A GP may offer a hospital referral to a patient for minor surgery. The patient may be resistant as they are not sure if they can afford to pay for this yet may not say so from embarrassment. The GP may have assumed that the patient is aware such treatment is free. An Interpreter could prompt this by stating there may be confusion over the issue and asking for clarification.

Northern Ireland Health and Social Services Interpreting Service (2004)

Interpreters need to be actively on the look-out for such clarification needs, and whether they (decide to) intervene or not clearly impacts on the way in which the discourse develops.

2.3.   Interpreter as cultural clarifier/informant/mediator

The California Healthcare Interpreters Association (2002) explains this third role of the interpreter as cultural clarifier/informant/mediator as follows:

> The cultural clarifier role goes beyond word clarification to include a range of actions that typically relate to an interpreter's ultimate purpose of facilitating communication between parties not sharing a common culture. Interpreters are alert to cultural words or concepts that might lead to a misunderstanding, triggering a shift to the cultural clarifier role.
>
> California Healthcare Interpreters Association (2002: 43–44)

Sometimes the interpreter may need to explain what lies behind the behaviour of one of the primary interlocutors, as the following two examples from the healthcare sector illustrate:

> *Chinese birth traditions:*
> A Chinese mother who has recently given birth may be resistant to coming into an appointment until a month after childbirth, due to a traditional cultural practice of the mother and baby remaining in the home for this period.
>
> Northern Ireland Health and Social Services Interpreting Service (2004)

> *A Spanish–English interpreter who is called to the 'Well-Baby Nursery'*
> Interpreting for the physician, I ask her whether she wants her baby boy circumcised. She nods, but then pauses and very seriously adds, "But my friend had a baby circumcised here, and they did it too much. I don't like how he looks. Can they just cut off a little bit?" To me, the woman clearly wants to decline the procedure but is having difficulty refusing what she considers an instruction from the physician. In general, Latinos feel they should agree with physicians out of politeness and respect, even when they really disagree or do not understand the issues involved. They expect physicians to make the decisions for them and do not understand why they are asked to make choices. They are used to, and seem to prefer, deferring to experts. These patients do not understand the American medical system and its notion of informed consent. Only when more acculturated do they start taking the level of responsibility for their own health that Americans routinely assume. Language and cultural issues once again are intermixed.
>
> Haffner (1992)

The latter example illustrates how interpreters may feel the need not only act as cultural clarifiers but also as cultural informants. In fact, this is how they are increasingly used in the business sector. A guide to Business Interpreting produced by the Regional Language Network (no date, 2001) in the UK says that the interpreter is often a business person's best source of information and advice. Similarly, Edwards (2002), discussing the role of interpreters in peace and relief mission negotiations, maintains that "The interpreter is your local specialist in public relations. An interpreter can give you suggestions on the best way to proceed with a person from a different cultural background, and may notice nuances that would otherwise be overlooked". Katan (cited by Kondo et al. 1997) takes this a step further and asserts that the interpreter should become a cultural mediator. He argues that many business people are turning away from using professional interpreters, partly because they are seen as intruders, and partly because they are perceived as not having enough understanding of corporate culture. So Katan suggests that interpreters should adjust their roles and become cultural mediators in business contexts: 1) working with business parties before events and preparing them for any intercultural problems that might emerge; 2) gaining permission to stop events if a misunderstanding is causing difficulty; 3) preparing materials on intercultural meetings to brief clients and to raise awareness of the cultural factors in communication. This, in effect, turns interpreters into intercultural trainers, and in fact this is an increasing trend. A growing number of universities provide training in both elements, and many agencies nowadays provide both interpreting and cultural briefing services.

However, acting as a cultural informant can also bring its problems. Kaufert (1999), who interviewed Aboriginal interpreters in Canada, reports that many complained they were inappropriately expected to provide various types of 'instant information', such as a summary of Aboriginal beliefs affecting individual and community responses to death and dying:

> Other dilemmas for the interpreters included being asked for information about the community care environment of a patient being considered for a home based palliative care option. … Interpreters complained that they experienced difficulty in providing information about environmental barriers to care when they did not know the community. They also emphasized that it was inappropriate to attempt to describe an individual or community's 'beliefs' in terms of both ethical considerations and their level of knowledge of the client. Two of the interpreters taking part in the study explained how these demands forced them into developing reductionist, decontextualized accounts of Aboriginal communities and descriptions of the ways in which Aboriginal people interpreted illness and death. Interpreters also stated that they recognized that the environment of communities was diverse and that responses to the experience of palliative care varied from individual to individual. One interpreter stated that it was dangerous to ask cultural mediators to provide "cultural formulas" characterising the perspectives of individuals or to develop generalisations about more inclusive cultural or linguistic groups.

Kaufert (1999: 407–408)

2.4.   Interpreter as client advocate

The California Healthcare Interpreters Association (2002) identifies a fourth possible role for interpreters – that of client advocate. Their rationale for this is as follows:

> Many immigrants may be unfamiliar with US healthcare system services available and their healthcare rights. Individuals with limited English proficiency find it difficult to advocate for their own right to the same level of care as English-speaking pa-

tients. Given the backdrop of such disparities, interpreters are often the only individuals in a position to recognize a problem and advocate on behalf of an individual patient. **However, the Patient Advocate role must remain an optional role for each individual healthcare interpreter in light of the high skill level required and the potential risk to both patient and interpreter.** [bold in original]

California Healthcare Interpreters Association (2002: 45)

Kaufert (1999) reports that Aboriginal language interpretation programmes in Canada vary in their official commitment to interpreters acting as advocates. However, he maintains that the interpreters in his study frequently worked informally as mediators, using their power as gatekeepers over the exact content of the message conveyed, and that sometimes they adopted a clear advocacy role. For example, he reports that many health professionals showed discomfort with the extended process of family decision-making that Aboriginal patients typically prefer, and thus tended to offer only a limited range of palliative care options. In these situations, the interpreters stepped into an advocacy role, telling patients that they had the right to make informed choices about the type of care they wanted to receive and explaining that they could refuse or delay treatment. The interpreters' involvement in mediation under these conditions was regulated, however, by their own professional code of ethics, which demanded objectivity and neutrality in the translation of messages.

3.   Using untrained interpreters

Many guidelines on the use of interpreters (e.g. the guidelines produced by The Office of Ethnic Affairs, Te Tari Matawaka, New Zealand) recommend strongly that only trained interpreters should be used, and warn of the risks of using untrained interpreters. Nevertheless, in practice, and especially in less formal situations of intercultural contact, people who are more or less bilingual in the languages involved frequently take up the role of interpreter. This section explores some of the hazards (as well as some of the advantages) associated with this practice that relate to cultural factors.

3.1.   Relatives as interpreters

In much public service or community interpreting, a family member takes on the role of interpreter. Sometimes this can work well, and it is what the family wants. For example, in the case (reported in section 1.1) of the 72-year-old Aboriginal man with urinary tract problems, Kaufert (1999: 418) reports that after he was found to have cancer, the man's son insisted on acting as the interpreter. When the official interpreter started to convey the diagnosis to the patient, the son immediately interrupted and would not allow him to continue. He explained that it was his responsibility to protect his father "from the 'bad news' of his cancer and his impending mortality" and insisted that he should act as interpreter.

In other circumstances, however, the use of a relative as an interpreter is highly problematic for cultural reasons, as Linda Haffner's (1992) personal experience as an interpreter illustrates:

> My next summons is from the Internal Medicine Clinic. The patient, a 50-year-old female peasant from Mexico, is accompanied by her 35-year-old son. Although the patient has been coming to the clinic for some time, she is new to me. Her son usually interprets, as he is reasonably fluent in both languages. This time I am called because the son has to leave to go to work.
>
> Before going into the room, the physician expresses to me his concern about whether the health problems claimed by this woman are real or imagined. She has been in the clinic three times before, each time with different vague and diffuse complaints, none of which make medical sense. As we learn, the poor woman has a fistula in her rectum. In her previous visits, she could not bring herself to reveal her symptoms in the presence of, and therefore to, her son as he interprets for her. She tells me that she has been so embarrassed about her condition that she has invented other symptoms to justify her visits to the physician. She confesses that she has been eager to have a hospital staff interpreter from the first visit, but her hope had not materialized until now.
>
> Haffner (1992: 256)

The problems of using relatives as interpreters are even more acute in the case of children. Haffner (1992) reports one situation where a pregnant woman was found to be having a stillbirth, and her 7-year-old daughter was used to tell her mother that the baby was dead. She then recounts the following incident, and reflects on culturally-related factors:

> I am reminded of the time when I was required for a family conference for a patient about to be discharged. When I arrive at the conference, present are a physician, a nurse, a physical therapist, a social worker, and several family members. The patient, the father, is absent. Everyone is sitting around a table except one. Standing by the physician is the patient's 9-year-old son, who is acting as the interpreter. The child looks frightened. The physician rather abruptly says to me, "We don't need you, the boy is doing fine". The boy, however, pleads with me to stay and take over, saying, "Please, *Señora*, can you help me? I don't know if I am doing it right". ... Being an interpreter is a heavy burden for a child, whose English is frequently marginal and certainly is not sophisticated. Disregard for these factors is hurtful to both the child and the family and threatens the effectiveness of the communication. The trauma to the unfortunate little girl (whose mother has a stillborn) is easily seen. I doubt anyone would consider using a child in this way if there were no language barrier. The situation in which the boy was used as an interpreter is similarly difficult, but the difficulty is perhaps a little more subtle.
>
> In rural Hispanic culture, the hierarchy is strict, with authority running from older to younger and from male to female. These relationships are for life, with parents in

control of adult children and older adults in control of their younger adult siblings. Traditionally in Latino culture, the head of the family is expected to make the decisions regarding any family member. The whole family looks to this person for support and advice. By using a young family member as an interpreter, the physician puts the child in control, with a much higher status than the child would otherwise have. This disrupts the family's social order.

Haffner (1992)

3.2.   'At hand' interpreters

In many situations, untrained interpreters are used because they are 'at hand' when an interpreter is needed. Knapp-Potthoff and Knapp (1987a, 1987b), in their research into 'non-professional' interpreting, found that the interpreters in their studies frequently functioned as independent individuals participating actively in the interactions. This quite often resulted in two problems: failure to interpret parts of what the primary interlocutors said, and the insertion of additional elements. In Knapp-Potthofff and Knapp's studies, some of this seemed to be due to personal concerns about face.

In our study of Chinese–British business meetings (Spencer-Oatey and Xing 2000, 2003, 2004, 2005) we found a similar situation during one (but not all) of the delegation visits. In this section we present some of the critical interactions that took place during this one particular trip. They illustrate the impact that intercultural factors can have on an (untrained) interpreter's performance and the problems that this can lead to.

In the trip concerned, six Chinese businessmen visited the headquarters of a British engineering company. They had already signed a contract with the British company in China to buy some engineering equipment, and the official purpose of the visit was to inspect the goods prior to shipping and to receive some end-user training. The British company concerned had previously hosted many Chinese delegations before, and on these previous occasions had nearly always used a PhD student (a native Chinese speaker) from a local university. This student was familiar with the technological aspects of the company's products, and the British company was very happy with his performance as an interpreter. However, at the time of this visit, this student was busy preparing for his PhD viva, and he recommended another Chinese PhD student from the same department to take his place. However, a number of problems arose as a result of his interpreting.

3.2.1.   A problematic intervention

The first meeting between the British staff and the Chinese visitors was an introductory welcome meeting. The British chairman welcomed the visitors and shortly afterwards he asked the British staff to introduce themselves. When they had done this, he invited each of the Chinese visitors to introduce themselves. This immediately caused confusion among the visitors. The delegation leader turned to consult the others, and one of them requested in Chinese that he do it on their behalf. It was almost a minute before the delegation leader responded to the chairman's request, and at this point he began reading out a speech. Immediately the interpreter interrupted him saying, in Chinese, that they should first introduce themselves. This resulted in further worried faces and discussion in Chinese, before the visitors started introducing themselves individually. This can be seen from the following extract. (All names of the participants have been changed in all the extracts.)

(1) Welcome Meeting, just after the British participants have finished introducing themselves. Int = Interpreter.

Jack: could could I now ask if if the members (.) could each introduce themselves so that we can learn (.) um (.) who they are and what their interests are.

Int: ta shuo jiushi rang nimen jiushi ziwo jieshao yixia jiushi yixie xingqu huozhe jiushi yixie er danwei ya yixie er zhege ziji de yixie xingqu aihao jieshao yixia??? [*he says that is he wants you that is to introduce yourselves that is your interests or that is something about your work unit or introduce some of your interests and hobbies.*]

Sun: [turns to colleagues and discusses with them and the interpreter in Chinese]

Sun: *we each introduce ourselves*

Shen: *it's best if you do it on our behalf*

Sun: [reading from a script] *first of all, to [X] Company=*

Int: bu shi bu shi. ta shuo xian jieshao yixia (.) wo shi jiushishuo shi jiushishuo wo shi gongsi de, wo shi danwei ?? [*no no. he said first you introduce yourself (.) I am that is I am that is I am from such and such a company, I am from such and such an organization*]

Sun: *I am [surname] from Company [name]*

Int: He is from [name of Company]

Chen: *say what you do*

Sun: *I'm involved in design*

Xu: *give your full name (.) full name (.) full name (.) say you're a design engineer*

Sun: *design engineer*

Int: His name is [name] and he is a design engineer.

Ma: *I am from [name of Company], and manager of the [product] Department*

Int: He is the manager of the [name of Department] of [name of Company] [Chinese delegation members continue to introduce themselves.]

The meeting was video-recorded, and afterwards we played the recording back to both the British and Chinese participants (separately), asking them to stop the tape when they wanted to comment on something significant to them. Both the Chinese and British participants commented on this part of the interaction. The Chinese visitors all pointed out that it was normal and polite for the head of the delegation to 'say a few words of appreciation' on behalf of the whole group, and then to introduce himself and each member of the delegation. They were clearly offended that he had not been given this opportunity:

(2) Interview and video playback with Chinese delegation

Sun: *According to our home customs and protocol, speech is delivered on the basis of reciprocity. He has made his speech and I am expected to say something. ... In fact I was reluctant to speak, and I had nothing to say. But I had to, to say a few words. Right for the occasion, right? But he had finished his speech, and he didn't give me the opportunity, and they each introduced themselves, wasn't this clearly implied that they do look down upon us Chinese.*

The delegation members then started discussing the extent to which the interpreter was responsible for the problem:

(3) Interview and video playback with Chinese delegation

Ma: *at moments like this [interpreter's name] shouldn't have interrupted*

Lin: *that's right*

Xu: *from the Chinese point of view, it's normal to say a few words*

Sun: *to say something out of courtesy*

Ma: *in fact, let me say something not so pleasant, [interpreter] was just a translator, nothing more. ... he shouldn't have taken part in anything else. whatever I said, he shouldn't have butted in, he should have just translated it, this was a formal occasion. ...*

Lin: *that's right, that's right. the key is to function as an interpreter ...*

Sun: *on the other hand, maybe they didn't want me to speak*

Ma: *it's true that they didn't ask you to speak*

Lin: *you could speak and you did (??)*

Ma: *you had the right to*

Sun: *I was speaking but if they [i.e. the British] didn't want me to he wasn't wrong. you and I are not familiar with things here, isn't it that the British look down on us Chinese? ... from this point of view, this was implied. in fact I was reluctant to speak, and I had nothing to speak about. but I had to, to say a few words. right for the occasion, right? but you had finished your speech and you didn't give me the opportunity, and you each introduced yourself, wasn't this clearly implied that we do look down upon you Chinese?*

   Ma: *no, no, in this whole thing I felt* [interpreter's name] *... played a very im-*
        portant role at this moment. ...
  Chen: *As far as [interpreter's name] is concerned, he went beyond his respon-*
        sibility didn't he
   Lin: *this is the point* [several chorus agreement]
  Chen: *[interpreter's name]'s interpreting is too brief, and sometimes he puts*
        his own opinions into his interpreting, that won't do. this is not the way
        of interpreting.

Presumably the interpreter felt that he needed to convey accurately the chairman's request for self-introductions, and that is why he interrupted the delegation leader when he started giving a brief speech. He ignored Chinese conventions regarding formal speeches in business meetings of this type, and
insisted on accurate adherence to what the British chairman had asked for. From
the British point of view, however, this was completely unnecessary. In the follow-up interview and video playback with the British chairman, he picked out
this 'chaotic' situation prior to the Chinese introductions and commented:

(4) Interview and video playback with Jack, the British chairman
 Jack: this was particularly funny this now. this is where I asked them to intro-
        duce themselves, and this is where they went into total chaos, and it just
        didn't work out. ... I thought, well, you know, and that's where you
        wonder well what did the translator say.
  Res: he was trying to give a return speech, he was expressing their thanks to
        [British company name], then he was cut short by the interpreter. the in-
        terpreter actually told them just to introduce themselves, just tell their
        names, their position, their interests ...
 Jack: and that's interesting, so it goes back to the point of our concern about
        interpretation, because if the interpreter said to me that they are just
        making a return speech, then it would have been fine.

So from the Chinese visitors' point of view, it was both appropriate and polite to
make a return speech before the introductions. From the British chairman's
comments, it is clear that he would have been quite happy with this. However,
from the interpreter's perspective, he wanted the British chairman's initial request to be carried out exactly, and he intervened to ensure that it was. His concern for accuracy, and his disregard for Chinese conventions regarding formal
speeches in business meetings of this type, not only caused unnecessary dis-
ruption to the natural flow of the event, but also caused some hard feelings on
the Chinese side.

3.2.2. Zero renditions of 'sensitive' requests

The day before the end of the visit, the British company was planning to take the visitors to London for some shopping and sightseeing, and wanted to know if there was anywhere in particular in London that they would like to visit. The Chinese visitors, however, wanted to be given their 'pocket money' so that they could use it during the shopping trip. On this and previous occasions, when the British company signed a contract in China, they would add the cost of the delegation visit to the contract price, and there was an unofficial understanding that any balance remaining at the end of the visit would be given to the visitors as personal 'pocket money'. The Chinese wanted to receive this money now, so that they could spend it in London. They were concerned that they would have no opportunity to use it if they did not receive it until just before they left for the airport. However, despite repeated requests by the Chinese visitors, the interpreter failed to interpret it on each occasion, until Xing (the researcher who was present) intervened. This is illustrated in the following extract:

(5) Meeting on the penultimate day of the visit. Int = Interpreter; Res = Researcher

Sajid: could you please ask them is there anything specific that they want to do in London because obviously we don't have much time left (gesturing to look at watch) (.) we must make plans (???)

   Int: ta shuo nimen shi bu shi you teshu de yaoqiu zai Lundun [*he asked if you have anything specific to do in London*]

Shen: tamen yao ba women de feiyong suan yi suan dei (.) yaoburan mingtian meiyou shijian le. [*they should work out our expenses otherwise there will be no time for it tomorrow.*]
       [not interpreted]

Sajid: (???) where do they want to go specifically? to Oxford Street (.) (???)

   Int: Lundun de hua tamen bijiao da yidian, Niujin Jie, yitiao shangyejie, [*well, London is a big city. Oxford Street, a shopping street*]

Sajid: because we want to make this visit as fruitful as possible for them. (???) but for now (.) what do they want to do specifically? they want to go to the Bank of China to change money? can you ask them?

   Int: ta de hua jiushishuo Lundun de hua, ye jiu shuo, yao zoulu de hua, cong zhe bian zou na bian de hua jiu shaowei yuan yidian, zheyang, ni ruguo xiang zai zhe er jiushishuo yige defang gouwu jiushishuo shi ba, zuo wan le zhi hou ta keyi kaiche, zai huan yige di'r [*in London, that is, if you walk, from this side to that side, it is a bit far. So if you decide to go shopping in one place, after you have finished, they can pick you up, and take you to another place.*]
       [Chinese visitors discuss among themselves]

Sun: jiu zheyang ba. tamen yao jiesuan, jiesuan wanle yihou ba qian na chulai tamen hao gouwu [*it's like this. they want to settle the expenses, after they've settled the expenses they can get the spending money so that they can go shopping*]
[not interpreted]

Xu: zou ba [*let's go*]

Chen: nimen buyao zou ta [pointing to Sajid] hai you hua shuo ne. hai dei suanzhang [*no wait a minute he* [pointing to Sajid] *hasn't finished yet. And we have to settle the expenses.*]
[not interpreted]

Sajid: so where do they want to go? what do they want to do? they want to go to the Bank of China (.) to change your money (.) yes? can you ask them?

Int: shi bu shi xian xiang dao Zhongguo Yinhang na'r? [*do you want to first go to the Bank of China?*]
[Chinese visitors discuss among themselves. Some say: suan le, *no, forget it*]

Sun: bu shi (.) tamen de yisi shi xianzai keyi suanzhang. (turning to other members) wo de yisi shi bu shi zhe ge yisi ya? jie le zhang zhi hou neng bu neng gou ba qian na chulai name tamen hao gouwu. shi bu shi zhe ge yisi? [*no (.) they want to settle the expenses now. (turning to other members) is this what you want to say? After the settlement could they have the money so they can go shopping with it. Isn't it what you wanted to say?*]
[Visitors chorus: shi ya, *yes*]
[not interpreted]

Res: [to interpreter] na ni jiu wenwen ta shi bu shi keyi xian na nage spending money. ni keyi wen ta (2) ruguo huan bu liao qian de hua. [*you could ask him if they could have their spending money. You can ask him that. (2) if they can't change their money.*]

Sajid: so they want to go to the Bank of China?

Int: no (.) they don't think they can change their money there.

Sajid: so what do they want to do?

Res: well actually they said if they can get eh (.) for example (.) the spending money now (.) today (.) so that they can do some shopping in London they don't need to change money.

As can be seen from this extract, the Chinese visitors asked four times if their 'expenses could be settled', which was an indirect way of asking to be given their spending money. However, the interpreter did not interpret any of these requests into English, and only translated the British host's question about which part of London they wanted to visit. Needless to say, Sajid, the British host, was extremely confused by the interaction and Xing, the on-the-spot researcher, felt so uncomfortable that he spoke directly to the interpreter, recommending that he translate the Chinese visitors' request. However, the interpreter still did not do so, and when Sajid asked again whether they would like to go to the Bank of China, he gave an unhelpful reply. Eventually the researcher stepped in to convey the Chinese visitors' request.

Why then did the interpreter fail to interpret the Chinese request? The visitors themselves clearly regarded it as an embarrassing request, partly perhaps because it involved money, and partly because their entitlement to the 'pocket money' was an informal, unofficial one. So they referred to it as 'settling expenses' rather than 'getting their pocket money', and Sun (the delegation leader) distanced himself further by using the pronouns 'they' and 'you' rather than 'we'. The interpreter's handling of these interchanges suggests that he too found it embarrassing, and in fact too face-threatening to interpret. However, the British host was not concerned by the request, and did not seem offended when it was finally conveyed. He commented that it might be difficult to get the money at short notice, but left instantly to see to the matter, and returned soon after with some cash.

The next day, in the close-out meeting before the delegation left for the airport, the problem of money surfaced again. When the visitors were handed the balance of cash, the Chinese visitors felt they were entitled to more and asked to see the full list of costs that the British had incurred. Once again, the interpreter failed to interpret their request. Over a period of 50 minutes, the visitors repeated their request fourteen times, using the following terms and phrases: list of costs, proof, proof of cost, the basis of the expense calculations, how they worked out the figure. Yet the interpreter did not convey this to the British until Sun, the delegation leader, lost his temper with the interpreter saying, *"this is not your business, you just translate what I say, translate what he says, don't worry about us, don't be afraid"*. Only then did he interpret what the Chinese were asking for.

A little later, when the interpreter again hesitated to interpret something, another of the Chinese visitors became extremely angry. He started blaming the British for cheating them out of the money that they felt they were due:

(6) Close-out meeting

Shen: *you just tell him. is it so easy to bully us Chinese (.) so easy to fool us around? this money is what we have been saving out of our mouth. we have had instant noodles every day just to save some money (.) and now they have grabbed it. how mean of them to do such a thing.*

Once again the interpreter failed to interpret this, and there was total silence for five seconds.

Needless to say, neither the Chinese nor the British were happy with the interpreter's performance. The visitors complained that his interpreting was too brief and that he interfered too much with the proceedings. They were unsure whether he was getting their message across clearly, either because of his language skills or else because he was afraid of offending the British company that was employing him and so did not speak clearly. The British staff were equally dissatisfied with the interpreter and had similar types of complaints. They commented that many of the interpretations were shorter than the original utterances, that he failed to interpret when they expected him to do so (and when their body language signalled that an interpretation was needed and expected), and that he seemed to act as an active participant rather than as a mediator between the primary interlocutors. The visit as a whole was highly problematic for everyone, and both the British and the Chinese felt that the interpreter's behaviour and performance contributed significantly to these problems. He ignored Chinese conventions when he had no need to (when he stopped the Chinese delegation leader from giving a return speech), and he avoided conveying sensitive information (perhaps in an attempt to maintain harmony – supposedly a highly valued Chinese principle) when both British and Chinese primary interlocutors wanted him to convey the visitors' request clearly.

4.   Concluding comments

The examples in this paper illustrate the very close interconnections between language and culture. They demonstrate the ways in which interpreters are active participants of an interaction, and how they exert influence on the development of the discourse. Interpreters have an extremely difficult task balancing accuracy and completeness on the one hand, with a range of cultural considerations on the other. We do not attempt to offer 'solutions' or practical advice for dealing with these matters; that would be too simplistic. However, we do call for more research and analysis to be carried out into this complex area, and we highlight the risk of using untrained interpreters for such a challenging task.

Transcription conventions

(.)	Pauses of less than one second
(3)	Pauses of the length indicated
=	Latching
(??)	Unintelligible speech
Word word	Words originally spoken in Chinese and translated into English by the authors

References

California Healthcare Interpreters Association
    2002   California Standards for Healthcare Interpreters. Ethical Principles, Pro-
            tocols, and Guidance on Roles and Interventions. Available at http://www.
            calendow.org/reference/publications/pdf/cultural/TCE0701-2002_Califor
            nia_Sta-pdf [Accessed 26 January 2007].

Edwards, Victoria
    2002   The role of communication in peace and relief mission negotiations. *Trans-
            lation Journal* 6(2). Available at http://accurapid.com/journal/20interpr.
            htm [Accessed 26 January 2007].

Haffner, Linda
    1992   Translation is not enough. Interpreting in a medical setting. *Western Jour-
            nal of Medicine* 157: 255–259. Available (with permission) at http://www.
            ggalanti.com/articles/articles_haffner.html [Accessed 26 January 2007].

Kaufert, Joseph M.
    1999   Cultural mediation in cancer diagnosis and end of life decision-making: the
            experience of Aboriginal patients in Canada. *Anthropology and Medicine*
            6(3): 405–421.

Knapp-Potthoff, Annelie and Karlfried Knapp
    1987a   Interweaving two discourses – the difficult task of the non-professional
            interpreter. In: Juliane House and Shoshona Blum-Kulka (eds.), *Interlingual
            and Intercultural Communication*, 151–168. Tübingen: Gunter Narr.

Knapp-Potthoff, Annelie and Karlfried Knapp
    1987b   The man (or woman) in the middle: Discoursal aspects of non-professional
            interpreting. In: Karlfried Knapp, Werner Enninger and Annelie Knapp-
            Potthoff (eds.), *Analyzing Intercultural Communication*, 181–211. Berlin:
            Mouton de Gruyter.

Kondo, Masaomi, Helen Tebble, Bistra Alexieva, Helle v. Dam, David Katan, Akira Mi-
            zuno, Robin Setton and Ilona Zalka
    1997   Intercultural communication, negotiation and interpreting. In: Yves Gam-
            bier, Daniel Gile and Christopher Taylor (eds.), *Conference Interpreting:
            Current Trends in Research*. Proceedings of the International Conference
            on Interpreting: What do we know and how? Turku, 25–27 August 1994.
            Amsterdam: John Benjamins.

Northern Ireland Health and Social Services Interpreting Service
    2004   Code of Ethics and Good Practice Guidelines for Interpreters. Available at:
            http://www.interpreting.n-i.nhs.uk/Code-of-Ethics-and-Good-Practice-
            Guidelines-for-Interpreters.doc [Accessed 26 January 2007].

Office of Ethnic Affairs, Te Tari Matawaka
    1995   Let's Talk. Guidelines for Government Agencies Hiring Interpreters. Available
            at: http://www.ethnicaffairs.govt.nz/oeawebsite.nsf/wpg_URL/Resources-
            Ethnic-Affairs-Publications-Lets-Talk-Guidelines-For-Government-Agencies-
            Hiring-Interpreters?OpenDocument&ExpandView [Accessed 26 January
            2007].

Regional Language Network (North West)
    no date Business Interpreting. A Guide to Commissioning an Excellent Service.

Available at: http://www.rln-northeast.com/Publications/Downloads/businessinterpreting.pdf [Accessed 26 January 2007].

Regional Language Network (North West)
2001   Interpreting for the Public Services. A Guide to Commissioning an Excellent Service. Available at: http://www.rln-northeast.com/Publications/Downloads/publicserviceinterpreting.pdf [Accessed 26 January 2007].

Roberts, Celia
this volume Intercultural communication in healthcare settings, Chapter 12.

Spencer-Oatey, Helen and Jianyu Xing
2000   A problematic Chinese business visit to Britain: issues of face. In: Helen Spencer-Oatey (ed.), *Culturally Speaking: Managing Rapport through Talk across Cultures*, 272–288. London: Continuum.

Spencer-Oatey, Helen and Jianyu Xing
2003   Managing rapport in intercultural business interactions: a comparison of two Chinese–British business meetings. *Journal of Intercultural Studies* 24(1): 33–46.

Spencer-Oatey, Helen and Jianyu Xing
2004   Rapport management problems in Chinese–British business interactions: a case study. In: Juliane House and Jochen Rehbein (eds.), *Multilingual Communication*, 197–221. Amsterdam: Benjamins.

Spencer-Oatey, Helen and Jianyu Xing
2005   Silence in an intercultural business meeting: Multiple perspectives and interpretations. *Multilingua* 24(1/2): 55–74.

Thielmann, Winfried
this volume Power and dominance in intercultural communication, Chapter 20.

Wadensjö, Cecilia
1998   *Interpreting as Interaction*. London: Longman.

III. Intercultural communication in different sectors of life

Editors' introduction

Section 3 explores intercultural communication issues within different sectors or aspects of life. A number of themes re-occur across the chapters:
- the contribution of research from other disciplines;
- the relative paucity of applied linguistic research;
- misunderstandings and awkward moments in intercultural communication;
- the relative impact of 'difference' in intercultural communication;
- intercultural communication training;
- intercultural communication and discrimination.

Chapter 12, by Roberts, focuses on the healthcare sector. At the beginning of the chapter, Roberts picks up the theme of Section 1 – that intercultural communication is informed by research from different disciplines – and explains the contribution made by medical anthropology and sociology research to our understanding of intercultural communication within the health sector. She then turns to the findings that have emerged from interactional sociolinguistic research. With the help of authentic examples, she analyses how conversational inferences are made and how conversational involvement is sustained in ethnically and linguistically heterogeneous communities. She illustrates how communicative misunderstandings and awkward moments can occur in such contexts, and considers the sources of such problems. Towards the end of the chapter, Roberts briefly explains how oral assessments of medical practitioners may have discriminatory outcomes for certain groups of ethnic minority candidates, and reports the positive contribution that applied linguistic research has made here – that many medical practitioners are now looking at oral examinations more from a discourse perspective and acknowledge that the interaction is jointly constructed by both candidate and examiner. Nevertheless, Roberts mentions several times that on the whole there is a dearth of applied linguistic research on intercultural communication in the health sector.

This is a theme that is reiterated by Franklin in chapter 13, in his consideration of intercultural issues in international business and management. He explains that most intercultural training in the European business sector is based on cross-national contrastive data of fundamental values and behavioural orientations, and he argues that this is unsatisfactory for a number of reasons:
- such differences are not necessarily noticed by managers in their intercultural interactions (i.e. difference is not equivalent to difficulty);
- some difficulties that the managers experience are not predicted or explained by such differences;
- the comparative data on values and behavioural orientations provide trainers with few insights into how people can improve their intercultural communication.

Franklin then reports a different research approach used by a few people in the intercultural field – the study of critical incidents to help identify *Kulturstandards*. He argues that such interactional research is more relevant and useful to intercultural trainers than contrastive quantitative data. However, he maintains that the analysis of authentic interaction data is even more useful because it has greater potential for illustrating how difficulties are experienced, dealt with and overcome. So Franklin ends his chapter by calling for more applied linguistic research into authentic intercultural interactions in the business sector.

Chapter 14, by Eades, focuses on intercultural communication in legal contexts. She provides some authentic interactional data of the kind that Franklin is calling for (in this case, in a legal context), and again focuses on the issue of difference. She starts by considering the use of silence in Aboriginal English, and illustrates and explains how its use differs from that in general Australian English. She reports how she developed an intercultural awareness handbook for lawyers that explained these and other differences in language use, and how in certain respects this helped to improve communication between lawyers and Aboriginal defendants and witnesses. However, she then argues that there is a major problem with such a 'difference' approach – that it ignores the impact of social inequality and power relations. Referring in detail to an authentic case study, she poignantly illustrates how knowledge of difference can be misused by powerful people to achieve their own purposes.

The next chapter, Chapter 15, by Scherr, continues the theme of cultural difference. It focuses on the various ways in which cultural differences can be handled in school education, and considers this at three levels: at the national policy level, at the community/local level, and within schools themselves. Referring particularly to France, Canada and Britain, Scherr compares the multicultural approach of Britain and Canada, which attempts to recognize and accept cultural diversity, with French republicanism, which postulates that social integration should be based on the acceptance by all citizens of French cultural values. Scherr explains how each approach has its own problems, and argues that each country's way of dealing with cultural differences in education needs to be understood within its broader social and political context.

Chapter 16, by Hinton, turns to the media sector and considers another aspect of difference: the extent to which people's interpretations of media communications are similar or different across cultures. Hinton points out that, in some people's view, the globalization of the media has led to a reduction of cultural difference in media interpretation. However, he takes the opposing view and argues that all media interpretation takes place within a specific cultural context, and that it is vital always to take this context into account. Hinton argues his case by examining two areas of media research: the impact of media violence on violence in society, and the extraordinary worldwide popularity of soap operas. At first glance, both these issues could seem to support the notion of universalism in media interpretation, but Hinton disputes this. He maintains that media interpretation is a dynamic process in which people actively make sense of media products in terms of their own cultural expectations.

The final chapter in this section, Chapter 17 by Piller, turns to a rather different topic: cross-cultural communication in intimate relationships. Focusing on couples from different national and/or linguistic backgrounds, she starts by illustrating how the number of international marriages has risen markedly in recent decades, and she considers possible reasons for this. She singles out three aspects of globalization that mediate cross-cultural intimate relationships: international mobility, international data flow (especially with the help of the Internet) and international cultural exchange. Using data from 'dating websites', she illustrates how people position themselves ideologically in terms of gender, race and family, often pitching themselves against other people of their own nationality.

12. Intercultural communication in healthcare settings

Celia Roberts

1. Introduction

Most of the literature on cultural issues in healthcare settings stems from medical anthropology and does not focus on the details of interaction. The sociological and sociolinguistic studies take a more interactional perspective but are concerned with asymmetrical encounters generally rather than with intercultural communication. The applied linguistic literature on intercultural communication in healthcare would make up only a slim volume, although it is growing. It is important, therefore, to make connections with the wider literature, not least because of the contributions anthropology and sociology have made to an understanding of discourse, identity and equality in healthcare settings. The work on healthcare discourse has concentrated on the health professional – patient interaction. Following Goffman, this is the "front stage" work of professionals. However, hospitals and other healthcare institutions are held together as much by "backstage" work: the talk and text between health professionals, managers and other staff in healthcare organizations (Atkinson 1995). And the institution of medicine and the professions within it are largely maintained by the education, training and selection work that prepares and develops health professionals. Much of this is carried out in high stakes gate-keeping encounters. So, this "backstage" work is also included in this chapter.

Migration and the diaspora continue to produce a changing communicative ecology in public life. Stable ethnic minority populations co-exist alongside relatively new groups of migrants and asylum seekers. As with other caring and social services, both the research and policies in the health arena chart the changes in practices produced as a result of multilingual and culturally diverse client populations. These include changes in the medical and nursing undergraduate curriculum and postgraduate training, concerns about fairness and equal opportunities in assessment and selection processes, and research and policies around interpreter mediated consultations.

2. Professional–patient communication

It is estimated that over ten thousand articles have been written about healthcare professional–patient communication. Most of these are written either by healthcare practitioners or psychologists (Ong, DeHaes, Hoos and Lammes 1995). In comparison, the output from linguistics has been small. Candlin and Candlin (2003: 135) with reference to the major applied and sociolinguistic journals remark that "one finds the occasional paper, but no real sense of ongoing commitment to the health care communication field". Only a very small fraction of these thousands of articles are focused on intercultural communication (Skelton, Kai and Loudon 2001).

3.   Difference as "cultural"

The research traditions of medical sociology and sociolinguistics, although not focused on ethnic notions of interculturality, conceptualize the health professional–patient encounter as one of difference in which the medical system is characterized as "a cultural system" (Kleinman 1988). The different perspectives and knowledge structures about, for example, AIDS or genetics, and managing social relations are broadly intercultural in that professionals and clients/patients are seen as voicing different world views (Mishler 1984). The sociolinguistic literature on healthcare settings has looked at inequalities in medical discourse (Freeman and Heller 1987), and healthcare generally (McKay and Pittam 2002) asymmetrical power relations (Ainsworth-Vaughn 1998, Wadak 1997) and how they are co-constructed in consultations (ten Have 1995) and, in particular, the gendered nature of such relations (Fisher 1995; West 1984), as well as social class (Todd 1984), the discursive representation of health and illness (Fisher and Todd 1983; Fleischman 2001; Hyden and Mishler 1999); and how different medical conditions shape the discourse of the consultation (Hamilton 2004).

The sociologically based studies of the consultation share with intercultural communication studies a concern with inferential processes and the potential for miscommunication which can feed into more structured social inequalities in healthcare. Cicourel (1983) examines the miscommunication when doctor and patient have different belief structures about the cause of an illness (see also Tannen and Wallet 1986). He argues that much of the misunderstanding that arises out of diagnostic reasoning stems from tacit clinical experience and from everyday understanding that is presumed to be shared knowledge. Similarly, Atkinson (1995) and Silverman (1987) drawing on seminal work on the ritual aspects of the consultation, analyse the powerful discourses that determine the patients' treatment.

As well as the cultural differences between health professional discourse and the lifeworld discourses of the patient, there are increasing tensions and instabilities between professional discourses and the wider institutional discourses of healthcare organization, as new types of communicative genres come into being (Iedema and Scheeres 2003; Cook-Gumperz and Messerman 1999).

Iedema (in press) describes the "interactive volatility" where there is increasing amount of talk in what might broadly be conceived of as intercultural encounters where professionals and others who inhabit different professional and organizational cultures now have to negotiate meanings together. This volatility is the result of new sites and practices where there are stuggles over how to interact, as professional roles and relationships have to be rethought. Research on the detailed interactional strategies of the consultation has been dominated by Conversation Analysis (CA). Although not addressed explicitly, Conversation Analysis looks at the differences in how professionals and patients communicate with each other. By looking at relatively large numbers of a particular phase of the consultation, CA has shown the patterns of turn design and their consequences for health professionals and their patients. CA studies in the USA, Finland and the UK, to name some of the main contributions to this tradition, have focused on particular phases such as openings, history taking and making a diagnosis (see Drew, Chatwin and Collins 2001 for an overview of CA in healthcare settings). CA, in pursuing the quest for general patterns, has not focused on ethnic/linguistic diversity in communication and so the unpredictable and less determinate qualities of consultations when patient and doctor draw on different ethno-linguistic resources (see Gumperz and Cook-Gumperz in this volume). However, CA methodology has influenced the interactional sociolinguistic research in healthcare settings described below.

It is not possible to look at all aspects of what Sarangi calls a developing "communicative mentality" (Sarangi 2004) in healthcare settings, nor to look at all the ways in which "diversity" affects interpretation in health encounters where diversity includes, as mentioned above, any difference in health professionals' and patients' perspectives.

The rest of the chapter will, therefore, focus on language and ethnicities in intercultural communication.

4.   Cultural differences and medical anthropology

Just as there are fuzzy boundaries between what is ethnically constituted as cultural difference and what is socially/institutionally constituted, as suggested, so the notion of "intercultural" is problematic. In other words "culture" can be conceived of too narrowly as *only* accounting for linguistic/ethnic differences or overused to explain *any* interaction where participants' ethnic/national origins differ. As Auer and Kern argue, an encounter is not intercultural just because people originate from different parts of the world and belong to different races and ethnicities. "Culture" can only be understood as part of action and interaction rather than standing outside it. Differences, difficulties and misunderstandings cannot be easily accounted for *because* people come from these different backgrounds. This may be the explanation but there are other reasons to do with "professional culture", individual differences, etc. which may account for differences (Auer and Kern 2000).

It is important to bear these arguments in mind when discussing the literature on health beliefs from medical anthropology. The significance of this approach in professional–patient consultations lies in the potential for misunderstandings when different explanatory models of illness, which patients bring to the encounter, clash with the diagnosis and explanation of the disease from the professional's perspective. Much of the early medical anthropology literature focused on non-western health beliefs and more recent studies have used this perspective to examine issues of cultural diversity in western healthcare settings (Kleinman 1988; Helman 1994), and in relation to mental illness (Rack 1991). These health beliefs may affect how the body is conceptualized, what is regarded as healthy and what causes disease and appropriate responses to it. Studies by medical anthropologists have also discussed different ways in which patients from different cultural backgrounds may present their symptoms, some highlighting objective signs and others the emotional or psychological aspects (Helman 1994). Another aspect of the cultural and linguistic relativity of health beliefs concerns pain and how it is responded to and expressed. Healthcare beliefs are also affected by different experiences of healthcare systems and this may affect practical issues such as adherence to treatment (Henley and Schott 1999). The culturally specific beliefs that patients bring to a consultation enter into the discourse of the encounter and cannot be ignored in a narrowly linguistic analysis. However, medical anthropology has not focused on the discursive and interactional aspects of the consultation (but see Manderson and Allotey 2003 for an exception). So, illuminating though this literature is, it tends to conceive of health beliefs as static sets of assumptions rather than active discourses which may be called up or not and which are mediated through different styles of self presentation. In contrast to much of the anthropological literature, recent studies in the UK suggest that patients from diverse backgrounds tend to use western medical models in their consultations with mainstream health professionals (Bhopal 1986).

Rather than fixed health beliefs, it is the discourse styles of relating to, and representing illness to the health professional that tend to make cultural issues relevant in the consultation (Anderson, Elfert and Lai 1989). As Pauwels (1991, 1994) indicates in her discussion of training health workers in Australia, broad differences in health beliefs were more readily available for comment than discourse and rhetorical features. So there is a tendency to focus on beliefs because they are easier to talk about than on ways of talking and interacting which are more hidden and require more technical understanding.

5.   Health professional–patient communication in linguistically and culturally diverse societies

In the clinical literature, cultural diversity tends to be treated in two different ways: either in terms of cultural awareness, drawing on the health beliefs literature described above or in terms of the "language barrier". Language and culture tend to be treated separately, rather than being "wired in together" (Agar 1994). While some research plays down language problems, most of the studies acknowledge them (Ahmad, Kernohan and Baker 1989; Ali 2003). And of these latter, nearly all are concerned with issues of interpreting; the majority with policy issues (Jacobs, Lauderdale, Meltzer, Shorey, Levinson and Thisted 2001) but others with the nature of mediated consultations and some of the drawbacks of them.

5.1.   Interpreter-mediated consultations

The linguistic and sociolinguistic studies on interpreter mediated encounters in healthcare settings argue that the interpreter is not a neutral tool (Putsch 1985) or a "walking bilingual dictionary" (Ebden, Carey, Bhatt and Harrison 1988) but a linguistic and social intermediary, dealing with discourse and social interaction and not just a narrow definition of language:

> "Interpreters do not merely convey messages they shape, and in some very real sense, create those messages in the name of those for whom they speak." (Davidson 2000: 382).

Davidson's work also clearly shows that as well as managing the conversational flow of the consultation, interpreters also act as gatekeepers, often editing and even deleting utterances of the patients for whom they are interpreting. To this extent, they are certainly not acting as advocates or ambassadors. Nor are they neutral since they act as social agents within the jointly constructed discourse (Bührig 2001). It is not surprising, therefore, that interpreter-mediated consultations are often less patient-centred than non-mediated ones (Rivadeneyra, Elderkin-Thompson, Silver and Waitzkin 2000).

In most medical settings, more informal interpreters are used than professional ones, including staff in the hospital or clinic and family and friends of the patients (Meyer 2001; Bührig and Meyer 2005). Yet there is a dearth of literature in this area. One area where there are some studies is in the use of children as informal interpreters for their family. This research has focused on the views of healthcare professionals and has identified several problems including limited language skills and the difficulties of interpreting complicated and sensitive subjects (Cohen, Moran-Ellis and Smaje 1999). The term "language brokering" is used, derived from the notion of cultural brokering (Kaufert and Koolage

1984) which suggests that a "broker" is more independent than an interpreter in initiating action in an encounter. The term "brokering" focuses on the consultation as an intercultural event and not just on narrow issues of linguistic translation. Although the role of children in these intercultural encounters can lead to the kind of problems mentioned above, research on children as brokers showed a more mixed picture (Green, Free, Bhavnani and Newman 2005). The child brokers often felt ignored and, contrary to good practice for professional interpreters, wanted to be treated as full participants in the consultation. But they also felt there were benefits to child brokering in terms of the responsibility it gave them and the help they could offer their families.

The interpreter-mediated consultation can produce its own misunderstandings and this may be in part due to the health professionals' own competence in working with interpreters (Blackford 1997). Some patients prefer to communicate directly with their doctor and there is some evidence that patients are suspicious of cultural mediators who may talk *for* them. Uncertainty about how talk is interpreted may lead to mistrust that can slide into negative assumptions about the group that speaks that language (Collins and Slembrouck in press).

Collins and Slembrouck's study looks at alternatives to the face-to-face interpreter-mediated consultation: the use of translated medical terms and phrases and the use of telephone interpreters. In this ethnographic linguistic study of a local community clinic in Belgium, Collins and Slembrouck show that there is considerable unease with all these different strategies among the staff of the clinic. A manual that consisted of key phrases, symptoms and diseases was translated into those languages where there were few or no informal interpreters. However, this was found to be cumbersome and created its own linguistic and interactional problems. Doctors preferred direct and unmediated consultation where possible.

6.   Intercultural communication in the majority language

While many of the broader cultural issues of a diverse society have been treated in the sociological and sociolinguistic literature on health settings (see above), the interactional dimension has received less attention. Discourse analysis methodology has been used to focus on interactional differences and on misunderstandings in Australian settings (Pauwels 1991; Cass, Lowell, Christie, Snelling, Flack, Marrnganyin and Brown 2002; Manderson and Allotey 2003), in South Africa (Crawford 1994) and in comparing doctor–patient communication in the USA and Japan using quantitative discourse analysis (Ohtaki, Ohtakia and Fetters 2003).

The rest of this chapter will draw on interactional sociolinguistics (Gumperz 1982, 1996, 1999, Gumperz and Cook-Gumperz in this volume) and on the detail of how conversational inferences are made and conversational involvement is sustained in ethnically and linguistically heterogeneous communities. Differences in communicative background enter into talk and affect how interpretations are made. Ways of talking are not separated from the socio-cultural knowledge that is brought along and brought about in the interaction or how social identity leaks out into the interaction through talk; for example, how to manage the moral self in consultations, what are allowable topics, how to structure an illness narrative; how direct to be in self-presentation or how to manage turns at talk with the professional. At a micro level, language and socio-cultural knowledge influence choice of words and idioms and a range of prosodic features, including intonation and rhythm. These are the "contextualization cues" (Gumperz 1982) which help to frame each phase of the consultation and channel the interpretive message of either professional or patient. Where these styles of speaking and conventions for interpreting the other's talk are not shared, misunderstandings frequently occur. Differences in communicative style can not only lead to overt misunderstandings but also to difficult or uncomfortable moments and to some of the small tragedies of everyday life (Levinson 1997); for example, if patients do not get access to scarce resources. Patients may be anywhere on a continuum of language ability in terms of lexico-grammatical accuracy, pragmatics and discursive strategies (Ali 2003). Patterns of language difference are situated and contingent rather than absolute and systematic, so:

> "We need to be able to deal with degrees of differentiation and ... learn to explore how such differentiation affects individuals' ability to sustain social interaction and have their goals and motives understood." (Gumperz 1982: 7).

7.   Patients with limited English and doctors in general practice

This final section is based on a series of studies drawn from a research project based at King's College London. The video data illustrated below form part of a corpus gathered for a programme of research on patient–family doctor interactions: Patients with Limited English and Doctors in General Practice: Education issues (the PLEDGE project), which used interactional sociolinguistic methods to explore how general practitioners (GPs) and patients negotiate meaning and collaborate to manage, repair or prevent understanding problems. 20% of the 232 video-recorded consultations were with patients from non-English speaking backgrounds or patients with a culturally specific style of communicating *and* featured frequent and profound misunderstandings.

Patients from these backgrounds ranged from those who had considerable difficulty conveying even their literal meaning, while others were more fluent, but have culturally different styles of communicating, influenced by their first languages.

The research looked at the potential for, and occasions of misunderstandings and awkward moments where the conditions for shared interpretation between patients and doctors cannot be created. The studies include: misunderstandings which occur when doctors fail to understand patients (Roberts et al. 2005), when the misunderstandings are caused by doctors and when both sides try to prevent and repair misunderstandings (Moss and Roberts 2005). We have also looked at phases in the consultation, for example, the opening phase (Roberts, Sarangi and Moss 2004) when differences in self-presentation can set the consultation off on the wrong footing.

Intercultural consultations challenge much of the received wisdom about good communication skills in the healthcare literature. The topsy-turvy, "looking glass" world of such consultations suggests that "patient-centred" models ("patients want their feelings elicited") and the idea that more talk is likely to mean less misunderstanding ("ask open questions") often do not work and even cause more confusion when talk itself is the problem. Communications research and textbooks argue that doctors should engage more with patients but in the PLEDGE data attempts to do so by the doctors through social chat and extended explanations were often closed down by the patients (Roberts, Moss, Wass, Sarangi and Jones 2005).

7.1.   Problems with patient-centredness

Data example one

In the following example, a young mother from Somalia has brought her baby daughter to see the family doctor because she has been suffering from diarrhoea. At this stage in the consultation, the doctor has already taken a brief history from the patient's mother and, before examining the baby, has asked her some initial questions about breast feeding her:

```
 1 D   little bit (.) right so you're virtually stopped (.)
 2     so what sort of questions have you got in your mind for me today (.)
 3     what do you want me to do
 4     (1)
 5 P   mm no: =she say=
 6 D   =today=
 7 P   eh: the lady she say if you want to contacting doctor eh:
       you want eh: talk him
 8 D   yeah= =
 9 P   = =I say yes I am happy with e- with =you=
10 D   =right= right ok= =
11 P   = =because (.) definitely when I am coming with you
12     when I go back I will go back happy
```

13 D ((laughs)) I hope so
14 P because I will look to see you and your doctor K (.)
15   I like it
16 D good= =
17 P = =[cos] when when I come in will come in the you know ((tut))
18   when I go back my home I'm happy
19 D right
20 P ((laughs))
21 D so you want me to- (.) check her over

At line one the doctor uses a number of contextualization cues to show that she is about to shift topic from discussing breast feeding. She pauses, uses the discourse marker "right" and sums up the patient's contribution. She then moves to a new frame, at line 2, to eliciting patient's concerns in classic patient-centred mode. The mother may well have missed the lexical and prosodic contextualization cues which mark the shift in topic and this exacerbates the difficulty in processing the questions in lines two and three. But the main difficulty seems to be that she cannot interpret the shift in frame marked by these open questions. She responds with a negative and then refers to the "lady" (probably the receptionist) and how she is happy to see this particular doctor. This is the beginning of a narrative account about coming in to see the doctor rather than an analytical account of her concerns. She then reformulates her perception of the doctor twice more. This repetition of how she likes this doctor and her colleague seems to shift the topic from the question she asked the receptionist (about seeing the doctor) to some general display of satisfaction. This may be because she is uncertain how to take the doctor's elicitation and/or because she sees it as culturally appropriate to praise her. This is not the footing which the doctor had anticipated in which the patient is offered a more equal social relationship with the doctor in indicating her concerns. The doctor's responses at lines 10, 16 and 19 are markers of possible change of frame rather than receipt tokens, particularly "right". However, the patient orients to them as the latter and on three occasions reiterates her positive evaluation of the doctor. When there is again a minimal response from the doctor at line 19 "right", the mother gives up on her praise and laughs, marking the closure of this unsuccessful attempt at patient-centredness. The doctor then speaks *for* the patient in line 21, thus undermining her original attempt to be patient-centred and shifting back to a more orthodox frame in which she pushes on with the next phase of the consultation (Roberts, Sarangi and Moss 2004).

Misunderstandings, as this example shows, are multi-causal and jointly accomplished: contextualization cues fail to be read; socio-cultural knowledge about patient roles is not shared and neither side has the appropriate linguistic resources to repair the misunderstanding. The origin of the problem may lie with the patient or with the doctor but together they either talk past each other or, in some cases, find other resources to repair and manage the interaction. Unsurprisingly, doctors had difficulties with patients' phonological differences, prosodic features, particularly contrastive stress and assessing speaker stance, and with grammatical and syntactical means of contextualizing. But the greatest difficulties were with patients' overall rhetorical style: with low self-display, with structuring their information and with two inter-related features of topic overload and overlapping/interrupting talk (Roberts, Moss, Wass, Sarangi and Jones 2005).

Topic management was also one of the elements of doctor talk which, on different occasions, either produced or prevented misunderstandings (see also Erickson and Rittenberg 1987). Rapid topic shift was a major cause of interactional difficulties. By contrast strategies for topic involvement and fostering chances of participation in which the patient could initiate the topic tended to prevent or help repair misunderstandings (Moss and Roberts 2005).

7.2.   Presentation of self and symptoms

It is a commonplace in the intercultural literature to find evidence of the illusion of understanding and of awkward moments where there is no overt breakdown but the sense of orderliness and the underlying rhythm of a typical institutional encounter fails to be established or maintained. This is illustrated in the opening phases of symptom telling where local English styles of self and symptom presentation contrast with those used by patients whose dominant language is not English. These issues and the next two examples are discussed in more detail in Roberts, Sarangi and Moss (2004). There are three aspects to the initial self-reporting by patients: the description of symptoms, the context in which the symptoms occurred and the patient's stance. By stance here we include both "affective stance" and "epistemic stance" (Ochs 1996).

Data example two
A young white woman who speaks a standard variety of English has brought her toddler to the surgery to have his infected eye checked out.

01 D   right so how can I help =you=
02 M   =o:h= =erm=
03 D   =I'm sorry= you've had to come
04 M   oh it's ok / (1) I think he's got conjuncti*vitis but =I'm not= sure
         (.) hes had
05 D   =oh dear=
06 M   it since la:st (0.5) he had a *gummy eye this side but {[ac]when he was
         born that was quite *gummy so I tolerated it}(.) then it *travelled to this

one and got {[dc]progressively worse (0.5) over the weekend we were in
Germany for a wedding so }= =

07 D   = =oh right (nice time)
08 M   yeah it was good
09 D   ok
10 M   erm it went *red underneath *there and *red just a*bove
11 D   right
12 M   {[dc]and it's been very *gunky}
13 D   mm= =
14 M   = = {[ac] [lo]as you can see I've sort of left it (.) erm }= =
15 D   = =so this is for how many days now

Through her use of prosodic features, the mother focuses on the symptom and
puts in the background the child's history of such infection. She does this by
putting emphatic stress on key syllables "conjunctiVITis", "GUMmy", "RED"
and so on and by speeding up her utterance at 6 when giving some of the background detail and then slowing down when she returns to the symptoms later in
turn 6 and 12. The repetition "red" and the rhythmic stress in this turn and the
next when she refers to the "gunky" eye reinforces the display of symptoms as
the most important information. This enables the doctor to attend to the presentation of symptoms, and the rest can be put in the background.

By making the child's symptoms the focus of her opening turns, and the context and stance the background, this patient aligns herself with the GP and the
medical model which she expects the GP to be working with. Since both doctor
and patient share the same cultural resources for making meaning, in this case
the same use of prosodic features to contextualise this phase of the consultation,
the indirect messages conveyed in these contextualisation cues are readily interpretable by the GP.

The mother's epistemic stance is a subtle blend of the agentive – she "tolerated" the gummy eye but also somewhat deferential – "I've sort of left it". The
patient's mother presents her "moral self" as a caring but not overly anxious
mother who does not want to over treat her child and she interweaves this moral
self with the medical model of symptom giving. As shown above, this is partly
accomplished through her prosodic management of the opening report.

Patients whose expert language is not English face linguistic, pragmatic and
rhetorical problems. Pragmatic and linguistic difficulties do not *necessarily* prevent such patients from managing the rhetoric of routine self-presentations.
However, many patients talk about their problems with resources which are
both linguistically and rhetorically different from those of the doctor.

In the next example, the patient focuses not on her symptoms but her inability to cope with them. She is an elderly woman of South Asian origin whose first
language is Gujarati.

Data example three

D   come in come in please come in [ ] good morning
P   good morning
D   have a seat
P   thank you
D   how are you today
P   oh: {[dc] [creaky voice]not very good}
D   not very good (.) what's happening
P   I *pain here (.) *too much (.) I can't cope you know
D   right
P   *yesterday (.) *whole day
D   right
P   and I eat (.) *three times (.) paracetamol
D   right
P   two three hours it will be *all *right and then (.) *come *pain again (.) I
    *can't cope (.) pain like
D   you can't cope with this pain
P   yeah very very bad (.) I don't know what's the wrong with me
D   sure how * long you have this
         /   \

The patient slows down her speech with "not very good" and speaks in a creaky, tremulous voice. It as if she is as acting out the pain in her talk. The rest of her initial self report is delivered in short quite sharply contoured units with little distinction made prosodically between the description of the symptoms, the context, the self-treatment and her stance. The doctor does not immediately ask her about her symptoms but instead repeats what she has said, "you can't cope with this pain", which elicits more affective talk. And when he does ask about the symptoms, the question is, prosodically, more like a comment than a question and does not seem to function as directing back the patient to the facts of the condition. One reason why this example may be different from the previous one is that the doctor is also of South Asian origin, a Panjabi speaker, and is willing to stay with the affective stance as the focus of this self report, rather than moving immediately to the question about how long she has had these symptoms.

Both the English mother and the Gujarati patient were able to create the conditions for shared negotiation and appropriate presentation of self and symptoms because they shared linguistic and cultural resources with the doctor. When this is not the case, the orderliness of the opening stage of the consultation is challenged. Unexpected aspects of self-reporting are put in the foreground and the expected focus is lost. Sometimes, patients cannot combine symptom telling with a stance which tells the doctor what kind of patient they have sitting opposite them. As a result openings become protracted and harder work interactionally. Doctors may make judgements about patients based on a style of self-reporting that does not meet the doctor's expectations. Patients become labelled as "difficult" or "passive" and these labels become social facts. These facts constructed out of the discourse of patient–healthcare professionals, can also lead to generalisations and stereotypes in the backstage work of healthcare encounters (Roberts,Sarangi and Moss 2004).

8.   Backstage work

As with the health professional–patient communication, the relatively little work by socio- and applied linguistics on backstage work has not focused on intercultural communication. Meetings (Cook-Gumperz and Messerman 1999), doctors' rounds (Atkinson 1995), interaction in operating theatres (Pettinari 1988) as well as talk, for example, in medical laboratories are all backstage work where the teams reflect the diverse multilingual nature of western urban societies. However, linguistic and ethnic diversity is rarely the focus of attention except in educational and selection processes where issues of disadvantage, language and indirect racial discrimination are increasingly matters of concern. These issues can manifest themselves in subtle ways. For example, Erickson's case study of an African-American inexperienced doctor presenting a case to his white preceptor (experienced attending doctor) shows how "racial" tension is an implicit resource which the young doctor uses to distance himself from the black "street" patient. But in so doing he uses a more formal medical register than is expected between two medical colleagues and so may come across as insufficiently socialized (Erickson 1999).

The preparation, training and assessment of ethnic minority healthcare professionals, particularly those educated and/or trained overseas, raises questions about the adequacy and fairness of these high-stake intercultural encounters. A recurrent theme is the gap between medical knowledge and socio-cultural knowledge. Both aspiring healthcare professionals and their educators and assessors tend to overemphasize medical knowledge and down-play or remain unaware of the socio-cultural knowledge which constructs these encounters. This is the case with healthcare workers in Canada (Duff, Wong and Early 2000), with professionals subjected to language testing in Australia (McNamara 1997) and in the London-based research projects which end this paper.

9.   Oral assessment and its potential for indirect discrimination

The first of these studies concerns the oral examination for membership of the Royal College of General Practitioners and the possibility of discriminatory outcomes for certain groups of ethnic minority candidates (Roberts and Sarangi 1999). Video recordings of the examinations were analysed using interactional sociolinguistic methods. The study concluded that the "hybrid discourses" of the exam were particularly problematic for non-traditional candidates especially those trained overseas. The exam consisted of three different modes of question: institutional, professional and personal. However the exam criteria were institutionally driven. For those candidates not used to the institutional discourses of gate keeping oral assessments, however proficient they were as doctors, the examination remained an unfair hurdle.

A similar concern with equal opportunities for certain groups of ethnic minorities, led to research in a large London medical school on the final year undergraduate clinical examination which consists of role-played consultations with actor-patients (Roberts et al. 2003). Candidates who were rated highly were compared with those that failed and three components of their performance were identified as shedding light on the contrast in their marks: communicative style in which highly situated talk was contrasted with a schema driven agenda; thematic staging in which candidates either staged their arguments to persuade or closed off negotiating too early; and ideological assumptions about "slippery areas" to do with beliefs and values. Ethnic minority candidates from overseas who had performed well in medical knowledge tests tended to be marked lower in these three areas.

10.   Conclusion

Discourse analysis and interactional sociolinguistics have started to look at the differences and misunderstandings which can occur in intercultural encounters in healthcare. Lack of shared assumptions about role-relations, differences in communicative style and a lack of resources on both sides to create conditions for negotiating understanding are fed by and feed into negative ethnic and linguistic ideologies. Inequalities in healthcare can result both for patients and for professionals working in healthcare settings. Studies of intercultural communication in such settings have made a contribution to the field of applied linguistics and shed new light on medical practices. Oral examinations are now looked at through the discourse analyst's lens. Judgements about candidates are no longer simply read off from their talk; and the interactional construction of the candidate by the examiner is now acknowledged (Roberts, Sarangi, Southgate, Wakeford and Wass 2000). Similarly, issues of language and ethnicity in doctor–patient communication are enriched by the applied discourse analyst's conceptual frameworks and analytic gaze. But there the contribution to medicine and health studies of interaction analysis is still only partially visible. The most important next step is for applied linguists to be widely published in mainstream medical and health journals.

Box 1: Transcription conventions

=word=	overlapping talk
word= =	latching (one speaker following another with no pause)
(.)	micro pause, less than one second
(2.0)	estimated length of pause of one second or more, to nearest 0.5 of a second
wor:d	segmental lengthening
wor-	truncation
[ ]	inaudible speech
[word]	unclear speech
((laughs))	non-lexical occurrence
{word}	talk overlaid by non-lexical occurrence
*	stressed syllable
[ac]	accelerated speech
[dc]	slown speech
[lo]	low pitch register
/ \	rising – falling pitch movement

References

Agar, Michael
    1994   *Language Shock*. New York: William Morrow.
Ahmad, Waqar, E.E. Kernohan and M.R Baker
    1989   Patients' choice of general practitioner: Influence of patients' fluency in English and the ethnicity and sex of the doctor. *Journal of the Royal College of General Practitioners* 39: 153–155.
Ainsworth-Vaughn, Nancy
    1998   *Claiming Power in Doctor–Patient Talk*. Oxford: Oxford University Press.
Ali, Nasreen
    2003   Fluency in the consulting room. *British Journal of General Practitioners* 53: 514–515.
Anderson, Joan, Helen Elfert and Magdalene Lai
    1989   Ideology in the clinical context: chronic illness, ethnicity and the discourse on normalisation. *Sociology of Health and Illness* 11(3): 253–278.
Atkinson, Paul
    1995   *Medical Talk and Medical Work*. London: Sage.

Auer, Peter and Friederike Kern
  2000   Three ways of analysing communication between East and West Germans
            as intercultural communication. In: Aldo di Luzio, Susanne Günthner and
            Franca Orletti (eds.), *Culture in Communication: Analysis of Intercultural
            Situations*, 89–116. Amsterdam: John Benjamins.
Bhopal Raj
  1986   Asians' knowledge and behaviour on preventative health issues: smoking,
            alcohol, heart disease, pregnancy, rickets, malaria prophylaxis and surma.
            Community Medicine 8: 315–321.
Blackford, Jeanine
  1997   Breaking down barriers in clinical practice. *Contemporary Nurse* 6: 15–21.
Bührig, Kristin
  2001   Interpreting in hospitals. In: Sara Cagada, Silvia Gilardoni and Marinette
            Matthey (eds.), *Communicare in Ambiente Professionale Plurilingue*. Lug-
            ano: USI.
Bührig, Kristin and Bernd Meyer
  2005   Ad-hoc interpreting and the achievement of common purposes in doctor-
            patient communication. In: Juliana House and Jochen Rehbein (eds.), *Multi-
            lingual Communication*, 43–62. Amsterdam: John Benjamins.
Candlin, Christopher and Sally Candlin
  2003   Healthcare communication: A problematic site for applied linguistics re-
            search. *Annual Review of Applied Linguistics* 23, 134–154.
Cass, Alan, Anne Lowell, Michael Christie, Paul Snelling, Melinda Flack, Betty Marrn-
            ganyin and Isaac Brown
  2002   Sharing the true stories: Improving communication between aboriginal pa-
            tients and health care workers. *Medical Journal of Australia* 176: 466–470.
Cicourel, Aaron
  1983   Hearing is not believing: Language and the structure of belief in medical
            communication. In: Sue Fisher and Alexandra D. Todd (eds.). 221–239.
Cohen, Suzanne, Jo Moran-Ellis and Chris Smaje
  1999   Children as informal interpreters in GP consultations: pragmatics and ideo-
            logy. *Sociology of Health and Illness* 21(2): 163–186.
Collins, Jim and Stef Slembrouck
  in press 'You don't know what they translate': language, contact, institutional pro-
            cedure, and literacy practice in neighbourhood health clinics in urban
            Flanders. *Journal of Linguistic Anthropology*.
Cook-Gumperz, Jenny and Lawrence Messerman
  1999   Local identities and institutional practices: Constructing the record of
            professional collaboration. In: Srikant Sarangi and Celia Roberts (eds.),
            145–181.
Crawford, Anne
  1994   Black patients white doctors: Stories lost in translation. Cape Town:
            National Language Project, Cape Town.
Davidson, Brad
  2000   The interpreter as institutional gatekeeper: The sociolinguistic role of inter-
            preters in Spanish–English medical discourse. *Journal of Sociolinguistics*
            4/3: 379–405.

Drew, Paul, John Chatwin and Sarah Collins
   2001   Conversation analysis: a method for research into interactions between pa-
             tients and healthcare professionals. *Health Expectations* 4/1: 58–70.
Duff, Patricia, Ping Wong and Margaret Early
   2000   Learning language for work and life: The linguistic socialisation of immi-
             grant Canadians seeking careers in health care. *Canadian Modern Lan-
             guage Review* 57(1): 9–57.
Ebden, Phillip, Oliver Carey, Arvind Bhatt and Brian Harrison
   1988   The bi-lingual consultation. *Lancet* 1: 347.
Erickson, Frederick
   1999   Appropriation of voice and presentation of self as a fellow physician: as-
             pects of a discourse of apprenticeship in medicine. In: Srikant Sarangi and
             Celia Roberts (eds.), 109–143.
Erickson, Frederick and William Rittenberg
   1987   Topic control and person control: A thorny problem for foreign physicians
             in interaction with American patients. *Discourse Processes* 10: 401–415.
Fisher, Sue
   1995   *Nursing Wounds: Nurse Practitioners/Doctors/Women Patients and the Ne-
             gotiation of Meaning.* New Brunswick, NJ: Rutgers University Press.
Fisher, Sue and Alexandra D. Todd (eds.)
   1983   *The Social Organisation of Doctor–Patient Communication.* Washington,
             DC: Centre for Applied Linguistics.
Fleischman, Suzanne
   2001   Language and medicine. In: Deborah Schiffrin, Deborah Tannen and Heidi
             Ehrenberger Hamilton (eds.), *Handbook of Discourse Analysis*: 470–502.
             Oxford: Blackwell.
Freeman, Sarah and Monica Heller (eds.)
   1987   *Medical Discourse.* Special Issue of *Text* 7(1).
Goffman, Erving
   1974   *Frame Analysis.* New York: Harper and Row.
Green, Judith, Caroline Free, Vanita Bhavnani and Anthony Newman
   2005   Translators and mediators: bilingual young people's accounts of their inter-
             preting work in health care. *Social Science and Medicine* 60: 2097–2110.
Gumperz, John
   1982   *Discourse Strategies.* Cambridge: Cambridge University Press.
Gumperz, John
   1996   The linguistic and cultural relativity of inference. In: John Gumperz and
             Stephen Levinson (eds.), 374–406.
Gumperz, John
   1999   On interactional sociolinguistic method. In: Srikant Sarangi and Celia
             Roberts (eds.), *Talk, Work and Institutional Order: Discourse in Medical,
             Mediation and Management Settings*, 453–471. Berlin: Mouton de Gruyter.
Gumperz, John and Stephen Levinson (eds.)
   1996   *Rethinking Linguistic Relativity.* Cambridge: Cambridge University Press.
Gumperz, John and Jenny Cook-Gumperz
this volume Discourse, cultural diversity and communication: a linguistic anthropologi-
             cal perspective. Chapter 2.

Hamilton, Heidi
  2004   Symptoms and signs in particular: The influence of the medical concern on the shape of physician–patients talk. *Communication and Medicine* 1/1: 59–70.
ten Have, Paul
  1995   Medical ethnomethodology: an overview. *Human Studies* 18: 245–261.
Helman, Cecil
  1994   *Culture, Health and Illness*, third edition. Bristol: Wright.
Henley, Alix and Judith Schott
  1999   *Culture, Religion and Patient Care in a Multi-ethnic Society: A Handlbook for Professionals*. London: Age Concern.
Hyden, Lars-Christer and Elliot Mishler
  1999   Language and medicine. *Annual Review of Applied Linguistics* 19: 174–192.
Iedema, Rick and Hermine Scheeres
  2003   From doing to talking work: Renegotiating knowing, doing and identity. *Applied Linguistics* 24: 316–337.
Iedema, Rick, Carl Rhodes and Hermine Scheeres
  in press   Surveillance, resistance, observance: exploring the teleo-affective intensity of identity (at) work. *Organization Studies*.
Jacobs, Elizabeth, Diane Lauderdale, David Meltzer, Jeanette Shorey, Wendy Levinson and Ronald Thisted
  2001   Impact of interpreter services on delivery of health care to limited English-proficient patients. *Journal of General Internal Medicine* 16(7): 468–74.
Kaufert, Joseph and William Koolage
  1984   Role conflict among 'cultural brokers': the experience of native Canadian medical interpreters. *Social Science and Medicine* 18(3): 283–286.
Kleinman, Arthur
  1988   *The Illness Narratives: Suffering, Healing and the Human Condition*. New York: Basic Books.
Levinson, Stephen
  1997   Contextualising contextualisation cues. In: Susan Eerdmans, C. Previgagno and Paul Thibault (eds.), *Discussing Communication Analysis 1: John Gumperz*, 24–30. Lausanne: Beta Press.
Manderson, Lenora and Pascale Allotey
  2003   Cultural politics and clinical competence in the Australian Health Service. *Anthropology and Medicine* 10(1): 71–85.
McKay, Susan and Jeffery Pittam
  2002   *Language and Health Care*. Special Issue *Journal of Language and Social Psychology* 21(1).
McNamara, Tim
  1997   Problematising content validity: The Occupational English Test as a measure of medical communication. *Melbourne Papers in Language and Testing* 6(1).
Meyer, Bernd
  2001   How untrained interpreters handle medical terms. In: Ian Mason (ed.), *Triadic Exchanges. Studies in Dialogue Interpreting*. Manchester: St Jerome.

Mishler, Elliot
    1984   *The Discourse of Medicine: Dialectics of Medical Interviews.* Norwood,
            NJ: Ablex.
Moss, Becky and Celia Roberts
    2005   Explanations, explanations, explanations: How do patients with limited
            English construct narrative accounts? *Family Practice* 22(4) 412–418.
Ochs, Elinor
    1996   Linguistic resources for socialising humanity. In: John Gumperz and
            Stephen Levinson (eds.), Rethinking Linguistic Relativity 407–437.
Ohtaki, Sachiko, Toshio Ohtakia and Michael Fetters
    2003   Doctor–patient communication: a comparison of USA and Japan. *Family
            Practice* 20(3): 276–282.
Ong, L.M., J.C. DeHaes, A.M. Hoos and F.B. Lammes
    1995   Doctor–patient communication: a review of the literature. *Social Science
            and Medicine* 40/7: 903–918.
Pauwels, Anne (ed.)
    1991   *Cross-cultural Communication in Medical Encounters.* Monash: Com-
            municative Languages in the Profession Unit.
Pauwels, Anne
    1994   Applying linguistic insights in intercultural communication to professional
            training programmes. An Australian case study. *Multilingua* 13 1/2:
            195–212.
Pettinari, Catherine
    1988   *Task, Talk and Text in the Operating Room: A Study in Medical Discourse.*
            Norwood, NJ: Ablex.
Putsch, R.W.
    1985   Cross cultural communication: The special case of the interpreters in health
            care. *Journal of the American Medical Association* 254: 3344–334.
Rack, Philip
    1991   *Race, Culture and Mental Disorder*, Second edition. London: Routledge.
Rivedeneyra, R., V. Elderkin-Thompson, R. Silver and H. Waitzkin
    2000   Patient-centredness in medical encounters requiring an interpreter. *Ameri-
            can Journal of Medicine* 108/6: 470–474.
Roberts, Celia and Srikant Sarangi
    1999   Hybridity in gatekeeping discourse: Issues of practical relevance for the
            researcher. In: Srikant Sarangi and Celia Roberts (eds.), 473–503.
Roberts, Celia, Srikant Sarangi, Lesley Southgate, Risheard Wakeford and Valerie Wass
    2000   Oral examinations, equal opportunities, ethnicity and fairness in the
            MRCGP. *British Medical Journal* 320: 370–374.
Roberts, Celia, Valerie Wass, Roger Jones, Srikant Sarangi and Annie Gillett
    2003   A discourse analysis study of 'good' and 'poor' communication in an OSCE:
            a proposed new framework for teaching students. *Medical Education* 37:
            192–201.
Roberts, Celia, Srikant Sarangi and Becky Moss
    2004   Presentation of self and symptoms in primary care consultations involving
            patients from non-English speaking backgrounds. *Communication and
            Medicine* 1/2: 159–169.

Roberts, Celia, Becky Moss, Valerie Wass, Srikant Sarangi and Roger Jones
2005   Misunderstandings: a qualitative study of primary care consultations in
          multilingual settings, and educational implications. *Medical Education* 39:
          465–475.
Sarangi, Srikant
2004   Towards a communicative mentality in medical and health care practice:
          Editorial. *Communication and Medicine* 1/2: 1–11.
Sarangi, Srikant and Celia Roberts (eds.)
1999   *Talk, Work and Institutional Order: Discourse in Medical, Mediation and
          Management Settings.* Berlin: Mouton de Gruyter.
Silverman, David
1987   *Communication and Medical Practice.* London: Sage.
Skelton, John, Joe Kai, and Rhian Loudon
2001 Cross-cultural communication in medicine: questions for educators. *Medical
          Education* 35/3, 257–261.
Tannen, Deborah and Cynthia Wallet
1986   Medical professions and parents: A linguistic analysis of communication
          across contexts. *Language in Society* 15, 295–312.
Todd, Alexandra Dundas
1984   The prescription of contraception. *Discourse Processes* 7: 171–200.
West, Candace
1984   *Routine complications: Troubles in talk between doctors and patients.*
          Bloomington: Indiana University Press.
Wodak, Ruth
1997   Discourse-sociolinguistics and the study of doctor–patient interaction. In:
          Britt-Louise Gunnarsson, Per Linell and Bengt Nordberg (eds.), *The Con-
          struction of Professional Discourse*, 173–2000. London: Longman.

13. Differences and difficulties in intercultural management interaction

Peter Franklin

1. Introduction

Those working in international business and management, in particular human resource development professionals, are increasingly interested in the study of intercultural communication for the way that it can provide (partial) solutions/ remedies for some of the problems or unsatisfactory states encountered in cross- and multicultural cooperation. These problems and unsatisfactory states may be found in all aspects of classical management. Decision making, project planning, conducting a meeting and giving feedback to a member of staff are examples of universal management activities, yet they all become more challenging when managers are working across corporate and/or national cultural borders because they may be achieved in culture-specific ways. When people encounter not just a foreign language and a different communication style but different ways of acting and managing, this can be very burdensome. In a tourist situation, interactional differences often result in only passing discomfort, but in business, much more is usually at stake. The success of the company's or client's business, the harmony of significant relationships, the jobs of staff and colleagues and/or indeed one's own, are among the things which may be endangered through culturally influenced, dysfunctional management interaction.

Solutions and remedies generated by the study of intercultural communication can be made available in the form of human resources and organizational development interventions, most frequently as intercultural training of one kind or another (cf. Rost-Roth, this volume; Newton, this volume). Increasingly, the study of intercultural communication is also being looked to as a source of assistance in tapping the potentially greater creativity and/or effectiveness assumed by companies, and to some extent demonstrated by research (e.g. Earley and Gibson 2002; Earley and Mosakowski 2000; Jackson, May and Whitney 1995; Watson, Kumar and Michaelson 1993) to be present in culturally diverse groups.

When it comes to the scientific underpinning of intercultural training in European business, approaches have generally tended not to rely on models of how to communicate effectively across cultures (e.g. Gudykunst 1998) or on studies of the competences of the successful intercultural communicator, which may explain the rarity of the term 'intercultural *communication* training' (cf. Rost-Roth in this volume). (At the time of writing, Google gives only 11,900 hits for 'intercultural communication training' as opposed to 125,000 for 'intercultural training'.)

Rather, training has generally sought support elsewhere. On the one hand, for culture-specific training, it has drawn to a certain extent on explicitly comparative, scientific studies of two (or more) cultures, often originating in management science, such as Stewart et al. (1994) and Ebster-Groß and Pugh (1996), or on more or less soundly based, implicitly comparative accounts of an individual culture, such as Nees (2000), the implicit reference culture unsurprisingly often being the U.S.A. On the other hand, both culture-specific and especially culture-general training has to an almost overwhelming extent depended on the pioneering work of Hall (1959, 1966, 1976, 1983) on behavioural orientations and communication styles across a range of national cultures and on the contrastive, value-oriented work of Hofstede (2001) and Trompenaars and Hampden-Turner (1997).

These scholars and writers dominate the intercultural (communication) training scene in business and management in Europe and probably worldwide. Berardo and Simons (2004), in their study conducted in collaboration with SIETAR Europa (European branch of the Society for Intercultural Education, Training and Research) among 261 intercultural trainers, record that these four writers together attracted 110 out of 170 responses from trainers when they were requested to name *culture models*. No other single scientist or author even reached double figures. Gudykunst was mentioned twice. All applied linguists taken together achieved a very small handful of mentions.

The studies by Hofstede and Trompenaars are hologeistic, nomothetic, quantitative investigations which supply insights about the values and varying expressions of those values to be found in society generally, in the family, at school and in the workplace in a large variety of national cultures. They concentrate on what Hofstede refers to as 'dimensions of culture', a dimension of a culture being "an aspect of a culture that can be measured relative to other cultures" (Hofstede 1994: 14) and thus yield information about differences among cultures.

Reference to such contrastive studies in culture-general training, such as is used to help build international teams or prepare young managers for international careers, can create awareness and understanding of the culturally determined, different values and phenomena encountered in international business and management situations. Given the lack of usable alternatives, in particular of insights from interactionist studies, they are also used in culture-specific training or in the training of bi-cultural groups, for example in post-merger integration training.

However, the differences which such etic studies highlight may not in themselves constitute all or any of the problems and unsatisfactory states in international business cooperation that have to be dealt with. They are relatively far removed from the daily communication situations and interactions of such co-operation and thus offer little help to international managers in the area of communication itself – in assisting managers actually to interact across cultures. Hofstede devotes only just over one page of 466 to the principles of intercultural communication and cooperation (2001: 423–425) and less than a page to language and discourse (2001: 425). Trompenaars and Hampden-Turner (1997: 74–76) deal with the topic in something under three brief pages.

More communication-oriented assistance is conventionally sought in the work of Hall (1959, 1966, 1976, 1983). As well as contributing insights on behavioural orientations which have found widespread acceptance in the intercultural trainers' repertoire of knowledge, Hall again offers a usefully contrastive, if under-researched, distinction in communication styles in different cultures. However, this work only serves to raise awareness and provide explanations in a single area of distinctiveness and does not claim to equip those taking part in training with techniques to promote effective communication across cultural borders.

These contrastive studies may make general behaviour patterns more understandable and predictable and therefore to some extent more manageable, but they are rather blunt instruments when it comes to preparing people for actually communicating in intercultural encounters in business. In particular, they cannot yield detailed insights into particular bi-cultural constellations. More critically, they do not move beyond creating awareness and understanding. They do not describe what kind of behaviour is successful in mastering intercultural management interaction and neither do they provide strategies and techniques for communicating and interacting across cultures, yet for the trainer these are perhaps the most crucial issues, given the trainees' understandable and frequent demand for solutions after being confronted with so many differences and difficulties!

Hofstede (1994: 138) memorably entitled a chapter on uncertainty avoidance *What is different is dangerous*. A similar belief underlies the approach of many trainers to such training; namely that, not unreasonably, what is different is not necessarily dangerous but at least potentially difficult and should therefore be highlighted and prepared for in intercultural training.

This unsatisfactory and almost exclusive reliance on Hofstede's and Trompenaars' contrastive, value-oriented approaches and on Hall's behavioural orientations and communication styles also in culture-specific, intercultural – or perhaps better in this case *cross*-cultural – training for business is the result, firstly, of a comparative lack of authentic interactionist data and, secondly, when the data is available, of a focus on other aspects of the communication.

It is the case that a limited amount of authentic data from business life has in fact been gathered, such as Spencer-Oatey and Xing (2000), Birkner and Kern (2000) and the investigations collected in Bargiela-Chiappini and Harris (1997) and in Ehlich and Wagner (1995) (although some of these latter studies investigate simulated or monocultural negotiations). However, it is often not acceptable for scholars to observe and/or record in business contexts. This difficulty in collecting authentic business and management interaction data means that intercultural trainers often do not know with any degree of certainty what kind of communication or interaction difficulties need to be prepared for in any particular cultural pairings.

The focus of the work on the little authentic data available has also tended not to help the management trainer. It is often either contrastive (e.g. Yamada 1997), or else it describes the characteristics of intercultural communication (e.g. Neumann 1997). More valuable from the training point of view is the limited amount of research which has collected both authentic data and also people's evaluations of it, such as Spencer-Oatey and Xing (2000) on a business meeting and Bailey (2000) on service encounters. Martin (2001) also uses the observations of experienced cross-cultural negotiators in her study of simulated Irish–German negotiation. It is such observations and evaluations which can be of special use to the cross-cultural trainer and which self-reports can also provide.

Given this comparative dearth of relevant research it is unsurprising then that cross-cultural trainers seeking to give scientific solidity and credibility to their work resort to major studies, even if these are not always able to give the help really needed. But is this reliance on 'big picture' studies really helpful to managers dealing mainly with only one other culture, as in the case of post-merger integration? In particular, the following questions arise, and the answers to them may cast doubts on the salience of the classical studies and the use to which they are put in much cross-cultural training:

1(a). Are the differences reported in the classical contrastive studies (Hofstede, Trompenaars and Hall) noticed as differences by managers in their intercultural interactions?

1(b). What differences are reported by managers but not described by the classical studies?

2. Do the differences described by the contrastive studies predict and explain the difficulties in intercultural management interaction?

3. What difficulties are reported by managers but are not predictable on the basis of the classical, contrastive studies?

4. Can the differences and difficulties experienced by practising managers be predicted more completely and explained more accurately by reference to insights from other studies which have received less attention than those by Hofstede, Trompenaars and Hall?

2.   The case study

This chapter aims to supply preliminary, tentative answers to these questions by referring to an example of intercultural management reality captured in a small qualitative case study[1] of 26 German and British human resources managers working together in the post-merger integration process subsequent to the take-over by the German parent company of its new British subsidiary company. The data discussed concerns the differences in the profiles, communication styles and management behaviour noted by the German managers about their British colleagues and vice versa, and the difficulties reported by the German managers about working with their British colleagues and vice versa. The self-report data was collected in a questionnaire using open questions and in focus-group activities prior to the designing and conducting of an intercultural training workshop for the managers concerned.

It should be emphasized that this is a small case study which yields a single snapshot of a complex reality and which makes no claims to completeness or conclusiveness in its description of Anglo-German management interaction. Rather the discussion of the data is to be understood more as a criticism of the prevailing research base and the (mis)use to which some of it is put in intercultural communication training in business and management. It should also be regarded as a suggestion for a more promising approach to designing targeted cross-cultural management communication training and indeed as an argument for more interactionist-based and self-report research insights.

Before examining the data yielded by the case study to answer question 1 above with respect to Anglo-German management interaction, we should perhaps recall what differences between British and German value-orientations can be derived from the Hofstede study and what differences between British and German communication styles can be derived from Hall's work.

The conventionally assumed differences lie firstly in the areas of German low-context communication (Hall and Hall 1990: 7) contrasted with British higher-context communication. According to Hall, high-context communication is characterized by large amounts of information which is not "coded, explicit [or] transmitted" (Hall 1976: 79) but is assumed or known to be shared and therefore accessible and understood by those involved in the communication process. This stored information, which Hall refers to as "context", plays a large part in high-context communication. Extreme high-context communication is located at one end of a continuum, and at the other end we find extreme low-context communication, in which "the mass of the message is vested in the explicit code" (Hall 1976: 79).

Low context communication is typically characterized by features such as a reliance on words rather than non-verbal signals to communicate, an emphasis on detail and exactness resulting in literalness, and verbal self-disclosure and directness, which are valued as showing honesty and straightforwardness. As far as the regulation of cooperation in business is concerned, low-context cultures tend to attach much importance to the written word of laws and regulations and written business documents such as contracts, minutes, memos and procedure handbooks.

High context communication is typically characterized by features such as a low reliance on explicit messages consisting of words, a correspondingly greater reliance on non-verbal signals, vagueness and tentativeness, a resulting tendency to interpret the intentions of the other party to the communication and low self-disclosure and indirectness, which are valued as showing consideration for the face of the other party. Cooperation in business is likely to be regulated in high-context cultures through personal and spoken undertakings, which offer security because they are based on sound interpersonal relationships and are guaranteed by the need to save face.

According to the assessments of Rösch and Segler (1987), Ferraro (1990) and others, cultures which typically display low-context communication behaviour are, for example, the Netherlands, the USA, the Scandinavian countries (except Finland) and Germany. Conversely, Japan, China, Arab countries, Latin America and southern Europe typically display high-context communication behaviour. Britain would occupy a middle position, somewhat higher than France but lower than southern European countries.

The difficulties in Anglo-German interaction resulting from these contrasting styles are widely reported in training and consultancy situations: German managers frequently describe their British colleagues as excessively polite, indirect and opaque to the point of lacking in straightforwardness and even honesty. British managers often describe their German colleagues as being direct and assertive to the point of being rude and aggressive.

The second major difference between Britain and Germany consists in the extremely low uncertainty avoidance of British management, which contrasts with the greater need for uncertainty avoidance of German management. Scoring 65 on Hofstede's (2001: 151) Uncertainty Avoidance Index (UAI) with a ranking of 29th of 53 countries and regions (according to the responses given by 116,000 members of the IBM company to questions on their work-related preferences), Germany is generally regarded as a mid-high uncertainty avoiding culture and Hofstede himself even refers to Germany as a culture in which uncertainty avoidance is high (2001: 178). According to the UAI, Britain, on the other hand, has an extremely low need to avoid uncertainty with a UAI score of 35 and a ranking of 47/48 (Hofstede 2001: 151).

For Hofstede, uncertainty avoidance is "the extent to which the members of a culture feel threatened by uncertain or unknown situations" (Hofstede 2001: 161). He characterizes low UAI cultures as ones in which "the uncertainty inherent in life is relatively easily accepted" (Hofstede 2001: 161), there is lower stress and less anxiety, emotions are suppressed and people are comfortable with ambiguity and chaos. High UAI cultures, on the other hand, are ones, according to Hofstede (2001: 161), "in which the uncertainty inherent in life is felt as a continuous threat that must be fought", there is higher stress and anxiety, emotions are not suppressed and there is a need for clarity and structure. Hofstede (2001: 146) regards technology, law and religion as the key domains which provide cultures with ways to cope with the uncertainty of life in societies at large.

For management situations in low UAI cultures, Hofstede (2001: 165–170) states that ambiguity in structures and procedures is tolerated, and precision and punctuality have to be learned. In the workplace, there is a belief in common sense and people with generalist knowledge, and the power of managers tends to depend on their position and the relationships they have with the people they work with.

This picture contrasts with high UAI cultures (Hofstede 2001: 165–170) in which highly formalized conceptions of management prevail and precision and punctuality come naturally. In the workplace, there is a belief in people with specialist knowledge and expertise, and the power of managers derives from an ability to control uncertainties. As the parallel domains to technology, law and religion in society at large, Hofstede (2001: 147) regards technology, rules and rituals as the domains which provide organizations and therefore managers with tools to cope with the uncertainty of life in organizations. Not only rules for behaviour contained, for example, in contracts and in company handbooks laying down procedures, but also formal structure, plans and reporting systems are likely to be salient features of management in higher uncertainty avoidance cultures such as Germany.

The difficulties in Anglo-German interaction predicted by these differences are borne out by experience. British managers often describe the rule-oriented behaviour of their German colleagues as being rigid, hierarchical and uncreative. When British managers fail to work in accordance with the given structures and do not keep to the plan agreed, German managers frequently experience their British colleagues as unpredictable, unreliable and even chaotic. 'Managing by muddling through' is one of the kinder epithets German managers sometimes use to describe British management practice.

2.1.   Question 1

Question 1a. Are the differences reported in the classical contrastive studies (Hofstede, Trompenaars and Hall) noticed as differences by managers in their intercultural interactions?
Question 1b. What differences are reported by managers but not described by the classical studies?

Table 1 summarizes the differences and difficulties reported by the British managers and their underlying regularities. Those reported by the German managers, and the regularities possibly underlying them, can be found in Table 2.

Table 1. Differences between German and British managers and difficulties in communication as reported by British managers and possible source of the difficulty as derived from Hofstede and Hall

	Reported as a difference	Reported as a difficulty	Possible source
Predicted differences			
specialization	yes	no	higher uncertainty-avoidance
process-orientation	yes	yes	higher uncertainty-avoidance
rule-orientation	yes	no	higher uncertainty-avoidance
data-orientation, precision	yes	no	higher uncertainty-avoidance, low context communication
directness	yes	no	low context communication
planning	no	yes	higher uncertainty-avoidance
Reported differences			
formality	yes	yes	
surnaming	yes	yes	
use of titles	yes	yes	
German-speaking, multilingual	yes	no	

Table 2. Differences between British and German managers and difficulties in communication as reported by German managers and possible source of the difficulty as derived from Hofstede and Hall

	Reported as a difference	Reported as a difficulty	Possible source
Predicted differences			
lack of structure	yes	yes	low uncertainty-avoidance
indirectness	yes	yes	higher context communication
lack of process-orientation	no	yes	low uncertainty-avoidance
Reported differences			
informality	yes	yes	
humour	yes	yes	
English-speaking, monolingual	yes	no	
lack of lingua franca skills	no	yes	

In the case study analysed here, the British reported that their German colleagues differed from themselves in their high degree of specialization, their process-orientation, rule-orientation, data-orientation and precision in their management work, behaviours which are conventionally attributed to a preference for uncertainty avoidance. The British managers also reported that a further difference concerned the directness of their German counterparts, a behaviour associated with low-context communication.

However, further differences were noted by the British managers which would not be predicted by Hofstede's and Hall's work. The most frequently reported difference concerned formality, surnaming and the use of titles. One British manager remarked, for example, 'I do not like formality [especially formal presentations]'; another noted 'I do not call my colleagues by their surname' and another observed 'I am never known by my title [Mrs] at work'. The second difference noted was the fact that their German colleagues were – unsurprisingly – German-speaking but multilingual.

These predicted and reported differences are listed in the second and third columns of Table 1, their possible causes in the fourth column.

The Germans reported that their British colleagues differed from themselves in their lack of structure in their management activity, a behaviour indicative of low uncertainty avoidance, and in their indirectness, a property associated with high-context communication.

However, further differences were noted by the German managers which would not be predicted by Hofstede's and Hall's work. These differences concerned the occurrence of humour and informality. A typical observation was 'I do not address my boss by his/her first name'. A further difference noted was the fact that their British colleagues were – unsurprisingly – English-speaking but generally monolingual.

These predicted and reported differences are listed in the second and third columns of Table 2, their possible causes in the fourth column.

In short, the conventional wisdom did not predict all the differences observed by the managers in this case study.

2.2.   Question 2

Question 2. Do the differences described by the contrastive studies predict and explain the difficulties in intercultural management interaction?

When asked to describe the difficulties in communicating and cooperating with their German colleagues, the British managers mentioned only two features of management behaviour which are also described by the contrastive studies, namely, their process-orientation and, related to this, the importance of planning, both features associated with higher uncertainty-avoidance. One manager noted, for example, '[my German colleagues] have rigid rules with a process to follow to achieve the required outcome'.

The equivalent question asked of the German colleagues also yielded two difficulties which could be predicted on the basis of the contrastive studies. The first was the lack of process-orientation in the behaviour of their British colleagues, a feature associated with low uncertainty-avoidance. Typical observations were, 'For the Germans, once something is agreed it is written in stone. For the British, changes are always possible'. The second difficulty predictable from Hall's work on differences in communication style, namely indirectness, was also reported as a difficulty by the German managers, a typical observation being 'Britons often say what they mean between the lines, which from a German perspective is difficult to understand'.

The case study would suggest that difficulties can be predicted to a certain but incomplete extent. It was especially the case for the British managers that many of the differences predicted by the contrastive studies were not reported as being problematical.

2.3.   Question 3

Question 3. What are the difficulties that are reported by managers but are not predictable on the basis of the classical, contrastive studies?

The German managers reported the informality and the use of humour by their British colleagues (cf. Marra and Holmes in this volume) as difficulties they experienced in their interaction, behaviours not predicted by Hofstede or Hall. For their part, the British managers reported the formality, surnaming and use of titles by their German colleagues as difficulties. All these features were among those mentioned by both British and German managers as differences.

One further difficulty reported by the German managers understandably remains unpredicted and unexplained by the major contrastive studies and this concerns what has been described in the table above as 'lack of lingua franca skills' (cf. Meierkord in this volume). The German managers reported that their British colleagues were unable or unwilling to take account of the fact that they (the German managers) did not have a native-speaker competence in English and did not adjust their use of their mother tongue to the lower level of competence in English of their German colleagues. For example, one German manager noted of his British colleagues: 'The English aren't always sympathetic to Germans when they speak English. To begin with, the English speak slowly, but then fall back into speaking the same speed and slang as if the listener is a native'.

These comments are typical of those made by German managers about Anglo-German interaction and are also recorded in other studies, e.g. Knapp (1998). This observation is also frequently made by managers of other nationalities who are not native speakers of English about their interaction with British and American colleagues in international management. Indeed, in complex conflict situations such as takeovers, assessment interviews or difficult client-supplier negotiations this lack of understanding may be seen as a deliberate attempt to put the non-native party to the communication at a disadvantage (Knapp 1998: 185).

2.4.   Question 4

Question 4. Can the difficulties experienced be explained more accurately by reference to insights from other studies which have received less attention than Hofstede, Trompenaars, Hall etc?

A more complete prediction of the difficulties reported on both sides (and also the explanation of those unexplained by conventional wisdom in the tables above) would have been achieved by an examination of the *Kulturstandards* or culture standards for Germany established by Thomas (2003), Schroll-Machl (2002a, 2002b, 2003), and complemented by those for Britain observed by Schmid (2003).

Explicitly taking as his point of departure definitions of culture formulated by Kroeber and Kluckhohn (1963) and Boesch (1980), Thomas (1988, 1996, 2003) sees culture as an orientation system typical of a society, an organization or a group. This system consists of symbols passed on within a society. It influences the behaviour of all the members of the group and defines their affiliation to the group. Culture as an orientation system allows its members to create their own ways of coping with their environment (Thomas 1988: 149).

According to Thomas, what he describes as culture standards are central features of a culture's orientation system. Perhaps similar in some ways to Spencer-Oatey and Jiang's (2003) concept of sociopragmatic interactional principles, they are defined by Thomas (1988: 153) as ways of perceiving, thinking, evaluating and acting that are regarded by the majority of the members of a culture as normal, typical and binding for themselves and others. According to Thomas, they serve to guide, regulate and assess one's own behaviour and that of others. An individual's and the group-specific application of culture standards to regulate behaviour may vary within an area of tolerance but behaviours outside this area are rejected.

In common with Hall, Hofstede and others, Thomas argues that members of a culture are mostly unaware of these culture standards and the behaviour-regulating function they have. They generally only become obvious to them in interactions with members of other cultures, frequently in what are known as critical incidents, or intercultural interactions which are experienced as problematical and conflict-bound by the interactants (Thomas 1996: 113). The orientation systems of the parties to the interaction break down because they are using differently calibrated sets of instruments in their cultural cockpit.

Culture standards are identified, their behaviour-regulating function determined and their origins described by scholars through the collection and analysis of critical incidents, unproblematical interaction situations and other data. Originated by Flanagan (1947, 1954) in his work on the training of U.S. pilots, critical incidents have long been used in the intercultural field as the basis for the creation of training instruments known as intercultural sensitizers or culture assimilators, as described, for example, by Fiedler, Mitchell and Triandis (1971), Albert (1983) and Rost-Roth in this volume.

Critical incidents can be collected and analysed and culture standards identified by applying a basic research procedure which exists in a number of varying forms. Thomas (2003) himself refers to procedures to identify culture standards described by Triandis (1995), Brislin et al. (1986), Landis and Bhagat (1996) and Thomas (2000). The description that follows here is based on the detailed description contained in Thomas (1996).

Semi-structured interviews were conducted both with members of the culture under investigation and with members of other cultures about their experiences of interaction with the other culture. In the research reported on here

(Thomas 1996: 118–122), which concerned German–Chinese interaction, the interviews were conducted after a three- to four-month period of residence in the host-culture under investigation, after the honeymoon period and at a time when adjustment to and integration in the new culture are required. Thomas assumes that in such a period the number of critical incidents is likely to increase because individual explanations, stereotypes, and special patterns for understanding the behaviour of members of the other culture have not yet been formed.

The interviews were conducted only with those with a high degree of interaction with the host culture, such as managers and teachers, took place in the first language of the interviewee and were recorded, transcribed and analysed.

The interviewees were asked to describe frequently occurring, task-related encounters in which their interaction partner reacted in a way they had not expected. The interviewee should have experienced the situation as conflict-bound or confusing or he/she should have misinterpreted the situation. The situation should be unambiguously interpretable for somebody with sufficient knowledge of the cultures involved. For each critical incident described they were also asked to indicate why their interaction partner had behaved so unexpectedly and to give their own explanation for the critical points in the incident they described.

The interviewees were also asked to describe encounters in which to their surprise they were able to interact without problems and without conflict and which took place smoothly and harmoniously.

The critical and harmonious incidents and the explanations given were translated into Chinese or German. The descriptions made by the Chinese were given to Germans who had lived for a long time in China and were experts on the country to assess and explain the critical incident. The descriptions made by the Germans were likewise given to Chinese experts to assess and explain.

With the help of these assessments and explanations, the descriptions of the interactions were analysed to identify the culture standards which determined the interaction process in the phase in which it was experienced as critical. The assumption was that the incidents were experienced as critical because behaviour was contrary to expectation. The member of one culture adheres to his/her own culture standards and thus shapes and interprets the interaction situation in a way unfamiliar to the other culture. A comparison of the assessments and explanations by the two sets of experts led to the determining of the culture standards significant for the critical incidents being investigated.

In a final step, the culture standards which emerged from this analysis were compared with knowledge and insights derived from research in the areas of cultural history and philosophy. Experts were asked to associate the culture standards established in the analysis with events and sources in the history of the culture concerned.

For the German culture, Schroll-Machl (2002a: 34) identified the following culture standards: *Sachorientierung* or 'task-orientation, objectivism', expressed in a focusing on the task in hand rather than the person with whom the interaction takes place; *Wertschätzung von Strukturen und Regeln* or 'valuing of structures and rules' and adhering to them; *Regelorientierte, internalisierte Kontrolle* or 'rule-oriented, internalized control' expressed through the application of universal guidelines that are valid for and applicable to all regardless of the people concerned and their relationships and of the situation concerned; *Zeitplanung* or 'time-planning' manifested in using time, which is regarded as a valuable resource, as efficiently as possible and in focusing on planning the use of time in advance, and on making and adhering to schedules; *Trennung von Persönlichkeits- und Lebensbereichen* or 'the separation of areas of personality and of living spheres' expressed in a differentiation of behaviour both according to the sphere in which members of the German culture are dealing with another person as well as according to how close they are to that person; *Direktheit der Kommunikation* or 'directness of communication' expressed in a task-focus, in frankness and honesty which make inference unnecessary; *Individualismus* or 'individualism' expressed in a high regard for personal independence and self-sufficiency.

This description of German culture standards would predict and explain more fully many of the differences and difficulties (specialization, process-orientation, rule-orientation, data-orientation, precision and directness) noted by the British managers under discussion here.

Unexplained by Schroll-Machl's list of German culture standards above are the difficulties encountered by the British described as formality, surnaming and the use of titles. However, Thomas' (2003: 26) description includes identical or similar terms, excluding individualism but adding *Interpersonale Distanzdifferenzierung* ('differentiation of interpersonal distance'). The formality, surnaming and use of titles reported by the British can be interpreted as ways of maintaining interpersonal distance where the British would expect the reverse.

Schmid (2003: 55–63) establishes the following culture standards for Britain: *Selbstdisziplin* ('self-discipline'), *Indirekte Kommunikation* ('indirect communication'), *Interpersonale Distanzreduzierung* ('reduction of interpersonal distance'), *Pragmatismus* ('pragmatism'), *Ritualisierte Regelverletzung* ('ritualized rule-abuse'), *Ritualsierung* ('ritualization'), and *Deutschenbild* ('stereotype of the Germans').

This description of British culture standards would predict and explain more fully than the contrastive studies the differences and difficulties (lack of structure, lack of process-orientation, indirectness, informality, humour) noted by the German managers under discussion here. Insights from comparative management studies such as Stewart et al. (1994: 114–115, 168–171) and Ebster-Groß and Pugh (1996: 147–148, 150–151, 156) would also have drawn attention to the last three of these features at least as differences.

The difficulties the German and British managers report can be seen to occur particularly when these culture standards do not merely differ but actually clash (German rule orientation vs. British pragmatism, British indirect communication vs. German directness of communication). Clearly, cultural differences alone are not necessarily difficult for both parties to the communication to handle in the interaction. Some people may find differences merely interesting or curious rather than problematical or threatening. It seems that it is when culture standards actually contradict each other that difficulties are reported. This is not surprising given the behaviour-regulating function that Thomas attributes to culture standards. When culture standards are in contradiction to each other, a member of one culture is confronted with ways of thinking and behaving which are directly contrary to what is regarded in his/her own culture as normal, typical and binding and which if manifested there would result in rejection.

Large differences in value orientations, such as Hofstede's five dimensions (i.e. low/high power distance, low/high uncertainty avoidance, individualism/ collectivism, masculinity/femininity, long-/short-term orientation) naturally may also impact on behaviour and lead to difficulties in interaction but the more clearly behaviour-oriented, less abstract nature of culture standards, their greater number and their generation from critical interaction make the culture standards approach particularly useful in the culture-specific training situation, where an understanding of potential difficulties is more useful than an understanding of mere differences.

The objection may be raised that the culture standards approach, rather like the maxim approach in politeness theory, may lead to the ascertaining of a large and unmanageable number of culture standards, something which does not possess the elegance of Hall's, Hofstede's or Trompenaars' work, which enables many cultures to be described and contrasted using a limited and thus manageable number of concepts. To counter this objection, three observations can be made.

Firstly, the elegance of Hall's, Hofstede's or Trompenaars' approaches is deceptive in that, although they may offer a contrastive description of a large number of cultures according to a small number of concepts, the description of individual cultures which emerges is far from comprehensive. Still less do they offer a description of the differences between individual cultures, things which Thomas's approach does. Hofstede (1994: 252), for example, admits: "Statistical handling of the data (...) produced the four dimensions described (...) The four together account for 49% of the country differences in the data, just about half. The remaining half is country specific: it cannot be associated with any worldwide factor, at least not in the data I had". This accounts for the small number of dimensions and the resulting incompleteness of the picture yielded by Hofstede's approach for describing an individual culture and the differences between it and another culture or cultures.

Secondly, Hofstede's and Trompenaars's approaches are, to use terms brought to anthropology by Pike (1966: 37–72) and defined for intercultural purposes by Berry (1980: 11–12), Gudykunst (2000: 293–294) and others, etic rather than emic in character. Etic studies contrast a large number of cultures according to criteria regarded as absolute or universal using structures devised by an expert looking at the object of investigation from the outside and applying quantitative methods. Thomas's approach is essentially emic in that it examines one culture or pair of cultures, studies behaviour in the culture from within the system using structures discovered by the analyst, the absence of an overall framework thus allowing cultures to be studied in their own right and using criteria that are "relative to internal characteristics" (Berry 1980: 12). Given these conditions, it is unsurprising that different studies dealing with slightly different contexts may produce slightly different sets of culture standards, as in the case of Schroll-Machl's and Thomas's culture standards for Germany reported above.

Thirdly, and most importantly for the applied linguist and the trainer interested in improving communication and cooperation across cultural borders, the culture standards approach uses a research procedure which is extremely valuable for identifying many types of cultural manifestations (behavioural orientations, communication styles and values) in as much as they are noticeable or difficult and thus for accessing key issues in intercultural interaction.

It is true that some of the culture standards described here may be seen as manifestations of Hofstede's dimensions (e.g. German rule orientation as an expression of higher uncertainty avoidance, British pragmatism and ritualized rule-abuse as expressions of British extreme low uncertainty avoidance) and some in turn may be similar to Hall's behavioural orientations and communication styles (e.g. German directness/honesty and British indirect interpersonal communication can be associated with Hall's low and higher context communication).

However, the culture standards approach allows us to predict and explain a significant difficulty experienced by both the British and German managers, namely that described by the British managers as formality, surnaming and the use of titles and by the German managers as informality and humour (cf. Kotthoff in this volume on ritual and style). What the British experience here as difficult can be regarded as an expression of German differentiation of interpersonal distance as reported by Thomas (2003: 26), and what the German report as difficult can be seen as an expression of British reduction of interpersonal distance, as recorded by Schmid (2003: 57–58).

In summary, the culture standards approach allows us to predict more completely some of the difficulties of British and German managers in their interaction with one another than the classical studies.[2]

The difficulties reported by the German managers concerning the lack of lingua franca skills of their British colleagues are features well-known to the experienced cross-cultural trainer but understandably are not predicted or explained by the classical contrastive studies which are used to such an overwhelming extent in cross-cultural training. Nor are they documented in the relatively few culture standards studies.

2.5.   Summary of the results of the case study

The managers in the case study reported some cultural differences that they experienced as difficulties; however, these could not be predicted and explained in their entirety through the work of Hall, Hofstede and Trompenaars alone, but only by reference to comparative studies of British and German management, and to work on culture standards. Perhaps equally significant for the intercultural training of the managers concerned, the case study also made clear that people do not necessarily experience cultural differences as difficult. Finally, it highlighted that many difficulties were connected more with communication than with culture – issues that could be readily solved through training.

3.   A role for applied linguistics?

Using self-reports, such as those discussed in this article, is one way in which cross-cultural trainers can to some extent compensate for the relative paucity of appropriate authentic, interactionist data provided by applied linguistics, and thus for the lack of knowledge about the nature of, and especially the perceived difficulties of, intercultural interaction in international management.

Cross-cultural training which addresses the difficulties that the trainees have experienced is immediately more credible to them, and therefore likely to be more successful. Inadequate though self-reports may be, they do provide a first access to the authentic intercultural business interaction that is so elusive to the investigator and trainer. In addition, they are – at least for the trainer – an easily applied means of collecting data which may yield knowledge and insights that are more useful for helping trainees to master the communication situation than the dominant contrastive, value- and behaviour-oriented approaches.

What self-report data probably cannot give the trainer – and what interactionist data derived from the management area and analysed by applied linguists may be able to provide – is knowledge of how the difficulties experienced are dealt with and, most useful of all, overcome (if at all) in the intercultural interaction; what behaviour and language co-occur with the difficulties experienced; and what behaviour and language co-occur with the absence of difficulties and thus may be conducive to effective or at least unproblematic intercultural management communication.

Experience of dysfunctional intercultural management communication suggests that other topics for applied linguistic investigation that are potentially fruitful for the intercultural training field include:

- the role of meta-communication in the creation of understanding;
- the negotiation of meaning in intercultural management interaction;
- how both of the above are realized in language, and in particular how interactants with higher or lower levels of competence in the language of the interaction can contribute to these processes – a need evidenced by the lack of lingua franca skills reported in the case study presented here.

Research into such questions could generate insights about intercultural interaction, regardless of the cultures involved, that could be useful for culture-general training, and – especially valuably – about interaction in particular cultural pairings.

Knowledge and insights of this kind generated by applied linguistics could be the source of the solutions and remedies for the training context which international managers and management development professionals quite rightly so urgently demand, and which go beyond awareness-raising and the creation of understanding of cultural differences. They would complement the scientific underpinning of intercultural training, making it more communication-oriented, and thereby contributing to the improvement of its results.

Such research and such data exist to a limited extent but, given the increasing global integration of business activity, there is an urgent need in intercultural management for much more. The insights generated from the research that exists have not generally found their way into intercultural training practice. For reasons which can be speculated on, the contribution of applied linguistics to the preparation of international managers and business people for their work sadly seems to be restricted, in Europe at least, largely to the admittedly significant one made by foreign language pedagogy.

Notes

1. Grateful acknowledgement is made of a grant awarded by the German Federal Ministry of Education and Research, of assistance given by Stephanie Frei and Ann Francis and of the support provided by the managers and companies that took part in the case study.
2. Incidentally, it is also perhaps important and certainly interesting to reflect on why the British reported the intercultural communication with their foreign colleagues to be relatively easy and the Germans reported considerably more difficulties. Do the British experience fewer problems because they are able to use their mother tongue? Or are the recognition of problems and their discussion a valued behaviour in German management culture in a way which is not the case in British management culture?

Is the making light of difficulties a valued behaviour in British culture and an expression of the self-discipline culture standard, as Schmid (2003: 55–56) would suggest? Or, in other words and more fundamentally, is not the use of self-report methods to gain access to the intercultural interaction also liable to be influenced like all methods of cross-cultural investigation not only by the cultural centredness of the instruments and the investigators but also by the culturally determined perceptual and behavioural patterns of the respondents? Or is that not precisely what the investigator wants to access?

References

Albert, Rosita D.
   1983   The intercultural sensitizer or culture assimilator. In: Dan Landis and Richard Brislin (eds.), *Handbook of Intercultural Training. Issues in Theory and Design*, Vol. 1, 186–217. New York: Pergamon Press.
Bailey, Benjamin
   2000   Communicative behaviour and conflict between African-American customers and Korean immigrant retailers in Los Angeles. *Discourse and Society* 11(1): 86–108.
Bargiela-Chiappini, Francesca and Sandra Harris
   1997   *The Languages of Business. An International Perspective*. Edinburgh: Edinburgh University Press.
Berardo, Kate and George Simons
   2004   *The Intercultural Profession: its profile, practices and challenges*. Internet: http://www.sietar-europa.org/about_us/ICP_Survey_Report.pdf [Accessed 30 January 2007].
Berry, John W.
   1980   Introduction to methodology. In: Harry C. Triandis and John W. Berry (eds.), *Handbook of Cross-Cultural Psychology. Methodology*, Vol. 2, 1–28. Boston: Allyn and Bacon.
Birkner, Karin and Friederike Kern
   2000   Impression management in East and West German job interviews. In: Helen Spencer-Oatey (ed.), *Culturally Speaking. Managing Rapport through Talk Across Cultures*, 255–271. London: Continuum.
Boesch, Ernst
   1980   *Kultur und Handlung*. Bern: Huber.
Brislin, Richard, Kenneth Cushner, Craig Cherrie and Mahealani Yong
   1986   *Intercultural Interactions: A Practical Guide*. Beverly Hills: Sage.
Earley, P. Christopher and Elaine Mosakowski
   2000   Creating hybrid team cultures: An empirical test of transnational team functioning. *Academy of Management Journal* 43(1): 26–49.
Earley, P. Christopher and Cristina B. Gibson
   2002   *Multinational Work Teams: A New Perspective*. Mahwah, NJ: Lawrence Earlbaum Associates.
Ebster-Grosz, Dagmar and Derek Pugh
   1996   *Anglo-German Business Collaboration*. Basingstoke: Macmillan.

Ehlich, Konrad and Johannes Wagner
  1995   *The Discourse of Business Negotiation.* Berlin: De Gruyter.
Ferraro, Gary P.
  1990   *The Cultural Dimension of International Business.* Englewood Cliffs: Prentice Hall.
Fiedler, Fred E., Terence Mitchell and Harry C. Triandis
  1971   The culture assimilator: An approach to cross-cultural training. *Journal of Applied Psychology* 55: 95–102.
Flanagan, John C.
  1947   *The Aviation Psychology Program in the Army Air Forces.* Washington, DC: Government Printing Office.
Flanagan, John C.
  1954   The critical incident technique. *Psychological Bulletin* 51(4): 327–358.
Gudykunst, William B.
  1998   *Bridging Differences. Effective Intergroup Communication.* Thousand Oaks, CA: Sage.
Gudykunst, William B.
  2000   Methodological issues in conducting theory-based cross-cultural research. In: Helen Spencer-Oatey (ed.), *Culturally Speaking. Managing Rapport through Talk Across Cultures,* 293–315. London: Continuum.
Hall, Edward T.
  1959   *The Silent Language.* New York: Doubleday.
Hall, Edward T.
  1966   *The Hidden Dimension.* New York: Doubleday.
Hall, Edward T.
  1976   *Beyond Culture.* New York: Doubleday.
Hall, Edward T.
  1983   *The Dance of Life: The Other Dimensions of Time.* Garden City, NY: Doubleday.
Hall, Edward T. and Mildred Reed Hall
  1990   *Understanding Cultural Differences.* Yarmouth, ME: Intercultural Press.
Hofstede, Geert
  1994   *Cultures and Organisations: Software of the Mind.* London: McGraw-Hill.
Hofstede, Geert
  2001   *Culture's Consequences. Comparing Values, Behaviours, Institutions, and Organizations Across Nations,* 2nd edn. Beverly Hills, CA: Sage.
Jackson, Susan E., Karen E. May and Kristina Whitney
  1995   Understanding the dynamics of diversity in decision-making teams. In: Richard A. Guzzo, Eduardo Salas and Associates (eds.), *Team Effectiveness and Decision-Making in Organizations,* 204–261. San Francisco: Jossey-Bass.
Knapp, Karlfried
  1998   Cultural, organisational or linguistic reasons for intercultural conflict? A case study. In: Jürgen Beneke (ed.), *Thriving on Diversity. Cultural Differences in the Workplace,* 173–190. Bonn: Dümmler.
Kotthoff, Helga
  this volume Ritual and style across cultures, Chapter 9.

Kroeber, Alfred L. and Clyde Kluckhohn
    1963   *Culture: A Critical Review of Concepts and Definitions.* New York: Vintage
             Books.
Landis, Dan and Rabi S. Bhagat
    1996   *Handbook of Intercultural Training*, 2nd edn. Thousand Oaks, CA: Sage
             Publications.
Mara, Meredith and Janet Holmes
    this volume Humour across cultures: joking in the multicultural workplace. Chapter 8.
Martin, Gillian S.
    2001   *German–Irish Sales Negotiation. Theory, Practice and Pedagogical Impli-
             cations.* Frankfurt: Peter Lang.
Meierkord, Christiana
    this volume Lingua franca communication in multiethnic contexts, Chapter 10.
Nees, Greg
    2000   *Germany: Unravelling an Enigma.* Yarmouth, ME: Intercultural Press.
Neumann, Ingrid
    1997   Requests in German–Norwegian business discourse: Differences in direct-
             ness. In: Francesca Bargiela-Chiappini and Sandra Harris (eds.), *The Lan-
             guages of Business. An International Perspective*, 72–93. Edinburgh: Edin-
             burgh University Press.
Newton, Jonathan
    this volume Adapting authentic workplace talk for workplace communication training,
             Chapter 24.
Pike, Kenneth
    1966   *Language in Relation to a Unified Theory of the Structure of Human Beha-
             vior.* The Hague: Mouton.
Rösch, Martin and Kay Segler
    1987   Communication with the Japanese. *Management International Review*
             27(4): 56–67.
Rost-Roth, Martina
    this volume Intercultural training, Chapter 23.
Schmid, Stefan
    2003   England. In: Alexander Thomas, Stefan Kammhuber and Sylvia Schroll-
             Machl (eds.), *Handbuch Interkulturelle Kommunikation und Kooperation.
             Band 2: Länder, Kulturen und Interkulturelle Berufstätigkeit*, 53–71. Göt-
             tingen: Vandenhoeck and Ruprecht.
Schroll-Machl, Sylvia
    2002a   *Die Deutschen – Wir Deutsche. Fremdwahrnehmung und Selbstsicht im
             Berufsleben.* Göttingen: Vandenhoeck and Ruprecht.
Schroll-Machl, Sylvia
    2002b   *Doing Business with Germans. Their Perception, Our Perception.* Göttin-
             gen: Vandenhoeck and Ruprecht.
Schroll-Machl, Sylvia
    2003   Deutschland. In: Alexander Thomas, Stefan Kammhuber and Sylvia
             Schroll-Machl (eds.), *Handbuch Interkulturelle Kommunikation und Ko-
             operation. Band 2: Länder, Kulturen und Interkulturelle Berufstätigkeit*,
             72–89. Göttingen: Vandenhoeck and Ruprecht.

Spencer-Oatey, Helen and Jianyu Xing
    2000   A problematic Chinese business visit to Britain. In: Helen Spencer-Oatey,
            (ed.), *Culturally Speaking. Managing Rapport through Talk across Culture*,
            272–288. London: Continuum.
Spencer-Oatey, Helen and Wenying Jiang
    2003   Explaining cross-cultural pragmatic findings: Moving from politeness
            maxims to sociopragmatic interactional principles (SIPs). *Journal of Prag-
            matics* 35(10–11): 1633–1650.
Stewart, Rosemary, Jean-Louis Barsoux, Alfred Kieser, Hans-Dieter Ganter und Peter
            Walgenbach
    1994   *Managing in Britain and Germany*. New York: St Martin's Press.
Thomas, Alexander
    1988   Untersuchungen zur Entwicklung eines interkulturellen Handlungstrain-
            ings in der Managerausbildung. *Psychologische Beiträge* 30(1–2): 147–165.
Thomas, Alexander
    1996   Analyse der Handlungswirksamkeit von Kulturstandards. In: Alexander
            Thomas, (ed.), *Psychologie interkulturellen Handelns*, 107–135. Göttin-
            gen: Hogrefe.
Thomas, Alexander
    2000   Forschungen zur Handlungswirksamkeit zentraler Kulturstandards. *Han-
            dlung, Kultur, Interpretation – Zeitschrift für Sozial- und Kulturwissen-
            schaften* 9(2): 231–278.
Thomas, Alexander
    2003   Kultur und Kulturstandards. In: Alexander Thomas, Eva-Ulrike Kinast and
            Sylvia Schroll-Machl (eds.), *Handbuch Interkulturelle Kommunikation und
            Kooperation. Band 1: Grundlagen und Praxisfelder*, 19–31. Göttingen:
            Vandenhoeck and Ruprecht.
Triandis, Harry
    1995   Culture-specific assimiliators. In: Sandra M. Fowler, and Monica G. Mum-
            ford (eds.), *Intercultural Sourcebook: Cross-Cultural Training Methods*,
            Vol. 1, 179–186. Yarmouth, ME: Intercultural Press.
Trompenaars, Fons and Charles Hampden-Turner
    1997   *Riding the Waves of Culture: Understanding Diversity in Global Business*.
            London: Nicholas Brealey.
Watson, Warren E., Kamalesh Kumar and Larry K. Michaelson
    1993   Cultural diversity's impact on interaction process and performance. *Acad-
            emy of Management Journal* 36(3): 590–602.
Yamada, Haru
    1997   Organisation in American and Japanese meetings: Task versus relationship.
            In: Francesca Bargiela-Chiappini, and Sandra Harris (eds.), *The Languages
            of Business. An International Perspective*, 117–135. Edinburgh: Edinburgh
            University Press.

14. Understanding Aboriginal silence in legal contexts[1]

Diana Eades

1. Introduction

> Speakers may have similar life styles, speak closely related dialects of the same language, and yet regularly fail to communicate.
>
> Gumperz and Cook-Gumperz 1982: 13

It is now more than 20 years since Gumperz and Cook-Gumperz drew attention to the subtle power of dialectal differences in intercultural misunderstandings. But there is still widespread misrecognition of communication differences between speakers who have quite similar dialects, but different worldviews, and different ways of using the same language. This misrecognition can have serious consequences for participants in intercultural interactions. In this paper we will consider this issue for Aboriginal English speakers in the Australian criminal justice system, particularly in lawyer–client interviews and courtroom examination and cross-examination.

When people speak closely related dialects of the same language, there is often a tendency to assume that utterances that sound the same must have the same meaning. But an understanding of the role of cultural context in interpretation, as well as the subtleties of pragmatic meaning, can shed light on how very similar, and at times identical, forms in related dialects do not necessarily have the same meaning (cf. Žegarac in this volume). A good example involves the use of silence. Silence sounds the same in any dialect (or language), but it does not always carry the same meaning.

Ethnographic research with Aboriginal English speakers has found that silence is often a positive and productive feature of many interactions (Eades 1988, 1991; Ngarritjin-Kessaris 1997). People often like to sit in silence with relatives, friends or acquaintances. This was explained to me many years ago as 'one way of getting to know people better'. It can also signal that people want to take time to think about an important issue. And when people are engaged in information seeking (not necessarily through direct questions, see Eades 1991), there are often considerable pauses before requested information is provided. While this research and the focus of the current paper is on Aboriginal people who speak varieties of English, similar ways of using silence are also reported among Aboriginal speakers of traditional languages (Walsh 1994).

This use of silence contrasts with a common western reaction that silence in a conversation, whether formal or informal, is an indication that something is going wrong. Indeed many Conversation Analysis studies of English conversations in western societies support Jefferson's (1989) finding that the 'standard average maximum tolerance for silence' is less than one second. By the time that there has been a silence of one second, or less, in many western conversations, participants are feeling uncomfortable, perhaps wondering if their interlocutor is offended, or socially awkward, or a snob. And many potential silences are filled well before the full one second time period. This is particularly noticeable in interviews and meetings, and even if the person 'filling the silence' is not ready to contribute anything of substance, people use verbal silence-fillers, such as *um, ah, let me see,* and so on.

It is not only Aboriginal Australians who have quite a different use and interpretation of silence compared to western speakers of English. There are some parallels between Aboriginal Australians and Native Americans (see Basso 1970; Philips 1993; Gumperz 2001). Other sociocultural groups whose different use of silence has been described include the Amish (Enninger 1987), Japanese (Lebra 1987) and Chinese (Young 1994).

The different uses and interpretations of silence have particular significance in interviews. The interview genre is typically a one-sided information exchange, where one party asks questions and the other provides answers. In intercultural communication workshops that I conducted throughout the 1990s, non-Aboriginal interviewers often reported that they experienced difficulty in eliciting information from Aboriginal interviewees, while Aboriginal interviewees often reported feeling rushed, pressured, and unable to take the time they needed to answer questions properly.

2.   Aboriginal silence in answer to lawyers' questions

Although the interview is a speech event not typically found in Aboriginal societies, it is central to the western legal system. Indeed, a basic assumption underlying the adversarial legal system is that repeated questions serve to elicit 'facts' or 'the truth'. So what happens when Aboriginal English speakers are interviewed in legal contexts?

The case of Robyn Kina in Brisbane shows how seriously the delivery of justice can be affected when Aboriginal silence in interviews is misinterpreted. Robyn Kina was an Aboriginal woman from southeast Queensland, who was found guilty in 1988 of the stabbing murder of her de facto husband in Brisbane, and was sentenced to life imprisonment. In her trial, no evidence was given, by Kina or by any other person, about the horrific circumstances which led to her stabbing the victim in self-defense and reaction to provocation. In 1993 Kina successfully appealed against the conviction, on the grounds that her lawyers did not find out the necessary information from her to run her defense (Pringle 1994). Her conviction was quashed and she was released from prison (having served the equivalent of the sentence she would be likely to receive for manslaughter).

In Kina's 1993 appeal, there were three types of expert evidence: from a psychiatrist on the issue of repressed memory, from a social worker on the 'battered woman syndrome', and from a sociolinguist (this author) about misunderstanding between Kina and her lawyers. The sociolinguistic evidence (which is discussed in detail in Eades 1996) showed how Kina's lawyers, who were not aware of Aboriginal English ways of speaking, lacked sufficient intercultural communication ability to find out her story and to adequately represent her at her trial. For example, not recognizing that Aboriginal answers to questions often begin with considerable silence, the lawyers had been unsuccessful in their attempts to elicit her story. They reported that she had been very difficult to communicate with, and she reported that they had asked her questions, and not waited for the answers! As a result of this serious miscommunication, the jury at her trial had convicted her of murder in the absence of important evidence which should have been used in her defense.

In finding that Kina's trial (in 1988) had involved a miscarriage of justice, the appeal court (in 1993) cited 'cultural, psychological and personal factors' which 'presented exceptional difficulties of communication between her legal representatives and the appellant' (*R v Kina* 35–6). In effect, the court accepted the sociolinguistic argument that Kina and her lawyers had suffered serious misunderstanding, which resulted in her wrongful murder conviction. This misunderstanding, it had been argued, was rooted in cultural differences in their uses of English, for example in the use of silence.

One of the shocking things about the wrongful conviction in Kina's case is that it was her own lawyers who failed her – it was not skilful manipulation of her evidence by an aggressive cross-examination. In fact she had given no evidence in her own defense, as her lawyers had not managed to find out her story, finding her 'extremely difficult to communicate with' (Eades 1996: 219).

3.   Intercultural communication awareness for lawyers

As the judges in Kina's successful appeal pointed out, her trial had taken place before there was any intercultural awareness training for legal professionals, and thus her lawyers could not have been expected to recognize the causes of miscommunication in their interviews with her. But in the early 1990s, intercultural awareness began to be provided for legal professionals, by means of workshops, and a handbook written to help lawyers in more effective communication with Aboriginal English speaking clients (Eades 1992; cf. Rost-Roth in this volume on intercultural training). This lawyers' handbook gave this advice about silence:

> Do not interpret silence as an Aboriginal speaker's admission of guilt or ignorance, or even as evidence of a communication breakdown. Remember that silence is often used positively by Aboriginal people to think about things and to get comfortable with the social situation.
>
> Eades 1992: 46

Research in a country town in the mid 1990s found that some lawyers were able to wait comfortably for their clients to provide an answer, while others were not. Example 1 below comes from a sentencing hearing in District (intermediate) Court in the case of an Aboriginal defendant who has pleaded guilty to assault. In answering questions which can help to establish grounds for minimizing the severity of his sentence, he is invited by his lawyer to show remorse for his actions to the judge:

(1)
29. DC: And do you tell His Honour that you know you shouldn't- and that you're sorry for having done that?
30. W: Uh well – yeah – I am – sorry (6.7) when we're not – oh sorry – when we're not drinkin' you know – we don't even fight or nothin' – you know – when we're drinking it's a bit of a problem – it's one of them things – drinking.

The witness answers with a formulaic apology, and the very long 6.7 silence which follows would not be allowed by many lawyers. But the power of the witness's silence, which is not interrupted by the lawyer (or judge), is evident, as it is followed by a personal, honest-sounding explanation which can be helpful to a typical defence strategy of suggesting that the most appropriate sentencing should include alcohol rehabilitation rather than a prison sentence.

In intercultural communication workshops with lawyers I have explained that a misunderstanding of Aboriginal ways of using silence can lead to lawyers interrupting an Aboriginal person's answer. Of course, we customarily define interruption as involving a second person starting to talk before the first speaker has finished talking. But if we accept that the first part of an Aboriginal answer often starts with silence, then to start the next question before the Aboriginal interviewee has had the time to speak, is in effect to interrupt the first part of the answer.

It seems obvious that lawyers, magistrates and judges need to be made aware of such cultural differences in communicative style. And in fact, in my experience, many legal professionals are excited to learn about this aspect of intercultural communication. A clear example of this comes from a 1992 hearing of the Queensland Criminal Justice Commission (CJC). This hearing was part of an investigation of an allegation of police misconduct, and I was asked to appear as an expert witness. In addition to explaining some of the subtle ways in which communication patterns differ between Aboriginal and non-Aboriginal speakers of English, I was asked to advise the Commission specifically on more effective ways of hearing the evidence of Aboriginal witnesses to this tribunal. As part of this process, I listened to an Aboriginal woman being questioned by lawyers. This woman had originally approached the Commission wanting to tell her story (related to her witnessing of police misconduct in the matter under investigation), and no disadvantage could occur to her as a result of her evidence. However, under questioning by the lawyers, she provided very little information. The lawyers asked her questions, and she appeared unable to provide answers. I was then asked to advise the Commission about communication with this witness, in her absence. I recommended that the lawyers should wait after each question, until the witness answered. I explained that this means asking a question and then 'shutting up'. Given the uncomfortable feeling that this leaves with many (non-Aboriginal) people, I suggested that the interviewing lawyer could shuffle papers, or say something like 'there's no need to rush'. In answer to the Commission's question about 'how long should we wait?' I replied, 'until after the answer'.

Following a short adjournment, the witness was asked to return to the witness stand, and this revised style of questioning took place, with remarkable results. The same witness who had earlier that day appeared shy, difficult to communicate with, and of little help to the Commission's investigation, was now an articulate witness with a clear and important story to tell the Commission. The only significant change was that the interviewing lawyers allowed time for the silence which began quite a few of her answers to their questions.

4.   Intercultural awareness is not enough

Experiences such as this CJC hearing, as well as Robyn Kina's case, seem to highlight the importance of intercultural awareness for legal professionals. An understanding of the possibility of different ways of using the same language, as well as specific details, appears to have the potential to lead to much more effective intercultural communication. This approach is consistent with much sociolinguistic work on intercultural communication, and can be called a 'difference' approach to linguistic and cultural diversity (see Pennycook 2001; Rampton 2001). This difference approach 'emphasizes the integrity and autonomy of the language and culture of subordinate groups, and the need for institutions to be hospitable to diversity' (Rampton 2001: 261). Thus in both the general lawyers' handbook and the specific example of the CJC hearing, differences between general Australian English and Aboriginal English ways of communicating were explained, and suggestions were made about how to accommodate Aboriginal English ways in order to facilitate more effective intercultural communication in the legal process. This difference approach underlies much sociolinguistic research as well as practical applications to intercultural communication. Driven to a considerable extent by a focus on linguistic equality, as well as cultural relativism and respect for different cultures, norms and ways of speaking, the view is that an understanding of cultural differences in communicative style can lead to more effective intercultural communication.

But there have been criticisms within sociolinguistics about this difference approach to linguistic and cultural diversity, in relation to studies of intercultural communication, as well as language and gender. The main criticism has been that it ignores social inequality and power relations, present in both intercultural and inter-gender encounters (for example Freed 1992; Meeuwis and Sarangi 1994; Meeuwis 1994; Shea 1994; Sarangi 1994; Singh, Lele and Martohardjono 1988; Pennycook 2001; Rampton 2001). Despite these criticisms, it is not clear to what extent studies of intercultural communication have taken up issues involving power relations (see Thielmann in this volume). We will now turn to another Queensland case, in which we see the explanatory inadequacy of the difference approach in the study of intercultural communication. We will see that intercultural awareness does not necessarily lead to successful communication, and further, that the communication difficulties in this case cannot be explained without a consideration of layers of power struggles.

4.1.   Pinkenba case

Some time after midnight on 10 May 1994, three Aboriginal boys aged 12, 13 and 14 were walking around a shopping mall near the Brisbane downtown area. The boys were approached by six armed police officers who told them to get into three separate vehicles. They were then driven 14 kilometers out of town and abandoned in an industrial wasteland in Pinkenba near the mouth of the Brisbane River, from where they had to find their own way back.

The boys were not charged with any offence, nor were they taken to any police station. According to police, the young people were 'taken down to Pinkenba to reflect on their misdemeanours' (ABC *Four Corners*, 8 March 1996). Following the boys' complaint to the Aboriginal Legal Service, an investigation was conducted by the Criminal Justice Commission. This investigation recommended that criminal charges be laid against the six police officers. As a result, the police officers were charged that they had unlawfully deprived each of the boys of 'his personal liberty by carrying him away in a motor vehicle against his will'.

In February 1995, the boys were prosecution witnesses in the committal hearing, which was the first stage in the trial process against the police officers. Most of the four day hearing consisted of evidence from the three boys, which included lengthy cross-examination by each of the two defense counsel who represented three of the police officers. The case centered on the issue of whether or not the boys had got into and travelled in the police cars against their will: no doubt was ever raised that they were approached and told to get in the police cars, and that they were taken to the industrial wasteland and abandoned there. The defense case was that the boys 'gave up their liberty' and that 'there's no offence of allowing a person to give up his liberty'.

The cross-examination of the boys was devastating: these three young Aboriginal part-time street kids, with minimal successful participation in mainstream Australian institutions, such as education, were pitted against the two most highly paid and experienced criminal barristers in the state. It is hardly surprising that the boys were unable to maintain a consistent story under the barrage of cross-examination, which involved so much shouting at times that many legal professionals in the public gallery were amazed that the lawyers were not restrained or disallowed from using this haranguing behaviour. Elsewhere (Eades 2002, 2003), I have written about the linguistic strategies used by these two defense counsel to manipulate and misconstrue the evidence of the three boys. These strategies succeeded in the magistrate accepting defense counsels' construction of these victim-witnesses as criminals with 'no regard for the community', and the reinterpretation of the alleged abduction as the boys voluntarily giving up their liberty while the police took them for a ride (both literally and metaphorically). As a result, the charges against the police officers were dropped.

Perhaps the most pervasive linguistic strategy used by defence counsel was their exploitation of the Aboriginal tendency to freely agree to propositions put to them in Yes-No questions, regardless of their actual agreement, or even their understanding of the question. Termed 'gratuitous concurrence' (Liberman 1981), this conversational pattern is widely found in intercultural interactions involving Aboriginal people, and is considered a major problem for the way in which Aboriginal people participate in the criminal justice system (Eades 1992, 2002).

A number of factors increase the likelihood of an Aboriginal witness in court using gratuitous concurrence, including interviewer hostility, for example shouting or haranguing. Example 2 occurred during the cross-examination of the oldest of the three boys, who was fifteen at the time. It typifies much of the cross-examination by the first of the two defence counsel, who used shouting and repeated question tags (such as *didn't you*), in response to answers that he did not accept. As we see in this example, the witness's response to such harassment (in Turn 4) often appears to be gratuitous concurrence.

(2)
1. DC1:   And you <u>knew</u> (1.4) when you spoke to these six police in the Valley that <u>you</u> didn't have to go anywhere with them if you didn't want to, didn't you?
2. BARRY: (1.3) No.

3. DC1:   You <u>knew</u> that, Mr (1.2) Coley I'd suggest to you, PLEASE DO NOT
LIE. YOU KNEW THAT YOU DIDN'T HAVE TO GO ANYWHERE if you
didn't want to, didn't you? (2.2) DIDN'T YOU? (2.2) DIDN'T YOU,
MR COLEY?

4. BARRY: (1.3) Yeh.

5. DC1:   WHY DID YOU JUST LIE TO ME? WHY DID YOU JUST SAY "NO" MR
COLEY?

Another factor which appears to lead to gratuitous concurrence is the asking of
difficult questions, through such syntactic strategies as double negatives, or
multiple questions, as we see in Example 3:

(3)
1. DC2:   You got <u>in</u> the car (2.1) without being forced – you went <u>out</u> there
without being forced – the <u>prob</u>lem began when you <u>were</u> <u>left</u>
there?

2. W1:   (1.5) [Mm.

3. PROS: [With respect Your Worship – there are <u>three</u> elements to that
question and I ask my friend to break them <u>down</u>.

4. M: Yes – just break it up one by one Mr Humphrey.

5. DC2:   You got in the car without being forced David – didn't you?
6. W1:   (1.5) No.

7. DC2:   You told us – you've told us a ((laughs)) number of times today
you did.
8. W1:   (1.3) They forced me.

In this example, the youngest witness, thirteen-year old David, is being cross-
examined by the less aggressive of the two defence counsel. In Turn 1, the lawyer puts three different propositions, all central to the defence argument, that the
boys went in the cars of their own free will, and thus were not unlawfully deprived of their liberty. David appears to agree to the question, in Turn 2. However, after the prosecutor succeeds in having defence counsel question just one
proposition at a time (Turn 5), David clearly disagrees, expressing his disagreement with the proposition in a complete sentence (Turn 8). This is a relatively
rare occurrence for this witness whose answers were overwhelmingly single
words, such as 'yeah' and 'no'.

    While the exploitation of gratuitous concurrence was central to the cross-
examination strategy, it was combined in many instances with the strategic ma-

nipulation of witness silence. In some instances defence counsel allowed little time between asking an initial question and following it up with pressured, often shouting, repetition of the verb phrase, as we see in Turn 5 of Example 2 above. In such examples we can see that the witness is given little chance to think about the question, or to use the lengthy silence which characterizes many Aboriginal conversations, and particularly interviews with Aboriginal people.

But there are a number of silences throughout the hearing. While the focus here is on witness silence in answer to a lawyer question, it is interesting to note the cross-examining lawyers' use of silence within a clause, seemingly for emphasis (in Example 2 Turn 1, Example 3 Turn 1, and Example 4 Turn 10). The lawyer silence in Example 2 Turn 3 is quite possibly caused by a memory lapse, as he remembers the boys' surname for sarcastic effect.

Consistent with the widespread Aboriginal use of silence at the beginning of an answer, we find silences of more than one second prefacing all of the witness answers in Example 2 and Example 3, as well as one of the answers in Example 4 (in Turn 11). But a number of other witness silences in answer to questions in these examples are not followed by witness answers. While these occurrences of silence might perhaps be seen as evidence that the legal system is accommodating Aboriginal ways of speaking, both defence counsel made sure, in two ways, that this is not how these silences would be interpreted. Firstly, such silences were invariably followed by some form of harassment as in Turn 3 of Example 2 above. And secondly, on at least two occasions defence counsel exploited the Aboriginal tendency to use gratuitous concurrence to get the witness to agree overtly to the proposition that his silence should be interpreted negatively, as we see below in Example 4, excerpted from the cross-examination of Albert by the second (less aggressive) defence counsel:

(4)
 1. DC2: And you told them lies to their faces, didn't you? (3.7) Didn't you Albert? (3.7) Didn't you Albert? (2.2) You lied in their face, didn't you? (3.6) Albert, answer my question, please=
 2. W: =I don't wanna.

 3. DC2: Well I'm sorry, but this isn't one that you can claim privilege on.
 4. W: I don't wanna.

 5. DC2: Pardon?
 6. W: I don't wanna.

 7. DC2: You don't want to answer?=

 8. M: =Well, I'm telling you, Albert, you have to answer this question, okay? You can't get out of this [one.

9. W: [(Inaudible).

10. DC2: Now, Albert (2.7) His Worship's told you to answer the question. Will
        you or won't you? (6.5) We have to take your silence as "no", don't
        we? (2.5) Albert?
11. W.:   (1.2) (p)Yes.

At this point in thirteen-year old Albert's cross-examination, he has been on the
witness stand for close to two and a half hours, most of it being cross-examination. Defence counsel is constructing Albert as a liar, in relation to the way in
which he had reported the incident in question to the lawyers at Aboriginal
Legal Service (ALS). Most of the extract is a metapragmatic discussion of
whether or not Albert will answer the question in Turn 1. Albert insists, in
Turns 2, 4 and 6, that he does not want to answer the question asked in Turn 1,
and defence counsel and the magistrate assert (in Turns 3 and 8 respectively)
that this is not a question that he can 'claim privilege on'. This refers to the rul-
ing (expressed to Albert six times by this stage) that a witness does not have to
answer any question that might incriminate him in relation to the commission of
a criminal offence. Much was made in the cross-examination of the three boys
of their criminal records (mainly for minor thefts). So, as many of the questions
asked about their 'criminal activities' the magistrate was obliged to pronounce
the warning about self-incrimination. The invocation of this right by a witness is
a tricky one, and it is hardly surprising that these young boys were unsure of
how and when to use this right. At this stage of his lengthy cross-examination,
Albert appears to be trying to invoke it as a way to avoid answering questions. It
is hardly surprising that this thirteen year old boy might see a question about
lying to a legal officer as having the same legal status and possible consequences as a question about throwing rocks at a street light (although in fact, the
former is not a criminal offence, unless it occurs in a courtroom).

    However, he is told that he can not avoid answering the question (about
whether he lied 'to [the] faces' of the ALS staff). But this is followed with a rid-
iculous question in Turn 10 – 'Will you or won't you?'. It is hardly surprising
that the witness uses a long silence at this point. The choice offered by this question seems to contradict the assertion by both defence counsel and the magistrate that Albert does not have this choice! By this stage, it is clear that the cross-
examination has moved beyond incrimination and harassment, to control and
disciplining which appears to be at the very least confusing, and much more
likely, senseless. Having got the witness to this state of confused (and senseless?) subjugation, as well as exhaustion, defence counsel moves in with the
powerful assertion 'We have to take your silence as "no"'. In this proposition,
defence counsel ignores widely available background knowledge which would
suggest other (non-incriminating) interpretations of the Aboriginal witness's si-

lence. From here it is very easy to get Albert to agree to the assertion (in Turn 11), in a context which strongly suggests that this is an answer of gratuitous concurrence.

The linguistic strategies, such as illustrated here in relation to silence and gratuitous concurrence were very overt and effective. Given the highly adversarial nature of the hearing and the fact that the two defence counsel were among the top criminal lawyers in the state, it would be safe to assume that these strategies were deliberately used to destroy the credibility of the witnesses (which is, after all, the major aim of cross-examination).

But it was disturbing to find out that the two defence counsel had at the Bar table a copy of the handbook for lawyers (Eades 1992). The handbook had been written to assist lawyers in more effective communication with Aboriginal witnesses. But, in the Pinkenba case, it appears to have been used upside-down, as it were. The provision of intercultural awareness for lawyers seems to have been used to make things worse in terms of intercultural communication. An understanding of cultural differences in communication, such as the use and interpretation of silence, appeared to provide the defence counsel with a powerful tool in the manipulation the evidence of the Aboriginal boys.

This situation realized my initial fears in writing the handbook, that information provided about cultural differences in communicative style, might be used against Aboriginal witnesses. But I had been reassured at the time that the adversarial balance would prevent such a situation. I now realize that this reassurance, and my acceptance of it, was based on a naively apolitical view of both the legal process, and the nature of intercultural communication. What happened to the adversarial balance in this case? If we examine the courtroom interaction, we find a situational power imbalance. The defence counsel (hired by the Police Union to defend the six police officers) were the most highly paid barristers in the state, while the prosecutor and the magistrate were considerably more junior is terms of experience and income. It has been suggested that the prosecutor and the magistrate were fearful of being exposed and ridiculed by the two top barristers.

But to analyse the intercultural communication in this hearing only in terms of the immediate context would be inadequate. Following Fairclough (1989), we need to go beyond the immediate situation of the courtroom in order to understand the power relations that were operating within the courtroom. This examination of 'power behind the discourse' in Fairclough's terms takes the sociolinguistic study of intercultural communication beyond a difference approach, to encompass the domination approach (or as it is generally called in language and gender studies, the 'dominance' approach, see Freed 2003). In this approach, "the focus shifts to larger structures of *domination*, and the need is stressed for institutions to combat the institutional processes and ideologies that reproduce the oppression of subordinate groups" (Rampton 2001: 261, emphasis in original).

Institutional processes and ideologies involved in reproducing the oppression of Aboriginal people are central to the understanding of this case. Indeed, this case highlights the importance of power relations in intercultural communication, representing, as it does, a climax in the 200-year struggle between the state and the Aboriginal community over the rights of police officers to remove Aboriginal young people. To briefly summarize this: since British invasion in the late 1700s, the police force has been used to control the movements of Aboriginal young people. Until the 1960s, this included the now widely known process of forcibly removing children from their families, as part of successive government attempts to deal with 'the Aboriginal problem'. Although this practice is no longer carried out, it is clear from the work of criminologists that current policing practices construct Aboriginal young people as a 'law and order problem'. Through selective policing, they are detained with much greater frequency than their non-Aboriginal counterparts. There has been increasing opposition from Aboriginal communities about the overpolicing of their young people, and the struggle between Aboriginal people and the police force is increasingly volatile.

Specifically in the city of Brisbane where the Pinkenba incident took place, several episodes in this struggle are noteworthy. In November 1993, an eighteen year old Aboriginal dancer died in police custody, after being arrested for disturbing the peace. Aboriginal outrage at his death escalated into a much publicized street riot. The Aboriginal community was further outraged when a Criminal Justice Commission inquiry into his death, found that it was due to natural causes, and that no fault would be attributed to any police officers. It was less than six months after this widespread outrage about the policing of Aboriginal young people, that the three boys were removed by police in the Pinkenba episode. But they were not charged with an offence, or taken to a police station, and indeed they were not in custody. This episode again stirred up considerable community outrage, and led to an investigation by the CJC. This investigation led to the six police officers involved being charged with unlawful deprivation of liberty, an offence which could attract a prison sentence. Thus, the committal hearing, in which the boys gave evidence, was charged with enormous political significance. The struggle between the police force and the Aboriginal community had moved from the streets to the courtroom, where language is a crucial weapon.

The political struggle at the heart of the Pinkenba case centred on several related questions: Do police officers have the right to remove Aboriginal young people from public places when they have not committed any offence? Do young Aboriginal people have the right to refuse to travel in police cars when told to do so by armed police officers, even if they are not under arrest? If they have this right, is it realistic to expect that they can exercise this right? These are questions about rights, freedom, the power of the police, and the role of the police in the exercise of neocolonial control over indigenous people (see Cunneen 2001). While these questions were discussed in the media, they were officially tested in the criminal justice process, through the committal hearing in this case. And this is where sociolinguistic analysis becomes central to the understanding of the reproduction of oppression, because the power struggle here is enacted through linguistic practices.

These linguistic practices are filtered through the laws of evidence. Thus the police officers, guilty until proven innocent by the prosecution, did not have to speak at all. And the Aboriginal boys had no protection, despite their youth, from the worst of cross-examination in an adult court. Further, most of their cross-examination was about their previous criminal records. Compounding these constraints on topic and participation structure, were the specific linguistic strategies used to manipulate the boys' evidence. This point takes us back to cultural differences in the use and interpretation of silence. As we have seen, it can *not* be argued that there was a misunderstanding or lack of awareness about cultural difference in communicative style. In fact, it appears most likely that a conscious knowledge of such issues was essential to the cross-examination strategy. Thus, a sociolinguistic explanation of the intercultural communication in this case requires an approach which examines power relations, both within the situation (or within the discourse), and in the wider society (or behind the discourse). Such an analysis fits with a third approach to linguistic and cultural diversity, termed the 'discourse' approach by Rampton (2001), and 'problematizing givens' by Pennycook (2001). What is important in this approach is 'viewing language as inherently political' and 'understanding power more in terms of its micro operations in relation to questions of class, race, gender, ethnicity, sexuality, and so on' (Pennycook 2001: 167; see also Conley and O'Barr 1998). Thus a sociolinguistic analysis of intercultural communication which uses this approach can examine actual linguistic strategies, such as the ways in which cultural differences in the use and interpretation of silence are exploited in cross-examination.

Of course, it can be argued that this was an extreme case, and certainly I have never seen cross-examination like it, either before or since. But the important point is that it happened, and it was allowed to happen. The cross-examination was so successful that the magistrate decided to drop the charges against the police officers. When the families of the boys complained, an appeal was launched against this decision. This resulted in a judge reviewing the magistrate's decision, and dismissing the appeal. So, it is clear that while the cross-examination of the three boys in this case may have been an aberration, it was still widely taken as 'due process' and the proper functioning of the justice system, and indeed it was legitimized by the judicial review. So the linguistic strategies, such as the ways in which cultural differences in the use and interpretation of silence were exploited in cross-examination, have effects far more wide-reaching than just the courtroom interaction in this case. Indeed such linguistic strategies are used as mechanisms by the state in the reproduction of its neocolonial control over the movements of Aboriginal young people.

Transcription conventions

- underlining indicates utterance emphasis
- CAPITALS indicate raised volume
- (p) before an utterance indicates that it is spoken in a low volume
- = indicates latched utterances, i.e. no pause between the end of one utterance and the start of the next
- a number in parentheses indicates the length of a pause in seconds, e.g. (3.2)
- a dash – indicates a very short untimed pause within an utterance
- a square bracket [indicates both the start of an interruption and the utterance which is interrupted
- the following abbreviations are also used in the transcripts:
  DC = defence counsel   M = magistrate
  P   = prosecutor   W = witness

All personal names in this paper are pseudonyms, with the exception of Robyn Kina, whose case has been widely discussed in the Australian media.

Notes

1. This paper draws on some of my previous work in Eades (1996, 2002, 2003, 2004a, 2004b). I am grateful to Michael Cooke for many helpful discussions about language and power in the legal system, and to Jeff Siegel for helpful comments on the draft.

References

Basso, Kenneth H.
  1970   'To give up on words': Silence in Apache culture. *Southwest Journal of Anthropology* 26(3): 213–230.
Conley, John M. and William M. O'Barr
  1998   *Just Words: Law, Language and Power.* Chicago: University of Chicago Press.
Cunneen, Chris
  2001   *Conflict, Politics and Crime: Aboriginal Communities and the Police.* Sydney: Allen and Unwin.

Eades, Diana
    1988   'They don't speak an Aboriginal language, or do they?' In: Ian Keen (ed.), *Being Black: Aboriginal Cultures in Settled Australia*, 97–117. Canberra: Aboriginal Studies Press.

Eades, Diana
    1991   Communicative strategies in Aboriginal English. In: Suzanne Romaine (ed.), *Language in Australia*, 84–93. Cambridge: Cambridge University Press.

Eades, Diana
    1992   *Aboriginal English and the Law: Communicating with Aboriginal English Speaking Clients: A Handbook for Legal Practitioners.* Brisbane: Queensland Law Society.

Eades, Diana
    1996   Legal recognition of cultural differences in communication: The case of Robyn Kina. *Language and Communication* 16(3): 215–227.

Eades, Diana
    2002   'Evidence given in unequivocal terms': Gaining consent of Aboriginal kids in court. In: Janet Cotterill (ed.), *Language in the Legal Process*, 162–179. Hampshire: Palgrave.

Eades, Diana
    2003   The politics of misunderstanding in the legal process: Aboriginal English in Queensland. In: Juliane House, Gabriele Kasper and Steven Ross (eds.), *Misunderstanding in Spoken Discourse*, 199–226. London: Longman.

Eades, Diana
    2004a   Beyond difference and domination? Intercultural communication in legal contexts. In: Christina Paulston and Scott Kiesling (eds.), *Intercultural Discourse and Communication: The Essential Readings*, 304–316. Oxford: Blackwell.

Eades, Diana
    2004b   Understanding Aboriginal English in the legal system: A critical sociolinguistics approach. *Applied Linguistics* 25(4): 491–512.

Enninger, W.
    1987   What interactants do with non-talk across cultures. In: Karlfried Knapp, Werner Enninger and Annelie Knapp-Pothoff (eds.), *Analyzing Intercultural Communication*, 269–302. Berlin: Mouton de Gruyter.

Fairclough, Norman
    1989   *Language and Power.* London: Longman.

Freed, Alice F.
    1992   We understand perfectly: A critique of Tannen's view of cross-sex conversation. In: Kira Hall, Mary Buchholtz and Birch Moonwomon (eds.), *Locating Power.* Proceedings of the Second Berkeley Women and Language Conference, 144–152. Berkeley, CA: Berkeley Women and Language Group, University of California.

Freed, Alice F.
    2003   Epilogue: Reflections on language and gender research. In: Janet Holmes and Miriam Meyerhoff (eds.), *The Handbook of Language and Gender*, 699–721. Oxford: Blackwell Publishing.

Gumperz, John
  2001   Contextualization and ideology in intercultural communication. In: Aldo Di
            Luzio, Suzanne Günthner and Franca Orletti (eds.), *Culture in Communi-
            cation: Analyses of Intercultural Situations*, 35–53. Amsterdam: John Ben-
            jamins.
Gumperz, John and Jenny Cook-Gumperz
  1982   Introduction: Language and the communication of social identity. In: John
            Gumperz (ed.), *Language and Social Identity*, 1–21. Cambridge: Cam-
            bridge University Press.
Jefferson, Gail
  1989   Preliminary notes on a possible metric which provides for a 'Standard
            Maximum' silence of approximately one second in a conversation. In:
            Derek Roger and Peter Bull (eds.), *Conversation: An Interdisciplinary Per-
            spective*, 166–96. Clevedon, PA: Multilingual Matters.
Lebra, Takie
  1987   The cultural significance of silence in Japanese communication. *Multilin-
            gua* 6(4): 343–357.
Liberman, Kenneth
  1981   Understanding Aborigines in Australian courts of law. *Human Organiz-
            ation* 40: 247–255.
Meeuwis, Michael
  1994   Leniency and testiness in intercultural communication: Remarks on ideo-
            logy and context in interactional sociolinguistics. *Pragmatics* 4(3): 391–408.
Meeuwis, Michael and Srikant Sarangi
  1994   Perspectives on intercultural communication: A critical reading. *Prag-
            matics* 4(3): 309–314.
Ngarritjan-Kessaris, Terry
  1997   School meetings and indigenous parents. In: Stephen Harris and Merridy
            Malin (eds.), *Indigenous Education: Historical, Moral and Practical Tales*,
            81–90. Darwin: Northern Territory University Press.
Pennycook, Alastair
  2001   *Critical Applied Linguistics: A Critical Introduction*. Mahwah, NJ: Law-
            rence Erlbaum Associates.
Philips, Susan
  1993   *The Invisible Culture: Communication in Classroom and Community on the
            Warm Springs Indian Reservation*. New York: Longman.
Pringle, Karen
  1994   Case notes: R v Robyn Bella Kina. *Aboriginal Law Bulletin* 3(67): 14–15.
Rampton, Ben
  2001   Language crossing, cross-talk and cross-disciplinarity in sociolinguistics.
            In: Nikolas Coupland, Srikant Sarangi and Christopher Candlin (eds.),
            Sociolinguistics and Social Theory, 261–296. London: Pearson Education
            Ltd.
Rost-Roth, Martina
this volume Intercultural training, Chapter 23.
Sarangi, Srikant
  1994   Intercultural or not? Beyond celebration of cultural differences in miscom-
            munication analysis. *Pragmatics* 4(3): 409–428.

Shea, David
    1994   Perspective and production: Structuring conversational participation across
                cultural borders. *Pragmatics* 4(3): 357–390.
Singh, Rajendra, Jayant Lele and Gita Martohardjono
    1988   Communication in a multilingual society: Some missed opportunities. *Language in Society* 17: 43–59.
Thielmann, Winfried
this volume Power and dominance in intercultural communication, Chapter 19.
Walsh, Michael
    1994   Interactional styles in the courtroom: An example from northern Australia.
                In: John Gibbons (ed.), *Language and the Law*, 217–233. London: Longman.
Young, Linda
    1994   *Crosstalk and Culture in Sino-American Communication.* Cambridge:
                Cambridge University Press.
Žegarac, Vladimir
this volume A cognitive pragmatic perspective on communication and culture,
                Chapter 3.

15. Schools and cultural difference

Albert Scherr

As a rule, intercultural communication takes place between individuals who have been educated in schools, and these will, to some degree, have inculcated in them an understanding of their national statehood and culture. For indeed schools are politically mandated to transmit the basic elements of citizenship and national identity, in order to ensure the continuity and endurance of the political community. This is true not only in those states that actively promote national history, culture and identity; it is also true where prevailing political values explicitly reject nationalistic programs and ideologies. At the same time, schools are institutions that provoke some portion of their pupils to distance themselves from the identity the schools seek to promote. Youthful rebellion and the development of youth sub-cultures arise not the least from confrontation with the norms of the dominant culture represented in school curricula and practices (Willis 1977, Eckert 2000).

For the transmission of national collective identity, and more generally for the formation, transmission and acquisition of collective identifications of all sorts, language obviously plays a central role; and just as the acceptance of a tendered national identity usually goes hand in hand with the acquisition of a national standard language, independent linguistic varieties often arise in connection with collectively felt non-national, regional, ethnic or youth-culture identities (Eckert 2000; Harris and Rampton 2003). As Ben Rampton (2003: 403) argues, the use of dialects by minority pupils and codeswitching in schools can "constitute acts of resistance within a racist society".

Thus, with respect to school as the institution which is centrally important for language acquisition and the development of individuals' construction of their cultural membership, both aspects are systematically intertwined.

This contribution addresses, from an international, comparative perspective, the questions of how schools as national, state-managed institutions bring forth collective identities and distinctions, and of how they establish perspectives on important features of non-national cultural identity (e.g., regional, ethnic, religious). It will reveal that how social and cultural heterogeneity are treated in the context of school-based socialization and education is closely related to influential socio-political programs, and that these can only be understood against the background of the given interlocking structures of social inequality and cultural identification.

1.   School, nation, culture and language

State-managed education of children and adolescents in schools is a fundamental characteristic of modern societies. Historically and socio-systematically, there is an intimate connection between industrial capitalism, nation-statehood, the establishment of state schools, and the enforcement of universal schooling, as has been pointed out by Talcott Parsons (Parsons 1971: 94.). On the one hand, the growth and enforcement of a state-managed educational system can be understood as a reaction to the social, spatial and temporal separations between family and wage-earning work that industrialization imposed, for industrial work meant that families were no longer in a position to give their children the knowledge needed to enter the work force. Thus, general education outside the family became the rule rather than the exception. On the other hand, however – and for the present purposes this is the decisive point – schools acquired essential significance in the effort to enforce the political idea of a unified national state with a homogeneous culture and language. Schools were to enable all future citizens to communicate in the standard national language, and they were meant to give them a historical and political understanding of themselves as citizens as well as a national identity (cf. Gellner 1983: Chapter 3).

The establishment and school-based transmission of a unified national linguistic standard, with a sharply drawn boundary to dialects and the linguistic standards of other nations, is by no means merely a response to functional demands of industrial capitalism or nation-state democracy. The "demand for the linguistically homogeneous nation and the clearly distinct national language" was, and for more than accidental reasons "remains a standard part of nationalist ideology" (Barbour 2000: 14). Calls to national patriotism and unity resonate most effectively with members of the national "imagined community" (Anderson 1991) when these, and no others, share the same common language. Seen in this light, the establishment of national languages is an essential part of the process that creates nation-states and national identities. Hence, it is hardly surprising that independence movements are often mingled with linguistic policies, and the development of new nations – as happened during the disintegration of Yugoslavia – is accompanied by efforts to emphasize and strengthen linguistic differences and boundaries (Barbour and Carmichael 2000).

Furthermore, to the extent that schools implement certain nationally oriented curricula (historical perspectives, national literary canons, geographic descriptions), they are made the means of instilling in children and adolescents a culture of the nation-state. From a socio-historical perspective the establishment of schools is part of the effort to establish a national culture and language and to marginalize traditional regional and class-specific cultures and languages, as well as to establish cultural boundaries to other nations (Hobsbawm 1990: 80). Out of a population excluded from political representation, living in local and regional frames of reference, schools are established to create citizens aware of their nation, who understand the language of their national government, feel themselves represented by it, are ready to serve in its armed forces, are willing to migrate within the national boundaries, and are prepared to accept the demands of working in its factories and living in its cities. Education is thus a key element in nation building, while schools and armies are an essential component of the state's communicative apparatus, meant "to spread the image and the heritage of the 'nation' and to inculcate attachment to it and to attach all to country and flag, often 'inventing traditions' or even nations for this purpose" (Hobsbawm 1990: 91).

Today, this patriotic amalgam of education with nation-state, national language and national culture still has its adherents, but world-wide it is by no means the only accepted model. To be sure, schools continue to be important socio-political institutions that must help to transmit a national language, as well as nationally significant knowledge, values and norms. Nevertheless, the experience of two world wars, the globalization of mass-media communications and trade, the social movements of the 1960s and 1970s and the large-scale, international migration of workers have led – especially in middle and northern Europe – to criticism of nationalist ideologies as well as to an influential re-examination of the idea that societies can only be conceived as nation-states, each with a uniform language and national culture. Processes of cultural pluralization, liberalization and differentiation, as well as the development of an increasingly trans-national culture, both popular and educated, have made the notion of autonomous national cultures less convincing. Additionally, the assertive political claims of migrants and minorities to an independent cultural status, the failure of the 'melting pot' in the USA and social developments in Canada have led to the political ideal of a 'multicultural society', that is, to the concept of a society still organized as a national state, distinguishing its citizens legally and politically from non-citizens and instituting a nationally defined legal system and standard language, but at the same time proclaiming linguistic, cultural and religious diversity as permitted or even welcome (Kymlicka 1995).

These developments have far-reaching consequences for the educational system and the schools of such states, as they change the socio-political norms to which pedagogical theory and practice are oriented. They tend to undermine the conception of the school as an institution meant to instill the values and norms of a national culture, and they lend more political and pedagogical weight to the goal of respecting cultural differences. This includes the discussion on the right of students to be instructed in their first language (Honeyford 2003). By no means, however, does this reduce the significance of national differences in educational practice, for the questions of what passes for 'culture and cultures', i.e., whether and in what sense education can claim to be founded on culture-neutral knowledge and universal values, and what place regional, religious and ethnic cultures can have in the educational program – these questions currently receive widely differing answers on political stages and in the resulting pedagogical discourses.

The following sections present some of the ways in which the schools and educational systems of three countries are approaching the treatment of culture and cultural differences. The interconnections of social policy, the reproduction of culture, and education will be discussed with reference to the educational systems of France, Britain and Canada, along with theories of intercultural pedagogy. The aim will be to show that the chosen socio-political frameworks not only have wide-reaching organizational and legal consequences, but that they also influence concrete behavioral features of the school environments.

2.   Education, reproduction of culture and multiculturalism

As social institutions, schools are charged with ensuring that all citizens acquire a common language as well as the knowledge, behavior patterns, value orientations and norms that are felt to be indispensable for life in their society. Universally mandatory schooling is an expression of this duty. Schooling thus is based, for one, on assumptions about the knowledge and skills necessary to meet the demands of industry and political life. Additionally, pedagogical theory and practice adopt assumptions about which skills, knowledge, moral and political convictions best fulfill current educational ideals. Now, pedagogically significant ideas about personality development and about worthwhile knowledge and skills are not autonomously derived from pedagogical theory, as has been repeatedly shown since the classic studies of Emile Durkheim (1922) and Siegfried Bernfeld (1973). Rather, they are expressions of socially dominant structures, models and norms, or of critical reactions to these in pedagogical theory and discourse. Accordingly, educational sociology regards the practice of schools as a constitutive element of societal reproduction, in the sense of its transmitting socially dominant values, norms and behavioral tendencies. Currently prominent theories and studies focus not only on the forms and content consciously known to their practitioners, but also on those structures and practices in which social demands reproduce themselves as self-evident and unquestioned background assumptions. This perspective displays educational practice as a component in the larger system that inculcates culture, in the sense of the restraining rules, norms, values, symbols, meanings and bodies of knowledge upon which the culture rests. Socio-historical, sociological and pedagogical studies have shown, furthermore, that school-induced socialization must be examined with respect to the question of how it contributes to enforcement of a particular social discipline and to the formation of personality structures typical of the culture (Apple 1982; Dreeben 1970; Foucault 1979; Holzkamp 1993).

Traditional pedagogical views have accordingly seen the task of schools as precisely that of upholding the basic postulates of the national culture, and they succeed to the extent that pupils acquire the conviction that these have no alternatives or are superior to those of other nations.

Seen this way, school-induced socialization has an enormous socio-political meaning, and as a result the forms and content of schooling are an enduring source of social conflict. School is thus not only the place where the hegemony of the dominant culture is played out and transmitted; it is also the scene of daily conflicts about legitimate vs. illegitimate behaviors and language, as well as about recognition of the social relevance of hegemonial values, norms and knowledge (Willis 1977, Gumperz and Cook-Gumperz in this volume). Here children from diverse cultural backgrounds come in contact and in conflict, and this alone demands an examination of the cultural norms of the schools' institutional frameworks as well as of their daily practice. Relevant questions concern the ways in which stereotypes of nation, race, ethnicity and religion affect communication in schools, how legitimate vs. illegitimate knowledge and language are distinguished, how normal and deviant behaviors are marked, and how national, religious, ethnic and sex-related identifications are established and represented. Discussions on the legitimate use of languages in schools in multilingual settings can so be linked to "struggles over the establishment of authority and legitimacy" (Heller and Martin-Jones 2003a: ix). One possibility of carrying out social conflicts is by means of the legitimate language and language uses (Heller and Martin Jones 2003b).

Hence theories and programs of multicultural education demand that pedagogical practice include sensitivity to cultural differences. They reject pedagogical models meant to enforce conformity to a nationally oriented culture and instead emphasize a perspective that accepts a multiplicity of differing and equally valuable nationally, religiously and ethnically formed cultures. In contrast to traditional social and pedagogical theories, they adopt a comparative view that sees the immediate social forms not as unquestionably given and natural, but rather as constitutive elements of various cultural frameworks. Adopting such a perspective imposes definite and pedagogically significant requirements for communication and understanding: individual knowledge and/or communicative activities must be interpreted within one of many possible cultural backgrounds. Accordingly, difficulties in mutual understanding among individuals and social groups are traced to differences among cultures. Problems and conflicts are likely when the participants in the intercultural dialogue – in contrast to scientific observers of the dialogue – remain naively caught in the perspective of their own culture, unable to adopt a larger view that would allow them to go beyond their own implicit assumptions and certainties. Thus, concepts for inter- and multicultural education attempt to instill awareness in all participants of the cultural embeddedness of individuals' experience and action. Further, multicultural education seeks to respond to the situation of socially disadvantaged migrants and minorities "so that students from diverse racial, ethnic, and social-class groups will experience educational equality" (Banks and Banks 2001: 3).

What is often overlooked in proposals for multicultural education is the difficulty of clearly and unambiguously identifying particular cultures and of assigning individuals or social groups to closed and clearly bounded cultural frameworks. Rather, it is necessary to look not just at cultures as a source of communicative problems, but also at the social conditions and practices by which cultures are created and differentiated from one another, not as closed communicative systems but as flexible interpretational frameworks; for every instance of 'intercultural' communication is in reality socially situated, that is, framed in a *single* encompassing system of social labellings and cultural differences, and the participants in intercultural communication operate with knowledge of their cultural membership, acquired in shared processes of socialization (Hall and du Gay 2002).

Educational socialization is relevant for the study of intercultural communication in four specific respects:

First, schools are institutions for the presentation and enforcement of national, ethnic and religious identifications – but also the locus of resistance against assimilation to the hegemonial culture.

Second, schools are the central agents of socialization, so that much of the cultural background and cultural identification which individuals bring into intercultural dialogue have been acquired not in autonomously native cultures but in the schools themselves.

Third, schools are social meeting points that are not isolated from the cultural differences, conflicts and adaptive dynamics found elsewhere; rather, they host a continuous background of 'doing culture', in which the interactions among pupils and teachers lead the participants to form ideas about various cultures and to differentiate themselves from others via cultural labels. Recognizing this, in pedagogical practice, 'culture' is often invoked as an explanatory scheme in reacting to difficult and irritating behavior, when it seems plausible to interpret the behavior as the expression of pupils' backgrounds and families.

Fourth, in observations and analyses of interactions it has been shown that attributions to cultural and ethnic factors, 'enlightened' by cultural theory, are often simplistic and that they tend to go hand in hand with projective and grossly simplifying explanations of the observed behavior (cf. e.g. Schiffauer et al. 2002).

By contrast, numerous and various criticisms of an inadequately thought-through multiculturalism have pointed out that individuals in modern societies cannot be intelligibly understood solely as products of a culture, which alone determines their experiences, thoughts and actions. Instead, it is necessary to take the multiplicity of cultural and social influences in individuals' lives into account, as well as the individual and collective forms of critical distancing and creative transformations of cultural givens that are characteristic of modern societies.

3.   Socio-political aspects and educational models for dealing with cultural differences

Despite a widespread expectation to the contrary, supported by sociological theories of modernization, cultural differences and identifications have in fact lost importance neither in the world community nor within nation-states. Such identifications are not merely holdovers from hierarchical societies, religions, ethnic and regional traditions that have successfully resisted the pressure of national leveling. In fact, in modern social conflicts, elements of shared national, ethnic, racial or religious identification have been introduced again and again as part of the social dynamic of conflict (Castells 1995). This is true not only of so-called ethnic conflicts, carried out openly and even violently, but also of social relations between natives and migrants or majorities and minorities. Even in societies lacking visible signs of ethnic, national or religious conflict, migrants are often socially disadvantaged and suffer discriminatory labeling with specific characteristics. Under these conditions, cultural, ethnic and religious identifications serve as a kind of collective self-assertion against the situation imposed by the host society.

Socialization and education in schools are, of course, not insulated from these conflicts, and it is worthwhile to study how social and cultural identifications play out within them. To this end we can distinguish three problem areas:

–   External social, political and legal conditions (including the economic, political, and legal status of migrants; dominant conceptions of national identity; linguistic and cultural policies; connections between cultural, ethnic and religious attributions and forms of social discrimination; prevalence of xenophobic or racial ideologies)
–   Within the community, the roles schools assume in the area of conflict over cultural supremacy (in particular, administratively propagated ideas, norms and curricula; treatment of language and cultural symbols; policies concerning the composition of classes and of the faculty; relations to the local community)
–   Within schools, how nationality, language, culture, race, ethnicity and religion are treated in the curricula and in the classroom, and how ethnic, cultural, linguistic, racial and religious attributions influence the evaluation and encouragement of pupils.

Comparative international studies (e.g., Schiffauer et al. 2002; Hormel and Scherr 2004) have shown factors in all of these areas to have important consequences.

Thus, teachers in Canadian schools are required to be sensitive to the ethnic and religious orientations of their pupils and to take these into account when choosing instructional materials and methods. In German schools, on the other hand, the dominant attitude requires teachers to give special attention to deficits in language and family background among immigrant children. French teachers, on the other hand, are deliberately not informed about the nationality and religion of their pupils, to promote equal treatment of all, unbiased by such factors. Further comparison of Canadian with German and French schools makes clear that assumptions about cultural 'stamps' are by no means independent of the social positions of immigrants and minorities, where the social and economic factors are frequently misunderstood as expressions of cultural difference – for example, when factors like social class and parents' formal education and occupation are ignored, and success or failure in school is attributed to cultural influences.

Studies of multicultural education have shown that in the interaction between teachers and pupils, popular ethnic, religious and cultural stereotypes shape teachers' expectations about the abilities of pupils who appear to come from corresponding backgrounds. In language education, for example, a recent German study shows that teachers tend to attribute linguistic deficits to children with immigrant backgrounds (Weber 2003). This phenomenon contributes to the judgment that immigrant children have low linguistic competence. Hugh Mehan et al. (2001) cite various studies demonstrating that in US schools, as well, deficiencies among minority pupils are attributed to cultural factors. With the introduction of multicultural approaches, with new forms of communication and new content, the effects of presumed cultural determinants disappeared, making evident the causal role of a particular combination of teaching approach with social and cultural backgrounds of the pupils.

Whether schools treat racism, xenophobia, and discrimination as challenges deserving a proactive effort, or as problems that can be neglected, is still a matter of great importance. Even where a commitment to facing the problems of multicultural education has been made, the various national approaches, which often derive from a nation-state's fundamental values and historical experience and support its claim to democratic legitimacy, lead to considerable differences in educational practice. Some of these will be sketched in the next section.

3.1.   Education for citizenship or multicultural education

In educational policy-making, cultural differences are seldom treated in the abstract but rather in reference to the situations of immigrants or in the framework of conflicts about adequate recognition of national, religious or ethnic minorities. This in itself establishes a problematic framework, insofar as imagined cultural differences among social groups can be projected onto the actual immigrants or minorities, while other potentially meaningful differences, like those between middle-class and working-class culture or between various political milieus, are neglected. Although a politically and pedagogically influential line of thought insists on recognizing the autonomy of national, ethnic and religious groupings, any discussion of cultural differences in an educational context cannot ignore the inevitable interdependency of cultural attributions and socioeconomic status. How educational practice recognizes and deals with these issues varies widely among states. Here we shall look at three representative approaches, in France, Britain and Canada.

One common feature of the policies in these countries is their goal of making schools places where pupils witness equality and fairness in the relationships between natives and immigrants, as well as between majorities and minorities. All, however, face one grave difficulty that repeatedly surfaces in sociological studies: unequal socio-economic backgrounds and resulting attitudes toward the educational system strongly affect pupils' relative chances for success, and the chances of the disadvantaged can be improved by compensatory schooling only to a limited degree (Bernstein 1977; Bourdieu and Passeron 1990; Dubet and Duru-Bellat 2000; McDonald 1999). The British and Canadian models differ from the French model, in that the former attempt to recognize cultural and social differences and implement compensatory measures, while the French system tries to insulate the educational system from differences in social status, nationality, religion and ethnicity. Simplified and idealized, France and Canada present a pair of maximally contrasting approaches – republican universalism vs. multiculturalism – in which the implications of the underlying assumptions can be seen with especial clarity. In France the ideal of a religiously, culturally and ethnically neutral state reigns, resting on consensually accepted ideals and values of the Enlightenment, of the Declaration of the Rights of Man and Citizen and of democracy, instituted in a republic of free and equal citizens. By contrast, Canada's population, long comprising two distinct national and linguistic groupings, has destined it to embrace most fully a multicultural conception of the national state, and with it, multicultural concepts of education.

3.2.   Fundamental differences between Canadian multiculturalism and
        French republicanism

Following Kymlicka (1995, 1997), Canada can be characterized as a liberal state and a 'civic nation', in which neither ethnic membership nor cultural identity play a role in defining citizenship. What matters are continuous residence and a willingness to acquire one of the national languages as well as elementary knowledge of Canadian history. All residents are granted formally equal political and social rights, access to state services and to the labor market. Citizens and landed immigrants enjoy equal legal status with the exception that only citizens have the right to vote and stand for office. The socio-economic situation of immigrants and minorities is quite heterogeneous, resulting from a selective immigration policy that favors highly qualified workers, and many immigrants belong to a relatively privileged class. Problems associated with disadvantaged classes are found most often in the indigenous population (Adam 2002; Geißler 2003: 24). Thus, in contrast to many European countries, Canadian immigrants are not typically socio-economically disadvantaged, and they do not have lower than normal rates of success in the educational system.

As in England, Canadian educational policy and pedagogical practice are multicultural and anti-racist (McLeod 1992; Moodley 1992, 1995). Since 1971 a national policy of multiculturalism has been implemented that aims not only to understand the cultural backgrounds of immigrants but also to orient and differentiate the school curricula accordingly, to the point of adapting styles and methods of teaching to pupils' backgrounds. Cultural multiplicity is not reduced to folkloristic enrichment of the dominant culture nor to helping immigrants to assimilate successfully. In fact, the goal of having culturally neutral schooling is fundamentally relativized, and schools are opened to local communities so as to let all cultural groupings participate in their development.

The educational system of France presents a stark contrast to that of Canada, and to that of Great Britain, as well. Its guiding principle is not that of social and cultural diversity but rather the ideal of *égalité*, the political and legal equality of all citizens. The republican cast of French immigration and integration policy shows itself in the conviction that French culture (*civilisation*) realizes universal modern values. It postulates that recognition of these values is the foundation upon which social integration, and therefore the relevant educational concepts and programs, must build (Dubet and Duru-Bellat 2000: 62ff.; Wieviorka 2003: 21). The historical background can be found in the belief of French political and intellectual elites in their own historical superiority:

> At bottom the *école publique* of Jules Ferry [beginning of the nineteenth century – A.S.] wanted to open the way to the universal for both children of the mother country as well those from the colonies. It led the former out of the narrow bounds of their dialects, their villages and towns, and the latter out of their savagery.
>
> Wieviorka 2003: 23

It follows from the aim of transmitting universal culture that multicultural and community-oriented education must be strictly rejected. In 2003 this principle was again invoked in the debate over the wearing of scarves as religious dress in schools; the winning side argued for the assumed culturally neutral republican principles, and against allowing culture-specific symbols. These, in contrast to the modern, universal cultural framework of the schools, are thus implicitly suspected of being primitive and pre-democratic, and for them there can be no place in a society of free and equal citizens.

A further corollary of this basic orientation is that deliberate, compensatory support for minorities is not compatible with the principle of equality and equal treatment of all citizens. Racism and discrimination are to be overcome by an appropriate form of education, emphasizing republican values, rather than by recognizing cultural differences. Education for citizenship and political autonomy are thus central themes, and it is expected that a citizen brought up with these enlightened, universal principles will reject racism and ethnic discrimination. French educational policy and practice are thus guided not by the goal of instilling acceptance of, and willingness to communicate with other cultures, but rather the goal of superseding cultural particularism, so that cultural differences lose their significance.

The traditional republican concepts of *Citoyenneté* and *Civilité* are also invoked as elements of social measures meant to react to social conflicts in cities and suburban slums, regional segregation and ethnic stereotyping of social inequality (Bourdieu et al. 2002; Dubet and Lapeyronnie 1992). Nevertheless, immigrants in France suffer high rates of unemployment, and, statistically seen, their chances for social advancement are meager. A significant portion of the children and adolescents have difficult school careers, and even those who obtain higher levels of education must reckon with considerable discrimination in the labor market. Social marginalization is the fate of many second-generation immigrants.

It will not be surprising that the basic differences between Canadian and French education have important consequences on all levels of educational politics and practice, as some selected aspects of these will reveal.

3.3.   Ethnic labeling in schools

In societies with sizable immigrant populations, the existence of and differences among various ethnic groups become topics of conversation, so that the society comes to postulate a number of distinct communities, each having a distinct history and culture, either claimed by the community or attributed to it by the others. The creation of ethnic differences and identifications is thus a social process, and schools are among the social participants. In Germany it can be shown that the social discrimination of pupils from immigrant backgrounds is a topic around which ethnically flavored group identities develop, finally being claimed as a positive point of reference in the groups' collective identities (Bommes and Scherr 1991; Tertilt 1996). Similar phenomena have been reported in France. In French schools, however, manifest symbolic references to religion or ethnicity are treated as illegitimate, so that ethnic symbols and labellings acquire an additional meaning they could not otherwise have: they signify rejection of the official program of ethnically neutral schooling.

In England and Canada, on the other hand, ethnic identification is seen in the political and educational spheres as a legitimate reference to distinctive cultural differences, and – differently from Germany and France – it can legitimately be invoked as an explanatory or justifying factor in official documents and proceedings. One reason for the acceptance of ethnicity in Britain is that immigrants from former colonies often possess British passports, and in Canada citizenship is attained with relative ease after immigration. Hence, immigrant groups cannot be excluded on the basis of legal status, and in Britain and Canada ethnicity tends to become a category that merely distinguishes groups within one and the same body politic.

In British schools ethnicity can be invoked in the context of proceedings that involve social inequality, social distance and racial discrimination. Pupils are categorized according to ethnically formulated criteria, which are also employed in gathering official statistics. The criteria are based on a heterogeneous set of attributes (race, nationality, religion, language, self-defined ethnicity) and are actually not strictly ethnic categories. A document from the Department for Education and Skills (DfES 2003: 8) prescribes the following set of categories: White, Mixed, Asian or Asian British, Black or Black British, Chinese. The category Asian is further sub-divided into Indian, Pakistani, etc. In schools such categories are used for collecting statistics on attendance, discrimination cases, and the treatment of racially motivated conflicts.

The guidelines established here for official and for self-classification are hardly suited for educational contexts, nor for characterizing actual cultural differences. They make evident a fundamental problem with proactive multicultural and anti-discriminatory programs: in order to observe and record specific difficulties that immigrants and minorities face, it is first necessary to obtain unambiguous categorizations or self-categorizations of all individuals who might be affected. This, however, indulges and confirms precisely the same categorizations that the programs are meant to overcome. No way out of this dilemma is visible, for all proactive measures must necessarily be directed to specific disadvantaged and discriminated groups.

3.4.   Compensatory and anti-discriminatory policies

In Canada and Britain schools participate in actively combating the disadvantaged status of immigrants and minorities. Special importance is given to measures directed at linguistic deficiencies. In the framework of an anti-discrimination program, the guidelines of the Ontario Ministry of Education for development of an 'inclusive curriculum' prescribe that pupils whose first language is neither English nor French shall receive adequate offerings to learn a school's language of instruction. Likewise, however, courses in the minority languages of the community are to be offered, and pupils are to be encouraged to develop their knowledge of their first language. Furthermore, the guidelines emphasize that dialects differing from Canadian Standard English are not to be stigmatized (Ministry of Education and Training Ontario 1993: 14). Thus, Canadian educational policies differ radically from the French program of ethnically blind equality, whose efforts are concentrated on measures directed against intentional discrimination and racial insults.

3.5.   Involvement and exclusion of communities

Opening schools to the communities they serve is a key measure in the school reforms that have been attempted in Canada and in Britain, one meant to draw the experience and concerns of immigrant and minority groups into the schools' development. The schools actively seek to improve communication with parents from immigrant populations, in order to compensate for these parents' underrepresentation in school activities, conferences and in the parent–teacher associations. Additional measures have been taken in Britain and Canada to overcome language barriers that hinder parents from participating in school affairs.

In France, on the other hand, schools are understood to be neutral institutions committed to republican universalism, and their task is therefore taken to be that of overcoming regional and ethnic identifications as well as cultural particularism. Pupils are to be perceived and treated above all as individuals and as citizens, not as members of groups, and this is meant to enable them to shake off traditional cultural and religious ties. This orientation brings with it the goal of insulating both pupils and educational practice from the parents' influence. Thus, in contrast to Britain and Canada, no special effort is made to involve parents in school affairs, as representatives of a community or of a culture of origin, and obtaining their participation is not a goal of French educational policy. Nevertheless, immigrants do join political initiatives that speak out on socially controversial issues, among them those that affect education. These attitudes toward schools' relationships to their immediate communities and their significant cultural symbols find expression in the architectural features of French schools, as a recent ethnographic study has shown (Schiffauer et al. 2002): they are typically isolated from their surroundings by walls, fences and closed gates, while British schools tend to lack such isolating elements.

3.6.   Curricula

Adopting the goal of transmitting an adequate representation of the knowledge and history of its minorities, Canadian educational policy has committed itself to multiculturalism and the abandonment of a Europe-centric, dominant culture in its school curricula. An additional goal is to scrutinize all educational materials for cultural stereotypes and prejudices. Schools not only permit but encourage pupils to express their identities with cultural and religious symbols and clothing. In all school subjects an effort is made to make reference to the traditions and cultural accomplishments of various groups. So, for example, the mathematics curriculum includes both Chinese arithmetic and that of the 'first nations'. Such curricula are seen not only as necessary for improving the motivation of minorities and improving their chances of success, rather, on a more fundamental level it is assumed that how the elements of knowledge are presented and transmitted has a significant influence on attitudes that the majority groups develop with respect to the minorities. To this end, members of the majority culture are compelled to learn about cultural accomplishments and important items of knowledge that stem from the minority cultures.

Multiculturalism on this pattern is vehemently rejected in France and therefore plays no role in curricular development. In the framework of citizenship education, cultural differences and variety are primarily discussed in terms of defining the boundaries between legitimate claims to cultural particularity and the demands imposed by republican values and civil rights. In emphasizing the supreme claims of democratic values and norms, as well as of human rights, French curricula try to present an orientation having universal validity, superior to all traditional cultures (Centre nationale de documentation pédagogique 2000a, b).

Like the French *Education à la Citoyenneté*, the British *Citizenship Curriculum* takes a skeptical view of the labellings implicit in naive multiculturalism. This position has nevertheless led to quite different consequences. The *Citizenship Curriculum* recognizes the positive importance of social and individual alliances, as well as the ways in which cultural and ethnic labelling can lead to discrimination (Department of Education and Skills 2002).

4.   Conclusions

The various ways of dealing with cultural differences in education can be understood adequately only against the background of each country's social and political situation and the goals underlying its national policies. These express socially influential assumptions about cultural differences and their significance which cannot be ignored in educational communication, and which are often felt by teachers, parents and pupils to be the correct view of their social reality.

Nationalistically oriented concepts of education have not lost favor and are still in force in many countries. However, programs like those of Canada and Britain, based on political and pedagogical multiculturalism and meant to encourage sensitive appreciation of cultural differences and to overcome social and economic disadvantages, have also become influential. These programs tend to distance themselves from the idea that cultural differences and problems in intercultural communication can be ignored in educational practice or overcome by assimilating all pupils to the same national culture. At the same time, multicultural education is by no means a panacea for social and cultural tensions, for the institutional recognition of ethnic differences goes hand in hand with tendencies to accept and fix ethnic labellings and prejudices (see Reisigl in this volume). This leads to the paradox of trying to overcome ethnicity as a mechanism of discrimination and repression by elevating ethnicity to the status of a legitimate category for steering social and educational practice. Thus, to reduce the importance of ethnic labelling, pupils are in fact ethnically labeled, in the end giving these labellings not a reduced, but a higher importance. Furthermore, by recognizing their ties to cultural groups, pupils are inhibited from achieving distance to these groups and individual autonomy, which can be of particular importance in conflicts with parents and 'members of one's own culture'. Growing up in modern, liberal societies, pupils are not compulsively bound to their ethnic-cultural backgrounds, and in accord with the values of these societies, they can legitimately free themselves from the claims of specific cultural traditions.

The contrary paradigm, represented in the policies of France, where they derive from a specific commitment to republican and democratic ideals, posits the essential unimportance of ethnicity and cultural difference. It, too, offers no complete answer to a situation in which social inequalities are merged with cultural differences and attributions, for the underlying premise of the school as an island that can be effectively insulated from disturbing social and parental influences is a fiction that cannot be upheld. Universalism and strict rejection of cultural particularity are not sufficient to overcome the drag of social disadvantage on individual aspirations, nor can a policy of equal treatment of all pupils, blind to ethnic and social groupings, react to the subtle forms of structural discriminated that are named and explicitly addressed in Canada and Great Britain. Against the background of the programmatic difficulties faced by both the multicultural and the republican orientations, intercultural research and pedagogical theory face the task of developing sensibility to forms of structural and institutional discrimination, and to the complex interaction of attributions, labellings and identifications with processes of distancing and achievement of personal autonomy.

References

Adam, Heribert
2002   Wohlfahrtsstaat, Einwanderungspolitik und Minderheiten in Kanada: Modell für Deutschland und Europa? [Welfare state, immigration politics and
minorities in Canada: A model for Germany and Europe]. In: Andreas
Treichler (ed.), *Wohlfahrtsstaat, Einwanderung und ethnische Minderheiten* [Welfare state, immigration and ethnic minorities], 327–344. Wiesbaden: Westdeutscher Verlag.

Anderson, Benedict
1991   *Imagined Communities. Reflections on the Origin and Spread of Nationalism*. London: Verso.

Apple, Michael W.
1982   *Education and Power*. Boston: Routledge.

Banks, James A. and Cherry A. McGhee Banks (eds.)
2001   *Handbook of Research on Multicultural Education*. San Francisco: Jossey-
Bass.

Barbour, Stephen
2000   Nationalism, Language, Europe. In: Stephen Barbour and Cathie Carmichael (eds.), *Language and Nationalism in Europe*, 1–17. Oxford: Oxford
University Press.

Barbour, Stephen and Cathie Carmichael (eds.)
2000   *Language and Nationalism in Europe*. Oxford: Oxford University Press.

Bernfeld, Siegfried
1973   *Sisyphus, or The Limits of Education*. Berkeley: University of California
Press.

Bernstein, Basil
1977   *Class, Codes and Control: Towards a Theory of Educational Trans-
missions*, Vol. 3, 2nd edn. London: Routledge Kegan Paul.

Bommes, Michael and Albert Scherr
1991   Der Gebrauchswert von Selbst- und Fremdethnisierung in Strukturen so-
zialer Ungleichheit [The usefulness of ethnicizing self and others in structures of social inequality]. *Prokla* 83(21): 291–316.

Bourdieu, Pierre et al.
2002   *Das Elend der Welt*. Konstanz: Universitätsverlag

Bourdieu, Pierre and Claude Passeron
1990   *Reproduction in Education, Society, and Culture*. London: Sage Publications.

Castells, Manuel
1995   *The Power of Identity*. Malden: Blackwell.

Centre national de documentation pédagogique (CNDP)
2000a   *Education Civique, Juridique et Sociale. Classe de Seconde*. Document
d'accompagnement. Paris: CNDP (http://www.cndp.fr/textes_officiels/
lycee/ecjs/sec/pdf/eseec001.pdf).

Centre national de documentation pédagogique (CNDP)
2000b   *Education Civique, Juridique et Sociale. Classe de Première*. Document
d'accompagnement. Paris: CNDP (http://www.cndp.fr/textes_officiels/
lycee/ecjs/pre/pdf/EPREC001.pdf).

Department of Education and Skills (DfES)
2002   *Citizenship. The National Curriculum for England.* London (http://www. dfes.gov.uk/citizenship).
Department of Education and Skills (DfES)
2003   *Minority Ethnic Attainment and Participation in Education and Training: The Evidence.* London: DfES (http://www.standards.dfes.gov.uk/ethnicminorities/links_and_publications/763003/RTP01-03_Amended).
Dreeben, Robert S.
1970   *Nature of Teaching: Schools and the Work of Teachers.* San Francisco: Scott Foresman.
Dubet, Francois and Marie Duru-Bellat
2000   *L'Hypocrisie Scolaire. Pour un Collège enfin Démocratique.* Paris: Editions du Seuil.
Dubet, Francois and Didier Lapeyronnie
1992   *Les Quartiers d'Exil.* Paris: Editions du Seuil.
Durkheim, Emile
1922   *Éducation et Sociologie.* Paris: Alain.
Eckert, Penelope
2000   *Linguistic Variation as Social Practice.* Oxford: Blackwell.
Foucault, Michel
1979   *Discipline and Punish: The Birth of the Prison.* London: Penguin.
Geißler, Rainer
2003   Multikulturalismus. In: Kanada – Modell für Deutschland [Multiculturalism in Canada – A model for Germany]. *Aus Politik und Zeitgeschichte* [From politics and current events] B26: 19–25.
Gellner, Ernest
1983   *Nations and Nationalism.* Oxford: Blackwell.
Gumperz, John and Cook-Gumperz, Jenny
this volume Discourse, cultural diversity and communication: a linguistic anthropological perspective. Chapter 2.
Hall, Stuart and Paul du Gay
2002   *Questions of Cultural Identity.* London: Sage.
Harris, Roxy and Ben Rampton (eds.)
2003   *The Language, Ethnicity and Race Reader.* London: Routledge.
Heller, Monica and Marilyn Martin-Jones
2003a   Introduction: symbolic domination, education and linguistic difference. In: Monica Heller and Marilyn Martin-Jones (eds.), *Voices of Authority,* ix–xi. Westport: Ablex Publishing.
Heller, Monica and Marilyn Martin-Jones
2003b   Conclusion: education in multilingual settings. In: Monica Heller and Marilyn Martin-Jones (eds.), *Voices of Authority,* 419–424. Westport: Ablex Publishing.
Hobsbawm, Eric J.
1990   *Nations and Nationalism since 1780: Programme, Myth, Reality.* Cambridge: Cambridge University Press.
Holzkamp, Klaus
1993   *Lernen. Eine subjektwissenschaftliche Grundlegung* [Learning. A subject-founded study]. Frankfurt: Campus.

Honeyford, Ray
   2003   The language issue in multi-ethnic English schools. In: Roxy Harris and
           Ben Rampton (eds.), *The Language, Ethnicity and Race Reader*, 145–160.
           London: Routledge.
Hormel, Ulrike and Albert Scherr
   2004   *Bildung für die Einwanderungsgesellschaft* [Education for the immigrant
           society]. Wiesbaden: Westdeutscher Verlag.
Kymlicka, Will
   1995   *Multicultural Citizenship: a Liberal Theory of Minority Right.* Oxford: Ox-
           ford University Press.
Kymlicka, Will
   1997   *States, Nations and Cultures.* Assen: Van Gorum & Co.
McDonald, Kevin
   1999   *Struggles for Subjectivity.* Cambridge: Cambidge University Press.
McLeod, Keith A.
   1992   Multiculturalism and multicultural education in Canada: human rights and
           human rights education. In: Kogila A. Moodley (ed.), *Beyond Multicultural
           Education*, 215–242. Calgary: Detselig Enterprises Ltd.
Mehan, Hugh et al.
   2001   Ethnographic studies multicultural education in classrooms and schools.
           In: James A. Banks and Cherry A. McGhee Banks (eds.), *Handbook of Re-
           search on Multicultural Education*, 129–144. San Francisco: Jossey-Bass.
Ministry of Education and Training Ontario
   1993   *Antiracism and Ethnocultural Equity in School Boards.* Toronto: Ministry
           of Education and Training Ontario (www.edu.gov.on.ca/eng/document/cur-
           ricul/antiraci/antire.html).
Moodley, Kogila A.
   1992   *Beyond Multicultural Education.* Calgary: Detselig Enterprises Ltd.
Moodley, Kogila A.
   1995   Multicultural education in Canada: historical development and current
           status. In: James A. Banks and Cherry A. McGhee Banks (eds.), *Handbook
           of Research on Multicultural Education*, 801–820. San Francisco: Jossey-
           Bass.
Parsons, Talcott
   1971   *The System of Modern Societies.* Englewood Cliffs: Prentice-Hall.
Rampton, Ben
   2003   Youth, race and resistance: a sociolinguistic perspective in micropolitics
           in England. In: Monica Heller and Marilyn Martin-Jones (eds.), *Voices of
           Authority*, 403–417. Westport: Ablex Publishing.
Reisigl, Martin
this volume Discrimination in discourses. Chapter 18.
Schiffauer, Werner, Gerd Baumann, Riva Kastoryano and Steven Vertovec (eds.)
   2002   *Staat, Schule, Ethnizität* [State, school, ethnicity]. Münster: Waxmann.
Tertilt, Hermann
   1996   *Turkish Power Boys.* Frankfurt/M: Suhrkamp.
Weber, Martina
   2003   *Heterogenität im Schulalltag* [Heterogeneity in day-to-day school life].
           Wiesbaden: Westdeutscher Verlag.

Wieviorka, Michel
   2003   *Kulturelle Differenzen und kollektive Identitäten* [Cultural differences and
            collective identities]. Hamburg: Hamburger Edition.
Willis, Paul
   1977   *Learning to Labour: How Working-class Kids get Working-class Jobs.*
            Farnborough: Saxon House.

16.   The cultural context of media interpretation

Perry Hinton

1.   Introduction

In this chapter I will be examining the role of culture in the interpretation of the media. With the globalization of the media we now have a number of interesting academic questions that arise when media communications cross cultural boundaries. To what extent is the interpretation of these communications unique to the home culture in which they are produced? Are there universal aspects of media interpretation that cross cultural boundaries? How do people in one culture interpret the media output of another culture? We can explore these by examining two areas that at first glance show a strong aspect of universality. First, the concern over children and media portrayals of violence and secondly, the extraordinary popularity of soap operas (particularly the South American genre of 'telenovelas'), which have enjoyed world-wide success. One possible explanation for culture not being a major determinant in media interpretation is that there is enough commonality in the audience impact across cultures so that key aspects of the communication have similar effects regardless of the culture. Furthermore, it has been proposed that globalization has brought about this homogeneity. One argument is that, with the globalization of media, the dominance of Western producers – particularly from the United States of America – has resulted in a reduction of cultural difference in media interpretation (see Tomlinson 1999, 2004, although it is not Tomlinson's view).

In this chapter, however, I will be taking the opposing view and arguing that an examination of the cultural context of both the academic research and the audience reception is important to gain a full picture of what is happening in media interpretation. Indeed, from a range of disciplines, such as anthropology (e.g., from the ideas of Geertz 1973, 2000), social psychology (Moscovici 1981), cultural psychology (Stigler, Shweder and Herdt 1990), and cultural studies (e.g., Alasuutari 1999), there has been a shift towards analysing communication in terms of a cultural analysis. The research in 'audience reception', for example, examines a more complex relationship of the audience with the programme – as an integrated element within their everyday lives – encompassing their culture and what it means to them within the discourse of their everyday lives (Alasuutari 1999). Globalization may not therefore result in a promulgation of a dominant (Western) ideology but one contested and negotiated within the social practices of the different cultures (Tomlinson 2004).

2.   Media effects

Firstly, it is interesting to note that much of the work on the effect of the media within Communication Studies – especially the impact of television on its audience – has been undertaken apparently without particular reference to culture. For example, it is quite possible to examine major modern texts on 'media effects' and not find the word 'culture' in the index at all (see Bryant and Zillman 1994; Potter 1999). Hence, there is an apparent separation of the cultural context in which the debate arises and the outcomes of the research indicating a media effect – with the resultant implication that the effect could well be universal. With the globalization of media messages we also have the attendant globalization of the concerns about the effect of the media on the audience, particularly children. Indeed, Carlsson states "Many people suspect a correlation between the rising level of violence in daily life, particularly, that committed by children and youth, and the culture of violence our children encounter on television, in video films, in computer games and via Internet" (Carlsson 1999: 9). We could therefore argue that the fact that Bryant and Zillman and Potter are writing in the United States of America and Carlsson in Sweden is irrelevant to the research in this area and that we are dealing with an issue of equal concern across cultures. However, I wish to question the extent to which we can we divorce this concern from its cultural origin and create a discourse around 'the violence of youth' devoid of its cultural setting.

Much of the academic debate on the effect of media violence was stimulated by the work of Bandura and his colleagues in the early 1960s in the United States of America (e.g., Bandura, Ross and Ross 1963)[1]. In their experiments, young children (3–6 years) were shown, in certain circumstances, to imitate an adult model whom they had observed punching and hitting a blow-up 'bobo' doll. This and subsequent studies refined the conditions under which modelling would or would not take place (Bandura 1977). As a result of these studies, television was seen as an exemplar role model in the shaping of children's imitative behaviour. Thus, the audience was viewed as susceptible under the right conditions (or wrong conditions depending on which way one looks at it) to the influence of the media. As a result, it was argued that watching violent televised behaviour could then lead to real-life violent behaviour. And we have evidence of an apparently universal effect.

Yet when we look for the context of the research on media effects, it often lies within a wider public discourse existing within the culture in which the research is based. There is no exception in this case. If we examine one of Bandura's early articles (Bandura, Ross and Ross 1963 – the first specifically on film mediation), we find right at the beginning, within the introduction, the following quote: "A recent incident (San Francisco Chronicle 1961) in which a boy was seriously knifed during a re-enactment of a switchblade knife fight the boys had seen on a televised rerun of the James Dean movie *Rebel Without a Cause*, is a dramatic imitative influence of film stimulation" (Bandura, Ross and Ross 1963: 3). Notice that here at the beginning of the journal article, prior to the presentation of the research, the link between a media presentation and violence is stated. It clearly establishes the cultural context of the research that follows – youth violence in American society. Thus, the research is developing the discourse that had been stated publicly in the newspaper. Furthermore, the findings develop the concerns of a society seeking an explanation for the violent behaviour of its youth, and focus those concerns on the role of the media.

The public concern about the violence of youth in the United States of America has pervaded both the research and the government's interest in the media (see, for example, the U.S. Surgeon General's Scientific Advisory Committee on Television and Social Behavior 1972, and underlying a number of references within Youth Violence: A Report of the Surgeon General 2001). We can see the same underlying context in a comprehensive review of the media violence research (Potter 1999). The book states in the very first sentence on page 1: "Violence in America is a public health problem". Statistics on murders and other violent crime in the United Sates of America are described, along with a particular focus on teenagers. Thus, Potter is explicitly concerned about "the problem of violence in *our* culture" (1999: 2, my italics). So we should not be surprised at the lack of an index entry for 'culture' in this book, and that of Bryant and Zillman (1994), as the focus of the book is within the specific context of youth violence in the United States of America.

Potter (1999) is expressing concerns that are part of a public debate within American society that engages the US administration as well. The Surgeon General's Report on Youth Violence (2001) also focuses on the violence of youth in American society as a problem for examination and explanation. The first paragraph of the preface to this report notes the events in the Columbine high school in April 1999 when two students used guns to kill twelve fellow students and a teacher before turning the guns on themselves. Thus, it is the discourse within the culture of the United States of America that provides the impetus for the report. Whilst the report is not specifically about media portrayals of violence, exposure to television violence at an early age (6–11 years) is seen as one of the risk factors in youth violence (see Chapter 4, Box 4.1 of the report).

The issue for the modern global media environment is that the cultural context may often be lost when a text enters a different culture. An American author writing for an American audience does not need to spell out the concerns about the effects of the media within their common society – although clearly Potter helpfully does. The difficulty is that this society is not necessarily the same society for the reader as the author, when the book enters the global market. Whilst gun crime is an issue in Britain, its scale is minimal in comparison to Potter's figures from the United States with many British people never having had access to a gun and never actually having held one in their lives (including myself). As I mentioned elsewhere (Hinton 2000), the focus on the crime statistics presented in the preface of Potter's book may not have resonance in cities with little street crime such as Tokyo or countries where ordinary citizens do not have access to guns, such as the United Kingdom.

Indeed, when we examine a contemporary text for the British market, Gunter and McAleer (1997: viii), in their preface, make reference to the concerns about television violence "in the United States" (my emphasis) and their statistics from Britain simply provide demographic data on the availability of television, rather than setting up an image of British youth. The conclusion to their preface is that parents are responsible (along with broadcasters) for their children's viewing. So, the issue of media and children is set up in a very different manner in the British, compared to the American, text – and this may lead to a different view of the audience reception of the media.

If the research arising from the specific concerns about the possible causes of youth violence in the United States of America then enters the globalized academic debate on media violence (e.g., Carlsson 1999), the specific cultural context of the concerns is at risk of being ignored. Yet the research shows clear cultural differences, with the Surgeon General's Report on Youth Violence (2001) acknowledging lower levels of youth violence in a number of other countries in comparison to the USA. Furthermore, there is clear evidence of cultural differences in reaction to media portrayals of 'violence'. For example, Weigman, Kuttschreuter and Baarda (1992), in a study lasting three years and encompassing a number of different countries, found that there were significant correlations between aggressive behaviour and watching violent television for both boys and girls in the United States of America but not in the Netherlands or Australia. Indeed, it is not necessarily the case that we have the same context for the 'media violence' debate within the cultures of other countries.

There is also the question of what is meant by 'media violence'. Indeed, it is often the definition that is seen as the central problem for researchers (Gunter and McAleer 1997; Gauntlett 1998; Livingstone 1990). In fact, the focus and definition will reflect an ideology (Gauntlett 1998) that itself will provide a cultural context in the way that the particular audience is viewed within the research. Within the United States of America there is a public debate about youth violence, which provides a framework to the research within which the authors reside (e.g. Potter 1999). It is not surprising, in this context, that the research seeks to examine the media in order to determine its potential effects on the youth of America.

However, outside of the specific concerns of the United States of America, maybe it is more appropriate, in the global media environment to conclude, as Gunter and McAleer (1997: 116), writing in the United Kingdom, state, "The debate around television violence will continue both in the public and academic spheres. Whether or not there is too much violence in programmes is a subjective question as much as it is a scientific one: the answer lies, to a large extent, in the prevailing public taste and opinion." These public opinions, I would suggest, are the representations we are communicating and negotiating within a particular cultural context. Taking the example of the Hong Kong kung fu movie genre, one interpretation is that these movies contain a series of violent incidents. However, this is not the only interpretation. Bruce Lee, the superstar of the genre, preferred to class his work as 'action' rather than 'violence' (Logan 1995). The performance of the other major star, Jackie Chan, is viewed by the audience as balletic and comedic (Clemetson 1996). Thus, we should not expect the same discourse of media violence for a community such as Hong Kong with its lower levels of youth violence and we would not expect the same connotation to be placed on children imitating their screen heroes.

If we look at the example of Japan, we can see that recently there have been public concerns about youth violence (e.g., Balasegaram 2001), particularly as a result of well-publicized murders by young people (despite Japan remaining a country with extremely low rates of crime, see Tamura 2004). Here, however, the debate about the causes of these crimes has focused on the nature of modern Japanese society, rather than specially on the media. It has been suggested that a social and economic system geared up for material success has led to a high degree of pressure on the young for academic success and many find it difficult to cope, becoming socially isolated (referred to as 'hikikomori'). Thus, the question of youth violence is contextualized within both the role of the education system and the nature of social relations within Japanese society in a period of change. Whilst there are discussions of how to deal with young people in the criminal justice system, much of the debate has focused on the social bonds and social control within the changing Japanese society and the spiritual and emotional well-being of the young within it (Japan Echo 2000a 2000b 2001 2005). Hence, in Japan, the recent publicity about youth violence has not led to an examination of the media per se, but rather to an examination of society itself.

3. Audience interpretation

As well as the considerable amount of work on media effects, there has been a second strand of research that has examined the active role an audience plays in interpreting the meanings of media messages (Livingstone 1990). Much of this work, interestingly, has focused on audience involvement with television dramas, commonly referred to as soap operas. In the modern global marketplace, television programmes from the United States of America have been exported to many countries round the world and these programmes (many of them soap operas such as *Dallas* and series such as *Friends*) have frequently achieved very high audience figures in the host country. This has set the context for public debates in a number of countries where their own audiences are seen as being influenced by the 'cultural imperialism' of these programmes, undermining their indigenous cultural values and replacing them with those of the many imported programmes, particularly from the United States of America (Schiller 1976; see Thielmann in this volume on dominance in other aspects).

One of the most remarkable audience figures for a television programme was the 200 million people who watched the final episode of the soap opera *The Rich Also Cry* in Russia in 1992 (O'Donnell 1999). Its regular audience for the 249 episode run was in excess of 100 million people. These figures are quite extraordinary, with up to 70% of the country watching the programme. However, one of the interesting features of this example is that the programme itself was not a Russian production at all, but a Mexican telenovela from 1979 with the original title of *Los Ricos También Lloran*, dubbed into Russian.

On the face of it we can see the phenomenal success of the programme as evidence for the wide appeal for certain television programmes, despite the transmission in a different country and many years after its original production. It could be that the Russians and the Mexicans share a common interest in the female-centred passionate, tragic love stories of the Mexican telenovelas (Arias-King 1998). Indeed, telenovelas, from Mexico, Brazil and a number of other South American countries, are watched in over one hundred countries world-wide, with estimates of a global audience of around two billion viewers (Schlefer 2004). Included in these are a range of countries from Eastern Europe, including the Czech Republic, Poland, Bulgaria and Russia (Sinclair 1999).

Yet the telenovelas are produced by different countries and are targeted to their home audience in their production. In Mexico, the two big producers are Televista and TV Azteca and in Brazil the major producer is TV Globo. The home audiences are large with 34% regularly viewing telenovelas in Mexico and 73% in Brazil, with the overall audience in Latin American countries of 54% of the population between 12 and 64 years (Soong 1999). Interestingly, telenovelas are very much part of the home culture in both their choice of subject and their relationship to the audience. The telenovela *Nada Personal* from Mexico dealt with issues such as political corruption. The similarity of aspects of the storyline to real events would not have been lost on the Mexican audience. Also, TV Globo monitors audience reaction to its programmes and may modify a particular storyline development within a telenovela as a result (Soong 1999).

We could argue that this intimate relationship with the audience provides a local product (as opposed to programmes from other parts of the world) that audiences prefer (Sola Pool 1977). Furthermore the cultural attributes and the language (Spanish and Portuguese) of the telenovelas can be seen as engaging the common culture of the Latin American audiences and providing ways of engaging with cultural issues (such as the position of women in the culture) common to those audiences. Wilkinson (2003) refers to this cultural setting as the 'cultural linguistic market'. Within this market, researchers have examined the role of the telenovela in issues of national and cultural identity and the role they play in the everyday life of the culture; and, indeed, how they are contributing to the public debate of social issues within a culture (Acosta-Alzuru 2003)

Yet the qualities of both language and culture are altered when a production is exported across both language and time. So we do not have the same cultural context for a Mexican programme produced for the home market in the late 1970s when it is shown dubbed in Russian in the early 1990s. Hence the question arises: what does the programme mean to the Russians in contrast to the Mexicans or is there simply enough common power of the storyline to engage audiences across time and culture?

We can examine two aspects of the way an audience interprets a programme. First, we can examine the meanings that they give to the programme. How, for example, do the Russians interpret the storyline of a Mexican soap opera? What happens when a television programme from one country is shown in a different country? Are their differences in audience interpretation? Secondly, we can examine the aesthetic enjoyment of the programme. It is possible that an audience in one country may thoroughly enjoy a programme from another country for different reasons, such as the exotic 'otherness' of it, compared to those of the audience in the original country, which may be reflecting their everyday concerns.

Within the analysis of communication, early models presented the flow of communication as a process that would result in an effect upon the audience member (based on the communication model of Shannon and Weaver, 1949). Developments of this model have been more sophisticated: for example, watching a lot of television is seen to have a 'cultivation effect', in that it provides material for shaping the beliefs of the viewer (Shanahan and Morgan 1999). For example, if television programmes showed a higher rate of youth crime than existed in the actual criminal statistics, then a heavy television viewing audience might, through cultivation, develop a belief that the rate of youth crime was higher than it actually is. We could argue that through the watching of television programmes from another country its values may be cultivated within the host nation. This would also provide a theoretical explanation for the concerns that through the export of its media a country could be engaging in cultural imperialism (e.g., Schiller 1976; Dorfman and Mattelart 1975).

Within cultural studies, however, it was argued that an audience might produce a number of alternative meanings to a programme. Hall's (1980) model focused on the way in which programmes were encoded (by the producers) and decoded (by the audience). In this model audiences may decode the messages within the programme in terms of the preferred meanings (i.e., presented in the encoding of the programme) or in oppositional terms. In his work on the audience of the British early evening current affairs programme, *Nationwide*, Morley (1980) identified the different readings of different groups, such as trade unionists or students, of the programme. He showed the audience members were not necessarily accepting the dominant ideology of the programme in their reception of it (Morley 1993).

This led to the audience being seen as an 'active audience', making their own meaning from the programme (Livingstone 1990). In her own work on the British soap opera *Coronation Street*, Livingstone (1989) showed that the explanations for events, such as a potential adulterous affair, proposed in the programme through the script were not necessarily the ones chosen by audience members. Indeed, the audience offered explanations (such as 'being carried away with their feelings') that were not presented in the programme itself. Thus, if a programme is shown in a different culture we may have a different interpretation to that of the home audience.

This was supported by Liebes and Katz (1990) in their analysis of the hugely popular US soap opera *Dallas* (concerning a rich oil-owning family) with different cultural groups. The studies involved focus groups of three couples who watched an episode of the programme followed by a discussion with the researchers. Fifty-five groups were tested, with around ten groups from each of different cultures within Israel (Israeli kibbutz members, Israeli Arabs, Jewish immigrants from Morocco and recent Jewish immigrants from Russia) as well as groups from Los Angeles in the United States. Katz and Liebes (1985) noted a range of differences and similarities in the interpretation by the different groups. A common point throughout was that the rich were unhappy. The researchers found that, in the discussions, the groups made sense of the different issues raised through their own cultural backgrounds. For example, the Russian viewers were more likely to cite the social roles (such as 'businessman') in their discussions of motivation within the programme whereas the Americans and kibbutz members tended to employ psychological explanations (Katz and Liebes 1986). Also, the Arabs saw immorality in the programme whereas the Russians focused on capitalism as the corrupting factor (Liebes and Katz 1989). The groups also differed in the way they discussed the programme: 'critically', in terms of the structure and conventions of the programme and 'referentially', in terms of their own experiences.

Interestingly, one country where *Dallas* was not popular was Japan, where it was only shown for six months before being cancelled. Employing the same methodology as earlier, Katz, Liebes and Iwao (1991) examined Japanese viewers' discussions of the programme. Here eleven focus groups were employed. The authors argued that the Japanese groups were very critical of the programme due to its 'inconsistency' or 'incompatibility' both in the story and the characters (Katz, Liebes and Iwao 1991: 102). They were the most critically distant, as opposed to involved (or 'referential'), of the groups examined – it was simply not a programme that they watched. Furthermore, it did not fit with the conventions of Japanese own locally produced 'doramas'. The Japanese did appreciate the aesthetic form of the programme – yet it did not appeal to them. Thus, in terms of an active audience approach, we should expect that the Russian viewers of *The Rich Also Cry* would differ in their interpretation of the programme in comparison to its original Mexican audience.

An active audience may have different interpretations of a programme but do they also gain different enjoyment from it? The 'uses and gratifications approach' (McQuaill 2001) proposes four reasons for a viewer choosing to watch a television programme: a need to find out what is happening around us, as a reference for our own sense of identity, as a form of relationship (with characters on the television), and as entertainment (diversion). Livingstone (1989) in her analysis of viewers of the British soap opera *Coronation Street*, found escapist entertainment was the major reason for watching and that four separate groups of viewers could be identified through the way they interpreted the characters' actions and motivations. These were linked to the viewers' relationships to the characters in the programme (through their experience of watching the programme) as well as factors such as age and gender. Livingstone (1990) draws on the proposal by Newcomb and Hirsh (1984) that television provides a 'cultural forum' – it is rich and complex and open to differences in interpretation. Yet the enjoyment of the programme can be both from the 'reality' of it (we can make references to our own lives) and the 'unreality' of it (it is exciting and glamorous).

In her work on the soap opera *Dallas*, Ang (1985) examined the written responses from Dutch viewers of the programme. The enjoyment these women viewers found in the programme was not its representation of American life as such but the pleasure in the wealth of the characters, the style of the programme, the luxury in the clothes, the cars and houses – all as features of melodrama. It was not the capitalist values that were presented within the programme (which personally the viewers may have opposed) but the dramatic playing out of the problems of the rich family at the centre that appealed to the viewers. The programme had an appeal as fantasy and as melodrama that led to an emotional enjoyment of it. Interestingly, her research led her to argue that television programmes should not be seen as presenting a dominant meaning (as would be argued from a 'cultural imperialism' stand-point) with a possible oppositional reading by the viewer. For Ang (1985) the 'effect' of the programme was much more 'local' and cultural (see also Ang 1990a) and hence more complex.

There has been some debate concerning the nature of the 'active audience' in its freedom of choice in constructing meanings (Morley 1993). The power of the media organizations which produce and distribute the programmes (producing their dominant meanings) is greater than that of the audience in interpreting and reinterpreting those messages (Morley 1993; Ang 1990b). Whilst the 'active audience' model undermines the view that audiences are pawns of powerful media effects in their making of meaning, they have little choice in the media production and delivery and therefore their enjoyment and interpretation of television programmes exists within the framework of the media industries. For example, the telenovela *The Rich Also Cry* was the first opportunity for a Russian audience to view this type of show after a diet of dull broadcasts (Baldwin 1995). Also Miller and Philo (2001) argue against the view that the audience can interpret a programme in any way: audiences usually can understand the intended message but they may accept or reject it. Their only exception is where language and culture are very different between the producers of the message and the audience.[2] As we shall consider below, the dubbing and the cultural differences between the Mexicans and the Russians could have led to differences in the interpretation of *The Rich Also Cry*. However, its focus on the life of its central female character could have the same appeal to Russian women as it had to the Mexican women thirteen years earlier.

One explanation for the global success of the telenovela is that, like Ang's analysis of *Dallas*, it provides the enjoyment of melodrama for a majority female audience (see Gledhill 1992). Telenovelas have a finite number of episodes (around 200) so, unlike some soap operas, they do have a conclusion. Traditionally, there is a romantic couple at the centre of the drama, with many difficulties providing obstacles to their love. Many telenovelas, such as the Mexican *Simplemente Maria* – a Cinderella story that was also successful in Russia – have a strong female lead at the heart of the story. Thus, the success of telenovelas across the world, both in their own countries of origin and in Russia or the Czech Republic lies in their emotional expression through melodrama. Their success in Bulgaria can be attributed to women's pleasure, in that they construct a feminine aesthetic that provides a validation of female emotional power and romantic relationships (Kotzeva 2001). However, we should be cautious in proposing an explanation that ignores the cultural context of the television experience. Baldwin (1995) argues that the success of *The Rich Also Cry* in Russia can be linked to the particular cultural context of Russia at the time of screening. Furthermore, there may be subtle culturally-specific features of the content within the programme that are only available to the knowing audience of the indigenous 'cultural-linguistic market' (Wilkinson 2003) and not to an audience from a different culture.

Acosta-Alzuru (2003) interviewed Venezuelan viewers of *El País de las Mujeres (The Country of Women)*, a non-traditional Venezuelan telenovela drawing on social issues current within the culture, including sexual harassment, domestic abuse, abortion and homosexuality. She found that issues such as domestic violence, which had been part of the public debate for some while, were accepted by the audience but other issues, such as abortion and homosexuality, which were problematic issues within Venezuelan culture, were much less acceptable, so the character choosing not to have an abortion was approved of by the viewers. Acosta-Alzuru (2003) argued that this showed the relationship between Venezuelan culture and the programme – and controversial issues, that were not part of the public debate, produced a concern in the audience. The stories and characters in the telenovelas are features of public discourse with friends and fellow workers, and hence the viewers felt discomfort when unspoken issues (such as sexual harassment) entered the public domain through the telenovela.

We can see a second example of the cultural links for the home culture in the Japanese drama, *Oshin* (the name of the central female character). This was highly successful in Japan in the 1980s and also in over forty other countries (Harvey 1995). The story spans the life of *Oshin* from her birth in 1901 to the 1980s, and charts her trials and tribulations through life. Thus, it can be enjoyed as the triumph of the female character over adversity during the most turbulent periods of the 20th century. However, as Harvey (1995) points out, there are covert meanings within the programme provided for a Japanese audience. The central character's strength, contrary to the Western stereotype of the Japanese woman, but clearly identifiable to the Japanese viewer, embodies the iconic quality of 'endurance', a quality that is seen as a key feature of the Japanese themselves in their progress though the 20th century. As Harvey (1995) shows, the central character *is* Japan and her life is a mirror of Japanese history. Within the programme the audience is provided with explanations for aspects of their own history through the experiences of *Oshin*.

Returning to the success of *The Rich Also Cry* in Russia, Baldwin (1995) links this to the contemporary culture of the host nation. "What the show's popularity can tell us about Russian culture in and on the post-communist stage is that the switch of a good/evil paradigm from that of communist/capitalist to capitalist/communist marks a radical change in the way knowledge about gender in contemporary Russia is socially constructed" (Baldwin 1995: 287). The programme was cheap to buy and came at a time when the Russian audience had little experience of this form of television. Yet the viewers took on the story of the female central character 'as their own'. As Kotzeva (2001: 78) acknowledges for the Bulgarian women viewers of telenovelas: "A post-communist reading of gender through construction of melodramatic identifications of female viewers could be further linked to the opening up of the nation to a consumerist global TV world".

In both Russia and Bulgaria the telenovela phenomenon extended beyond the personal in that the arrival of actors from the programmes led to huge numbers of fans turning out to see them and politicians meeting them (Kotzeva 2001; Baldwin 1995). Even the Russian President Boris Yeltsin met Veronica Castro, star of *The Rich Also Cry* when she visited the country in 1992 (Baldwin 1995). This, in itself, becomes an interesting cultural phenomenon in its own right. Hence, the success of the telenovelas outside their countries of origin can be seen as the host nation taking them into their own culture. They become part of the communication within the culture, the subject of everyday discussion and a vehicle for engaging in issues such as gender and relationships in a changing society.

4.   Concluding comments

In conclusion, we should not view globalization as a mechanism that necessarily leads to a homogeneity of media interpretation, but rather as "a process of complex connectivity" (Tomlinson 2004: 26). It is a dynamic process by which media products interact with their home culture to structure the discourse around such societal concerns as youth violence or gender roles. When media messages, such as television programmes are exported to other cultures, we should not expect this audience to interpret the programmes in the same way but to actively make sense of them in terms of their own cultural expectations.

Traditionally, the academic analysis of the media has focused on individuals and the effect that the media message can have upon them, leading to a tendency to ignore cultural differences or to see them as a 'backdrop' to experience. However, the development of a more cultural focus in analysis, such as in cultural psychology within the field of psychology (e.g., Stigler, Shweder and Herdt 1990), has placed culture at the heart of understanding audience interpretation. Rather than examining cultural difference, as cross-cultural psychology does, cultural psychology examines the interrelationship between the mind and culture (Shweder 1991) and the set of cultural practices that develop within a culture. Thus, the focus of study is the involvement of culture in interpretation and understanding. We can examine this through an examination of cultural products such as beliefs, traditions and the interpretation of the media.

One way of viewing this process is through Moscovici's theory of social representations (Moscovici 1981, 1998). He argues that people within a culture share common representations, such as the English view of the French. This idea of representation bears similarity with the idea of schema in cognitive psychology (Augostinos and Innes 1990); however, Moscovici (1998) emphasizes that representations are not static features in the individual mind but are dynamic and that representations are being constantly developed through communication within a culture. So newspapers, television and everyday conversations within a culture provide the forum for the negotiation of the cultural representations. Moscovici (1998) uses the analogy with money to explain this. I have 'my' money in 'my' pocket but I can give it to you. I will happily exchange two £5 notes for one £10 note. So the specific notes are not the important feature. Just like the exchange of money, ideas flow within a culture, developing these cultural models. Thus, both home-produced and foreign media products

provide communications that can enter the discourse of the audience and interpretation becomes a complex process of structuring and developing that discourse within their culture.

Whilst concepts such as 'media violence' or 'women's consumption of
melodrama' can be examined without reference to the cultural setting, a focus
on the cultural context reveals a richer understanding of an audience's engagement with the media. With respect to both media violence and television soap
operas, they are more than simply different media communications. Rather they
are cultural products. A key feature of soap operas or telenovelas is that they become part of the communication within the culture, both through magazines and
television reporting on them, and through the everyday conversations of the
audience. Within the original culture the specific cultural references, as in *Oshin*
or *The Country of Women*, can offer representations that are linked to ideas that
develop the viewer's sense of national and cultural identity (Acosta-Alzuru
2003). To the host culture, some programmes may be rejected (such as *Dallas* in
Japan) but others may be used within the culture to develop their own representations of themselves, within the frameworks of their own lives (Kotzeva 2001).
Across cultures there may be shared concerns about, and pleasures in, the media
products but media interpretation takes place within a cultural context.

Notes

1. The research interest in media violence goes back to the 1920s with the public concerns about the effect of the cinema in the United States of America (Gunter 1994).
2. Stone (1993) cites an example of a Chinese film comedy that was viewed by Western
critics and audiences as a melodrama.

References

Acosta-Alzuru, Carolina
    2003   Tackling the issues: meaning making in a *telenovela*. *Popular Communi-
            cation* 1(4): 193–215.
Alasuutari, Pertti
    1999   Introduction: three phases of reception studies. In: Pertti Alasuutari (ed.),
            Rethinking the Media Audience, 1–21. London: Sage.
Ang, Ien
    1985   *Watching Dallas: Soap Opera and the Melodramatic Imagination*. New
            York: Methuen.
Ang, Ien
    1990a   Melodramatic identifications: television fiction and women's fantasy. In:
            Mary E. Brown (ed.), *Television and Women's Culture*, 75–88. London:
            Sage.

Ang, Ien
  1990b   The nature of the audience. In: John D.H. Downing, Ali Mohammadi and
           Annabelle Sregerny-Mohammadi (eds.), *Questioning the Media: A Critical
           Introduction*, 155–165. Newbury Park: Sage Publications.
Arias-King, Fredo
  1998   Is it power or principle? A footnote on Clinton's Russia policy. *Johnson's
          Russia List*. http://www.cdi.org/russia/johnson/2475.html [Accessed 31 Ja-
          nuary 2007].
Augoustinos, Martha and John M. Innes
  1990   Towards an integration of social representations and social schema theory.
          British Journal of Social Psychology 29: 213–231.
Balasegaram, Mangai
  2001   Violent crime stalks Japan's youth. *BBC News Online*. http://news.bbc.co.
          uk/1/hi/asia-pacific/1377781.stm [Accessed 31 January 2007].
Baldwin, Kate
  1995   Montezuma's revenge: Reading Los Ricos También Lloran in Russia. In:
          Robert C. Allen (ed.), *To be Continued ... Soap Operas Around the World*,
          285–300. London: Routledge.
Bandura, Albert
  1977   *Social Learning Theory*. Englewood Cliffs, NJ: Prentice Hall.
Bandura, Albert, Dorothea Ross and Sheila A. Ross
  1963   Imitation of film-mediated aggressive models. *Journal of Abnormal and
          Social Psychology* 66(1): 3–11.
Bryant, Jennings and Dolf Zillman (eds.)
  1994   *Media Effects: Advances in Theory and Research*. Hillsdale, NJ: Lawrence
          Erlbaum Associates.
Carlsson,Ulla
  1999   Foreword. In: Cecilia von Feilitzen and Ulla Carlsson (eds.), *Children and
          Media: Image, Education, Participation*, 9–11. Göteborg: The UNESCO
          International Clearinghouse on Children and Violence on the Screen at Nor-
          dicom.
Clemetson, Lynette
  1996   Return of the dragon. *Far Eastern Economic Review* March: 46–47.
Dorfman, Ariel and Armand Mattelart
  1975   *How to Read Donald Duck: Imperialist Ideology in the Disney Comic*. New
          York: International General Editions (originally published 1971).
Gauntlett, David
  1998   Ten things wrong with the effects model. In: Roger Dickinson, Ramaswami
          Harindrath and Olga Linné (eds.), *Approaches to Audiences – A Reader*,
          120–130. London: Arnold.
Geertz, Clifford
  1973   *The Interpretation of Cultures*. New York: Basic Books.
Geertz, Clifford
  2000   *Available Light: Anthropological Reflections on Philosophical Topics*.
          Princeton, NJ: Princeton University Press.
Gledhill, Christine
  1992   Speculations on the relationship between soap opera and melodrama.
          Quarterly Review of Film and Video 1–2(14): 103–124.

Gunter, Barrie
 1994   The question of media violence. In: Jennings Bryant and Dolf Zillman
           (eds.), *Media Effects: Advances in Theory and Research*, 163–211. Hills-
           dale, NJ: Lawrence Erlbaum Associates.
Gunter, Barrie and Jill McAleer
 1997   *Children and Television*, 2nd edn. London: Routledge.
Hall, Stuart
 1980   Encoding/decoding. In: Stuart Hall, Dorothy Hobson, Andrew Lowe and
           Paul Willis (eds.), *Culture, Media, Language*, 128–138. London: Hutchinson.
Harvey, Paul A.S.
 1995   Interpreting *Oshin* – war, history and women in modern Japan. In: Lise
           Skov and Brian Moeran (eds.), *Women, Media and Consumption in Japan*,
           75–110. Richmond: Curzon Press.
Hinton, Perry R.
 2000   Review of 'W.J.Potter, On Media Violence'. Thousand Oaks, CA: Sage,
           1999. 304pp. *European Journal of Communication* 15(3): 434–436.
Japan Echo
 2000a   Juvenile crime. *Japan Echo*, 27 5. http://www.japanecho.co.jp/sum/2000/
           270510.html [Accessed 31 January 2007].
Japan Echo
 2000b   Educational reform. *Japan Echo* 27, 6. http://www.japanecho.co.jp/sum/
           2000/270603.html [Accessed 31 January 2007].
Japan Echo
 2001   A new class of drifters. *Japan Echo* 28, 5. http://www.japanecho.co.jp/sum/
           2001/280515.html [Accessed 31 January 2007].
Japan Echo
 2005   Japan's new misfits. *Japan Echo* 32, 1. http://www.japanecho.co.jp/sum/
           2005/320103.html [Accessed 31 January 2007].
Katz, Elihu and Tamar Liebes
 1985   Mutual aid in the decoding of Dallas: preliminary notes from a cross-cul-
           tural study. In: Phillip Drummond and Richard Patterson (eds.), *Television
           in Transition*, 187–198. London: British Film Institute.
Katz, Elihu and Tamar Liebes
 1986   Patterns of involvement in television fiction: A comparative analysis. *Euro-
           pean Journal of Communication* 1(2): 151–171.
Katz, Elihu, Tamar Liebes and Sumiko Iwao
 1991   Neither here nor there: Why 'Dallas' failed in Japan. *Communication* 12:
           99–110.
Kotzeva, Tatyana
 2001   Private fantasies, public policies: Watching Latin American telenovelas in
           Bulgaria. *Journal of Mundane Behavior* 2(1): 68–83.
Liebes, Tamar and Elihu Katz
 1989   On the critical abilities of television viewers. In: Ellen Seiter, Hans Bor-
           chers, Gabrille Kreutzner and Eva-Maria Warth (eds.), *Remote Control:
           Television, Audiences and Cultural Power*, 204–222. London: Routledge.
Liebes, Tamar and Elihu Katz
 1990   *The Export of Meaning: Cross-Cultural Readings of Dallas*. Oxford: Ox-
           ford University Press.

Livingstone, Sonia M.
   1989   Interpreting a television narrative: how different viewers see a story. *Journal of Communication* 40(1): 72–85.
Livingstone, Sonia M.
   1990   *Making Sense of Television: The Psychology of Audience Interpretation* Oxford: Butterworth-Heinemann.
Logan, Bey
   1995   *Hong Kong Action Cinema.* New York: Overlook.
McQuaill, Dennis
   2001   With more hindsight: conceptual problems and some ways forward for media use research. *Communications* 26(4): 337–350.
Miller, David and Greg Philo
   2001   The active audience and wrong turns in media studies. *Soundscapes – Journal on Media Culture.* http://www.icce.rug.nl/~soundscapes/VOLUME04/ Active_audience.html [Accessed 1 February 2007].
Morley, David
   1980   *The Nationwide Audience:Structure and Decoding.* British Film Institute Television Monograph no. 11. London: British Film Institute.
Morley, David
   1993   Active audience theory: Pendulums and pitfalls. *Journal of Communication* 43(1): 13–19.
Moscovici, Serge
   1981   On social representations. In: Joseph P. Forgas (ed.), *Social Cognition: Perspective on Everyday Understanding*, 181–209. London: Academic Press.
Moscovici, Serge
   1998   The history and actuality of social representations. In: Uwe Flick (ed.), *The Psychology of the Social*, 209–247. Cambridge: Cambridge University Press.
Newcomb, Horace and Paul J. Hirsch
   1984   Television as a cultural forum: Implications for research. In: William D. Rowland and Bruce Watkins (eds.), *Interpreting Television: Current Research Perspectives*, 58–73. Beverly Hills,CA: Sage.
O'Donnell, Hugh
   1999   *Good Times, Bad Times: Soap Operas and Society in Western Europe.* London: Leicester University Press.
Potter, W. James
   1999   *On Media Violence.* Thousand Oaks, CA: Sage.
Schiller, Herbert I.
   1976   *Communication and Cultural Domination.* New York: International Arts and Sciences Press.
Schlefer, Jonathan
   2004   Global must-see TV. *Boston Globe* 04. 01. 2004. http://www.boston.com/ news/globe/magazine/articles/2004/01/04/global_must_see_tv/ [Accessed 31 January 2007].
Shanahan, James and Michael Morgan
   1999   *Television and its Viewers: Cultivation Theory and Research.* Cambridge: Cambridge University Press.

Shannon, Claude E. and Warren Weaver
  1949   *The Mathematical Theory of Communication.* Urbana, IL: University of Illinois Press.
Sinclair, John
  1999   *Latin American Television: A Global View.* New York: Oxford.
Sola Pool, Ithiel de
  1977   The changing flow of television. *Journal of Communication* 27(2): 139–179.
Soong Roland
  1999   Telenovelas in Latin America. http://www.zonalatina.com/Zldata70.htm [Accessed 31 January 2007].
Stigler, James W., Richard A. Shweder and Gilbert S. Herdt (eds.)
  1990   *Cultural Psychology: Essays in Comparative Human Development.* New York: Cambridge University Press.
Stone, Alan A.
  1993   Comedy and culture. *Boston Review* September/October. http://www.boston review.net/BR18.5/alanstone.html [Accessed 31 January 2007].
Shweder, Richard A. (ed.)
  1991   *Thinking Through Cultures: Expeditions in Cultural Psychology.* Cambridge: Harvard University Press.
Surgeon General's Report on Youth Violence
  2001   *Youth Violence: A Report of the Surgeon General.* U.S. Department of Health and Human Services. http://www.surgeongeneral.gov/library/youthviolence/report.html [Accessed 31 January 2007].
Tamura, Masahiro
  2004   Changing Japanese attitudes towards crime and safety. *Japan Echo* 31, 4. http://www.japanecho.co.jp/sum/2004/310406.html [Accessed 31 January 2007].
Thielmann, Winfried
this volume Power and dominance in intercultural communication, Chaper 20.
Tomlinson, John
  1999   *Globalisation and Culture.* Cambridge: Polity Press.
Tomlinson, John
  2004   Globalisation and national identity. In: John Sinclair and Graeme Turner (eds.), *Contemporary World Television*, 24–28. London: British Film Institute.
U.S. Surgeon General's Scientific Advisory Committee on Television and Social Behavior
  1972   *Television and Growing Up: The Impact of Televised Violence*, DHEW Publication No. HSM 72–9086. Washington, DC: U.S. Department of Health and Human Services.
Weigman, Oene, Margot Kuttschreuter and Ben Baarda
  1992   A longitudinal study of the effects of television viewing on aggressive and prosocial behaviours. *British Journal of Social Psychology* 31: 147–164.
Wilkinson, Kenton T.
  2003   Language differences in the telenovela trade. *Global Media Journal* 2(2). http://lass.calumet.purdue.edu/cca/gmj/sp03/gmj-sp03-wilkinson.htm [Accessed 31 January 2007].

17. Cross-cultural communication in intimate relationships

Ingrid Piller

1. Introduction

In this article I will attempt to provide an overview of recent research in cross-cultural intimate relationships. Of course, such an undertaking immediately poses the question: what is a cross-cultural intimate relationship? I will focus on only one type of intimate relationship, namely romantic and sexual couple relationships with various degrees of duration, commitment and exclusivity, ranging from life-long monogamous marriage on the one hand to short-lived prostitution encounters on the other. It could be argued that couple communication can never be cross-cultural as each couple forms their own personal 'mini-culture' no matter where the partners come from. Alternatively, it has also been suggested that men and women each have their gender-specific cultures (Maltz and Borker 1982; Tannen 1986, 1990), and in this view each and every heterosexual couple would engage in a cross-cultural relationship. For the purposes of this paper, I will engage with neither of these two extremes on the definitional cline [see the Intoduction by Spencer-Oatey and Kotthoff]. Rather, I will consider an endogamous relationship one in which the partners share the same national and linguistic background, and, conversely, a cross-cultural couple one in which the partners come from different national and/or linguistic backgrounds. I will thus ignore couple relationships where the partners come from different class, racial, regional or religious backgrounds although many studies of intermarriage focus on these (e.g., Stoltzfus 1996; Breger and Hill 1998; Ata 2000; Sollors 2000).

The paper is organized as follows: in the next section I will explore beliefs about exogamy and endogamy, as these provide the context in which cross-cultural communication in intimate relationships occurs. I will then provide demographic evidence for a sharp increase in international intimate relationships over the past 30 years and will discuss some of the reasons for this trend. I will argue that globalization in its various forms has facilitated meetings for partners from diverse backgrounds. Three aspects of globalization in particular are relevant, and I will discuss each in turn: increased international mobility, increased international data flow, and increased international cultural exchange. Throughout, I will concentrate on cross-cultural communication during the "early days" of an intimate relationship, i.e. when the relationship is considered or is just being established. I do so for two reasons: first, I have explored communication issues once a cross-cultural relationship has been established elsewhere (Piller 2001a, 2001b, 2002, in press), particularly language choice, the assumption that communication in cross-cultural intimate relationships is a "problem" per se, arguments, and the bilingual education of children in such relationships. Second, and more importantly, it would be wrong to assume that an intimate relationship is characterized by cross-cultural communication for an extended period just because the partners come from different national and/or linguistic backgrounds. As elsewhere, cross-cultural communication cannot be defined on the basis of the identities of the interactants, but rather on the basis of what it is that interactants orient to: only if they orient to cultural difference and culture as a category is actively constructed, can a communicative event be considered cross-cultural (Piller 2000; Scollon and Scollon 2001, Spreckels and Kotthoff in this volume). The more established a cross-cultural intimate relationship becomes, the rarer cross-cultural communication will be.

2.   Endogamy and exogamy

Many societies around the world see endogamous relationships – marriage within one's own group – as the norm, and intermarriage as the exception from the norm that is in need of explanation. By contrast, a relatively small number of societies routinely practice exogamy, and consider intra-cultural marriage a deviation from what is typically done. Examples of traditional societies that consider intermarriage the norm include the Banoni on the Solomon Islands (Lincoln 1979) and the Tucanoan in the Vaupés region in the North West Amazon Basin of Brazil and Colombia (Jackson 1983). The Tucanoan have a strong taboo against endogamy, and group membership is defined on the basis of one's "native" language. Residence is patri-local and language usage is dual-lingual, i.e. each partner speaks their "native" language and receives the partner's "native" language back. A child grows up hearing the father's language spoken widely, but also the language of the mother, and those of other female relatives, all of whom would be in-married. Thus, children grow up multilingual but consider their father's language their "native" language. Intermarriage is also fast becoming the predominant practice in some non-traditional societies such as Australia, where a 2004 newspaper article reported that "love is changing the face of Australia" (Gibbs and Delaney 2004). According to Gibbs and Delaney (2004), 22 % of the Australian population claimed more than one ancestry in the 2001 national census – a figure that reflects the intermarriage rate of previous generations, and is presumably significantly higher today.

It is against this background of different ideologies about intermarriage that intimate cross-cultural communication occurs. Ideology may be clearly stated as societal rules or taboos as in the Tucanoan case, or it may be implicit in practice as in the Australian case. Clearly, ideologies that consider intermarriage the norm are the exception globally. Even if ideology is implicit in practice, assumptions about intermarriage as exceptional may continue to exist simultaneously. Gibbs and Delaney (2004) provide an example: after having reported on the demographic findings regarding increased intermarriage in Australia, the authors go on to note with a certain air of surprise that "it appears that intermarriage is well-received". The interview excerpts with partners in cross-cultural relationships that follow clearly indicate that the interview question was regarding any negative experiences, and are summed up as follows: "The *Herald* talked to a dozen couples who said they experienced negligible racism in Sydney. They searched in vain to find examples of a hostile look or whispered taunt".

Therefore, in the following I will concentrate on cross-cultural intimate communication in contexts where intermarriage is exceptional and/or regarded as exceptional (usually both).

3.   Cross-cultural intimate relationships and globalization

In 1960, 19,458 German citizens married a non-citizen in a state-registered ceremony in Germany. By 1995, that number had risen to 50,686 (Statistisches Bundesamt 1997: 22). An even steeper increase can be observed in Japan: in 1965, 3,500 marriages between a Japanese citizen and a non-citizen were registered. By 1997, that number had risen to 27,000 (Radford and Tsutsumi 2004). The figures for the USA provide the same picture of an increase in international marriages: in 1992, 128,396 immigrants were admitted as spouses of US citizens. Ten years later, in 2002, 294,798 spouses of US citizens were admitted.[1] These three examples must suffice to prove the point that international marriages have, on a world-wide scale, increased enormously over the past decades. Furthermore, it must be borne in mind that marriage is only one form of an intimate cross-cultural relationship: it is difficult, if not impossible, to provide statistics on intimate relationships other than those sanctioned by the state. Intimate cross-cultural relationships not included in the marriage statistics take many different forms, and would, *inter alia*, include gay and lesbian couples, cohabitation and de facto relationships, and short-term relationships. Statistics that can be considered indicators of these types of relationships further confirm the finding of a tremendous increase in intimate cross-cultural relationships in recent decades. For instance, an indicator would be the figures of women who enter a country on an "entertainer visa" in countries where such a visa class exists, as it does in Japan. In the 1990s around 60,000 "entertainers" annually entered Japan from the Philippines (Radford and Tsutsumi 2004) to work in bars, cabarets and nightclubs, in other words to provide some form of "intimate labor", be it sexual or non-sexual companionship.

This increase in cross-cultural intimate relationships is directly linked to globalization. Globalization can be defined as "a social change, an increased connectivity among societies and their elements [...]; the explosive evolution of transport and communication technologies to facilitate international cultural and economic exchange".[2] Three aspects of globalization in particular can be isolated that have facilitated cross-cultural intimate relationships: increased international mobility; increased international data flow; and increased international cultural exchange. I will discuss each in turn.

4.   Increased international mobility

Globalization is characterized by unprecedented numbers of people moving around the world, be it for the purposes of study, employment, pleasure, or to flee from persecution, to name but a few. Obviously each instance of international mobility increases the chances for people to meet and find a partner from elsewhere. For instance, in my research with English-and-German-speaking couples (Piller 2002), I found that the majority of participating couples had met while one partner was abroad as an exchange student. Others met while one or both partners were working abroad, where "work" includes military service. Indeed, statistical evidence that the mere fact of overseas residence increases cross-cultural relationships comes from marriages between male US citizens and female German citizens registered in Germany (Statistisches Bundesamt 1997: 23). This is the only group of international marriages registered in Germany that saw a significant decrease in the period from 1960 to 1994. In 1960, 6,062 German women married a US national (which was then by far the largest group of foreign men to enter marriage with a German woman in Germany; the second largest group were Italian men with 1,215 registered marriages). However, in 1994, only 1,728 German women married a US national. As it happens this decrease – during a period where international marriages overall increased around 2.5 times (see above) – runs parallel to the stationing and eventual drawdown of US troops (Herget, Kremp and Rödel 1995). In another example, Walters (1996) points out that a number of the Anglophone wives of Tunisian men in his study first met their partner while they served as Peace Corps volunteers in Tunisia. Waldis' (1998: 196) research with Swiss–Tunisian couples where the female partner is Swiss and the male partner is Tunisian found that there were three circumstances in which the partners had met: while the Tunisian men studied overseas in Switzerland, while the Tunisian men worked overseas in Switzerland, while both partners studied or worked abroad in France, or while the Swiss women holidayed in Tunisia as overseas tourists.

In addition to the fact that increased international mobility for a range of purposes creates chances for cross-cultural intimate relationships to emerge, people may actually engage in international travel with the express aim of entering an intimate relationship as is the case in travel for sex and romance. Travel for sex and romance is not in itself a new phenomenon: the scarcity of women in the American West in the 19th century, for instance, saw many Chinese women migrate to the US for relationship reasons (White-Parks 1993). They either came as "picture brides" of Chinese men, where the marriage had been arranged by their families back in China, or they came as prostitutes, often having been sold or forced into the sex trade. Old as the practice may be, travel for sex and romance has exploded in recent decades. It is useful to make a distinction between travel for sex, or, less euphemistically, "prostitution travel", which is illegal in many contexts and oftentimes involves slavery and human trafficking, and romance travel, which centers around the mail-order bride industry and where both partners choose to enter a cross-cultural intimate relationship under legitimate circumstances. At the same time, there is a fine line between the two, as has become apparent, for instance, in cases of internet relationship scams. Given that the demand and supply countries for both sex and romance travel tend to be the same, it could also be argued that sex and romance travel are two sides of the same coin.

The extent of international prostitution travel can be gleaned from websites devoted to the fight against the sexual exploitation of women and children.[3] These show that throughout the 1990s the international mobility of both prostitutes and their clients increased tremendously. For instance, approximately 500,000 women annually are trafficked as prostitutes into Western Europe (Hughes et al. 1999). In many Western European countries, migrant prostitutes significantly outnumber local prostitutes, as for instance in Germany, where 75 % of prostitutes are foreigners (Hughes et al. 1999). At the same time, an estimated 200,000–400,000 German men annually travel abroad as prostitution tourists, with the Philippines, Thailand, South Korea, Sri Lanka and Hong Kong as their main destinations (Hughes et al. 1999). Figures for other industrialized countries show a similar picture of high demand for international prostitution, both as regards in-bound prostitutes and out-bound clients: Japan, for instance, has about 150,000 foreign women in prostitution, and Japanese men constitute the largest group of prostitution tourists in Asia (Hughes et al. 1999). The suppliers in this global division of sexual labor come from impoverished nations in Asia and Latin America, and, since the end of the Cold War, Russia and Eastern Europe.

Global economic inequality similarly underlies the legitimate side of the business od romance travel, which centers around the mail-order bride industry. Kojima (2001) analyses the mail-order bride industry as a system for the global division of reproductive labor. Women in industrialized countries have on an individual level been successful in freeing themselves from the imperative to marry and have children, but they have not succeeded in changing the underlying system of capitalism and patriarchy which depends upon gendered unpaid work for social and human reproduction. Consequently, the gap is being filled by migrant wives and mothers. Like prostitution travel, romance travel is immensely gendered: men from industrialized nations go on "romance tours" to choose an overseas bride, while women from underdeveloped nations migrate to join their overseas husbands and take up residency with them. A "romance tour" is a form of package tourism where a mail-order bride agency organizes for a client to meet a number of available women in a given destination with the aim of marriage. The package typically includes airfare and hotel, arranged meetings with individual women or parties with a number of women, marriage contracts and legal assistance, and wedding arrangements. "Cherry Blossoms", a US-based international marriage agency, for instance, offers romance tours to Shenzhen (China), Lima (Peru), Cebu City (Philippines), Bangkok (Thailand), and Ho Chi Min City (Vietnam), where the agency introduces the client to five women per day for a period of up to seven days "or as needed if you do not need so many. Most of our men go for at least two weeks so once they have time to get to know some of the women they have met better before returning home". "Cherry Blossoms" claims on their website that over 90% of the men who use their tour services get engaged and then marry within a year of their tour.[4] Instead of or along with individual introductions, agencies also organize "socials" for the men to attend along with a number of local women seeking marriage. The male–female ratio in some such socials is 12:2,000 (O'Rourke 2002). Indeed, many of the clients who provide testimonies about their experience with the US-based agency "Russian Brides" gush about the wide selection, as this correspondent: "I picked four that I liked the best, Sveta, Maria, Natasha, and Nadia. I had a wonderful time with all four. It was hard to choose between them. In the week I spent in Moscow, I had more dates and fun than I've had in the past ten years with American women".[5] Romance tours, as well as the mail-order bride industry more generally, have been enormously facilitated, if not enabled, by the internet, and it is to this medium that I will now turn.

5.   Increased international data flow

It is not only increased international travel that has resulted in the tremendous increase in cross-cultural intimate relationships, but also increased international data flow, using such technologies as the Internet. Today, virtual meetings are as common as physical meetings. My students, who are in their 20s often tell me stories of how they met their partners online, or that they are conducting virtual relationships, with only very limited actual physical encounters – something I, in my late 30s, still find remarkable. The internet has removed some, even if not all, of the constraints of space on love. It is in this space that dating and matchmaking agencies of all kinds are booming, including mail-order bride services. The modern mail-order bride industry began in the early 1970s with personal ads and print mail-order catalogues (O'Rourke 2002). However, it was only with the spread of internet access that the industry started to boom. In 2002, O'Rourke (2002) estimated that, at the time, there were around 2,700 agencies worldwide, with around 500 based in the US. From the mid-1980s onwards an estimated 5,000 mail-order brides from the Philippines alone entered the US each year, a total of 55,000 as of 1997 (Hughes et al. 1999). The advantages of the web-based agency over newspaper ads or print catalogues are obvious: To begin with, the database can be kept up-to-date at all times, so that customers do not need to worry that the prospective partners they are interested in might already have been taken. Most sites emphasize this fact in their advertising, for instance:

> If you watch our site closely, you will notice that 50 beautiful women are added to it every week. But what you might not notice, unless you bookmarked many ladies' profiles, is that we also de-activate many profiles every week. Approximately 5–25 such deactivations each week result from daily client requests and contacts from ladies asking to be removed from our site as they have entered a serious relationship. We honor these requests without hesitation.[6]

Furthermore, the genre of the personal ads has changed with the new medium. Personal ads are no longer a minimalist genre where the advertiser has to be concise because they are paying per word or even per letter (Bruthiaux 1996). Web-ads typically include a closed list of attributes (age, physical measurements, ethnicity, religion, smoking status, etc.), plus a photo, and two open-ended sections where the advertiser can describe themselves and their desired other.

Finally, prospective partners do not have to rely on the personal ad in isolation, rather the membership system of many sites offers an opportunity for instantaneous communication. If a client is interested in an advertiser they can initiate a chat session with them. Cristina, whose "real-life success story" is featured on "Filipina Heart" describes the process as follows:

> I dont know where to start my fairytail like story. I was in filipinaheart only to chat with my friends but i did not expect that i will meet the man that will give me happiness, love, and everything to me. one day, i go to the internet cafe to close my profile in filipinaheart because i am so busy studying but there is this man named garry that popped up in my computer screen only a few minutes before i can close my profile. i am not really interested to talk that day but i felt something for him and that talk last for hours and we promised to talk everyday either in filipinaheart or phone. we communicate everyday […][7]

If a site does not offer a membership system (where the men pay for access to the data of all the women advertising on a site), the client can purchase the contact details of the women they are interested in on a case-by-case basis ("add to shopping cart"), usually with discounts for bulk buyers. The liberalization of the telephone market has also meant that even frequent and long international telephone calls to conduct a romantic relationship have become affordable from many industrialized countries. Indeed, some mail-order bride websites also offer telephone deals: "[W]e have found a pre-paid phone card company that offers incredibly low rates for all of your domestic and foreign calling needs. Calling the Philippines used to be very expensive to say the least. Now, it can be done at a very attractive price. Do your wallet a favor, and take a moment to check out these cards through our link."[8]

Thus, websites offer far greater choice to their customers, both quantitatively (number of potential partners) and qualitatively (extended basis on which a choice is being made). While the internet offers many advantages for cross-cultural intimate communication, it also has well-known dangers. Mail-order bride sites often function as "shop-fronts" for organized crime and lure women into prostitution, and even if they do not, the danger of entering an abusive relationship is high. The mail-order bride industry is poorly regulated, and most of the regulations aim to prevent immigration fraud rather than protecting the women who enter a country as mail-order brides, and who are oftentimes dependent on their new husband in many ways, not least for their residency status. Unsurprisingly, the incidence of domestic violence in such marriages is higher than in marriages resulting from other encounters (O'Rourke 2002). Intimate cross-cultural encounters on the internet can thus easily become a vehicle of exploitation as in this case of a Russian mail-order bride in the US:

> My internet meeting with Ed led to my being victimized in three ways. I was a victim of domestic violence, of sexual assault, and trafficking … There were no pimps or organized crime rings. In my case, the internet was the vehicle for my sexual exploitation. It enabled Ed, a sexual predator, to lure me across the world into a situation in which I had no choice but to submit to his sexual demands. I was not his first victim, and I will not be his last. I have heard that he has a new Russian bride, and my heart bleeds for her.[9]

6.   Increased international cultural exchange

Globalization is also characterized by an increase in international cultural exchange, in particular through cultural exports emanating from "cultural centers" such as the movie industry in Hollywood and Bollywood, or the music industry in London, New York, and Hong Kong. Increased international mobility and increased international data flow explain the increase in cross-cultural intimate relationships as a function of increased chances for cross-cultural encounters. However, at the same time, the fact remains that some people actively seek out a partner from a different cultural background as the mail-order bride phenomenon makes abundantly clear. Therefore, in this section, I will argue that it is globalization as increased international cultural exchange that is instrumental in encouraging an increasing number of people to actively seek out a cross-cultural intimate relationship. Cross-cultural desires in this view are not some kind of inner state, but rather a discursive construction (see Cameron and Kulick 2003a, 2003b for a full discussion of desire as a discursive construction). In this understanding public discourses – be they a Hollywood movie or a pop song – provide structures that individuals can draw on.

In previous work (Piller 2002, in press), I have described that a number of the partners in long-standing cross-cultural intimate relationships I interviewed explained that, at the beginning of their relationship, the fact that their partner came from another culture was part of the attraction. One German woman, for instance, said of her US-American husband, "I always wanted to marry a cowboy". Another German woman has the following exchange with her British partner:

```
Erika¹⁰   @and if you weren't an Englishman, you wouldn't stand no
          chance. not like a snowball in hell, so.@ @@@ das hat
          fuer mich ne grosse Bedeutung, dass du Englaender bist.
          ((that is very important for me that you are an English-
          man.))
Michael   immer noch? ich glaube am Anfang war das mal.
          is that still the case? I think that used to be so in the
          beginning.
```

My data show that partners in a cross-cultural intimate relationship may initially see each other as a representative of their culture. The more established the relationship is the less partners see each other as cultural representatives, and the more they see each other as individuals. In her study of Russian–American marriages, Visson (1998: 102) similarly observes that partners tended to see themselves as individuals, but their spouses in cultural terms, "as products of a 'foreign' culture".

Takahashi's PhD research provides a further important contribution to our understanding of cross-cultural desire as a discursive construction within a specific context: this researcher shows that some Japanese women actively seek out an English-speaking partner because they take them to be good-looking and considerate ladies' men, similar to the media images of celebrities such as David Beckham, Tom Cruise or Brad Pitt (Piller and Takahashi 2006; Takahashi 2006). There are numerous sources from which these images of Western men as attractive, caring, loving, and giving emanate: there are of course Hollywood movies and numerous other US cultural products, but, more crucially for our discussion, international cultural interconnectedness has reached such levels that these images also emanate from Japanese cultural products, such as *manga* and *anime*, Japanese pop songs (as opposed to American ones, which are available simultaneously), women's magazines, and the advertising for the English-language-teaching industry. As Takahashi's (2006) ethnographic research shows it is particularly in situations where Japanese women experience serious dissatisfaction with Japanese society, and particularly Japanese men, as for instance the experience of severe bullying or divorce from a cheating husband, that they decide to actively pursue the possibility of meeting a Western partner.

Dissatisfaction with Western women also emerges as the main reason that mail-order bride websites give for American men to pursue a partner from outside their own culture. I will now shift away from the focus on women that has previously dominated research in cross-cultural desires (as in most language-and-gender-related enquiry; see, e.g. Piller and Pavlenko 2004), and explore the cross-cultural desires expressed by Western men on these sites in greater detail. There are four aspects to these discursive constructions: representations of what Western men are like and what they desire in a relationship; representations of what Western women are like and why these "default partners" are not being considered; representations of foreign women – I will concentrate on Filipinas – and what makes them desirable; representations of Filipino men, their "default partners", and what makes them undesirable or unsuitable partners for Filipinas. I will briefly discuss each. To begin with, it is important to bear in mind that categories such as "Western man" and "Filipina" are member categorizations (Sacks 1992; Antaki and Widdicombe 1998, Spreckels and Kotthoff in this volume) on the websites. One site, for instance, has the following slogan: "Western Man + Filipina = Happiness. You do not have to be good with Algebra to know that is a winning equation!!"[11] In this example, as in numerous others, the categorization is a member categorization as it is used on the site, and it also provides evidence for the fact that advertisers on this website (be they Western men or Filipinas) approach each other (initially) in cultural categories, i.e. as representatives of their respective cultures.

Western men

According to O'Rourke (2002: 477), surveys have repeatedly shown the following characteristics of US-American men who seek the services of a mail-order bride agency:

> [A] median age of 37, where ninety-four percent were white; fifty percent had two or more years of college, while less than one percent lacked high school diplomas; fifty-seven percent had been married at least once before; and seventy-five percent hoped to father children through the mailorder marriage. Additionally, the men surveyed were, for the most part, politically and ideologically conservative and financially successful.

In her analysis of 60 personal ads placed by men on the "Filipinaheart" site in early 2004, Mooring (2004a) also found – on the basis of their demographic details which form part of a check-list on this site, as they do on most – that the majority of these advertisers (75 %) were 36 years or older (up to 65). Most were Christians (only 22 % identified as "Other", "No Religion", "Buddhist" or "Jewish", in this order). In their open-ended self-descriptions the most frequently occurring attributes, in descending order, were: "attractive/good looking", "honest", "financially secure/successful", "great sense of humor", "loving", "caring", "romantic", "family-oriented", "religious/god-fearing", "fun-loving", "understanding", "simple", "faithful", and "open-minded". The composite picture produced from those 60 ads is one of a traditional head-of-the-family, breadwinner husband-and-father. This is also the image espoused in the marketing statements of the websites themselves. The following is an example:

> This site caters to the classical American gentlemen. Men who understand that man and women are different, and someone a lot smarter than us made us different for very good reasons. What you are looking for is someone 100 % loyal and who fulfills all the other roles a traditional wife fills. What I found is that women from the Philippines meet that criteria and are more compatible with American gentlemen than American women. […] I've seen an understanding of the social order from Philippine people I've not seen in any American younger than 60 to 70 years old. What this means is **the Philippine people teach social and family skills that Americans have abandoned**. But not all Americans. There are still plenty of American men who appreciate and desire those skills and understanding.[12]

Western women

The above quotation also mentions that American women lack compatibility with American men. Negative representations of Western women are pervasive on these websites and their frequency testifies to the fact that the writers see endogamy as the norm, and feel they need to justify their search for a foreign partner (see above). Western women are represented as "liberated" (which is always used in quotation marks), selfish, aggressive, and materialistic. Statements such as this one abound:

> I know many of you are tired of the US or Canadian singles scene like I was. You know … insincere girls who like to play games or expect constant material gifts. But these Asian ladies are honest, faithful, rarely lose their figures as they age, are extremely supportive, and care more about your heart than your wallet. For them, nice guys finish first! I know that is a new concept to many who are reading this … I know it was for me. Don't settle for a demanding and unappreciative woman. The age of the internet has opened up a whole new world of opportunity. It's time you meet the woman you truly deserve! Life is too short to settle for a "6" when you can have a "10"![13]

Much of what is said about Western women is said by implication, through contrasting them, implicitly or explicitly, with Filipinas, as in "they rarely lose their figures when they age", which implies that Western women do.

Filipinas

Foreign women are everything that Western women are not, or are no longer. They are the ideal of conventional femininity: beautiful, petite, devoted, religious, obedient, submissive, and sexy. Previous research has shown that Orientalist images (Said 1978, 1993; Spurr 1993) predominate in the images of Asian women in the West, and particularly in the US (Marchetti 1993; Uchida 1998). The image of Asian women is dominated by the "Madame Butterfly", or, more recently, "Miss Saigon" stereotype, which portrays Asian women as exotic, sexually available, submissive, obedient, domestic, sweet and passive. For her honours thesis, Mooring (2004b) collected generalizations about Filipinas from six different mail-order bride sites,[14] and found that they largely coincide with the image described by Uchida (1998). The following is typical:

> Filipina women are renowned for their beauty, femininity and traditional family values. They are sincere, devoted and they believe in a lasting marriage. The majority of our members are in the Philippines. Our personal opinion reflects the fact that Filipina women stand out among Asian women in terms of charm, openness, intelligence, education and trustworthiness. In addition, Filipina women make excellent wives, and they excel and value their husbands as their priority. They are very affectionate and romantic, and their focus and goals is giving their man tender loving care, surpasses all the women in South East Asia. They are well educated in their different respective professions and you'll find them very mature in their thinking. They are mature for their age and view older men as more stable and responsible partner. These ladies are very feminine and gentle, cultured and passionate. They enjoy the outdoors as much as indoor activities. Their outer physical beauties coupled with their wonderful personality, high level of intelligence, sense of humor and sincere devotion to their man creates one of the strongest relationships you could ever hope to find.[15]

On many sites, as on this one, there is also evidence of defending the "Filipina brand" against competitors, namely other Asian women. The strongest "selling points" in this respect are their English ability and their Christianity, but other differences that make Filipinas more attractive to Western men than other Asian women are mentioned as well:

> We are different from most Asian cultures. We are loyal to family unit more than country. We are comfortable loving and marrying men of other race, while most Asians "lose face" if marry outside their on culture. [...] Marry a Filipina, and you not have to eat with chopsticks or bow all time.[16]

The same competition can be observed on Russian mail-order bride websites, where Russian women, who are relative newcomers to the scene, with the industry only dating from the end of the Cold War, are positioned vis-à-vis Asian women: "Western men see Russian women as more mature and usually more educated than their Asian counterparts".[17] However, their main competitive edge seems to be their race: Russian women are similarly exoticized as Asian women, but they have the added bonus of being White: they "have a European face but the patience of an Asian".[18] Similarly, a feature in the *Sydney Morning Herald Magazine* entitled "Reds in the beds" (Phelan 2000) described Russian mail-order brides as "sexy, willing [...] Olgas, Svetlanas, and Natashas." The "earthy, exotic soul of Russian women [is said to be] very attractive, partly because the Russians have a much more traditional approach to relationships and forming a comfortable home life". In sum, "here are exotic white women who know their place".

Filipinos

The emasculation of Asian men is a frequent trope in Orientalist discourse (Marchetti 1993; Spurr 1993; Pennycook 1998), and mail-order bride websites are no exception. In the same way that Filipinas are everything that Western women are not, Western men are everything that Filipinos are not, as in this example:

> We, being Filipinas in general, think of Western gentlemen, particularly Western European and North American men as God-fearing, hardworking, and deserving of much love, respect, and admiration. Please understand this the right way, but frankly we take pleasure in being submissive to the reasonable demands of our husband. Western men make us feel comfortable, and even protected, as we naturally look to Western men for high moral and spiritual integrity. Ok, so we like taller guys and Western features, maybe because of movie heroes. Too many boys here playboy, drinker, gambler, and abuser. American (USA & Canada) man have reputation of treating wife in good manner.[19]

Indeed, the fear of (sexual) abuse and violence which the anonymity of the internet engenders, and which is well-founded given the high incidence of international sexual exploitation (see above), is always present on these websites. However, it is banished in two ways: either it is projected on scamming competitor websites or, more frequently, on foreign men. In addition to projecting fears, negative representations of non-Western men also allow the Western suitor to take up another traditional male subject position, namely that of the knight-in-shining-armor who comes to the rescue of the damsel-in-distress. Numerous male advertisers mention their abhorrence of women being mistreated, for example: "I am searching for a Life Partner. I can and will offer her my understanding and love. I am very responsible and loving and I don't like it when a man mistreats a woman. I am looking for a woman that I can give all of my love to [...]".[20]

Summary: increased international cultural representations

Orientalist discourses that emerged with the colonial expansion of European nations and, later the USA, continue to persist. However, while Said's (1978) original analysis focused on representations of "high culture" such as novels and academic scholarship, they are now well and truly engrained and almost universally disseminated through pop culture. The "Madame Butterfly" stereotype is a good example: while the Puccini opera (first performed in 1904) is a typical product of high-culture with the limited distribution that entails, the "Miss Saigon" musical ran for over 10 years each in both London and on Broadway and toured internationally, ensuring a much wider distribution. It has always been one feature of Orientalist discourse to represent the relationship between the colonizer and the colonized as a sexual one where the colonizer is associated with masculinity and the colonized with femininity (Hyam 1990; Spurr 1993). The expanded dissemination of Orientalist discourses has also led to an expansion of sexual relationships between men from industrialized countries, and women from underdeveloped ones. In the era of globalization, a Western man no longer has to be a colonialist to enjoy "exotic" romance.

While I have focused on the desires expressed by Western men, my discussion would be incomplete without a short mention of the desires expressed by the women, even if only to avoid the impression that the women are passive victims of neo-colonial relations. They are not. Like the men they are part of a similar international cultural realm, and many of the women actually mention movie stars in describing some desired traits of their prospective partners. Many of the women advertisers are college-educated and, technologically speaking, they have internet access. It is apparent that it is precisely those Filipinas who have access to international cultural exchange who choose to seek a partner from elsewhere.

7.   Conclusion

Intimate communication is often perceived as an immensely private space that is not accessible to observation and research. Like others (e.g. Dryden 1999; Gubrium and Holstein 1987, 1990; McElhinny 1997), my analysis here, as well as my previous work with cross-cultural couples (particularly Piller 2002, in press; Piller and Takahashi 2006) demonstrates that the private–public distinction cannot hold. The positioning of a cross-cultural intimate relationships occurs within a societal space in which intermarriage is either seen as the norm, or – usually – as an exception that needs to be justified and accounted for. Furthermore, large societal-level processes such as globalization provide the structure within which individuals can agentively develop and pursue cross-cultural desires. I have here focused on the ways in which globalization as a macro-process is interlinked with cross-cultural intimate relationships (see also Reisigl in this volume). I have singled out three aspects of globalization that mediate cross-cultural intimate relationships and have exemplified those with data from previous research and, particularly, mail-order bride websites. These aspects of globalization are increases in three domains: international mobility, international data flow, and international cultural exchange. These provide increased chances for partners from different cultural backgrounds to meet but they also turn on the desires of individuals to meet a cross-cultural partner. Internationally disseminated ideologies of gender, race, and family pitch (in the present case study) American men against American women, and Filipinas against Filipinos, and other Asian women. These positionings find their parallel in international economic relationships: in the same way that other forms of labor have been outsourced from industrialized countries, sexual, reproductive and emotional labor is being outsourced. In the same way that other international outsourcing has removed employment regulations from the control of the state and the unions and has weakened workers' rights internationally, "intimate outsourcing" is weakening the cause of gender equality internationally. It is within this larger framework that individuals pursue their personal happiness.

Notes

1. http://uscis.gov/graphics/shared/aboutus/statistics/; last accessed on 29/09/2004.
2. http://en.wikipedia.org/wiki/Globalisation; last accessed 29/09/2004; see also Bouchara in this volume.
3. E.g. *End Child Prostitution, Child Pornography and Trafficking of Children for Sexual Purposes* at http://www.ecpat.com/eng/index.asp; *Coalition Against Trafficking in Women* at http://www.catwinternational.org/.
4. http://www.blossoms.com/cgi-bin/htmlos.cgi/28173.1.418454620598222596; last accessed on 30/09/2004 All quotes from mailorder bride websites are verbatim.
5. http://www.russianbrides.com/client_comments8.html; last accessed on 30/09/2004.
6. http://www.russianbrides.com/faq1.htm; last accessed on 30/09/2004.
7. http://www.filipinaheart.com/success.cfm; last accessed on 30/09/2004.
8. http://www.manilabeauty.com; last accessed on 01/10/2004.
9. http://action.web.ca/home/catw/attach/catw2003report.pdf; last accessed on 30/09/2004.
10. All the names are pseudonyms. The transcription conventions are as follows:
    Intonation and tone units
    ,   clause final intonation ("more to come")
    .   clause final falling intonation
    Paralanguage
    @   laughter (one @ per syllable, i.e. @@@ = "hahaha")
    Translation
    italics translations of speech that was originally in German are in italics.

11. http://www.everlastinglove.com/match.htm; last accessed on 30/09/2004.
12. http://www.filipinalove.com/offer.shtml; last accessed on 01/10/2004; emphasis in the original.
13. http://www.manilabeauty.com; last accessed on 01/10/2004; my emphasis.
14. http://www.filipina-ladies-personals.com; http://www.filipinaconnection.net/; http://www.filipinacupid.com; http://www.filipinalove.com; http://www.manilabeauty.com/; http://www.everlastinglove.com.
15. http://www.filipina-ladies-personals.com/new/meetfilipina.htm; last accessed on 30/09/2004.
16. http://www.everlastinglove.com/match.htm; last accessed on 01/10/2004.
17. http://www.american.edu/TED/bride.htm; last accessed on 01/10/2004.
18. http://www.american.edu/TED/bride.htm; last accessed on 28/09/2004.
19. http://www.everlastinglove.com/match.htm; last accessed on 01/10/2004; my emphasis.
20. http://www.blossoms.com/cgi-bin/htmlos.cgi/30505.19.9369808260016707861; last accessed on 28/09/04; my emphasis.

References

Antaki, Charles and Sue Widdicombe S. (eds.)
  1998   *Identities in Talk*. London: Sage.
Ata, Abe W.
  2000   *Intermarriage between Christians and Muslims: A West Bank Study*. Ringwood, Victoria: David Lovell Publishing.
Breger, Rosemary and Rosanna Hill (eds.)
  1998   *Cross-cultural Marriage: Identity and Choice*. Oxford and New York: Berg.
Bruthiaux, Paul
  1996   *The Discourse of Classified Advertising: Exploring the Nature of Linguistic Simplicity*. New York and Oxford: Oxford University Press.
Cameron, Deborah and Don Kulick
  2003a   Introduction: Language and desire in theory and practice. *Language and Communication* 23: 93–105.
Cameron, Deborah and Don Kulick
  2003b   *Language and Sexuality*. Cambridge: Cambridge University Press.
Dryden, Caroline
  1999   *Being Married, Doing Gender: A Critical Analysis of Gender Relationships in Marriage*. London: Routledge.
Gibbs, Stephen and Brigid Delaney
  2004   Mix and match. *Sydney Morning Herald*, 14 June 2004.
Gubrium, Jaber F. and James A. Holstein
  1987   The private image: experiential and method in family studies. *Journal of Marriage and the Family* 49: 773–786.
Gubrium, Jaber F. and James A. Holstein
  1990   *What is Family?* Mountain View, CA: Mayfield.
Herget, Wilfried, Werner Kremp and Walter G. Rödel (eds.)
  1995   *Nachbar Amerika: 50 Jahre Amerikaner in Rheinland-Pfalz [Neighbor*

America: Americans in Rhineland-Palatinate, 1945–1995]. Trier: WVT Wissenschaftlicher Verlag Trier.

Hughes, Donna M., Laura Joy Sporcic, Nadine Z. Mendelsohn and Vanessa Chirgwin
1999   *The Factbook on Global Sexual Exploitation.* Coalition Against Trafficking in Women. Retrieved 29/09/2004 from the World Wide Web: http://www. uri.edu/artsci/wms/hughes/factbook.htm

Hyam, Ronald
1990   *Empire and Sexuality: The British Experience.* Manchester: Manchester University Press.

Jackson, Jean E.
1983   *The Fish People: Linguistic Exogamy and Tukanoan Identity in Northwest Amazonia.* Cambridge: Cambridge University Press.

Kojima, Yu
2001   In the business of cultural reproduction: theoretical implications of the mail-order bride phenomenon. *Women's Studies International Forum* 24(2): 199–210.

Lincoln, Peter C.
1979   Dual-lingualism: passive bilingualism in action. *Te Reo* 22, 65–72.

Maltz, Daniel and Ruth Borker
1982   A cultural approach to male-female miscommunication. In: John J. Gumperz (ed.), *Language and Social Identity,* 196–206. Cambridge: Cambridge University Press.

Marchetti, Gina
1993   *Romance and the "Yellow Peril": Race, Sex, and Discursive Strategies in Hollywood Fiction.* Berkeley: University of California Press.

McElhinny, Bonnie
1997   Ideologies of public and private language in sociolinguistics. In: Ruth Wodak (ed.), *Gender and Discourse,*106–139. London: Sage.

Mooring, Ylana
2004a   Attractive Western man seeks honest Filipina mail order bride: ideology of gender relationships in advertisements seeking Filipina mail order brides. Unpublished Honours Essay, University of Sydney, Sydney.

Mooring, Ylana
2004b   The discourse of Filipina mail-order bride websites. Unpublished Honours Thesis, University of Sydney, Sydney.

O'Rourke, Kate
2002   To have and to hold: A postmodern feminist response to the mailorder bride industry. *Denver Journal of International Law and Policy* 30(4): 476–498.

Pennycook, Alastair
1998   *English and the Discourses of Colonialism.* London: Routledge.

Phelan, A.
2000   Reds in the beds. *Sydney Morning Herald Magazine*, 1 April 2000, 49–52.

Piller, Ingrid
2000   Language choice in bilingual, cross-cultural interpersonal communication. *Linguistik Online* 5(1) http://www.linguistik-online.com/1_00/index.html.

Piller, Ingrid
2001a   Linguistic intermarriage: language choice and negotiation of identity. In:

Aneta Pavlenko, Adrian Blackledge, Ingrid Piller and Marya Teutsch-Dwyer (eds.), *Multilingualism, Second Language Learning and Gender*, 199–230. Berlin and New York: Mouton de Gruyter.

Piller, Ingrid
2001b   Private language planning: the best of both worlds? *Estudios de Socioling-üística* 2(1): 61–80.

Piller, Ingrid
2002   *Bilingual Couples Talk: The Discursive Construction of Hybridity.* Amsterdam: Benjamins.

Piller, Ingrid
in press   "I always wanted to marry a cowboy": bilingual couples, language and desire. In: Terry A. Karris and Kyle Killian (eds.), *Cross Cultural Couple Relationships*. Binghampton, NY: Haworth.

Piller, Ingrid and Aneta Pavlenko
2004   Bilingualism and gender. In: Tej K. Bhatia and William C. Ritchie (eds.), *The Handbook of Bilingualism*, 489–511. Oxford: Blackwell.

Piller, Ingrid and Kimie Takahashi
2006   A passion for English: desire and the language market. In: Aneta Pavlenko (ed.), *Languages and Emotions of Multilingual Speakers*, 59–83. Clevedon: Multilingual Matters.

Radford, Lorraine and Kaname Tsutsumi
2004   Globalization and violence against women – inequalities in risks, responsibilities and blame in the UK and Japan. *Women's Studies International Forum* 27: 1–12.

Sacks, Harvey
1992   *Lectures on Conversation*. Oxford: Blackwell.

Said, Edward W.
1978   *Orientalism*. London: Routledge & Kegan Paul.

Said, Edward W.
1993   *Culture and imperialism*. London: Vintage.

Scollon, Ronald and Suzanne W. Scollon
2001   Discourse and intercultural communication. In: Deborah Schiffrin, Deborah Tannen and Heidi Ehrenberger Hamilton (eds.), *The Handbook of Discourse Analysis,* 538–547. Malden, MA, and Oxford: Blackwell.

Sollors, Werner (ed.)
2000   *Interracialism: Black–White Intermarriage in American History, Literature, and Law.* New York: Oxford University Press.

Spreckels, Janet and Kotthoff, Helga
this volume Identity in intercultural communication. Chapter 20.

Spurr, Davis
1993   *The Rhetoric of Empire: Colonial Discourse in Journalism, Travel Writing, and Imperial Administration*. Durham: Duke University Press.

Statistisches Bundesamt
1997   *Strukturdaten über die ausländische Bevölkerung*. Wiesbaden: Metzler & Poeschel.

Stoltzfus, Nathan
1996   *Resistance of the Heart: Intermarriage and the Rosenstrasse Protest in Nazi Germany*. New York: W.W. Norton.

Takahashi, Kimie
  2006   Akogare and English language learning: Japanese women in Australia. Un-
            published PhD, University of Sydney, Sydney.
Tannen, Deborah
  1986   *That's not what I Meant! How Conversational Style Makes or Breaks Rela-
            tionships.* New York: Ballantine Books.
Tannen, Deborah
  1990   *You Just don't Understand: Women and Men in Conversation.* New York:
            Ballantine Books.
Uchida, Aki
  1998   The orientalization of Asian women in America. *Women's Studies Inter-
            national Forum* 21(2): 161–174.
Visson, Lynn
  1998   *Wedded Strangers: The Challenges of Russian–American Marriages.* New
            York: Hippocrene.
Waldis, Barbara
  1998   *Trotz der Differenz: Interkulturelle Kommunikation bei maghrebinisch–eu-
            ropäischen Paarbeziehungen in der Schweiz und in Tunesien. [Despite the
            difference: Intercultural communication in Maghrebine-European relation-
            ships in Switzerland and Tunisia]* Münster: Waxmann.
Walters, Keith
  1996   Gender, identity, and the political economy of language: Anglophone wives
            in Tunisia. *Language in Society* 25: 515–555.
White-Parks, Annette
  1993   Journey to the golden mountain: Chinese immigrant women. In: Bonnie
            Frederick and Susan H. McLeod (eds.), *Women and the Journey: The Fe-
            male Travel Experience,* 101–117. Pullman, WA: Washington State Univer-
            sity Press.

IV. Issues and debates

Editors' introduction

Section 4 focuses on a number of key concepts and issues in intercultural communication that are subject to ongoing discussions within the field. Three of the chapters deal with issues that are ethically important: discrimination (chapter 18), power and dominance (chapter 19) and stereotyping (chapter 20). Two of the chapters deal with concepts that are analytically important: identity (chapter 20) and communities of practice (chapter 21). The authors write from different standpoints, illustrating the range of viewpoints and interests that exist within the field. However, all four chapters try to incorporate both broad and narrow conceptions of culture, and illustrate how social and cultural analyses can be combined at the micro and macro levels.

A special feature of Martin Reisigl's chapter on discrimination (chapter 18) is that it goes beyond verbal communication, drawing attention to other aspects of semiotic processes, in particular, visual communication. Reisigl defines various subtypes of discrimination, such as depersonalization, separating, distancing, accentuating differences, devaluing and many more. Discrimination is very often implicit and indirect; for example, many immigrants are faced with indirect discrimination in the labour market by not having the same chances as natives. He takes into consideration economic, political and historical factors and the related structures of hegemony and dominance. Like Gunther Kress and Theo van Leeuwen, he addresses the imaginary relationship between visually represented individuals and viewers. Visual discrimination by symbolic distanciation, for example, means to depict specific persons or groups of persons in relation to the viewers as if they were not 'close' to the viewers, 'strangers'. Comparisons of the representations of in-groups and out-groups permit a diagnosis of whether there is discrimination or not.

In chapter 19, Winfried Thielmann draws special attention to conflicts of interest and perspectives in institutions. Adopting as a starting point the concept of cultural apparatus developed by Konrad Ehlich and Jochen Rehbein, he shows how conflicts within institutions result from knowledge asymmetries, differing use of language, and varying interests. Because of institutional power structures and role-specific behaviour, institutional agents often do not become aware of the failure of intercultural communication. Even when agent and client belong to the same society and speak the same language, communication between an institutional member and a member of the general public is already intercultural communication in the narrow sense. Thielmann also delves into the highly asymmetrical relationship of first world donor countries and third world recipients of foreign aid. Intercultural science transfer often runs the risk of being a silent instantiation of dominance in intercultural communication. He discusses the successful development of the Grameen bank in Bangladesh through Yunus' efforts to overcome inbuilt ethnocentricity in Western economic theory. Finally, Thielmann also discusses the interconnection of language politics and the cultural apparatus taking, as an example, the Shuar in the Ecuadorian Amazon region.

Spreckels and Kotthoff discuss identity in chapter 20, and argue that the core elements of our identity – national and ethnic identity, gender and body identity – have lost their quasi-'natural' quality as guarantors. Concepts from sociology, anthropology and social psychology show identity as a construction of "us and others." Accordingly, representations of self and other are embedded in processes of social categorization, as developed in ethnomethodology, positioning theory and discursive psychology. Although categorization processes are unavoidable in our everyday interactions, this can lead to stereotyping. The authors go into semiotic details that fashion a cultural habitus. In many contexts categorization works with flexible demarcation lines, such as East-West. The space in which normalities go unchallenged can range from a close 'community of practice' to diffuse communities with comparable consumption habits, lifestyles, attitudes and values. Spreckels and Kotthoff carefully examine various constructions of 'us' and 'them,' for example, women's headscarves as a nonverbal formation of a multi-vocal cultural boundary marker.

A fundamental question for all intercultural research is how cultural groups can be defined and identified. In chapter 21, Saskia Corder and Miriam Meyerhoff explore the notion of a community of practice as a cultural group. Drawing especially on the work of Lave and Wenger (1991), they discuss the criterial features of a community of practice, and then compare it to related concepts such as speech community and social network. They demonstrate how communities of practice each have their own sets of practices and shared repertoires (cf. the chapters in section 2 of this Handbook) and hence can be regarded as cultural groups. Through fine-grained interactional analyses, they illustrate how power and subordination in the workplace are created linguistically, through speakers' knowledge or lack of knowledge of the shared repertoire and locally shared history in the community of practice they are participating in. Nevertheless, the authors warn against using the concept of community of practice too loosely, and being too lenient in applying the criterial features.

18.   Discrimination in discourses

Martin Reisigl

1.   Introduction

Discrimination has become an issue that discourse analysis increasingly focuses on, especially critical discourse analysis and the research on intercultural communication. "Discrimination" means to put individuals, who are considered to be different from others, at a disadvantage. The word prototypically refers to "negative discrimination" and relates to an ethical, normative dimension, to a political as well as legal evaluation and judging against the background of democratic principles of justice and the conviction of the validity of human rights. In this respect, "discrimination" means to treat a specific social group or single members of the group, who are set apart from other groups or members of other social groups, unfairly, unjustly, for example by repressing or suppressing them, decrying them, discrediting them, debasing them, degrading them, defaming them, keeping political rights from them and establishing unjustifiable social, political, economic, educational or other inequalities, by segregating them, excluding them, etc.

In my article, I will primarily be concerned with various forms of verbal discrimination, i.e. with discrimination by language use, and with visual discrimination. Apart from this introduction, the chapter is divided into five sections. Section 2 aims to explain the concept of "social discrimination" from a general and a disciplinary point of view. Section 3 offers an overview of different types of social discrimination. Section 4 contains a brief delineation of various concepts of "discourse" that are relevant for the issue in question. Section 5 presents a discourse analytical framework that allows the approach to discursively realized social discrimination in a methodical way. Furthermore, section 5 considers various strategies of discrimination in the area of visual communication. In the final section, I argue that a critical analysis of verbal and visual discrimination is best accomplished from an interdisciplinary approach and can be an important means of anti-discrimination policy and politics.[1]

2.   Concepts of "social discrimination"

The action verb "to discriminate" originates from the Latin "discriminare". The Latin verb derives from the noun "discrimen", which means "distinction", "difference", "separating" and "sorting out". Accordingly, "discriminare" originally denotes "distinguish", "differentiate", "separate", "set apart", and this is – so to say – the "harmless" original meaning of the word which does not yet automatically represent negative social exclusion and segregation. The English expression is first recorded to assume the negative denotation of "debasement" and "disadvantaging" in 1866, when the word related to the making of distinctions prejudicial to people of a different "color" or "race" in the USA (The Oxford English Dictionary 1989: 758).

The notion of social discrimination is connected with the infringement of justice. Thus, it serves first and foremost as a legal and political concept, although it has, among others, also been adopted by sociology, social-psychology and discourse analysis. It follows from the concept's social-ethical implications that a discourse analysis and analysis of intercultural communication concerned with the linguistic and visual realization of discrimination should become social analysis.

In discourse analytical studies and analyses of intercultural communication, the term "discrimination" is at times applied in a rather undifferentiated way, as an unquestioned term of scientific everyday language. A close look brings to the fore that "social discrimination" is a relational concept which includes at least five elements. The concept's three main constituents can be explicated as: "Someone discriminates against somebody else by doing something". "Doing something" (including "omitting doing something" and "letting something happen") stands for the discriminating action or process, which includes the two further conceptual components of "on the basis of a specific feature" and "in comparison to somebody else". In other words: "Discrimination" implies (1) social actors as perpetrators that belong to a specific social or cultural group, (2) specific persons or groups of persons affected by the discrimination (i.e. victims or beneficiaries), (3) the discriminating action or process, (4) the "distinguishing feature" or peg on which to hang the discrimination (for example "race", "gender", "language" or "sexual orientation"), and (5) a comparative figure or group in comparison to which or to whom somebody is discriminated.

(1) "Discriminators" are social actors who commit – as perpetrators – the social action of discrimination. Discriminators generally have the power to discriminate against others, or empower themselves (at least temporarily) to discriminate against others, often by the discriminatory action itself. Power asymmetry normally prevents the less powerful to discriminate against the more powerful, except for situations in which the more powerful are absent and cannot exert their power (discrimination *in absentia* is sometimes called "indirect discrimination"; see Graumann and Wintermantel 1989: 199, and see below, section 3). A differentiated analysis has to take into account that social beings adopt very different social roles and can, thus, be discriminators in a specific situation and respect (e.g. as "white" against "black" people, as men against women, as heterosexuals against homo- and bisexuals, as citizens against non-

citizens or "foreigners", as adults against children, as young people against seniors, as healthy people against the disabled or those with special needs), whereas they may become victims of discrimination in another situation and respect. Even though some forms of discrimination (like racism, nationalism and sexism) are kept alive by rather stable social structures in specific social, political and historical contexts, and are thus rather permanent in kind, discrimination is never an absolute, but always a relative matter.

(2) Victims or beneficiaries of discrimination are very often (members of) minorities or socially marginalized groups, and minoritization as well as marginalization themselves are frequently the result of discrimination. Sometimes, as in the case of sexism, in which the victims of discrimination are usually women, discriminated individuals do not belong to a numerical minority, but to a socially widely suppressed group. In certain social contexts, victims of a specific form of social discrimination can sometimes themselves become discriminators, and some victims often turn out to be manifold victims of different forms of discrimination. This latter fact has been neglected in social research for some time. Since the late 1980s and in the beginning of the 1990s, however, feminist African American scholars introduced the concepts of "multiple discrimination" and "intersectional discrimination" into the debate about particular forms of discrimination of African American women, which both differed from discrimination against other groups of women (e.g. "white" women) and from discrimination against African American men (see Fredman and Szyszak 1993: 221; Makkonen 2002: 57, 2003: 14).

"Multiple discrimination" is conceived of as complex discrimination on the basis of different distinguishing features and for different (e.g. racist, sexist, ageist, religious fundamentalist) reasons, which operate separately and subsequently, i.e. independently, in different social fields and situations at different times: "A disabled woman may be discriminated against on the basis of her gender in access to highly skilled work and on the basis of her disability in a situation in which a public office building is not accessible to persons with wheelchairs." (Makkonen 2002: 10).

"Intersectional discrimination", in contrast, is considered to be a complex discrimination on the basis of different distinguishing features and for different (e.g. racist, sexist or religious fundamentalist) reasons, which operate simultaneously and concurrently in one and the same social field and situation: "One example of such discrimination would be unjustified subjection of disabled women to undergo forced sterilization, of which there is evidence around the world: this kind of discrimination is not experienced by women generally nor by disabled men, not at least anywhere near to the same extent as disabled women." (Makkonen 2002: 11).

Makkonen also distinguishes a third form of complex discrimination, which he terms "compound discrimination" (Makkonen 2002: 11). According to him, "compound discrimination" relies on several grounds of discrimination which add to each other *in a particular situation*: "An illustrious example would be, to continue along the intersection of origin and gender, a situation in which the labor market is segregated on multiple basis: some jobs are considered suitable only for men, and only some jobs are reserved particularly for immigrants. In such a situation, the prospects of an immigrant woman to find a job matching her merits are markedly reduced because of compound discrimination." (Makkonen 2002: 11).

The recognition of complex discriminatory phenomena such as multiple, intersectional and compound discrimination should prevent analysts of intercultural communication from explaining discrimination simplistically by taking "culture" or "subculture" as an essentialized and homogenous category. Only a multi-factorial analysis becomes aware of the many different facets of discrimination.

(3) The third conceptual component is the discriminating action or process itself, by which justice or human rights are infringed. It is realized in various social sectors or fields (such as legislation, work, education, housing, public services, mass media, sports) and can take the form of a (physical) action or non-action, of an active exclusion and segregation, a denial of opportunities and equal rights, different treatment, an act of ignoring, an omission, etc. It may be realized verbally or in writing (e.g. by a degrading insult, a derision or a banning) or visually (e.g. by a humiliating depiction). It can be direct or indirect, explicit or implicit, etc.

(4) The concept of discrimination always includes a "distinguishing feature" or peg on which to hang the discrimination. The distinguishing features that are taken for the dissimilation and separation are frequently related to social identity markers, for instance to gender, "race", skin colour, birth, hereditary factors, age, disability, the ethnic, national or social background, the membership of a (for example national) minority, language, religion or belief, ideology, political affiliation, sexual orientation and economic situation. The distinguishing criteria on the basis of which people are treated differently, negatively and adversely are often interpreted as stigmata that are considered to indicate a negative deviancy from a positive "normality" (see Goffman 1963).

Unfortunately, the reasons for discrimination are very often identified by exclusive reference to these real or fictitious features, and this is rather misleading, since it is not "race" which is the reason for the discrimination against a specific group of persons, but racism, which lies behind the social construction of "race" categories (see Reisigl and Wodak 2001: 2–5). In most legal texts, be it on a national or an international level, one reads about "discrimination on the grounds of 'race', gender, age, etc." Such "grounds" are often conflated with "reasons", the phrase "on the grounds of" being interpreted as "for the reasons that." At this point, linguistic critique should ask for a more accurate language use that does not risk a fallacious inversion, that is to say, the identification of the reasons for discrimination on the side of the victims, instead of identifying the reasons on the side of the perpetrators. Nationalism and not nation or nationality, sexism and not sex or gender, ageism and not age are the reasons for the respective forms of discrimination.

(5) The concept of discrimination finally comprises a comparative element or figure, strictly speaking, a person or group of persons, in comparison to whom someone is considered to be discriminated against. The comparison with another person in a similar situation like the one in which discrimination is carried out, but with different identity markers as distinguishing features (e.g. a different skin colour, ethnic origin, age, gender, religion, sexual orientation), is required to clearly prove an unequal, less favourable treatment. Such a comparison is most important in legal conceptions of discrimination. To draw a comparison is un-complicated, if "direct discrimination" is in question, and rather difficult, if dis-crimination is "indirect". Sometimes, persons serving as comparative figures are taken from the past (e.g. previous tenants, lodgers or employees), sometimes they are participating investigators (who control, for instance, the accessibility of a restaurant or pub for different social groups remaining incognito), and in cases in which direct comparison is impossible, they can be hypothetical figures employed in comparisons by analogy.

There are no clear-cut terminological distinctions of different forms of so-cial discrimination, nor are there homogeneous conceptualizations on an inter-national level and across the disciplines of legal studies, political science, soci-ology, social-psychology and discourse analysis. Just to mention two diverse attempts of differentiation:

In his socio-cognitive approach to prejudices in discourse, Teun A. van Dijk differentiates mnemotechnically among "seven Ds of discrimination". They are dominance, differentiation, distance, diffusion, diversion, depersonalization or destruction and daily discrimination. Van Dijk considers them to be general and specific action plans which are part of so-called "ethnic situation models" and which, as such, pre-shape consciously or unconsciously social interactions and the organization of social interests of ingroups. Van Dijk's heterogeneous list encompasses phenomena which do not mutually exclude each other. "Daily dis-crimination", for instance, is a category which runs across the other "Ds of dis-crimination" (see Van Dijk 1984: 40).

Cross-cutting categories are a characteristic of the social-psychological approach proposed by Graumann and Wintermantel (see Graumann and Winter-mantel 1989: 184–194) too, whose model is discussed in works on "intercultural communication" (see, for instance, Lüsebrink 2005: 106–108). Graumann and Wintermantel distinguish among five major functions or subfunctions of dis-crimination and of the perception of others: separating, distancing, accentuating differences, devaluating, and fixating (by assigning traits or by (stereo)typing). Their typology is insightful, although it could probably be re-organized more systematically. Actions or processes of accentuating differences, of devaluating and of (stereo)typing are realized by the explicit or implicit assignment of traits. In this respect, assigning traits – which I call "predication" in section 5.2. – is a more basic operation than accentuating differences, devaluating and stereotyping. On the other hand, assigning traits presupposes the discursive construction of social actors who can be endowed with attributes. This construction – which I discuss in my own approach in section 5.1. under "nomination" – may, among others, be realized by typing. Separating and distancing – two operations which I subsume under "perspectivation" in section 5.4. – also presuppose that there are social actors, i.e. someone who can be separated from someone else.

In the given context I deliberately refrain from trying to offer a unifying proposal that aims to put an end to the terminological muddle across and within the different disciplines, since such a suggestion can only, if it can at all, be successful if it is elaborated in a differentiated interdisciplinary discussion. Given that the terminological difficulties related to the concept of "discrimination" have not yet been appreciated in most of the disciplines concerned with the problem, the explication of terminological differences gets more space in the present chapter than most readers of a handbook of applied linguistics and intercultural communication would probably expect. Both the previous section and the following section are designated to increase the awareness of conceptual distinctions, dissimilarities and similarities.

3.   Types of social discrimination

Among the – mostly binary – differentiations of "discrimination" are "intended" versus "non-intended discrimination", "direct" versus "indirect discrimination", "explicit" versus "implicit discrimination", "active" versus "passive discrimination", and "individual" versus "structural" or "institutional discrimination". Some of these categories cross-cut, overlap and are thus not neatly separable from each other.

The theoretical distinction between "intentional" and "unintentional discrimination" – which is especially relevant in legal discussions – as well as between "active" and "passive discrimination" seem to be rather palpable differentiations that need no long explications, although it is often difficult to prove concretely that someone discriminates against somebody else purposely. The other three binary distinctions, however, are characterized more inconsistently and disputed more controversially in the relevant literature.

As for the distinction between "direct" and "indirect" as well as "explicit" versus "implicit discrimination", conflicting suggestions are to be found in different disciplines. The psychologists Graumann and Wintermantel propose to speak of *"direct discrimination"* in the realm of verbal discrimination if the discriminated individuals are communication partners of the producers of "discriminatory speech acts", whereas they consider a *"nondirect discrimination"* to be a verbal discrimination of a person who is not present in the situation of discrimination. In this respect, the form of interpersonal relationship is their distinguishing criterion, whereas they further distinguish between "explicit" and "implicit discrimination" according to the form of verbal expression. They regard verbal discrimination as being explicit, if the discriminatory function can be identified with the utterance taken out of the speech situation. In contrast, Graumann and Wintermantel judge verbal discrimination to be implicit, if the discriminatory function cannot be understood without knowing the conditions of the situation, the presuppositions and contextual implications of the utterance (see Graumann and Wintermantel 1989: 199).[2]

The concepts of "direct" and "indirect discrimination" play an important role in legal contexts too. Legal approaches consider an act of discrimination to be *"direct"*, if a person is treated less favourably than another person in a comparable situation has been or would be treated on the basis of a legally prohibited "ground" of discrimination, i.e. of a distinguishing feature such as sex/gender, "race", age, ethnic origin, religion, sexual orientation, etc. Examples of "direct discrimination" are an employer's categorical refusal to hire immigrants due to foreign nationality or to hire women due to potential pregnancy or motherhood (see Makkonen 2002: 4). Discrimination is legally considered to be *"indirect"*, if an apparently equal treatment or a neutral provision, decision, criterion, procedure or practice is discriminatory in its effects, that is to say, if it puts a person having a particular characteristic at a particular disadvantage without legal justification. If an employer hires employees on the condition of their perfect fluency in the official language of the state, although the work does not in itself necessitate such fluency, many immigrants are faced with "indirect discrimination" in the labour market (see Makkonen 2002: 4–5). In cases of "indirect discrimination" in the legal sense, it is often difficult, if not impossible (and, thus, legally not necessary) to prove that there is or has been an intention to discriminate against somebody, whereas in many cases of direct discrimination such a proof is legally required.

"Institutional discrimination" is conceptualized as practices or procedures in a company or an institution, which have been internally structured in a way that they tend to have discriminatory effects. This form of discrimination is often unintentional. If it is deliberate, as in the case of the former Apartheid regime in South Africa, Makkonen proposes to call it *"institutionalized discrimination"* (Makkonen 2002: 4; see also Makkonen 2003: 12). A special case of "institutionalized discrimination", strictly speaking of "positive institutionalized discrimination", is *"affirmative action"* or "positive discrimination" (the latter term is sometimes rejected as being inappropriate and, thus, replaced by "positive action"; see Makkonen 2002: 5). It aims to arrive at equality via tem-

porary unequal, i.e. preferential treatment. For this purpose, distinctions on "grounds" of the above-mentioned social features are legally justified.

"Structural discrimination" is considered to be a type of intersectional discrimination (see Makkonen 2002: 14). It can take the form of "institutional discrimination" and is frequently not deliberately produced, though it can sometimes be intentionally effectuated by a short-sighted policy or institutional practice. It usually concerns members of groups in vulnerable social positions – in many societies, for example, women – and is often rendered invisible by naturalization and backgrounding. To give just one example taken from Crenshaw and referred to in Makkonen: "Structural discrimination" is actuated in states with immigration laws that try to prevent marriage fraud and require an immigrant to stay in the new state for several years and to remain "properly married" before she or he can apply for a permanent status. This legal regulation has the consequence that immigrant women who have married a national and become a victim of domestic violence have either the option to divorce and get subsequently deported or to suffer continuing violence (see Crenshaw 1991: 1247; Makkonen 2002: 15–16; see also Piller in this volume).

As the above explanations of the disciplinarily distinct concepts of "direct" and "indirect" as well as "explicit" and "implicit" discrimination show, we have to be aware of the problem that different disciplines and analytical approaches only seemingly speak about the same things when they use the same words. This problem has scarcely been recognized in the relevant literature on social discrimination until now. Thus, it is explicated rather extensively in the present chapter, without jumping to a one-sided terminological proposal. My overview leads to at least four conclusions, which could be taken as a basis for further attempts to elaborate conceptual distinctions which could possibly be interdisciplinarily valid: (1) Discrimination in the negative sense of the word represents an infringement of principles of justice. (2) Discrimination can either be committed by unequal treatment, where equal treatment would be just, or by equal treatment, where differentiation would be fair. (3) The distinction between "direct" and "indirect" links up with the relationship between discriminators and discriminated. (4) The distinction between "explicit" and "implicit" relates to the way discrimination is semiotically realized.

4.   Concepts of "discourse" in approaches to verbal discrimination

The analytical focus of the following sections lies on verbal forms of discrimination. Whereas Graumann's and Wintermantel's (1989) as well as Wagner's (2001) approach to verbal discrimination are primarily "speech act" oriented and therefore try to analyse "discriminating as speech acting" and to identify "discriminatory speech acts" (see Graumann and Wintermantel 1989: 193–201), the approaches to be presented in the following are first and foremost discourse oriented. If one speaks about "discrimination in discourse", however, "discourse" can assume different meanings. Here, I want to focus on five approaches to discourse relevant for the analysis of discrimination.

I personally take a "discourse" as a complex topic-related unity of semiotic action, which, among others, involves argumentation about validity claims such as truth and normative validity. In contrast to mono-perspectivist conceptualizations of "discourse" (e.g. Fairclough 1995: 14), I consider pluri-perspectivity, i.e. different points of view, to be a constitutive feature of a "discourse" (Reisigl 2003: 92). In this sense, "discourses" are pluri-perspective semiotic bundles of social practices that are composed of interrelated, simultaneous and sequential linguistic as well as other semiotic acts and that are both socially constitutive and socially constituted. In this view, discursive practices manifest themselves within, and across, social fields of action as thematically interconnected and problem-centred semiotic (e.g. oral, written or visual) tokens that belong to particular semiotic types (i.e. communicative action patterns, genres or textual types), which fulfil specific social purposes (see Reisigl and Wodak 2001: 36). Following Girnth (1996), I conceive "fields of action" as institutionalized frameworks of social interaction structured to serve specific social aims (for more details, see Reisigl 2003: 128–142). Discourses cross between fields, overlap, refer to each other, or are in some other way sociofunctionally linked with each other (Reisigl and Wodak 2001: 36–37).

Although this concept of "discourse" is taken as a basis of the present chapter, there are several other concepts of "discourse" which have been introduced into the discussion about "discrimination in (intercultural) discourses". At least four of them must be mentioned:

Teun A. van Dijk was one of the first critical discourse analysts who dealt with the relationship between social discrimination (especially racist and ethnicist discrimination) and discourse (see van Dijk 1984; Smitherman and van Dijk 1988). His socio-cognitive approach conceives "discourse" as part of a conceptual triangle formed by cognition, discourse and society (see van Dijk 2001a: 98). Van Dijk understands "discourse" in a broad sense as a "'communicative event', including conversational interaction, written text, as well as associated gestures, facework, typographical layout, images and other 'semiotic' or multimedia dimensions of signification". For van Dijk, one of the most urgent tasks of critical research on discourse is the study of and fight against various forms of discrimination – first and foremost of discriminatory gender inequality, ethnocentrism, antisemitism, nationalism and racism – in discourses (see van Dijk 2001b: 358–363). In his numerous studies on discrimination, he especially focuses on the socio-cognitive, discursive and social conditions of the production, reproduction and transformation of prejudices and stereotypes that link up with discrimination (see, e.g., van Dijk 1984, 1987, 1993).

Researchers studying "intercultural communication" usually presuppose a very general understanding of "discourse". The interactional sociolinguist John J. Gumperz was one of the first to connect discourse analysis and intercultural communication (see Scollon and Scollon 2001: 540; see also Hinnenkamp 1991, 2001, 2003). He adopts a rather broad understanding of "discourse" and regards it as language (first and foremost, as spoken language) used in social contexts. Gumperz discussed early on the relationship between intercultural misunderstanding and social discrimination. He found out that various breakdowns in intercultural communication are due to inferences based on undetected differences in contextualization strategies (see Gumperz 1982: 210; see also Gumperz and Cook-Gumperz in this volume), and that cultural misunderstandings can lead to discrimination, or are sometimes read as discrimination, even though they may be misinterpretations resulting from unrecognized cultural differences (see Gumperz 1982: 174). Gumperz draws the conclusion that if more people begin to understand culture- and language-bound differences in contextualization cues, discrimination will be lessened. He further concluded that conversation analysis can serve as the diagnostic tool to determine whether there are communicative differences among members of different cultures.

The results of Gumperz' investigations are less relevant for the analysis of "overt discrimination" against minorities, which in western industrialized societies has significantly decreased (see Gumperz 2001: 226), than for the analysis and assessment of "covert", non-intentional, indirect, implicit or structural discrimination associated with unobserved linguistic diversity which causes difficulties in social interactions. An explanation exclusively concentrating on this cultural or linguistic diversity would, however, sometimes be too simplistic, as critics of Gumperz' approach state (see, for instance, Singh, Lele and Martohardjono 1996; see also Scollon and Scollon 2001: 540), and as Gumperz himself notes in more recent works (see, e.g., Gumperz 2001: 225, where he also focuses on factors such as language ideology).

Rajendra Singh, Jayant Lele and Gita Martohardjono (1996: 238) argue that beyond the uncovering of and training to recognize cultural and linguistic differences there is a need to take into consideration economic, political and historical factors and the related structures of power asymmetry, hegemony and dominance when analysing discrimination in intercultural encounters. They maintain that miscommunications in multiethnic, industrialized societies is often based on institutionally encouraged violations of principles of cooperation, charity and humanity. This observation goes beyond the analytical scope of Gumperz' approach. It is especially important for the study of "institutional discrimination", but also of "intersectional discriminations" characterized by the simultaneous and concurrent intersection of different discriminating factors in one and the same social field and situation.

Ron and Suzie W. Scollon, who have also extensively worked on intercultural communication, distinguish among different ways to use the word "discourse". In their introductory textbook on "intercultural communication", they differentiate among three meanings of the noun (see Scollon and Scollon 2003a: 107). The first and technically most narrow meaning of "discourse" refers to a linguistic unit composed of sentences that are connected by grammatical and other relationships, which constitute cohesion and are reconstructed by inferential processes. The second meaning sees "discourse" as a functional entity relating to the social environment and functions of language use, as situated social practice. The third and broadest meaning of "discourse" is linked to a whole self-contained system of communication with a language or jargon shared by a particular social group, with a particular ideological position and with specific forms of interpersonal relationships among members of the group. This third denotation is more adequately named "discourse system" rather than just "discourse".[3]

Ron and Suzie W. Scollon's approach is known as "interdiscourse communication" approach (see Scollon and Scollon 2001: 544). According to them, language users position themselves in every instance of actual communication multiply within an indefinite number of discourses or, as they prefer to say, of "discourse systems", such as the so-called "gender discourse system", "generation discourse system", "professional discourse system", "Utilitarian discourse (system)" and "voluntary discourse system" (see Scollon and Scollon 2003a). The two discourse analysts assume that each of these "discourse systems" is realized in a complex network of different forms of discourse, face systems, socializations and ideologies – the four basic elements of "discourse systems" (see also Scollon and Scollon 2003a: 108). In contrast to other approaches to intercultural communication, Scollon and Scollon avoid presupposing cultural membership and identity as given concepts. In their "mediated discourse analysis", as they also call their approach, they aim to analyse how, under which circumstances, for which purpose and with what consequences categories such as culture, social identity and social membership are produced in social interactions as relevant categories for the participants. They take social and cultural groups to be outcomes of social interactions and social change and argue against attributing to them the status of direct causal factors (see Scollon and Scollon 2001: 244–245). This implies that social discrimination in intercultural communication should not only be analysed by plain reference to categories of culture, subculture, identity and social group membership as simple explanatory concepts, but that discrimination, just as these culture- and identity-categories, arises in social interactions, which have to be understood as mediated (inter)actions.

One of the most prominent German groups of researchers dealing with discourse and discrimination is the "Duisburg group", directed by Siegfried and Margret Jäger. This team of critical discourse analysts is strongly influenced by Michel Foucault and Jürgen Link. Siegfried Jäger conceives "discourse" as "the flow of knowledge – and/or all societal knowledge stored – throughout all time [...], which determines individual and collective doing and/or formative action that shapes society, thus exercising power" (Jäger 2001a: 130, 2001b: 34). Within this approach, "discourses" are understood as historically determined, transindividual, institutionalized and regulated social practices that become material realities *sui generis*. The "Duisburg group" especially focuses on racist, ethnicist, "xenophobic" and nationalist discrimination against foreigners since the unification of West and East Germany in 1989 and 1990 until now. A specific research interest of this approach relates to the linking up of discourses or "discourse strands". The latter are conceptualized as thematically interrelated sequences of "discourse fragments" (i.e. texts or parts of texts that deal with a specific topic) which manifest themselves on different "discourse levels" (e.g. science, politics, the media, education, everyday life, business life, administration). The Duisburg discourse analysts are also engaged in proposing strategies against discrimination, for instance, against verbal discrimination in the media press coverage (see Jäger, Cleve, Ruth and Jäger 1998; Duisburger Institut für Sprach- und Sozialforschung 1999).

This short overview shows that to speak, write or read about "discrimination in discourse" can imply a variety of things, since "discourse" functions as a broad cover-term for very different meanings, which can at best be inferred from the respective contexts. Researchers on "discrimination in discourses" often are not aware of this conceptual heterogeneity.

The following section will primarily build on my own understanding of "discourse" outlined at the beginning of the section. In accordance with other approaches to discourse sketched out above, I consider "discourse" to be a social-semiotic practice. More precisely than most of the above-mentioned approaches, I take topic-relatedness, problem-centeredness, argumentativity and pluri-perspectivity as basic constituents of a "discourse". Explicitly introducing these constitutive features, I hope to conceptualize "discourse" empirically more comprehensibly than many discourse approaches do.

5.   The realization of discrimination in discourses

The relationship between "language and discrimination" (see, e.g., Roberts, Davies and Jupp 1993) can generally be analysed from at least two viewpoints. On the one side, language is employed as a means of social discrimination (see, e.g., Billig 2006). On the other side, language becomes an object of discrimination (see, e.g., Skuttnabb-Kangas and Phillipson 1994; Skuttnabb-Kangas 2000; Bough 2006). The two forms of discrimination often overlap, as in cases in which discrimination is directed against a language (for example, by language prohibition) and, therefore, also against the group or community of speakers who use this language. However, one difference between the two forms of discrimination just mentioned draws on the distinction between "object language" and "metalanguage": If language is an object of discrimination, the object language becomes a metalinguistic matter of discrimination, especially with respect to language policy or language policies and language planning. In contrast to this, the use of language as a means of discrimination does not normally involve such a straightforward metalinguistic status.

Several discourse studies on racism, antisemitism, nationalism and right-wing populism have been done on the example of Austria by the Viennese group of critical discourse analysts (see, among others, Wodak et al. 1990, 1994, 1999; Gruber 1991; Wodak and van Dijk 2000; Reisigl and Wodak 2001; Reisigl 2002, 2003). The analytical and methodological framework of this approach combines, among others, discourse analysis, argumentation theory, rhetoric and systemic function linguistics. It has been elaborated for the analysis of racist, antisemitic and ethnicist language, but can also be employed in and adapted to the analysis of other forms of social discrimination. In the following, this approach lays the theoretical and methodical foundations for analysing the realization of discrimination in discourses.

5.1.   Discrimination by nomination

The first discourse analytical aspect of verbal discrimination I want to especially focus on relates to the question of how persons are named and referred to linguistically, if they are discriminated against by means of discursive practices (nomination strategies). Discrimination by nomination can take many different forms, some of them being very explicit, as in the case of racist, ethnicist, nationalist, sexist and antisemitic slurs employed in insulting speech acts or verbal injuries, others being more implicit, as is the case of discrimination by simple non-nomination or linguistic deletion.

There are numerous linguistic and rhetorical means and ways to realize discrimination by nomination. These means are not discriminatory as such, but depending on the concrete discursive context in which they are used (the following list being far from complete):

(1) Phonological and prosodic features are sometimes employed as means of intentional prosodic disparagement and slighting alienation of proper names. This is the case if proper names are purposely articulated with a distorting pronunciation (for an example see section 5.6).

(2) Among the potential morphological or morphosemantic means to realize discriminatory nomination are degrading diminutives, depreciatory morphemes and debasing antonomastic semisuffixes (such as German "-heini" in *"Provinz-heini"*, meaning "provincial guy", or "-susi/e" in *"Heulsuse"*, meaning "cry-

baby"). A special example for sexist diminutive titulation is the German form of address *"Fräulein!"* (literally: "little woman"), which refers to an unmarried woman, in contrast to German *"Frau"*, which is used for married women. Here, the discrimination lies in the patriarchal distinction of whether a women is still "free" for marriage or not, whereas an analogous distinction of unmarried and married men has not been lexicalized. Similar examples can be found in languages such as French (*"Mademoiselle!"*), Spanish (*"Senorita!"*) or Italian (*"Signorina!"*). The analysis of intercultural communication has to take into account that such sexist nominations are nowadays judged to be politically incorrect in some speech communities, whereas there is less linguistic sensitivity for this sexism in other speech communities.

(3) Syntactic means relating to discriminatory nomination are passivation and nominalization (see already Sykes 1985: 88–94). They are, strictly speaking, syntactic means of non-nomination. If a politician claims that "immigration must be stopped", those whom the politician wants to be hindered from immigrating, i.e. potential immigrants, are callously backgrounded (see below) by nominalization, and those who the politician wants to reject the immigrants, i.e. those who make, implement and execute a rigid anti-immigration act, are backgrounded by passivation.

(4) Numerous semantic means can potentially serve discrimination against members of specific social groups (see already Sykes 1985: 94–99). Just to mention a few of them: (a) There are various negatively connoted general anthroponyms, e.g. "genderonyms" and "gerontonyms", such as the sexist German *"Weib"*, pejoratively used for "woman", or the ageist German *"Balg"* or *"Göre"* for English "brat". (b) "Ethnonyms" are often employed as debasing antonomasias such as *"Jude"* used in antisemitic idioms like *"So ein Jude!"*, meaning "Such a usurious profiteer!". (c) Synecdochic-metaphoric slurs are frequently based on the names of more or less tabooed body parts and bodily activities, (e.g. sexual practices), for instance "asshole", "cunt", "motherfucker" and "whore". They reduce persons to a socially tabooed part of the body or bodily activity. In many (though not all) contexts, they become discriminatory nominations. (d) Animal metaphors are regularly used as insulting swearwords, for instance, "pig/ swine", "rat", "parasite" (employed, among others, as antisemitic metaphors by the Nazis), cow and dog. (e) Proper names are sometimes employed as generalizing antonomasias, i.e. as appellative nouns. Several examples can be mentioned here: (i) A specific first name is used as a debasing antonomastic epithet for a specific person, for instance, "Heini" or "Susi"; or a specific first name is used as a collective androcentric antonomasias for a whole social group, for instance, English "Fritz" for all Germans, German *"der Ali"* for all Turks, or German *"der Ivan"* for all Russians. (ii) A specific first name is used as antonomastic antisemitic slur, such as "Judas" denoting "traitor"; or a specific first name

is used as a discriminating marker of "Jewishness", for instance the two compulsory first names "Sara" and "Israel" prescribed by the Nazis on August 17, 1938 for all female and male Jews in Nazi Germany (see Berding 2003: 177); (iii) Specific surnames are used as antonomastic ethnicist slurs such as "Piefke", a pejorative anthroponym for Germans, especially referring to Germans from the North of Germany.

(5) Among the pragmatic means of discriminatory nomination are deictic expressions. They may relate to personal deixis, such as distancing and debasing "they" and "those", to local deixis such as "down there" or "out there", or to "social deixis" such as condescending asymmetrical personal address with the German *"du"*-form (for instance in "foreigner talk"). Metalinguistic comments or puns on allegedly alien first names or surnames are also potential pragmatic means of discrimination connected with nomination too.

Van Leeuwen's (1996) concepts relating to the representation of social actors allow us to analytically grasp some of the more subtle forms of discriminatorily constructing, identifying or hiding social actors:

The social actors' exclusion from linguistic representation is often employed to veil persons responsible for discriminatory actions. It becomes implicit discrimination by non-nomination in cases such as the sexist non-naming of women (pretending, for example, that the so-called "generic masculine" in languages like German would linguistically include them), or in cases of linguistic under-representation of ethnic minorities by not giving them sufficient access to and voice in mass media and by not reporting about them to an adequate extent. The linguistic exclusion can be a radical, total one which leaves no lexical or grammatical traces in the discursive representation of specific social actors. Van Leeuwen calls this form of linguistic exclusion "suppression" (Van Leeuwen 1996: 38). If the exclusion is partial and leaves some traces that enable readers or hearers to infer the excluded social actors with more or less certainty, van Leeuwen speaks about "backgrounding" (Van Leeuwen 1996: 38). The passive is a syntactic means of backgrounding.

If persons are nominated, i.e. linguistically included, the inclusion is not always an indicator of fair and just representation and treatment, but can sometimes have a disguising, relativizing or averting function. Such is the case, if the linguistic inclusion pretends that there is equal treatment, whereas inequalities and injustices remain in effect. Strategies of linguistic inclusion which can become discriminatory are (according to van Leeuwen):

(1) "genericization", i.e. the general nomination of a whole group of persons (e.g. "Germans"),
(2) "assimilation", i.e. the reference to social actors as groups, which can be realized by

(a) "collectivization", i.e. the nomination of social actors by collectives or mass nouns (e.g. "the crowd"), or

(b) "aggregation", i.e. the statistical quantification of groups of participants (e.g. "10,000 are too many"), and

(3) "impersonalization", i.e. the nomination of persons as if they were not really human beings, which can be realized by

(a) "abstraction", i.e. the representation of social actors by means of a quality assigned to them (e.g. "the unskilled", "illegals"), or

(b) "objectivation", i.e. the nomination of persons by means of reference to a place or object (e.g. by metonymies like "the foreign countries") (Van Leeuwen 1996: 47–59).

There are myriads of lexicalized discriminatory anthroponyms in any language which are employed as discriminatory nominations in different social fields and subfields of action such as policy and politics, economy, religion, military, science, education, sexuality, housing, media, health service, arts, etc. Many of them are tropes, and especially metaphors, metonymies and synecdoches (including antonomasias). They cannot be discussed in the present chapter (for a selection of such anthroponyms, see Reisigl and Wodak 2001: 48–52; for discriminating metaphors, see also El Refaie 2001). Whether a specific anthroponym has a discriminatory effect or not, is, in concrete casas, determined by the pragmatic context or co-text.

5.2.   Discrimination by predication

The second discourse analytical aspect of verbal discrimination I want to selectively focus on relates to predication strategies employed to discriminate against people by ascribing debasing traits, characteristics, qualities and features to them. Such predications are usually connected with social prejudices and stereotypes – the latter being understood as fixed, uniform, reductionist, overgeneralizing schemes or schematic modi operandi which are mostly acquired by socialization, are frequently distributed via mass media and show a high degree of recognizability (see Reisigl in print).

Discriminatory predications in discourses are linguistically or visually more or less explicit or implicit and – like nomination and argumentation – specific or vague. Predicational strategies are mainly realized by specific forms of nomination (based on explicit denotation as well as on more or less implicit connotation), by attributes (in the form of adjectives, appositions, prepositional phrases, relative clauses, conjunctional clauses, infinitive clauses and participial clauses or groups), by predicates or predicative nouns/adjectives/pronouns, by collocations, by explicit comparisons, similes, metaphors and other rhetorical figures (including metonymies, hyperboles, litotes, euphemisms) and by more or less implicit analogies, allusions, evocations, and presuppositions or implications. The visual predication of discriminatory stereotypes is realized by strategies characterized below in section 5.5.

Two short examples must suffice for illustrating discriminatory predications ascribed to social groups who are often discriminated against in discourses with an intercultural dimension.

Among the most frequent discriminatory traits explicitly or implicitly predicated to so-called *"Ausländer"* ("foreigners") in the discourse about migrants and migration in countries such as Austria and Germany, we find the predications that "foreigners" would be bad, uncooperative work colleagues and workmates, "socio-parasites", unwilling to assimilate and integrate, different in culture and religion, culturally immature, less civilized and more primitive, careless, dirty, infectious, backward, conspicuous, loud, inclined to sexual harassment, sexism and patriarchal oppression, physically different, aggressive, criminal, etc. (see Karl-Renner-Institut 1990; Reisigl and Wodak 2001: 55). And discourses about gypsies, for example in Germany and Austria, contain discriminatory predications against gypsies such as being tattered and ragged, roguish and wicked, thieving, vagrant, unreliable and antisocial, false and mendacious, superstytrous, inclined to cursing and witchcraft, and so on.

Empirical discourse studies lead to analogous overviews of corresponding discriminatory stereotypes directed against other social minorities and marginalized groups (e.g. against Jews, see Wodak et al. 1990; Gruber 1991; Reisigl and Wodak 2001: 91–143).

A potent discursive resource for fighting such stereotypes and the related prejudices is argumentation. Argumentation, however, also represents a widespread technique of discrimination.

5.3.   Discrimination by argumentation

Social discrimination against others is often justified and legitimized by means of arguments and argumentation schemes (argumentation strategies). In discourses containing arguments for and against discrimination, argumentation does not always follow rules for rational dispute and constructive arguing such as the freedom of speech, the obligation to give reasons, the correct reference to previous utterances by the antagonist, the obligation to "matter-of-factness", the correct reference to implicit premises, the respect of shared starting points, the use of plausible arguments and schemes of argumentation, logical validity, the acceptance of the discussion's results and the clarity of expression and correct interpretation (see van Eemeren and Grootendorst 1992). Numerous violations of these rules, i.e. many fallacies, can be identified in discourses on ethnic or intercultural issues, where racist, ethnicist or nationalist legitimizing strategies are employed in order to justify unequal treatment and the violation of basic democratic principles and human rights.

Among these fallacies are the *argumentum ad baculum* (a verbal threat or intimidation instead of using plausible and relevant arguments), the *argumentum ad hominem* (a verbal attack on the opponent's personality and character instead of trying to refute the opponent's arguments), the *argumentum ad populum* (an appeal to "masses" of people, often aiming to justify prejudiced emotions and opinions of a social group, instead of relevant arguments), the *argumentum ad verecundiam* (the misplaced appeal to deep respect and reverence for – allegedly – competent, superior, sacrosanct or unimpeachable authorities, instead of relevant arguments), the *argumentum ad nominem* (a fallacious argumentation scheme based on the conclusion rule that the literal meaning of a person's name, a thing's name or an action's name applies to the person, thing or action themselves, just in the sense of "nomen est omen"), the *post hoc, ergo propter hoc* (this fallacy consists in mixing up a temporally chronological relationship with a causally consequential one, in the sense of "A before B, therefore B because of A"), the *argumentum ad consequentiam* (a fallacious causal argumentation scheme that stresses the consequences of a (non-)decision or (non-)action, without these consequences being plausibly derivable from the (non)-decision or (non)-action), the hasty generalization (an argumentation scheme based on an empirically, statistically unconfirmed over-generalization; in fact, many racist, ethnicist, nationalist and sexist prejudices rely on this fallacy, which takes a part for the whole), etc. (for more details and examples of these fallacies, see Reisigl and Wodak 2001: 71–74).

In discourses related to problems of social discrimination it is sometimes difficult to distinguish between fallacious and more or less plausible argumentation schemes, which, in argumentation theory, are designated as "topoi". "Topoi" are those obligatory parts of argumentation which serve as "conclusion rules". They link up the argument or arguments with the concluding claim (see Kienpointner 1992: 194). A typical topos in the discourse about migrants and migration is the topos of danger or topos of threat. It means that if a political action or decision bears dangerous, threatening consequences, one should not perform or do it, or if there is a specific danger and threat, one should do something against it. This topos is often fallaciously realized, if immigrants are "xenophobically" depicted as a threat to national identity and culture against which the government should proceed. This and other content-related topoi and the respective content-related fallacies to be found in the discourses about migrants and asylum seekers (e.g. the discourse about migration and the discourse about asylum) are, among others, analysed in Kienpointner and Kindt (1997), Wengeler (1997), Reeves (1983) and Reisigl and Wodak (2001: 75–80).

5.4.   The perspectivation, intensification and mitigation of discrimination

Two further types of discursive strategies closely linked with argumentation strategies and thus to be taken into consideration in the analysis of social discrimination are *perspectivation strategies* and *intensification* or *mitigation strategies*. The one group of strategies relates to the position or point of view a speaker or writer assumes with respect to discriminating language, i.e. to the perspective from which discriminating arguments – but also nominations and predications – are expressed, and to the method of framed discriminatory language. Discriminatory nominations, predication and argumentations, can, for instance, be realized from an I-perspective, she-/he-perspective or we-perspective; they can be framed by direct quotation, indirect quotation or free indirect speech, and so on. The other group of strategies links up with the question of whether utterances containing discriminating nominations, predications and argumentations are articulated overtly or covertly, whether the respective speech acts are intensified or mitigated. The former can, among others, be realized by hyperboles or amplifying particles like "very" and "absolutely". The latter can be realized by questions instead of assertions or by procataleptic concessions like "yes, but" (for more details on these two types of discursive strategies, see Reisigl and Wodak 2001: 81–85; Reisigl 2003: 214–237).

5.5.   Visual discrimination

Social discrimination is not just realized in the multiple semiotic modes of verbal language, but also in other semiotic modes, including visual modes. Theo van Leeuwen (2000) approaches "visual racism" with the help of two complementary methods, combining (a) the method of analysing the "grammar of visual design" (see Kress and van Leeuwen 1996), which, among others, allows to grasp the imaginary relationship between visually represented individuals and viewers, with (b) his functional-systemic model of the representation of social actors (see van Leeuwen 1996). Although van Leeuwen focuses on the problem of "racism" (although he does not explicate his concept of "racism"), his approach offers a far more general framework, which enables the analysis of diverse forms of social discrimination (especially of implicit discrimination).

Without any claim of completeness, van Leeuwen distinguishes among eight strategies of "visual racism", which, taken more generally, represent eight strategies of various forms of visual discrimination. They are (1) symbolic distanciation, (2) symbolic disempowerment, (3) symbolic objectivation, (4) exclusion, (5) representation as agents of negatively valued actions, (6) homogenization, (7) negative cultural connotation and (8) discriminatory stereotyping.

The first three strategies are differentiated on the basis of criteria such as distance, angle and gaze, which constitute three key factors that are involved in each visual representation and can be integrated into a system network.

Different degrees of distance are visually represented within a continuum of close shots and long shots. Visual discrimination by *symbolic distanciation* means to depict specific persons or groups of persons in relation to the viewers as if they were not "close" to the viewers, as if they were "strangers" far from the observers (see van Leeuwen 2000: 339). Such a representation entails an undifferentiated, de-individualizing portrayal without any details. Long shots, however, are not a means of visual discrimination per se, but – since any form of discrimination is a relational issue that involves a comparative figure – become discriminatory against specific persons or social groups only if there are other persons or groups, which, in comparison to those preferentially depicted by long shots, are preferentially represented by close-ups, which imply greater nearness, differentiation and the possibility to perceive more individual characteristics. Kress and Van Leeuwen discovered in a case study on the Australian school book *Our Society and Others*, that in the chapter on Aboriginal people, all Aborigines except one were represented by long shots, whereas the book's depictions of non-Aboriginal people did not follow this pattern (see van Leeuwen 2000: 337). Comparisons like this one permit a diagnosis of whether there is discrimination at work or not. Such a comparison of the representation of in- and outgroups has to draw on representative empirical findings, since symbolic distanciation is predominantly part of a pattern or syndrome not recognizable at first glance, and thus part of implicit discrimination.

The angle from which a person is depicted can tell both (a) about the relation of power between the viewer and the represented person (this aspect regards the vertical angle from above, from below or on eye level), and (b) about the relation of involvement between the viewer and the represented person (this aspect concerns the horizontal angle, i.e. the frontal or oblique representation). Presupposing that looking up at someone from a low angle in many social contexts means to be less powerful, that looking at someone from eye-level denotes a symmetric power relationship or equal social position, and that social superordination or domination is related to a relatively high, more elevated point of view (one may just think of the "boss's chair"), to visually represent somebody as below the viewer, as "downtrodden" (van Leeuwen 2000: 339), can mean to symbolically disempower the depicted person. *Symbolic disempowerment* becomes implicit discrimination, if specific social groups and their members (e.g. outgroup and minority members) are systematically more often "objects" of a perspectivation from above or a bird's eye view than other social groups (e.g. ingroup and majority members).

The relation of involvement and detachment, which concerns the apparent social interaction between depicted figures and viewers, is visually expressed on the horizontal axis and by the gaze. If a visually represented person looks at the picture's viewer and the depicted body is angled towards the viewer, this bodily orientation suggests a high degree of interactional involvement, since both the frontal posture and the direct gaze are highly phatic and sometimes also conative (e.g. demanding). If the gaze and the posture of a depicted figure are not directed at the viewer, but represented from an oblique angle, the appellative quality is rather low, and the viewers assume the roles of "voyeurs" who are looking at somebody who is not aware of being looked at (see van Leeuwen 2000: 339). It is within such relational contexts that *symbolic objectivation* can become visual discrimination. Such is the case if persons of specific social groups are – in contrast to other social groups – systematically represented "as objects of our scrutiny, rather than as subjects addressing the viewer with their gaze and symbolically engaging with the viewer in this way" (van Leeuwen 2000: 339). We are faced with such a form of discrimination if women are shown as available sexual commodities.

The other five strategies of discrimination distinguished by Theo van Leeuwen do not primarily relate to the interpersonal metafunction, but to the ideational metafunction. They generally correspond to the above-mentioned strategies of verbal discrimination, if one disregards the differences of semiotic modes.

5.6.   An example of indirect and implicit discrimination

In the present context, I just analyse one concrete example of indirect and implicit discrimination in order to illustrate a specific discriminatory argumentation strategy in connection with discriminatory nomination, predication, perspectivation and intensification strategies.

The example gives an idea about coded antisemitism in the Austrian postwar era (see Wodak and Reisigl 2002 for a detailed analysis of the example). It documents how Jörg Haider, the former leader of the far-right Austrian Freedom Party, employs the fallacious topos of name-interpretation in order to attack the head of Vienna's Jewish community, Ariel Muzicant, during a polemic "beer hall speech" on February 28, 2001. The primary audience of Haider's speech were mostly party followers and party sympathizers. The secondary audience was composed of those who saw and heard the speech extract transmitted in the radio and TV news. The tertiary audience consisted of those who read the transcribed speech (extract) in print media and the internet. Haider uttered his discriminatory attack against Muzicant in the campaign period preceding the regional elections in Vienna in March 2001, and in a political and historical situation in which, among others, two discourses were intensely present in public: the discourse about the so-called "sanctions" of the 14 EU member states against the participation of the Austrian Freedom Party in the coalition government and the discourse about the restitution of Jewish spoils robbed by Austrian

National Socialists. Ariel Muzicant was engaged both in the critique and warning of the FPÖ's participation in the government and in the negotiations about the restitution. In his polemic speech, Haider insulted Muzicant as follows:

> Mister Ariel ((0.5 sec)) Muzicant. ((*1.0 sec*)) I don't understand at all how ((*1.0 sec*)) if someone is called Ariel [he] can have so much dirt sticking to him ((*fervent applause and beginning laughter*)) this I really don't understand, but ((*Haider looks below at his manuscript*)) I mean ((*2 sec of applause and laughter*)) this is another thing. ((*7 sec of applause, during which Haider seizes a beer mug standing at the desk before him and takes a swig*))
> ((Transcript of an extract of the TV news *Zeit im Bild 2* (*Time in Pictures 2*) of March 1, 2001; underlining stands for stressing))

> [Der Herr Ariel ((*0.5 sec*)) Muzicant. ((*1.0 sec*)) I versteh überhaupt net, wie ((*1.0 sec*)) wonn ana Ariel haßt, so viel Dreck am Steckn haben kann ((*starker Applaus und Lachen setzen ein*)) des versteh i überhaupt net, oba ((*Haider blickt nach unten auf das Manuskript*)) i man ((*2 sec langer tosender Applaus und Lachen*)) des is a ondere Soche. ((*7 sec lang anhaltender Applaus, während dessen Haider zum Bierkrug greift, der vor ihm auf dem Podium steht, und einen Schluck Bier trinkt*))]

For those among the primary, secondary and tertiary audience who have a respective historical background knowledge, Haider's criminalizing insult of Muzicant bears high allusive potential of coded antisemitism. Within the specific context, Haider's slur alludes to at least four prejudiced predications discriminating against Jews, viz. (a) the stereotype of "the Jewish traitor to the Fatherland.", (b) the stereotype of "the Jew as criminal world conspirator against Austria", (c) the stereotype of "the dirty, impure Jew" and (d) the stereotype of "the business-minded, tricky, fraudulent, criminal Jew". In addition, some of the Jewish listeners and readers of the secondary and tertiary audience associated Haider's offense with the historically unproven assertion that National Socialists processed bodies of murdered Jews in order to make soap. These recipients argued that Haider metaphorically transformed Jews once again into soap.

Haider expresses the stereotypes (a) and (b) in the speech sequence immediately preceding the quotation. He claims in this "pre-sequence" that Muzicant had a share of the responsibility for the so-called "sanctions" against Austria and sent a letter with the World Jewish Congress "throughout America" (please note the exaggerating intensification) in which he stated that Jews were again in dire straits and had to leave Austria. In order to vividly and persuasively construct his insinuating assertion that Muzicant would complain about a growing antisemitism in Austria, Haider makes use of pseudo-authentic direct speech. He puts the following words into Muzicant's mouth: "Now we must already collect, because our fellow citizens are again being badgered and must leave Austria. [Jetzt müssen wir schon sammeln, weil unsere Mitbürger sind wieder bedrängt und müssen Österreich verlassen.]" A syntactic indicator for the fact that this perspectivation strategy recurs to fictitious quotation is the word order in

the subordinate causal clause: a verb-second position after the German subjunc-
tion *"weil"* ("because") would be typical for spoken language, but is not for a
letter like the one Haider ascribed to Muzicant (apart from the fact that such a
letter would have been written in English).

The third and fourth stereotypes are implicitly verbalized in the allusive
predication of criminality contained in the quoted extract. Among the discursive
features which support discriminating associations with these two antisemitic
prejudices are four peculiarities: (1) The first one relates to nomination and perspectivation. Haider phonetically distorts the surname of the Jewish president,
articulating "Muzicant" with [ts] instead of [s]. This distancing perspectivation
by alienating nomination is combined with the syntactic realization of *"Der
Herr Ariel Muzicant"* as an isolated "free topic" that is segmented by two relevance pauses. Both of these features are suited to open for the audience a potential space of associations with the name of the Jewish president, all the more
since the determining article *"der"* in Austrian German suggests that the person
named "Ariel Muzicant" is well-known. This nomination is followed (2) by the
allusive homonymic and antithetic play on words based on a fallacious topos of
name interpretation, i.e. *argumentum ad nominem*. In a syntactically not well-
formed conditional formulation, Haider plays with the contrast between the
proper name "Ariel", which is both a male Jewish first name and the name of a
detergent (i.e. an ergonym) that connotes cleanness, purity, and the criminalizing German idiom *"Dreck am Stecken haben"* meaning "to have dirt (sticking)
on the stick", with the implication of having a shady, criminal past. The implicit
fallacious argumentation scheme can generally be explicated by the conditional
paraphrase: If a person carries a specific proper name, the (denotative or conno-
tative) meaning of this proper name also applies to the person her- or himself. In
the concrete case, the *argumentum ad nominem* means: If a male's name is
"Ariel", he should be a person with a pure, clean character. (3) The third linguistic particularity of the quoted passage is the strategic intensification of the
criminalizing predication by "so much". In the given context, the deictic expression "so" points to an undefined, sensually not perceptible aspect in the
speaker's and listeners' mental "space of imagination". If the listeners' space of
imagination" contains allusive paths leading to antisemitic prejudices, the allegedly large amount of dirt ("much") is de-coded in a way as to be associated with
the stereotypes of "the dirty, impure Jew" and "the business-minded, tricky,
fraudulent, criminal Jew". (4) The fervent applause as an indicator of agreement
with the content of Haider's insult and the laughter of the primary audience as a
sign of being amused by Haider's utterance show that the speaker's message
well reaches his first addressees in the room. In view of the fact that these listeners are first and foremost followers and sympathizers of the far-right party
which is the successor organization of the "Verband der Unabhängigen" (VdU;
"Association of Independents"), a political melting pot for former National So-

cialists in Austria, it is reasonable to suspect that many of the primary auditors associated Haider's insult with the two discriminatory stereotypes. Several additional factors (both linguistic and contextual ones) which further increased the probability of Haider's primary audience to develop discriminatory antisemitic associations are discussed in Wodak and Reisigl (2002).

6.   Conclusion

Many supplementary questions and aspects of social discrimination in discourses cannot be dealt with in the present chapter, for example the relationship between discrimination and propaganda, instigation and ridiculation, the question of whether there are specific "genres" or "text types" (e.g. transgressive inscriptions in public space, jokes, caricatures and satires) which are more frequently employed for discrimination than other "genres" or "text types", and the question of whether there are culture-dependent and legal norms that variably delimit the boundaries between verbal discrimination and joking, caricaturing and lampooning backed by freedom of speech. A critical analysis must also take them into consideration.

Such a critical analysis of discursive practices that aim at discriminating against specific social groups or at disguising discrimination has both theoretical as well as practical relevance. Linguistic critique or language critique can be a means of anti-discrimination policy and politics (see Reisigl and Wodak 2001: 263–271). Its controlling and sensitizing contributions consist (1) in the narrow text- and discourse-related reconstruction and description of the use of semiotic means of discrimination (e.g. in the accurate linguistic and interactional analysis of Haider's utterance and the reactions of the primary audience); (2) in the socio-diagnostic integration of the linguistic analysis into a broader, trans- or interdisciplinarian framework that uncovers socio-political functions of discriminatory discursive practices that are performed at a specific time in a specific place, i.e. in a specific historical situation (e.g. in the analytical embedding of Haider's speech in the actual political situation of the election campaign and of the controversial discussions about the so-called "sanctions" and the restitution of Jewish spoils, as well as in the embedding in the historical context of coded antisemitism in the Austrian post-war era); and (3) in prospective practical critique which aims to contribute to the solution of discrimination-related social problems, for example, by attempting to improve the communicative relations between different (sub)cultural groups within the political system of a democracy, by attempting to sensitize speakers and writers of a specific society with respect to discriminating semiosis, and by offering, for example, discourse analytical knowledge in the area of anti-discriminating argumentation and media coverage (e.g. in writing a specialist linguistic report for the legal proceedings started by Muzicant against Haider).

As the article and especially the analysis of the example in section 5.6. have shown, the problem of social discrimination in discourses is far too complex to be grasped comprehensively by an exclusive analysis of intercultural communication in a strict sense. Verbal and visual discrimination are topics which are best approached in interdisciplinary analyses that combine the analysis of intercultural communication with critical discourse analysis and, possibly, also with politological analysis, social-psychological analysis, legal analysis and economic analysis.

Notes

1. I would like to thank Helga Kotthoff and Ingrid Piller for constructive comments on an earlier version of the article and Maura Bayer for correcting my English.
2. See Wagner (2001: 12–13) for a slightly different terminological distinction of "direct" and "indirect" as well as "explicit" and "implicit discrimination".
3. In comparison to Scollon and Scollon (2003a), Scollon and Scollon (2003b) mention just two meanings of "discourse". In the narrow sense – they explain – "discourse" means "language in use". In a broader sense, they regard "discourse" as "a body of language use and other factors that form a "social language" such as the discourse of traffic regulation, commercial discourse, medical discourse, legal discourse." (Scollon and Scollon 2003b: 210).

References

Berding, Dietz
  2003   Gutachten über den antisemitischen Charakter einer namenpolemischen Passage aus der Rede Jörg Haiders vom 28. Februar 2001. In: Anton Pelinka and Ruth Wodak (eds.), *Dreck am Stecken: Politik der Ausgrenzung*, 173–186. Vienna: Czernin.
Billig, Michael
  2006   Political rhetorics of discrimination. In: Keith Brown (ed.), *The Encyclopedia of Language and Linguistics,* Volume 9, 2nd edition, 697–699. Oxford: Elsevier.
Bough, John
  2006   Discrimination and language. In: Keith Brown (ed.), *The Encyclopedia of Language and Linguistics*, Volume 3, 2nd edition, 694–696. Oxford: Elsevier.
Crenshaw, Kimberlé
  1991   Mapping the margins: intersectionality, identity politics, and violence against women of color. *Stanford Law Review* 43 (6): 1241–1299.
Van Dijk, Teun A.
  1984   *Prejudice in Discourse*. Amsterdam: Benjamins.

Van Dijk, Teun A.
  1987   *Communicating Racism. Ethnic Prejudice in Thought and Talk.* Newbury
          Park, CA: Sage.
Van Dijk, Teun A.
  1993   *Elite Discourse and Racism.* Newbury Park, CA: Sage.
Van Dijk, Teun A.
  2001a   Multidisciplinary CDA: a plea for diversity. In: Ruth Wodak and Michael
          Meyer (eds.), *Methods of Critical Discourse Analysis*, 95–120. London et
          al.: Sage.
Van Dijk, Teun A.
  2001b   Critical discourse analysis. In: Deborah Schiffrin, Deborah Tannen and
          Heide Hamilton (eds.), *Handbook of Discourse Analysis*, 352–371. Oxford:
          Blackwell.
Duisburger Institut für Sprach- und Sozialforschung (eds.)
  1999   *Medien und Straftaten. Vorschläge zur Vermeidung diskriminierender Be-*
          richterstattung über Einwanderer und Flüchtlinge. Duisburg: DISS.
Van Eemeren, Frans H. and Rob Grootendorst
  1992   *Argumentation, Communication, and Fallacies. A Pragma-Dialectical Per-*
          spective. Hillsdale, NJ et al.: Laurence Erlbaum Associates.
El Refaie, Elizabeth
  2001   Metaphors we discriminate by: naturalized themes in Austrian newspaper
          articles about asylum seekers. *Journal of Sociolinguistics* 5/3: 352–371.
Fairclough, Norman
  1995   *Critical Discourse Analysis. The Critical Study of Language.* London, New
          York: Longman.
Fredman, Sandra and Erika Szyszak
  1993   The interaction of race and gender. In: Bob Hepple and Erika M. Szysczak
          (eds.), *Discrimination: The Limits of Law*, 214–226. London: Mansell Pub-
          lishing.
Girnth, Heiko
  1996   Texte im politischen Diskurs. Ein Vorschlag zur diskursorientierten Be-
          schreibung von Textsorten. *Muttersprache* 1/1996: 66–80.
Goffman, Erving
  1963   *Stigma: Notes on the Management of Spoiled Identity.* Englewood Cliffs,
          NJ: Prentice Hall.
Graumann, Carl Friedrich and Marget Wintermantel
  1989   Discriminatory speech acts: A functional approach. In: Daniel Bar-Dal,
          Carl Friedrich Graumann, Arie W. Kruglanski and Wolfgang Stroebe (eds.),
          Stereotyping and Prejudice: Changing Conceptions, 183–204. New York/
          Berlin: Springer.
Gruber, Helmut
  1991   *Antisemitismus im Mediendiskurs: Die Affäre "Waldheim" in der Tages-*
          presse. Wiesbaden/ Opladen: Deutscher Universitätsverlag/Westdeutscher
          Verlag.
Gumperz, John J.
  1982   *Discourse Strategies.* Cambridge: Cambridge University Press.
Gumperz, John J.
  2001   Interactional sociolinguistics: A personal perspective. In: Deborah Schiff-

rin, Deborah Tannen and Heidi Hamilton (eds.), *The Handbook of Discourse Analysis*, 215–228. Malden, MA/Oxford, UK: Blackwell.

Gumperz, John and Jenny Cook-Gumperz
this volume   Discourse, cultural diversity and communication: a linguistic anthropological perspective. Chapter 2.

Hinnenkamp, Volker
1991   Talking a person into interethnic distinction: A discourse analytic case study. In: Jan Blommaert and Jeff Verschueren (eds.), *Intercultural and International Communication: Selected Papers from the 1987 International Pragmatics Conference (Part III) and the Ghent Symposium on Intercultural Communication*, 91–109. Amsterdam/Philadelphia: John Benjamins.

Hinnenkamp, Volker
2001   Constructing misunderstanding as a cultural event. In: Aldo di Luzio, Susanne Günthner and Franca Orletti (eds.), *Culture in Communication: Analyses of Intercultural Situations*, 211–243. Amsterdam/Philadelphia: John Benjamins.

Hinnenkamp, Volker
2003   Misunderstandings: Interactional structure and strategic resources. In: Juliane House, Gabriele Kasper and Steven Ross (eds.), *Misunderstanding in Social Life: Discourse Approaches to Problematic Talk*, 57–81. Harlow, UK: Longman/Pearson Education.

Jäger, Siegfried
2001a   *Kritische Diskursanalyse: Eine Einführung*. Duisburg: DISS.

Jäger, Siegfried
2001b   Discourse and knowledge: Theoretical and methodological aspects of a critical discourse and dispositive analysis. In: Ruth Wodak and Michael Meyer (eds.), *Methods of Critical Discourse Analysis*, 32–62. London: Sage.

Jäger, Margret, Gabriele Cleve, Ina Ruth and Siegfried Jäger
1998   *Von deutschen Einzeltätern und ausländischen Banden: Medien und Straftaten: Mit Vorschlägen zur Vermeidung diskriminierender Berichterstattung*. Duisburg: DISS.

Karl-Renner-Institut (eds.)
1990   *Fremdenangst und Ausländerfeindlichkeit – Gegenargumente*. Vienna: Karl-Renner-Institut.

Kienpointner, Manfred
1992   *Alltagslogik: Struktur und Funktion von Argumentationsmustern*. Stuttgart-Bad Cannstatt: Frommann-Holzboog.

Kienpointner, Manfred and Walther Kindt
1997   On the problem of bias in political argumentation: An investigation into discussion about political asylum in Germany and Austria. *Journal of Pragmatics* 27: 555–585.

Kress, Gunther and Theo van Leeuwen
1996   *Reading Images*. London: Routledge.

Van Leeuwen, Theo
1996   The representation of social actors. In: Carmen Rosa Caldas-Coulthard and

Malcom Coulthard (eds.), *Texts and Practices: Readings in Critical Discourse Analysis*, 32–70. London/New York: Routledge.

Van Leeuwen, Theo
2000   Visual racism. In: Martin Reisigl and Ruth Wodak (eds.), *The Semiotics of Racism: Approaches in Critical Discourse Analysis*, 333–350. Vienna: Passagen.

Lüsebrink, Hans-Jürgen
2005   *Interkulturelle Kommunikation*. Stuttgart/Weimar: Metzler.

Makkonen, Timo
2002   Multiple, Compound and Intersectional Discrimination – Bringing Experiences of the Most Disadvantaged to the Fore. *Institute for Human Rights Research Reports* No. 11 (April 2002): (http://www.abo.fi/instut/imr/norfa/timo.pdf).

Makkonen, Timo
2003   Hauptursachen, Formen und Folgen von Diskriminierung. In: Internationale Organisation für Migration (IOM) and Regionalbüro für die Baltischen und Nordischen Staaten (eds.), *Handbuch zur rechtlichen Bekämpfung von Diskriminierung*, 8–31. Helsinki: International Organisation for Migration (IOM).

The Oxford English Dictionary
1989   *The Oxford English Dictionary*. Volume IV, *Creel–Duzepere*. Second Edition. Prepared by J.A. Simpson and E.S.C. Weiner. Oxford: Clarendon Press.

Piller, Ingrid
this volume Cross-cultural communication in intimate relationships. Chapter 17.

Reeves, Frank
1983   *British Racial Discourse: A Study of British Political Discourse about Race and Race-Related Matters*. Cambridge: Cambridge University Press.

Reisigl, Martin
2002   "Dem Volk aufs Maul schauen, nach dem Mund reden und angst und bange machen" – Von populistischen Anrufungen, Anbiederungen und Agitationsweisen in der Sprache österreichischer PolitikerInnen. In: Wolfgang Eismann (ed.), *Rechtspopulismus. Österreichische Krankheit oder europäische Normalität?*, 149–198. Vienna: Cernin.

Reisigl, Martin
2003   *Wie man eine Nation herbeiredet. Eine diskursanalytische Untersuchung zur sprachlichen Konstruktion der österreichischen Nation und österreichischen Identität in politischen Fest- und Gedenkreden*. Vienna: unpublished PhD.

Reisigl, Martin
in print Stereotyp. In: Gert Ueding (ed.), *Historisches Wörterbuch der Rhetorik (HWRh)*. Volume 8, Tübingen: Niemeyer.

Reisigl, Martin and Ruth Wodak
2001   *Discourse and Discrimination: Rhetoric of Racism and Antisemitism*. London/New York: Routledge.

Roberts, Celia, Evelyn Davies and Tom Jupp
1993   *Language and Discrimination: A Study of Communication in Multi-Ethnic Workplace*. London/New York: Longman.

Scollon, Ron and Suzie Wong Scollon
2001   Discourse and intercultural communication. In: Deborah Schiffrin, Deborah Tannen and Heide Hamilton (eds.), *Handbook of Discourse Analysis*, 538–547. Oxford: Blackwell.
Scollon, Ron and Suzie Wong Scollon
2003a   *Intercultural Communication: A Discourse Approach*. Malden, MA/Oxford, UK: Blackwell.
Scollon, Ron and Suzie Wong Scollon
2003b   *Discourses in Place*. London/New York: Routledge.
Singh, Rajendra, Jayant Lele and Gita Martohardjono
1996   Communication in a multilingual society: some missed opportunities. In: Rajendra Singh (ed.), *Towards a Critical Sociolinguistics*, 237–254. Amsterdam: Benjamins.
Skuttnabb-Kangas, Tove and Robert Phillipson (eds.)
1994   *Linguistic Human Rights: Overcoming Linguistic Discrimination*. Berlin/New York: Mouton de Gruyter.
Skuttnabb-Kangas, Tove
2000   *Linguistic Genocide in Education – Or Worldwide Diversity and Human Rights*? Mahwah, NJ/London: Lawrence Erlbaum Associates.
Smitherman, Geneva and Teun A. van Dijk (eds.)
1988   *Discourse and Discrimination*. Detroit: Wayne State University Press.
Sykes, Mary
1985   Discrimination in Discourse. In: Teun A. van Dijk (ed.), *Handbook of Discourse Analysis. Volume 4: Discourse Analysis in Society*, 83–101. London et al.: Academic Press.
Wagner, Franc
2001   *Implizite sprachliche Diskriminierung als Sprechakt: Lexikalische Indikatoren impliziter Diskriminierung in Medientexten*. Tübingen: Narr.
Wengeler, Martin
1997   Argumentation im Einwanderungsdiskurs: ein Vergleich der Zeiträume 1970–1973 und 1980–1983. In: Matthias Jung, Martin Wengeler and Karin Böke (eds.), *Die Sprache des Migrationsdiskurses: Das Reden über "Ausländer" in Medien, Politik und Alltag*, 121–149. Stuttgart: Westdeutscher Verlag.
Wodak, Ruth and Teun A. van Dijk (eds.)
2000   *Racism at the Top: Parliamentary Discourses on Ethnic Issues in Six European States*. Klagenfurt-Celovec: Drava.
Wodak, Ruth and Martin Reisigl
2002   "Wenn einer Ariel heißt" – Ein linguistisches Gutachten zur politischen Funktionalisierung antisemitischer Ressentiments in Österreich. In: Anton Pelinka and Ruth Wodak (eds.), *"Dreck am Stecken". Politik der Ausgrenzung*, 134–172. Vienna: Czernin Verlag.
Wodak, Ruth, Johanna Pelikan, Peter Nowak, Helmut Gruber, Rudolf de Cillia and Richard Mitten
1990   *"Wir sind alle unschuldige Täter!" Diskurshistorische Studien zum Nachkriegsantisemitismus*. Frankfurt am Main: Suhrkamp.

Wodak, Ruth, Florian Menz, Richard Mitten and Frank Stern
  1994   *Die Sprachen der Vergangenheiten: öffentliches Gedenken in österreichischen und deutschen Medien.* Frankfurt am Main: Suhrkamp.
Wodak, Ruth, Rudolf De Cillia, Martin Reisigl and Karin Liebhart
  1999   *The Discursive Construction of National Identity.* Edinburgh: Edinburgh University Press.

19. Power and dominance in intercultural communication

Winfried Thielmann

1. Introduction and overview

The treatment of non-native speakers within legal proceedings, linguistic expansion of indigenous languages in post-colonial societies, and science transfer to developing countries – these quite heterogeneous phenomena have two things in common: they are, somehow, matters of intercultural communication and they are, somehow, linked to the issues of power and dominance. Linguistic analysis of these phenomena faces a serious difficulty: Best linguistic evidence available consists of authentic *speech* and authentic *texts*. Hence there is a tendency to interpret elements of the linguistic surface as manifestations of, say, power and dominance – much in the way of text-immanent literary interpretation (e.g. Fairclough in print). Any attempt to go beyond the linguistic surface implies, however, that one has to make assumptions about people's intentions – for which there is no ultimate evidence in the material (McIlvenny 1992: 89–91).

In the first section of this chapter I shall argue that one can get out of this conundrum if one acknowledges that *extralinguistic phenomena* play a crucial role in societal interaction. Societal interaction consists in routine pursuits of systems of purposes. These routines are results of societal problem-solving processes and manifest themselves in *institutions* and in *interactional patterns* such as the *question-answer-pattern* – a specific, non-universal, purpose-driven structure for knowledge-processing (Ehlich and Rehbein 1979). In a pragmatic sense, these routine pursuits are already "cultural". Thus, intercultural issues systematically arise when people interact who – as a matter of societal routine – do things differently, even though they may speak the same language (Redder and Rehbein 1987). Issues of power and dominance within intercultural communication come into play when, for instance, institutional asymmetries such as the agent-client relationship are compounded by asymmetries of knowledge (Günthner and Luckmann 1995, Günthner in this volume). Hence for an understanding of power and dominance in intercultural communication, societal organization and actants' knowledge are crucial factors to be considered in the analysis. If linguistics takes these matters seriously, analysis of authentic intercultural discourse – or of texts and concepts from the intercultural sphere – may be able to dissolve issues of power and dominance into the question of how and in which systematic way people deal with asymmetrical situations while pursuing their purposes. Such analyses may be able to expose the pivots of such communication and thus provide the basis for concrete suggestions of improvement.

In the second section of this chapter I shall attempt to examine – with due brevity – three authentic situations of intercultural communication occurring under the constraints of particular asymmetries:

– Intercultural communication within legal proceedings (Mattel-Pegam 1985)
– Conceptual aspects of intercultural science and knowledge transfer that inspired the "grassroots" Grameen banking system in Bangladesh (Yunus and Jolis 1998)
– Linguistic expansion of an indigenous language in a post-colonial situation (Kummer 1985).
   All translations are mine.

2.   Language, cultural knowledge and extralinguistic reality – some theoretical reflections on intercultural communication and power

In this section I intend to unfold, motivate and exemplify the notion of *cultural apparatus* developed in Redder and Rehbein (1987), as this concept has proven to be a helpful analytical tool in dealing with intercultural communication phenomena.

2.1.   The concept of culture and its history

The concept of culture has a complex history of which I shall only mention a few crucial stages. For a critical discussion see Redder and Rehbein (1987: 7–8) and Ehlich (1996).

The Latin verb *colere* 'to farm', its past participle *cultus* and the noun *cultura* are initially almost exclusively tied to the agricultural sphere (e.g. Cato: De agricultura). Through *colere*, Romans differentiated themselves from other societies that did not farm, for instance nomadic tribes. It appears that the discriminating potential of the concept was the driving force for Cicero's metaphor of the *cultura animi* (Tusculanae disputationes) through philosophy – the 'farming of the mind' to overcome the state of "barbarism". Despite its discriminatory aspects, the Roman concept is essentially dynamic. It is the concept of an *activity*. During enlightenment, the concept – while maintaining its dynamic aspects – was expanded to also comprise other activities through which human societies can overcome the *status naturalis* and gain comfort: crafts, technology as well as politeness. Herder, for instance in his reflections on the origin of language ([1772] 1997: 120), then links the concept to the development and improvement of nations and thus provides the basis for a more static interpretation:

culture as a *way of being*. Promulgated by highly influential scholars such as Humboldt, this static concept of culture dominates in the 19th century and also remains powerful throughout the twentieth century: Culture is understood not as an activity, but as a product of activity, a system of achievements through which a society defines itself. The contradiction between *activity* and *entity*, however, never completely disappears: The change from assimilationism to multiculturalism in post-war Australian immigration policy may be taken as evidence of a recognition of the dynamic elements of the culture concept, yet the actual results of this change remain doubtful. In their sceptical but sympathetic history of post-war Australian immigration, Bosworth and Wilton (1984: 36–37) suggest that even modern Australian multiculturalism is hardly more than a public celebration of a multiplicity of cultural icons whilst immigrants' different ways remain unrecognized.

2.2.   The cultural apparatus and its role in intercultural communication

Is it possible to scientifically instrumentalize and bring to fruition a concept that is – because of its complex tradition – rather an *explanandum* than an *explanans*? Drawing on Gramsci (1983), who reinstated the dynamic aspects of the culture concept and conceived of it as the practice of critical awareness of societal processes, Redder and Rehbein (1987) advocate a *pragmatic* concept of culture. They conceive of culture as an *apparatus*, a "functional aggregate of essentially different action paths determined by certain purposes". Punctuality, for instance, is part of the cultural apparatus, an "organised ensemble of societal [and therefore transindividual; W.T.] experience, ways of thought, forms of representation and practices" (Redder and Rehbein 1987: 16). The cultural apparatus is the basis for the societal reproduction of the respective domain (for instance punctuality). At the same time, however, it is the basis for criticism and change when actants become aware of its structure. Because of its importance for societal reproduction, a cultural apparatus may also be externalized. Then it takes the form of a *societal apparatus*, an *institution*.

Intercultural communication occurs when the differences between two people's cultural apparatus become apparent to them (Redder and Rehbein 1987: 18). Due to the aggregate nature of the cultural apparatus, these differences can lie in the areas of societal experience, practice and language. Intercultural communication in a *narrow sense* occurs when actants of the same society who speak the same language encounter a problem that results from differences in their cultural apparatus. Intercultural communication in a *broader sense* occurs when this kind of problem is encountered by actants from different societies who speak different languages.

What is the systematic place of the cultural apparatus within our daily activities ? Consider this quasi-empirical example:

Helga (five years old,
looking into the fridge):   Mum, where's the juice?
Mother: It's still on the table where you left it.

Helga has a need and tries to use her own resources to locate the item that fulfils the need. But she encounters an obstacle. She can categorize this obstacle as a specific *knowledge* deficit ("where") within what she already knows ("that the juice must be somewhere"). She also knows that her mother usually knows where things are. She asks her mother a question, and her mother supplies the knowledge element Helga needs. This exchange of words will have consequences in extralinguistic reality: juice will be consumed.

The *question-answer-pattern* (Ehlich and Rehbein 1979) is a societal problem solution for the purpose of knowledge management the child has already learned. At school, however, she will encounter an unfamiliar usage of this pattern: It is usually the teachers who ask questions, and they do not do so because they want to know something, but because they want to know if one knows. Helga will have to make the transition from a child to a student within an *institution* and will have to learn how to handle an institutional transformation of the question-answer pattern that serves a completely different kind of knowledge management. She will have to modify and expand her *cultural apparatus*.

2.3.   Intercultural communication in a narrow sense: power and dominance within intercultural communication at school

School is a cultural apparatus turned institution: Schools exist in societies that – to ensure their reproduction – need to pass on a complex ensemble of *standard problem solutions* to the next generation (Ehlich and Rehbein 1986: 11, Scherr in this volume). Because of this very purpose, schools suffer from an inherent contradiction. They have to pass on standard solutions to problems that are not problematic for their clientele. As Ehlich and Rehbein demonstrate (1986: 11–13), the core of problem-solving consists of an *interest-driven lack of understanding*, the productive bafflement arising from a blockage of an action path. Schools, however, have to pass on a great number of standard problem solutions very quickly. Because of this, they have to:

a) leave out crucial stages of the actual problem-solving process (especially the stage of productive bafflement)
b) as a consequence of a), abstract from the "reality out here" and generally pass on knowledge through language only.

To overcome these inherent contradictions, schools have developed specific solutions, for instance the *task-solution pattern* (Ehlich and Rehbein 1986: 14) and the *teacher's presentation with parts assigned to students*, during which the teacher elicits parts of knowledge from the class in order to ensure that students maintain involvement and participate in the presentation of new knowledge (Ehlich and Rehbein 1986: 81–87).

By the time children go to school, they have developed a cultural apparatus that allows them to manage their lives in the social situations they have encountered so far. Once they are at school, they become *clients* of an institution. There they encounter teachers, institutional *agents* with a very different cultural apparatus. Communication between students and teachers at school is, to a certain degree, *intercultural communication* in the narrow sense outlined above, i.e. it is intercultural communication whenever students and teachers encounter a problem that is due to a difference in their cultural apparatus.

Within the institution, the onus is on the students to modify – via intercultural communication in an *asymmetrical* situation – their cultural apparatus in a way that they become "proper" clients. The following admonition is a typical authentic example of this type of intercultural communication:

T[eacher]: People who are wriggling are not looking. (Thwaite 2004: 83)

From the perspective of the institution, students are not expected to use the critical potential of their cultural apparatus (except for institutionally provided valves such as school newspapers), but rather its potential for adaptation and expansion.

This not only comprises the acquisition of, say, punctuality, but also the ability to manage the client-side of institution-specific interactional patterns such as the task-solution pattern, the exam-question or the teacher's presentation with parts assigned to students. In terms of knowledge management, students' institutional survival is virtually guaranteed when they can memorize the linguistic side of knowledge regarding standard solutions to problems that are not their own. Kügelgen (1994), an empirically based study of school discourse, paints a dark picture of what actually arrives in students' minds apart from mere words to be uttered at the right time.

Students' expanded cultural apparatus also comprises a cultural sub-apparatus, so to speak, of institutional survival consisting, for instance, of tactical questions (to pretend interest and thus escape the teacher's attention for a while) and maxims ("Cheat where you can but don't get caught!") (Ehlich and Rehbein 1977: 66), etc.

To sum up: Communication between agents of an institution and their clients has – because of their different cultural apparatus – *per se* an intercultural dimension whenever a problem occurs that points to these differences. Since the communicative situation in institutions is asymmetrical, the onus is usually on the clients to adjust, modify and expand their cultural apparatus to make this communication work. As we have seen, the very fact of institutionalization of areas essential to a society's reproduction may lead to intrinsic contradictions the institution can only partially overcome: Knowledge acquired at school cannot have the same quality as knowledge acquired through the individual, interest-driven solution of an authentic problem, even though pedagogical refinement of, say, the task–solution pattern may give students the illusion that they have done so. While the institutional agents have developed routines to at least partially overcome the institution's inherent contradictions on their part, clients have to absorb the interactional consequences of these contradictions into their cultural apparatus.

Of course, these issues can be discussed in the terms of power and dominance. Students are in the teacher's *domain of power* (Ehlich and Rehbein 1977: 22), they have to do – within the institutional limits, of course – what the teacher wants. Students and teachers are at the bottom of a hierarchy topped by, say, a minister – a hierarchy that, frequently in mysterious ways, decides on the content of what is being taught. Power is also – somehow – embodied in the *ideological knowledge* (i.e. a representation of society's structure that is inadequate but necessary for the society's reproduction as it is [Ehlich and Rehbein 1986: 167–168]) schools have to pass on by virtue of being schools.

I hope that I have been able to demonstrate, however, that it is the structure and dynamics of institutions themselves that require the most crucial – and often painful – changes on the part of the individual. And institutions are something no complex society can do without.

3.   Asymmetrical intercultural communication in a broader sense

In this section I shall examine three very different authentic examples of asymmetrical intercultural communication in a broader sense, i.e. with actants belonging to or deriving from different societies.

3.1.   Ethnocentrism – the failure of intercultural communication in prison

The particular asymmetries of legal institutions and their impact on communication have for some time been in the focus of linguists' attention (Hoffmann [1989] offers a collection of mostly empirically based studies from various perspectives). Aspects investigated include discourse types and strategies in the court room (Hoffmann 1983, 2002), the impact of class on legal proceedings (Wodak 1985), and problems of understanding resulting from the disfunctionality of discourse types within the institution (Hoffmann 1980). Koerfer's study of interpreter-mediated discourse in the court room (1994) deals explicitly with intercultural communication in the broader sense (for an account of the state of research in this area see Schröder 2000 and also Eades and Meierkord in this volume).

The following reflections are based on the material and analysis in Mattel-Pegam (1985). The material consists of a transcription of the discourse at a German prison between an Italian prisoner, his German lawyer and an interpreter of German nationality. The Italian has been sentenced to seven years in prison for robbery. The lawyer is preparing an appeal. The consultation occurs at the client's request. In the following section of the transcript, the Italian client is – for about the third time – trying to get across the reason for which he wanted to see his lawyer: As the appeal is not looking too good, the Italian wishes to inquire whether there is the possibility of a *provvedimento*, an extra-judicial means that could be used in his favour. (I: Interpreter; L: Lawyer; C: Client):

(39)   I: Un altro avvocato non/
              Another lawyer, not/

(40a)   C: Ma io non ho detto altro avvocato
              but I haven't said different lawyer

(40b)   C: di prendere <u>provvedimento</u>
              use a means

(40c)   C: Capisce provvedimento.che signific/
              Do you understand provvedimento.what that mean/

(41)   I: No.
              No.

(42a)   C: Di fare ancora qualcosa.
              To do something else.

(42b)   C: Di scrivere a qualche pubblico ministero più interessante
              To write to some public ministry that's more interested

(43)   I: I see ... a mediator.

(44)   L: The only one to decide about this is the Fourth Panel of the Federal
              Court and nobody else, isn't it?

(45)   I: C'è soltanto la corte suprema ... nessun altro.
              There's only the Supreme Court ... nothing else.

The interpreter – whose performance throughout the exchange is not impressive – does not understand the crucial term *provvedimento* (see Spencer-Oatey and Xing in this volume on interpreter behaviour). This has – prior to the section quoted here – already caused some annoyance on the lawyer's part, who came to believe that his client wanted a *second* lawyer. In this section, the client can finally identify the problem, raise it *as a problem* (40c) and provide some knowledge to make the term less problematic (42a–42b). The interpreter begins to understand (43), but the lawyer, who has got some Italian too, cuts the conversation short by stating that there is only the institutionally provided path and no other. Mattel-Pegam writes (1985: 312; her emphasis):

The prisoner clearly has some idea about the meaning of the term [i.e. *provvedimento*]. But in his view *it is up to the expert to give the term precise mean-*

ing, i.e. up to the lawyer, whom the prisoner not only sees as a legal expert, but also as a helper. Hence it would have been necessary for the interpreter to give some explanation.

Within the framework of Redder and Rehbein (1987), this is an example of failed intercultural communication in a *broader sense*: The prisoner on the one side, and the lawyer and the interpreter on the other not only belong to different groups of actants, but also to different societies. They encounter a problem that points to differences in their cultural apparatus (here: knowledge about institutional paths and alternatives as well as about the function of institutional agents). The actants on the institutional side and their client act *ethnocentrically* in that they assume mutual validity of their presuppositions. Otherwise the client would not have readily assumed the existence of a *provvedimento*, and the lawyer and the interpreter would have expected some reference to alternative remedies. The three interactants make no use of the critical potential of their cultural apparatus. None of them reaches their goal: The client, instead of a proper explanation, receives what can only be called a *rebuff* in illocutionary terms (44). The lawyer and the interpreter are not quite sure why the client wished to consult them in the first place.

Since all interactants act ethnocentrically, why does the transcript seem to transmit a strong sense that the client is being treated unfairly? This is due to the institutional asymmetry: The agents can afford to act ethnocentrically. Their client, however, cannot. As he does, the agents can make him "[…] accept what he has not understood" (Mattel-Pegam 1985: 322). Mattel-Pegam aligns herself with Gumperz (1978) when she concludes that because of institutional power structures and role-specific behaviour institutional agents usually do not all become aware of the failure of intercultural communication (Mattel-Pegam 1985: 322, Gumperz and Cook-Gumperz in this volume).

In the light of the discussions above, I feel that this point can be elaborated: Even when agent and client belong to the same society and speak the same language, institutional communication is already intercultural communication in the narrow sense. And because of this it has a similar potential of failure. Research into institutional communication (e.g. Ehlich 1980; Rehbein 1985b; Löning and Rehbein 1993; Redder and Wiese 1994) reveals that agents have a very strong tendency to act "ethnocentrically" also with clients belonging to their own society – i.e. with the majority who considers this as "normal". An (ethnic) minority, however, is *qua se* not yet part of societal normality – otherwise it would not be perceived as such. Hence it is more likely that institutional change is, in the long run, brought about by the ramifications of intercultural communication failure in the broader sense. Ironically, society as a whole is likely to profit from the pain its institutions cause (ethnic) minorities.

3.2.   Dominant knowledge – a productive failure of intercultural science transfer

The relationship between first world donor countries and third world recipients of foreign aid is – for obvious reasons – highly asymmetrical. Foreign aid can be used as an instrument of power (for the complex interrelation between political and economic interests behind foreign aid see Schmidt [2003]). It is even more disturbing, however, when measures undertaken "within a responsible and constructive approach to the question of development aid" (Schmidt 2003: 507) seem to backfire. The steel plant at Rourkela, India, which was built with German aid, is a case in point: While this technology transfer has generated growth and employment, its impact on the region has resulted in substantial environmental and social problems such as the displacement of tribal populations (Meher 2003).

Science and knowledge transfer to developing countries is technology transfer's silent companion. Science transfer appears to be devoid of the interests behind foreign aid, and – because it involves scientists on both sides – to be somehow even immunized against intercultural communication problems. Yet the following brief case study may show that intercultural science transfer has the potential of being a silent instantiation of dominance in intercultural communication.

In the late 1960s, Muhammad Yunus from Bangladesh – on whose book (Yunus and Jolis 1998) this section is based – completed his doctorate in Economics at Vanderbilt University in Nashville, Tennessee. In 1972 he returned to Bangladesh as a lecturer for economics at the University of Chittagong. The great famine of 1974 made him aware of the limits of his knowledge: "I remember very well the enthusiasm with which I taught my students the solutions economic theories provided for all sorts of economic problems. I was enthralled by the beauty and elegance of these theories. But all of a sudden I realised the futility of my efforts. What was their point when everywhere, on the pavements and in front of the doors, people were dying from starvation?" (Yunus and Jolis 1998: 17). Yunus stopped teaching equations of economic theory. Instead, he and his students began to study empirically the reasons for poverty in their country. They soon found out three things: Most of the poor of their country ran small businesses. They stayed poor because in order to set up their businesses they had to borrow money from money lenders who charged ursurious rates. The poor would not be eligible for a bank loan, however, because they had nothing to offer as a material collateral. Yunus realized that the concept of "collateral" could be reinterpreted: "Collateral" did not have to be anything material, it could also consist of the clients' economic potential within their social network. This was the principle upon which Yunus developed his – profit making – Grameen bank, which meanwhile operates successfully in more than fifty thousand villages in Bangladesh.

The conceptual implications of this productive failure of intercultural science transfer are very intricate (for a detailed analysis see Thielmann [2004: 296–302]). Here I shall focus on the intercultural dimension, which – on a large scale – displays parallels to what has been said in Section 2.3. about power and dominance within intercultural communication at school.

Yunus studied economics in a Western country. In the terms of the previous analyses, he started out as a client of a foreign university and returned as a lecturer, as an institutional agent. As a client, he did not act ethnocentrically. On the contrary, he embraced the new knowledge. He willingly expanded his cultural apparatus. As an agent, being "enthralled by the beauty and elegance" of the theories he had studied, he passed this knowledge on. He acted as a multiplier within global science transfer – and he, unknowingly, was instrumental in imposing Western societal problem solutions on a society that worked differently. I shall argue that Yunus' initial ethnocentrism was due to the tacit assumptions behind the theories he studied in America.

As Toulmin (2001: 47–66) demonstrates in his insightful chapter "Economics or the physics that never was", Western economic theory formation was highly influenced by early modern physics, especially by Newton's theory of planetary motion. Yet by the beginning of the 19th century, physicists already knew that the solar system is much less stable than Newtonian law suggests. Economists of the 20th century, however, were still modelling their theories in the tradition of their predecessors, i.e. after a physics "that never was". In accordance with an early interdisciplinary science transfer gone sour without their knowledge, they expected their theories to hold, like a natural law, everywhere at any point in time. They did not expect them to be subject to variations of societal makeup. This had major consequences for intercultural science transfer: The knowledge that economic laws possess a status close to natural laws formed an integral part of economists' cultural apparatus. They tended to conceive of economic laws as universally applicable problem solutions, as a *set of recipes* that could be readily passed on as such.

Within intercultural science and knowledge transfer, the ethnocentricity that lies in passing on knowledge based on such a presupposition is, however, not likely to reveal itself: The appeal of recipes that supposedly hold for any society makes multipliers uncritically reproduce their inbuilt ethnocentricity – with potentially disastrous consequences for the society that imports solutions to problems that are not its own.

The powerful corrective of 1974's famine made Yunus fall back on another part of his education: empirical methodology. His studies yielded economic laws specific to his society, on the basis of which concrete measures for improvement could be put into place.

I have conducted this discussion without any reference to powerful institutions such as the World Bank or interest-driven policies of donor countries, etc. The reason why I could do so is, I believe, quite evident: Even if these players had behaved genuinely altruistically, they would still have been prone to act on the basis of a knowledge the ethnocentricity of which they were not aware of.

3.3.   Linguistic expansion (Sprachausbau) under postcolonial duress

santa Maria   nijéit – chu
                fuck   neg.
(*virgo intacta* in Shuara; from Kummer 1985: 127)

Nowhere perhaps are power and dominance in intercultural communication felt more strongly about than in the area of – to put it neutrally – language maintenance. "Languages differ in their linguistic devices and purposes. Beyond this they differ in the forms of representation and practices, i.e. in the cultural apparatus, tied to them." (Redder and Rehbein 1987: 19). This complex interrelation is the basis for nation building via aggressive language policy (e.g. Hill 2002; Mikula 2002), maintenance of minority languages (e.g. Aklif 1999; Clyne 2004; Hatoss 2004) and issues of language planning and "ecology" (e.g. Gundara 1999; Mühlhäusler 2000; Liddicoat and Muller 2002b). As can be seen from most of these studies, linguists and policy makers alike make frequent use of the concept of *identity* – which is unfortunate, as this concept is as much of an *explanandum* as the culture concept. For if one just takes "identity" in a minimalist sense, say, "that which holds out against another", the concept can be applied to the major part of the material world as well as to mental entities such as thoughts in the sense of Frege (1967). Also the ecological metaphor tends to lose its descriptive merits very quickly when it is used to re-introduce, after the Darwinist speculations of the 19th century, biological notions to societal and linguistic processes (Finke 1996).

I therefore believe that an understanding of these issues is facilitated by trying to look at the purposes that generate them:

Nation building usually occurs amongst societies that are very similar. Its purpose is territorial and is best achieved by making political and linguistic borders coincide in people's minds (Auer 2004). Dragosavljevič (2002) illustrates how aggressive language policy instrumentalizes the tiny differences between Ijekavian and Ekavian to ultimately create different countries within former Yugoslavia.

The issue of language maintenance frequently arises in postcolonial societies that comprise – very different – indigenous societies. Tradition and communication in these societies are mostly oral. If they lose their languages, they do not lose "identity", they lose their cultural apparatus. They lose society as such. "If people don't have their land and language, they will be lost. They won't know the names of the hills or waterholes, the trees or the animals. They won't know the dreaming stories for their country." (Deegan 1999: v).

For an indigenous society within a postcolonial environment there are three principal paths of further development:

a) It survives intact, i.e. its members can survive in the traditional way.
b) Part of the tradition is lost, the rest is maintained. The truncated indigenous society is supported as a resource (e.g. for tourism) by the postcolonial society and/or by members who are also integrated in the postcolonial society.
c) The indigenous society is completely absorbed by the postcolonial society.

I shall now focus on a society that has taken a fourth, alternative route of *linguistic expansion* ('Sprachausbau'): the Shuar of the Ecuadorian Amazon. My reflections are chiefly based on Kummer (1985).

After the Shuar had successfully resisted colonization attempts until the late 19th century, Salesian missionaries succeeded in establishing schools and administration, which in turn brought more and more colonists to the Shuar territory. While the major part of the acephalous Shuar society retained its language and traditional ways, a smaller part was integrated in the colonial society. Further change occurred when the Ecuadorian government required land for more colonists during the 1960s. The missionaries, whose contract with the government was cancelled in 1966, ensured their institutional survival by assisting the Shuar in setting up their own administration: the *Federación de los Centros Shuar*. The Shuar language, whose status had suffered during the first colonization period, became an important instrument to unify the Shuar against the new colonists. It was also made a language of instruction in the Federation's bilingual school system. Missionaries and their former Shuar students designed lessons in accordance with Ecuador's curriculum. These lessons were then radio broadcast to the remote *Centros*. There they were passed on to children by assistant teachers. According to Almeida (2004), the Catholic influence has been meanwhile reduced and the Bi-cultural Shuar Radio Education System (SERBISH) "provides education for about 7,500 children – out of a Shuar population of 70,000 – in 297 schools teaching from primary to the end of the secondary level". During this process, the Shuar language had to be linguistically expanded to render concepts of the modern, Spanish speaking postcolonial society.

As can be seen from the brief example at the beginning of this section, first attempts at the linguistic expansion of Shuara were made by missionaries – who were also the first to write the language. "Holiness" and "virginity" were not part of the Shuar's cultural apparatus; thus *santa* was left as part of the name and "virginity" was rendered via the neutral concept of intercourse, *nijéit* – for which there does not seem to be a neutral term in Western languages (Kummer 1985: 127).

The modern linguistic expansion of Shuara occurred within a few decades. Kummer discusses various sections from Shuar school books, from which I have compiled a small word list to show some examples of expansion of the lexicon (the numbers in brackets refer to the pages of Kummer's article):

Table 1. Expansion of the lexicon in Shuara

Shuar word	Literal translation	Intended meaning	Reference
tuntui	drum	radio	(131, 133)
tsuramta	fit, seizure	electricity	(132, 133)
uunt kunkuim	big turtle	truck	(132, 133)
chikich kunkuim	small turtle	car	(132, 133)
irun-mia-yi	there lived	there were	(136, 137)
jiru (from Span. 'hierro')	iron	iron	(145, 146)
mahin	machine	machine	(145, 146)
mahin tante	machine that turns	turbine	(145, 146)
entsa kya aaniun katsurman	something strong that is similar to a rock in water	dam	(145, 146)
takamtiktai	a means that is made work	slave	(140, 142)
nekainiachiat (for Span. 'inculto')	someone who knows nothing	uneducated person	(140, 142)

Apart from the loan words *jiru* and *mahin*, the linguistic devices employed to render new concepts are exclusively Shuar. The strategies include metaphorization ("drum" for "radio") and paraphrase ("something strong that is similar to a rock in water" for "dam"). These terms and phrases are *motivated* (Ricken 1995) in that the new concept is, however vaguely, linked to knowledge already there – which facilitates recollection. The form *takamtiktai* 'slave' is the result of word formation: "(…) the suffix -tai (…) designates a person or a thing that is used as a means for an action. This suffix is one of the most important productive elements to derive terms for appliances that are new to the culture from the activities characteristic for these appliances." (Kummer 1985: 143). Another structural device used frequently by the translators is the verbal suffix -iti which allows the attribution of processes to entities. This new and frequent usage of structural devices "leads to new syntactic registers that – to ensure accessibility of the new text types – need to remain close to the traditional registers." (Kummer 1985: 147).

At a first glance none of the linguistic expansion strategies discussed here is in any way surprising. When European vernacular languages were expanded for the purpose of doing science, all of these strategies were used in one way or another (for German see Wolff [1733] 1973, [1713] 1978; Ricken 1995; Ehlich 1995; for Italian Thielmann 2003). But these expansions were not only a slow process, they also occurred on the basis of concepts that were already known to the scientific community by their Latin terms.

Yet the Shuar language was expanded within a few decades to accommodate the complete cultural apparatus of postcolonial Ecuador as it is represented by the National Curriculum. New concepts were rendered by new terms in a language of instruction stretched to the limits. The language was made "do the splits". So were – presumably – the students when in this language they learned about societal solutions to problems alien to their society. As for the linguistic difficulties during the process of linguistic expansion, Kummer writes (1985, 141): "Within the analytical sections of the school book texts, the shift in the frequencies of certain syntactic connection devices and their unusual combination results in a syntax the average speaker of Shuar cannot decode. (…) Even teachers who have to work with these texts can only reproduce the parts of a complex sentence, but not the complex sentence as a whole. As a result, students taught by these teachers do not understand these complex sentences either. It would require a larger study to determine whether the new syntactic registers created in the school book language are gradually going to be accepted by the ethnic community, or whether education in their own language is going to fail for reasons such as the large distance between traditional syntax and the new register."

According to Almeira (2004) the experiment has worked and enjoys the Shuar's full support: "In the search for an alternative to modernization imposed from above, the Shuar have managed to reduce semi-illiteracy to seven per cent and total illiteracy to two per cent." "Relying on their organizational strength, they now have some very ambitious projects, including one for an educational television station, for which they are seeking foreign technical assistance and funding."

The Shuar survived as a society because they codified, institutionalized and expanded their language. Stretched to its very limits, this language at least partially mediates and reconciles two extremely different cultural apparatus in a way that gives the society a genuine opportunity to determine its own future within postcolonial Ecuador.

Even in the light of this, it is still possible to argue that the linguistic expansion of Shuara is equivalent to the Shuar's final colonization and that the society's traditional ways will suffer. But such a view would presuppose authenticity as desirable for indigenous societies in a postcolonial context. It would neglect the fact that the only authentic indigenous societies are those still un-known. The only way to preserve the "authenticity" of a known indigenous so-ciety is to limit contact and to make sure they cannot communicate their own in-terests in a world that to them will never be the same nevertheless.

4.   Conclusion

Power and dominance within intercultural communication are due to asymmetri-cal constellations within three different instances of reality: societal structure, actants' knowledge and language. I have discussed three particular asymmetries with regard to these instances: the agent-client asymmetry of institutions; tacit ethnocentrism of knowledge within intercultural science transfer; and linguistic expansion of an indigenous language under postcolonial duress.

Interaction within institutions is paradigmatic for intercultural communi-cation in a narrow sense: Even when agents and clients speak the same language, their cultural apparatus differ. School, which is concerned with the expansion of its clients' cultural apparatus, is an extreme example of an institution whose in-trinsic contradictions make it perpetuate its permanent intercultural communi-cation failure. Institutional asymmetries compound the difficulties for intercultu-ral communication in a broader sense: As agents can get away with behaving ethnocentrically, their clients may not find advice, but encounter a rebuff.

Intercultural science transfer is a complex process in institutional terms, as multipliers are former clients turned agents. If the knowledge they are meant to spread is based on ethnocentric presuppositions, they will act ethnocentrically in spreading it – which will have ramifications for the society intended to profit from this knowledge.

Indigenous languages are usually not equipped to render the cultural appar-atus of the postcolonial administrative languages they are in competition with. This puts them in a fragile position.

The problems of power and dominance in intercultural communication thus analysed cannot be resolved by "removing" power and dominance. As far as institutions can at all reconcile their intrinsic contradictions, ethnocentric behaviour of agents can be overcome by intercultural training and guidelines. Intercultural science transfer should, on principle, be perceived as intercultural communication in a broader sense, i.e. the knowledge transferred should be con-ceived of as a problem solution specific to the society that solved the problem for itself. On principle, indigenous languages can be expanded to mediate and rec-oncile the cultural apparatus of both the indigenous and the postcolonial society, so that the indigenous society has a genuine opportunity to determine its own fu-ture. As the case of the Shuar has shown, this necessitates circumstances and pre-requisites that enable the indigenous society to design its own language policy.

References

Aklif, Gedda
  1999   *Ardiyooloon Bardi Ngaanka. One Arm Point Bardi Dictionary*. Halls
          Creek,WA: Kimberly Language Resource Centre.
Almeida, Marcos
  2004   Shuara, a language that refused to die. In: *UNESCO Courier* 2004: 4
          (http://www.unesco.org/courier/2000_04/uk/doss23.htm, 7. 12. 04).
Auer, Peter
  2004   Sprache, Grenze, Raum. *Zeitschrift für Sprachwissenschaft* 23(2): 149–179.
Bosworth, Richard and Janis Wilton
  1984   *Old Worlds and New Australia. The Post-War Migrant Experience*. Ring-
          wood (Australia): Penguin.
Brünner, Gisela and Gabriele Graefen (eds.)
  1994   *Texte und Diskurse. Methoden und Forschungsergebnisse der Funktionalen
          Pragmatik*. Opladen: Westdeutscher Verlag.
Clyne, Michael
  2004   Languages taken at school and languages spoken in the community – a com-
          parative perspective. *Australian Review of Applied Linguistics* 27(2): 1–17.
Deegan, Bonnie
  1999   Foreword to the One Arm Point Bardi Dictionary. In: Gedda Aklif (ed.),
          Ardiyooloon Bardi Ngaanka. One Arm Point Bardi Dictionary. Halls Creek,
          WA: Kimberly Language Resource Centre.
Dragosavljevič, Andjelija
  2002   Language and politics in the Republika Srpska. In: Anthony Liddicoat and
          Karis Muller (eds.), *Perspectives on Europe. Language Issues and Lan-
          guage Planning in Europe*, 141–152. Melbourne: Language Australia.
Eades, Diana
  this volume Understanding Aboriginal silence in legal contexts. Chapter 14.
Ehlich, Konrad (ed.)
  1980   *Erzählen im Alltag*. Frankfurt a. M.: Suhrkamp.
Ehlich, Konrad
  1995   Die Lehre der deutschen Wissenschaftssprache: sprachliche Strukturen,
          didaktische Desiderate. In: Leo Kretzenbacher and Harald Weinrich (eds.),
          Linguistik der Wissenschaftssprache (Akademie der Wissenschaften zu
          Berlin. Forschungsbericht 10), 325–352. Berlin: de Gruyter.
Ehlich, Konrad
  1996   Interkulturelle Kommunikation. In: Hans Goebl and Peter H. Nelde (eds.),
          *Kontaktlinguistik. Ein internationales Handbuch zeitgenössischer For-
          schung*, 920–931. Berlin/New York: de Gruyter.
Ehlich, Konrad and Jochen Rehbein
  1977   Wissen, kommunikatives Handeln und die Schule. In: Herma C. Goeppert
          (ed.), *Sprachverhalten im Unterricht. Zur Kommunikation von Lehrer und
          Schüler in der Unterrichtssituation*, 36–114. München: Fink.
Ehlich, Konrad and Jochen Rehbein
  1979   Sprachliche Handlungsmuster. In: Hans Georg Soeffener (ed.), *Interpreta-
          torische Verfahren in den Sozial- und Textwissenschaften*, 243–274. Stutt-
          gart: Metzler.

Ehlich, Konrad and Jochen Rehbein
    1986   *Muster und Institution. Untersuchungen zur schulischen Kommunikation.*
            Tübingen: Narr.
Fairclough, Norman
    (in print) Critical discourse analysis in researching language in the new capitalism:
            Overdetermination, transdisciplinarity and textual analysis. In: Claire Har-
            rison and Lynne Young (eds.), *Systemic Functional Linguistics and Critical
            Discourse Analysis.* London/New York: Continuum.
Finke, Peter
    1996   Sprache als *missing link* zwischen natürlichen und kulturellen Ökosystemen.
            Überlegungen zur Weiterentwicklung der Sprachökologie. In: Alwin Fill
            (ed.), *Sprachökologie und Ökolinguistik*, 27–48. Tübingen: Stauffenburg.
Frege, Gottlob
    1967   Begriff und Gegenstand. In: Ignacio Angelleli (ed.), *Gottlob Frege, Kleine
            Schriften*, 167–178. Hildesheim: Olms.
Goeppert, Herma C. (ed.)
    1977   *Sprachverhalten im Unterricht. Zur Kommunikation von Lehrer und Schü-
            ler in der Unterrichtssituation.* München: Fink.
Gramsci, Antonio
    1983   *Marxismus und Kultur. Ideologie, Alltag, Literatur* (transl. and ed. by Sa-
            bine Kebir). Hamburg: VSA.
Gumperz, John
    1978   The conversational analysis of interethnic communication. In: E. Lamar
            Ross (ed.), *Interethnic Communication. Proceedings of the Southern An-
            thropological Society*, 305–325. University of Georgia Press.
Gumperz, John and Jenny Cook-Gumperz
    this volume Discourse, cultural diversity and communication: a linguistic anthropologi-
            cal perspective. Chapter 2.
Gundara, Jagdish
    1999   Linguistic Diversity, Globalisation and Intercultural Education. In: Joe
            Lo Bianco, Anthony J. Liddicoat and Chantal Crozet (eds.) *Striving for the
            Third Place. Intercultural Competence through Language Education*,
            23–42. Melbourne: Language Australia.
Günthner, Susanne and Thomas Luckmann
    1995   *Asymmetries of Knowledge in Intercultural Communication: The Relevance
            of Cultural Repertoire of Communicative Genres.* Konstanz: Fachgruppe
            Sprachwissenschaft der Universität Konstanz, Arbeitspapier Nr. 72.
Günthner, Susanne
    this volume Gumperz, John and Cook-Gumperz, Jenny in this volume Discourse, cul-
            tural diversity and communication: a linguistic anthropological perspec-
            tive. Chapter 2.
Harrison, Claire and Lynne Young
    2004   *Systemic Functional Linguistics and Critical Discourse Analysis.* London/
            New York: Continuum.
Hatoss, Anikó
    2004   Mother tongue maintenance and acculturation in two vintages of the Hun-
            garian diaspora in Queensland. *Australian Review of Applied Linguistics*
            27(2): 18–31.

Herder, Johann Gottfried
1997 [1772] *Abhandlung über den Ursprung der Sprache.* Stuttgart: Reclam.
Hill, Peter M.
2002   Language and national identity. In: Anthony Liddicoat and Karis Muller
        (eds.), *Perspectives on Europe. Language Issues and Language Planning in
        Europe*, 11–20. Melbourne: Language Australia.
Hoffmann, Ludger
1980   Zur Pragmatik von Erzählformen vor Gericht. In: Konrad Ehlich (ed.), *Er-
        zählen im Alltag*, 28–64. Frankfurt a. M.: Suhrkamp.
Hoffmann, Ludger
1983   *Kommunikation vor Gericht.* Tübingen: Narr.
Hoffmann, Ludger (ed.)
1989   *Rechtsdiskurse.* Tübingen: Narr.
Hoffmann, Ludger
2002   Rechtsdiskurse zwischen Normalität und Normativität. In: Ulrike Haß-
        Zumkehr (ed.), *Sprache und Recht*, 80–100. Berlin/New York: de Gruyter.
Koerfer, Armin
1994   Interkulturelle Kommunikation vor Gericht. Verständigungsprobleme beim
        fremdsprachlichen Handeln in einer kommunikationsintensiven Institution.
        In: Gisela Brünner and Gabriele Graefen (eds.), *Texte und Diskurse. Metho-
        den und Forschungsergebnisse der funktionalen Pragmatik*, 351–373. Opla-
        den: Westdeutscher Verlag.
Kügelgen, Rainer v.
1994   *Diskurs Mathematik. Kommunikationsanalysen zum reflektierenden Lernen*
        (Arbeiten zur Sprachanalyse 17). Frankfurt a. M.: Lang.
Kummer, Werner
1985   Probleme der Funktionserweiterung von Sprachen: Der Sprachausbau bei
        den Shuara in Ecuador. In: Jochen Rehbein (ed.), *Interkulturelle Kommuni-
        kation*, 166–174. Tübingen: Narr.
Liddicoat, Anthony and Karis Muller (eds.)
2002a   *Perspectives on Europe. Language Issues and Language Planning in Eu-
        rope.* Melbourne: Language Australia.
Liddicoat, Anthony and Karis Muller
2002b   Language issues and language planning in Europe. In: Anthony Liddicoat
        and Karis Muller (eds.), *Perspectives on Europe. Language Issues and Lan-
        guage Planning in Europe*, 1–10. Melbourne: Language Australia.
Lo Bianco, Joe, Anthony Liddicoat and Chantal Crozet (eds.)
1999   *Striving for the Third Place. Intercultural Competence through Language
        Education.* Melbourne: Language Australia.
Löning, Petra and Jochen Rehbein (eds.)
1993   *Arzt-Patienten-Kommunikation. Analysen zu interdisziplinären Problemen
        des medizinischen Diskurses.* Berlin/New York: de Gruyter.
Mattel-Pegam, Gesine
1985   Ein italienischer Strafgefangener konsultiert einen deutschen Rechtsan-
        walt. In: Jochen Rehbein (ed.), *Interkulturelle Kommunikation*, 299–323.
        Tübingen: Narr.
McIlvenny, Paul
1992   Missing an important transition relevance point: Towards a critical conver-

sation analysis. In: Leena Kuure and Paul McIlvenny (eds.), *Text and Talk. Proceedings of the 4th Discourse Analysis Seminar*, Oulu, October 1992, 87–112. Oulu (Finland): University of Oulu.

Meher, Rajkishor
  2003   The social and ecological effects of industrialisation in a tribal region: The case of the Rourkela Steel Plant. *Contributions to Indian Sociology* 37(3): 429–457.

Meierkord, Christiane
this volume Lingua franca communication in multiethnic contexts. Chapter 10.

Mikula, Maja
  2002   Croatia's independence and the language politics of the 1990s. In: Anthony Liddicoat and Karis Muller (eds.), *Perspectives on Europe. Language Issues and Language Planning in Europe*, 109–123. Melbourne: Language Australia.

Mühlhäusler, Peter
  2000   Language planning and language ecology. *Current Issues in Language Planning* 1(3): 306–367.

Redder, Angelika and Jochen Rehbein
  1987   Zum Begriff der Kultur. *Osnabrücker Beiträge zur Sprachtheorie (OBST)* 38: 7–21.

Redder, Angelika and Ingrid Wiese (eds.)
  1994   *Medizinische Kommunikation: Diskurspraxis, Diskursethik, Diskursanalyse*. Opladen: Westdeutscher Verlag.

Rehbein, Jochen
  1997   *Komplexes Handeln. Elemente zur Handlungstheorie der Sprache*. Stuttgart: Metzler.

Rehbein, Jochen (ed.)
  1985a   *Interkulturelle Kommunikation*. Tübingen: Narr.

Rehbein, Jochen
  1985b   Medizinische Beratung türkischer Eltern. In: Jochen Rehbein (ed.), *Interkulturelle Kommunikation*, 349–419 Tübingen: Narr.

Ricken, Ulrich
  1995   Zum Thema Christian Wolff und die Wissenschaftssprache der deutschen Aufklärung. In: Leo Kretzenbacher and Harald Weinrich (eds.), *Linguistik der Wissenschaftssprache* (Akademie der Wissenschaftssprachen zu Berlin. Forschungsbericht 10), 41–90. Berlin: de Gruyter.

Scherr, Albert
this volume Schools and Cultural Difference. Chapter 16.

Schmidt, Heide-Irene
  2003   Pushed to the front: The foreign assistance policy of the Federal Republic of Germany. *Contemporary European History* 12(4): 473–507.

Schröder, Hartmut
  2000   Sprachliche Aspekte der Kommunikation von Ausländern vor Gerichten. In: Gerhard Wolf (ed.), *Kriminalität im Grenzgebiet. Bd. 3: Ausländer vor deutschen Gerichten*, 269–284. Berlin/Heidelberg/New York: Springer.

Spencer-Oatey, Helen and Jianyu Xing
this volume The impact of culture on interpreter behaviour. Chapter 11.

Thielmann, Winfried
2002   The problem of English as the *lingua franca* of scholarly writing from a German perspective. In: Anthony Liddicoat and Karis Muller (eds.), *Perspectives on Europe. Language Issues and Language Planning in Europe*, 95–108 Melbourne: Language Australia.
Thielmann, Winfried
2003   Wege aus dem sprachpolitischen Vakuum? Zur scheinbaren wissenschaftskulturellen Neutralität wissenschaftlicher Universalsprachen. In: Konrad Ehlich (ed.), *Mehrsprachige Wissenschaft – europäische Perspektiven. Eine Konferenz im Europäischen Jahr der Sprachen.* www.euro-sprachen-jahr.de/.
Thielmann, Winfried
2004   Begriffe als Handlungspotentiale – Überlegungen zu einer Klärung des Phänomens der 'Bedeutung' einiger fach- bzw. wissenschaftssprachlicher Symbolfeldausdrücke. *Linguistische Berichte* 199: 287–311.
Thwaite, Anne
2004   Classroom discourse of an experienced teacher of indigeneous children. *Australian Review of Applied Linguistics* 27(2): 75–91.
Toulmin, Stephen
2001   *Return to Reason.* Cambridge, MA: Harvard University Press.
Van Dijk, Teun (ed.)
1985   *Handbook of Discourse Analysis.* Volume 4. *Discourse Analysis in Society.* London: Academic Press.
Wodak, Ruth
1985   The interaction between judge and defendant. In: Teun A. Van Dijk (ed.), *Handbook of Discourse Analysis.* Volume 4. *Discourse Analysis in Society*, 181–191. London: Academic Press.
Wolff, Christian
1978 [1713] *Ausführliche Nachricht von seinen eigenen Schriften, die er in deutscher Sprache heraus gegeben* (Facsimile of the edition from 1733; Gesammelte Werke 1. Abt. Bd. 9). Hildesheim: Olms.
Wolff, Christian
1973 [1733] *Vernünfftige Gedanken von den Kräften des menschlichen Verstandes und ihrem richtigen Gebrauch in Erkenntniß der Wahrheit (Deutsche Logik).* Hildesheim: Olms.
Yunus, Muhammad and Allan Jolis
1998   *Grameen – eine Bank für die Armen der Welt.* Bergisch Gladbach: Lübbe.

20. Communicating Identity in Intercultural Communication

Janet Spreckels and Helga Kotthoff

When studying intercultural communication, the question automatically arises of the identities through which individuals encounter each other and how this encounter can be analyzed. When an Italian and a Swedish surgeon jointly perform an operation in Zurich, their national identities are not necessarily important. What is relevant under the given circumstances is that both are surgeons, can communicate with each other, and who has more experience in performing particular surgical procedures. In order to discuss, in the second part of the article, the various procedures which set cultural categorization as relevant, in the first part the conceptualization of "identity" will be outlined.[1]

1. Social identity

The concept of *social identity* arose in social psychology and was, among others, developed by the social psychologists Henri Tajfel, Joseph Forgas and Jim Turner. Tajfel (1982: 2) defines the concept of social identity as follows:

> Social identity will be understood as that *part* of the individuals' self-concept which derives from their knowledge of their membership of a social group (or groups) together with the value and emotional significance attached to that membership.

Social identity is thus the part of an individual's self-concept that is derived from her/his knowledge of her/his membership in social groups and from the emotional significance with which this membership is endowed. Tajfel's emphasis on "part" can be understood if one considers the other part of the self-concept, 'personal' identity. The concept of this division of the 'self' into two parts goes back to the social psychologist George Herbert Mead. In his major work, *Mind, Self and Society* (1934), he developed an interactionist paradigm of identity that contains the reflexive ability of the subject to behave toward himself and toward others. Identity accordingly has two components:

i. a social component, the so-called 'me' and
ii. a personal component (also the personal, individual, subject or self) component, the 'I'

Mead thereby paved the way for the later concept of the 'social' vs. the 'personal' identity, without, however, himself using these terms. The social component of identity worked out by Mead develops through the growth of the individual into his socio-cultural surroundings and is derived from identification with various social collectivities, such as, e.g., a family, sport association or peer group of which the individual understands himself to be a part. Social identity is thus a part of the self worked out in the socio-cultural life context. Personal identity, to the contrary, refers to the uniqueness of the individual in connection with his unmistakable life history (Hillmann 1994: 350–53) and is "something like the continuity of the I" (Habermas 1968). Krappmann (1978: 39) summarizes this dichotomy as follows:

> Obviously, identity is both simultaneously: the anticipated expectations of the other and the individual's own answers. G.H. Mead took this dual aspect of identity into account in his concept of the self, which contains a "me" that is the adopted attitudes of the other, and an "I," the individual's answer to the expectations of the others.

Although most authors usually speak of 'identity' in the singular, "each social identity is just one among many [...] which each individual possesses" (Schwitalla & Streeck 1989: 237), because "the uniqueness of individuals lies in their blend of multiple social and personal identities" (Meyerhoff 1996: 215). We all take various roles in everyday life (as daughter, girlfriend, member of a sport club, etc.), affiliate with various social groups and thereby mark out a variety of social identities. Individuals construct their social identities on the basis of various socially and culturally relevant parameters, such as nationality, gender, age, profession, lifestyle, etc. (Duszak 2002: 2 and Keupp et al. 2002: 68). The concept of social identity must therefore be understood as multi-sided and very dynamic.

Today it is commonplace in social psychology to think of identity as the processual and never-ending task of each person (see Brabant, Watson and Gallois in this volume), but this was not always the case. In the older literature there were occasionally static concepts which portrayed biography and identity "as something stable, permanent and unchangeable" (Keupp et al. 2002: 22). Such approaches, which portray identity as a sort of goal to be achieved, can however not be upheld in view of empirical studies and an increasingly multi-facetted society. Already Mead (1934) pointed in his interactionist approach to the constructive and negotiated character of social identity and emphasized that identity is by no means a quantity that is set once and for all, but rather is constantly being negotiated in interaction. More recently, this important aspect has often been emphasized, thus, e.g., Duszak (2002: 2) has written, "social identities tend to be indeterminate, situational rather than permanent, dynamic and interactively constructed."

1.1.   Modern patchwork identities

If the construction of identity, as described above, is a lifelong process, this dynamism and changeability simultaneously pose the danger of an inconsistent identity. Our modern world is marked by accelerated processes of change, greater geographic and social mobility, freedom to form attachments, the pluralization of life forms and worldviews, and progressive individualization. Thereby each individual's possible identity spectrum has considerably increased: "While earlier the development of identity was much more strongly marked by the position into which one was born, modern man is forced to choose among many possibilities, and this struggle of youth with the required choice of a self-definition is […] referred to as an identity crisis" (Oerter and Dreher 1995: 348; Baumeister 1986; Luckmann et al. 1981).

A key term in the contemporary process of finding an identity is 'possibility of choice': "modernity confronts the individual with a *complex diversity of choices* and … at the same time offers little help as to which options should be selected" (Giddens 1991: 80, emphasis added). Where previously there was little possibility of choice, today individuals face a life-world variety of experiences that on the one side frees them, but on the other side leaves them deeply insecure and partly overtaxed. Schäfers (2001: 92) points out that identity problems only arise in social systems like the present ones. Giddens (1991: 81) aptly describes this situation with the insight: "[W]e have no choice but to choose."

Certain basic, self-evident aspects of our society are being put in question and shaken by new alternatives. Today there are, e.g., various models of the most important social group upon which society is based: the family. The emancipation movement brought about the possibility for the classical role models of the devoted mother and housewife and the father as family breadwinner to be challenged and revised. Certainly there are still a large number of families with traditional role assignments, but besides this, today there are also some families where the wife 'brings home the bacon' while the husband takes a parental leave of absence. In addition, there are single mothers and fathers, commuter families, homosexual couples with children, so-called 'patchwork families' that result from the founding of families after respectively terminated partnerships, etc. Family relationships are today anything but clearly defined and therefore no longer serve to the same degree as previously as stable references for identity. The family is only one area of societal life that has lost stability in the course of socio-cultural change; besides it one can name class membership, nation, professional world, religion, gender and generational relationships, sexuality and many others. Keupp et al. (2002: 87) therefore speak of the "dissolution of guarantees of coherency" and affirm that "even the core stocks of our identity constructions – national and ethnic identity, gender and body identity [have lost] their quasi-'natural' quality as guarantors of identity."

In the 1960s James Marcia, a student of Erikson, developed the identity model of his teacher, by constructing a differentiated model with four different identity states, the "identity status model" (Marcia 1966). He distinguishes among a) "achievement," i.e., an earned or developed identity, b) the "moratorium," a currently ongoing struggle with various value questions, c) "foreclosure," the adopted identity, mostly through the adoption of the value conceptions of the parents, and finally d) "identity diffusion," a state in which individuals have not yet reached a firm position on values. In order to grasp a person's current identity status, Marcia posed youthful subjects a series of questions in the frame of an "identity status interview" (concerning professions, religion, politics, etc.). His empirical studies (Marcia 1989) showed that the share of youth with diffuse identities had increased after ca. 1984 from 20% to ca. 40%. Marcia thereby offered an early proof that youth are becoming less inclined to "commit themselves to stable, binding and obligating – and in this sense identity-giving – relationships, orientations and values." (Keupp et al. 2002: 81).

This tendency has increased in recent years. In the so-called 'fun society' of today hedonistic, media-, experience- and consumer-oriented values play a commanding role, which simultaneously entails a large number of new possible identifications. Penelope Eckert (2000: 14) describes the situation of youth in modern times as a "marketplace of identities," and Baacke (1987) describes the life worlds of youths as "surfing between various experiential worlds." The result of these expanded possibilities of choice are modern identities that Elkind (1990) refers to as "patchwork identities." Such an identity is, as the metaphorical concept reveals, pieced together from individual "patches," namely partial-identities, and possesses no unified identity core. Oerter and Dreher (1995: 354) point out that persons with patchwork identities can be very successful, but no longer fulfill "the 'classical' criteria of a worked-out, integrated identity." In a patchwork-self, "value attitudes and customs are juxtaposed with no ties and in part contradict each other." (ibid.) The classical question of identity research, namely of how the individual succeeds in achieving a consistent identity from a variety of possibilities and thereby experiences herself, despite all the differences, as not torn, but rather coherent, thus is becoming increasingly important in modern times. Keupp and other psychologists take up Elkind's concept in a study entitled *The Patchwork of Identities in Late Modernity* and come to the conclusion that in many situations individuals by no means achieve a unified self (2002: 196). This is, however, neither possible nor necessary, since, "the constancy of the self does not consist in resolving all differences, but rather in enduring the resulting tensions and mastering constantly recurring crises." Modern identities are thus, on the one side, marked by more possibilities, to which the virtual communities of the internet have made a not inessential contribution, and, on the other side, however, also by more uncertainties. The construction of identity in youth can therefore take the form of an "open and often chaotic process of search." (Eckert et al. 2000: 17).

1.2.   Social categorization

Besides the so far presented complexity and changeability of social identity, the meaning of the 'other' forms the second central aspect for the constitution of the 'self'. As the initially formulated definition of social identity by Tajfel and others and the discussions above have made clear, this part of individual identity is derived from simultaneous membership in specific groups and demarcation from other groups: the development of a person's identity must be understood as "interdependent and inter-subjective" (Keupp et al. 2002: 138). We develop our identity not in a vacuum, but rather in and through the constant comparison of the self with other individuals and groups: "Only by comparing ourselves with others can we build up our affiliations and our non-alignments" (Duszak 2002: 1). Turner (1982: 17) therefore brings the concept of social identity together with a further central concept of identity research, social categorization:

> Social identification can refer to the process of locating oneself, or another person, within a system of social categorizations or, as a noun, to any social categorization used by a person to define him- or herself and others. [...] The sum total of the social identification used by a person to define him- or herself will be described as his or her *social identity*. Social categorizations define a person by systematically including them within some, and excluding them from other related categories. They state at the same time what a person is and is not.

Identity can thus only be grasped in a social context. Anyone who wants to do research on the social identities of individuals must therefore of necessity also take into account the relationships of these individuals to other persons and groups (Keupp et al. 2002: 67, Oerter and Dreher 1995: 361, Strauss 1969: 44), for from an "anthropological perspective identity is a *relationship* and not, as everyday language supposes, an individual characteristic" (Goussiaux cited in Keupp et al. 2002: 95). Identity and alterity are inseparably bound to one another, and hence Goussiaux formulates the question of identity not as 'Who am I?', but rather as "[W]ho am I in relationship to the others, who are the others in relationship to me?" Tajfel & Forgas (1981: 124) express this relationship with the intuitive formula: "We are what we are because they are not what we are." This fundamental aspect of relationships of social identity is constantly being emphasized in identity and categorization research. Since creating affinity with or respectively demarcation from others is often achieved using linguistic means, it is especially linguistic studies that have been dedicated to these processes (recently, e.g., Duszak 2002, Hausendorf and Kesselheim 2002, Androutsopoulos and Georgakopoulou 2003). Already in 1959, Anselm Strauss asserted: "Central to any discussion of identity is language" (1969: 15). Articles with titles like: "We, They and Identity" (Sebba and Wootton 1998), "Us and Others" (Duszak 2002), and "Us and Them" (Zhou 2002) point to the fact that without the 'they' no 'we' can exist.

Representations of self and other are embedded in processes of social categorization. Already Goffman (1963: 2) linked the term social identity and the concept of social category together: "When a stranger comes into our presence, then, first appearances are likely to enable us to anticipate his *category* and attributes, his *'social identity'*." He thus refers to the individual's category membership as social identity. In every interaction individuals consciously and unconsciously place themselves in relation to others and thereby perform a stranger- and self-categorization. Duszak (2002: 2) even speaks of the "impossibility of *non-othering*" (emphasis in original) and refers to social identities as the products of categorization processes "that fulfill the human needs of organizing experience for future access and use."

The concept of social categorization goes back to the sociologist Harvey Sacks. In the mid-1960s Sacks studied interaction processes, which he referred to as *social* or *membership categorization*. His *Lectures on Conversation* (and related topics from the social sciences), held in the 1960s and 1970s at the University of California, were first published by Gail Jefferson in 1992, after Sacks's death, and thereby stimulated new interest in categorization research. Sacks defines "membership categories" very broadly (but also very statically) as "known things," as units of societal knowledge.

1.3.   Category variety

There are a great variety and number of categories. Sacks (1992) refers to a small number of category collections that are applicable to everyone, such as gender, age/generation, confession, nation, etc., as basis collections. Some categories are more persistent than others: for example, individuals, other than transsexuals, usually retain their congenital biological gender for their entire lifetime, and we usually never change our nationality. Besides this, there are many categories to which people belong for only short periods of their lives. Between the ages of ca. 13 and 19 years persons belong to the age category "teenager," which, however, only constitutes a transitional stage and is followed by other age-related categories. Unlike such transitional categories, there are permanent ones which people keep for a lifetime, e.g., ethnic membership ("Asian"). In everyday life we encounter special categories that can be traced back to lifestyle preferences, as for example, heavy metal fan, environmentalist, inline-skater, and sexual preferences (heterosexual, homosexual, transvestite) and many others (Spreckels 2006).

There are categories that, without contextual knowledge, are neutral or at least can be (Portuguese, student, barber) and those whose designation can by definition contain an evaluation, thus, e.g., derogatory designations and invectives like Wog, Pollack or suck-up, idiot, slut, etc. This type of category, in which societal evaluations are anchored, are of particular interest to Jayyusi (1984) in her study *Categorization and the Moral Order*.

Often it makes a difference whether it is a matter of a self- or strangers' categorization. The category *greenie* (*Öko*), which is often named in the group communication of the girls in Spreckels's study (2006), is more of a strangers' categorization. Even if a dictionary merely refers to this short word as a 'humorous' term for a 'supporter of the ecology movement', the particular designation is often used in a derogatory sense. Members of the category would therefore probably not categorize themselves as *greenies*. The politically incorrect word 'nigger', if used by a white, is an expression of racism, while the same word, if used by a black, is a playful adaptation of the racist expression and a conscious profession of his ethnic origin (see chapter 18 by Reisigl in this volume). A jocular adoption of a strangers' attribution observed from outside was also studied by Schwitalla & Streeck (1989: 249) in a group of working-class youth who are viewed by adults as bothersome and unpleasant. By identifying with this strangers' attribution ("mir falle iwwerall uff" – "we stand out everywhere") they are performing an inversion of values. Categories can thus be used for discrimination, but they can also be played with.

1.4.   Social categories versus social groups

It is important to differentiate between the two concepts of 'social category' and 'social group', which are sometimes used as synonymous. Sacks himself emphasizes this difference (1979: 13).

> We're dealing [...] with a category. They're not groups. Most of the categories (women, old people, Negroes, Jews, teenagers, etc.) are not groups in any sense that you normally talk about groups, and yet what we have is a mass of knowledge known about every category, any member is seen as a representative of each of those categories; any person who is a case of a category is seen as a member of the category, and what's known about the category is known about them [...].

Besides Sacks, other researchers point to the important distinction between groups and categories. Thus, e.g., Turner writes (1982: 169): "In general ... [a] group has been conceptualized as some (usually) small collection of individuals in face-to-face relations of interaction, attraction and influence [...]" and demarcates from it social categories that he, drawing on Tajfel, refers to as the result of "discontinuous divisions of the social world into distinct classes" (Turner 1982: 17).

Often it cannot be determined to what extent categories coincide with reality, for in a certain sense we only create reality through categorization (Kesselheim 2003: 72). But this is exactly where we confront the danger of social categories. Kesselheim (p. 72) points out that categories are not completely arbitrary just because they are "created," "for they must prove themselves in societal action."

Each category is related, according to the respective circle of usage, to various "category-bound activities" (Sacks 1992: 568), thus 'typical' activities for all members of the category. We expand the Sacksian concept to the term "category-bound features," proposed by Jayyusi (1984: 35), thus category-bound characteristics that besides activities and modes of behavior also include aspects such as category-bound external appearance (clothing, hairstyle, political symbols, etc.), convictions, competencies, rights, etc.

Besides such categories, which refer back to a societal knowledge stock, there are also categories that are only understood by a narrow circle of persons (e.g., a community of practice, see Meyerhoff and Marra in this volume). Such categories that are accessible only to a limited extent arise in the frame of common experiences. Hausendorf (2000: 14) points out that making links with existing categories and creating one's own categories are often closely linked.

Tajfel (1959) has pointed out that categorization processes can occur not only inductively, but also deductively, i.e., "the assignment to a category of some attribute perceived to characterize an exemplary member." The categorization thus occurs deductively, if one knows that an individual belongs to a specific category and on the basis of this knowledge imputes to him certain 'typical' attributes. Conversely, it occurs inductively, if one assigns a person to a category on the basis of certain category-typical attributes. Both sequence directions of categorization often unavoidably include stereotyping.

1.5.   Stereotyping as part of categorization

Whether we want to categorize or not: Categorization processes are unavoidable in our everyday interactions. We continually and automatically categorize our environment, i.e., we assign persons, animals or also objects to larger units in order to structure the complexity of our experiences: "There is nothing more basic than categorization to our thought, perception, action, and speech. Every time we see something as a *kind* of thing, for example, a tree, we are categorizing." (Lakoff 1987: 5) In his study *Women, Fire and Dangerous Things*, George Lakoff goes even further when he asserts that, "without the ability to categorize, we could not function at all, neither in the physical world nor in our social and intellectual lives" (1987: 6). That means that we must categorize in order to make the world understandable, for categorization means simplification. But it is precisely in this simplification that we find a danger of stereotyping and thereby as a consequence the danger of developing prejudices.

Categories are often very large units that of necessity entail reducing individuals to one or a few attributes, equating them with other representatives of the category and thereby robbing them of their individuality. Such a large category as, e.g., 'women' or 'blacks' or 'Italians' makes it clear how problematic it can be to subsume individuals under a unit on the basis of an individual attribute, even though they differ from one another on the basis of countless other attributes. By categorizing we decide which attributes of persons are to be set as relevant and which are not: "The way in which things [or respectively persons] are classed together reveals, graphically as well as symbolically, the perspectives of the classifier" (Strauss 1969: 20).

Categorizations are especially problematic when persons are refused certain rights merely on the basis of their membership in a specific category, when, e.g., women receive lower salaries for the same work merely on the basis of their biological sex, or when people are treated as potential criminals on the basis of their skin color. Lakoff (1987: 85) writes in this regard: "[... social stereotypes] are used in reasoning and especially in what is called 'jumping to conclusions'. [...] Stereotypes are used in certain situations to define expectations, make judgements, and draw inferences." If social categories are linked with stigmata, these are automatically transferred to each individual member. But just as categorization is unavoidable in human interactions, so is stereotyping: "it is useless to talk of trying to eradicate from the human mind the tendency to stereotype, to designate nastily, and to oversimplify," writes Anselm Strauss (1969: 21). With Lakoff, he regards this tendency, however, as typically human: "This is not to say that humans are brutish, but that they are thoroughly human".

Harvey Sacks himself linked his concept of "category-bound activities" with that of "stereotypes" (1992: 568). With both concepts it is a matter of the generalizing ascription of behavioral modes to individuals as representatives of specific larger units. Although Sacks sees the dangers that such a generalization can entail, he emphasizes a certain value of categorizations (1992: 577). Many other scientists besides Sacks have emphasized the connection between categories and stereotypes and offered various definitions, of which a few will be briefly summarized.

Thus, e.g., Allport writes (1979: 191): " ... *a stereotype is an exaggerated belief associated with a category.* [...] A stereotype is not identical with a category; it is rather a fixed idea that accompanies the category". This means that Allport also sees the proximity of both concepts, but separates them. Two other definitions of 'stereotype' neglect the concept of 'category' and instead introduce other central concepts. Schwarz and Chur (1993: 52) conceive the term "stereotype" as "a mental representation in which aspects of an area of reality are crudely generalized and strongly reduced to a few (in part not even applicable) attributes."

After a critical discussion of various approaches, Quasthoff formulates a definition that shifts the linguistic realization of stereotypes to the center of attention:

> A stereotype is the verbal expression of a conviction applied to social groups or individual persons as their members that is widespread in a given community. It has the logical form of a judgment that in an unjustifiably simplifying and generalizing

way, with an emotionally valuing tendency, ascribes or denies to a class of persons certain qualities or modes of behavior. Linguistically it is describable as a sentence (1973: 28).

According to this definition, a stereotype therefore represents a verbal form of stating a conviction. Thereby the first important step was taken to making a formerly entirely social-psychological concept of stereotype for the first time understandable from a linguistic perspective. Twenty-five years later the author herself criticized her concept, however, insofar as it was presumably too static, and demanded the "dynamization of stereotype research" (Quasthoff 1998). Since she, similar to Sacks, understands "stereotypifications as components of social categorizations" (1998: 47), this more dynamic approach likewise applies to categorization research. The goal of more recent categorization research has been to work with a process-oriented concept of stereotypes that makes it possible to empirically understand stereotypes and categories with the aid of conversation analysis as interactively produced constructs.

In categorization it is always a matter of more than a pure assignment of persons to larger units and of the thereby achieved structuration, or respectively simplification, of the world. Interactants often categorize with a specific intention, which can be conversation-organizationally conditioned. Thus Sacks (1992: 40) already stated that categorization questions often appear at the beginning of a conversation, because they are suitable, as an important component of everyday knowledge, for starting conversations with strangers. Categorizations can, however, be employed beyond the discourse level for the purpose of social organization. Quasthoff (1998: 47), e.g., points out that connected with stereotypifications and social categorizations are "processes of alliance formation or respectively of the demarcation and exclusion of those present or absent." Categorization processes thus crucially determine the social framework of a group; they are a possibility for 'social positioning' (Davies and Harré 1990; Wolf 1999). Interactants can categorize cooperatively or dissent from categorizations. The cooperative negotiation of a negatively connoted 'other category' usually leads to alliance formation against it. Simultaneously, these processes influence the interactive formation of group identity.

Kesselheim (2003: 57) names two essential lines of tradition that pursue such a more dynamic conceptualization of categorization: For one thing, he mentions the British Manchester School, which has further developed the concept from a sociological (and social-psychological) perspective. As representatives of this research approach he names, among others, Antaki, Edwards, Hester, Jayyusi, Widdicombe. On the other hand, he names linguistic work on categorization in the German-speaking countries, such as the Bielefeld "National Self- and Other Images in East-European States – Manifestations in Discourse" project and the "Communication in the City" project of the Institute for the German Language (IDS) in Mannheim (Kallmeyer 1994). From the first research strand arise concepts such as "identity-in-interaction" (Antaki & Widdicombe 1998), which, in the frame of linguistic research on social identity, has proved to be an extremely fruitful instrument.

"The student of identity must necessarily be deeply interested in interaction for it is in, and because of, face-to-face interaction that so much appraisal – of self and others – occurs," writes Anselm Strauss (already in 1969: 44). If one wishes to study a complex phenomenon like identity with the aid of conversation analysis as an interactively produced phenomenon, identity must be conceptualized differently than was for a long time the case in social psychology. Deppermann and Schmidt point out that earlier social scientific concepts of identity cause great problems for the empirical study of identity in conversations, because they often refer to "abstracting constitutional dimensions of identity which can not or can only in a highly rudimentary form be drawn into the study of everyday action episodes" (2003: 27). "The current concepts of identity thus seem to have too many assumptions, to be too macroscopic and too much weighted with empirically irredeemable implications to offer a foundation appropriate for the subject-matter to use in the study of everyday interactions" (2003: 28).

For this reason, ethnomethodological conversation analysis and discursive psychology (Edwards and Potter 1992; Potter and Wetherell 1987) developed an interactionist concept of identity that can be much better grasped empirically. Stuart Hall points out that identities are positions that interactants take in discourse (1996: 6). Identities are accordingly understood as everyday world resources with the help of which individuals can better position themselves. Already in 1990 Davies and Harré introduced the concept of "positioning" as a more dynamic representation of identities in conversation. They define "positioning" as "the discursive process whereby selves are located in conversations as observably and subjectively coherent participants in jointly produced story lines" (1990: 48). In conversations we assign various positions to ourselves and to others, and from them we observe and evaluate the world. "Position" appears to the authors as "the appropriate expression to talk about the discursive production of a diversity of selves" (1990: 47) and they therefore propose this term as an alternative to more static models such as that of the 'role', or Goffman's concepts of "frames" and "footing" (Goffman 1974, 1981).

Like Davies and Harré, the social psychologists Antaki and Widdicombe (1998) emphasize in their concept of 'identity-in-interaction' the importance of discourse or respectively interaction in doing research on identities. Already the title of their collection *Identities in Talk*, which gives an overview of various constructivist theories of identity, points to the discursive negotiation of identity. Widdicombe summarizes, "the important analytic question is not [...] whether someone can be described in a particular way, but to show *that* and *how* this identity is made relevant or ascribed to self or others" (1998: 191). Thus it is not a matter of studying who conversational partners are in terms of their demographic data, but rather of studying locally identifiable, discursively produced identities which interactants select from a broad spectrum of possibilities and set as relevant. At the center of this new concept of identity is who or what conversational participants locally identify each other as being in the microcosm of the interaction, why and in what manner (with what linguistic means) they do this. Identity is thereby "regarded as an everyday world resource with which societal members themselves perform identity work, categorize and interpret their social world and thereby also construct their own identity" (Deppermann and Schmidt 2003: 28).

A source of orientation for identity research from a linguistic viewpoint is in addition the concept of 'acts of identity' of Le Page and Tabouret-Keller (1985), which up to the present has been widely received. This approach, developed in the frame of (socio-linguistic) Creole research, regards linguistic practice as 'acts of identity' and thereby produces the important connection between speech variation and identity (P. Eckert 2000). According to this, individuals adopt linguistic patterns as an expression of their identification with specific reference groups. Youths can thus express their membership in specific youth cultural groups and scenes by employing the appropriate vocabulary. In a newer study, Auer and Dirim (2003) show how non-Turkish youth perform various 'acts of identity' by acquiring Turkish.

2.   Communicating identity in intercultural encounters

Intercultural scenarios have a variety of effects on the communication of identity. Ethnic and national identities can be set as relevant simply because the way a behavioral mode is marked by culture first becomes clear in a foreign culture. Whereas, for example, for many Germans punctuality represents an inconspicuous aspect of normality, in a foreign cultural context it suddenly becomes a characteristic of one's own 'being German'. Besides that, there is the influence of specific national stereotypes that belong to active knowledge stocks. The ethno-comedies that are currently popular in some Western countries play with the knowledge of such stereotypes by humorously exaggerating them (Kotthoff 2004).

Many identity categories are interwoven in their cultural typification. Thereby the space-time scope of the categories is in each case hard to determine. What is regarded today as the typical manner of a young woman lawyer from Munich will not differ in many contexts from that of a woman lawyer in London, Stockholm or Chicago. Gender, class, profession, age, and style influence each other and together with nationality and ethnicity produce a context-dependent type. The young urban professionals who serve as an example here can show their individual identity through a specific styling as more or less fashion-conscious, more or less status-conscious and much more. In Russia such a woman will possibly be immediately identified as coming from the West. Wearing low-heeled shoes and not using much makeup can, for example, become symbolic difference markers for this type of woman, indices of a cultural membership that is not in a strict sense national. West-East could become a flexible demarcation line for the female yuppie. Such habitus phenomena of clothing and body presentation are sometimes divested of their status as normality in the foreign culture. Something that does not attract attention at home suddenly indicates elsewhere cultural difference. The space in which normalities go unchallenged can range from a close 'community of practice' to diffuse communities with comparable consumption habits, lifestyles, attitudes and values (e.g. 'Asian cultures' or 'the West').

In this section we wish to go into the communication of national and ethnic identity. Language plays a role in the attribution of ethnic and national identity. As was pointed out in the first part of this chapter, we do not view identity as something constructed through institutions, individuals and 'discourse' within an 'imagined community', but as situated in the life world. In many sciences, national identity is utilized as a category for causal and/or variable analysis, often generating important statistical data for various policy requirements and institutional actors. As Hester and Housley (2002: 2) point out, the emergence of national identities has been located within important social and economic transformations, developments and historical fissures. They regard the work of Billig (1995) on the everyday routines and practices of 'banal nationalism' as the most notable attempt to move beyond the theoretical matrix surrounding the social reproduction of nationalism and identity. The two authors also recommend Bechhofer, McCrone, Kiely and Steward (1999) as a study which investigated national identity among Scottish landowners and the Scottish cultural elite. Bechhofer et al. (1999: 530) state:

> It is relatively straightforward to argue that national identities are not essentially fixed or given. This is usually taken to mean that such identities are open to manipulation, most obviously by the state and its institutions so that people come to think of themselves as 'nationals' in a fairly unproblematic way [...] Our argument, on the other hand, is that national identities depend critically on the claims which people themselves make in different contexts at different times. But the processes of identity work rest not simply on the claims made, but on how such claims are received, that is validated or rejected by significant others.

Nationality and ethnicity can overlap. Often there are political disputes about which ethnic group can imagine itself as bearing the state. Right-wing circles often avail themselves of such slogans as 'France for the French' and thereby contribute to the marginalization of immigrants (see chapter 18 by Reisigl in this volume).

Below we attempt to further illuminate a few linguistic and non-linguistic forms of communicating cultural identity and alterity.

2.1.   Formations of 'us' and 'them' by national identity categorization

Koole and Hanson (2002) examine the display and use of national identity categories in classroom interaction in the Netherlands. 'Moroccan' is the teacher's membership categorization (outlined above), which is challenged by the pupils. The teacher adopts the position of a knowledgeable actor in discussions of topics from the everyday experience of her students. Koole and Hanson in particular show how the teacher employs the national identity category 'Moroccan' in a deterministic, deductive manner. In response, Moroccan students challenge not so much the national identity category as such, but its meaning in terms of category-bound activities. They also show how difficult it can be for a teacher to participate successfully in the student-centered approach that is advocated for multi-ethnic classes today. The interactional practices and competencies required for such participation appear to be largely incompatible with the teacher's acting as the one who knows (2002: 212). The authors show in detailed transcriptions that even when all participants recognize a category such as 'Moroccan', this does not imply that they agree on all the attributes of this category. In one lesson, the class discusses the practice of bathing and taking showers, and the teacher claims that, in contrast to Dutch children, Moroccan and Turkish children are taught that boys and girls should do this separately. A Moroccan girl challenges the teacher's category predicate that Moroccan boys and girls never bathe together. She tells about her family in which she (seven years old) had a bath together with her eight year old brother. The teacher sets her counter-example apart as an exception to the rule. Her family is more liberal.

In another case (2002: 221), the teacher works with a category that links wearing headscarves to religion. This category knowledge allows the teacher to select an answer from the children that is in line with her knowledge, and to neglect answers ("we wear them at home") that are potentially, or actually, not in agreement with this knowledge. She seems to aim at having her category knowledge confirmed, rather than at having the students relate their experiences with headscarf practices, as the authors discuss. Teachers such as the one presented by Koole and Hanson have often been trained from a transfer perspective and have received their education from knowledge-transferring teachers, not from a construction model of learning and education. The authors conclude that they faced a problem of interactional competence in the school environment (see chapter 16 by Scherr in this volume).

2.2.   Formations of "us" and "them" by communicative style

Communicative style (see chapter 9 by Kotthoff in this volume) is another possibility to index and/or symbolize a certain social identity. There are many studies of how young people in urban settings use vernacular, linguistic creativity, playfulness, polyphony, and bricolage as resources for "acts of identity" (Le Page and Tabouret-Keller 1985, Irvine 2001). Distinctive patterns of bilingual speech among adolescents frequently make use of stylized immigrant speech varieties that function as group consolidating resources (Androutsopoulos and Georgakopoulou 2003). In contemporary multi-ethnic urban environments 'language crossing' can be observed, i.e. the use of minority languages or language varieties which do not belong to the speaker, e.g. German youths using English or Turkish (Auer and Dirim 2003), Anglo youths using varieties of Jamaican Creole in England or African-American vernacular English in the USA (Rampton 1995, Cutler 1999). As an interactional practice, language crossing foregrounds ethnic group relations and at least partially challenges traditional conceptions of ethnicity.

As an example of the development of a socio-cultural identity through a communicative style, we summarize an ethnographic and interaction analytic study of a group of Turkish girls made by Keim (2003, 2004, forthcoming). The girls, who grew up in a typical Turkish migrant neighborhood in the inner city of Mannheim, Germany, categorize themselves as 'power-girls'. On the basis of biographical interviews with group members and long-term observation of group interactions, Keim reconstructs the formation of an ethnically-defined ghetto clique and the group's development into educated, modern German-Turkish young women. She describes a change in the stylistic repertoire of the girls that is closely related to key experiences of their social life relevant to the group's changing socio-cultural identity.

Keim (forthcoming) summarizes that many migrant families have been living in Germany for over 30 years, and most of their children view Germany as their home country. In the course of time, migrant 'ghettos' emerged and stabilized in many inner city districts. Preschool institutions and schools were and still are badly equipped for the instruction of children from various cultural and linguistic backgrounds (see chapter 16 by Scherr in this volume). Many teachers in Germany saw, and still see, migrant children as double semi-linguals with serious deficits. A high percentage of migrant children are not successful in school and have few opportunities in the German job market. Out of frustration with their children's educational and professional failure and out of fear that they would become more and more estranged from 'their culture', many Turkish parents tried to educate their children with increasing rigidity in their own traditional norms and values. One of the central problems for young migrants has been coming to terms with their parents' traditional demands and, at the same time, experiencing failure in and exclusion from more advanced educational and professional worlds in Germany. Keim shows the children's ability to cope with often contrasting traditions and demands from different social worlds as fundamental in the process of forming their own socio-cultural identity.

Ghetto children who, at the age of ten, have the chance to go to the *Gymnasium* or the *Realschule* (only 10–20 % of an age-group attend these prestige schools) develop quite different social orientations. Since both types of schools are situated outside the ghetto, the children have to enter German educational worlds where migrants are a small minority. They experience the negative image of the Turkish migrants in terms of abuse such as *scheiß Ausländer* ('damn foreigner') and *dreckiger* ('filthy') or *dummer Türke* ('stupid Turk'). In these schools they have to cope with new educational, linguistic, and social standards for which they are usually not prepared. A typical reaction to these experiences is the organization of an ethnically-defined peer group, along with dissociation from or the upgrading of ethnic features.

Keim observed the stylistic development of the 'power-girls' in two processes of differentiation: the girls' emancipation from the traditional Turkish female role and their opposition to the German school world. The 'power-girls' created a specific style that contrasted on all stylistic dimensions with the Turkish style of their parents and of the 'traditional young Turkish woman', as well as with that of the German *Gymnasium*. Both contrasts made the girls fall back on features taken from the behavior of young Turkish males in their surroundings in their early phase. They used many vulgar expletives, a German-Turkish language mixture, and pidginized morphosyntax, for example.

The 'power-girl' style was rigorously rejected by German educational institutions. These experiences led them to transform their style in order to become socially and professionally successful in German society. Stylistic elements that had been evaluated by the peer-group as 'not belonging to us' were accepted in later biographical phases when the processing of new experiences effected a change in social orientations and aspirations.

In the case of the 'power-girls', a mixing of German and Turkish was preferred in in-group communication, especially in everyday interactions, such as in narration and argumentation. In mixing, the girls use their bilingual competence for discursive and socio-symbolic functions, as Keim shows. Turks of the parental generation, as well as Germans (the girls' teachers and German peers), were excluded from mixing. Since Keim could not find another group that had developed such a highly elaborate mixing style, she assumes that mixing, as well as its discursive functions, are part of the 'power-girls'' peer-group style.

Those 'power-girls' who had to leave the ghetto early in the course of their educational careers had – when Keim met them – already acquired a high level of competence in mono-lingual German. But in in-group communication, mixing was their preferred code of interaction. The mixing of these girls differed slightly from that of the others in the higher proportion of German structures and elements. In some interactions – for example, discussions about their school affairs – German was their dominant language. This shows, according to Keim, that in the course of their educational careers outside the ghetto, the girls' linguistic competences and preferences had changed: in specific constellations, together with specific topics, the relevance of mixing had decreased, and the relevance of German had increased.

When all girls attended schools outside the ghetto, they acquired a high competence in mono-lingual German. For the oldest girls, who had just started university study, German had become the central means of expression in all professional domains. But in in-group communication, all the girls still preferred mixing. At this later time of Keim's study, it had become a means of symbolizing their affiliation with the category of the 'German-Turk' and their dissociation from the Turkish-speaking world, as well as from the German-speaking majority. When Keim asked them about their ideal life-partner, they spontaneously answered that they would only marry a German-Turk, a man who could mix languages. Thus, the formation of German-Turkish mixing, as well as the use of monolingual German, are closely related to the speakers' processing of social experiences and to their construction of a genuine socio-cultural identity.

Besides language, clothing is also an important resource for indexing or symbolizing cultural identity.

2.3.   Non-verbal formation of 'us' and 'them'

2.3.1.   Women's headscarves as a boundary marker

We deal in this section with the symbolic discourse about the headscarves worn by Muslim women and their potential to arouse controversy. Clothing is one of the cultural signs that have an effect at first glance and convey meaning in a variety of ways. Clothing can mark the boundaries of age, sex/gender, status, religion and many other dimensions. Its symbolic significance is thus "multivocal" (Korff 1990). Schöning-Kalender (2000) shows Islamic discourse as significant in two regards: for one thing, as a body of religious rules and regulations that does or does not prescribe the clothing of confessing Muslims, for another, as a political ideology that is symbolized by specific forms of clothing. If Turkish, German or French state and school authorities point out that Islam does not absolutely prescribe that women wear veils, they can thereby draw on a rich literature of Islamic experts (Mernissi 1989 Bilgin 1997). On the basis of the Turkish constitution, there are strict clothing requirements for public institutions that are oriented to basic secular principles (i.e. prohibition of wearing headscarves). As a second dimension, Schöning-Kalender (2000: 191) describes political Islam, for which the veiling of women has become a public symbol on the basis of a veiling requirement in some countries. In its various and especially in its radical forms, political Islam in Iran, Afghanistan and Algeria is very present in Western media. As well in Turkey a conflict is smoldering over university attendance for women students wearing headscarves.

In 1998, a teacher named Fereshta Ludin was forbidden to wear a headscarf when teaching in German schools. She insisted that wearing a headscarf was just an expression of her personality. Schöning-Kalender points out that thereby a sign was also selected that in the meantime has come to be seen almost everywhere in the world as a sign of political Islamization. The type of scarf and especially the way of tying it, as well as generally all the other clothing worn by Ludin in public indicated that it was not a matter of the traditional headscarf worn, e.g., by her grandmother. In Turkey a variant consisting of a long coat and headscarf that falls over the shoulders, leaves the face free but covers all the hair and the neck, has since the early 1980s been referred to as *Türban*. With this reinterpretation, according to Schöning-Kalender, this way of wearing a headscarf is also set apart from all traditional ways of wearing a headscarf. In the course of the dispute in Turkey this has resulted in the concept of *Türban* itself becoming a symbol of political Islam.

Another discursive context for Ludin's headscarf is constituted through the perception of cultural difference as an instrument for codifying social inequality. The critique points to the fact that Turkish women wearing a headscarf were allowed for decades to do janitorial work in German schools, but a woman wearing a headscarf is not suitable as a teacher. Young Turkish women of the second or third generation living in Germany suspect that the prohibition of the headscarf expresses a fear of the majority society of the rise of the minority. Some of them wear a headscarf with pride: "Look here, you Germans. Someone who wears a headscarf is not born to be a cleaning lady." Schöning-Kalender introduces as a third perspective gender discourse. A few young women wear headscarves in Turkey and in Western countries not due to pressure from their fathers, but rather reinterpret it as a confession of the Muslim significance of physicality and feminine identity against Western gender ideals that favor particularly for young women the maximal display of sexual attributes. With the headscarf they demonstrate that a female identity continually focused on self-eroticization is not their ideal. The multi-vocality of such symbols makes it necessary to trace their location in different contexts. The dispute does not end there; the voices of the dispute are, however, better recognizable.

2.3.2. *Symbols of national identity*

In conclusion, we will take a look at newly arising national identities and their symbolization. Although ethnic labeling had never been entirely absent in postwar Europe, its status was relatively modest. The collapse of the communist regimes in Eastern Europe in the late 1980s, however, saw the resurgence of eth-nicity in an unsuspected and brutal way. Also, the process of globalization in-vokes or stimulates certain strategies for constructing and managing one's 'own' national, regional, local or non-territorially bound identities.

As an example of newly arising national identities we take a look at a former Republic of the Soviet Union: Lithuania. Cepaitiene (2000) studied the creation and meaning of Lithuanian national symbols in the press and memoirs of Li-thuanian national revival leaders in the first half of the 20th century and at the end of 20th century. Flags as well as crests, currencies, monuments, mottoes, etc. are seen as carefully constructed and projected images of identity that result from a conscious decision-making process. The intention to create the Lithua-nian national flag emerged during the First World War, when the political inde-pendence of Lithuania was becoming a reality. In the summer of 1988, after al-most half a century of Soviet occupation, the Lithuanian national flag, which was banned by the Soviet Union, appeared openly at demonstrations organized by political movements. Cepaitiene describes (2000: 466) how the banned national symbol, displayed in public, implied the idea of a recovering nation and an independent state. The publicity of the national flag crystallized previously disseminated national feelings. The legalization of the national flag was initi-ated by authorities who were influenced by Gorbachev's *perestroika*. But people could perceive and experience different meanings of the banned national sym-bol – and such was the case. When it was proclaimed as a Lithuanian national flag by the Lithuanian Communist party authority at one of the first rallies, the Sajudis press reported the next day: "That evening in the Vingis park we finally experienced our power. Sajudis (political mass movement for a restoration of Lithuania) and all Lithuanians are awakening to the new moral life" (p. 469). More and more the flag became an icon of pride in a new state and nation and emotional affiliation with the ethnic community. In conclusion and finally, the flag also became a symbol of demarcation from Russia.

2.4.   Conclusion: identity in a globalized world

Intercultural encounters make it clear that identity constitutes itself in relation-ships rather than being merely a characteristic of individuals. Even when we grant that modern identities are patchwork constructions and that a complex communicative management is needed to make a certain identity accountable, it is all the same evident that these identities also need a certain stability and coher-ence within their respective cultures. For persons, groups or larger social con-figurations like states it is often the case that the respective identities have to be asserted in the face of external opposition. Thus, for any unity, a part of the as-sociated politics of identity will consist in the search for an environment in which the social identity can solidify and assert itself, secure from outside incursion.

In this age of globalization we must bear in mind that the construction of identity is no longer bound to locality (Giddens 1990). The essence of globalization is the intensification of world-wide social relations, at the expense of formerly local activities and relations. Along with economic and cultural globalization, the globalization of social relationships has far reaching consequences for individuals' life goals and identity formation. "The advent of modernity increasingly tears space away from place by fostering relations between 'absent' others, locationally distant from any given situation of face-to-face interaction." (Giddens 1990: 18). Appadurai (1995) posits that modern configurations of space, time and culture overlap with 'imagined worlds' and 'imagined communities'. Each of these landscapes is assembled by social actors on the basis of the cultural images and possibilities for identity that are presented to them. Tourists, migrants and refugees produce new 'ethnoscapes' that, in turn, overlap with the 'technoscapes' of transnational enterprizes and the 'mediascapes' of globalized sources of information, images and symbols.

Identity and otherness are still driving forces between social conjunctions and disjunctions, and in a globalized world ever more social knowledge is required to understand their manifestations. Not only for this reason will the field of study called 'communicating identity' remain interdisciplinary, drawing together sociology, linguistics, psychology, political science and anthropology, as this article has attempted to show.

Notes

1. This first part is based on Janet Spreckels's discussion of identity concepts in her book *Britneys, Fritten Gangschta und wir*: Identitätskonstitution in einer Mädchengruppe. Eine ethnographisch-gesprächsanalytische Untersuchung (2006).

References

Allport, Gordon W.
    1979   *The Nature of Prejudice*. Reading MA et al.: Addison-Wesley.
Androutsopoulos, Jannis K. and Alexandra Georgakopoulou (eds.)
    2003   *Discourse Constructions of Youth Identities*. Amsterdam/ Philadelphia: Benjamins.
Antaki, Charles and Sue Widdicombe (eds.)
    1998   *Identities in Talk*. London: Sage.
Appadurai, Arjun
    1995   The Production of Locality. In: Richard Fardon (ed.), *Counterworks: Managing the Diversity of Knowledge*, 204–225. London: Routledge.

Auer, Peter and Inci Dirim
  2003   Socio-cultural orientation, urban youth styles and the spontaneous acquisi-
          tion of Turkish by non-Turkish adolescents in Germany. In: Jannis K. An-
          droutsopoulos and Alexandra Georgakopoulou (eds.), *Discourse Construc-
          tions of Youth Identities*, 223–246. Amsterdam/ Philadelphia: Benjamins.
Baacke, Dieter
  1987   *Jugend und Jugendkulturen*. Weinheim: Juventa.
Baumeister, Roy F.
  1986   *Identity: Cultural change and the struggle for self*. New York: Oxford Uni-
          versity Press.
Bechhofer, Frank, David McCrone, Richard Kiely and Robert Steward
  1999   Constructing National Identity: Arts and Landed Elites in Scotland. *Sociol-
          ogy* Volume 33, N° 3, 515–534.
Bilgin, Beysa
  1997   Das emanzipatorische Potential des Islams. In: Claudia Schöning-Kalender,
          Ayla Neusel and Mechthild Jansen (eds.), *Feminismus, Islam, Nation: Frau-
          enbewegungen im Maghreb, in Zentralasien und in der Türkei*, 199–216.
          Frankfurt: Campus.
Billig, Michael
  1995   *Banal nationalism*. London: Sage.
Brabant, Madeleine, Watson, Bernadette and Gallois, Cindy
this volume Psychological perspectives: social psychology, language and intercultural
          communication. Chapter 4.
Cepaitine, Auksule
  2000   Lithuanian national symbols. In: Decker, Ton/Helslot, John/Wijers, Carla
          (eds.), *Roots & Rituals. The Construction of Ethnic Identities*, 465–476,
          Amsterdam: Het Spinhuis.
Cutler, Cecilia
  1999   Yorkville Crossing: White teens, hip hop, and African American English.
          Journal of Sociolinguistics 3:4, 428–442.
Davies, Bronwyn and Rom Harré
  1990   Positioning: The Discursive Production of Selves. *Journal for the Theory of
          Social Behaviour 20:1*, 43–63.
Deppermann, Arnulf and Axel Schmidt
  2003   "Vom Nutzen des Fremden für das Eigene: Interaktive Praktiken der Kon-
          stitution von Gruppenidentität durch soziale Abgrenzung unter Jugend-
          lichen. In: Hans Merkens and Jürgen Zinnecker (eds.), *Jahrbuch Jugend-
          forschung 3/2003*, 25–56. Opladen: Leske und Budrich.
Duszak, Anna
  2002   Us and Others: An introduction. In: Anna Duszak (ed.), *Us and Others:
          Social Identities across languages, discourses and cultures*, 1–28. Amster-
          dam/ Philadelphia: Benjamins.
Eckert, Penelope
  2000   *Linguistic Variation as Social Practice*. London: Blackwell.
Eckert, Roland, Christa Reis and Thomas Wetzstein
  2000   *"Ich will halt anders sein wie die anderen": Abgrenzung, Gewalt und Krea-
          tivität bei Gruppen Jugendlicher*. Opladen: Leske und Budrich.

Edwards, Derek and Jonathan Potter
  1992   *Discursive Psychology.* London et al.: Sage.
Elkind, David
  1990   *Total verwirrt: Teenager in der Krise.* Bergisch Gladbach: Bastei Lübbe.
Giddens, Anthony
  1990   *The Consequences of Modernity.* Cambridge: Polity Press.
Giddens, Anthony
  1991   *Modernity and self-identity: Self and society in the later modern age.* Oxford: Polity Press.
Goffman, Erving
  1963   *Stigma: Notes on the Management of Spoiled Identity.* Englewood Cliffs NJ: Prentice-Hall.
Goffman, Erving
  1974   *Frame Analysis.* New York: Harper and Row.
Goffman, Erving
  1981   *Forms of Talk.* Oxford: Blackwell.
Habermas, Jürgen
  1968   *Erkenntnis und Interesse.* Frankfurt a.M.: Suhrkamp.
Hall, Stuart
  1996   Introduction: Who Needs Identity? In: Stuart Hall and Paul du Gay (eds.), *Questions of Cultural Identity,* 2–17. London: Sage.
Hausendorf, Heiko
  2000   *Zugehörigkeit durch Sprache: Eine linguistische Studie am Beispiel der deutschen Wiedervereinigung.* Tübingen: Niemeyer.
Hausendorf, Heiko and Wolfgang Kesselheim
  2002   The communicative construction of group relationships: A basic mechanism of social categorization. In: Anna Duszak (ed.), *Us and Others: Social identities across languages, discourses and cultures,* 265–289. Amsterdam/ Philadelphia: Benjamins.
Hester, Stephen and William Housley (eds.)
  2002   *Language, Interaction and National Identity: Studies in the social organisation of national identity in talk-in-interaction.* Burlington: Ashgate.
Hillmann, Karl-Heinz
  1994   *Wörterbuch der Soziologie.* Stuttgart: Alfred Kröner.
Irvine, Judith
  2001   "Style" as distinctiveness: the culture and ideology of linguistic differentiation. In: Penelope Eckert and John Rickford (eds.), *Style and sociolinguistic Variation,* 21–43. Cambridge: University Press.
Jayyusi, Lena
  1984   *Categorization and the Moral Order.* Boston et al.: Routledge and Kegan Paul.
Kallmeyer, Werner (ed.)
  1994   *Kommunikation in der Stadt: Teil 1.* Berlin/ New York: de Gruyter.
Keim, Inken
  2003   Social style of communication and bilingual speech practices: Case study of three migrant youth groups of Turkish origin in Mannheim/ Germany. *Turkic Languages* 2003, Vol. 6/2, 284–298.

Keim, Inken
2004   Linguistic variation and communication practices in migrant children and youth groups. In: C.B. Dabelsten and N.J. Jorgensen (eds.), *Languaging and Language Practices. Copenhagen Studies in Bilingualism*, Vol. 36, 78–94. Copenhagen.

Keim, Inken
forth-   Socio-cultural identity and communicative style: a case study of a group of
coming   German-Turkish girls in Mannheim/ Germany. In: Peter Auer (ed.), *Social identity and communicative styles – An alternative approach to linguistic variability.* Berlin: de Gruyter.

Kesselheim, Wolfgang
2003   Prozesse der Gruppenkonstitution: Die konversationelle Herstellung von Gruppen im aktuellen argentinischen Einwanderungsdiskurs. Bielefeld: un-published dissertation.

Keupp, Heiner, Thomas Ahbe, Wolfgang Gmür, Renate Höfer, Beate Mitzscherlich, Wolfgang Kraus and Florian Straus
2002   *Identitätskonstruktionen: Das Patchwork der Identitäten in der Spätmoderne.* Reinbek: Rowohlt.

Koole, Tom and Mylène Hanson
2002   The Category 'Moroccan' in a Multi-ethnic Class. In: Stephen Hester and William Housley (eds.), *Language, Interaction and National Identity: Studies in the social organisation of national identity in talk-in-interaction.* Burlington: Ashgate.

Korff, Gottfried
1990   Rote Fahnen und Bananen: Notizen zur politischen Symbolik im Prozess der Vereinigung von DDR und BRD. *Schweizerisches Archiv für Volkskunde* 86, 130–160.

Kotthoff, Helga
2004   Overdoing culture: Über Typenstilisierung bei Kaya Yanar. In: Karl Hörning and Julia Reuter (eds.), *Doing culture*, 184–201. Bielefeld: Transcript.

Kotthoff, Helga
this volume Ritual and style across cultures. Chapter 9.

Krappmann, Lothar
1978   *Soziologische Dimensionen der Identität.* Stuttgart: Klett.

Lakoff, George
1987   *Women, fire and dangerous things: What categories reveal about the mind.* Chicago: Chicago University Press.

LePage, Robert B. and André Tabouret-Keller
1985   *Acts of Identity: Creole-based approaches to language and ethnicity.* Cambridge: Cambridge University Press.

Luckmann, Thomas et al.
1981   Anonymität und persönliche Identität. In: Franz Böckle, Franz-Xaver Kaufmann and Karl Rahner (eds.), *Christlicher Glaube in moderner Gesellschaft*, Volume 25, 6–38. Freiburg i.B. et al.: Herder.

Marcia, James E.
1966   Development and validation of ego identity status. *Journal of Personality and Social Psychology 3,* 551–558.

Marcia, James E.
    1989   Identity diffusion differentiated. In: Mary Ann Luszcz and Ted Nettelbeck
            (eds.), *Psychological development: Perspectives across the life-span*, 289–
            295. North Holland: Elsevier Science Publishers.
Mead, George Herbert
    1934   *Mind, Self and Society.* Chicago et al.: Chicago University Press.
Mernissi, Fatema
    1989   *Der politische Harem.* Frankfurt: Campus.
Meyerhoff, Miriam
    1996   Dealing with gender identity as a sociolinguistic variable. In: Victoria Berg-
            vall, Janet Bing and Alice Freed (eds.), *Rethinking language and gender
            research: theory and practice*, 202–227. New York: Longman.
Oerter, Rolf and Eva Dreher
    1995   Jugendalter. In: Rolf Oerter and Leo Montada (eds.), *Entwicklungspsycho-
            logie*, 310–395. Weinheim: Beltz.
Potter, Jonathan and Margret Wetherell
    1987   *Discourse and Social Psychology: Beyond attitudes and Behaviour.* Lon-
            don et al.: Sage.
Quasthoff, Uta
    1973   *Soziales Vorurteil und Kommunikation – eine sprachwissenschaftliche
            Analyse des Stereotyps.* Frankfurt a. M.: Athenäum Fischer.
Quasthoff, Uta
    1998   Stereotype in Alltagskommunikationen: Ein Beitrag zur Dynamisierung
            der Stereotypenforschung. In: Margot Heinemann (ed.) *Sprachliche und so-
            ziale Stereotype,* 47–72. Frankfurt/M.: Lang.
Rampton, Ben
    1995   *Crossing: Language and ethnicity among adolescents.* London: Long-
            man.
Reisigl, Martin
    this volume *Discrimination in intercultural communication.* Chapter 18.
Sacks, Harvey
    1979   Hotrodder: A Revolutionary Category. In: George Psathas (ed.), *Everyday
            Language – Studies in Ethnomethodology*, 7–14. New York: Irvington.
Sacks, Harvey
    1992   *Lectures on Conversation.* Edited by Gail Jefferson. Cambridge MA:
            Blackwell.
Schäfers, Bernhard
    2001   *Soziologie des Jugendalters.* Opladen: Leske und Budrich.
Scherr, Albert
    this volume *Schools and cultural difference.* Chapter 15
Schöning-Kalender, Claudia
    2000   Textile Grenzziehungen: Symbolische Diskurse zum Kopftuch als Symbol.
            In: Judith Schlehe (ed.), *Zwischen den Kulturen – zwischen den Geschlech-
            tern*, 187–198. Munich: iudicium.
Schwarz, Monika and Jeannette Chur
    1993   *Semantik – ein Arbeitsbuch.* Tübingen: Narr.
Schwitalla, Johannes and Jürgen Streeck

1989   Subversive Interaktionen: Sprachliche Verfahren der sozialen Abgrenzung
           in einer Jugendlichengruppe. In: Volker Hinnenkamp and Margret Selting
           (eds.), *Stil und Stilisierung: Arbeiten zur interpretativen Soziolinguistik*,
           229–251. Tübingen: Niemeyer.
Sebba, Mark and Tony Wootton
1998   We, they and identity: Sequential versus identity-related explanation in
           code-switching. In: Peter Auer (ed.), *Code-switching in conversation: Lan-
           guage, interaction and identity*, 262–286. London: Routledge.
Spreckels, Janet
2006   *Britneys, Fritten, Gangschta und wir*: Identitätskonstitution in einer Mäd-
           chengruppe. Eine ethnographisch-gesprächsanalytische Untersuchung.
           Frankfurt, Bern, New York: Lang.
Strauss, Anselm L.
1969   *Mirrors and Masks: The Search for Identity*. Mill Valley CA: Sociology.
Tajfel, Henri
1959   Quantitative judgement in social perception. *British Journal of Psychol-
           ogy 50*, 16–29.
Tajfel, Henri (ed.)
1982   *Social Identity and Intergroup Relations*. Cambridge: Cambridge Univer-
           sity Press.
Tajfel, Henri and Joseph Forgas
1981   Social categorization: cognitions, values and groups. In: Joseph Forgas
           (ed.), *Social Cognition: Perspectives on everyday Understanding*, 113–140.
           London: Academic.
Turner, John C.
1982   Towards a cognitive redefinition of the social group. In: Henri Tajfel (ed.),
           Social Identity and Intergroup Relations, 15–40. Cambridge: Cambridge
           University Press.
Wolf, Ricarda
1999   Soziale Positionierung im Gespräch. *Deutsche Sprache 27: 1*, 69–94.
Zhou, Minglang
2002   Us and Them in Chinese: Use of *lai* (come) and *qu* (go) in the construction
           of social identities. In: Anna Duszak (ed.), *Us and Others: Social Identities
           across languages, discourses and cultures*, 51–68. Amsterdam: Benjamins.

21. Communities of practice in the analysis of intercultural communication

Saskia Corder and Miriam Meyerhoff

1. Introduction

Increasingly, there is a need for sociolinguists to engage and be familiar with the notion of the 'community of practice'. In the last fifteen years, it has spread from its roots in the fields of language and gender, and variationist socioling-uistics, so that in a recent volume on applied linguistics, work using methods as diverse as conversation analysis, focus group discussions and corpus analysis have been gathered together as studies in 'communities of practice' (Sarangi and Van Leeuwen 2003). The approach has found favour outside the English-speaking world: the term has been translated into Portuguese as *comunidades de prática* (Ostermann 2003, in press), in Spanish as *comunidades de práctica*, in Italian as *comunità di pratiche* or *comunità di prassi* and it is usually translated into German as *Praxisgemeinschaft(en)* (the English term is also used in the German literature, as is *Handlungsgemeinschaft*) (Grünhage-Monetti 2004a, 2004b). The sudden popularity and currency of the term is undoubtedly due to many factors – some methodological, some sociological and some philosophi-cal. One characteristic of communities of practice that touches on all three di-mensions is the fact that a community of practice focuses neither solely on the individual, nor solely on the community. Instead, it provides a framework for analysing the process by which sociolinguistic meaning emerges in which the individual and community are interdependent and inextricably linked. That is, "the value of the concept is in the focus it affords on the mutually constitutive nature of the individual, group, activity and meaning" (Eckert 2000: 35).

Nevertheless, we feel that familiarity with the term has spread faster than familiarity with the analytic presuppositions and methods that are fundamental to a community of practice analysis. Where the term is deployed as if it were simply a (more fashionable) synonym for the 'speech community', 'social net-work' or 'social/cultural group', important differences about speaker agency and the relationship between local and supra-local social categories or meaning are blurred and even effaced. We contend that this effacement is non-trivial. We would argue that a proper appreciation of how the community of practice differs from other frameworks for analysing language variation and use enhances our ability to provide meaningful sociolinguistic explanation. In taking this posi-tion, we follow Penelope Eckert, who has been the principal exponent of the community of practice in sociolinguistics.

Consequently, the goals of this chapter are two-fold. First, we provide a description of what communities of practice are. What are their defining characteristics? What excludes certain groups of speakers from being members of a community of practice? This will serve as an introduction to the concept for those who are not already familiar with the term, and will re-establish the essential parameters of discussion for those who are acquainted with it. Part of this will entail explicit contrast between the community of practice and other, pre-existing constructs such as the speech community and social networks.

Second, we demonstrate how the community of practice might impact on studies of intercultural communication. Is it possible to use studies of different communities of practice to frame questions about intercultural (mis)communication? Would such studies lend themselves to being transformed into programmes for intervention or for highlighting best practice in intercultural communication? What generalizations emerge from community of practice-based research and what limitations are there in the use of the community of practice for sociolinguistic research, particularly in the field of intercultural communication?[1]

The organization of the chapter reflects these interdependent goals. We begin with a discussion of what communities of practice are and where sociolinguistics has borrowed the concept from. We go on to locate communities of practice in relation to other ways of analysing groups of speakers, focusing on the importance of speaker agency, the notion of 'performativity' and the emergent nature of speech norms and communicative competence. We provide examples of research illustrating these points, and suggest ways in which such research or similar work might be directed more specifically to intercultural communication research.

2.   Definitions

2.1.   Culture and intercultural communication

Other papers in this volume are better placed to provide detailed discussion of how the term *culture* is used in lay conversation and in academic discourse. We will be operating with a very loose sense of *culture* (and hence *intercultural communication*) that reflects very closely our interests in the dynamics of interaction between speakers and the emergence and (re)negotiation of relationships through talk.

We will take *culture* to refer to a way of life shared by a group of people. We will assume that this way of life consists of cultivated, i.e. learnt, behaviours, and that these – as well as the experiences that underlie them, and the knowledge or values they are understood to validate – are accumulated over a period of time and reproduced even as the members of the group might change. In this way, the *culture* of a group ultimately becomes a set of practices, beliefs and values which are accepted relatively unthinkingly by the members of the group.

It follows, therefore, that *intercultural communication* describes a situation in which people who have acquired different ways of life (as defined above) find themselves in a position where they need to communicate with each other, and the differences and similarities between the behaviours they have learnt may facilitate or impede their interaction.

We note that the word *culture* itself is heavily laden with cultural meaning. Kuper (1999) discusses how, even among Western European languages, the denotation of *culture*, French *civilisation*, German *Kultur* or *Bildung* all differ from each other in ways that reflect the development of local intellectual and political traditions.[2]

It will become clear in this chapter that these definitions cleave fairly closely to the theoretical framework we will be discussing, the community of practice.

2.2.   Communities of practice: a social theory of learning

Lave and Wenger's (1991) formulation of the community of practice was originally framed as part of a more general social theory of learning. Their own research had focused (respectively) on describing and understanding how professional communities of tailors and insurance company employees are inducted and trained as new members of the workplace community of practice. They were interested in understanding better how emergent patterns of participation may perpetuate and reify routines for accomplishing specific tasks.

The adoption of communities of practice as a framework for describing and analysing socially significant linguistic variation has been led by the feminist linguists Penelope Eckert and Sally McConnell-Ginet (e.g., 1992, 1999). Eckert and McConnell-Ginet persuasively articulated the additional point, that an individual is a member of multiple communities of practice. Behaviours that characterize members of an individual community of practice may receive their most informative interpretation as part of a constellation of overlapping and interrelated, socially meaningful, learned behaviours. Identities are mutually dependent and multifaceted (Spreckels and Kotthoff in this volume). For example, gendered behaviour (acting 'girlish' or 'masculine') takes on its gendered meaning not solely because of its iteration within individual communities of practice, but also because of the echoes or interactions between those behaviours and others that cross-cut, or are shared by, other communities of practice. This intersection of identities and practices is explicitly activated when people talk about 'working class' culture as being more 'masculine' than 'middle class' culture, or 'British men' being more 'feminine' than 'North American men'.

To date, a lot of sociolinguistic research within a community of practice framework has focused on using the methods and theory associated with the community of practice to better understand how gender identities emerge and what their relationship is with other social identities, as well as dynamics of power and subordination. Many of the case studies focus on communities of practice that are corporeally defined, and readily accessible by the researcher – either teenagers (who are corralled in schools for a large part of the day) or workplaces (where staff are corralled in offices). In principle, however, a community of practice might be mediated with the mutual engagement taking place on-line or through text messaging.

The community of practice's genesis as a theory of social learning, therefore, establishes two presumptions: norms are *emergent*, and norms are part of the social matrix. To analyse interaction and language within a community of practice framework is to study the emergence of norms and the gradual fixing of their social meaning through the dual dynamics of *participation* and *reification*.

2.3.   Criterial features of the community of practice

Wenger (1998: 76) defines three features as being criterial to a community of practice. These are *mutual engagement* of members, members' *jointly negotiated enterprise*, and members' *shared repertoire*. Clearly, the three criteria are not themselves wholly independent; a shared repertoire will be learnt through mutual engagement, and joint negotiation of an enterprise requires engagement. A shared repertoire (whether linguistic or non-linguistic communicative norms) may be further circumscribed by the enterprise members negotiate for themselves.

The following definition concisely bundles these factors and has been widely-cited in sociolinguistics: "A community of practice is an aggregate of people who come together around mutual engagement in an endeavor ... practices emerge in the course of this mutual endeavor." (Eckert and McConnell-Ginet 1992: 464).

2.3.1.   *Importance of maintaining a focus on the criterial features*

It is extremely important to be sure that all three criteria are satisfied in order to speak of a community of practice. This has been argued elsewhere (Holmes and Meyerhoff 1999, Meyerhoff 2002), but it is worth restating the point, since without all three, crucial aspects of the socially situated theory of learning that underpins the community of practice are ignored. (Differences between the community of practice and other constructs are explored in more detail in section 3.) There are a number of analytic frameworks which can be mobilized for the analysis of intercultural communication. All of Wenger's criterial features are required to ensure that the community of practice offers something that is clearly different, since any one of the features in the definition proposed may be shared by other analytical frames.

For example, mutual engagement may define a social network, a joint enterprise may define a group (as in intergroup theory), and a shared repertoire defines membership in a speech community. In characterizing the speech community in this manner, we follow Labov's (1972) definition of a speech community most closely, with its emphasis not only on shared norms but shared evaluations of those norms. Evaluations of the norms admit the possibility that some members of a speech community will select and some will avoid specific forms.[3] A shared repertoire may emerge as a consequence of mutual engagement – this is the basic assumption of Communication Accommodation Theory (Giles and Coupland 1991, Gallois et al. 1995, and see Brabant et al. in this volume) after all – but principles of intergroup theory may be operative without a jointly negotiated enterprise.

These three criterial features provide more than just descriptive clarity. Note, in particular, the importance of the jointly negotiated enterprise in defining a community of practice. They also have theoretical and methodological significance. The combination of these three criteria provides a theoretical focus on speaker agency and historicity. It also means that the methods most naturally suited to collecting and analysing data within a community of practice involve the researcher's own longitudinal, ethnographic engagement with the community of practice (see Kotthoff in this volume; Gumperz and Cook-Gumperz in this volume). This in turn imposes limits on the kinds of communication and sociolinguistic questions it will be most useful for answering (we return to this point in section 4).

2.3.2.   Core vs. peripheral membership

It is useful in communities of practice to make a distinction between core (expert) members of communities of practice and members who are more peripheral to the community of practice, either because they are novices in the community, or because they choose not to adopt all the practices associated with core membership. Cheshire (1982) recorded a number of adolescents for her sociolinguistic study of the Reading vernacular, and she grouped the speakers into core, secondary and peripheral members. Though she framed her analysis in terms of a social network (the core vs. secondary/peripheral membership division was made partly on the classic network measure of reciprocal naming of 'friends'), she also made the division based on how actively individuals participated in typical social practices. In this way, her work foreshadows the community of practice turn in sociolinguistics. Cheshire found neat analogues of the core/non-core distinction in the teenagers' linguistic practices, with core members using more of the regional vernacular forms (in negation, subject–verb agreement, and complementizers in relative clauses) and non-core members using more of the supra-local, standard variants.

The community of practice's emphasis on the gradual learning of norms provides a framework that readily accommodates individuals shifting from peripheral membership in a community of practice to core membership. Fiona Moul (2004) worked with a tutorial in a first year university course over a semester. A clear, dominant culture was established for patterns of interaction in the tutorial from the start (this was partly defined by the tutor's teaching style and partly by the previous experience that some second year students who were taking the course brought into the tutorial from Week 1). Moul showed how the participation patterns of one young woman, Maria, moved from being peripheral (in Weeks 1–3), to patterning like a core member of the tutorial (in Weeks 9–10). This was measured in terms of how often Maria contributed to tutorial discussions and the range of speech acts she used in making her contributions.

Moul's study focused not only on what individuals *do* in the tutorials (the extent to which members share a repertoire), but also on the extent to which they become involved in defining the goals of the tutorial and the success or appropriateness of each other's contributions, e.g. how being funny or supportive interrelate with being a leader or core member of a tutorial. She showed how a community of practice approach to studying variation can illuminate not just how core membership is enacted but also what it means to the group and individuals within the social space of that particular tutorial.

Taking a more longitudinal perspective on the distinction between core and peripheral membership in communities of practice leads us to another aspect of the framework, which perhaps resonates particularly with researchers in intercultural communication. This is the extent to which members of a community of practice can be said to have a shared history.

2.4.   'Locally shared histories' and 'biographies'

Wenger points out that within a community of practice "learning and the negotiation of meaning are ongoing within the various localities of engagement, and this process continually creates *locally shared histories* [emphasis ours]" (1998: 125). As we noted above, Moul found that previous experience of tutorials and previous experience in the subject area affected the level of an individual's participation and the kind of role they adopted as members of the emergent tutorial community of practice (2004: 35). In other words, we see evidence in her study for the relevance of shared histories that are highly local (i.e. form part of the culture of the tutorial) and those which may belong to the larger culture (i.e. here, the university).

Holmes and Stubbe (2003: 168) discuss how workplaces constitute communities of practice, acquiring their own locally shared history and patterns of communication. They also examine how humour plays a role in the construction of distinctive workplace cultures (see Marra and Holmes in this volume, for an extended discussion). They show that in some workplaces, small talk plays an important role in constituting membership in the community of practice. In one example, they discuss how a woman they call 'Mary' began working in a new organization in which workers regularly shared fairly intimate details of their personal life. Mary initially felt uncomfortable with this; it would have been considered unprofessional in her previous workplace. However, their longitudinal perspective showed that she eventually became accustomed to it, and came to value it as an important bonding and support mechanism amongst staff. This shows how new members of a community of practice must gain knowledge of the linguistic practices that are part of the locally shared history in order to fit in (Holmes' work has more recently referred to this as 'doing relational practice', see Marra and Holmes in this volume). Linguistic norms play a critical part in creating specific workplace cultures, and these norms are negotiated over time amongst colleagues.

Corder (2004) examined the communicative patterns of four football (soccer) teams (two women's and two men's) for a period of several months at the start of the football season, exploring commonalities and differences between the four communities of practice constituted by the teams. The study was intended to illuminate how, within the stereotypically masculine social frame of football, players, especially female players, create a space for themselves. Corder found that the four teams studied all followed a similar 'script' in the changing room and during match breaks and there was considerable overlap in the topics they discussed before, during and after their matches. However, like workplaces, the teams had all negotiated meanings specific to the locally shared history of each team. For example, Corder found that having what we might call a football 'biography' played an important role in defining the communities of practice each team constituted. That is, she found that the locally shared histories of the different teams' communities of practice were coloured by whether or not team members could draw on previous experience with and integration in football culture.

Since participation in some communities of practice over an individual's lifespan is highly constrained according to sex – the vast majority of boys play football in the UK; the vast majority of girls do not – Corder felt that this required the women's teams to work out exactly how they would respond to their lack of a typical boy's football-dominated biography.[4]

Corder compared discussion of team tactics in a casual male team, 'Your Mum', and the casual women's team, 'Studmuffins'. Your Mum's extensive experience of football is clear from their use of highly specific tactical words, and lucidity of expression in terms of prior and next move, e.g.

(1) Player 1:   Use the lines boys ... right wings and left wings get them in the
                game coz they're fucking shit down the lines boys
    Player 2:   Aye they're lost at the cross balls.

                                                                (8. 11. 03, 004, 00:55)

This is in direct contrast to Studmuffins who analyse the game on a superficial
level, e.g.

(2) Sonia: Yeh, yeh. Or Jen, what I was thinking sometimes Jen ... if you
                stand completely still and just give me an arm I'll just throw the
                ball in that direction and then hope ... (laughter)

                                                                (7. 11. 03, 001, 01:55)

(3) Laura: I like just kind of **toot** around at the back [of the pitch].

                                                                (20. 11. 03, 007, 02:55)

Corder contextualizes this difference in terms of more long-term issues of identity, what other communities of practice they are members of, and how these are
interleaved, making up their gendered biography. Although Studmuffins have
taken themselves out of the traditional feminine marketplace by playing a male
dominated sport, this team of women are not interested in re-packaging themselves as part of the masculine marketplace. The lack of a typical boys' biography that gradually and cumulatively incorporates experience with playing
football helps to maintain the essential femaleness of their identities. Corder
found they reinforce their identity as 'girls' playing football[5] in several ways,
drawing on a 'gossipy' style when discussing team tactics, as seen in (2), and in
changing room discussions more generally. This is how Studmuffins have
jointly negotiated a response to the double-bind of being female participants in a
hegemonically male culture.

    Examples 2–3 illustrate how the locally shared history of a community of
practice may be partly dependent on patterns that exist beyond the community
of practice. In this case, the style Studmuffins have converged on for discussing
football tactics is constrained by other factors such as how society expects
women to talk, and how it constrains their movements and experiences – that is,
their biographies – as children and adults.

    This discussion of the criterial features of a community of practice and the
framework's emphasis on historicity and agency indicates ways in which communities of practice overlap but also differ from other widely-used frameworks
for analysing language in use. In the next section, we provide a more explicit
comparative focus.

3.   Relating communities of practice to other theory and methods

Eckert's (2000) discussion of communities of practice within a U.S. high school discusses the way in which she sees her use of the community of practice as complementing, rather than replacing, well-established notions like social network analysis and the speech community as the basis for analysing (socio)linguistic variation. Eckert has argued that the explanatory power of the community of practice is derived from the analyst acquiring close familiarity with the community of practice itself, and also that part of its power is derived from being able to see how very local meanings for actions and practices relate to and articulate with supra-local social identities. We may only understand the power dynamics within the very local domain of a community of practice if we also see how the local dynamics challenge or reaffirm power dynamics within society at large. This means a researcher's analysis will always benefit from both the bird's-eye view (provided, for example, by the study of a speech community) and the high degree of empathy gained through familiarity with a community of practice.

In the following sections we spell out what seem to us the crucial dimensions on which the community of practice differs from the speech community, social networks, and intergroup theory–all of which the community of practice has formally or informally been analogized to. We believe such analogies are ill-informed, and we hope that by providing this summary we will provide a ready source of information that may save others from going down possible garden paths. Earlier work (Holmes and Meyerhoff 1999; Meyerhoff 2002) discusses the overlap and difference between communities of practice and the speech community, intergroup theory and network analysis, hence, we principally focus in this chapter on the relationship between the community of practice and social constructionist views of language. In particular, we look at how the community of practice relates to Judith Butler's notion of *performativity*.

3.1.   Speech community

There are numerous definitions of *speech community* in sociolinguistics. Some emphasize the role played by shared behaviours and shared attitudes or evaluations of differences in behaviour, while others focus more on the creative tension behind conflict, or lack of convergence. As has long been recognized in psychology, defining what is Other can (paradoxically) serve the important function of clarifying what is Self. Here, when we talk about the speech community, we will be thinking about it in terms of shared (or divergent) practices, since this provides the closest basis for comparison with the community of practice.[6]

One of the principal criticisms levelled at the way in which Labovian social dialect surveys operationalize the speech community is that they impose external perceptions about what the relevant social categories are within the community. Even where the social categories represent distinctions that the community seems to consider salient (such as middle vs. working class; women vs. men; urban vs. rural), it has been argued that large-scale groupings mask internal variability within the groups, and impose a deterministic view of social identities on the subsequent analysis.

Another source of concern is that the methods associated with defining and analysing variation in a speech community actually hinder meaningful interpretation of any variability that the research uncovers. Take for example, the widely-recognized generalization that if a variant is more frequently used by speakers from higher socio-economic strata, then it is also more frequently used by all speakers (regardless of their socio-economic class) in careful or out-group-directed speech. An analysis of a speech community can describe this, and the researcher may suggest various reasons for this correlation between style and class. For example, one explanation for the correlation might be that people want to suggest they come from a high social class when they are talking to strangers or in a formal context. Another explanation might be that people believe higher class speakers usually hold positions in the wider community which license them to speak in the most formal social contexts, and individuals draw on this generalization when they have to speak formally. Yet another explanation might be that formal contexts remind people of being at school, where use of formal and standard varieties is explicitly taught.

Within the framework of the analysis of the speech community, we can do no more than postulate what social motivations underlie the facts we observe. We certainly cannot choose between any one of these accounts when we are analysing speakers in the large groups associated with studies of speech communities. And increasingly, sociolinguists would argue that the causes of the widespread correlation between style and class are most likely to be a combination of all these factors (and perhaps more).

On the other hand, within the closer community of practice analysis of speakers' attitudes and how they orient to and interpret social meaning through a wide range of linguistic and non-linguistic behaviours, sociolinguists acquire an understanding of what it means to be 'middle class', or what it means for particular ways of speaking to be 'careful' or 'good'. Bucholtz (1999) provides a nice example of this in her study of an all-female community of practice of high school students who self-identified as 'nerds'. This community of practice constructed a range of linguistic (and non-linguistic) resources that marked them out from other communities of practice in the school, for instance by using low frequency and technical vocabulary, avoidance of swearing, and an adherence to more standard-like syntax. (In section 4, we return to the uses that analyses of this level of detail might have for applied sociolinguists.)

3.2.   Social networks

The most significant difference between being a member of a social network and a member of a community of practice is whether or not that membership is actively or passively defined. Membership in some social networks may be defined by (relatively) conscious choices, but social networks can also be defined passively. That is, you might think, "I like the way she talks to her daughter. I'd like to get to know her better", and this conscious choice could establish a network of parents at a kindergarten. On the other hand, more passive patterns of association can define you as a member of a network, for example, by regularly attending regional meetings of a political party. Not all members of this network would necessarily have interpersonal engagement. In other words, while all communities of practice are a kind of social network, not all social networks are communities of practice.

3.3.   Social identity theory

Tajfel's (Tajfel and Turner 1986, see also Spreckels and Kotthoff in this volume) social identity theory contends that we all possess many identities, some of which are defined largely in interpersonal terms and some of which are defined largely in intergroup terms. This distinction between personal and group identities is a structural idealization; it is hypothesized that all identities are defined as being more or less interpersonal and intergroup. In addition, Tajfel indicates that he suspects there is no such thing as a purely personal identity, even in interactions where interlocutors believe they are focusing on the idiosyncracies of their mood, personalities, or the immediate context, their responses will be conditioned by previous experiences that they have subsequently generalized over groups.

Social identity theory proposes that comparison between individuals and groups is a fundamental cognitive and social process. Moreover, comparisons of this nature are seen as highly functional, since typically the process serves to assert positive aspects of one's ingroup identity. This can be seen in the following examples from the Studmuffins, the casual women's team whose members in some respects (we have seen) are happy to emphasize aspects of their femininity. In example (4), Sonia invokes an explicit contrast between the way Studmuffins approach their matches and "a boy's [game]". Example (5) provides an interesting counter-point to this, in which Jo makes it clear that for all their "tooting" around the pitch (see example 3), their identity is not a stereotypically female one. They are emphatically not the kind of women who play netball.

(4) Sonia: They're the most aggressive team we've played ...
    Jo: That girl just knocked you
    Sonia: Yeh no they're really aggressive, they're playing much more of a
              boy's [game]

                                                        (7. 11. 03, 002, 00:50)

(5) Jo: It's not fucking netball.

                                                        (16. 10. 03, 006, 01:30)

Social identities may be perceived or well-established through practices. A lot
of intergroup research has found significant effects based on group memberships which have been assigned to people solely for the purposes of the experiment. In the experiments, it is common to provide members of these evan-
escent groups with an externally-imposed, shared goal in order to create
cohesiveness and provide a commonality for the members to focus on. But
this is a convenience for the lab. In real life, a social group may not share a
jointly negotiated goal, other than that of contrasting themselves with other
groups.

    Another important difference between social groups and communities of
practice is (again) the nature of engagement between co-members. Much of the
research on intergroup relations has been an attempt to understand (and then intervene in) situations of religious or ethnic prejudice. The groups being considered in this kind of research (Jews, Whites, Muslims, etc.) are clearly not
ones that require (or even allow) exhaustive mutual engagement. (There are parallels here between the often-cited "imagined communities" of nationalism introduced by Anderson 1991.)

    Although it is possible for social identities to be circumscribed in such a way
that they can be isomorphic with communities of practice, as we saw with social
networks, the community of practice is necessarily more exclusive. It necessarily involves shared practices and activities and necessarily involves interpersonal contact among the members.

3.4.   Social constructionism and performativity

Social constructionism is a theory that holds that our identities are not part of
our biological make-up, but that they are constructed through the social activities in which we participate. That is, no identity is pre-cultural, all are highly
cultural constructs. Like social networks, social groups may be compatible with
a social constructionist analysis of interaction. However, the community of
practice inherently falls within the scope of social constructionism. In this section we consider how communities of practice articulate with the idea that identities are created through cultural performances.

This social constructionist approach is in direct contrast to the type of sociolinguistic variation highlighted by traditional speech community studies, known as the 'social factors approach'. That is, "identif[ying] SOCIAL FACTORS that divide a speech community: age, sex, ethnicity and social class ... By this model, a person is an intersection of social groups" (Hazen 2002: 240).

The philosopher Judith Butler's theory of performativity meshes easily with theories of learned social behaviour, which are basic to the community of practice. Butler (1990) proposed that gender is based on the performance of a stylized repetition of acts, to which members of society have ascribed a gendered meaning. Hence, "gender is not a fact, the various acts of gender create the idea of gender and without those acts, there would be no gender at all" (Butler 1990: 140). In order to show how we employ the iterability of certain codes to signify gender, Butler draws on Austin's concept of performative speech acts, utterances that actually do something in the act of being uttered, for example 'I bet', 'I promise'.

Cameron and Kulick (2003) further clarify the notion of performativity, pointing out that it does not entail the speaker 'performing' in terms of self-conscious play-acting. Rather, it entails the conscious or unconscious repetition of acts that represent conventional notions such as 'femininity' or 'masculinity'. Deborah Cameron (1996) develops the notion of performativity in a social science context, showing that the notion is directly related to the community of practice. She states that "throughout our lives we go on entering new communities of practice: we must constantly reproduce our gendered identities by performing what are taken to be the appropriate acts in the communities we belong to – or else challenge prevailing gender norms by refusing to perform those acts" (Cameron 1996: 45). Corder's study of the two female football teams showed that each team created a unique gender identity for themselves. Corder argued that the casual and more social team, Studmuffins, negotiated masculine and feminine styles of interaction to create a gender identity which was neither exclusively male nor female. By contrast, the Female Firsts team performed a gender identity through their shared repertoire, which more actively placed them in a social marketplace that values masculinity.

We noted that Butler based her notion of performativity on Austin's theory of speech acts, and in particular the idea that some speech acts are performatives. Corder's analysis of the discursive repertoires used by Studmuffins and Female Firsts shows that the teams do not differ markedly at the larger level of what they talk about and what they do; the telling differences in their repertoires emerge at the level of specific linguistic strategies that are associated with each group. So both teams (like the men's teams) covered very similar topics in pre- and post-match conversation and during half-time breaks: the opposing team was always abused during half-time (regardless of who was winning), match tactics would be discussed pre-match and during half-time, post-match discussion always turned to cigarettes and alcohol.

However, the manner in which match tactics, for example, were discussed differed radically and involved the performance/iteration of linguistic routines that are associated with very different groups of speakers in the community as a whole. Discussion of tactics in Studmuffins very often used phrases that would more typically index casual conversation between intimates or indicate lightheartedness:

(6) Julie: That was funny that was quite an amusing game Sam every time you went for the ball I was like "it's your ball baby"
    Sam: (laughter)
    Julie: I stink
    Wanda: Woo hoo I fouled I was like "whoops".

                                                (16. 10. 03, 006, 00:25)

Phrases like "'it's your ball baby" and "I was like 'whoops'" do not occur in the Female Firsts' discussion of match play and were a Studmuffins player to come into Female Firsts and use them she would be ridiculed as too feminine and left a peripheral member of the team. Female Firsts exercise strong sanctions against behaviour that seems too 'girly', as shown in (7)–(8), and sometimes refer to each other with male terms of address (9) or using "chick" to refer to non-present women (10):

(7) [Sandy the goalkeeper for Female Firsts is defending herself for having let through two goals]
     Sandy: I had approximately two touches in the game
     Player 2: and they were SHITE (laughter)
     Player 1: she cost us two goals
     Sandy: and I fell in the bun
     Player 2: <on tiptoes, backing Sandy into the changing room wall> YOU DIDN'T FALL YOU /?/ JUST CHUCK IN THE BUN YOU KNEW YOU WERE DOING IT "<high pitch> I fell I fell in the bun I really hurt myself"

                                                (12. 11. 03 B, 002, 10:35)

(8) [Anna, in Female Firsts, is bleeding profusely from a very bad cut]
     Player 1: Anna how's your knee? <smiling>
     Anna: Alright … Oh right yeh it's really sore, <pretending voice> ahhhh

                                                (12. 11. 03 A, 004, 02:38)

(9) Player 1: Good one son.

                                                (12. 11. 03, 002, 12:20)

(10) Player 1: Baldy – who was that chick you introduced me to?

                                                (12. 11. 03, 005, 06:00)

The use of the term 'bun' in example (7) refers to the football net, and was exclusively coined as a reference term by the Female Firsts. It is worth some independent comment because it seems to appropriate part of the jargon of femininity (analogizing the goal net to a hair net around a bun). In other words, the use of it both iterates the feminine history and life stories of the Female Firsts and contests and redefines them as stereotyped displays of femininity.

In order to function in the Female Firsts, or in a community of practice in general, knowledge of such specialized, technical terms is essential. It is this knowledge that sets apart the 'peripheral' members from the 'core' members within a community of practice and (purposefully) differentiates communities of practice from each other. As Holmes and Stubbe (2003: 123) state "members of a CofP [community of practice] ... share a repertoire of resources which enables them to communicate in a kind of verbal shorthand which is often difficult for outsiders to penetrate".

In this sense, using the notion of performativity within the community of practice can help us appreciate the importance of linguistic practices in (re)creating power, status and subordination in the workplace. Cultural facts, such as whether speakers do or do not have certain activities or strategies as part of their repertoire, and their claim to appropriate shared history, all have an impact on where the individual will be located in social space. Heydon (2003) provides a particularly potent analysis drawn from interaction in police interrogations in Australia. She first uses conversation analysis to identify conscious and unconscious routines in police officers' and suspects' talk, and then draws on insights from the communities of practice framework to discuss how the iteration of some linguistic routines can be skillfully deployed by interrogating officers to constitute a suspect as a 'criminal' within the culture of the police force (see also Eades in this volume). We discuss the potential larger-scale implications of this kind of research and what societal benefit it could have in Section 4 below.

4.   Seeing the bigger picture: potential and limitations

In the first three sections of this article we have examined how communities of practice are defined. We have then explored examples of the ways in which social practices, especially linguistic practices, provide evidence for specific communities of practice and we have tried to illustrate how these very local behaviours intersect with other identities that members may have and how the community of practice approach enables sociolinguists to construct a bridge linking the local and the supra-local.

This seems to us an aspect of the community of practice approach that must be attractive to researchers and practitioners working in the area of intercultural communication. Assuming a definition of *culture* as in section 2.1, intercultural communication necessarily involves contact between individuals who have accumulated different sets of *practices* and beliefs which are important for how they define themselves. The detailed, and generally longitudinal, nature of the analysis required for a study of a community of practice is very similar to the work of an anthropologist. With this kind of descriptive detail, comparisons between communities of practice can be quite specific. As Corder showed in her work with Studmuffins and Female Firsts, the salient details are often found not at the level of what general activities the members of different communities of practice engage in, but at the level of how the members of different communities of practice actualize those activities (cf. Marra and Holmes in this volume).

This presents both opportunities and challenges to researchers who might be interested in using sociolinguistics as the basis for engaging with and planning interventions in institutions such as schools, in order to combat bullying, or in order to break cycles of chronic under-performance by working class students and widen their participation in the social and economic marketplace. Community of practice studies such as those done by Peck (2000) and Holmes (2000), and Heydon's conversation analytic approach, show that through micro-level analysis of language within a community, linguists can expose interactional patterns that create institutional power asymmetries, and hence are able to make tangible suggestions for macro-level or societal improvement.

Furthermore, community of practice studies have allowed for important suggestions to be made in the promotion of gender equality, particularly in the area of the workplace. As Stubbe et al. (2000: 250–251) discuss, by focusing on a social constructionist or performative model of language, and by analysing individual interactions, we can break down unhelpful gender stereotypes which impose oppositional categorizations such as 'Men are from Mars and Women are from Venus'.[7]

Nevertheless, we see reason to be cautious in our enthusiasm. While there is always something refreshing and emancipatory about a new approach to studying and analysing old questions and problems, we see the community of practice as being an addition to sociolinguists' tool kit, rather than a substitution for all the old tools. Just as there are inherent areas of potential, there are inherent limitations to the kinds of situations and questions which can be addressed using the community of practice approach. It is due to these limitations that we felt it necessary to discuss in Section 2.3.1 the importance of Wenger's criterial features being fulfilled in order to speak of a community of practice.

5.   Conclusions

Overall, we have discussed how and why the community of practice has become such a popular analytical framework. We have proposed that the usefulness and attractiveness of this construct must not make the researcher lenient in applying the criterial features that Wenger outlined at its conception. We have discussed the limits of communities of practice, and shown how their potential may be maximized if they are used in conjunction with other theoretical constructs, rather than in place of them.

We have examined how the notion of the community of practice is fundamentally connected to the theory of social constructionism and performativity, and how this helps us observe micro cultural details in order to understand and unpackage macro cultural 'norms' and even make suggestions for societal progress.

In particular, this discussion has shown that the CofP is useful in understanding how power and subordination in the workplace are created linguistically, through speakers' knowledge or lack of knowledge of the shared repertoire and locally shared history in the community of practice they are participating in.

Using the community of practice helps the researcher show that culture is not fixed or static, but rather is negotiable, mutable and often goal-directed. It highlights the fact that "Members of societies are agents of culture rather than merely bearers of a culture that has been handed down to them and encoded in grammatical form ... the relationship between person and society is dynamic and mediated through language" (Ochs 1996: 416).

Notes

1. To the best of our knowledge, the use of communities of practice as the basis for intercultural communication research is – so far – limited to Grünhage-Monetti's work. However, as sociolinguists, we are aware that this may reflect our limited knowledge of the field of ICC. It strikes us that one of the benefits of interdisciplinary dialogues – such as this volume – is that it enables researchers to identify overlaps in method or approach which may be masked by different naming conventions in different fields. We welcome information on parallels in other disciplines.
   The authors thank the editors of this volume for their comments, encouragement and flexibility while we were writing this chapter. This chapter draws extensively on Corder's (2004) unpublished Masters dissertation. We gratefully thank the team members of Studmuffins, Female Firsts, Your Mum and Male Firsts for being so helpful and accommodating.
2. We are grateful to Niko Besnier for drawing this to our attention.
3. Not all definitions of the speech community focus on these two factors, and the notion

of 'shared evaluations' of norms is frequently misunderstood as meaning shared appreciation for and use of a standard variant. Neither of these factors can be reviewed in detail here. See Patrick (2002) for more details.

4. Garfinkel's (1967) discussion of the pre-operative transsexual Agnes, highlighted the importance of biography for claiming a particular social identity. Sidnell (2003) gives a very nice example of how this notion can be elaborated using the methods of conversation analysis.

5. The teams refer to themselves as 'girls' and 'boys', see example (1) above.

6. It does not imply that definitions giving primacy to attitudes are worse; it simply acknowledges that in a short review article they are tangential.

7. This refers to John Gray's (1992) bestselling book *Men are from Mars, Women are from Venus* which dichotomizes male and female interactional styles representing them virtually as polar opposites.

References

Anderson, Benedict
    1991   *Imagined Communities: Reflections on the Origins and Spread of Nationalism.* London: Verso.

Brabant, Madeleine, Bernadette Watson and Cindy Gallois
    this volume Psychological perspectives: social psychology, language and intercultural communication, Chapter 4.

Bucholtz, Mary
    1999   'Why be normal?': Language and identity practices in a community of nerd girls. *Language in Society* 28: 203–223.

Butler, Judith
    1990   *Gender Trouble: Feminism and the Subversion of Identity.* New York: Routledge.

Cameron, Deborah
    1996   The language–gender interface: challenging co-optation. In: Victoria Bergvall, Janet Bing and Alice Freed (eds.), *Rethinking Language and Gender Research: Theory and Practice*, 31–53. London: Longman.

Cameron, Deborah and Don Kulick
    2003   *Language and Sexuality.* Cambridge: Cambridge University Press.

Cheshire, Jenny
    1982   *Variations in an English Dialect: A sociolinguistic study.* Cambridge: Cambridge University Press.

Corder, Saskia
    2004   Negotiating and performing gender role expectations through discourse: a study of the community of practice of a female football team. MA dissertation, Department of Linguistics, University of Edinburgh.

Eades, Diana
    this volume Understanding Aboriginal silence in legal contexts, Chapter 14.

Eckert, Penelope
    2000   *Linguistic Variation as Social Practice.* Oxford: Blackwell.

Eckert, Penelope and Sally McConnell-Ginet
    1992   Think practically and look locally: Language and gender as community-based practice. *Annual Review of Anthropology* 21: 461–490.
Eckert, Penelope and Sally McConnell-Ginet
    1999   New generalizations and explanations in language and gender research. *Language in Society* 28: 185–201.
Gallois, Cindy, Howard Giles, Elizabeth Jones, Aaron C. Cargile and Hiroshi Ota
    1995   Accommodating intercultural encounters: elaborations and extensions. In: Richard L. Wiseman (ed.), *Intercultural Communication Theory*, 115–147. London: Sage.
Garfinkel, Harold
    1967   *Studies in Ethnomethodology.* Englewood Cliffs, NJ: Prentice Hall.
Giles, Howard and Nikolas Coupland
    1991   *Language: Contexts and Consequences.* Milton Keynes: Open University Press.
Gray, John
    1992   *Men are from Mars, Women are from Venus.* New York: Harper Collins.
Grünhage-Monetti, Matilde
    2004a   Erkenntnisse, Ergebnisse und Perspektiven des GRUNDTVIG-Projekts EICP: Interkulturelle Kompetenz und ziviler Dialog in der Stadtgesellschaft. *Bildung für Europa*, Volume 2.
Grünhage-Monetti, Matilde
    2004b   Language provision in the workplace for speakers of other languages: a democratic and economic imperative, reality or Zukunftsmusik for Europe? In: Cherry Sewell (ed.), *Language Learning for Work in a Multicultural World*, 54–64. London: CILT.
Gumperz, John and Jenny Cook-Gumperz
    this volume Discourse, cultural diversity and communication: a linguistic anthropological perspective, Chapter 2.
Hazen, Kirk
    2002   Identity and language variation in a rural community. *Language* 78(2): 240–257.
Heydon, Georgina
    2003   'Now I didn't mean to break his teeth': applying topic management to problems of power asymmetry and voluntary confessions. In: Srikant Sarangi and Theo van Leeuwen (eds.), *Applied Linguistics and Communities of Practice,* 81–97. London: Continuum International Publishing Group.
Holmes, Janet
    2000   *Gendered Speech in Social Context.* Wellington: Victoria University Press.
Holmes, Janet and Miriam Meyerhoff
    1999   The community of practice: theories and methodologies in language and gender research. *Language in Society.* 28: 173–185.
Holmes, Janet and Maria Stubbe
    2003   *Power and Politeness in the Workplace.* London: Longman.
Kotthoff, Helga
    this volume Ritual and style across cultures, Chapter 9.

Kuper, Adam
  1999   *Culture: the Anthropologists' Account.* Cambridge, MA/London: Harvard
          University Press.
Labov, William
  1972   *Sociolinguistic Patterns.* Philadelphia: University of Pennsylvania Press.
Lave, Jean and Etienne Wenger
  1991   *Situated Learning: Legitimate Peripheral Participation.* Cambridge: Cam-
          bridge University Press.
Marra, Meredith and Janet Holmes
this volume Humour across cultures: joking in the multicultural workplace, Chap-
          ter 8.
Meyerhoff, Miriam
  2002   Communities of practice. In: J. K. Chambers, Peter Trudgill and Natalie
          Schilling-Estes (eds.), *The Handbook of Language Variation and Change,*
          526–548. Oxford: Blackwell.
Moul, Fiona
  2004   Investigating differences between participation of Scottish and English stu-
          dents in tutorial interaction: an ethnographic study of an emergent commu-
          nity of practice. MA dissertation, Department of Linguistics, University of
          Edinburgh.
Ochs, Elinor
  1996   Linguistic resources for socializing humanity. In: John Gumperz and
          Stephen Levinson (eds.), *Rethinking Linguistic Relativity,* 407–437. Cam-
          bridge: Cambridge University Press.
Ostermann, Ana Cristina
  2003   Localizing power and solidarity: pronoun alternation at an all-female police
          station and a feminist crisis intervention center in Brazil. *Language in So-
          ciety* 32(3): 351–381.
Ostermann, Ana Cristina
  2006   Comunidades de práctica: Gênero, trabalho e face. In: Viviane M. Heberle,
          Ana Cristina Ostermann and Débora de Carvalho Figueiredo (eds.), *Lin-
          guagem e gênero no trabalho, na mídia e em outros contextos,* 15–47. Flo-
          rianópolis: Editora da UFSC.
Patrick, Peter L.
  2002   The speech community. In: J. K. Chambers, Peter Trudgill and Natalie
          Schilling-Estes (eds.), *The Handbook of Language Variation and Change,*
          573–597. Oxford: Blackwell.
Peck, Jennifer J.
  2000   The cost of corporate culture: linguistic obstacles to gender equity in Aus-
          tralian business. In: Janet Holmes (ed.), *Gendered Speech in Social Con-
          text,* 211–230. Wellington: Victoria University Press.
Sarangi, Srikant and Theo van Leeuwen (eds.)
  2003   *Applied Linguistics and Communities of Practice.* London: Continuum In-
          ternational Publishing Group.
Sidnell, Jack
  2003   Constructing and managing male exclusivity in talk-in-interaction. In: Janet
          Holmes and Miriam Meyerhoff (eds.), *The Handbook of Language and
          Gender,* 327–352. Oxford: Blackwell.

Spreckels, Janet and Kotthoff, Helga
this volume Communicating identity in intercultural communication. Chapter 20.
Stubbe, Maria, Janet Holmes, Bernadette Vine and Meredith Marra
    2000   Forget Mars and Venus, let's get back to earth!: Challenging gender stereo-
           types in the workplace. In: Janet Holmes (ed.), *Gendered Speech in Social
           Context*, 231–258. Wellington: Victoria University Press.
Tajfel, Henri and John Turner
    1986   The social theory of intergroup behaviour. In: Stephen Worchel and Wil-
           liam G. Austin (eds.), *The Psychology of Intergroup Relations*, 7–24. Chi-
           cago: Nelson Hall.
Wenger, Etienne
    1998   *Communities of Practice: Learning, Meaning, and Identity.* Cambridge:
           Cambridge University Press.

V. Assessing and developing intercultural competence

Editors' introduction

The final section of this Handbook, Section 5, turns to a key practical issue associated with intercultural communication: how people's intercultural (communicative) competence can be assessed and developed.

Chapter 22, by Prechtl and Davidson Lund, starts by exploring the complex question of what intercultural competence is. It briefly reviews a number of different frameworks for delineating intercultural competence, and then presents the INCA framework, which was developed by a pan-European consortium of academic experts and engineering employers. It discusses the complex issue of assessing intercultural competence, and describes the grid of competences and assessment tools that the INCA team developed.

Assessment of intercultural competence is needed for a variety of purposes, and one of the most important of these to help identify intercultural training needs. Chapter 23, by Rost-Roth, deals with this issue of intercultural training. It starts by explaining the need for training that has been identified (especially in business contexts), and the range of different target groups that need training. It thus builds on some of the chapters in Section 3 of this Handbook, which deal with intercultural communication issues in different sectors (see, for example, the chapters in this volume by Franklin on the business sector, by Roberts on the health sector, and by Eades on the legal sector). Rost-Roth then presents some approaches and methods that are widely used for providing such training.

Intercultural competence entails a number of components (e.g. the INCA framework identifies six: tolerance for ambiguity, behavioural flexibility, communicative awareness, knowledge discovery, respect for otherness and empathy), and intercultural communicative competence is just one of them. This is a crucially important aspect of intercultural interaction, and yet much training focuses on 'cultural knowledge' and/or different values. Applied linguists and experts in modern foreign language teaching have tried to draw attention to the importance of language awareness (see, for example, the work by Müller-Jacquier, described in this volume by Rost-Roth), but more needs to be done, and this is an area where applied linguistics has the potential to make a major contribution to the field.

Chapter 24, by Newton, takes a step in this direction. Drawing on authentic data collected by the Language in the Workplace Project at Victoria University of Wellington, Newton describes a programme they have developed to raise people's awareness of sociocultural aspects of language use. The aim is to improve people's skills in applying such awareness in their communication at work. As one of the reviewers of Newton's chapter pointed out, many 'traditional' intercultural trainers would not regard this as 'intercultural training', and would see it either as simply 'language use' or at best, a communication element of intercultural training. Yet the reality is that much intercultural interaction founders, either directly or indirectly, because of communication problems. There is, therefore, a clear need for linguists to present their insights in a way that is of practical relevance for intercultural training, and Newton's chapter illustrates an attempt to do this.

22. Intercultural competence and assessment: perspectives from the INCA Project

Elisabeth Prechtl and Anne Davidson Lund

1. Introduction

This chapter explores the nature of intercultural competence and ways of assessing it. It focuses on the insights gained through the INCA Project, a project which was funded by the Commission of the European Communities under their Leonardo da Vinci II programme and which ran from 2001 to 2004. The INCA project involved academic experts and engineering employers from Austria, the Czech Republic, Germany and the UK, and its aim was practical: to develop a valid framework of intercultural competence and robust instruments for assessing intercultural competence to meet the needs of employers.

In the 1990s in the UK, the Languages National Training Organisation (LNTO),[1] who had the remit of 'promoting a greater national capacity in language [linguistic] competence for business and employment purposes', found limited interest among employers for development of language skills, but a keen interest in 'cultural awareness'. Employers identified a need for a better understanding of ways of working with colleagues, suppliers, customers, etc. in other countries but had difficulty articulating the concept. Further, a number had invested in training (see Rost-Roth in this volume), supposedly to improve employees' competences in this area, but had been disappointed by the outcomes.

There was thus a clear demand from employers for work on intercultural competence and assessment, and the specific impetus for the INCA project came from engineering companies with multinational operations and with multi-ethnic teams. It was agreed that some form of cross-sector quality assurance matrix for this skill area, which is severally referred to as 'cultural awareness', 'cross-cultural understanding', 'intercultural awareness', etc., would be helpful. There is a need for a standardized, objective means of knowing, for example, how one person's 'satisfactorily completed day's training in intercultural awareness' equates to a university degree module in 'intercultural management'; how one person might be profiled in terms of strengths and weaknesses in the (to be identified) different areas making up intercultural competence and what this could mean for recruitment, personnel development, team-building and career progression. Furthermore, there is a need for some form of benchmarking for the evaluation and quality improvement of training in this field.

In addition, employers in the UK have been looking for an objective quality assurance tool, ideally set out as a series of levels, a grid of sorts, like those used for competence-based assessment in other disciplines (and conceivably forming the basis for an eventual suite of occupational standards). Such a matrix would not be sufficient on its own; it would need to be accompanied by some means of testing the employee's level of competence against the grid, and a recording mechanism for the results of those tests and any other successful improvement in the individual's intercultural competence.

The INCA project aimed to address these practical needs. While the INCA project ended in October 2004, it has led to a series of associated developments in each of the partner countries concerned and beyond, and the framework and assessment tools are still being tested, evaluated and further refined.

2.   What is intercultural competence?

Intercultural communication is not yet fully recognized as a discipline in its own right, and there are many areas of debate around intercultural competence, including the extent to which it is possible to distinguish intercultural competence from intercultural communicative competence, and what the relationship of both is with linguistic competence. Research into intercultural competence is housed in disciplines as disparate as Behavioural Psychology, Management Science and Linguistics, to name but a few.

Researchers and practitioners from these various disciplines have explored intercultural communication and cross-cultural competences from a variety of angles (see Dinges and Baldwin 1996; Kealey 1996 for an overview). Experts on foreign language teaching have stressed the importance of combining linguistic and cultural competencies (Byram 1997, 2001); cross-cultural researchers have focused on the similarities and differences between cultures; international human resource managers have looked at the selection and training of expatriates; communication theorists have focused on intercultural communication processes (Gudykunst 1993; Müller-Jacquier 2000; Kim 2001). Since the 1960s, foreign assignments have been analysed; for instance technical advisors (Ruben and Kealey 1979) or students on foreign assignments (Furnham and Bochner 1982) have been researched. Recent studies have focused on the personnel and environmental factors contributing to expatriates' success on foreign assignments (Ward and Chang 1997; Selmer and Leung 2003), as well as factors predicting successful collaboration within multinational teams (Podsiadlowski 2002).

There are many different approaches to describing and explaining people's experiences of crossing cultures. Ward (2001) identifies three theoretical approaches: the 'stress and coping' approach, the 'culture learning' approach and the 'social identity' approach. The stress-and coping approach "conceptualizes cross-cultural transitions as a series of stress-provoking life changes" (Ward

2001: 413). In contrast, the 'culture learning' approach assumes that problems arise when managing everyday interactions, and that when dealing with persons from different cultures at work, one needs to be aware of the different cultural approaches. The 'social identity' approach focuses on people's self-identifications as members of cultural groups.

According to Brislin (1994: 23), one of the routes to success in international encounters is "good intercultural interaction". This refers to "a genuine interest in working with people from other countries as well as the ability to do so" (Brislin 1994: 23). The interest in working with others depends on the way one sees other cultures. So Bennett (1993) describes a developmental model of intercultural sensitivity that is based on the idea that "as one's experience of cultural difference becomes more complex and sophisticated, one's potential competence in intercultural relations increases" (Hammer, Bennett, and Wiseman 2003). An individual can develop greater intercultural sensitivity by moving away from a worldview in which his/her culture is central to all reality, and can reach a stage of ethno-relativism where s/he considers different cultures to be equally valid.

So what *does* 'intercultural competence' entail? Different theorists have proposed different answers.

2.1.   Insights from the Council of Europe

According to the Council of Europe, "intercultural skills and knowledge include

- the ability to bring the culture of origin and the foreign culture into relation with each other;
- cultural sensitivity and the ability to identify and use a variety of strategies for contact with those from other cultures;
- the capacity to fulfil the role of cultural intermediary between one's own culture and the foreign culture and to deal effectively with intercultural misunderstanding and conflict situations;
- the ability to overcome stereotyped relationships." (Council of Europe, n.d.: 104–105).

2.2.   Insights from foreign language education

Michael Byram and his colleagues (Byram 1997; Byram, Nichols and Stevens 2001), whose expertise is in foreign language education, include the following five components in their model:

- intercultural attitudes: curiosity and openness, readiness to suspend disbelief about other cultures;
- knowledge: of social processes and knowledge of illustrations of those processes;

- skills of interpreting and relating, on interpreting and documents are events from another culture and relating in them to one's own;
- skills of discovery and interaction: acquiring new knowledge of a culture and cultural practices, communicate and interact;
- critical cultural awareness: of criteria, perspectives, practices and products in one's own an other cultures.

These five theoretically derived components have been subject to empirical validation through fieldwork with language learners.

2.3.   Insights from management science

In the world of international assignments and 'culture shock', technical and managerial employees have been involved in empirical studies to derive components of a theory of intercultural competence. Several factors that contribute to success in intercultural encounters have been identified.

According to Kealey (1996), three interrelated 'soft' or personal skills are required for effective intercultural collaboration:

- adaptation skills
- cross-cultural skills
- partnership skills

Adaptation skills relate to the ability to cope with experiences resulting from crossing cultural boundaries; they entail competences such as flexibility and stress tolerance. Cross-cultural skills, such as cultural sensitivity, realism and political astuteness, enable an individual to participate in a host culture. Partnership skills, such as openness to others and perseverance, facilitate the establishment of effective working relationships with colleagues from different cultures.

In order to describe important intercultural variables, Kühlmann and Stahl (1998) asked expatriates about "critical incidents" encountered during their overseas assignment (Stahl 2001). They derived seven factors critical to success in an international working environment:

- Tolerance for ambiguity
- Behavioural flexibility
- Goal orientation
- Sociability and interest in other people
- Empathy
- Non-judgmentalness
- Meta-communication skills (Kühlmann and Stahl 1998; Stahl 2001: 201)

According to Stahl, these factors represent "the minimum requirements for an international assignment" (2001: 203). They represent key components of the 'intercultural personhood' (Kim 2001) and are called intercultural competences. Gelbrich (2004) conducted a study of the impact of intercultural competence, and found that it influences successful workplace interaction for individuals on overseas assignments. In her study with a student sample, intercultural competence explained more than 40% of successful interactions in that context.

3.   INCA's framework of intercultural competence

3.1.   The situation at the outset of the project

The INCA model assumes that intercultural competence is needed in situations of 'cultural overlap', in which people from different cultures, with specific sets of values, beliefs and behaviours, interact. This can occur anywhere; it is not restricted to overseas encounters. For example, one of the INCA development partners, the Engineering Employers' Federation in the West Midlands region of England, provided a rich test bed for theory and practice in intercultural competence because of the large number of different cultures and languages represented among young employees in the locality.

The INCA model is generic, in that it applies to all cultural groups. It identifies the range of competences needed in intercultural encounters, whatever the cultural groups involved. Although there may be different ways of exhibiting the competences (Lustig and Koester 1999: 329) within each cultural group, from a practical point of view, it is not feasible to acquire the specific norms of every different cultural group (Spencer-Oatey 2006: 2544). Intercultural competence must therefore be seen as a generic competence. Nevertheless, assessment instruments need to be validated for different cultural groups (Matsumoto et al. 2003: 545; Matsumoto, You and LeRoux in this volume).

3.2.   Components of intercultural competence

As shown in Table 1, the INCA framework of intercultural competence comprises six components, each of which has three elements. The six components are based to a large extent on Kühlmann and Stahl's (1998) research. However, Byram's (1997) "knowledge discovery" component was added, because the world is constantly changing, and it is important not only to focus on one's actual knowledge but also to be able to enlarge one's sphere of knowledge, and in particular, knowledge about other cultures.

Table 1. The six components and three elements of the INCA model

	A. Motivation	B. Skill / Knowledge	C. Behaviour
i. Tolerance for ambiguity (TA)	Readiness to embrace and work with ambiguity	Ability to handle stress consequent on ambiguity	Managing ambiguous situations
ii. Behavioural flexibility (BF)	Readiness to apply and augment the full range of one's existing repertoire of behaviour	Having a broad repertoire and the knowledge of one's repertoire	Adapting one's behaviour to the specific situation
iii. Communicative awareness (CA)	Willingness to modify existing communicative conventions	Ability to identify different communicative conventions, levels of foreign language competencies and their impact on intercultural communication	Negotiating appropriate communicative conventions for intercultural communication and coping with different foreign language skills
iv. Knowledge discovery (KD)	Curiosity about other cultures in themselves and in order to be able to interact better with people	Skills of ethnographic discovery of situation-relevant cultural knowledge (including technical knowledge) before, during and after intercultural encounters	Seeking information to discover culture-related knowledge.
v. Respect for otherness (RO)	Willingness to respect the diversity and coherence of behaviour, value and belief systems.	Critical knowledge of such systems (including one's own when making judgements).	Treating equally different behaviour, value and convention systems experienced in intercultural encounters.
vi. Empathy (E)	Willingness to take the other's perspectives	Skills of role-taking de-centring; awareness of different perspectives	Making explicit and relating culture-specific perspectives to each other

The three elements (motivation, skill/knowledge and behaviour) relate to Ward's (2001) 'ABC' (affective, behavioural, cognitive) model of intercultural competence. An intercultural individual should be willing to engage in inter-cultural interaction ('motivation', the affective component), should have the necessary skills and knowledge ('skills/knowledge', cognitive component) for doing so, and should show those resources in his or her behaviour ('behaviour'). As Bennett (1993) points out, developing one's intercultural competence is based on a process and includes developing all three components. It is possible to conceive of a developmental path from motivation, through skills/knowledge, to behaviour, as the outward manifestation of acquired competence in one or more of the elements, and this is what the INCA model proposes.

3.3.   Levels of intercultural competence

Having specified an agreed set of elements for the INCA model, and having cat-egorized them as shown in Table 1, the project team then endeavoured to refine the model by creating a series of 'levels' of competence. It was agreed that it is not possible to define a threshold below which an individual cannot be charac-terized as being interculturally competent.

Two examples are given here (see Table 2) of the outcomes of the debates the teams engaged in concerning 'levels' of an individual's competence in the components of the INCA model.

Table 2. Descriptive definitions of two of the INCA Intercultural Competence Compo-nents and their levels

Tolerance for ambiguity
As members of cultures other than one's own behave differently, have different standards and different opinions, a lot of uncertainty and unpredictability emerges for people in in-tercultural situations. An individual often does not know what kind of behaviour is ex-pected and how his/her behaviour is being evaluated. For instance, sequencing and tim-ing of actions, modes of delegation, acceptable standards of quality – all differ from those in one's own culture.

A high degree of competence in the dimension of tolerance for ambiguity means that the individual is able to accept such uncertainties and ambiguities, and to find solutions to the problems of interaction that arise. So, in simple terms, the individual is motivated to be alert to the possibility of ambiguities ('motivation'); has acquired the knowledge and the skills to know how to deploy a range of tactics in such circumstances ('knowl-edge/skills'); and approaches such situations in a relaxed and confident manner ('behav-iour').

By contrast, people with *a low degree of tolerance for ambiguity* experience unstruc-tured and ambiguous situations as unpleasant and threatening. They either try to avoid such situations or to move out of them. If this is impossible, they are visibly uncomfort-able, prone to misinterpreting unclear situations and simplifying ambiguities. When try-ing to solve problems of interaction, they will often neglect a part of the problem and search for simple solutions. When confronted with contradictory and ambiguous opinions they will search for a compromise and prefer a very clear and definite way of proceeding.

Behavioural flexibility
In their own culture people usually know the behaviour that is expected of them and that is considered appropriate, and this generally encompasses a small spectrum of possible ways of behaving. When people from different cultures meet, an individual's usual behaviour might not be appropriate for others, and they in turn might not react to behaviour in the way the other person would expect. Thus it is essential in intercultural situations to be able to expand and adapt one's own repertoire of behaviour.

People with *a high degree of behavioural flexibility* know how to use, and are able to use a broad spectrum of behaviours ('knowledge/skills'). In the same situation they are able to act in different ways (behaviour'). They are motivated to look for and be sensitive to even weak signals in situations ('motivation') and are able to adapt their behaviour accordingly. They also take into account how their own behaviour influences others, and are able to adopt different patterns of behaviour.

People with a *low degree of behavioural flexibility* always act in the same way, even when they meet people from other cultural backgrounds. They are unable to consider different ways of proceeding in a situation and will not deviate from a previously determined behavioural procedure. An inflexible person will not notice the negative effects of their own behaviour on others. Thus they cannot adapt their own behaviour to specific situations or adopt patterns of behaviour from others. This competence can be illustrated by referring to a first contact situation between someone from a task-oriented culture and someone who prefers getting to know the other person first. The task-oriented person may simply move quickly to the task, without adapting his behaviour by first spending time on relationship building.

Having developed the INCA model, agreed the 6 components of intercultural competence, and agreed that between 'high' and 'low' there was most probably an 'intermediate' level of competence, the team then agreed 3 'levels' – Basic, Intermediate, and Full. In line with the National Language Standards of the LNTO, which comprise a calibration grid of 'can do' statements identifying an individual's competence in each of the four different language skills (reading, listening, speaking, writing), the INCA team then operationalized the Intercultural Competence grid as a series of descriptors, or 'can do' statements. These are shown in Table 3.

Table 3. The INCA grid of competences and levels

Level ⇧ Dimension ⇨	Level 1 Basic	Level 2 Intermediate	Level 3 Full
Overview of competence	I am already willing to interact successfully with people of other cultures. I tend to pick things up and learn from them as I go along, but I haven't yet the experience to have worked out any system of dealing with intercultural situations in general. I respond to events, rather than having planned for them. At this stage I am reasonably tolerant of other values, customs and practices although I may find them odd or surprising and approve or disapprove.	As a result of experience and/or training, I am beginning to view more coherently some of the aspects of intercultural encounters I used to deal with in a 'one-off' way. I have a mental 'map' or 'checklists' of the sort of situations I am likely to need to deal with and am developing my skills to cope with them. This means that I am more prepared for the need to respond and adapt to the needs of unfamiliar situations. I am quicker to see patterns in the various experiences I have and I am beginning to draw conclusions without having to seek advice. I find it easier to respond in a neutral way to difference, rather than approving or disapproving.	Many of the competences I developed consciously at level 2 have become intuitive. I am constantly ready for situations and encounters in which I will exercise my knowledge, judgement and skills and have a large repertoire of strategies for dealing with differences in values, customs and practices among members of the intercultural group. I not only accept that people can see things from widely varying perspectives and are entitled to do so, but am able to put myself in their place and avoid behaviour I sense would be hurtful or offensive. At this level of operation I am able to intercede when difficulties arise and tactfully support other members of the group in understanding each other. I am confident enough of my position to take a polite stand over issues despite my respect for the viewpoint of others.

Level Dimension	Level 1 Basic	Level 2 Intermediate	Level 3 Full
Tolerance for ambiguity	**TA1.1** When uncertainty arises from cultural difference, I adopt a tolerant attitude as long as the issue is not a sensitive one for me	**TA2.1** I now see the uncertainties that can arise from intercultural encounters as an interesting challenge, provided that the issues involved are not sensitive for me	**TA3.1** I am aware of ways of coping with ambiguous situations even when these give rise to inner moral conflicts that are serious for me
Behavioural flexibility	**BF1.1** I take events as they come, doing what seems right at the time **BF1.2** I hope that others will eventually adapt t to the way I do things	**BF2.1** I adapt my behaviour in new situations, taking account of lessons learnt in previous intercultural situations. I sometimes adopt the behaviour patterns of others, rather than waiting for them to adopt mine **BF2.2** My behaviour is now influenced by principles that guide me and I often plan for eventualities.	**BF3.1** I make use of my knowledge and understanding to inform tactfully, support and encourage others in an intercultural group. I consistently adopt behaviour that minimizes the risk of offending or hurting others' feelings **BF3.2** I do adapt my behaviour to different situations and interaction partners.
Communicative awareness	**CA1.1** I know that others may communicate in ways I am not familiar with **CA1.2** When people communicate in ways I do not understand I try in an unsystematic way to take part.	**CA2.1** I am aware of a number of useful strategies for dealing with common communication problems. **CA2.2** I seek to achieve good communication both by making my own conventions clearer and by adopting those of others. When there is, or might be, a problem with communication, I quite often find ways around it, e.g., using gesture, re-explaining, simplifying etc.	**CA3.1** I have a good overall understanding of the kinds of communicative difficulties that can arise in an intercultural context and of a wide range of strategies for resolving them **CA3.2** I use my communication strategies to prevent, solve and mediate problems arising from differences in language or other communication conventions

Knowledge discovery	**KD1.1** I have some general knowledge about the cultures of those I work with. This knowledge consists of facts that are not always connected and I don't yet have an overall picture of the relevant cultures **KD1.2** I learn from intercultural experiences and add to my previous knowledge	**KD2.1** I take the trouble to find out about the cultures I am likely to be working with, paying attention not only to isolated facts, but to values, customs and practices common in those cultures **KD2.2** When I experience new values, customs and practices I use the knowledge to develop into an overall system of principles	**KD3.1** I have a deep understanding of cultures I encounter frequently. When involved in new intercultural situations I strive to acquire the best possible available knowledge and understanding both through prior research and by seeking regular clarification within the group **KD3.2** I have acquired a system of principles that can be applied reliably to almost any intercultural encounter
Respect for otherness	**RO1.1** Sometimes I may jump to conclusions about different behaviour or norms that I later realize were not entirely correct	**RO2.1** I react neutrally to cultural differences, rather than hastily categorizing them as good or bad	**RO3.1** I fully respect the right of those from other cultures to have different values from my own and can see how these values make sense as part of a way of thinking
Empathy	**E1.1** Although I often find culturally different behaviour curious, I try to make allowances for it	**E2.1** I have developed a mental checklist of how others may perceive, feel and respond differently to a range of routine circumstances This supports my concern to put others at ease and avoid upsetting them	**E3.1** I often imagine myself in the place of those from different cultures when trying to understand all aspects of a work problem.

4.   Assessing intercultural competence

The INCA project needed tangible product outcomes for use with employees, trainees and apprentices. So, having developed the INCA model of 18 component competences, a way had to be devised to map and record people's levels of competences against the INCA grid.

4.1.   Controversial issues

Intercultural assessment is a complex process fraught with controversy. Problematic questions include:
- Should assessment be for selection/evaluative purposes, or for diagnosis that can support an iterative learning process?
- What exactly should be assessed?
- Should assessment be of current performance or of potential for development and change?

Questions such as these have been debated for many years and the views of the project team members, who came from very different academic cultures and workplace practices, mirrored these different perspectives.

It was eventually agreed that the INCA tests should be appropriate for initial diagnosis – a 'snapshot in time' of performance – but also for recognizing a candidate's potential for development. This would be achieved by scoring the test participants' results against the INCA grid and using the score and associated comments for constructive feedback – an essential component of the assessment process – and to work out with participants next steps for developing competence. It was also agreed that even participation in one of the INCA tests would constitute an intercultural learning experience, and that therefore the tests, combined with essential feedback, might contribute to the participants' iterative process of intercultural competence development.

The aim of any external assessment is to draw a picture of the potential a person has for managing intercultural encounters effectively. Assessing their competence as potential does not mean that there is no way to develop that competence. On the contrary, beyond the assessment, intercultural competence can be developed through training and other actions. In this sense, initial assessment is seen as a first step. The INCA tests really only aimed to serve this first step. Further steps, such as subsequent training and development, were not addressed by the INCA project. However, it was agreed that behavioural measurement would be included in the assessment process, because as Lustig and Koester (1999) argue, the evidence for intercultural competence is behaviour:

> What you really do, rather than your internalized attitudes or projections of what you might do, is what others use to determine whether you are interculturally competent.
> Lustig and Koester (1999: 329)

4.2.   Existing tools

The comprehensive list of tools revealed by desk research at the outset of the INCA project was current at the time and comprised a wide range of examples of different tests. Some examples are given in Table 4. However, they had a number of weaknesses: 1) most tests were relatively newly-developed and there was no evidence to hand of their validity or reliability; 2) most were contextualized to bicultural settings and were not therefore of great value to the project, and 3) of the examples given in Table 4, most are self-assessment tools, and a basic premise of the INCA project is that behavioural assessment is crucially important. As Kealey (1996: 97) points out:

> It is not uncommon for an individual to be exceptionally well versed on the theories of cross-cultural effectiveness, possess the best of motives, and be sincerely concerned about enacting the role accordingly, yet still it be unable to demonstrate those understandings in their own behaviour.
>
> Kealey (1996: 97)

In addition, given the close connection between the INCA project and the Council of Europe, there was an expectation that the project would draw on the existing language proficiency assessment model of the European Language Portfolio.

5.   INCA tools for recording and assessing intercultural competence

5.1.   The European Language Portfolio and other
Portfolio-type developments

The Council of Europe developed and promotes the concept of the European Language Portfolio (ELP). Consistent with all other European Language Portfolio models endorsed by the Council of Europe, the ELP model, as developed in the UK and appropriate for use by adult language learners and vocational/professional purposes in any of the Council of Europe member states, comprises three sections:

– Biography
– Passport
– Dossier of evidence

The language learner uses the Biography to make a personal record of his/her language learning experiences, whether formal/informal, in the home, on holiday, in an educational environment and/or at work; the Passport records the learner's competence, mapped against the Common European Framework and the National Language Standards, and the Dossier provides a structure for evidence to support the learner's record of progress and can include certificates of achievement, test results, statements from peers, examples of successfully completed language tasks, and so on.

One intention of the INCA project was to align its products as far as possible with those already in the field. It was therefore felt helpful that the INCA portfolio should mirror the three-section structure of the ELP. The ultimate aim is to bring the two portfolios, the ELP and the INCA Portfolio, together into one.

Table 4. A selection of existing tools and scales for assessing intercultural competence

	Behavioral Assessment Scale for Intercultural Competence ('BASIC')[2] (Koester and Olebe 1988)	Intercultural Readiness Check (Van der Zee and Brinkmann 2002)	Intercultural Adjustment Potential Scale (Matsumoto et al. 2001)	The International Profiler (World Work Limited n.d.)
A. Dimensions	– display of respect – orientation to knowledge – empathy – task role behaviour – interaction management – tolerance for ambiguity – interaction posture	– intercultural sensitivity – intercultural communication – intercultural relationship building – conflict management – leadership – preference for certainty	– emotion regulation – openness – flexibility – critical thinking	– openness – flexibility – personal autonomy – emotional resilience – perceptiveness – listening orientation – transparency – cultural knowledge – influencing – synergy
B. Aim	This tool identifies certain skills valuable in intercultural communication. The BASIC descriptions of behaviours are culture-general.	This tool is a 60-item questionnaire which assesses how participants currently deal with cultural differences.	The scale measures individual differences in the four constructs considered necessary for intercultural adjustment.	The 10 international competences describe in a clear professional context what is required by highly effective operators to transfer skills from a domestic to an international context.

	Behavioral Assessment Scale for Intercultural Competence ('BASIC')[2] (Koester and Olebe 1988)	Intercultural Readiness Check (Van der Zee and Brinkmann 2002)	Intercultural Adjustment Potential Scale (Matsumoto et al. 2001)	The International Profiler (World Work Limited n.d.)
C. 'Studies'		The Intercultural Readiness Check was tested by combining it with another questionnaire, the Multicultural Personality Questionnaire (MPQ), which assess five personality traits (Cultural Empathy, Openmindedness, Flexibility, Social Initiative, Emotional Stability).	Sojourners from Japan (2001)	

The Council of Europe concept is that the ELP is a personal and portable record, not intended for use for purposes of recruitment, diagnosis or assessment. The pure intention is that the language learner should use the ELP as an entirely personal document, and as a means of reflecting on his/her language learning experiences, achievements, goals and preferred learning styles, whenever and wherever the individual's learning takes place. The Council of Europe Common European Framework, on which the ELP is based, lends itself to exploitation as the basis for assessment and testing purposes, and since the ELP was first developed, parallel developments in the field of competence-based assessment have produced other passports and portfolios (e.g., Europass, UK e-passport) which are designed for wider application and are indeed used not only as a portable personal record of learning and achievement, but also as the basis for diagnostic testing, presentation of evidence for recruitment, and records held for human resource management purposes, with sophisticated online tools allowing different levels of privileged access to the record for the individual record 'owner' and for other interested parties. This pragmatic potential for the INCA portfolio was taken into account.

5.2.   The INCA Portfolio

The INCA Portfolio provides the structure to record the progress an individual makes along a path to more highly developed intercultural competence. The Passport and Biography sections of the Portfolio allow the individual to keep a record of significant intercultural experiences. The Dossier, as for the ELP, is a 'receptacle' for evidence to support the individual's assertions.

The INCA Portfolio allows the individual to evaluate his/her own experiences, learning and progress in that it includes the INCA grid: the six elements of intercultural competence plus three "levels", and examples of level descriptors that relate to intercultural situations encountered at work (see Table 3). The individual may plot his/her "level" against each element of competence, on one occasion, and revisit that, amending the self-evaluation as his/her competence develops. The individual is encouraged to note events and situations in which there has been an intercultural element and to reflect and comment on how the event or situation contributed to his/her intercultural development. The Passport contains space for independent verification by a supervisor, peer or other, of successful intercultural competence in a given work situation. The Passport, which is supported by a self-assessment element, also has space to include information about the results of external assessments, whether carried out by visiting assessors, through participation in an assessment centre, or through online assessments. The INCA Portfolio thus offers the individual a comprehensive means of recording his/her developing intercultural competence.

5.3.   The INCA suite of assessment tests

The creation of the INCA model was in part informed by feedback from participating engineers, trainees, apprentices and graduates, and their employers, who all wanted an objective means of assessing intercultural competence. This is not surprising in a context where an appreciation of one's level of intercultural competence can add value at recruitment, especially if it can be used to predict one's potential in intercultural situations. So, to verify the validity of the INCA intercultural competence elements and levels, and for the benefit of those learners seeking external assessment of their competence, a suite of assessment tests was a further product of the INCA project.

There was a considerable range of opinion within the project team concerning the format of tests to be administered. It was agreed that, in order to have merit as a stand-alone testing instrument, the INCA testing suite needed to produce a profile of an individual's intercultural competence based on a range of different types of evidence. While instruments such as biographical interviews or personality questionnaires are simple to administer (Prechtl and Kühlmann 2004), many of the team felt that this form of assessment was insufficient on its own. Such questionnaires mainly focus on the subject's own assessment of his or her competence, and therefore run the risk of producing socially desirable answers. Also, a problem with the self-assessment scales commonly used with such questionnaires is their inability to assess behaviour itself. In addition to a biographical questionnaire, the INCA team therefore also chose to include behaviour-oriented test types in the final suite.

Moreover, the way one sees oneself is not always the same as the way one is seen by others. So in order to have a balanced and more objective view of a person's competence, the INCA team felt it necessary to complement the self-evaluation with assessment tests based on external assessors' evaluations. An assessment centre approach was therefore chosen to form part of the INCA suite of tests.

Further, it was recognized that the assessment centre requires a considerable dedication of time and resource, so the team created a number of on-line tests, tests that might, in theory, be available for use whenever and wherever a participant should choose, and that also offered the capacity for on-line external assessment, very much in the spirit of other competence-based assessment approaches (e.g., the UK e-passport).

The INCA team produced two types of test:

1. cognitive/affective-oriented written exercises for completion on- or off-line;
2. behaviour-oriented group exercises.

For the written exercise items, candidates are presented with critical incidents, along with a series of open-ended questions, such as: 'What advice would you give the teams involved for improving their communication?'. A trained assessor scores the responses against the INCA grid. For the group exercises, since the best predictor of behaviour is behaviour (Kealey 1996), the assessees work together in a team with counterparts from another culture. They are observed by trained assessors, who score their behaviour against the INCA grid. (For examples of the different test types and content, see the INCA website, http://www.incaproject.org/)

Devising the tests was one major task; a second was preparing assessors to make judgments about participants' responses to the tests. The INCA grid descriptors (see Table 3) serve as the basis for observational guidelines for external assessors. Each test item explores some or all of the identified six elements of intercultural competence. External assessment is carried out by element, and according to a detailed description of the assessee's response. The assessor marks each aspect of the response as either positive or negative according to the guideline statements. The aggregate score of negative/positive for that element of intercultural competence is then set against the descriptors for the range for that element, from Basic to Full competence, and the assessee's level of competence determined.

Table 5 shows what a completed assessment sheet could look like following an assessee's participation in a test requiring one-to-one interaction with an individual from another cultural environment. The number of pluses (+) or minuses (–) obtained in the final total score equates to a score in terms of the 3-point range from Basic to Full competence as set out in the INCA grid at Table 3.

Table 5. Sample completed INCA assessment sheet

Element of intercultural competence	Respect for Otherness (RO)	Score
Positive indicators shown by assessee response	Shows respect for values and norms of both discourse partners	+
	Describes the behaviour of both persons in neutral/ positive terms	+
	Avoids prejudiced statements	+
	Takes into account the views of both parties	+
Negative indicators shown by assessee response	Describes one person's behaviour as negative	
	Insults the interlocutor	–
	Makes prejudiced statements	
	Total	3+

It was recognized that assessors might be biased because of their own cultural backgrounds, and so as much effort as possible was made to minimize this through the creation of teams/pairings of assessors from different countries, and through moderation of assessments. It was also recognized that an individual might be capable of showing socially desired behaviour (i.e. 'pretending') in an assessment setting. Further research would be required to ascertain whether this was a frequent occurrence.

5.4.   Piloting the INCA model: grid, tests, assessment, portfolio

At the very outset of the project, research was carried out to ascertain in each country and work setting the practical parameters concerning assessment. The differences in practices across the 5 countries and across the different pilot settings reinforced the wide range of different constraints under which a generic assessment tool would have to operate. While some assessees were permitted to take a day off for participation in the pilots, some were not. Some employers insisted on "on-the-job" assessment. *INCA On-line*[3] offered the opportunity for a number of the assessment tests to be undertaken whenever the assessee wished, yet the pilots confirmed that a mix of computer-based and other forms of assessment produced the most balanced results. The interaction-oriented exercises (role-plays and a group exercise) were also necessary to provide the assessor with behavioural data as well as theoretical responses.

In the summer of 2003, more than 50 assessees from five countries (Austria, Czech Republic, Germany, Netherlands, UK) participated in the pilot exercises to evaluate the assessment tests. The process also offered feedback on the INCA grid and the appropriateness of the INCA Portfolio. Alongside the tests for intercultural competences, the INCA project team created a manual for use by assessors as well as a separate, less detailed manual for assessees. Assessors for the pilot exercise were trained by INCA team members and gave their feedback on the manuals.

The on-line tests types were tested both online and, where resources did not permit, using 'pencil and paper'. Tests in the form of role-plays were also conducted. While the assessment process, tests and assessment guidelines were standardized, the tests were localized to the testing environment.[4] Care was taken to ensure that the tests and assessment formats were sufficiently generically applicable to be appropriate for each country. While some of the tests dealt with a specific culture (e.g., one test set in China), some focused on non-culture-specific knowledge or behaviour (cf. Matsumoto et al. 2003).

Modifications were made to all aspects of the INCA products as a consequence of the pilot exercises. The pilot exercises offered a limited amount of empirical data against which to validate the INCA grid, although validation did not prove conclusive at this stage.

Managing the multinational administration of a multi-faceted assessment process proved a very challenging endeavour! At the outset of the INCA project the intention was to develop an assessment tool generically applicable for all participating countries, localized as necessary. In the pilot phase, the different exercises were approached in a different way in the various pilot groups, which supported the principle of localization. So, while the exercises can be undertaken in all countries, a localization to the prevailing context is required. Further localization is necessary to ensure that the process and tools are appropriate to local or company requirements.

The pilots revealed "national" preferences for different kinds of tools, no doubt a consequence of the richness of the national heritage concerning education, training, and assessment expectations and current practices. Whereas UK apprentices responded well to the open-ended questions associated with the written exercises, German students found this test type too undemanding. Employees in technical or professional roles who deal with management issues every day appreciated a combination of managerial and technical information in the scenarios while apprentices and students not experienced in managerial issues found this combination of information challenging. On the other hand, the interaction required for the group exercises was appreciated by all those involved in the pilots. The administration of the pilots was in itself a lesson in intercultural competence.

The recommendation arising from the pilots was that any assessment should consist of a combination of self-assessment exercises and scenarios with open-ended answers – both of which might be computerized, as well as exercises based on face-to-face interaction. It was encouraging to note that pilot participants felt that the *INCA On-line* computerized assessment package offered an element of flexibility not hitherto associated with the assessment centre approach.

6.   Final comments

There is a range of possible applications for the products of the INCA project. While the project's test bed was in the engineering sector, and some of the test content was developed with a focus on the engineering sector, adaptation of the tests to other sectors has already proved possible. There has been interest in the INCA products from professionals and academics working in fields as diverse as health care and logistics, business, linguistics and public service, as well as from trainers in cultural matters and in languages. The INCA products lend themselves for application for a number of functions including diagnostic testing, recruitment, selection, continuing professional development and the evaluation of intercultural development programmes (Kinast 2003).

Project team members had different intentions for the end use of the INCA products, and many of the associated aims were met. From a diagnostic point-of-view, the INCA products can be seen as a stable, competence-based assessment requiring a one-point measurement. From a developmental point-of-view, the results from such an assessment can be used to develop competences and skills further (cf. Trickey no date). The appraisal of an individual's intercultural capacity is also helpful in the planning of international careers and training programs (Stahl 2001). When all assessments are calibrated to a matrix, and taken as an initial assessment of intercultural competence, appropriate follow-up training and development can be devised to target particular elements and to help develop an individual's capacity, which – in time – may be calibrated a second time against the framework to measure improvement.

For the moment, the present INCA model, the grid and the assessment exercises, require more extensive testing, in particular to check their validity and to investigate their wider applicability and usefulness. Colleagues from the University of Bayreuth are exploring whether a reduction in the number of components of the INCA model would be valid.[5] They are also interested in finding out the extent to which the INCA assessment results can assist in *predicting* intercultural success, i.e. intercultural adjustment or co-operation in an international team, and a study to this end is underway. In the UK, the INCA grid is the object of a feasibility study into the development of National Occupational Standards in intercultural competence and the INCA Portfolio is being linked explicitly to the UK Adult and Vocational European Language Portfolio as that is reviewed. Projects are also underway in the public services and manufacturing sectors to explore the extent to which the INCA model can be applied more generically. Further research into the intercultural competence framework, the assessment exercises and the practical benefits of the model are thus needed and are currently being carried out.

The instruments, as developed by the completion date for the INCA project, may be seen at http://www.incaproject.org/ [Accessed 1 February 2007]

Notes

1. In 2003, LNTO merged with the Centre for Information on Language Teaching and Research to form CILT, the National Centre for Languages.
2. For a description of BASIC, see Graf and Harland (2005) and Lustig and Koester (1999).
3. The computerized testing and assessment vehicle developed as part of the project.
4. 'Localization' entails not only a good translation of texts but also checks on the appropriateness – and frames of reference – for such elements as place names and names of characters in role-plays etc.
5. A qualitative analysis has already been conducted to this end at the University of Bayreuth (Armann 2004).

References

Armann, Susanne
    2004   Entwicklung und Erprobung eines Interkulturellen Assessment Centers für Ingenieure [Development and Trialling of an intercultural assessment centre for engineers]. Diplomarbeit [diploma thesis], University of Bayreuth, Germany (Unpublished).
Bennett, Milton J.
    1993   Towards ethnorelativism: a developmental model of intercultural sensitivity. In: Michael Paige (ed.), *Education for the Intercultural Experience*, 21–72. Yarmouth: Intercultural Press.

Brislin, Richard W.
1994   Working cooperatively with people from different cultures. In: Richard Brislin and Tomoko Yoshida (eds.), *Improving Intercultural Interactions. Modules for Cross-Cultural Training Programs*, 17–54. Thousand Oaks: Sage Publications.
Byram, Michael
1997   *Teaching and Assessing Intercultural Communicative Competence*. Clevedon: Multilingual Matters.
Byram, Michael, Adam Nichols and David Stevens
2001   *Developing Intercultural Competence in Practice*. Clevedon: Multilingual Matters.
Council of Europe
n.d.   The Common European Framework in its political and educational context. http://www.coe.int/T/DG4/Portfolio/documents/0521803136txt.pdf [Accessed 1 February 2007]
Dinges, Norman G. and Kathleen D. Baldwin
1996   Intercultural competence. In: Dan Landis and Rabi S. Bhagat (eds.), *Handbook of Intercultural Training*, 2nd edn, 106–123. Thousand Oaks: Sage.
Furnham, Adrian and Stephen Bochner
1982   Social difficulty in a foreign culture: an empirical analysis of culture shock. In: Stephen Bochner (ed.), *Cultures in Contact*, 161–198. Oxford: Pergamon Press.
Gelbrich, Katja
2004   The relationship between intercultural competence and expatriate success: a structural equation model. *Die Unternehmung* 58(3–4): 261–277.
Graf, Andrea and Lynn Harland
2005   Expatriate selection: evaluating the discriminant, convergent and predictive validity of five measures of interpersonal and intercultural competence. *Journal of Leadership and Organizational Studies* 11: 46–62.
Gudykunst, William
1993   Toward a theory of effective interpersonal and intergroup communication. In: Richard Wiseman and Jolene Koester (eds.), *Intercultural Communication Competence*, 33–71. Newbury Park: Sage.
Hammer, Mitchell, Milton Bennett and Richard Wiseman
2003   Measuring intercultural sensitivity: The intercultural development inventory. *International Journal of Intercultural Relations* 27(4): 421–443.
INCA Project. Project website: http://www.incaproject.org [Accessed 16 August 2006].
Kealey, Daniel J.
1996   The challenge of international personnel selection. In: Dan Landis and Rabi S. Bhagat (eds.), *Handbook of Intercultural Training*, 2nd edn, 81–105. Thousand Oaks: Sage.
Kim, Young Yun
2001   *Becoming Intercultural. An Integrative Theory of Communication and Cross-Cultural Adaptation*. Thousands Oaks: Sage.
Kinast, Eva-Ulrike
2003   Diagnose interkultureller Handlungskompetenz [Diagnosing intercultural competence for action]. In: Alexander Thomas, Eva-Ulrike Kinast and Syl-

via Schroll-Machl (eds), *Handbuch Interkultureller Kommunikation und Kooperation. Band 1 [Handbook of Intercultural Communication and Co-operation, Vol. 1]*, 167–180. Grundlagen und Praxisfelder. Göttingen: Vandenhoeck *and* Ruprecht.

Koester, Jolene and Margaret Olebe
    1988   The behavioral assessment scale for intercultural communication effectiveness. *International Journal of Intercultural Relations* 13: 333–347.

Kühlmann, Torsten and Günter Stahl
    1998   Diagnose interkultureller Kompetenz: Entwicklung und Evaluierung eines Assessment-Centers [Diagnosing intercultural competence: Development and evaluation of an assessment centre]. In: Christoph Barmeyer and Jürgen Bolten (eds.), *Interkulturelle Personalorganisation [Intercultural Personnel Management]*, 213–224. Sternenfels: Verlag für Wissenschaft und Praxis.

Lustig, Myron W. and Jolene Koester
    1999   *Intercultural Competence*. New York: Longman.

Matsumoto, David, Jeffery LeRoux, Charlotte Ratzlaff, Haruyo Tatani, Hideko Uchida, Chu Kim and Shoko Araki
    2001   Development and validation of a measure of intercultural adjustment potential in Japanese sojourners: the Intercultural Adjustment Potential Scale (ICAPS). *International Journal of Intercultural Relations* 25: 483–510.

Matsumoto, David, Jeffery LeRoux, Mariko Iwamoto, Jung Wook Choi, David Rogers, Haruyo Tatani and Hideko Uchida
    2003   The robustness of the intercultural adjustment potential scale (ICAPS): the search for a universal psychological engine of adjustment. *International Journal of Intercultural Relations* 27(5): 543–562.

Matsumoto, David, Seung Hee You and Jeffery LeRoux
this volume Emotion and intercultural adjustment, chapter 5.

Müller-Jacquier, Bernd
    2000   Linguistic Awareness of Cultures-Grundlagen eines Trainingsmoduls [Bases for a training module]. In: Jürgen Bolten (ed.) *Studien zur internationalen Unternehmenskommunikation [Studies of Intercultural Communication in Companies]*, 20–49. Leipzig: Popp.

Podsiadlowski, Astrid
    2002   *Multikulturelle Arbeitsgruppen in Unternehmen [Multicultural Teams in Companies]*. Münster: Waxmann.

Prechtl, Elisabeth and Torsten Kühlmann
    2004   Experten für den Auslandseinsatz auswählen [Selecting experts for an overseas assignment]. *Personalmanager* 6: 34–35.

Rost-Roth, Martina
this volume Intercultural training, chapter 23.

Ruben, Brent D. and Daniel J. Kealey
    1979   Behavioral assessment of communication competency and the prediction of cross-cultural adaptation. *International Journal of Intercultural Relations* 3: 15–47.

Selmer, Jan and Alicia Leung
    2003   Personal characteristics of female vs. male business expatriates. *International Journal of Cross Cultural Management* 3(2): 195–212.

Spencer-Oatey, Helen
  2006   Sociolinguistics and intercultural communication. In: Ulrich Ammon, Nor-
          bert Dittmar, Klaus J. Mattheier and Peter Trudgill (eds.), *Sociolinguisitics.
          An International Handbook of the Science of Language and Society*, Vol. 3,
          2537–2545. Berlin: Walter de Gruyter.
Stahl, Günter
  2001   Using assessment centers as tools for global leadership development: an ex-
          ploratory study. In: Mark Mendenhall, Torsten Kühlmann and Günter Stahl
          (eds), *Developing Global Business Leaders*, 197–210. Westport/ London:
          Quorum Books.
Trickey, David
  n.d.   Diversity management competencies and the development challenge.
          http://www.tco-international.com/articles.aspx [Accessed 1 February 2007].
van den Zee, Karen I. and Ursula Brinkmann
  2002   Assessments in the intercultural field: The Intercultural Readiness Check
          and the Multicultural Personality Questionnaire. *IBI Quarterly* 1(2). Avail-
          able at: http://www.ibinet.nl/ [Accessed 1 February 2007]
Ward, Colleen
  2001   The A, B, Cs of acculturation. In: David Matsumoto (ed.), *The Handbook of
          Culture and Psychology*, 411–445. Oxford: Oxford University Press.
Ward, Colleen and Weining C. Chang
  1997   'Cultural fit': A new perspective on personality sojourner adjustment. *In-
          ternational Journal of Intercultural Relations* 21(4): 525–533.
World Work Limited
          The International Profiler. Download: http://www.worldwork.biz/legacy/
          www/downloads/Introduction.pdf/ [Accessed 1 February 2007]

23. Intercultural Training[1]

Martina Rost-Roth

Intercultural training is of increasing importance and has already tradition. The *Handbook of Intercultural Communication,* edited by Asante, Newmark and Blake, was published in 1979 and contains many useful contributions on training methods. A few years later, Landis and Brislin's (1983) *Handbook of Intercultural Training* was published, and the papers and overviews in this three-volume work show how extensive and versatile the training programs on offer at this point were.

Another sign of the increasing importance of the training area is the setting up of professional organizations. SIETAR, the 'Society for Intercultural Education, Training and Research', was founded in the USA in 1974, and unites the activities of those working in the area of training. 'SIETAR Europa' was founded in 1991 and 'SIETAR Deutschland' in 1994. The SIETAR homepages offer various services, providing information on the organization, journals and other publications, and training programs on offer.[2]

1.   Need for training

The literature on internationalization in the business world frequently refers to the necessity of preparing employees for intercultural contact (Scherm 1995: 249–250), yet companies have long been aware that many expatriate assignments are unsuccessful. Vance and Ensher (2002: 447) point out that 16 to 40 % of managers posted abroad return home prematurely, either because their performance is inadequate, or because they or their families have problems adjusting to the new culture.[3] Additionally, intercultural training is becoming more important not only with regard to postings abroad, but also for business travellers and multicultural teams. The costs of insufficient preparation can have a negative effect not only in the case of premature returners, but also in the form of poor negotiation outcomes. For example, Lanier (1979: 178) makes the point that an estimated 50 % of employees sent abroad do not work efficiently, due to inadequate cultural adjustment. Trimpop and Meynhardt make an even stronger claim:

> The companies assess the success of their foreign postings at less than 30 %. That means they admit that over 70 % of all postings abroad are failures! The number of assignments which thus worked well or very well is likely to be around the 10 % mark. (Trimpop and Meynhardt 2003: 188, translation by the author)

According to Black and Mendenhall (1992: 178), the annual costs of insufficient preparation are estimated to be from 50,000 to 150,000 US dollars in individual cases and several tens of millions of dollars for a company with several hundred expatriate employees.

Black and Gregersen (1999: 53) see an increasing need for training, in view of the fact that 80% of medium-sized and large companies send employees abroad, and 45% of these companies plan to increase this figure. Yet the need for intercultural training is rarely adequately recognized. According to Black and Mendenhall (1992: 178), 70% of US employees who are sent abroad, and 90% of their families, go overseas without any prior intercultural training; similarly, according to a Price Waterhouse study (1997), only 13% of companies offer cultural awareness training for all their staff on a regular basis. Black and Mendenhall (1992) complain that in some cases, companies still maintain the basic assumption that managers who work well at home will also deliver good performance abroad. Nevertheless, the number of shorter intercultural preparation courses (briefings for culturally 'challenging' postings) did increase to 47%, compared to 21% in 1995 (Dowling et al. 1999: 156).

International mergers are also frequently unsuccessful (Niedermeyer 2001: 65). An increasing need for training is thus seen in cross-border mergers and joint ventures. In recent years, there has been a rise in the number of mergers with companies from Eastern Europe. In such cases, difficulties arise because these companies, on the one hand, want 'new' Western know-how, but on the other hand are returning to their own traditions more strongly. Companies can be more successful in this context if they "sensitize their managers to intercultural issues", because conflicts arising from the "implementation of Western management methods" are anticipated and better dealt with (Thomas and Hagemann 1992: 197; Bolten and Dahte 1995).

According to Bolten and Schröter, the wave of mergers and acquisitions since the late 1990s "has led to changes in the international corporate landscape". In their experience, these corporate mergers are "very sensitive and susceptible to disturbance" (Bolten and Schröter 2001: 9). With this in mind, Kammhuber (2001: 78) describes merger consulting as a new working area, and also refers to experiences from the Daimler/Chrysler merger in this context.

Finally, to plan effective intercultural training, it is useful to examine how successful postings are handled. Black and Gregersen (1999) take this approach, and study what characterizes companies with successful outcomes of foreign postings and employees working abroad. They identify three key factors: 1. "knowledge creation and global leadership development", 2. intercultural competence, and 3. well-designed reintegration programs (Black and Gregersen 1999: 54).

2.   Target groups

Gudykunst and Hammer (1983: 143) discuss the question of who should be trained. In the business world, the following areas of application can be distinguished:
–   intercultural training for management,
–   intercultural training for integration of foreign employees and the building of multinational teams,
–   intercultural training for staff in marketing, product management and PR divisions,
–   intercultural training for international negotiation,
–   intercultural training for family members.

Marketing, product management and public relations are becoming increasingly important areas. Problems of intercultural contact arise in these fields in particular, due to the fact that many symbols are dependent on culture, and thus cannot be 'exported' directly. For example, whereas a stork is a symbol of the (happy) birth of a child in Germany, in Singapore it symbolizes death in childbirth. Colour symbolism is also highly dependent on culture (see Kotthoff in this volume). For instance, the colour white is connected with cleanliness and hygiene in western countries, but with mourning and death in Asian cultures. Taking account of such differences is not only absolutely crucial for the success of advertising, but is also important for corporate image representation. In the case of creating a uniform corporate identity, it is essential that the elements chosen do not have a counterproductive effect due to cultural differences.

Intercultural training for multinational teams is also essential for other areas, such as international administration, or for teams of doctors or nursing staff in the medical field (see Roberts in this volume). Thomas and Hagemann (1992) maintain that more problems and conflicts arise in groups comprising three or more cultures than in less culturally diverse groups, and that more time is needed to carry out tasks.

Yet multicultural teams can also provide the potential for creative problem-solving. Adler (2002), for example, demonstrates how intercultural teams can be used to develop valuable synergies. So one task of culture-oriented training programs is to promote appreciation of other cultural approaches.

Another area which is subject to increasing attention is negotiations in international and multicultural contexts (Thomas and Hagemann 1992: 196; Bolten 1992; Ehlich and Wagner 1995).

Family members of staff posted abroad are also receiving increasing attention, as experience shows that the success of the actual employee's work depends crucially on the well-being and support of his or her family. As family members are usually less well integrated, they can experience particular problems. Children over 13 years tend to have particular difficulties. Another frequently occurring problem is that partners have no possibility of being able to work. Referring to the findings of Tung and Andersen (1997) and the Price Waterhouse study (1997–1998), Dowling et al. (1999: 163–164) establish that increasing awareness of the need to involve families is evolving. Thus, for example, training material for children has also been developed (Kaltenhäuser and Swol-Ulbrich 2002).

3.   Types of training

There have been a number of attempts to systematize the range of approaches to intercultural training that now exist in the literature. Brislin, Landis and Brandt (1983: 181) distinguish six different approaches, according to type of learning or training:
- Information or fact-oriented training
- Attribution training (culture assimilator or intercultural sensitizer, learning about values)
- Cultural awareness
- Cognitive behavior modification
- Experiential learning (emphasis on learning through actual experience)
- Interaction training
    Another way in which training programs can be categorized is in relation to their timing, with the following threefold classification:
- (Pre-departure) Orientation training
- Training abroad
- Reintegration training (Thomas 1996).
    Gudykunst and Hammer (1983: 126) distinguish training programmes in two ways, firstly, according to whether they are based primarily on the presentation of information ("didactic") or on an experiential approach ("experiential"), and secondly, on whether they prepare participants for encountering other cultures in general or for dealing with specific individual cultures. Using this system, Gudykunst, Guzley and Hammer (1996) differentiate between four types of training:
I   Experiential culture-general training
II   Experiential culture-specific training
III Didactic culture-general training
IV   Didactic culture-specific training
    The authors provide numerous examples of training techniques for these different types, and also discuss studies evaluating them.
    References to this classification can be found frequently throughout the more recent literature. For instance, Bolten (2001) discusses the advantages and disadvantages of various training concepts with reference to this categorization:

Table 1. Training concepts (Bolten 2001: 9–10, translation by the author)

Culture-general informative training concepts	Culture-specific informative training concepts
– Culture-general assimilator – Seminars on intercultural communication theory, cultural anthropology and comparative cultural psychology – Training videos – Discourse-analysis-based training – Case study analysis	– Culture-specific assimilator – Language classes – Culture-specific seminars on history, everyday history and changing values of a cultural area – Case study analysis
Positive: High cognitive learning effect in relation to the understanding of intercultural communication processes. Negative: Mainly rather academic approach, which is regarded as too abstract by management staff.	Positive: Thorough understanding in relation to the development of a specific cultural system is possible, as long as the approach is not only descriptive but also explanatory. Negative: With a descriptive or fact-based historical approach, reduction to Do's and Taboos; thus a risk of intensifying stereotypes.
Culture-general interaction-oriented training concepts	Culture-specific interaction-oriented training concepts
– Intercultural workshops (multicultural groups) – Simulations, role plays for intercultural sensitization – Self-assessment questionnaires	– Bicultural communication workshops – Culture-specific simulations – Negotiation role plays – Sensitivity training
Positive: Mixed groups can experience interculturality directly. Negative: Simulations etc. are often fictitious and are not taken seriously by the participants.	Positive: Semi-authentic experience of business-related intercultural actions, as long as the training group is bi-cultural. Negative: Culture-specific knowledge is not passed on as a rule.

There is not enough scope in this context to describe all the forms of training in detail (for an overview of further types of training, see also Fowler and Mumford 1999, Cushner and Brislin 1997, and Newton in this volume). However, examples of different conceptions will be provided below.

4.   Simulations and role plays

Simulations and role plays with various guidelines are among the 'classics' in the field of intercultural training. Gudykunst and Hammer (1983) and Gudykunst, Guzley and Hammer (1996) provide an overview of various approaches, concepts and estimations of their effectiveness.

One of the most well-known is certainly 'Bafa Bafa'. This is an experience-oriented method used as general preparation for other cultures. Participants are divided into two groups, which stand for different cultures. Each group initially has to learn certain rules which are crucial for their own culture. Observers are then sent into 'the other culture' to find out its rules. Finally, 'visitors' are exchanged.

> In Bafa Bafa participants simulate two hypothetical cultures: Alpha culture, a male dominated, collectivist culture, and Beta culture, a female dominated, individualistic culture. Trainees typically spend 30 minutes learning the rules to their respective cultures before engaging in brief exchanges between the two. After every one has had a chance to interact with the other culture, trainees attempt to describe and explain what it is that they experienced. Debriefing can explore such issues as attribution formation, anxiety, verbal and nonverbal communication, culture shock, a feeling of 'home' on return to one's 'own group', and so forth. A minimum of three hours is typically required to carry out the simulation with a debriefing. Two trainers are required.
>
> (Cushner and Brislin 1997: 5)

As with many other training programs, Bafa Bafa was first developed as an instrument for the military (Gudykunst and Hammer 1983: 133). Another well-known simulation is the 'Albatros'. The Albatros aims at bringing the participants into a situation in which they are confronted with behaviour and experiences new to them. It serves to show that many things are interpreted wrongly at first sight.

There are also approaches that make use of language learning experience in intercultural training programmes: 'Piglish: A Language Learning Simulation' is regarded as useful, not only for sensitizing individuals without previous language learning experience, but also for experienced language teachers (Hartley and Lapinsky 1999).

Gudykunst et al. (1996) and Fowler and Mumford (1995: 17–126) describe a large number of role plays and simulation games which are used repeatedly in modified forms in various training concepts. For an overview of the possibilities of using simulation games, see also Sisk (1995).

Finally, experimental games and video conferences are also of interest as simulations, and are described below along with other recent developments (see section 9).

5.   Critical incidents and culture assimilator

The 'culture assimilator' – also known as the 'intercultural sensitizer' – was developed in the 1960s. The first assimilator was based on a study of Arab students in the USA, who were questioned on cultural conflict situations. Dealing with such conflict-relevant situations, referred to as 'critical incidents', forms the central content of the training programs.[4]

The training program is provided as written material, which can be either used as it is or integrated as an element of a course program. The objective is to prepare participants for encountering their own and other cultural orientation systems by means of cognitive insights.

Albert (1983: 196) provides an overview of early 'culture assimilators'. Firstly, there are culture assimilators for preparing participants for specific target cultures. Target groups and cultures in this area include, for example, Iran, Honduras and Thailand. Secondly, there are also programs for individual target groups and for dealing with minorities.[5] There are also cultural assimilators that aim to sensitize participants in general (Brislin et al. 1983).

The material is divided into sections, each focusing on specific 'critical incidents' as case studies. There are alternative explanations for every case study. Both adequate explanations from the perspective of the host country are offered as well as false interpretations typical of the participants' own culture or ignorance of cultural influences. Participants select which explanations apply. The programs then set out why certain alternatives can be regarded as correct and others not. Thomas (1996) gives the following example:

"*1. Critical interaction situation 'computer training'*
Due to my working focus on the computer sector, I also hold computer training courses in China. I always ask the participants repeatedly during the courses whether they have understood everything, so that I can carry on with the material. They all answer 'yes'. However, when I then ask a specific question, no one can answer it. I now assume that many participants have not understood the material, although they nod in reply to my question as to whether they have understood. This behaviour on the part of the Chinese always surprises me.

Why don't the Chinese students admit that they haven't understood something? Read through all the possible answers below. Then tick one of the four scale points given for every alternative.

2. Alternative explanations

a) The Chinese students don't want to admit to not understanding because they are afraid of punishment

       most applicable – quite applicable – not very applicable – least applicable.

b) In this learning situation, the pupils don't tell the truth because they want to conceal their weakness and don't want to criticize the teacher.

       most applicable – quite applicable – not very applicable – least applicable

c) [...]

d) [...]

3. Justification of the explanations

Explanation a) This answer is not quite correct. A German teacher is unlikely to want or be able to make Chinese students so scared of punishment that they therefore don't admit to not understanding. [...]

   Explanation b) This answer is correct. For us, too, it is difficult to admit that we haven't really understood something that we ought to. In China teachers are very well respected. Especially if they teach such important subjects as computing it is particularly difficult for students to admit that they do not understand. [...]

                       (Thomas 1996: 122–123, translation by the author)

At the end of each individual unit, information is given on basic 'cultural standards', at a higher level of abstraction. Thomas understands cultural standards as norms and benchmarks for producing and evaluating behavior, whereby the aim is to differentiate various orientation systems. The basic assumption is that cultural standards can be reconstructed via the analysis of critical incidents (Thomas 1996 and 1999: 115; see also Franklin in this volume). In the training material, the description of cultural standards is included. For example, the following standards are seen as significant for dealing with the Chinese culture:

- social harmony (HE)
- hierarchy
- relationships ('GUANXI' and 'RENQING', 'RENJI GUANXI')
- 'work unit', 'unit where you live' ('DANWEI')
- face (MIANZI)
- respect, Politeness ('QIANGONG XING')
- 'relativism of rules'(Liang/Kammhuber 2003: 171–182, translation by the author)

In most cases, around 10 standards are listed per target culture. The descriptions in the materials are frequently found useful as an initial orientation. However, critics also see a risk that the descriptions of cultural standards in the training material become absolute. The authors Müller and Thomas (1991: 12) themselves refer to the critical aspect that differences are emphasized, whereas common factors tend to remain in the background.

6.   Linguistic Awareness of Cultures

Training programs that prepare participants not only for specific target cultures, but also for more general problems in contact situations with other cultures, centre on differences in behaviour. Programs such as 'Linguistic Awareness of Cultures' make reference to discourse and more subtle linguistic areas. This training program was essentially initiated by Müller-Jacquier, and was developed as part of the research project 'Intercultural Behavioral Training' (Helmolt and Müller 1991: 518), whereby the program also makes reference to Gumperz (Müller-Jacquier 2000: 33).[6]

The term *'Linguistic* Awareness of Cultures' (abbreviated hereafter as LAC) refers back to the term 'Cultural Awareness Training'. One key aspect of this training concept is that it attempts to make participants aware of differences in communicative behavior. Another crucial point is that it is not only concerned with passing on knowledge of individual differences in communication habits, but also aims to teach strategies for deriving cultural differences. Here, Müller-Jacquier opposes normative problem-solving strategies, such as those that principally form the basis of the culture assimilators, and the explanatory patterns these offer, which primarily emphasize psychological insights and differing value orientations (Müller-Jacquier 2000: 20–22). In contrast, he attempts to make participants aware that there are often (only) differences in conventions. This approach is based on teaching linguistic categories to describe typical intercultural interaction problems, which arise from differing communication rules. The program illustrates how individual linguistic and communicative areas can be influenced by culture and determined by different conventions and behavioral expectations.

Different linguistic areas are illustrated with the help of examples, which are also presented to a certain extent as 'critical incidents'. However, the objective is not to carry out 'isomorphic attributions' and ascriptions, but to make cross-culturally functioning mechanisms visible (Müller-Jacquier 2000: 8). The overriding learning target is a more general sensitization to everyday communication and problems of intercultural communication, and the following linguistic areas are addressed (Müller-Jacquier 2000: 27–39):

1) The program illustrates that *lexical items and social meanings* often cannot be transferred directly from one language or culture to another, as they reflect cross-sections of social reality in each case, and these can be very different in different cultural contexts. Examples of terms which show such differing culturally influenced conceptions include *Sunday, friend, friendliness, coziness, order, school, church, going for a walk.* It also points out that sometimes there is no equivalent in other languages for certain words, or that different terms 'coincide'. The Japanese word *'kyaku'* is used as one example of differing concep-

tualizations; the term covers the German or English/American words *'Kunde'/ 'customer'* and *'Gast'/'guest'*.

2) *Speech acts* may be realized in different forms, and speech acts that appear identical may be based on differing interpretations. Different conventions are illustrated, for example, by means of responses to compliments, and conventions for giving invitations in which different formulations imply different levels of commitment (Müller-Jacquier 2000: 28–29).

3) *Conversational organization and conventions of discourse sequence:* In this context, the program thematizes differences in the organization of speaker exchanges (rather long silent phases in Japanese; different realizations of overlapping and interruption in French and German), or different realizations of conversational conditions (see Günthner in this volume). Differences are also displayed in overriding structures and expectations of the course of conversations. For example, Spanish people may not be used to German expectations that points on an agenda should be discussed in a fixed order and should not be taken up or questioned later on (Müller-Jacquier 2000: 29–31).

4) The program shows that there are also differing taboo *subjects*, and that tabooization may differ depending on situations or points in time.

5) Training approaches that do not simply contrast two cultures, but refer to several cultures in comparison, have a decisive advantage in sensitizing participants to differing *levels of directness*:

> If one establishes comparatively that, for example, Germans are direct with regard to communicative disclosure of speech intentions, and Swedes are indirect [...], it is easy to forget to point out – as in many comparative approaches – that these statements are to be regarded as relational, and that, for example, a number of Asian speakers would describe Swedes as very direct. (Müller-Jacquier 2000: 31)

This makes it clear that contrasts and qualifications do not exist as absolute quantities, but that qualifications and assessments arise from different starting points and perspectives.

6) Participants are made aware of *register differences* and that speakers select language variants and speech styles depending on the situation, status of conversational partners, etc. Differing formality grades play a particular role in this register selection. This is shown, for example, in differing forms of greetings and address and their evaluation for defining the situation and relationship (see Kotthoff in this volume).

7) *Paraverbal communication* is an extremely interesting area, which is neglected in most other training programs. The objective is to clarify the differing effects of intonation and prosodic phenomena. For instance, Japanese intonation often sounds monotonous to German listeners. Germans often find that a certain high tone of voice frequently heard among French native speakers sounds affected. Differing assessments are also displayed with regard to speech volume.

Speaking quietly is seen as an expression of control over one's emotions in Japan, and positively evaluated. Pauses in speech are also valued positively, as they are seen as a sign of reflection. However, in other cultures, speaking quietly with long pauses may be interpreted as an expression of insecurity, and judged negatively.

8) The field of *nonverbal communication*, which is particularly prone to false interpretation in cultural comparisons as it is rarely perceived consciously, is also integrated into the training program. There are considerable differences, for example, in the area of eye contact. In Japan, speakers tend to make eye contact less frequently and for shorter periods than in Germany. Gestures also show differences in cultural conventions.

There are differing expectations and interpretations in relation to posture and body language, too: in Japan, a calm position is assessed as an expression of good manners, and women who fold their arms are often seen as arrogant. With regard to aspects of facial expressions such as smiling, there are also considerable differences. Thus, smiling is also used in Japan, for example – unlike in Western societies – to conceal anger. Differences in the area of proximity are also critical, as bodily closeness or distance is often interpreted psychologically.

9) The program shows that *value orientation and attitudes* are manifested in the form of interaction. It quotes, e.g., the dimensions introduced by Hofstede – i.e. individualism/collectivism, high/low power distance, high/low uncertainty avoidance, masculinity/femininity, long-term/short-term life planning. The aim is to illustrate that differences only appear via contrasts, and that such orientations affect all the other areas of speech behavior described here.

10) As a further area, *rituals* in the various life domains are also thematized (Kotthoff in this volume). Thus, for example, representatives of other cultures find it strange that guests knock on the table of a public house or bar in Germany, or that adults shake children's hands to congratulate them on their birthdays.

By means of cross-linguistic and cross-cultural comparison for these communication areas, 'Linguistic Awareness of Cultures' attempts to make participants aware that linguistic behavior may be based on diverse conventions.

The training is delivered through interactively designed presentations, group work and self-learning phases. Recently, video material has also been made available. The objectives include practicing 'proposing alternative explanatory hypotheses' and promoting meta-communicative skills.

"The following case illustrates our points:
Dr. Greiner has just been appointed department head in a German company's branch office in Seoul, Korea. After he arrives, he calls his first team meeting. He prepared questions in advance to help him get oriented to the work at that branch, to gather im-

portant information, and, at the same time, to begin to "socialize" with his future colleagues. However, not very long into the meeting, he realizes that his Korean colleagues' answers are very vague. Indeed, they seem to become increasingly vague and even evasive the more precisely he phrases his questions. To ensure that they understand his English, he repeats his questions whenever the answers are provided reluctantly. He smiles and attempts to make eye contact. Finally, he states that if his colleagues have any questions, he would be very happy to answer them. But there are none. After the meeting he does not know much more than he did before and is quite irritated. He assumes they have hidden agendas and want something from him. He resolves to gather some of the needed information in formal and informal face-to-face conversations (in his office and also at the lunch table) and to phrase his questions even more precisely at the next meeting.

Many leaders would, like Dr. Greiner, attempt to find culturally oriented explanations and solutions to their experience; however, the results would be limited. We propose that a truly effective leader will also generate hypotheses about the different linguistic conventions that might explain the situation. A linguistic analysis would yield a number of additional hypotheses. For example, relying on a linguistic explanation of directness and indirectness, leaders might consider that the Korean colleagues are giving contextualized answers to the questions. However, they would note that Dr. Greiner seems to be misinterpreting these context-sensitive statements as vague even though, according to Korean conventions, they are quite clear. Therefore, he cannot understand why he was not provided with concrete information. Linguistically sensitive leaders might also propose that speech acts explain the situation. They might hypothesize that Dr. Greiner posed questions in a way that seemed to be calling for a decision or yes/no response without realizing that in a high-context culture (...) like Korea, such questions may be seen as requiring a face-threatening commitment that the Koreans want to avoid.

Third, they could propose that Dr. Greiner was not introduced according to Korean discourse conventions. Because proper introductions may be an important prerequisite for communication in first-contact situations, the Koreans may have been hesitant to respond to his questions.

Relying on the linguistic perspective of nonverbal communication, leaders might contemplate that Dr. Greiner wrongly interpreted his colleagues' lowered eyes as a sign of embarrassment or ignorance. He may not have recognized it as a gesture of politeness towards their superior.

Global leaders would also benefit from analyzing Dr. Greiner's reactions to the Koreans' responses using a linguistic-interactionist point of view. Considering the effects of foreign behavior on the situation and relying on the linguistic notion of speech acts, they might propose that Dr. Greiner's reaction to his interpretation of the Korean answers of asking even more concrete decision questions was unsuitable for the situation. Thereby, he provoked his colleagues to give even vaguer answers and avoid eye contact more strongly, interactively causing even more misunderstanding. In addition, they may analyze the nonverbal communication, noting that Dr. Greiner reacted to the Korean's convention of avoidance of eye contact by trying even harder to obtain it. Thereby, he might have provoked an even more intense avoidance of eye contact.

Finally, linguistically savvy leaders would analyze the conventions of discourse and observe that Dr. Greiner caused further insecurity in the response behavior of his co-participants by repeating questions that had been understood and even answered already. This analysis illustrates how important it is to come up with multiple explanations for reconstructed critical incidents (regardless of whether they are personal experiences or documented in the literature). All the explanatory hypotheses have the potential of being accurate, for the given case study as well as for other German-Korean or U.S.-Korean interactions." (Müller-Jacquier and Whitener 2001: 236–238)

The program is further characterized by an interactionist perspective, which takes the interculturality of conflict situations into account. The authors work on the assumption that participants in intercultural encounters not only act on the basis of the principles of their own cultural socialization, but also display new forms as they react and adjust to their interlocutors.

One factor worth remarking on is that the ability to form alternative and multiple explanatory hypotheses is seen as the basis for fostering intercultural competence (see also Wiseman 2002); it is a skill that is more helpful overall for intercultural contact situations than the need for knowing correct solutions.

7.   Discourse analysis-based training

Training programs based on discourse analysis explicitly target communication problems in everyday working life. The aim is to promote behavioral changes through participants reflecting on their own practical work. This approach requires relatively intensive advance preparation, as participants deal with case studies from their own work. The basic principles are presented in Liedke, Redder and Scheiter (1999). The first aim is to reveal fundamental communicative problems, not to pass on "magic recipes" (Liedke, Redder and Scheiter 1999: 158). The second aim is to attempt to generate behavioural changes principally by analyzing situations occurring in sound transcripts or video recordings, and by extending these in role plays. This training concept has been put into practice mainly in the field of governmental communication and training for public administration staff who deal with foreign clients.

Ten Thije (2001) also presents a discourse analysis-based training program. It is worth noting in this context that the selection of case studies and discussions is not limited to dealing with misunderstandings,[7] but also seeks to focus on other aspects of intercultural situations, such as creating common ground (see also Koole and ten Thije 1994 on the theoretical foundation of this aspect). Reflecting on the scope for action is regarded as particularly important. For a program adapting authentic workplace talk for training purposes, see Newton in this volume.

8.   Coaching, consulting, training on the job – recent tendencies in intercultural competence training

The terms 'coaching' and 'consulting' are gaining increasing significance (see particularly Bolten 2001). Bolten attributes the demand for such new forms of training to the fact that preparation time prior to foreign assignments, and thus the time available for preparatory 'off-the-job' measures and training is being reduced.

Furthermore, findings such as those of Stahl (1998: 157 and 171) indicate that many problems that occur during periods abroad do not decrease with longer lengths of stay. This can also be seen as one reason why 'on-the-job' training – in contrast to outsourced 'off-the-job' courses – is gaining in importance. Correspondingly, Dowling et al. (1999: 157) and Oechsler (2002: 876–878) cite support in everyday work as an important component for supporting foreign assignments and a prerequisite for success.

Bolten (2001) compares 'on-the-job' and 'off-the-job' training schemes:

Table 2. Training schemes (Bolten 2001: 3, translation by the author)

off-the-job	on-the-job
Intercultural training as conventional cognitive and awareness training; *Intercultural experimental games* Professionally oriented experimental games, in which intercultural on-the-job situations are simulated	*Intercultural mediation* Mediating activity in open and concealed conflicts in multicultural teams
Intercultural consulting Providing intercultural advice to management personnel on issues of staffing international teams and in assignment and reintegration processes	*Intercultural coaching* Coaching and supervising multicultural teams with the aim of making them aware of their own culture-specific actions, and formulating synergy potentials as targets

One prime advantage of on-the-job programs, in comparison to traditional off-the-job training, is that they enable more direct reactions to dysfunctional situations. Bolten (2001) sees two main roles for coaches: firstly, the coach as a metacommunicator, supervisor and moderator who has high-level analytic skills for understanding communication and interaction processes, and secondly, the coach as a moderator and expert, who also helps to implement the suggestions of consultants. The job of consultants, in turn, consists mainly of providing advice for making decisions over staffing teams, foreign assignments or re-integration programs.

The use of mediators is a further 'on-the-job' measure. Mediators, as independent persons, can be used to facilitate communication and to work with parties involved in conflicts. The mediator attempts to take all the different interests into account, in order to come up with mutually agreed solutions (Bolten 2001 and Mayer and Boness 2005).

A further tendency that can be observed is an increase in efforts to integrate experience in the location itself (Vance and Ensher 2002). Thus, companies attempt to use the 'Host Country Workforce (HCW)' as an additional source of information and potential. This opens up possibilities for passing on critical incidents and information on workplace standards directly, as a resource for mentoring and on-the-job coaching.

A further recent tendency is experimental games training for staff (usually managers) involved in foreign assignments, or in bi-national or multinational groups, along with representatives of the target country. Training can also take place via video conference. Participants are set tasks which they have to solve jointly with representatives of the other culture or other company. The trainers intervene to point out cultural differences and initiate behavioral modification. 'Interact' (Bolten 1999) is an experimental game specifically related to the participants' everyday work. The participants form groups which differ according to the cultural origin and native languages of the members. The groups are placed in different places or rooms with one trainer each. One task of the game is to enter into cooperative negotiations. This training method uses work-related tasks and highly specialized demands to create a 'semi-authentic scenario', enabling participants and trainers to recognize typical behavior patterns in intercultural interactions, which are supposed to be reflected in the context of the training.

9.   Video Material, CD ROMs and Websites

There are an increasing number of training programs in the form of video material. One well known and relatively widespread example is Copeland und Griggs' (1985) *Going International*. This program covers the following elements:
- Bridging the culture gap
- Managing the overseas assignment
- Beyond culture shock
- Welcome home, stranger
- Working in the USA
- Living in the USA

–   Going international – safely
–   Cross-cultural relationships and workshops

Each tape includes critical incidents, interviews with experts, and advice. Gudykunst, Guzley and Hammer (1996) comment that particularly *Bridging the Cultural Gap, Beyond Culture Shock* and *Welcome Home Stranger* can be put to good use to illustrate intercultural communication processes. Information on these programs can be found at http://www.griggs.com/videos/giser.shtml/ (accessed 12. 02. 2006). This site promotes video products by stating an increasing need for training due to increasing globalization, and estimating the cost to the economy ("each year billions of dollars are lost"). The video material is supplemented by a users' guide. The site also recommends using the series *Global Contrasts* as an additional resource.

The series *Valuing Diversity*[8] is also well known. These films primarily aim to make viewers aware of the dynamics underlying encounters between individuals with different backgrounds. The series also aims to promote self-reflection.

Another set of training material is *Diversophy*, developed by George Simons International, which is available as a card game set or in an online version and as *Tele-diversophy* for mobile phones. It is aimed at varied occupational groups, and is developed for different cultural contexts. Its objective is to create "a low-risk environment where participants feel free to confront their prejudices and increase awareness".[9]

Summerfield (1993) provides references to numerous film and video material. More recent examples are the video materials produced under the direction of Trickey and Ewington, which aim "to illustrate cultural diversity in multicultural teams"[10] and to specify "competencies required for managing in an international context"[11] or Jonamay, Myers and Simons (2000) as a CD-ROM assisted handbook of training exercises for professionals.

There is also increasing interest in instruments that assess competences and provide profiles of people who work in intercultural and international settings. For example, *The International Profiler* questionnaire, developed by interculturalists and psychometricians at WorldWork Ltd., London, and available in various languages, supplies licensed consultants with a respondent's profile across 'a set of of ten competencies (with 22 associated skills, attitudes and areas of knowledge) that define the special capabilities required to transfer leadership, managerial and professional skills to an international context'.[12] The *INCA project* assessment tools, which are also designed to be used by different cultural groups, are available online in English, German and Czech.[13] For more information on assessment and self-assessment of intercultural competence, see also Prechtl and Davidson Lund in this volume.

For further up-to-date information on this steadily growing field, readers should consult the relevant journals,[14] which are also represented on the internet, and the homepage and links of SIETAR.[15] Instructions for the development and use of video programmes in different contexts can be found in Fowler and Mumford (1999). For opportunities to develop CD-Roms and online materials, see especially Simons and Quappe (2000).

10.   Selection criteria for training programs

Since intercultural training courses are based on very different training approaches, the question of what criteria to use in practice for selecting a training program is complicated. Scherm (1995), with reference to other studies, regards three criteria as important:
– Length of the foreign assignment;
– Extent of the interaction in the foreign culture, i.e. frequency and intensity of contacts to the cultural surroundings;
– Divergence between the host and the home culture (degree of unfamiliarity). (Scherm 1995: 248, translation by the author).

Black and Mendenhall (1992) also address the question of what criteria should be used for selecting training programs. They initially establish that up to now, there is no systematic way of comparing different intercultural training courses and their characteristics. So they regard the question of how to determine different forms of training intensity (i.e. 'rigour') as central. The intensity is partly determined by the way in which the training concepts integrate learners. The learning theory assumption that the level of difficulty of grasping something is partly dependent on how new or unfamiliar the behavior to be learned is, is translated into contact with other cultures. Linguistic contrasts and the previous experience of the parties are also taken into account. Further factors are the length of the assignment and 'job novelty'.

11.   Effectiveness of intercultural training

The evaluation of training is a broad-based area of research, to which this article can only make a marginal reference. Problems of evaluating training programs are described in the first volume of Landis and Brislin's *Handbook of Intercultural Training* (1983). There has also been a great deal of literature dealing with the problem of evaluation since then (see particularly Blake and Heslin 1983; Kinast 1998: 20–54 for methodological problems; see also Trimpop and Meynhardt 2003; Morris and Robie 2001). Blake and Heslin discuss the following research methods and data sources:
1. self reports;
2. judgments of significant others […];
3. archival/objective measures;

4. evaluator observations; and
5. measures of one's overt behavior.

Assessing training effectiveness often entails using the model developed by Kirkpatrick. According to Kirkpatrick (1994) evaluation of training should explore reactions of trainees, learning, transfer/behaviour and results at successive levels, each level providing information important for the next level:

1. reactions (measures how participants react to the training program),
2. learning (attempts to assess the amount of learning, e.g. skills, knowledge, attitude),
3. transfer (how the newly acquired skills, knowledge, or attitude are being used),
4. results (improved quality, decreased costs?).

Brislin et al. (1983) maintain that the possible positive effects of training fall into three areas:
– Changes in thinking,
– Changes in feelings,
– Changes in behavior. (Brislin et al. 1983: 7–8)

Black and Mendenhall (1992) summarize findings on the effect of intercultural training programs from various studies as follows:

> 9 out of 10 studies that examined the relationship between training and self-confidence in the ability to behave effectively in intercultural situations, established a positive connection; 16 out of 16 found positive correlations with more suitable perceptions in intercultural contact; 9 out of 9 found a positive correlation with adjustment processes (for a summary of the findings, see Black and Mendenhall 1992: 179).

Hammer (1999) also provides an overview of the effects of intercultural training, and lists the following factors as being significant for success:

> There are three fundamental outcomes that indicate the success or failure of expatriate adaptation and that guide the development of cross-cultural training efforts: personal/family adjustment and satisfaction, intercultural interaction, and professional effectiveness (Hammer 1999: 9).

Drawing on the findings from Black and Mendenhall's studies, Hammer summarizes them as follows:

> In short, cross-cultural training has been shown to develop cross-cultural skills that affect subsequent success in an overseas assignment, improve expatriates' psychological comfort and satisfaction with living and working in a foreign culture, and improve task accomplishment in the cross-cultural environment. (Hammer 1999: 8)

Of course, the effectiveness of training programs is highly dependent on the trainer's abilities.[16]

To conclude, 'intercultural competence' is an extremely complex phenomenon, and a combination of different training methods seems desirable, because combining different training approaches makes optimal use of their advantages while compensating for their shortcomings.

Notes

1 I am greatly indebted to Helen Spencer-Oatey for her editorial advice and Peter Franklin for helpful comments and hints.
2 http://www.sietar-europa.org/, 12. 02. 2006
3 See also Black and Gregersen (1999) and Black and Mendenhall (1992: 178), who refer to various studies.
4 On the original idea of 'culture assimilators', see Fiedler and Triandis (1971). The technique of centering discussion on critical incidents originates from Flanagan (1954). Ideal critical incidents for culture assimilators are seen as fulfilling the following criteria (in this case formulated for Americans as the addressees of the training): a) a common occurrence in which an American and a host national interact, b) a situation which the American finds conflictful, puzzling, or which he is likely to misinterpret and c) a situation which can be interpreted in a fairly unequivocal manner, given sufficient knowledge about the culture. (Fiedler, Mitchell, Triandis 1971: 97)
5 See for example Slobodin et al. (1992) *The Culture Assimilator: For Interaction with the Economically Disadvantaged* or Landis and Miller (1973) *The Army Culture Assimilator: Interacting with Black Soldiers* or Müller and Thomas (1991) *Interkulturelles Orientierungstraining für die USA,* or Brüch and Thomas 1995 *Beruflich in Südkorea. Interkulturelles Orientierungstraining für Manager, Fach- und Führungskräfte.*
6 See also Knapp/Knapp-Potthoff (1990) for general strategies for enhancing mutual understanding.
7 For literature on miscommunication and misunderstanding see Coupland, Wiemann and Giles [sic!] (1991) and Rost-Roth (2006).
8 http://www.griggs.com/videos/vdser.shtml, 12. 02. 2006
9 http://www.diversophy.com, 12. 02. 2006
10 http://www.tco-international.com/team.asp, 12. 02. 2006
11 http://www.tco-international.com/competencies.asp, 12. 02. 2006
12 http://www.worldwork.biz/legacy/www/downloads/Introduction.pdf, 12. 02. 2006
13 http://www.incaproject.org, 12. 02. 2006
14 See for instance the *European Journal of Intercultural Studies* (http://www.intercultural.at/, 12. 02. 2006), *Interculture-Online* (http://www.interculture-online.info/index.php?bereich=backissues&ausg=1&inhalt=1&lang=deu, 12. 02. 06, or '*International Journal of Human Resource Management*' (http://www.tandf.co.uk/journals/titles/09585192.asp, 12. 02. 2006).
15 http://www.sietar.de/SIETARproject/3.0Interculturale-learning.html, 23. 11. 2005
16 Paige (1996) goes into more detail on the required skills for trainers.

References

Adler, Nancy J.
2002   *International Dimensions of Organizational Behavior.* 4th edition. Cincinnati Ohio: South-Western.

Albert, Rosita D.
1983   The intercultural sensitizer or culture assimilator. In: Dan Landis and Richard Brislin (eds.), *Handbook of Intercultural Training Volume I: Issues in Theory and Design,* 186–217. New York: Pergamon.

Asante, Molefi Kete, Eileen Newmark and Cecil A. Blake (eds.)
1979   *Handbook of Intercultural Communication.* London: Sage.

Bennett, Milton and Jane Bennett
1992   *Audio-Visual Resources: Selected Reference Materialis for Using Films and Videos.* [http://www.iaccp.org/teaching/films/bennett.pdf, 12. 02. 2006].

Black, J. Stewart and Mark Mendenhall
1992   A practical but theory-based framework for selecting cross-cultural training methods. In: Mark Mendenhall and Gary Oddou (eds.): *International human resource management,* 177–204. Boston: PWS-Kent.

Black, J. Stewart and Hal B. Gregersen
1999   The Right Way to Manage Expats. *Harvard Buisness Review,* 52–63.

Blake, Brian F. and Richard Heslin
1983   Evaluating Cross-Cultural Training. In: Dan Landis and Richard Brislin (eds.): *Handbook of Intercultural Training Volume I: Issues in Theory and Design,* 203–223. New York: Pergamon.

Bolten, Jürgen
1992   Interkulturelles Verhandlungstraining [Intercultural Negotiation Training]. *Jahrbuch Deutsch als Fremdsprache,* 18, 269–287. München: iudicium.

Bolten, Jürgen
1999   InterAct: Zur Konzeption eines interkulturellen Unternehmensplanspiels [Interact: The Conception of an Intercultural Business Simulation]. In: *InterAct: Ein wirtschaftsbezogenes interkulturelles Planspiel für die Zielkulturen Australien, Deutschland, Frankreich, Italien, Großbritannien, Niederlande, Ostasien, Rußland, Spanien und USA, [InterAct: The Conception of an Intercultural Business Simulation Game for the Target Cultures Australia, Germany, France, Italy, Great Britain, The Netherlands, East Asia, Russia, Spain and the USA],* 94–99. Sternenfels: Wissenschaft und Praxis.

Bolten, Jürgen
2001   Interkulturelles Coaching, Mediation, Training und Consulting als Aufgaben des Personalmanagements internationaler Unternehmen [Intercultural Coaching, Mediation, Training and Consulting as Tasks for Human Resources Managers in International Corporations]. In: Alois Clermont, Wilhelm Schmeisser and Dieter Krimphove (eds.), *Strategisches Personalmanagement in Globalen Unternehmen [Strategic Human Resource Management in Global Corporations],* 1–16. München: Vahlen. [http://www2. uni-jena.de/philosophie/iwk/forschung/Publikationen/Coaching.pdf, 30. 1. 2005].

Bolten, Jürgen and Marion Dahte (eds.)
1995   *Transformation und Integration: Aktuelle Probleme und Perspektiven west-/ost-europäischer Wirtschaftsbeziehungen* [*Transformation and Integration: Western/Eastern European Business Relations: Current Problems and Perspectives*], Sternenfels: Verlag Wissenschaft und Praxis.

Bolten, Jürgen and Daniela Schröter (eds.)
2001   *Im Netzwerk interkulturellen Handelns.* [*In the Network of Intercultural Action*] Sternenfels: Verlag Wissenschaft und Praxis.

Brislin, Richard, Dan Landis and Mary E. Brandt
1983   Conceptualizations of Intercultural Behavior and Training. In: Dan Landis and Richard Brislin (eds.), *Handbook of Intercultural Training. Volume I: Issues in Theory and Design*, 1–35. New York: Pergamon.

Brown, Penelope and Stephen Levinson
1978   Universals in Language Usage: Politeness Phenomena. In: Esther N. Goody (ed.), *Questions and Politeness: Strategies in Social interaction*, 56–289. Cambridge: Cambridge University Press.

Brüch, Andreas and Alexander Thomas
1995   *Beruflich in Südkorea: Interkulturelles Orientierungstraining für Manager, Fach- und Führungskräfte* [*On business in South Korea: Intercultural Orientation Training for Managers, Professionals, and Executives*]. Heidelberg: Roland Asanger.

Copeland, Lennie and Lewis Griggs
1985   *Going International.* New York: Random House.

Coupland, Nikolas, Howard Giles and John M. Wiemann (eds.)
1991   *Miscommunication and Problematic Talk.* Newbury Park/ London/ New Delhi: Sage.

Coupland, Nikolas, John M. Wiemann and Howard Giles
1991   Talk as 'Problem' and Communication as 'Miscommunication': An Integrative Analysis. In: Nikolas Coupland, Howard Giles, and John M. Wiemann (eds.): *Miscommunication and Problematic Talk*, 1–49. Newbury Park/ London/ New Delhi: Sage.

Cushner, Kenneth and Richard W. Brislin
1996   *Intercultural interactions: A practical guide*, Thousand Oaks: Sage.

Cushner, Kenneth and Richard W. Brislin
1997   *Improving Intercultural Interactions: Modules for Cross-Cultural Training Programs.* Volume 2. Thousand Oaks: Sage.

Dowling, Peter J., Denice E. Welch and Randall S. Schuler
1999   *International Human Resource Management: Managing People in a Multinational Context.* Cincinnati: South Western College Publishing.

Ehlich, Konrad and Johannes Wagner (eds.)
1995   *The Discourse of Business Negotiation.* Berlin/ New York: Mouton de Gruyter.

Fiedler, Fred E., Terence Mitchell and Harry C. Triandis
1971   The Culture Assimilator: An Approach to Cross-cultural Training. *Journal of Applied Psychology*, 55, 95–102.

Flanagan, John C.
1954   The Critical Incident Technique, 327–358. In: *Psychological Bulletin*, 51.

Fowler, Sandra M. and Monica G. Mumford
 1995   *Intercultural Sourcebook: Cross-Cultural Training Methods*, Volume 1,
         Yarmouth: Intercultural.
Fowler, Sandra M. and Monica G. Mumford
 1999   *Intercultural Sourcebook: Cross-Cultural Training Methods*, Volume 2,
         Yarmouth: Intercultural.
Franklin, Peter
this volume Differences & difficulties in intercultural management interaction.
         Chapter 13.
Gudykunst, William B. and Mitchell Hammer
 1983   Basic Training Design: Approaches to Intercultural Training. In: Dan
         Landis and Richard Brislin (eds.): *Handbook of Intercultural Training, Vol-
         ume I: Issues in Theory and Design*, 118–154. New York: Pergamon.
Gudykunst, William B., Ruth Guzley and Mitchell Hammer
 1996   Designing Intercultural Training. In: Dan Landis and Rubi Bhagat (eds.),
         Handbook of Intercultural Training. 2nd edition, 61–80. Thousand Oaks:
         Sage.
Gudykunst, William B. and Bella Mody (eds.)
 2002   *International and Intercultural Communication*. Thousand Oaks: Sage.
Günthner, Susanne
this volume *Intercultural communication and the relevance of cultural specific reper-
         toires of communicative genres*. Chapter 7
Gumperz, John J.
 1982   *Discourse Strategies*. Cambridge: Cambridge University Press.
Gumperz, John J., Tom Jupp and Celia Roberts
 1979   *Crosstalk: A Study of Crosscultural Communication*. Southall: NCILT
         National Centre for Industrial Language Training.
Hammer, Mitchell R.
 1999   Cross-Cultural Training: The Research Connection. In: Sandra M. Fowler
         and Monica G. Mumford (eds.), *Intercultural Sourcebook: Cross-Cultural
         Training Methods*. Volume 2, 1–18. Yarmouth: Intercultural.
Hartley, Cay and Terri Lapinsky
 1999   Piglish: A Language Learning Simulation. In: Sandra M. Fowler and Mon-
         ica G. Mumford (eds.), *Intercultural Sourcebook: Cross-Cultural Training
         Methods*. Volume 2, 131–141. Yarmouth: Intercultural.
Helmolt, Katharina v. and Bernd-Dietrich Müller
 1991   Zur Vermittlung interkultureller Kompetenzen [Teaching Intercultural Skills].
         In: Bernd-Dietrich Müller (ed.), *Interkulturelle Wirtschaftskommunikation*
         [*Intercultural Business Communication*], 509–548. München: iudicium.
Inman, Marianne
 1985   Language and Cross-Cultural Training in American Multinational Corpor-
         ations. *The Modern Language Journal*, 69, 3, 247–255.
Jonamay, Lambert, Selma Myers and George Simons
 2000   *Global Competence: 50 Training Activities for Succeeding in International
         Business*. Amherst MA: Human Resource Development.
Kaltenhäuser, Bettina and Hilly v. Swol-Ulbrich
 2006   *Andere Länder, andere Kinder* [*Other Countries. Other*]. Frankfurt a. M.:
         VAS Verlag.

Kammhuber, Stefan
  2001   Interkulturelle Trainingsforschung: Bestandsaufnahme und Perspektiven
          [Intercultural Training Research: Overview and Perspectives]. In: Jürgen
          Bolten and Daniela Schröter (eds.), *Im Netzwerk interkulturellen Handelns*
          [*In the Network of Intercultural Action*], 78–93. Sternenfels: Verlag Wis-
          senschaft und Praxis.
Kinast, Eva-Ulrike
  1998   *Evaluation interkultureller Trainings* [*Evaluation of intercultural training*],
          Berlin: Papst Science.
Kirkpatrick, Donald L.
  1994   *Evaluating Training Programs: The Four Levels.* San Francisco CA: Ber-
          rett-Koehler.
Knapp, Karlfried and Knapp-Potthoff, Annelie
  1990   Interkulturelle Kommunikation, *Zeitschrift für Fremdsprachenforschung*
          [Journal of Foreign Language Research], 1: 62–93
Koole, Tom and Jan D. ten Thije
  1994   *The Construction of Intercultural Discourse.* Amsterdam/ Atlanta: Editions
          Rodopi.
Kotthoff, Helga
this volume Ritual and Style in Intercultural Communication. Chapter 9.
Landis, Dan and Richard W. Brislin (eds.)
  1983   *Handbook of Intercultural Training Volume I: Issues in Theory and Design.*
          Volume 2. *Issues in Teaching Methodology. Volume 3. Area Studies in In-
          tercultural Training.* New York: Pergamon.
Landis, Dan and Radhika Baghat (eds.)
  1996   *Handbook of Intercultural Training.* 2nd edition. Thousand Oaks CA:
          Sage.
Landis, Dan and Miller, A. (sic)
  1973   The Army Culture assimilator. Lukeacting with black soldiers. Philadel-
          phia: Center for Social Development.
Lanier, Alison R.
  1979   Selection and Preparation for Overseas Transfers. *Personnel Journal*, 58,
          160–163.
Liang, Yong and Stefan Kammhuber
  2003   Ostasien: China [East Asia: China]. In: Alexander Thomas, Stefan Kamm-
          huber and Sylvia Schroll-Machl (eds.), *Handbuch Interkulturelle Kom-
          munikation und Kooperation. Vol. 2: Länder, Kulturen und Interkulturelle
          Berufstätigkeit* [*Handbook of intercultural communication and Cooper-
          ation. Vol. 2. Countries, Cultures, and Intercultural Employment*], 171–185,
          Göttingen: Vandenhoeck & Ruprecht.
Lieberman, Simma, George Simons and Kate Berardo
  2003   *Putting Diversity to Work: What to know and do to get the best out of a di-
          verse workforce.* Canada: Crisp.
Liedke, Martina, Angelika Redder and Susanne Scheiter
  1999   Interkulturelles Handeln lehren – ein diskursanalytischer Trainingsansatz
          [Teaching Intercultural Action – A Discourse Analytic Approach]. In:
          Gisela Brünner, Reinhard Fiehler and Walther Kindt (eds.), *Angewandte*

Diskursforschung, Bd. 2. Methoden und Anwendungsbereiche [*Applied Discourse Research. Vol. 2. Methods and Areas of Practice*], 148–179. Opladen: Westdeutscher Verlag.

Macharzina, Klaus and Michael-Jörg Oesterle (eds.)
2002   *Handbuch Internationales Management: Grundlagen – Instrumente – Perspektiven* [*Handbook of International Management: Basics – Instruments – Perspectives*]. 2nd edition. Wiesbaden: Gabler.

Mayer, Claude-Hélène and Christian M. Boness
2005   *Intercultural Mediation & Conflict Resolution*, Stuttgart: ibidem.

Morris, Mark A. and Chet Robie
2001   A meta-analysis of the effects of cross-cultural training on expatriate performance and adjustment. *International Journal of Training and Development*, 5, 112–125.

Müller, Andrea and Alexander Thomas
1991   *Interkulturelles Orientierungstraining für die USA* [*Intercultural Orientation Training for the USA*]. Saarbrücken: Breitenbach (new edition: Asanger).

Müller, Bernd-Dietrich
1991   Die Bedeutung der interkulturellen Kommunikation für die Wirtschaft [The importance of intercultural communication for Business]. In: Bernd-Dietrich Müller (ed.), *Interkulturelle Wirtschaftskommunikation* [*Intercultural Business Communication*], 27–42. München: iudicium.

Müller-Jacquier, Bernd
2000   Linguistic Awareness of Cultures: Grundlagen eines Trainingsmoduls [Linguistic Awareness of Cultures: Basics of a Training Modul]. In: Jürgen Bolten (ed.), *Studien zur internationalen Unternehmenskommunikation* [*Studies in International Business Communication*], 27–51. Leipzig: H. Popp.

Müller-Jacquier, Bernd and Ellen M. Whitener
2001   Effective Global Leadership: The Role of Linguistic Analysis of Intercultural Communications. In: Torsten Kuhlmann, Mark Mendenhall and Gunter L. Stahl (eds.), *Developing Global Business Leaders: Policies, Processes, and Innovations*, 225–241. Westport CT: Quorum Books.

Newton, Jonathan
this volume   Adapting authentic workplace talk for workplace communication training. Chapter 24.

Niedermeyer, Manfred
2001   Interkulturelle Trainings in der deutschen Wirtschaft: eine Bestandsaufnahme [Intercultural Training in the German Business Sector: An Overview]. In: Jürgen Bolten and Daniela Schröter (eds.), *Im Netzwerk interkulturellen Handelns* [*In the Network of Intercultural Action*], 62–77. Sternenfels: Verlag Wissenschaft und Praxis.

Oechsler, Walter A.
1997   Verfahren zur Auswahl, Vorbereitung und Entsendung von Stammhausdelegierten ins Ausland [Procedures for the Selection, Preparation, and Assignment of Company Delegates Abroad]. In: Klaus Macharzina and Michael-Jörg Oesterle (eds.), *Handbuch Internationales Management:*

Grundlagen-Instrumente-Perspektiven [*Handbook of international management: Principles, Instruments, Perspectives*], 771–784. Wiesbaden: Gabler.

Oechsler, Walter A.
2002   Verfahren zur Auswahl, Vorbereitung und Entsendung von Stammhausdelegierten [Procedures for the Selection, Preparation, and Assignment of Company Delegates Abroad]. In: Klaus Macharzina and Michael-Jörg Oesterle (eds.), *Handbuch Internationales Management: Grundlagen – Instrumente – Perspektiven* [*Handbook of international management. Principles, Instruments, Perspectives*]. 2nd edition, 865–880. Wiesbaden: Gabler.

Paige, Michael R.
1996   Intercultural Trainer Competencies. In: Dan Landis and Rubi Bhagat (eds.), *Handbook of Intercultural Training*. 2nd edition, 149–161. Thousand Oaks: Sage.

Prechtl, Elisabeth and Anne Davidson Lund
this volume Intercultural competence and assessment: perspectives from the INCA Project. Chapter 22.

Price Waterhouse
1997–1998 *International Assignments: European Policy and Practice*, Europe. Berlin: Price Waterhouse.

Roberts, Celia
this volume Intercultural Communication in Healthcare Settings. Chapter 12.

Rost-Roth, Martina
2006   Intercultural Communication in Institutional Settings: Counseling Sessions. In: Kristin Bührig and Jan D. ten Thije (eds.), *Beyond misunderstanding. The linguistic analysis of intercultural communication*, 189–215. Amsterdam/ Philadelphia: Benjamins.

Scherm, Ewald
1995   *Internationales Personalmanagement* [*International Human Resources Management*]. München, Wien: Oldenbourg Verlag.

Simons, George F., Carmen Vázquez and Philip R. Harris
1993   *Transcultural Leadership: Empowering the diverse workforce*. Houston Texas: Gulf Publishing Company.

Simons, George F. and Stephanie Quappe
2000   *Four books, four websites & four games later ... What we have learned about working across cultures in a virtual world*.
        A paper presented at the SIETAR Europa Congress, Bruxelles, March 17, 2000, [http://www.diversophy.com/gsi/Articles/4bks.pdf, 12. 02. 2006].

Sisk, Dorothy
1995   Simulation Games as Training Tools. In: Sandra Fowler and Monica Mumford (eds.), *Intercultural Sourcebook: Cross-Cultural Training Methods*. Volume 1, 81–92. Yarmouth: Intercultural.

Slobodin, L. et al.
1972   *Culture Assimilator. For Interaction with the economically disadvantaged*. Washington D.C.: Department of Health, Education and Welfare.

Stahl, Günter
1998   *Internationaler Einsatz von Führungskräften* [*International Assignment of Executives*]. München/ Wien: Oldenbourg.

Stahl, Günter
1999   *Geschäftlich in den USA: ein interkulturelles Trainingshandbuch* [*On Business in the USA: An Intercultural Training Handbook*]. Wien: Wirtschaftsverlag Ueberreuter.

Stüdlein, Yvonne
1997   *Management von Kulturunterschieden: Phasenkonzept für internationale strategische Allianzen* [*Managing Cultural Differences: A Phase Concept for International Strategic Alliances*]. Wiesbaden: Gabler.

Summerfield, Ellen
1993   *Crossing Cultures Through Film.* Yamouth Maine: Intercultural.

ten Thije, Jan D.
2001   Ein diskursanalytisches Konzept zum interkulturellen Kommunikationstraining [A Discourse Analytic Concept of Intercultural Communication Training]. In: Jürgen Bolten and Klaus Schröter (eds.), *Im Netzwerk interkulturellen Handelns: Theoretische und praktische Perspektiven der interkulturellen Kommunikationsforschung* [*In the Network of Intercultural Action: Theoretical and practical perspectives on Intercultural Communication Research*], 176–204. Sternenfels: Wissenschaft und Praxis.

Thomas, Alexander
1996   Analyse der Handlungswirksamkeit von Kulturstandards [Analysis of the Effectiveness of Cultural Standards]. In: Alexander Thomas (ed.), *Psychologie interkulturellen Handelns* [*Psychology of Intercultural Action*], 107–135. Göttingen: Hogrefe.

Thomas, Alexander
1999   Kultur als Orientierungssystem und Kulturstandards als Bauteile [Culture as an Orientation System and Cultural Standards as Components]. *IMIS-Beiträge*, 10, 91–130.

Thomas, Alexander and Katja Hagemann
1992   Training interkultureller Kompetenz [Training of Intercultural Competence] In: Niels Bergemann and Andreas L. J. Sourisseaux (eds.), *Interkulturelles Management* [*Intercultural Management*], 173–199. Heidelberg: Physica.

Thomas, Alexander, Eva-Ulrike Kinast and Sylvia Schroll-Machl (eds.)
2003   *Handbuch Interkulturelle Kommunikation und Kooperation. Vol. 1: Grundlagen und Praxisfelder* [*Handbook of Intercultural Communication and Cooperation. Vol.: Principles and Areas of Practice*]. Göttingen: Vandenhock & Ruprecht.

Thomas, Alexander, Stefan Kammhuber and Sylvia Schroll-Machl (eds.)
2003   *Handbuch Interkulturelle Kommunikation und Kooperation. Vol. 2: Länder, Kulturen und Interkulturelle Berufstätigkeit* [*Handbook of intercultural communication and Cooperation. Vol. 2. Countries, Cultures, and Intercultural Employment*]. Göttingen: Vandenhoeck & Ruprecht.

Trimpop, Rüdiger M. and Timo Meynhardt
2003   Interkulturelle Trainings und Einsätze: Psychische Kompetenzen und Wirkungsmessungen [Intercultural Training and Assignments: Psychological Skills and Measurements of Efficacy]. In: Klaus Götz (ed.), *Interkulturelles Lernen/ Interkulturelles Training* [*Intercultural Learning/ Intercultural Training*]. 5th edition, 187–220. München: Rainer Hampp.

Tung, Rosalie L. and Arthur Andersen
  1997   *Exploring International Assignees' Viewpoints: A Study of the Expatri-
          ation/ Repatriation Process*. Chicago: Arthur Andersen Worldwide.
Vance, Charles and Ellen A. Ensher
  2002   The Voice of the host country workforce: A key source for improving the
          effectiveness of expatriate training and performance. *International Journal
          of Intercultural Relations*, 448–461.
Wiseman, Richard L.
  2002   Intercultural Communication Competence. In: Gudykunst, William B. and
          Bella Mody (eds.), *International and Intercultural Communication*,
          207–224. Thousand Oaks: Sage.
Wottawa, Heinrich and Heike Thierau
  2003   *Lehrbuch Evaluation [Textbook of Evaluation]*. third edition. Bern et al.:
          Hans Huber.

24. Adapting authentic workplace talk for workplace intercultural communication training

Jonathan Newton

1. Introduction

This paper describes the challenge of selecting and adapting recordings of authentic workplace interactions for use in a workplace language programme. The programme is designed to assist migrants to acculturate to the communicative practices of the New Zealand workplace. Authentic interactions were taken from a large corpus of recordings made in a wide range of blue and white collar workplaces. While the interactions are largely intracultural, using this authentic language allows us to identify important sociopragmatic features of workplace language that are rarely highlighted in artificial materials used in intercultural communication training and provides participants with resources that are directly relevant to their needs.

2. Using transcripts of authentic workplace talk to develop intercultural communication skills[1]

The use of authentic language in second language instruction has attracted lively discussion and debate. The relevant issues are captured in a recent article by Richard Day (2003), *Authentic materials, a wolf in sheep's clothing*. Debate on the topic is wide-ranging, encompassing areas such as: the nature of authenticity (Widdowson 1978; Breen 1985); distinctions between text and task authenticity (Guariento and Morley 2001); the role of corpora of authentic language in materials design and curricula (Carter 1998; Cook 1998; Kennedy 2003) – as exemplified in the COBUILD project (Sinclair 1987); the value of simplification and simplified materials for reading instruction (Widdowson 1978; Lynch 1996, Nation and Wang 1999); and classroom uses of authentic material (Burns, Gollin and Joyce 1997; and detractors Cook 1997; Day 2003).

Among those who argue the case for authentic materials, Burns, Gollin and Joyce (1997) claim that authentic spoken texts provide an important link to interaction outside the classroom, and prepare students for the unpredictability of everyday communication. Carter (1998) uses corpus data to demonstrate how frequently occurring features of authentic conversation such as three-part exchanges, vague language, ellipsis, hedging, widespread use of discourse markers and interruptions, are absent from scripted dialogues in published ELT materials.

On the other hand, Day (2003) argues that authentic materials are too difficult for many typical language students and can have a damaging effect on motivation and attitude. Day suggests that instead of a concern with authenticity, teachers should focus on *appropriateness,* that is, materials that match the needs and level of the learners. Cook (1997: 230) also warns against overvaluing authentic language, arguing that the language classroom is a "play world in which people can practice and prepare" and not "a real world where behaviour has serious consequences".

While Day and Cook are right to caution against authenticity for its own sake (what has been referred to as 'the cult of authenticity'), I believe that their concerns are largely unfounded within the context of workplace communication training (and the general field of language for specific purposes). Here, the goal of preparing participants for the workplace calls for a closer alignment rather than a disjuncture between language training programmes and worksites (the play world and the real world in Cook's terms).

One obvious way to accentuate this alignment is through using authentic language from the workplace in the training context, the topic that I explore in this chapter. And yet authentic spoken interaction is rarely used in commercially published materials for workplace training (Holmes 2005). Instead, recourse to invented interactions and scenarios is widespread. From a practical point of view this is hardly surprising since recordings of authentic conversational workplace language are not easy to obtain. Not least among the challenges is identifying and gaining permission from workers in appropriate and willing worksites, and carefully managing ethical matters and confidentiality. Even when recordings are obtained, transcribing interactional data and extracting useful and useable material for instruction is a time-consuming process.

Workplace interactions are embedded in localized contexts reflecting the discourse history of particular communities of practice and referring to contextual artifacts or shared procedures not accessible to a listener or the reader of a transcription. Further, a single interaction, even when framed with opening and closing moves, is typically shaped by its role as a small part of a much larger and ongoing conversation involving past and future interactions between interlocutors (Vine 2004). The relevance of the larger conversation is frequently signaled in comments that pick up on previous conversations. When a conversation is transcribed, these and other features of the conversation can make for complex, idiosyncratic, unruly conversational artifacts that belie the perceived ease with which we all carry out conversations in our native language.

In sum, while authentic spoken interaction offers unique opportunities to look 'inside' workplace talk and to bring the workplace and training programmes together, the task of making such material useable is logistically challenging. As Dumitrescu (2000: 22) argues, "while authentic materials hold great promise for trainees who are focused on practical language use, the use of authentic language contexts does not relieve the instructor's burden of materials development".

3.   The data source and workplace training context

This challenge provides the impetus for the current chapter. The corpus of workplace interactions which provides the raw data for the chapter was collected by the Language in the Workplace Project (LWP)[2] at Victoria University of Wellington which, since 1996, has been developing a large corpus of transcribed recordings of workplace talk from a range of blue and white collar workplaces. More than 2500 interactions have been recorded from twenty one worksites, and involving around 5000 participants. This material has been used extensively for research purposes (see Holmes and Stubbe 2003; see also Marra and Holmes in this volume), but until recently it has been relatively underused as a resource for workplace language training (although see Stubbe and Brown 2002; Holmes and Fillary 2000; Malthus, Holmes and Major 2005).

We saw an opportunity to address this gap when, in 2005, the university was contracted to provide language-focused training courses for skilled migrants who had been unable to find work in their chosen professions in New Zealand for at least two years. Applicants for the courses are required to be proficient in English at a level comparable to at least an IELTS score of 6.0 (roughly equating to intermediate proficiency) and to be trained and experienced in a profession. Professions represented by participants in the programme include law, stock broking, finance and economics, teaching, academia, design, economics, accountancy, and IT and telecommunications consultants. Applicants reported a number of barriers to employment prior to joining the course. Primary among these are limited language proficiency (especially in relation to job interviews) and the need for professional work experience in the New Zealand context before many employers will consider employing them.

The twelve-week course is divided into a five-week in-class component followed by a six-week workplace placement (with each Friday spent back in class) and concludes with a final week in class. The initial five week block focuses on job interview technique and other aspects of finding employment as well as on developing awareness of critical aspects of communication in the NZ workplace in preparation for the six week work placement and it is to this end that we harnessed the LWP corpus. Using such a large quantity of workplace talk for intercultural communication training requires careful planning around three critical issues:[3]

1. Identifying pragmatic targets for instruction;
2. Selecting suitable samples of workplace talk;
3. Choosing appropriate instructional methods to exploit authentic workplace talk.

The remainder of this chapter addresses each of these issues in turn, and in so doing provides guidelines for approaching intercultural communication training through the use of authentic materials.

4.   Identifying pragmatic targets for instruction

Workplace interaction contains a wealth of sociopragmatic features suitable for intercultural communication training as examples (1) and (2) in following sections illustrate. But as Montgomery (2003: ix) notes, " … cultures are boundless and it is difficult to anticipate what features of context will be significant for communication." To resolve this difficulty and approach the data in a coherent way, we identified the following general sociopragmatic principles that not only provided instructional targets but also guided the search for suitable interactions:

a. talk is functionally complex; an utterance performs more than one function at the same time and one form often has many layers of meaning (e.g., informative, relational, attitudinal);
b. expressing degrees of politeness involves selecting contextually appropriate discourse strategies;
c. interpreting polite and impolite behaviour involves taking account of appropriateness in context;
d. language provides a range of strategies and devices for boosting and softening the strength of an utterance;
e. language provides direct and indirect ways of expressing meaning.

The generality of the principles is useful in programmes involving participants from a range of nationalities who are preparing for a range of types of work. The intercultural dimension of these principles is not explicit here, but is an essential part of the application of the principles to targeted interactions. Participants are always encouraged to be mindful of their culture of origin, aware of "the possibility of difference" (Corbett 2003: 24) and prepared for the "decentring from one's own taken-for-granted world" (Byram and Flemming 1998: 7, cited in Corbett 2003: 24). We see this in Task 4 discussed later in the chapter where participants are asked to imagine an interaction that they have just studied taking place in their culture of origin and to identify ways in which the communication might differ in the two contexts.

Principles (b) and (c) stress the importance of context for judging appropriateness. Context involves not only the broad cultural context as represented in the work of social psychologists and management scientists such as Hofstede (2001) but also features of micro-context such as the physical environment and shared histories of participants (Lo Bianco 2003: 29; cf. Gumperz and Cook-

Gumperz in this volume). It is essential that study of the sociopragmatic features of an authentic interaction takes these factors into account, although such exploration may be somewhat speculative given the limited availability of this kind of information. Let me use example (1) to illustrate this point.

(1) Context: Tom enters Greg's office to request a day's leave

  Tom: can I just have a quick word
  Greg: yeah sure, have a seat
  Tom: [sitting down] great weather, eh?
  Greg: mm
  Tom: yeah, been a good week did you get away skiing at the weekend
  Greg: yeah, we did now how can I help you
  Tom: I was just wondering if I could take Friday off and make it a long weekend
  Greg: mm I don't see any problem with that + you will have finished that report by then won't you

In this example Tom uses small talk and an informal communicative style in his approach to a superior to request a day's leave. Without more information about the worksite and the interlocutors in this conversation it is a question of speculation whether the level of informality we see here reflects a particularly friendly relationship between Tom and Greg that overrides status differences, a workplace in which informality is encouraged, or a more general feature of the New Zealand culture within which this interaction takes place.

5.   Selecting suitable samples of workplace talk

In order to define our data search and to address the most obvious needs of intercultural communication training we narrowed the materials to a focus on face-threatening speech acts (often referred to as 'difficult talk' in ESOL teaching materials). Face threatening speech acts are particularly problematic in intercultural communication because of the role culture plays in constructing face and in shaping the strategic and linguistic realizations of politeness and face work (Brown and Levinson 1987; Blum-Kulka, House and Kaspar 1989; Kasper and Blum-Kulka 1993; Trosberg 1995; Gass and Neu 1996; Spencer Oatey 2000; Kasper and Rose 2003). Furthermore, for the purposes of instruction in sociopragmatic competence, face threatening speech acts are likely to furnish plenty of examples of the sociopragmatic principles identified in the previous section and of indirectness, hedging, boosting and softening strategies which often cause difficulty in intercultural communication.

Face threatening speech acts encompass a broad but finite set of speech acts, and in order to manage the scope of the materials for instruction we restricted our attention to the following four broad categories of such speech acts:

1. Making requests, giving and receiving instructions, and refusing;
2. Making and receiving complaints, and giving and receiving feedback;
3. Expressing opinions, making suggestions and disagreeing;
4. Giving and receiving apologies.

The decision to organize the programme around particular groupings of face-threatening speech acts made first stage data sorting relatively straightforward since the corpus was also coded by speech act. We were thus able to extract from the data base of 2500 interactions a smaller sample of the targeted speech acts and their surrounding conversational moves. In order to select a finite set of useable interactions from these large data sets our two primary criteria were first, that an interaction contain salient examples of the sociopragmatic principles identified in the previous section, and second, that the speech act occurred within a coherent bounded speech event that would be comprehensible as a stand-alone episode. Example (1) discussed above clearly meets these criteria. It is not particularly difficult or complex but nevertheless displays some revealing pragmatic choices around the use of small talk and downsizers in a request made by a subordinate to a superior.

Clear cut interactions such as this were the exception rather than the rule however. As the data search continued, it quickly became clear that relatively few episodes would meet the second criterion of being stand-alone episodes that made sense to an external reader without needing to supply an extensive description of the background and context. The highly situated and contextualized nature of spoken discourse produces meanings that emerge from shared physical context, shared histories and previous conversations, all of which are difficult for a third party reading a transcript to access. It was immediately apparent just how different this authentic material was from artificial interactions constructed for instructional purposes. While it could be claimed that selective sampling of 'ideal' authentic interactions leads to similar distortions, I would argue that the features of interaction that can be lost in the selection process (e.g., widespread exophoric reference, lack of boundedness) are not those that deserve attention in intercultural communication training. We finally selected material which resembled as closely as possible the workplace contexts of the students on our language-focused training courses for skilled migrants.

6.   Choosing appropriate instructional methods to exploit authentic workplace talk

There is considerable support for an approach to second language instruction which emphasizes awareness rather than performance as the critical factor in successful second language acquisition (Schmidt 1990; Gass 1997; Ellis 1999).

'Awareness' in this case refers both to "forming some kind of explicit representation of a target form" (Ellis 1999: 15) and to *noticing* formal qualities of the
input (Gass 1997). While Ellis is referring here to grammar instruction, Kasper
and Rose (2003) propose that such an approach is a valid starting point for instruction in interlanguage pragmatics. As they note,

> [t]eachers can explicitly model and guide students in their use of target practices, en-
> gage students in awareness-raising activities of L2 pragmatics, and provide feedback
> on students' productions. Peer activities enable students to collaboratively work on
> tasks and support each other's development of pragmatic ability through using the
> target language and metapragmatic discussion
>
> Kasper and Rose (2003: 233)

Their extensive review of empirical research on acquiring pragmatic competence in a second language shows convincingly that learners provided with
metapragmatic information ('explicit representation of a target form' in Ellis's
formulation) outperform those without this information (Kasper and Rose
2003: 268).

'Awareness' is approached somewhat differently, though compatibly, in
Tomlinson and Masuhara (2004). The authors distinguish *cultural awareness*
from *cultural knowledge*, the former defined as "a gradually developing inner
sense of the equality of cultures, an increased understanding of your own and
other people's cultures, and a positive interest in how cultures both connect and
differ" (Tomlinson 2001: 5, cited in Tomlinson and Masuhara 2004: 7). Instruction focused on cultural awareness makes use of probing, exploring, reflecting
and comparing, with the ultimate goal of raising sensitivity to cultural differences and producing learners more able to navigate intercultural encounters.
Typically, this awareness is internal, dynamic, variable, multidimensional and
interactive (Tomlinson and Masuhara 2004: 6).

In contrast, they define *cultural knowledge* as static and stereotypical generalizations about the cultural norms that distinguish different cultures (e.g.
Germans are direct, the English are reserved). This is the conventional view of
cultural knowledge as external, static, articulated, stereotypical, and reduced
(Tomlinson and Masuhara 2004: 6), a view which *essentializes* culture. While
cultural knowledge is quick and efficient to dispense in intercultural communication training, the authors note that such an approach to culture all too easily
overlooks the heterogeneity and dynamic nature of culture (Tomlinson and Masuhara 2004: 6).

In choosing an instructional method that best utilizes authentic spoken interactions we sought to give primacy to the goal of awareness-raising both in the
sense of awareness used in the SLA literature and in Tomlinson and Masuhara's formulation discussed above. Communicative practice also plays an integral role, both emerging from and priming opportunities to reflect on prin-

ciples of intercultural communication and to apply these principles to the interpretation of authentic workplace interactions. The integral connections between performance, awareness-raising and text interpretation can be seen in the materials discussed below. The materials refer to the following scenario:

The Scenario

The workplace: A ministry of the New Zealand Government

The people:
- Sara (53) is the manager of a team within this ministry.
- Ripeka (48) is communications manager for the ministry.
- Ella (42), Simon (37), and Marisse (34) are all report writers who work in the team.
- The team have worked together for about one year.

The situation:
Sara is holding a weekly meeting with her team. She has noticed an increasing number of writing errors in documents produced by the team. These documents include letters sent to the public, and reports posted on the ministry website and sent to government officials.

6.1.   Communicative practice

Performative practice (i.e. role play) plays an essential role in awareness raising (Swain 1995) and fulfils this role particularly well when it precedes awareness-raising and interpretation activities. Positioned thus, practice primes participants to *notice the gap* between their performance of a difficult workplace communicative event and the performance of the original interaction. Task 1 provides an example of this approach based on the scenario presented above. In this task the participants are asked to analyse a short, constructed segment of talk (deliberately designed to portray ineffective and inappropriate communication strategies) and then to work with others to produce improved versions of the talk (they will later listen to and analyse the original interaction).

Task 1
   Here is one way that Sara could raise the problem:
   "Look, I'm very unhappy with the quality of your writing. It's full of mistakes and I'm really embarrassed by it. It gives us all a bad name. You need to do something about it or else there might be consequences."
a. What could be wrong with this approach? Find at least three possible problems with the way Sara communicates here.
b. Now work together with another participant and role-play ways Sara could address this problem more effectively.

Communicative practice can also be facilitated by providing trainees with a scenario along with a partial transcript of the original interaction containing either the initial turn(s) or with critical turns omitted and with the requirement that they work in pairs or groups to complete the interaction. Various versions can then be presented by the trainees and discussed and compared with the original interaction. Mak et al. (1999: 84–85) discuss the advantages of such role-based approaches to developing sociopragmatic competence. These include opportunities for diagnosis by a facilitator, opportunities for observing a range of ways of managing a speech event, opportunities for obtaining feedback from other group members, and opportunities for supported experimentation with different ways of managing communication.

6.2.   Awareness-raising and interpretation tasks

Awareness-raising and interpretation tasks are concerned with awareness both as attention to *explicit knowledge* and as *noticing*. These two dimensions of awareness are discussed below.

6.2.1.   Awareness as attention to explicit knowledge

We can distinguish two forms of explicit knowledge for attention in intercultural communication training: knowledge of broad principles of culture and language (sociopragmatic knowledge), and knowledge of appropriate and polite linguistic forms and strategies (pragmalinguistic knowledge). Both are addressed in the principles outlined in section 4 above. At a sociopragmatic level, trainees reflect on their interpretation and performance of linguistic action with reference to first language values. At a pragmalinguistic level, they instantiate their sociolinguistic knowledge in the form of particular communication strategies and linguistic devices.

Analysis of Sara's talk from the interaction provided in the appendix illustrates a number of these principles. Sara's two main turns in the interaction are also presented below in example (2) as a single stretch of discourse.

(2)

Sara: and that's the um issue of writing [deep breath]. Um when, um whenever you – er – we're drafting, well, I've noticed a couple of mistakes creeping into our work. That's stuff that, that even that *I've* looked at. I notice it because the letters go through – all the letters that go out of the ministry go through what's called the day file. They also go through, er, each manager as well as our own staff. Sometimes suddenly as I'm re-reading I spot a spelling mistake which I didn't see the first time or a grammatical mistake. I really ask for all of you to make sure that you take it to one other person at least to, um, to look at before you, before you post it. Even when you send it to me to look at it must also be checked by others. Of course when you're doing a big chunk of work then that's normal for us t- – we always do that checking. Even with just simple letters make sure that they're looked at. It's so easy to overlook just a simple mistake and the less mistakes we send out the better

Sara is a team leader (i.e. manager) in a Government department, and her gentle way of giving the team a directive as well as negative feedback about their writing reflects a 'team' culture in this particular workplace. Sara manages by consensus and collaboration rather than coercion and directive. At a pragmalinguistic level we see this in features of her talk such as the use of inclusive third person pronouns ('we're drafting'), downsizers ('a *couple* of mistakes'), indirect speech acts ('I really ask for all of you to …'), expressions of understanding ('It's so easy to overlook just a simple mistake'), and extended explanation leading up to the negative feedback and directive. These are all potentially valuable targets for awareness-raising that highlight culturally specific ways of doing workplace talk.

6.2.2.   Awareness as noticing

Analysis of Sara's talk leads us to the second formulation of awareness: awareness as noticing. Tasks which require learners to analyse and interpret authentic workplace talk encourage awareness as *noticing* of salient sociopragmatic features of talk. As noted above, noticing of features in input is facilitated by practice opportunities that make learners aware of a gap between their performance and the performance that they are exposed to in an authentic interaction. It is also aided by the provision of explicit knowledge which makes non-obvious or ambiguous features of input more salient.

Prompt questions are a simple yet effective way of encouraging noticing since the questions themselves require learners to take a critical look at communication and to become more aware of the processes involved in identifying and interpreting the multiple meanings bound up in everyday interactions. The following prompt questions lend themselves to interpretation of a range of sociopragmatic features of workplace talk:

– What is the basic proposition?
– What other social meanings are being communicated? (e.g., disapproval, surprise)
– How are these meanings being communicated (wording, tone, non-verbal language)?
– What does the way people are talking to each other tell you about their relationship with each other?

- How would you interpret the [speech act/episode]?
- How does the addressee interpret the [speech act/episode]?
- How would you rate the politeness of the [speech act/episode]?
- How would you rate the appropriateness of the [speech act/episode]?

The following tasks (Tasks 2 to 4) require participants to interpret the interaction provided in the Appendix. (Note that the numbering of the tasks reflects the sequence in the original materials.) In Task 2, participants assess the sociopragmatic qualities of the interaction which they have listened to, and then in Task 3 look for evidence of pragmalinguistic strategies and forms that realize politeness and directness in the interaction and that support the interpretations they made in the previous task. The question *'How would you rate the effectiveness of Sara's communication style?'* in Task 2 is particularly interesting in that it encourages participants to consider the qualities that make communication effective or ineffective, thus drawing attention to the face-work being done by Sara as she seeks to address the sensitive issue of the poor quality writing produced by her team.

Task 2
Listen to the interaction and rate how Sara communicates with her team on the scales below (circle a number in each scale).

How polite was Sara?

Polite			Impolite
1	2	3	4

How direct was Sara?

Direct			Indirect
1	2	3	4

How would you rate the effectiveness of Sara's communication style?

Very effective			Not at all effective
1	2	3	4

To answer this third item you need to define *effectiveness* You can do this by identfying the outcomes that would you expect from "effective" communication. What might these be?

Task 3
Now read the interaction as you listen again. Underline words or phrases that Sara uses to convey her message *constructively* and *effectively*. Note also any

other ways that she communicates effectively (e.g., pausing, use of voice quality, the structure of the message).

Task 3 provides a series of prompt questions that mirror the generic questions provided above, but with encouragement for participants to consider the interaction in the light of their cultural background.

Task 4
a. What does Sara ask her team to do to reduce the number of mistakes that they make in their writing? What words does Sara use to soften this instruction?
b. Compare Sara's complaint with the complaint you created [see sample tasks 4 below]. What differences do you notice?
c. Imagine the same situation in your culture of origin.
   Would you expect a manager to communicate in the way that Sara has communicated here?
   In what ways might the situation and the communication be different?
d. Work with a partner to identify five ways to communicate effectively based on your analysis of Sara's communication.

The various options for awareness-raising and text interpretation described above combined with communicative practice offer a varied but integrated approach to using authentic talk in intercultural communication training for the workplace.

7.   Conclusions

Our research in a wide range of workplaces indicates that the sociolinguistic and sociopragmatic demands of integrating into a new workplace are often very daunting. Learning ways of interacting which are appropriate and normal in a workplace is an important aspect of fitting in and becoming an integrated member of the workplace as a community of practice. Sociopragmatic competence is an often underestimated aspect of workplace success.

Even those born and brought up in an English-speaking speech community may find the process of learning how to do things appropriately with words at work very challenging. Fitting into the workplace involves learning the sociolinguistic and sociopragmatic rules of expression which are particular to the specific community of practice one is joining. Managing workplace discourse, knowing how to make a complaint appropriately, how to make a joke, how to disagree without causing offence, and how to refuse effectively – these are examples of areas which can present pitfalls to people from cultures with different norms from those of their co-workers.

Our use of authentic workplace talk in an intercultural communication training course strongly supports an approach to teaching and training which is rooted in real workplace language. Our analyses of the complexities of authentic workplace interaction suggest that teaching materials need to move beyond formulaic phrases and artificially constructed text book dialogues, which bear little relation to genuine workplace talk. The evidence surveyed in this paper indicates that distinctive ways of doing things develop in particular communities of practice. Our experience suggests that teachers therefore need to make use of multi-media resources for work-oriented communications skills courses, based, preferably, on authentic interaction in the organizations and worksites in which their students will be working.

In conclusion, authentic materials are a valuable resource for assisting migrants to become more informed, sensitive, flexible, and strategically equipped communicators in their second language (Tomlinson and Masuhara 2004: 7). Such materials can be instrumental in encouraging critical awareness of the assumptions and values that lie beneath utterances and behaviour, and in developing the ability to assess situations and recognize multiple interpretations. Most importantly for intercultural communication training purposes, such materials can help alert trainees to likely areas of cultural difference thus enabling them to better negotiate the distance between their own and the new culture. In sum, our work on authentic materials provides evidence that the expensive and complex business of collecting and analysing authentic workplace interaction has worthwhile practical outcomes for those engaged in preparing people for the communicative demands of the workplace.

Appendix

'Mistakes creeping into our work'

The workplace: A ministry of the New Zealand Government

The people:
– Sara (53) is the manager of a team within this ministry.
– Ripeka (48) is communications manager for the ministry.
– Ella (42), Simon (37), and Marisse (34) are all report writers who work in the team.
– The team have worked together for about one year.

The situation:
  Sara is holding a weekly meeting with her team. She has noticed an increasing number of writing errors in documents produced by the team. These documents include letters sent to the public, and reports posted on the ministry website and sent to government officials.

The interaction

Sara   ... which leads me onto one other item which I haven't got on the um agenda ah is it alright if I ...?

Ripeka yep, sure

Sara   and that's the um issue of writing [deep breath]. Um when, um whenever you – er – we're drafting, well, I've noticed a couple of mistakes creeping into our work. That's stuff that, that even that *I've* looked at. I notice it because the letters go through – all the letters that go out of the ministry go through what's called the day file. They also go through, er, each manager as well as our own staff. Sometimes suddenly as I'm re-reading I spot a spelling mistake which I didn't see the first time or a grammatical mistake

Simon/Ella/Ripeka   mm, yeah

Sara   I really ask for all of you to make sure that you take it to one other person at least to, um, to look at before you, before you post it. Even when you send it to me to look at it must also be checked by others. Of course when you're doing a big chunk of work then that's normal for us t- – we always do that checking. Even with just simple letters make sure that they're looked at. It's so easy to overlook just a simple mistake and the less mistakes we send out the better

Ella   I'm doing that eh [laughs]

Simon   yeah, kia ora

Ripeka   I'd like to take that a bit further too cos if we're going to use other languages in the letters, make sure they are also checked as well okay

Sara   Kia ora

Notes

1. I am a member of the Wellington Language in the Workplace Project (LWP). All references to 'we' and 'us' refer to fellow team members. I would like to thank in particular, Janet Holmes and Meredith Marra for assistance with preparing this paper for publication. Nicky Riddiford assisted with valuable comments and insights on the teaching programme which forms the basis for the analysis in this paper. LWP transcribers made the material available for analysis. Finally, I thank those who allowed their workplace interactions to be recorded. This research was supported by a Victoria University Research Fund Grant.

2. For more details, see the Language in the Workplace website, http://www.vuw.ac.nz/lals/lwp [Accessed 31 January 2007]

3. A fourth critical issue is, of course, monitoring and assessment of the effectiveness of instruction. This however, lies beyond the scope of this chapter.

References

Blum-Kulka, Shoshana, Juliane House and Gabriele Kasper (eds.)
    1989   *Cross-cultural Pragmatics: Requests and Apologies.* Norwood, NJ: Ablex.
Breen, Micheal P.
    1985   Authenticity in the language classroom. *Applied Linguistics* 6(1): 60–70.
Brown, Penelope and Stephen C. Levinson
    1987   *Politeness. Some Universals in Language Usage.* Cambridge: Cambridge
            University Press.
Burns, Ann, Sandra Gollin and Helen Joyce
    1997   Authentic spoken texts in the language classroom. *Prospect* 12(2): 72–86.
Byram, M and M. Flemming (eds.)
    1998   *Language Learning in Intercultural Perspective: Approaches through Drama
            and Ethnography.* Cambridge: Cambridge University Press.
Carter, Ronald
    1998   Orders of reality: CANCODE, communication, and culture. *ELT Journal*
            52(1): 43–56.
Cook, Guy
    1997   Language play, language learning. *ELT Journal* 51(3): 224–231.
Cook, Guy
    1998   The uses of reality: a reply to Ronald Carter. *ELT Journal* 52: 57–63.
Corbett, John
    2003   *An Intercultural Approach to English Language Teaching.* Clevedon:
            Multilingual Matters.
Day, Richard
    2003   Authentic materials: A wolf in sheep's clothing. *Guidelines* 25(2): 21–24.
Dumitrescu, Valeriu
    2000   Authentic materials: Selection and implementation in exercise language
            training. *English Teaching Forum* 38(2): 20–23.
Ellis, Rod
    1999   The place of grammar instruction in the second/foreign language curricu-
            lum. *New Zealand Studies in Applied Linguistics* 5: 1–21.
Gass, S.
    1997   *Input, Interaction and the Second Language Learner.* Mahway, NJ: Law-
            rence Erlbaum.
Gass, Susan and Joyce Neu (eds.)
    1996   *Speech Acts across Cultures: Challenges to Communication in a Second
            Language.* Berlin/New York: Mouton de Gruyter.
Guariento, William and John Morley
    2001   Text and task authenticity in the EFL classroom. *ELT Journal* 55(4):
            347–52.
Gumperz, John and Jenny Cook-Gumperz
    this volume Discourse, cultural diversity and communication: a linguistic anthropologi-
            cal perspective, chapter 2.
Hofstede, Geert
    2001   *Culture's Consequences. Comparing Values, Behaviors, Institutions, and
            Organizations Across Nations*, 2nd edn. Beverly Hills, CA: Sage.

Holmes, Janet
    2005   Socio-pragmatic aspects of workplace talk. In: Yuji Kawaguchi, Susumu
            Zaima, Toshihiro Takagaki, Kohji Shibano and Mayumi Usami (eds.), *Lin-
            guistic Informatics – State of the Art and the Future: The First International
            Conference on Linguistic Informatics*, 196–220. Amsterdam: John Benja-
            mins.
Holmes, Janet and Rose Fillary
    2000   Handling small talk at work: Challenges for workers with intellectual dis-
            abilities. *International Journal of Disability, Development and Education*
            47(3): 273–291.
Holmes, Janet and Maria Stubbe
    2003   *Power and Politeness in the Workplace. A Sociolinguistic Analysis of Talk
            at Work*. London: Pearson Education.
Kasper, Gabriele and Shoshana Blum-Kulka (eds.)
    1993   *Interlanguage Pragmatics*. Oxford: Oxford University Press.
Kasper, Gabriele and Kenneth R. Rose
    2003   Pragmatic development in a second language. *Language Learning* 52:
            Suppl. 1.
Kennedy, Graeme
    2003   Amplifier collocations in the British National Corpus: Implications for
            English language teaching. *TESOL Quarterly* 37(3): 467–489.
Lo Bianco, Joseph
    2003   Culture, visible, invisible and multiple. In: Joseph Lo Bianco and Chantal
            Crozet (eds.), *Teaching Invisible Culture: Classroom Practice and Theory*,
            11–38. Melbourne: Language Australia.
Lynch, Tony
    1996   *Communication in the Language Classroom*. Oxford: Oxford University
            Press.
Mak, Anita, Marvin Westwood, F. Ishu Ishiyama and Michelle Barker
    1999   Optimising conditions for learning sociocultural competencies for success.
            International Journal of Intercultural Relations 23(1): 77–90.
Malthus, Caroline, Janet Holmes and George Major
    2005   Completing the circle: Research-based classroom practice with EAL nurs-
            ing students. *New Zealand Studies in Applied Linguistics* 11(1): 65–91.
Marra, Meredith and Janet Holmes
this volume Humour across cultures: joking in the multicultural workplace, chapter 8.
Montgomery, Martin
    2003   Forward: In: John Corbett (ed.), *An Intercultural Approach to English Lan-
            guage Teaching*, ix–x. Clevedon: Multilingual Matters.
Nation, I.S. Paul and Karen Ming-Tsu Wang
    1999   Graded readers and vocabulary. *Reading in a Foreign Language* 12(2):
            355–380.
Schmidt, Richard
    1990   The role of consciousness in second language learning. *Applied Linguistics*
            11(2): 17–46.
Sinclair, John M.
    1987   *Looking Up: An Account of the Cobuild Project in Lexical Computing*. Lon-
            don and Glasgow: Collins.

Spencer Oatey, Helen (ed.)
    2000   *Culturally Speaking: Managing Rapport in Talk Across Cultures.* London: Continuum.
Stubbe, Maria and Pascal Brown
    2002   *Talk That Works. Communication in Successful Factory Teams: A Training Resource Kit.* Wellington: School of Linguistics and Applied Language Studies, Victoria University of Wellington.
Swain, Merill
    1995   Three functions of output in second language learning In: Guy Cook and Barbara Seidlhofer (eds.), *Principles and Practice in Applied Linguistics*, 125–144. Oxford: Oxford University Press.
Tomlinson, Brian and Hitomi Masuhara
    2004   Developing cultural awareness. *Modern English Teacher* 13(1): 5–11.
Trosberg, Anna
    1995   *Interlanguage Pragmatics.* Berlin: Mouton de Gruyter.
Vine, Bernadette
    2004   *Getting Things Done at Work.* Amsterdam: John Benjamins.
Widdowson, Henry G.
    1978   *Teaching Language as Communication.* Oxford: Oxford University Press.

Contributors

Madeleine Brabant
is an organizational psychologist in Brisbane, Australia. Her research focuses on intergroup processes, particularly the language used across gender, generational, and organizational roles.

Jenny Cook-Gumperz
is Professor of Education at University of Californa, Santa Barbara. A sociologist and sociolinguist, she is well known for her work on literacy theory and the social context of children's language learning. She has also published about gender and language socialization.

Saskia Corder
graduated with a 1st class MA (Hons) in English Language and Linguistics from The University of Edinburgh in 2004, which included a year studying at UCLA in Los Angeles. She went on to do Consular work for The Foreign and Commonwealth Office in Beijing until September 2005 and is now in a fundraising and marketing graduate training programme at Cancer Research UK in London.

Anne Davidson Lund
is Assistant Director of CILT, The National Centre for Languages, the English government's centre of expertise for languages. A graduate linguist, Anne has worked in education and business in Europe, the USA and Northern Africa. Anne's doctoral research was in intercultural competence.

Diana Eades
(University of New England) has published widely on Aboriginal English in the legal system, contributed to the education of legal professionals, and given expert linguistic evidence. Currently Secretary of the International Association of Forensic Linguists (IAFL), she has previously served as President and Vice-President.

Peter Franklin
is Professor of Business English and Intercultural Business and Management Communication at HTWG Konstanz University of Applied Sciences, Germany, where he is also Co-Director of the KIeM Institute for Intercultural Management, Values and Communication.

Cindy Gallois
is Professor of Psychology at the University of Queensland in Brisbane, Australia. Her research interests encompass intergroup language and communication in health, intercultural, and organisational contexts.

John J. Gumperz
Professor Emeritus of Anthropology, University of California, Berkeley, is one of the founders of sociolinguistics. The ethnographic approach to language, language and social interaction, intercultural communication, contextualization – these are some of the key terms he introduced. His work is introduced in *Language and Interaction. Discussions with John Gumperz.* 2003

Susanne Günthner
is Professor of German Linguistics at the University of Münster, Germany. Her research interests include interactional linguistics, syntax in conversation, genre analysis, intercultural communication, and anthropological linguistics.

Perry Hinton
is a psychologist and Academic Director of the Human Development and Learning programmes at the Westminster Institute of Education, Oxford Brookes University, Oxford, England. He is interested in the relationship between cognition and culture. His publications include *Stereotypes, Cognition and Culture*.

Janet Holmes
is Professor of Linguistics at Victoria University of Wellington, where she teaches a variety of sociolinguistics courses. She is Director of the Language in the Workplace Project. Her publications include *An Introduction to Sociolinguistics*, *Women, Men and Politeness*, *Power and Politeness in the Workplace*, and *Gendered Talk at Work*.

Helga Kotthoff
is Professor at the German Department of University of Education, Freiburg, Germany. She has published on sociolinguistics, intercultural communication, German grammar, anthropological linguistics, humour and gender studies. She teaches in these fields.

Jeffrey LeRoux
received his doctorate in Psychology from UC Berkeley. He taught at Scipps College, the University of Hawaii at Hilo and San Francisco State University before becoming president of the Center for Psychological Studies in Berkeley, California.

David Matsumoto
is Professor of Psychology and Director of the Culture and Emotion Research Laboratory at San Francisco State University. His main areas of research are in culture, emotion, and nonverbal behavior.

Meredith Marra
is a lecturer in the School of Linguistics and Applied Language Studies at Victoria University of Wellington. As Research Officer for the Language in the Workplace Project, her research interests include the language of meetings and the use and function of humour in workplace interactions.

Christiane Meierkord
is Professor in the English department (applied linguistics section) at University of Münster, Germany. Her research interests include World Englishes, spoken English, intercultural communication, and interlanguages. She currently investigates Englishes in post-apartheid South Africa.

Miriam Meyerhoff
is Professor of Sociolinguistics at the University of Edinburgh. She works on language and gender, and variation in creoles. She is co-editor with Janet Holmes of the *Handbook of Language and Gender.*

Jonathan Newton
is a senior lecturer in the School of Linguistics and Applied Language Studies (LALS), Victoria University of Wellington, New Zealand and an associate in the Language in the Workplace Project.

Ingrid Piller
is Pofessor at the Macquarie University Australia. She is an applied sociolinguist, who works on English as a global language, multilingualism and language learning. She is currently writing a textbook on *Intercultural Communication* for Edinburgh University Press.

Elisabeth Prechtl
studied psychology at the University of Bamberg (Germany) and Université Catholique de l'Ouest (Angers, France) 1995–2001, after which she worked at an SME institute associated to the University of Bayreuth. Since November 2005 she has been a consultant within the Audi Academy (Ingolstadt, Germany). She is currently doing PhD research on the validation of an intercultural assessment centre.

Martin Reisigl
teaches applied linguistics at the University of Vienna and works on a research project supported by research fellowships of the German Alexander von Humboldt Foundation and the Austrian Academy of Sciences (APART). His research interests include discourse analysis, text linguistics, sociolinguistics, rhetoric and semiotics.

Celia Roberts
is Senior Research Fellow at King's College London. Her research interests are institutional discourse, medical communication, second language socialisation and linguistic ethnographic methodology. Her publications include *Language and Discrimination*, *Talk Work and Institutional Order* and *Language Learners as Ethnographers*.

Martina Rost-Roth
is a reader in Linguistics/German at the Free University Berlin, has been a Visiting Scholar at the UC Berkeley (Department of Anthropology/Gumperz) and has held an acting professorship of intercultural communication at Chemnitz Technical University, among other positions. Her work focuses on conversational analysis, second language acquisition and intercultural communication.

Albert Scherr
is Professor of sociology at the University of Education Freiburg/Germany. His main fields of interest include sociology of education, intercultural and anti-racist education, theory of social work.

Helen Spencer-Oatey
is Director of the Centre for English Language Teacher Education at the University of Warwick. She is interested in the impact of culture on language and interaction, especially in relation to the management of rapport. Previously she was manager of the MA Intercultural Communication degree at the University of Bedfordshire. Her publications include *Culturally Speaking* (Continuum) and *Intercultural Interaction* (Palgrave, forthcoming).

Janet Spreckels
is Junior Professor at the German Department of Freiburg University of Education, Germany. She received her PhD from Heidelberg University with a sociolinguistic study on communication among adolescent girls.

Winfried Thielmann
is a lecturer/researcher at the Institute of German as a Foreign Language of the Ludwig Maximilian University in Munich. Previously he taught German and German linguistics at the Australian National University in Canberra.

Nathalie van Meurs
is a research fellow at the Open University, U.K., investigating national and organizational culture. Previously she lectured in cross-cultural psychology and empirical methods at Oxford Brookes University.

Bernadette Watson

is a postdoctoral fellow in psychology at the University of Queensland. Her research encompasses health psychology and communication, focusing on inter-role interactions among health professionals and between them and patients.

Jianyu Xing

is an associate Professor in the School of International Studies at the University of International Business and Economics, Beijing, China. His lecturing and research interests include EFL, Business English and Intercultural (Business) Communication. He completed his PhD at the University of Bedfordshire in applied linguistics.

Seung Hee Yoo

is a graduate student in social psychology at Yale University. She received her BA from Yonsei University in Korea and MA from San Francisco State University.

Vladimir Žegarac

is a reader in Language and Communication at the University of Bedfordshire, UK. His main research interest is in the implications of relevance-theoretic pragmatics for understanding social aspects of human communication.

Index